FUTURES GUIDE 2019

The Top Prospects For Every MLB Team and more

Edited by Brendan Gawlowski and Craig Brown

Nathan Bishop, Ben Carsley, Kevin Carter, Zack Crizer, Scott Delp, Victor Filoromo, Brendan Gawlowski, Aaron Gleeman, Nathan Graham, Jon Hegglund, Wilson Karaman, David Lee, Jay Markle, Tyler Oringer, Jeffrey Paternostro, Keith Rader, Jen Mac Ramos, Alex Rosen, Bret Sayre, Jarrett Seidler, Collin Whitchurch

Dave Pease, Consultant Editor
Rob McQuown, Statistics Editor
Scott Orgera, Associate Editor

Library of Congress Cataloging-in-Publication Data:
paperback
ISBN-10: 1732355568
ISBN-13: 978-1732355569

Project Credits
Cover Design: Kathleen Dyson
Interior Design and Production: Jeff Pease, Dave Pease
Layout: Jeff Pease, Dave Pease

Cover Photos
Front Cover: Vladimir Guerrero Jr. © Aaron Doster-USA TODAY Sports
Back Cover:
Forrest Whitley. © Mark J. Rebilas-USA TODAY Sports
Eloy Jimenez. © Rick Scuteri-USA TODAY Sports
Victor Robles. © Amber Searls-USA TODAY Sports

Baseball icon courtesy of Uberux, from https://www.shareicon.net/author/uberux

Manufactured in the United States of America
10 9 8 7 6 5 4 3 2 1

Table of Contents

Arizona Diamondbacks

The State of the System:

It's not the deepest system in the world, but we are on one straight year of it being an okay system, and man does that feel weird to type.

The Top Ten:

1 Jazz Chisholm SS

OFP: 60 Likely: 50 ETA: Early 2020

Born: 02/01/98 Age: 21 Bats: L Throws: R Height: 5'11" Weight: 165 Origin: International Free Agent, 2015

YEAR	TEAM	LVL	AGE	PA	R	2B	3B	HR	RBI	BB	K	SB	CS	AVG/OBP/SLG	DRC+	VORP	BABIP	BRR	FRAA	WARP	PF
2016	MSO	RK	18	270	42	12	1	9	37	19	73	13	4	.281/.333/.446	81	15.4	.363	0.6	SS(60) 2.5, 2B(1) 0.0	0.3	105
2017	KNC	A	19	125	14	5	2	1	12	10	39	3	0	.248/.325/.358	93	6.4	.371	0.7	SS(29) 0.8	0.4	98
2018	KNC	A	20	341	52	17	4	15	43	30	97	8	2	.244/.311/.472	101	17.7	.303	-1.4	SS(75) -0.3	0.9	106
2018	VIS	A+	20	160	27	6	2	10	27	9	52	9	2	.329/.369/.597	139	21.0	.443	0.5	SS(36) -0.7	0.9	98
2019	*ARI*	*MLB*	*21*	*252*	*26*	*6*	*1*	*8*	*23*	*9*	*94*	*3*	*1*	*.163/.193/.297*	*28*	*-12.3*	*.220*	*0.2*	*SS 1*	*-1.2*	*96*

Breakout: 6% Improve: 11% Collapse: 1% Attrition: 8% MLB: 12% *Comparables: Trevor Story, Joel Guzman, Javier Guerra*

The Report: Look, I already spent an entire blurb this year debating the role of aesthetics in prospect evaluation, so there is no way I am not going to be enamored with a dude who dresses up like Black Panther to hit huge batting practice dingers. Jazz—I'm invoking the Bartolo rule from the style guide here—had me long before that, though. He's a quick-twitch, potential plus-or-better shortstop. That's a pretty big box checked off in the heart of any prospect writer. With plus actions, plus arm, plus range, and uh, plus raw (and that's not power in this case), Jazz is never boring on any ball hit in his vicinity, and he's capable of the spectacular.

At the plate? Well, Jazz is more Pharoah Sanders than John Coltrane at present. He swings hard and generates more power than you'd think out of his wiry frame, although he pays for it with substantial swing and miss. He might have to find a compromise between the natural fluidity of his swing and his aggressive, power-minded approach. But even Coltrane recorded *Om* eventually (though I don't suggest Jazz take the same approach with his pre-game preparations) and if the hit tool doesn't come around, he might not have enough of a career to merit any future critical reevaluation.

The Risks: High. There's still a fair bit of risk in the bat, and Double-A will provide a crucial test for the profile.

Ben Carsley's Fantasy Take: As you can likely tell already, Jazz is a much better IRL than fantasy prospect. That being said, there's enough to like here since we're dealing with a dude who's a lock to stay at short, who can hit for some power, and who might only be a year-and-a-half away. In short, I wouldn't ever expect Chisholm to ever perform as a top-10 shortstop, but he might be able to hit for enough power and steal just enough bases to become a top-20 option. This is not the most exciting fantasy system…

2 Jon Duplantier RHP   OFP: 60   Likely: 50   ETA: 2019

Born: 07/11/94 Age: 24 Bats: L Throws: R Height: 6'4" Weight: 225 Origin: Round 3, 2016 Draft (#89 overall)

YEAR	TEAM	LVL	AGE	W	L	SV	G	GS	IP	H	HR	BB/9	K/9	K	GB%	BABIP	WHIP	ERA	DRA	WARP	PF
2017	KNC	A	22	6	1	0	13	12	72^{2}	45	4	1.9	9.7	78	52%	.240	0.83	1.24	3.41	1.6	98
2017	VIS	A+	22	6	2	0	12	12	63^{1}	46	2	3.8	12.4	87	53%	.324	1.15	1.56	2.58	2.0	98
2018	WTN	AA	23	5	1	0	14	14	67	52	4	3.8	9.1	68	56%	.282	1.19	2.69	4.70	0.5	103
2019	*ARI*	*MLB*	*24*	*1*	*1*	*0*	*3*	*3*	*15*	*12*	*2*	*4.9*	*9.6*	*16*	*44%*	*.297*	*1.38*	*4.21*	*4.86*	*0.1*	*96*

Breakout: 10% Improve: 23% Collapse: 22% Attrition: 42% MLB: 51%   *Comparables: Brian Johnson, P.J. Walters, Chris Reed*

The Report: The old Good/Bad format would work well for this dude. Duplantier has a lot of good—a full four-pitch mix where each could become average with upside from there. There's a lively low-to-mid-90s fastball that hitters beat into the ground, and the trendy hard slider works well in concert for swings-and-misses. His curve flashes plus too, and he also throws a changeup that might get to average or slightly better. As you'd imagine for an advanced true four-pitch guy, he's run into little trouble so far in the minors through Double-A.

So what's the bad? We've noted in the past that he's a control-over-command guy, but he's started walking people more than we anticipated. There's effort and violence in the delivery, and 2017 is the only season in college or pro ball that he's stayed healthy while starting. You could very easily see him consolidating the repertoire down to feature the fastball and slider, transitioning to a relief role, and never looking back.

The Risks: High. "Starting pitcher from Rice" is its own entire category of red flag. Duplantier missed about two months this summer with biceps tendinitis. He has also had significant elbow trouble earlier in his career, and battled shoulder problems in college. So there's a lot of injury risk here on top of the scouty reliever risk.

Ben Carsley's Fantasy Take: I want to like Duplantier from a dynasty perspective because I think he'll be fun to watch, but I'm comparatively low on him as a fantasy guy. As noted above, there probably isn't elite strikeout potential here, and now it looks less likely to come with a sparkly WHIP to mitigate the lack of Ks. Add in the durability/reliever concerns and you get a guy who I think is fairly overvalued in dynasty. He's a solid prospect to be sure, and one who may still fight his way onto the 101, but I think he's a touch overrated in our world right now.

3 Kristian Robinson OF   OFP: 60   Likely: 50   ETA: 2023

Born: 12/11/00 Age: 18 Bats: R Throws: R Height: 6'3" Weight: 190 Origin: International Free Agent, 2017

YEAR	TEAM	LVL	AGE	PA	R	2B	3B	HR	RBI	BB	K	SB	CS	AVG/OBP/SLG	DRC+	VORP	BABIP	BRR	FRAA	WARP	PF
2018	DIA	RK	17	182	35	11	0	4	31	16	46	7	5	.272/.341/.414	128	9.5	.351	1.3	CF(26) -5.3, LF(6) -0.9	0.1	91
2018	MSO	RK	17	74	13	1	0	3	10	11	21	5	3	.300/.419/.467	119	5.9	.405	0.5	CF(10) -2.3, LF(7) 0.4	0.0	108
2019	*ARI*	*MLB*	*18*	*252*	*18*	*7*	*0*	*6*	*22*	*5*	*94*	*3*	*1*	*.156/.172/.253*	*5*	*-20.3*	*.220*	*-0.2*	*CF -1, LF 0*	*-2.3*	*96*

Breakout: 0% Improve: 0% Collapse: 0% Attrition: 0% MLB: 0%   *Comparables: Adalberto Mondesi, Wilmer Flores, Tommy Brown*

The Report: Jarrett Seidler waxed about Bahamian prospects in our Angels list, but Robinson is the crown jewel of that talented 2017 class. With a frame (and tools profile) that is essentially a Jo Adell starter kit, we were always going to be smitten with him. There's explosive bat speed and his approach improved throughout his first pro season. He's a good bet to stick in center field even if he fills out in his late teens and twenties. He's potentially plus-or-better in the four tools you really care about (the arm is light). Robinson offers the kind of upside you dream about in an outfield prospect; you don't have to squint hard to see a 20/20 center fielder.

He's also another prospect who fits well in our old Good/Bad format. There's significant swing-and-miss. He can get a little out of control at the plate. He's still likely four or more years away from paydirt. Conversely, he's still a prospect who doesn't fall all that well into our OFP/Likely format because of the rigidness of our application. I also don't get to punt it for another year. Let's just say the positive and negative risk here stretches well beyond what's below and reconvene this time next year—where it's entirely possible I will be making the same apologies I made for being a year late on (insert complex league breakout prospect of choice). Unlike Vladito, I will at least make sure he's *on* the 101 this time.

The Risks: High. He spent all of 2018 in short-season ball as a 17-year-old. As good as the tools are here, the delta is gonna be high.

Ben Carsley's Fantasy Take: The odds may be long, but anytime you get an athlete with Robinson's power/speed combination you have to pay attention as a fantasy owner. Robinson already had some buzz last year, so he may be owned already in more serious leagues. But if you're looking for an all-upside flier or your leaguemates haven't caught on yet he's a fine addition in formats with 150-plus prospects rostered.

4 Daulton Varsho C   OFP: 60   Likely: 50   ETA: Late 2020

Born: 07/02/96 Age: 22 Bats: L Throws: R Height: 5'10" Weight: 190 Origin: Round 2, 2017 Draft (#68 overall)

YEAR	TEAM	LVL	AGE	PA	R	2B	3B	HR	RBI	BB	K	SB	CS	AVG/OBP/SLG	DRC+	VORP	BABIP	BRR	FRAA	WARP	PF
2017	YAK	A-	20	212	36	16	3	7	39	17	30	7	2	.311/.368/.534	161	24.1	.338	2.4	C(36) 0.8	1.5	94
2018	VIS	A+	21	342	44	11	3	11	44	30	71	19	3	.286/.363/.451	132	30.4	.341	2.5	C(55) 1.4	1.8	97
2019	*ARI*	*MLB*	*22*	*252*	*27*	*9*	*1*	*9*	*30*	*12*	*64*	*5*	*1*	*.214/.252/.375*	*68*	*1.5*	*.249*	*0.5*	*C 0*	*0.2*	*96*

Breakout: 12% Improve: 40% Collapse: 0% Attrition: 34% MLB: 47% *Comparables: Hank Conger, Francisco Mejia, Chance Sisco*

The Report: In addition to sounding like a protagonist from a *Walking Tall* direct-to-video sequel, Varsho carries the requisite big stick. Despite his cold-weather catching pedigree, he handled the Cal League with little issue and projects for above-average power with enough facility with the bat to get most of it into games. The biggest question with Varsho was a familiar one to anyone who spends too much (any) time thinking about catching prospects: Will he stick? The frame is more Joe Don Baker than The Rock, which is the only instance that isn't a demerit, and he has an easy plus arm. His receiving has improved throughout his pro career, although it still remains fringy for now. The upper minors will give us a better idea if Varsho is an A-List catching prospect or just another Kevin Sorbo. For now, the audition tape is promising.

The Risks: High. Catchers are weird. Cold weather catchers with glove questions are just risky.

Ben Carsley's Fantasy Take: Varsho would be a good dynasty catching prospect if they existed, but, as we've chronicled many, many times, they really don't. Hopefully Varsho still has catching eligibility a few seasons into his career when he's ready to hit MLB pitching. If so, he could easily be a top-7 catcher. He could also be a Quad-A first baseman at that point, a la Peter O'Brien. He should be owned in TDGX-sized leagues with 200-plus prospects rostered, but he shouldn't be on our dynasty top-101.

5 Taylor Widener RHP   OFP: 55   Likely: 50   ETA: 2019

Born: 10/24/94 Age: 24 Bats: L Throws: R Height: 6'0" Weight: 195 Origin: Round 12, 2016 Draft (#368 overall)

YEAR	TEAM	LVL	AGE	W	L	SV	G	GS	IP	H	HR	BB/9	K/9	K	GB%	BABIP	WHIP	ERA	DRA	WARP	PF
2016	STA	A-	21	2	0	1	6	1	15^{1}	2	0	2.3	14.7	25	57%	.095	0.39	0.00	2.14	0.5	94
2016	CSC	A	21	1	0	3	7	1	23	15	2	1.2	13.3	34	38%	.289	0.78	0.78	2.00	0.8	98
2017	TAM	A+	22	7	8	0	27	27	119^{1}	87	5	3.8	9.7	129	45%	.273	1.15	3.39	3.37	2.6	99
2018	WTN	AA	23	5	8	0	26	25	137^{1}	99	12	2.8	11.5	176	37%	.275	1.03	2.75	3.06	3.6	101
2019	*ARI*	*MLB*	*24*	*1*	*1*	*0*	*3*	*3*	*15*	*12*	*2*	*3.4*	*10.4*	*17*	*38%*	*.291*	*1.18*	*3.77*	*4.35*	*0.2*	*96*

Breakout: 16% Improve: 28% Collapse: 22% Attrition: 32% MLB: 61% *Comparables: Yefrey Ramirez, Jharel Cotton, Jake Arrieta*

The Report: This was my 2018 sleeper prospect coming out of the EL playoffs, so you can't say we didn't try to give you a heads up. Suffice to say, the sleeper woke up big after a spring trade to Arizona, decimating the Southern League and working his way into the 101 conversation. As we've noted often in the past, the Yankees grow major-college sleeper pitchers on trees—they found Widener as a 12th-round college swingman out of South Carolina.

Widener works consistently in the low-to-mid-90s with the fastball. He commands and manipulates the pitch extremely well, which is the basis for most successful starting pitching prospects. He also has a potential plus slider, although it gets a little slurvy occasionally, and a change that flashes average. The command of his secondary offerings lags behind the fastball at present, although he's getting better here. He could end up in the rotation or the bullpen longer term.

The Risks: Medium. He's a converted reliever, but he's stayed healthy and pitched well in the rotation for two years now. He's on the smaller side and will need more consistency with his secondaries to start in the big leagues. He's a bit of a matched pair with Duplantier.

Ben Carsley's Fantasy Take: Well, on the one hand it's fair to call Widener underrated from a dynasty POV, because I feel like lots of people have barely heard of him. On the other hand, there isn't a ton of upside to get excited about here. So in deep leagues with 200-plus guys owned? Sure, Widener makes a nice pickup. In shallower formats? You can probably wait until he's in the majors to make him a streaming option.

6 Alek Thomas OF

OFP: 55 Likely: 45 ETA: 2022

Born: 04/28/00 Age: 19 Bats: L Throws: L Height: 5'11" Weight: 175 Origin: Round 2, 2018 Draft (#63 overall)

YEAR	TEAM	LVL	AGE	PA	R	2B	3B	HR	RBI	BB	K	SB	CS	AVG/OBP/SLG	DRC+	VORP	BABIP	BRR	FRAA	WARP	PF
2018	DIA	RK	18	138	24	3	5	0	10	13	18	8	2	.325/.394/.431	167	15.2	.381	1.6	CF(13) -2.1, LF(11) -2.4	0.4	93
2018	MSO	RK	18	134	26	11	1	2	17	11	19	4	3	.341/.396/.496	160	7.8	.392	-1.0	CF(21) 0.1, LF(7) 0.5	0.8	110
2019	*ARI*	*MLB*	*19*	*252*	*21*	*2*	*4*	*4*	*18*	*6*	*69*	*2*	*1*	*.184/.203/.276*	*24*	*-13.0*	*.236*	*1.3*	*CF 0, LF 0*	*-1.5*	*96*

Breakout: 5% Improve: 6% Collapse: 0% Attrition: 3% MLB: 8% *Comparables: Carlos Tocci, Engel Beltre, Franmil Reyes*

The Report: Despite not signing their first-round pick, Arizona came away from the 2018 draft far from empty-handed. Thomas was a football and baseball commit to TCU and you can see it in his sturdy, athletic frame. Despite being a multisport star in high school, his baseball skills are quite advanced for his age and profile. He's also a bit of a bloodlines prospect, as his father Allen is the strength and conditioning director for the White Sox and played a couple seasons in the minors himself. The junior Thomas is a quick-twitch up the middle type with a loose and pretty left-handed swing. He has good wrists and plus bat speed, as well as some innate feel for hitting. It's a line-drive oriented swing that's not going to project for much game power, so Thomas fits best as a top-of-the-order, slash-and-dash type center fielder. He makes a useful matched set with Jake McCarthy; Thomas offers more in the way of upside, but also a bit more variance and risk. Like I always say, it's good to diversify your center fielders.

The Risks: High. There is a limited pro track record. Power projection might limit the ceiling.

Ben Carsley's Fantasy Take: Thomas is a solid watch-list guy as a toolsy project who's too raw and far away to get truly excited about right now, but who could shoot up lists if the bat looks good against more legit competition.

7 Jake McCarthy OF

OFP: 55 Likely: 45 ETA: 2021

Born: 07/30/97 Age: 21 Bats: L Throws: L Height: 6'3" Weight: 195 Origin: Round 1, 2018 Draft (#39 overall)

YEAR	TEAM	LVL	AGE	PA	R	2B	3B	HR	RBI	BB	K	SB	CS	AVG/OBP/SLG	DRC+	VORP	BABIP	BRR	FRAA	WARP	PF
2018	YAK	A-	20	241	33	17	3	3	18	22	40	20	8	.288/.378/.442	143	20.3	.341	-0.5	CF(44) 8.0, LF(11) -2.3	1.5	104
2019	*ARI*	*MLB*	*21*	*252*	*28*	*13*	*0*	*6*	*21*	*10*	*66*	*7*	*3*	*.172/.219/.308*	*35*	*-10.1*	*.209*	*0.4*	*CF 3, LF 0*	*-0.8*	*96*

Breakout: 1% Improve: 2% Collapse: 0% Attrition: 2% MLB: 2% *Comparables: Abraham Almonte, Xavier Avery, Raimel Tapia*

The Report: McCarthy is another in the recurring series of "good center field gloves with a chance to hit" that we have all come to know and love (well, maybe less love from Ben). The comp-round pick plays aggressively in center field, with good instincts on the grass and the closing speed to go get it in the gaps. The glove is going to be the carrying tool here but it is potentially plus.

McCarthy isn't a zero at the plate either. Like many UVA hitters, his approach and swing is geared toward hitting line drives up the middle. He lacks the leg drive or lift to project for much pop, but may add enough strength to run into a few pull side. The more likely scenario is that he sprays the gaps and uses his plus speed to take a few extra bases. The other scenario we have to consider is that better velocity, sequencing, and positioning erode enough of his hit tool to make him more of a useful fourth outfielder than a regular.

The Risks: Medium. The defensive skills make for a nice base but he has run himself into some injuries with his style of play. While I don't expect a college performer like McCarthy to struggle in full-season ball, he hasn't hit there yet.

Ben Carsley's Fantasy Take: Less love from Ben is right. McCarthy's only path to fantasy value is to become an accumulator, which means we shouldn't have interest in him until and unless it looks like he'll be playing often. His glove is good enough that such a future is possible, but if it does come to fruition it won't be terribly exciting.

8 Blaze Alexander SS   OFP: 55   Likely: 45   ETA: 2022

Born: 06/11/99 Age: 20 Bats: R Throws: R Height: 6'0" Weight: 160 Origin: Round 11, 2018 Draft (#339 overall)

YEAR	TEAM	LVL	AGE	PA	R	2B	3B	HR	RBI	BB	K	SB	CS	AVG/OBP/SLG	DRC+	VORP	BABIP	BRR	FRAA	WARP	PF
2018	DIA	RK	19	118	25	10	2	2	25	19	21	7	3	.362/.475/.574	218	21.5	.438	-0.9	2B(11) 0.5, SS(10) -3.5	0.9	91
2018	MSO	RK	19	129	27	9	3	3	17	12	31	3	0	.302/.364/.509	113	11.4	.386	1.5	SS(24) 3.6, 2B(4) 0.9	0.9	110
2019	*ARI*	*MLB*	*20*	*252*	*25*	*11*	*1*	*5*	*22*	*17*	*81*	*1*	*1*	*.195/.248/.320*	*50*	*-6.4*	*.269*	*-0.2*	*SS 0, 2B 0*	*-0.7*	*96*

Breakout: 3% Improve: 3% Collapse: 0% Attrition: 0% MLB: 3% *Comparables: Amed Rosario, Tyler Wade, Tim Beckham*

The Report: I suppose with his above-average speed you can chalk one up to nominative determinism here, but really the more appropriate appellation would be "Canon" Alexander. I guess if we really want to stretch things, we could suggest that the blaze refers to the smoke trail left behind by his throws. But however you hamfistedly describe it, Alexander has a gun for an arm. It's a plus-plus rocket launcher (there, that was easy enough in the end). The rest of the tools play well at the six too. He's a plus athlete with good hands and actions. The arm is just as sturdy on the move as it is planted deep in the hole, and his lean frame could add plenty of good weight while sticking at shortstop. The question with Alexander coming into June was the bat. While you'd think his post-draft performance would assuage those concerns, he did most of his damage in the Pioneer League, which offers about as much gravitational pull on baseballs as the surface of the moon. This is a bit of an oversimplification of the results/run environment, but Alexander's .873 OPS for Missoula was only good for a 101 DRC+. We don't scout the (advanced) statline here, but I do worry that Alexander lacks a bit of physicality at the plate and can overswing and lose barrel control. There's pretty good bat speed though, and I wouldn't be surprised if he develops sneaky pop either. This 2018 draft troika represents a neat little tier for me and I'd be amenable to any order depending on what you want to emphasize. Alexander would definitely top the tier on name value (though not the system—Jazz Chisholm is the easiest 80-grade I'll give out all winter).

The Risks: High. Like most IMG guys, Alexander is a little bit older for a prep bat, if that matters to you. He also has a limited pro track record and there are questions about the ultimate projection with the bat.

Ben Carsley's Fantasy Take: Ah, so he is… a worse offensive version of Jazz Chisholm. Tempting, but watch list at best for now.

9 Pavin Smith 1B   OFP: 50   Likely: 45   ETA: 2020

Born: 02/06/96 Age: 23 Bats: L Throws: L Height: 6'2" Weight: 210 Origin: Round 1, 2017 Draft (#7 overall)

YEAR	TEAM	LVL	AGE	PA	R	2B	3B	HR	RBI	BB	K	SB	CS	AVG/OBP/SLG	DRC+	VORP	BABIP	BRR	FRAA	WARP	PF
2017	YAK	A-	21	223	34	15	2	0	27	27	24	2	1	.318/.401/.415	166	15.3	.363	-1.8	1B(42) 1.0	0.7	93
2018	VIS	A+	22	504	63	25	1	11	54	57	65	3	2	.255/.343/.392	112	9.5	.275	-1.1	1B(109) 9.0, RF(1) -0.1	0.6	97
2019	*ARI*	*MLB*	*23*	*252*	*22*	*9*	*0*	*6*	*26*	*18*	*49*	*0*	*0*	*.195/.252/.315*	*49*	*-11.4*	*.216*	*-0.6*	*1B 2*	*-1.0*	*96*

Breakout: 9% Improve: 15% Collapse: 0% Attrition: 6% MLB: 15% *Comparables: Alex Romero, David Cooper, Jake Smolinski*

The Report: This may be a bit harsh on Smith, who did about what you'd expect given the pre-2018 report when he ranked second in the system. Arizona's farm is much better though, while Smith's range of outcomes has seemingly narrowed after he slugged .392 in the California League. The good remains the same. Smith has great bat control and can cover just about any part of the zone. He also understands the strike zone well and passes on offerings that would send most others fishing. He's a natural hitter. He's also a first baseman and, aye, there's the rub.

There's some natural inside-out to Smith's swing and not much loft. It's only average bat speed, despite his feel for hitting. He's got a lean frame, but lacks the innate athleticism of the similarly-profiled Evan White. And ultimately, he posted a sub-.400 slugging in the Cal as a college first baseman. So yes, it might be a bit harsh, but there is cause for concern here.

The Risks: Low. I don't think anyone doubts that Smith can hit for average and get on base at a decent clip. The concern is that it won't be a high enough average or OBP for a first baseman with limited pop.

Ben Carsley's Fantasy Take: Yeah you can skip out on this "I'll have the Matt Thaiss special, but milder"-ass first baseman.

10 Domingo Leyba 2B

OFP: 50 Likely: 45 ETA: Late 2019

Born: 09/11/95 Age: 23 Bats: B Throws: R Height: 5'11" Weight: 160 Origin: International Free Agent, 2006

YEAR	TEAM	LVL	AGE	PA	R	2B	3B	HR	RBI	BB	K	SB	CS	AVG/OBP/SLG	DRC+	VORP	BABIP	BRR	FRAA	WARP	PF
2016	VIS	A+	20	374	48	25	1	6	40	29	62	5	1	.294/.346/.426	120	26.5	.341	2.1	SS(66) -3.3, 2B(17) -1.9	1.0	100
2016	MOB	AA	20	174	21	7	1	4	20	17	22	4	2	.301/.374/.436	143	14.7	.331	0.8	SS(39) -2.6, 2B(5) 0.1	1.0	97
2017	YAK	A-	21	32	4	1	0	1	6	4	2	0	0	.286/.375/.429	124	2.0	.280	0.1	SS(6) 2.0	0.3	105
2017	WTN	AA	21	64	11	4	0	2	9	5	6	0	0	.276/.344/.448	118	5.5	.280	1.9	SS(14) -2.2	0.2	104
2018	WTN	AA	22	358	43	17	2	5	30	35	46	5	2	.269/.344/.381	114	14.0	.300	-1.7	2B(72) -2.9, SS(8) 0.5	0.5	101
2019	*ARI*	*MLB*	*23*	*252*	*28*	*10*	*1*	*6*	*24*	*16*	*45*	*1*	*0*	*.235/.286/.368*	*75*	*1.0*	*.264*	*-0.2*	*2B -2, SS 0*	*-0.1*	*96*

Breakout: 10% Improve: 32% Collapse: 0% Attrition: 11% MLB: 35% *Comparables: Johnny Giavotella, Eric Sogard, Daniel Descalso*

The Report: Leyba bounced back well from his 2017 season-ending shoulder surgery and resumed being extremely Domingo Leyba. I shouldn't like this profile as much as I do, and you can feel free to prefer the toolsier dudes in the next five (or the major-league-ready relievers, if that floats your boat). He's a hit-tool driven second baseman without much in the way of big tools. He's always been more solid than spectacular. His bat control is excellent, but can also lead to suboptimal contact, since he isn't a big power guy; he might scrape double-digit home runs on occasion.

Leyba's a reliable hand at second who could stand at short once a week for you in a pinch. It's a thoroughly uninteresting profile, but for some reason I like it. He's a switch-hitter with good bat control on both sides. He'll work some walks just by virtue of being pesky and fouling off pitches. Leyba may not ever start for a good team, but he's a useful player and he's about ready for the majors.

The Risks: Low. Leyba is healthy, hitting, and unlikely to change much for good or for ill before he is ineligible for a prospect list.

Ben Carsley's Fantasy Take: You don't really need me on this one. You know what (not) to do.

The Next Five:

11 Geraldo Perdomo SS

Born: 10/22/99 Age: 19 Bats: B Throws: R Height: 6'2" Weight: 184 Origin: International Free Agent, 2016

YEAR	TEAM	LVL	AGE	PA	R	2B	3B	HR	RBI	BB	K	SB	CS	AVG/OBP/SLG	DRC+	VORP	BABIP	BRR	FRAA	WARP	PF
2017	DDI	RK	17	278	42	3	2	1	11	60	37	16	8	.238/.410/.285	136	20.0	.282	1.4	SS(63) 11.9	3.1	97
2018	DIA	RK	18	101	20	4	2	1	8	14	17	14	1	.314/.416/.442	173	14.9	.382	2.6	SS(14) 2.6, 2B(8) 0.5	1.3	92
2018	MSO	RK	18	29	3	0	1	0	2	7	4	1	1	.455/.586/.545	248	6.6	.556	0.4	SS(5) 0.3, 2B(1) -0.2	0.5	107
2018	YAK	A-	18	127	20	3	2	3	14	18	23	9	4	.301/.421/.456	148	16.1	.359	1.4	SS(30) 3.9	1.3	103
2019	*ARI*	*MLB*	*19*	*252*	*26*	*0*	*0*	*6*	*17*	*24*	*70*	*5*	*2*	*.138/.221/.213*	*18*	*-23.1*	*.167*	*-7.5*	*SS 5, 2B 0*	*-2.0*	*96*

Breakout: 11% Improve: 13% Collapse: 0% Attrition: 9% MLB: 15% *Comparables: Gleyber Torres, Jurickson Profar, Elvis Andrus*

Perdomo isn't that far off the toolsy 19-year-old up-the-middle draftees in the top 10, but his rawness bleeds through a bit more. He's tall and lean, bordering on thin, but projects for average raw power if and when he fills out. He's not quite as fast-twitch as Alexander—and the arm's about two grades lighter—but he's a solid middle infielder with clean actions and footwork. The defensive profile may play better at the keystone than at shortstop, which is why he's just off the main list for now, but his upside with the bat makes his overall upside similar to Thomas and Alexander.

12 Yoan Lopez RHP

Born: 01/02/93 Age: 26 Bats: R Throws: R Height: 6'3" Weight: 185 Origin: International Free Agent, 2015

YEAR	TEAM	LVL	AGE	W	L	SV	G	GS	IP	H	HR	BB/9	K/9	K	GB%	BABIP	WHIP	ERA	DRA	WARP	PF
2016	MOB	AA	23	4	7	0	14	14	62	67	10	4.6	5.2	36	42%	.285	1.60	5.52	4.18	0.7	97
2017	VIS	A+	24	2	0	4	20	0	30^{2}	16	2	2.6	16.4	56	49%	.298	0.82	0.88	1.86	1.1	100
2018	WTN	AA	25	2	6	12	45	0	61^{2}	38	4	3.8	12.7	87	37%	.258	1.04	2.92	2.78	1.6	100
2018	ARI	MLB	25	0	0	0	10	0	9	7	2	1.0	11.0	11	56%	.238	0.89	3.00	3.84	0.1	103
2019	*ARI*	*MLB*	*26*	*2*	*1*	*0*	*35*	*0*	*37^{2}*	*29*	*4*	*4.3*	*11.1*	*46*	*40%*	*.298*	*1.26*	*3.85*	*4.43*	*0.3*	*96*

Breakout: 12% Improve: 25% Collapse: 8% Attrition: 19% MLB: 35% *Comparables: Daniel Stumpf, Barrett Astin, Ryan Brasier*

Lopez has been dominant since a move to the pen in 2017. A 98-and-a-slider guy, the fastball has explosive life up in the zone and it pairs well with a power slider around 85 with good late tilt, although it can get a little slurvy and flat at times. The righty even has a slightly better change than you'd expect—although it can be quite firm, it has a 10+ mph gap that he sells well. The control isn't always ideal, but Lopez moves the ball around the zone well enough given that he's throwing 98 with a plus slider. He's probably not going to throw quite enough strikes to make you feel entirely comfortable with him in the highest leverage roles, but he's a major-league-ready setup option nonetheless.

13 Marcus Wilson OF

Born: 08/15/96 Age: 22 Bats: R Throws: R Height: 6'3" Weight: 175 Origin: Round 2, 2014 Draft (#69 overall)

YEAR	TEAM	LVL	AGE	PA	R	2B	3B	HR	RBI	BB	K	SB	CS	AVG/OBP/SLG	DRC+	VORP	BABIP	BRR	FRAA	WARP	PF
2016	YAK	A-	19	177	24	5	2	0	15	38	40	18	3	.252/.418/.319	148	15.3	.351	1.9	CF(41) -1.3, RF(2) -0.1	0.7	93
2016	KNC	A	19	115	11	8	1	1	5	13	32	7	2	.253/.357/.384	110	6.1	.364	1.0	CF(25) -2.0	0.2	103
2017	KNC	A	20	447	56	21	5	9	54	55	90	15	7	.295/.383/.446	139	32.8	.361	2.2	CF(61) 2.5, LF(33) 0.0	3.0	99
2018	VIS	A+	21	502	60	26	2	10	48	44	141	16	6	.235/.309/.369	82	15.3	.316	0.9	CF(109) 4.8	0.0	96
2019	*ARI*	*MLB*	*22*	*252*	*27*	*7*	*0*	*7*	*22*	*19*	*79*	*4*	*1*	*.176/.237/.299*	*43*	*-7.6*	*.227*	*0.0*	*CF 1, LF 0*	*-0.7*	*96*

Breakout: 5% Improve: 16% Collapse: 0% Attrition: 9% MLB: 21% *Comparables: Daniel Fields, Jake Cave, Ryan Kalish*

I really figured I'd be penciling Wilson somewhere on our 101 this year. While he's not markedly different from the cavalcade of speed-and-glove center fielders you've already read about multiple times on the list and many others, sometimes you just get a feeling. Instead, Wilson struggled mightily in the Cal League in 2018 as he tried tapping into more power and instead merely upped his strikeouts. There are still center-field tools here. He's an above-average runner with good instincts and an average arm. He should add more strength and maybe some fringy pop develops on its own. And he'll only be 22 next season, even if he will likely be repeating Visalia. I'm not giving up yet, even if Wilson needs an overhaul, or at least a reset in the batter's box. Your dudes are your dudes.

14 Jimmie Sherfy RHP

Born: 12/27/91 Age: 27 Bats: R Throws: R Height: 6'0" Weight: 175 Origin: Round 10, 2013 Draft (#300 overall)

YEAR	TEAM	LVL	AGE	W	L	SV	G	GS	IP	H	HR	BB/9	K/9	K	GB%	BABIP	WHIP	ERA	DRA	WARP	PF
2016	VIS	A+	24	0	0	8	12	0	12^{1}	5	0	4.4	15.3	21	68%	.263	0.89	0.00	1.36	0.5	100
2016	MOB	AA	24	2	0	10	16	0	19^{2}	6	1	2.3	14.2	31	51%	.147	0.56	0.46	1.38	0.8	100
2016	RNO	AAA	24	1	4	12	24	0	23^{1}	20	5	5.0	10.4	27	42%	.288	1.41	6.17	3.74	0.3	100
2017	RNO	AAA	25	2	1	20	44	0	49	37	6	1.8	11.2	61	35%	.279	0.96	3.12	3.21	1.1	100
2017	ARI	MLB	25	2	0	1	11	0	10^{2}	5	0	1.7	7.6	9	54%	.192	0.66	0.00	6.00	-0.1	100
2018	RNO	AAA	26	5	1	15	38	0	45	31	1	4.0	11.6	58	36%	.283	1.13	1.60	2.75	1.2	100
2018	ARI	MLB	26	0	0	0	15	0	16^{1}	8	1	5.5	9.4	17	40%	.179	1.10	1.65	6.54	-0.3	105
2019	*ARI*	*MLB*	*27*	*2*	*1*	*0*	*30*	*0*	*32*	*25*	*4*	*4.1*	*10.4*	*37*	*40%*	*.291*	*1.25*	*3.93*	*4.54*	*0.1*	*96*

Breakout: 12% Improve: 29% Collapse: 29% Attrition: 22% MLB: 63% *Comparables: Cory Gearrin, Blake Parker, Spencer Patton*

What does Sherfy have to do to get an extended shot in a major league pen? He turned 27 at the end of the year and has dominated the PCL the last two seasons in one of its more unfriendly pitching climes. His fastball is down a tick nowadays, but it's still a lively offering. Sherfy adjusted by leaning heavily on his curveball which is a potential plus offering. That's usually a winning formula for major league relievers nowadays, and it's unclear why Sherfy has toiled away in Reno for so long. He's a bit of a personal cheeseball of mine, but he's also basically a major-league-ready setup guy. That's not without value, even if it doesn't usually set the prospect writer's heart a flutter.

15 Taylor Clarke RHP

Born: 05/13/93 Age: 26 Bats: R Throws: R Height: 6'4" Weight: 200 Origin: Round 3, 2015 Draft (#76 overall)

YEAR	TEAM	LVL	AGE	W	L	SV	G	GS	IP	H	HR	BB/9	K/9	K	GB%	BABIP	WHIP	ERA	DRA	WARP	PF
2016	KNC	A	23	3	2	0	6	6	28^{2}	24	1	1.6	7.5	24	32%	.277	1.01	2.83	3.50	0.5	95
2016	VIS	A+	23	1	1	0	4	4	23	19	3	2.7	8.6	22	31%	.262	1.13	2.74	4.36	0.3	98
2016	MOB	AA	23	8	6	0	17	17	97^{2}	99	9	1.9	6.6	72	38%	.297	1.23	3.59	3.26	2.1	99
2017	WTN	AA	24	9	7	0	21	21	111^{1}	94	7	3.2	8.6	107	40%	.292	1.19	2.91	4.52	0.9	106
2017	RNO	AAA	24	3	2	0	6	6	33^{2}	29	8	3.5	8.3	31	34%	.231	1.25	4.81	4.67	0.4	113
2018	RNO	AAA	25	13	8	0	27	27	152	149	12	2.6	7.4	125	40%	.302	1.27	4.03	4.24	2.2	116
2019	*ARI*	*MLB*	*26*	*1*	*1*	*0*	*3*	*3*	*17*	*16*	*3*	*3.0*	*8.0*	*15*	*38%*	*.288*	*1.26*	*4.50*	*5.20*	*0.0*	*96*

Breakout: 7% Improve: 16% Collapse: 8% Attrition: 18% MLB: 40% *Comparables: Kendry Flores, Chris Stratton, D.J. Mitchell*

Like Pavin Smith, Clarke is a victim of a vastly improved system, because he was very much Taylor Clarke once again in 2018. Working in the low-90s from his long, 6-foot-7 frame and high-three-quarters slot, Clarke creates a tough plane on his heater. While it's far from an overpowering pitch, he will cut it at times and work it in and out to keep it off of barrels. Despite his large humanness, Clarke has above-average command and control.

What Clarke doesn't have is an obvious out pitch. He relies primarily on a low-80s slider, which can get a bit loose and lacks ideal depth. He's comfortable commanding it to either side and can spot it for a strike, but he struggles to entice swings and misses with it out of the zone, and gets hit hard when up and out over the plate. He also offers a mid-70s curveball that has inconsistent shape (although the best ones are solid 11-6 breakers) and a changeup which has 10 mph or so of velo separation but not much fade. The stuff is generally fringy, the command a bit better than that. Clarke ultimately profiles as a backend starter or swing type, albeit not the ideal one for Chase Field, humidor or no.

Others of note:

Andy Yerzy, C, Short-Season Hillsboro

Yerzy is more The Rock than Joe Don Baker and that's a more unusual frame to stick behind the plate. There are some other logical points of divergence with Varsho as well, considering Yerzy was a prep catching pick. There will always be more questions about the glove, given the gap between catching high school arms and pro pitchers. Like many prep catchers, Yerzy got drafted as high as he did because of his bat, specifically the raw pop here. It's second deck, plus raw, but the swing has limited it to occasional pull-side power so far as a pro. Behind the plate, his size limits his lateral agility. Both his receiving and footwork on throws are works in progress. He has the ingredients for an everyday catcher, but that baking time is going to be significant, like a soufflé. And also like a soufflé, there are a lot of ways this could fall flat.

Top Talents 25 and Under (born 4/1/93 or later):

1. Ketel Marte
2. Jazz Chisholm
3. Jon Duplantier
4. Luke Weaver
5. Kristian Robinson
6. Carson Kelly
7. Daulton Varsho
8. Taylor Widener
9. Alek Thomas
10. Jake McCarthy

Arizona doesn't have Taijuan Walker or Archie Bradley young (or in Walker's case healthy) enough to kick around anymore on this list, so the spotlight shifts to last year's fifth-ranked youngin', Ketel Marte. It's coming, that big breakout. He's been creeping towards the day steadily over a 400-game career now, with last year's three-win effort his best big-league season to date. A broad base of skills translates into positive value in all three phases of the game, and the team has floated the idea of deploying him in center next season. Wherever he lands on the defensive spectrum, it's likely to remain an up-the-middle assignment of some kind for the foreseeable future, and with a massively team-friendly deal locking him in place through 2024, he's emerged as one of the more valuable assets around.

From there, the team took its first two steps in the long journey into post-Goldschmidtian viability when they acquired Luke Weaver and Carson Kelly for the former franchise cornerstone. After titillating with a curiously-high strikeout rate as a rookie in St. Louis, Weaver's command regressed and the performance plummeted accordingly in his sophomore campaign. The secondaries both got tattooed too often, and there isn't enough fastball there for him to lean on the pitch as much as he does without exquisite command. The raw material is there for mid-rotation value, and he'll certainly have a longer leash to explore that space in Arizona than he would have in St. Louis.

Kelly's bat has yet to flash big-league utility through three start-and-stop tours now, but stop-and-starts aren't particularly conducive to such pursuits. He's got precious little left to prove in Triple-A, as the glove looks as promising as ever and he's posted a 115 DRC+ with a double-digit walk rate across his last two seasons in Memphis. He should be able to hold down a big-league job for a long time thanks to the leather, and if the bat nudges its way into respectability, I'll have undersold him on this list.

With a transitional period looming it should surprise no one if this list is much more flush with on-the-brink talent this time next year.

Atlanta Braves

The State of the System:

Even as Atlanta enters their contention cycle, their system remains one of the best in baseball, if still very pitching-heavy.

The Top Ten:

1 Ian Anderson RHP OFP: 70 Likely: 55 ETA: Early 2020

Born: 05/02/98 Age: 21 Bats: R Throws: R Height: 6'3" Weight: 170 Origin: Round 1, 2016 Draft (#3 overall)

YEAR	TEAM	LVL	AGE	W	L	SV	G	GS	IP	H	HR	BB/9	K/9	K	GB%	BABIP	WHIP	ERA	DRA	WARP	PF
2016	BRA	RK	18	1	0	0	5	5	18	14	0	2.0	9.0	18	59%	.304	1.00	0.00	5.04	0.1	100
2016	DNV	RK	18	0	2	0	5	5	21^{2}	19	1	3.3	7.5	18	60%	.290	1.25	3.74	3.31	0.6	97
2017	ROM	A	19	4	5	0	20	20	83	69	0	4.7	11.0	101	50%	.345	1.35	3.14	4.00	1.2	103
2018	BRV	A+	20	2	6	0	20	20	100	73	2	3.6	10.6	118	47%	.282	1.13	2.52	3.25	2.4	96
2018	MIS	AA	20	2	1	0	4	4	19^{1}	14	0	4.2	11.2	24	48%	.304	1.19	2.33	3.14	0.5	94
2019	*ATL*	*MLB*	*21*	*6*	*6*	*0*	*21*	*21*	*94^{2}*	*82*	*11*	*4.7*	*9.6*	*101*	*46%*	*.301*	*1.38*	*4.27*	*4.96*	*0.4*	*94*

Breakout: 5% Improve: 19% Collapse: 5% Attrition: 13% MLB: 26% *Comparables: Chris Tillman, Archie Bradley, Kyle Crick*

The Report: The conceit of Anderson's Annual comment is our confusion over how he ended up so high on the 101. I've always liked him since the draft, but he'd pitched sparingly in both his post-draft summer and first full pro season. Well, the reins loosened in 2018 and his results were excellent. Anderson sat mid-90s with movement, his curve tightened into a plus 12-6 out pitch, and his change again made progress. Add in a starter's frame and delivery and you have one of the better pitching prospects in baseball.

It's easy for even Anderson to get lost in the obscene depth of arms that Atlanta has, but he was the third overall pick in the draft and you'd expect the development of a cold-weather arm to be a bit more of a slow burn than the Allards and Sorokas of the world. But none of this should really be as much of a surprise as it was. In the end, he tops a very good system, and a very good group of arms. Anderson has the highest upside here, and he isn't even all that far off anymore.

The Risks: Medium. The cameo in Double-A went fine. The changeup is improving. He threw ~120 innings. Everything is proceeding well, but he's still a pitcher.

Ben Carsley's Fantasy Take: Well then. Anderson got enough hype late last season that he's almost assuredly owned in your dynasty league, but that doesn't mean people are valuing him correctly yet. I think the point about Anderson getting lost in Atlanta's absurd pitching depth is a very good one, because if you took out name/organization and just looked at the write-up above, you'd think of a top-20 dynasty prospect, no? Anderson may fall just short of that, but he's an easy top-35ish guy who could develop into an exciting fantasy SP2/3 in the Jameson Taillon mold. Now is the time to buy, if it's not too late already.

2 Austin Riley 3B   OFP: 70   Likely: 55   ETA: 2019

Born: 04/02/97 Age: 22 Bats: R Throws: R Height: 6'3" Weight: 220 Origin: Round 1, 2015 Draft (#41 overall)

YEAR	TEAM	LVL	AGE	PA	R	2B	3B	HR	RBI	BB	K	SB	CS	AVG/OBP/SLG	DRC+	VORP	BABIP	BRR	FRAA	WARP	PF
2016	ROM	A	19	543	68	39	2	20	80	39	147	3	3	.271/.324/.479	130	33.9	.341	-2.6	3B(122) 3.1	2.4	100
2017	BRV	A+	20	339	43	10	1	12	47	23	74	0	2	.252/.310/.408	109	12.9	.289	-0.4	3B(80) -2.5	0.3	102
2017	MIS	AA	20	203	28	9	1	8	27	20	50	2	0	.315/.389/.511	148	20.1	.393	-0.5	3B(47) -1.6	1.1	95
2018	MIS	AA	21	109	17	10	3	6	20	8	28	0	0	.333/.394/.677	175	19.1	.415	1.0	3B(27) 1.2	1.3	95
2018	GWN	AAA	21	324	41	17	0	12	47	26	95	1	0	.282/.346/.464	123	24.1	.374	1.1	3B(71) -0.3	1.5	98
2019	*ATL*	*MLB*	*22*	*47*	*5*	*2*	*0*	*2*	*6*	*3*	*16*	*0*	*0*	*.235/.291/.418*	*79*	*0.0*	*.319*	*-0.1*	*3B 0*	*0.0*	*94*

Breakout: 16% Improve: 41% Collapse: 0% Attrition: 15% MLB: 47% *Comparables: Chris Carter, Chris Davis, Andy Marte*

The Report: Over the summer, I got a chat question concerning whether or not I was worried about Austin Riley's strikeout rate. I don't remember exactly what he was slugging at the time, but it was probably over .500. For the year it was .522. Yes he struck out a quarter of the time; it's 2019, baby. He's likely never going to win a batting title, sure. The swing can get a little leak-and-lift, and he can lose balance. Riley is just a big dude with long levers, so there's going to be swing and miss. But it comes with massive raw power as well. He's getting it into games now too and has improved enough at third base to at least be average there. Riley can make all the plays and his plus arm is more than enough for the hot corner.

Ironically, I was the last person on staff to buy in; there is no zealot like the convert I suppose. Before the season Scott Delp pegged Riley as a next year's 101 guy writing: "[He] doesn't have to hit more than .270 or so to be a solid major league third baseman. The power is there. His defense is there. I expect him to build on the improvements he has made and dominate Double-A in 2018. That should get even the doubters to relent."

I'm a doubter no longer. So no, I'm not worried.

The Risks: Medium. Riley is basically a Josh Donaldson injury away from being the everyday third baseman. There may be a bit of a rough adjustment period as major-league arms front-foot him with better secondary stuff, but I expect the tools to win out in the end here.

Ben Carsley's Fantasy Take: I became a Riley convert last season, and he's developed into one of my favorite fantasy prospects in the game. Sure, he might not carry your team in batting average, but Riley has big-boy power and should earn top-10 finishes at the position many times. Look at what Mike Moustakas did last year—.251/.319/.459 with 28 bombs—and consider that Riley's floor. If you're looking for a closer approximation to his ceiling, you need to shop in the 2018 Matt Carpenter aisle—.257/.374/.523 with 36 bombs and 100-plus RBI. Get excited.

3 Mike Soroka RHP   OFP: 60   Likely: 50   ETA: Debuted in 2018

Born: 08/04/97 Age: 21 Bats: R Throws: R Height: 6'5" Weight: 225 Origin: Round 1, 2015 Draft (#28 overall)

YEAR	TEAM	LVL	AGE	W	L	SV	G	GS	IP	H	HR	BB/9	K/9	K	GB%	BABIP	WHIP	ERA	DRA	WARP	PF
2016	ROM	A	18	9	9	0	25	24	143	130	3	2.0	7.9	125	52%	.305	1.13	3.02	3.17	3.2	99
2017	MIS	AA	19	11	8	0	26	26	153^{2}	133	10	2.0	7.3	125	49%	.275	1.09	2.75	4.13	1.9	95
2018	GWN	AAA	20	2	1	0	5	5	27	20	0	2.0	10.3	31	70%	.299	0.96	2.00	2.64	0.9	96
2018	ATL	MLB	20	2	1	0	5	5	25^{2}	30	1	2.5	7.4	21	45%	.345	1.44	3.51	4.64	0.2	91
2019	*ATL*	*MLB*	*21*	*4*	*4*	*0*	*13*	*13*	*69*	*60*	*7*	*2.8*	*8.7*	*67*	*48%*	*.297*	*1.18*	*3.57*	*4.15*	*0.9*	*94*

Breakout: 6% Improve: 14% Collapse: 11% Attrition: 23% MLB: 31% *Comparables: David Holmberg, Jacob Turner, Tyler Skaggs*

The Report: Soroka debuted a few months before his 21st birthday, a fitting early arrival for a player intelligent and mature beyond his years. His elite makeup shows on the mound, as he goes after hitters and gets the most out of his stuff, which may not jump off the page but is deep enough with sufficient command to portend a mid-rotation profile.

Soroka's fastball has plus sink and creeps into the mid-90s. He pounds the knees to both sides and pitches to contact efficiently when he's spotting well. The breaking ball rides the middle ground between a curve and slider, but it spins like crazy with solid bite; it's at least an above-average offering. He struggled to find his breaker and changeup on the same day a couple seasons ago, but he has a feel for both consistently now, giving the changeup a similar 55 potential grade.

Soroka's greatest strengths are makeup and durability. The latter came into question in 2018 when a shoulder concern cut his season short, but he came back strong by the end of the year to quiet any lingering doubts.

The Risks: Medium. The shoulder—and the fact that he's a pitcher—are the only reasons the word "risk" should be applied here. He proved his shoulder was healthy in workouts toward the end of the season, but a full year of production in 2019 would be nice to see. His initial major-league taste showed he belongs, and he should permanently belong as soon as spring 2019.

Ben Carsley's Fantasy Take: Soroka really puts the general consensus that there's no such thing as a safe pitching prospect to the test, as he's about as sure a bet to be a worthwhile fantasy SP4/5 starter as exists. That being said, the lack of big-time strikeout stuff makes him a *slightly* better IRL prospect than fantasy arm. Still, add up Soroka's very high floor, fairly favorable contextual factors, and fantasy-friendly ETA and you get an arm that should fight its way inside the top-50 dynasty prospects. See, we're not always negative about pitchers!

4 Kyle Wright RHP

OFP: 60 Likely: 50 ETA: Debuted in 2018

Born: 10/02/95 Age: 23 Bats: R Throws: R Height: 6'4" Weight: 200 Origin: Round 1, 2017 Draft (#5 overall)

YEAR	TEAM	LVL	AGE	W	L	SV	G	GS	IP	H	HR	BB/9	K/9	K	GB%	BABIP	WHIP	ERA	DRA	WARP	PF
2017	BRV	A+	21	0	1	0	6	6	11^{1}	8	0	3.2	7.9	10	61%	.258	1.06	3.18	4.53	0.1	104
2018	MIS	AA	22	6	8	0	20	20	109^{1}	103	6	3.5	8.6	105	56%	.311	1.34	3.70	3.84	1.9	94
2018	GWN	AAA	22	2	1	0	7	4	28^{2}	15	2	2.5	8.8	28	51%	.183	0.80	2.51	4.19	0.4	98
2018	ATL	MLB	22	0	0	0	4	0	6	4	2	9.0	7.5	5	41%	.133	1.67	4.50	4.98	0.0	92
2019	*ATL*	*MLB*	*23*	*3*	*3*	*0*	*18*	*8*	*51*	*43*	*5*	*3.7*	*8.6*	*49*	*51%*	*.286*	*1.25*	*3.91*	*4.54*	*0.4*	*94*

Breakout: 16% Improve: 27% Collapse: 20% Attrition: 40% MLB: 60% *Comparables: Brett Marshall, Jake Thompson, Giovanni Soto*

The Report: If you draw up the ideal pitching prospect, you may end up with someone who looks a lot like Wright. He has the total package of height, length, velocity, depth to stuff, feel, and a major-league debut under his belt. The margin between the top few notches in the current Braves system is thin, and Wright was in the conversation for the top spot.

Wright's best pitch is a plus slider that flashes a tick more with hard, late bite and downward low-80s action. It's a true swing-and-miss offering and he'll lean on it heavily. He's capable of holding 94+ throughout an outing and sits 92-96 with above-average life and plane but present 4 command that should get a little better from there. He mixes a deep curveball with 12-6 action as a third pitch of at least above-average potential. The changeup tends to only flash because of inconsistent command, but it shows above-average and is very serviceable as a fourth pitch.

Wright would be the top prospect in many other systems, and Atlanta's depth shouldn't push him to the shadows. Wright is the type of pitching prospect organizations covet and he'll compete for a big-league job this spring.

The Risks: Medium. Wright unsurprisingly rocketed through the system and reached Atlanta by the end of 2018, so he's not exactly a risky prospect. He mostly repeats his arm slot, but his command isn't where you'd like it to be and the fastball can get hit at times.

Ben Carsley's Fantasy Take: We cautioned last year that Wright didn't have the insane upside some prefer from the first college arm popped in a draft—and the same was true this year with Casey Mize—but that doesn't make Wright a bad prospect by any stretch. He surprised even his most optimistic supporters by reaching the majors in his first full season, and while he faces stiff competition for playing time in Atlanta, he's got the talent to lock down a spot. Wright has a slightly higher ceiling and slightly lower floor than Soroka, but also profiles as a potential well-rounded fantasy SP4. Expect a little less than that type of performance for 2019, but it shouldn't be too long before you can bank on Wright as one of your rotation stalwarts. He's another easy top-101 (and potential top-50) choice.

5 Bryse Wilson RHP OFP: 60 Likely: 50 ETA: Debuted in 2018

Born: 12/20/97 Age: 21 Bats: R Throws: R Height: 6'1" Weight: 225 Origin: Round 4, 2016 Draft (#109 overall)

YEAR	TEAM	LVL	AGE	W	L	SV	G	GS	IP	H	HR	BB/9	K/9	K	GB%	BABIP	WHIP	ERA	DRA	WARP	PF
2016	BRA	RK	18	1	1	0	9	6	26^{2}	16	0	2.7	9.8	29	66%	.250	0.90	0.68	3.10	0.7	96
2017	ROM	A	19	10	7	0	26	26	137	105	8	2.4	9.1	139	54%	.272	1.04	2.50	3.70	2.5	101
2018	BRV	A+	20	2	0	0	5	5	26^{2}	16	0	2.4	8.8	26	60%	.229	0.86	0.34	3.83	0.5	94
2018	MIS	AA	20	3	5	0	15	15	77	77	3	3.0	10.4	89	44%	.347	1.34	3.97	3.82	1.4	93
2018	GWN	AAA	20	3	0	0	5	3	22	20	6	1.2	11.5	28	45%	.280	1.05	5.32	3.15	0.6	98
2018	ATL	MLB	20	1	0	0	3	1	7	8	0	7.7	7.7	6	29%	.381	2.00	6.43	5.37	0.0	94
2019	*ATL*	*MLB*	*21*	*1*	*1*	*0*	*2*	*2*	*10*	*9*	*1*	*3.9*	*9.1*	*10*	*48%*	*.298*	*1.31*	*4.23*	*4.91*	*0.0*	*94*

Breakout: 6% Improve: 17% Collapse: 5% Attrition: 16% MLB: 27% *Comparables: Carlos Martinez, John Lamb, Jesse Biddle*

The Report: Every year has its share of pop-up prospects, and 2018 was Wilson's time to shine. He has plus-plus makeup and that may have helped him morph from a future middle reliever to a possible major-league starter with the stuff to thrive in a valuable multi-inning role.

Wilson's fastball is clearly his best pitch. He consistently hits the mid-90s and he's capable of holding it through an outing. His stuff plays up when he pops the four-seamer above the hands and breaks off an above-average slider down and away. His changeup has also grown by leaps and bounds over the past year or two. It can be the better secondary depending on the day and could also reach above-average if everything clicks. Wilson is a bulldog on the mound, and while he's not a budding ace, he could be a serviceable mid-rotation arm or a weapon out of the bullpen.

The Risks: Low. He reached the majors in 2018 and has a high floor. There's nothing left for him in the minors and he's durable.

Ben Carsley's Fantasy Take: It's pretty crazy that a prospect this good is perhaps the worst bet to make the fantasy top-101 among the first seven players on this list. Such is life when you "only" profile as a fantasy SP5/6, but considering that Wilson is just about ready now and can miss bats, he's got a solid argument for inclusion on the list. One factor that's out of his control and may give us pause–as Wilson is one of the lesser options in this totally loaded list, he'd seem to be perhaps the most likely bullpen convert.

6 Cristian Pache OF OFP: 60 Likely: 50 ETA: Mid-2020

Born: 11/19/98 Age: 20 Bats: R Throws: R Height: 6'2" Weight: 185 Origin: International Free Agent, 2015

YEAR	TEAM	LVL	AGE	PA	R	2B	3B	HR	RBI	BB	K	SB	CS	AVG/OBP/SLG	DRC+	VORP	BABIP	BRR	FRAA	WARP	PF
2016	BRA	RK	17	114	16	2	4	0	11	6	11	7	3	.283/.325/.377	114	1.7	.313	-0.1	CF(25) 7.4, RF(1) 0.1	0.8	97
2016	DNV	RK	17	122	12	2	3	0	10	7	13	4	2	.333/.372/.404	145	10.1	.376	1.1	CF(27) 10.1, RF(2) -0.8	1.5	98
2017	ROM	A	18	514	60	13	8	0	42	39	104	32	14	.281/.335/.343	100	22.4	.360	5.8	CF(116) 27.8, RF(2) 0.0	4.3	102
2018	BRV	A+	19	387	46	20	5	8	40	15	69	7	6	.285/.311/.431	114	14.8	.330	-1.1	CF(93) 3.9	1.3	98
2018	MIS	AA	19	109	10	3	1	1	7	5	28	0	2	.260/.294/.337	72	-0.6	.347	-0.5	CF(28) 1.3	-0.1	97
2019	*ATL*	*MLB*	*20*	*252*	*20*	*3*	*1*	*5*	*23*	*5*	*65*	*3*	*2*	*.202/.215/.285*	*28*	*-11.9*	*.249*	*0.3*	*CF 6*	*-0.7*	*94*

Breakout: 8% Improve: 8% Collapse: 0% Attrition: 3% MLB: 8% *Comparables: Anthony Gose, Gorkys Hernandez, Justin Williams*

The Report: Pache's defense is well-chronicled at this point. He gets double-plus grades on his glove and arm, and he has a chance to be the best defensive center fielder in the game. He also has 70 speed, and his prowess in the field gives Pache a major-league future all by itself.

The question is how much he'll hit. He's made solid strides over the past year to stay back and incorporate his lower half better, helped in large part by a leg kick. While his mechanics have improved, he's still too aggressive at the plate, to the point where his approach could be debilitating if it doesn't develop further. He'll only be 20 this year, so there's time.

If Pache can develop an average hit tool, and in turn tap into his solid-average power, he's going to be a star. Because the approach is what it is, something along the lines of a defense-first, everyday center fielder with solid-average value is a more realistic projection. There's certainly nothing wrong with that.

The Risks: High. 2019 will tell us a lot about where Pache is at the plate. It'll be his first full season at Double-A and we'll presumably know much more about his bat by year's end.

Ben Carsley's Fantasy Take: Are you feeling lucky, punk? Forget about the power for a second—even if Pache hits enough to make use of his 70 speed on a regular basis, he's a potential OF3. If he also grows into 15-20 homer pop? We're approaching OF2 territory. Of course there's also the chance his hit tool collapses enough that he doesn't play every day, at which point he's a fantasy bench guy you sneak into your UTIL spot now and then in the hopes of grabbing some steals. So how do you reconcile all that on a top-101 list? A guy with top-50 player upside, top-150 player median projections and a fantasy bench floor? No seriously, I'm asking, because I don't know.

7 Drew Waters OF

OFP: 60 Likely: 50 ETA: Mid-2020

Born: 12/30/98 Age: 20 Bats: B Throws: R Height: 6'2" Weight: 183 Origin: Round 2, 2017 Draft (#41 overall)

YEAR	TEAM	LVL	AGE	PA	R	2B	3B	HR	RBI	BB	K	SB	CS	AVG/OBP/SLG	DRC+	VORP	BABIP	BRR	FRAA	WARP	PF
2017	BRA	RK	18	58	13	3	1	2	10	7	11	2	1	.347/.448/.571	126	7.7	.417	0.8	CF(9) -1.6, RF(3) 0.7	0.1	106
2017	DNV	RK	18	166	20	11	1	2	14	16	59	4	2	.255/.331/.383	81	5.6	.409	-1.3	CF(35) -4.6	-0.8	92
2018	ROM	A	19	365	58	32	6	9	36	21	72	20	5	.303/.353/.513	140	31.6	.362	3.9	CF(83) -0.6	2.4	99
2018	BRV	A+	19	133	14	7	3	0	3	8	33	3	0	.268/.316/.374	93	4.7	.363	0.0	CF(30) -1.5, RF(1) -0.1	-0.1	97
2019	*ATL*	*MLB*	*20*	*252*	*24*	*11*	*1*	*6*	*21*	*5*	*88*	*3*	*1*	*.173/.187/.298*	*26*	*-12.4*	*.237*	*0.4*	*CF -1, RF 0*	*-1.4*	*94*

Breakout: 5% Improve: 6% Collapse: 0% Attrition: 3% MLB: 6% *Comparables: Kyle Tucker, Alex Verdugo, Clint Frazier*

The Report: The Braves were surely thrilled when they were able to nab Waters in the second round in 2017. The center fielder showed the aptitude to translate his standout prep tools to the professional ranks, and it paid off with a big full-season debut. It should be a steady climb up the rankings both organizationally and across baseball for Waters.

Waters or Pache was a popular debate in Braves prospect circles this past season. Some gave the edge to Pache for his defense and bigger upside. Some prefer Waters, due to a higher floor and greater likelihood of utilizing all five tools at the big-league level. The hit tool has at least average potential and could reach higher from the left side based on plus bat speed and solid barrel awareness. He'll grow into consistently plus raw power and should tap into it enough for at least above-average in-game pop, if not plus, based on his lofty exit velocity numbers. He's a plus runner at present and should remain at least above-average, while his instincts and speed will keep him in center; his arm is plus. The one concern here is that Waters is dramatically better at the plate from the left side, to the point where he might need to abandon switch-hitting.

The Risks: High. His first full season was a success, but he probably won't taste the higher levels until at least mid-2019, so the road ahead is still fairly long.

Ben Carsley's Fantasy Take: Waters was one of Bret's dynasty darlings last offseason. It turns out our Internet Dad was right, and if you bought in on Waters before the hype you're a happier person for it. Waters' upside isn't sky-high, but his solid floor and proximity to the majors should push him into the top-75 or so on our top-101 list this offseason. From a fantasy perspective, he's kinda what Blake Rutherford was supposed to be? Also his name literally means "prepared a bath," so factor that in for what it's worth.

8 Touki Toussaint RHP

OFP: 60 Likely: 50 ETA: Debuted in 2018

Born: 06/20/96 Age: 23 Bats: R Throws: R Height: 6'3" Weight: 185 Origin: Round 1, 2014 Draft (#16 overall)

YEAR	TEAM	LVL	AGE	W	L	SV	G	GS	IP	H	HR	BB/9	K/9	K	GB%	BABIP	WHIP	ERA	DRA	WARP	PF
2016	ROM	A	20	4	8	0	27	24	132^{1}	105	13	4.8	8.7	128	40%	.263	1.33	3.88	5.17	-0.3	100
2017	BRV	A+	21	3	9	0	19	19	105^{1}	101	8	3.6	10.5	123	45%	.324	1.36	5.04	3.50	2.2	101
2017	MIS	AA	21	3	4	0	7	7	39^{2}	30	3	5.0	10.0	44	38%	.276	1.31	3.18	4.23	0.4	94
2018	MIS	AA	22	4	6	0	16	16	86	66	7	3.8	11.2	107	48%	.284	1.19	2.93	3.93	1.4	95
2018	GWN	AAA	22	5	0	0	8	8	50^{1}	35	0	3.0	10.0	56	44%	.280	1.03	1.43	3.37	1.2	100
2018	ATL	MLB	22	2	1	0	7	5	29	18	1	6.5	9.9	32	47%	.254	1.34	4.03	4.69	0.2	92
2019	*ATL*	*MLB*	*23*	*7*	*6*	*0*	*34*	*18*	*112*	*88*	*12*	*4.5*	*9.8*	*122*	*41%*	*.284*	*1.29*	*4.05*	*4.69*	*0.7*	*94*

Breakout: 12% Improve: 23% Collapse: 17% Attrition: 34% MLB: 54% *Comparables: Mauricio Robles, Archie Bradley, Keyvius Sampson*

The Report: You're excused for having prospect fatigue when it comes to Toussaint. He's been a prospect since the First Goldstein Age, and one could write a book on his development at this point. It'd be a good read, because Toussaint has worked his butt off to turn into the legitimate starting pitching prospect we all hoped he'd become.

Toussaint's ceiling may not be as stratospheric as it was a few years ago, but his floor is much higher. In part, that's because he found the right arm slot in Mississippi last summer. It's lower now and he's found a motion that helps him repeat better, which means that his command is now more consistent. The walk rate is still high, perhaps lofty enough to portend a shift to the bullpen, but he's managing it better. His fastball still sits mid-90s and bumps 98, but he's learned to work 92-95 effectively by manipulating the pitch with sink or cut. He'll still draw a few oohs and ahhs with a 70-grade curveball each outing, but it tends to sit plus with more three-quarters tilt than in the past. His changeup has jumped multiple grades the past couple years and is now a viable third pitch, even flashing plus with good arm speed and hard sink to resemble a splitter.

It's always been about control and command for Toussaint. He hasn't developed them so much that he's now a lock to be a No. 2/3 starter, but it's come so far that we can at least have the conversation. He's repeating better, dialing the stuff back and locating much more consistently, and he looks the part of a major-league starter a lot more often now. He still may end up as a high-level reliever pumping 97 with a 70 curve, but damn if he hasn't given the Braves a reason to keep him in a rotation for the time being.

The Risks: Medium. He had bright moments in his first major-league stint and has little left to prove in the minors, regardless of his future role.

Ben Carsley's Fantasy Take: They got there in entirely different ways, but from a fantasy perspective it seems like Wilson and Toussaint are pretty equal at this point. The bet here is that Touki is even *more* likely to end up in the bullpen, so he might just miss our 101, but he's got enough raw stuff to appear on it once more. I can't believe I'm being this positive about pitchers?

9 **Kyle Muller LHP** OFP: 55 Likely: 50 ETA: Early 2020

Born: 10/07/97 Age: 21 Bats: R Throws: L Height: 6'6" Weight: 225 Origin: Round 2, 2016 Draft (#44 overall)

YEAR	TEAM	LVL	AGE	W	L	SV	G	GS	IP	H	HR	BB/9	K/9	K	GB%	BABIP	WHIP	ERA	DRA	WARP	PF
2016	BRA	RK	18	1	0	0	10	9	27^2	14	0	3.9	12.4	38	55%	.233	0.94	0.65	1.50	1.3	96
2017	DNV	RK	19	1	1	0	11	11	47^2	43	5	3.4	9.3	49	40%	.284	1.28	4.15	4.93	0.6	98
2018	ROM	A	20	3	0	0	6	6	30	24	3	2.4	6.9	23	54%	.253	1.07	2.40	4.86	0.1	98
2018	BRV	A+	20	4	2	0	14	14	80^2	80	2	3.6	8.8	79	42%	.350	1.39	3.24	4.73	0.6	98
2018	MIS	AA	20	4	1	0	5	5	29	22	3	1.9	8.4	27	40%	.244	0.97	3.10	4.21	0.4	94
2019	*ATL*	*MLB*	*21*	*5*	*8*	*0*	*21*	*21*	99^2	*95*	*17*	*4.9*	*8.5*	*94*	*43%*	*.300*	*1.50*	*5.29*	*6.14*	*-0.9*	*94*

Breakout: 10% Improve: 12% Collapse: 6% Attrition: 15% MLB: 19% *Comparables: Caleb Ferguson, Nick Adenhart, J.C. Ramirez*

The Report: Muller prompted a few nervous glances when he showed up with less velocity after signing and then lost a good portion of the 2017 season as well. He gained it back this past spring and took off from there to essentially make up for the previous season. He's now on track as a potential major-league starter or strong back-end lefty reliever.

Muller is a big dude with a maxed frame. He isn't notably athletic on the mound but has surprisingly solid arm speed. He gets on hitters with quality extension to a fastball that consistently sits 91-95 with some riding life. He'll flash a plus changeup with good arm replication, and it should settle into above-average territory. He also throws two breaking balls that could both reach average. The stuff doesn't pop, but Muller does a good job using his length to jump on batters and throws strikes at a solid rate. His command won't develop beyond average, but big lefties with three average or better pitches tend to find work.

The Risks: Medium. Muller has the stuff and physicality to move quickly, but he hasn't pitched a full season beyond A-ball yet. It'll also be good to see another full season at his current velocity.

Ben Carsley's Fantasy Take: Between his status as a pop-up prospect and the likelihood that he'll continue to remain somewhat anonymous thanks to the five-thousand more notable arms ahead of him, Muller has a good argument as one of fantasy's more underrated prospects. He's not a top-101 guy, but he's likely in the top-150, making him a nice grab for fantasy owners in deeper leagues looking to fill out the bottom of their minor league rosters. There's some poor man's Eduardo Rodriguez potential here if one of the breaking balls steps up a half-grade, which is more of a compliment than it sounds like.

10 Joey Wentz LHP

OFP: 55 Likely: 45 ETA: 2020-21

Born: 10/06/97 Age: 21 Bats: L Throws: L Height: 6'5" Weight: 210 Origin: Round 1, 2016 Draft (#40 overall)

YEAR	TEAM	LVL	AGE	W	L	SV	G	GS	IP	H	HR	BB/9	K/9	K	GB%	BABIP	WHIP	ERA	DRA	WARP	PF
2016	BRA	RK	18	0	0	0	4	4	12	3	0	3.8	13.5	18	33%	.167	0.67	0.00	1.31	0.6	96
2016	DNV	RK	18	1	4	0	8	8	32	31	0	5.6	9.8	35	26%	.365	1.59	5.06	3.96	0.6	99
2017	ROM	A	19	8	3	0	26	26	131^{2}	99	4	3.1	10.4	152	41%	.293	1.10	2.60	2.80	3.8	102
2018	BRV	A+	20	3	4	0	16	16	67	49	3	3.2	7.1	53	46%	.250	1.09	2.28	4.15	0.9	97
2019	*ATL*	*MLB*	*21*	*4*	*5*	*0*	*14*	*14*	*62^{1}*	*58*	*9*	*5.3*	*8.1*	*56*	*37%*	*.293*	*1.51*	*5.13*	*5.96*	*-0.5*	*94*

Breakout: 3% Improve: 9% Collapse: 5% Attrition: 8% MLB: 15% *Comparables: Sean Reid-Foley, Mauricio Robles, Mike Montgomery*

The Report: The ERA is still shiny, but this wasn't an encouraging year for our Cole Hamels cosplaying protagonist (seriously, the mannerisms are uncanny). His control imploded around Earth Day, and Wentz started missing significant time with various injuries after a May start in which he walked six without escaping the second inning. Wentz sat out more than a month two separate times last summer, and ultimately just wasn't on the mound a whole lot from mid-May on.

When healthy, Wentz features a low-90s fastball that we've debated on at great length. Despite its merely average velocity, it tends to play up due to plane and command. The out pitch is a classic big hook, and he also features a change that's flashed. He has a large frame and a smooth motion.

There's a lot to like here, but that "when healthy" caveat looms large. The key is staying on the mound; he could pop right back into the middle of the 101 with a healthy Double-A campaign, or fall off the list entirely if things go south again.

The Risks: High. He ended up missing almost half the 2018 season. He's a pitcher whom we keep hearing about shoulder owies with (and other owies, too). His velocity remains a bit down as a pro from amateur reports that had him more consistently in the mid-90s. So there's a bit more than your generic A-ball pitching prospect risk here, and that's why we're a bit more down on him than we were.

Ben Carsley's Fantasy Take: Wentz was one of our favorite low-minors fliers a year ago, and while there's still some cause for optimism it's also time for us to cool our jets a bit. Do I still like Wentz enough to include him on a top-200 list? For sure. But he's nowhere close to the top-101 arm I'd hoped he'd be by this point, and the upside is a touch more modest than in my dreams as well. Still, don't discount him entirely just because he's 10th on this loaded list.

The Next Five:

11 Greyson Jenista OF

Born: 12/07/96 Age: 22 Bats: L Throws: R Height: 6'4" Weight: 210 Origin: Round 2, 2018 Draft (#49 overall)

YEAR	TEAM	LVL	AGE	PA	R	2B	3B	HR	RBI	BB	K	SB	CS	AVG/OBP/SLG	DRC+	VORP	BABIP	BRR	FRAA	WARP	PF
2018	DNV	RK	21	47	10	1	0	3	7	6	9	0	1	.250/.348/.500	133	2.2	.250	0.0	RF(7) 2.6, LF(2) 0.6	0.4	99
2018	ROM	A	21	130	20	5	3	1	23	10	17	4	1	.333/.377/.453	141	7.5	.373	0.2	RF(30) -0.4	0.5	100
2018	BRV	A+	21	74	3	3	1	0	4	7	15	0	0	.152/.230/.227	39	-5.8	.192	-0.6	RF(14) -0.8, CF(1) 0.0	-0.7	97
2019	*ATL*	*MLB*	*22*	*252*	*19*	*6*	*1*	*5*	*23*	*10*	*60*	*1*	*0*	*.180/.213/.281*	*28*	*-14.8*	*.214*	*0.0*	*RF 0, LF 0*	*-1.5*	*94*

Breakout: 3% Improve: 4% Collapse: 0% Attrition: 3% MLB: 4% *Comparables: Lorenzo Cain, Jorge Bonifacio, Victor Reyes*

In his first taste of pro ball, Jenista looked like a raw teenager, not a 21-year-old fresh off a successful college career. His results were hit-and-miss over three levels between short-season ball and eventually the Florida State League. Partly, that stemmed from inconsistencies in mechanics and approach. His swing was out of sync when I saw him in Rome, to the point that the three-game look was a waste. To his credit, he figured some things at that level and earned his way to Florida for the final few weeks, although he again struggled in a new uniform.

Jenista's carrying tool is obviously the huge raw power. He's physically maxed with a big frame and strength for days, and it shows in batting practice. The question is how much of that raw he'll find in games, because the swing has quite a few moving parts and tends to get long. He has decent athleticism for his size and will steal a bag or two, but it's not a part of his game and his future appears to be in left field. If Jenista struggles to translate his power from 5 to 7 p.m., he's ticketed for a Triple-A future. It's tough to turn down that kind of strength, though, and it's easy to see why the Braves gave him a chance in the second round.

12 William Contreras C

Born: 12/24/97 Age: 21 Bats: R Throws: R Height: 6'0" Weight: 180 Origin: International Free Agent, 2015

YEAR	TEAM	LVL	AGE	PA	R	2B	3B	HR	RBI	BB	K	SB	CS	AVG/OBP/SLG	DRC+	VORP	BABIP	BRR	FRAA	WARP	PF
2016	BRA	RK	18	82	8	5	0	1	8	7	15	0	1	.264/.346/.375	109	2.5	.321	-1.1	C(28)-0.7	0.0	97
2017	DNV	RK	19	198	29	10	1	4	25	24	30	1	0	.290/.379/.432	140	18.7	.326	-0.4	C(35)-0.5	0.8	94
2018	ROM	A	20	342	54	17	1	11	39	29	73	1	1	.293/.360/.463	135	23.3	.351	-0.9	C(43)-0.3	1.6	98
2018	BRV	A+	20	90	3	7	0	0	10	6	16	0	0	.253/.300/.337	103	2.5	.309	-0.3	C(20)-0.4	0.1	97
2019	*ATL*	*MLB*	*21*	*252*	*18*	*6*	*0*	*7*	*25*	*9*	*72*	*0*	*0*	*.162/.189/.272*	*18*	*-15.0*	*.196*	*-0.6*	*C 0*	*-1.6*	*94*

Breakout: 13% Improve: 14% Collapse: 0% Attrition: 13% MLB: 14% *Comparables: Francisco Mejia, Christian Vazquez, Travis d'Arnaud*

If you've caught a glimpse of Contreras behind the plate, in the box or both, you'll understand that it's not a huge risk to say he's the next big thing among catching prospects. You can't teach the athleticism that he offers at the position. His defense is raw, his receiving particularly so, but his actions are incredibly athletic. He shifts side to side with ease and has quick feet. He can struggle squaring up his body to block pitches in the dirt, but his technique should improve with reps. He shows the aptitude and athleticism to develop into at least an average defender. He pops between 1.95-2.05 with quick actions and plus carry on the throws for an above-average arm.

In the box, Contreras has an excellent power-based swing with quick hands and an explosive lower half. He lifts very well and compensates for deep hands at load with above-average bat speed. His approach is on par with his age and he should develop into an average hitter to go with above-average power based on loud contact to all fields. He projects for impact power for the position. Put it all together and Contreras has the potential to be a solid everyday catcher, with some star potential if everything clicks.

13 Jasseel De La Cruz RHP

Born: 06/26/97 Age: 22 Bats: R Throws: R Height: 6'1" Weight: 175 Origin: International Free Agent, 2015

YEAR	TEAM	LVL	AGE	W	L	SV	G	GS	IP	H	HR	BB/9	K/9	K	GB%	BABIP	WHIP	ERA	DRA	WARP	PF
2016	DBR	RK	19	2	0	0	12	3	26^{1}	23	1	4.8	6.8	20	54%	.293	1.41	3.42	3.61	0.5	121
2016	BRA	RK	19	2	0	0	6	0	15	4	0	0.6	7.2	12	46%	.114	0.33	0.00	2.05	0.6	100
2017	BRA	RK	20	2	1	0	4	4	19	13	1	3.3	8.1	17	49%	.231	1.05	1.89	3.44	0.5	97
2017	DNV	RK	20	0	2	0	7	6	23^{2}	25	1	4.2	7.2	19	57%	.316	1.52	5.32	3.39	0.7	93
2018	ROM	A	21	3	4	0	15	13	69	65	6	4.4	8.5	65	64%	.309	1.43	4.83	4.14	0.8	98
2019	*ATL*	*MLB*	*22*	*3*	*3*	*1*	*25*	*9*	54^{1}	*53*	*6*	*5.8*	*7.2*	*43*	*51%*	*.302*	*1.61*	*5.14*	*5.98*	*-0.6*	*94*

Breakout: 4% Improve: 6% Collapse: 1% Attrition: 5% MLB: 8% *Comparables: Yoervis Medina, Drew VerHagen, Dean Deetz*

De La Cruz's 2018 season was a transitional campaign. He flashed the stuff of a top-10 system prospect and, at his best, was on a similar level as Atlanta's better arms. He struggled staying healthy, though, and sometimes was pulled early after failing to adjust to setbacks. At this point, he's best labeled as a raw power arm who could go in a million directions. When healthy, he pumps a heavy 93-97 and carries it to the middle innings. His best slider is a plus pitch in the mid-80s with hard, late bite, but it's generally short and inconsistent, and his command could hold it back to solid-average. He also tosses in hard changeups in the upper-80s with enough arm replication and feel to make it worthwhile, maybe enough to flash average. He has an average frame, if not a little slight, but he can appear tough on right-handers by throwing across his body and getting decent extension with above-average arm speed. If De La Cruz can stay healthy and learn to battle on the mound, the Braves have another notable arm, likely as a power reliever.

14 Patrick Weigel RHP

Born: 07/08/94 Age: 24 Bats: R Throws: R Height: 6'6" Weight: 240 Origin: Round 7, 2015 Draft (#210 overall)

YEAR	TEAM	LVL	AGE	W	L	SV	G	GS	IP	H	HR	BB/9	K/9	K	GB%	BABIP	WHIP	ERA	DRA	WARP	PF
2016	ROM	A	21	10	4	0	22	21	129	92	7	3.3	9.4	135	46%	.264	1.08	2.51	3.18	2.9	97
2016	MIS	AA	21	1	2	0	3	3	20^{2}	9	2	3.5	7.4	17	45%	.143	0.82	2.18	3.05	0.5	94
2017	MIS	AA	22	3	0	0	7	7	37^{1}	32	2	2.7	9.2	38	37%	.300	1.15	2.89	3.16	0.9	93
2017	GWN	AAA	22	3	2	0	8	8	41	42	5	3.7	6.6	30	44%	.301	1.44	5.27	4.75	0.4	95
2019	*ATL*	*MLB*	*24*	*2*	*2*	*0*	*7*	*7*	*36^{1}*	*29*	*3*	*4.3*	*9.2*	*37*	*41%*	*.290*	*1.28*	*3.73*	*4.32*	*0.4*	*94*

Breakout: 8% Improve: 17% Collapse: 10% Attrition: 25% MLB: 36% *Comparables: Tyler Beede, Nick Pivetta, Alex Colome*

The Braves system is still very, very good, if not quite as deep as it's been in years past. That's what happens when you graduate top end talent into the core of a division winner and/or lose an entire IFA class for rampant violations of the CBA. Anyway, Weigel returns to the Braves list in part due to the new shallowness. He popped back up in the complex in August after missing more than a full year after Tommy John surgery. He was knocking on the door of the majors in early 2017 on the strength of his above-average command of mid-90s heat and a potential above-average slider, but it remains an open question what will come back in more extended pro action. There was already a fair bit of reliever risk in the profile when healthy, and if you look above him, uh, there may not be a ton of room in the Braves rotation in future years. Still, Weigel is an intriguing arm and one that might be closer than you think if it looks as good in April 2019 as it did in April 2017.

15 Freddy Tarnok RHP

Born: 11/24/98 Age: 20 Bats: R Throws: R Height: 6'3" Weight: 185 Origin: Round 3, 2017 Draft (#80 overall)

YEAR	TEAM	LVL	AGE	W	L	SV	G	GS	IP	H	HR	BB/9	K/9	K	GB%	BABIP	WHIP	ERA	DRA	WARP	PF
2017	BRA	RK	18	0	3	0	8	8	14	11	0	1.9	6.4	10	36%	.250	1.00	2.57	6.56	-0.1	101
2018	ROM	A	19	5	5	0	27	11	77^{1}	70	5	4.8	9.7	83	40%	.297	1.44	3.96	3.97	1.0	93
2019	*ATL*	*MLB*	*20*	*3*	*4*	*1*	*32*	*10*	*58^{2}*	*59*	*10*	*5.1*	*7.5*	*49*	*37%*	*.301*	*1.58*	*5.60*	*6.51*	*-1.2*	*94*

Breakout: 0% Improve: 0% Collapse: 1% Attrition: 1% MLB: 1% *Comparables: Eric Hurley, Wilmer Font, German Marquez*

The Braves threw a million-and-a-half in Tarnok's direction to get him to sign as a pitcher, and the results so far have been promising. He has an ideal, projectable pitcher's frame and the type of premium athleticism you'd expect in a two-way guy. His fastball is mostly low-90s at present but he can run it up higher in short bursts—and Tarnok did much of his work in short bursts in 2018. His power curve can get a little slurvy at times, but will flash plus 11-5 tilt. There's effort in the delivery and some head whack which can affect his command and control, but you'd think that gets ironed out with more reps. Atlanta has brought him along slowly as he didn't really get stretched out until late in the year and tossed only 77 innings. There's already a fair bit in the profile that points towards a bullpen future, but the Braves have done well with this profile recently. Tarnok is likely to be more of a slow burn than the arms listed above, but he's certainly worth monitoring.

Others of note:

Huascar Ynoa, RHP, High-A Florida

Ynoa and Tarnok make for fairly neat points of comparison. They are similar ages and pitched at similar levels. They have similar listed height/weights (although Ynoa is clearly larger and stockier now). Ynoa has more fastball at present, sitting in the mid-90s with good run. His slider is also more advanced as a primary breaker and is a projectable plus. He's more likely to be a reliever though, due to a delivery that can be described as "torquey" at the best of times and "tornadic" at most others. The command and control (or the curve and change) are unlikely to ever be good enough to start, but this is deeper than you usually start finding the 95-and-a-slider guys in most systems. And Ynoa is a better version of it than most of them.

Tucker Davidson, LHP, High-A Florida

We pegged Davidson as a potential breakout Top Ten guy on last season's list. That didn't quiiiiiite happen. He didn't consistently sustain mid-90s velocity over his first full year as a starter, and the curveball wasn't quite as sharp. A return to the pen might be in the offing at some point, despite having an ideal starter's frame. The delivery has some effort and the change hasn't developed as much as you'd like. There's still plenty of time, and Davidson could use another year of starter's reps anyway, but his future might be as a plus fastball/curve lefty pen arm. That's quite a useful piece though, so there's still plenty to like.

Kolby Allard, LHP, Atlanta Braves

We ranked Kolby Allard as the 24th best prospect in baseball coming into the season. That was—checks notes—higher than everyone else. In 2018 his velocity backslid further, his potential plus-plus hook looked fringy, and the changeup... well, that was better at least. He was only 21 and mostly fine in Triple-A. He did pitch in the majors—briefly and incredibly poorly. He's still left-handed. But yeah, we'd like that one back. Oh well...

Top Talents 25 and Under (born 4/1/93 or later):

1. Ronald Acuna Jr.
2. Ozzie Albies
3. Ian Anderson
4. Austin Riley
5. Mike Soroka
6. Kyle Wright
7. Johan Camargo
8. Dansby Swanson
9. Bryse Wilson
10. Cristian Pache

Sometimes, baseball fans do this thing where we anoint a movie as our new favorite before it even hits theaters, then wait to be disappointed. We do this mostly because we are dumb, but also because sometimes Ronald Acuna Jr. shows up and buries our good sense under a barrage of homers. After a brief, injury-interrupted adjustment period, he slashed .304/.380/.589 from June 29 on and carried the Braves to a surprise division title that he couldn't legally buy bubbly to celebrate. It looked like Ozzie Albies might require a similar paean, but an aggressive approach and weakness against righties dragged him down in the second half. Still, this is a Jose Ramirez starter kit. He's a lock for premium defense and baserunning, and a refined approach could lead to a more steady, star-level performance.

If a new youngster cements himself in the Braves core in 2019, it will likely be a pitcher. Mike Soroka and Kyle Wright are readymade No. 3 starters with the chance for more. Soroka stands out for his sturdy frame and advanced ability to manipulate and command two fastballs and a strong slider. It wouldn't be a huge shock if he blossomed into a Jameson Taillon-type presence near the front of this rotation.

Johan Camargo's defensive metrics may weigh on his WARP readouts as he moves into a Marwin Gonzalez role, but his bat is the important part. Having just turned 25 in December, he has 780 plate appearances on the ledger to prove he strikes out less often than average while connecting for consistent extra-base power. It's possible that he doesn't become a standout in the traditional sense, but wielding this strong a stick while manning the infield portends a long, useful career ahead.

That competence against the world's best pitchers lands Camargo ahead of Dansby Swanson. With his prospect pedigree fading in the rearview mirror, we're fast approaching reassessment time for the former No. 1 pick. While Swanson posted 2.4 WARP in 2019, it was mostly a credit to solid play at shortstop. Heaven knows the team will never regret acquiring him, but if his defense is the only calling card, we're always going to wonder about his longevity and consistency. So, until his DRC+ touches 90, it's probably time to view him as a failsafe more than a cornerstone.

It's not hard to formulate an argument that Swanson's present reality is one of Cristian Pache's worst-case scenarios. The latter is nearly a lock to play superb defense in center field—an increasingly sought-after skill given the game's batted ball tendencies—and he certainly has the raw physical ability to make huge strides at the plate. That leaves quite a few likely 2019 contributors—A.J. Minter and Touki Toussaint and Sean Newcomb and Luiz Gohara—off this arbitrarily conceived top 10, as role players will have a tough time grabbing headlines in this organization. Minter and Toussaint's bat-missing abilities are probably the best bets to rise up and stake a claim to stardom, but all these arms could eventually present a welcome quandary for the Braves: In the shifting pitching landscape, is a solid arm best used as a No. 4 starter, a relief ace, or trade bait?

Baltimore Orioles

The State of the System:

The rebuild has begun. It's, uh, gonna take a while.

The Top Ten:

1 Yusniel Diaz OF   OFP: 60   Likely: 55   ETA: Late 2019

Born: 10/07/96   Age: 22   Bats: R   Throws: R   Height: 6'1"   Weight: 195   Origin: International Free Agent, 2015

YEAR	TEAM	LVL	AGE	PA	R	2B	3B	HR	RBI	BB	K	SB	CS	AVG/OBP/SLG	DRC+	VORP	BABIP	BRR	FRAA	WARP	PF
2016	RCU	A+	19	348	47	8	7	8	54	29	71	7	8	.272/.333/.418	100	8.7	.326	-2.1	CF(34) -6.1, RF(15) -0.7	-0.9	100
2017	RCU	A+	20	374	42	15	3	8	39	35	73	7	9	.278/.343/.414	96	8.9	.328	-1.0	CF(29) 1.8, RF(26) -1.2	-0.3	108
2017	TUL	AA	20	118	15	8	0	3	13	10	29	2	5	.333/.390/.491	151	6.6	.434	-0.8	RF(26) -0.6, CF(5) -0.1	0.4	101
2018	TUL	AA	21	264	36	10	4	6	30	41	39	8	8	.314/.428/.477	159	21.5	.360	1.8	CF(29) -1.7, RF(28) -1.6	1.5	110
2018	BOW	AA	21	152	23	5	1	5	15	18	28	4	5	.239/.329/.403	97	4.6	.267	-0.5	RF(29) 0.3, CF(6) -0.5	-0.1	99
2019	*BAL*	*MLB*	*22*	*252*	*26*	*7*	*1*	*7*	*27*	*16*	*64*	*3*	*3*	*.214/.264/.348*	*63*	*-3.6*	*.259*	*-0.6*	*RF 0, CF -1*	*-0.5*	*108*

Breakout: 11%   Improve: 35%   Collapse: 1%   Attrition: 21%   MLB: 36%   *Comparables: Domonic Brown, Billy McKinney, Caleb Gindl*

The Report: Diaz's bat carried him to the top of this list. He has excellent hand-eye coordination and solid quick-twitch which allows him to barrel the ball even though his swing can lengthen at times. The longer swing allows him to tap into his average raw power, although his swing plane is a bit flat and his hardest contact comes on low line drives. He has a patient approach with an excellent feel for the zone and quality pitch recognition. He could be a fine hitter without any further adjustments, but the flat plane seems exactly the type of swing that the Dodgers would have tweaked to unlock more XBH power. Now he's with the Orioles in a transitory time; it will be interesting to see if the player development staff has any adjustments in mind.

Diaz is an average runner and, as he's completely filled out, he will likely remain one for a while. He has solid instincts in the outfield and an above-average arm, which should allow him to be fringy in center or above average in right. Diaz can be too aggressive on the basepaths and he probably won't be much of a base-stealing threat.

Even with a solid defensive profile in right, Diaz will need to hit to provide significant value. Fortunately for O's fans, he's a good bet to do so. His fluid athleticism and hand-eye coordination should fuel above-average production with room for more if a swing adjustment unlocks more pop.

The Risks: Low. Diaz is about ready for prime time, although there's a small chance that big-league pitchers will exploit his lengthy swing enough to limit him to platoon duty. His power needs to play at least fringe-average for him to be an above-average regular, and there's a chance that that adjustment never happens.

Ben Carsley's Fantasy Take: Diaz is a good fantasy prospect, but his valuation should fluctuate pretty heavily based on your league size. Do you play in The Dynasty Guru Experts (TDGX) League-sized formats with 20-plus teams? If so, Diaz is an easy top-50 dynasty prospect as someone who's a safe bet to become an everyday regular. In shallower formats, Diaz may end up as more of just A Guy, albeit one who contributes solidly across the board. From a fantasy perspective, we've compared his ceiling to prime Melky Cabrera in the past, and that still feels apt. He's got a very clear path to playing time to boot.

2 Ryan Mountcastle 3B OFP: 60 Likely: 50 ETA: 2020

Born: 02/18/97 Age: 22 Bats: R Throws: R Height: 6'3" Weight: 195 Origin: Round 1, 2015 Draft (#36 overall)

YEAR	TEAM	LVL	AGE	PA	R	2B	3B	HR	RBI	BB	K	SB	CS	AVG/OBP/SLG	DRC+	VORP	BABIP	BRR	FRAA	WARP	PF
2016	DEL	A	19	489	53	28	4	10	51	25	95	5	4	.281/.319/.426	111	25.2	.331	-1.7	SS(105) -21.1	-1.0	95
2017	FRD	A+	20	379	63	35	1	15	47	14	61	8	2	.314/.343/.542	135	28.9	.343	1.5	SS(76) -12.1	1.1	108
2017	BOW	AA	20	159	18	13	0	3	15	3	35	0	0	.222/.239/.366	57	-0.4	.265	0.5	3B(37) -1.1	-0.6	106
2018	BOW	AA	21	428	63	19	4	13	59	26	79	2	0	.297/.341/.464	117	22.2	.339	-1.5	3B(81) -4.9	0.8	100
2019	*BAL*	*MLB*	*22*	*252*	*22*	*12*	*1*	*8*	*30*	*5*	*61*	*0*	*0*	*.224/.240/.376*	*64*	*-5.3*	*.265*	*-0.3*	*3B -3*	*-0.8*	*108*

Breakout: 16% Improve: 30% Collapse: 6% Attrition: 25% MLB: 36% *Comparables: Josh Vitters, Brandon Laird, Renato Nunez*

The Report: A scouting cliché we reference often on the prospect team: "When in doubt, just pick the best hitter." His power may or may not come. He may or may not stick up the middle. But if he hits, who cares, really? Ryan Mountcastle can hit. His swing gets long from time-to-time, usually when he's trying to add leverage to get his plus raw power into play, but when everything is working it just looks right. We do think the power will come, and if he's a 60 hit/55 power bat, so what about the rest, really?

I suppose we do have to cover it though. So, the rest: Mountcastle has a well-below-average arm, so third base is unlikely to work out any better than shortstop did, despite adequate instincts and hands for the hot corner. It's possible Mountcastle could handle second, but he could grow off the keystone as well, making left field or even first base a more likely long-term defensive home. That puts significant pressure on the bat to play to projection.

The Risks: Medium. We love the bat, and he conquered Double-A at 21, but it's unclear where Mountcastle will end up on the defensive spectrum.

Ben Carsley's Fantasy Take: For my money, Mountcastle is the best fantasy prospect in the system and one of my favorite pure bats in all the minors. There are some warts, sure, but it's also easy to see Mountcastle following the Nick Castellanos career path and blooming into a top-10 fantasy third baseman or top-25 fantasy outfielder. Count any years you get 3B/CI eligibility out of him as a blessing, and bank on a .280-plus average with 20 bombs and solid R/RBI totals for the long haul.

3 DL Hall LHP OFP: 60 Likely: 50 ETA: Late 2020

Born: 09/19/98 Age: 20 Bats: L Throws: L Height: 6'2" Weight: 195 Origin: Round 1, 2017 Draft (#21 overall)

YEAR	TEAM	LVL	AGE	W	L	SV	G	GS	IP	H	HR	BB/9	K/9	K	GB%	BABIP	WHIP	ERA	DRA	WARP	PF
2017	ORI	RK	18	0	0	0	5	5	10^{1}	10	1	8.7	10.5	12	58%	.360	1.94	6.97	4.79	0.1	114
2018	DEL	A	19	2	7	0	22	20	94^{1}	68	6	4.0	9.5	100	46%	.262	1.17	2.10	3.69	1.7	90
2019	*BAL*	*MLB*	*20*	*2*	*7*	*0*	*14*	*14*	57^{2}	*62*	*11*	*7.6*	*8.1*	*52*	*44%*	*.304*	*1.91*	*6.89*	*6.85*	*-0.9*	*108*

Breakout: 2% Improve: 2% Collapse: 1% Attrition: 3% MLB: 4% *Comparables: Josh Hader, Sean Gallagher, Jeurys Familia*

The Report: Baltimore's 2017 first-round pick had a strong full-season debut and spent the entire year as a 19-year-old in the South Atlantic League. Beyond the eye-popping top line stats, Hall looks every bit the part of a high-ranking lefty prospect arm. His fastball sits in the mid-90s and can touch higher. It's a heavy pitch which he will also cut, and it shows late life when he wants to elevate it for a strikeout. He pairs it with a power curve that flashes plus. It's a big, tight breaker that he can start in the zone and entice chases, or drop in for a strike.

Hall's slider and change lag behind at present. The slider is shorter and shows a different look with average depth at times, but is too often a flat 10-4 offering. The straight change benefits from his deceptive arm action, but is well below average at present, and hangs in the zone too often.

Mechanically, Hall has some things to iron out as well. It's an uptempo but inconsistent delivery that leaves his upper and lower halves out of sync at times. He'll throw across his body with slingy arm action and a bit of crossfire. That adds deception to the fastball, but also makes the command projection more average than plus. He won't always finish his pitches off and will miss armside and up here and there. If you guessed that Hall is a mid-rotation starting pitching prospect who needs to improve his command and third pitch, congratulations, you've been here before. Did you remember your punch card? There will be plenty more arms like this to come over the next couple hundred of pages as well.

The Risks: High. I believe we used the "He's an Orioles pitching prospect named "DL" joke a fair bit last year. So this year I will just point out that a pre-draft comp I got from a prospect team member was Scott Kazmir. So yeah, those risks...

Ben Carsley's Fantasy Take:

The thing about Hall is that he's an Orioles pitching prospect. Maybe the front office overhaul in Baltimore will lead to better results for this particular breed of dynasty asset, but I'll believe it when I see it. There's enough upside and a short enough timeline here that you can make Hall a top-200 guy if you want to. I won't, because I'm a cynic.

4 Grayson Rodriguez RHP   OFP: 60   Likely: 45   ETA: 2023

Born: 11/16/99 Age: 19 Bats: L Throws: R Height: 6'5" Weight: 220 Origin: Round 1, 2018 Draft (#11 overall)

YEAR	TEAM	LVL	AGE	W	L	SV	G	GS	IP	H	HR	BB/9	K/9	K	GB%	BABIP	WHIP	ERA	DRA	WARP	PF
2018	ORI	RK	18	0	2	0	9	8	19^{1}	17	0	3.3	9.3	20	43%	.321	1.24	1.40	2.91	0.7	97
2019	*BAL*	*MLB*	*19*	*1*	*3*	*0*	*11*	*8*	*31*	*36*	*6*	*6.2*	*7.1*	*24*	*42%*	*.314*	*1.85*	*6.53*	*6.46*	*-0.4*	*108*

Breakout: 0% Improve: 0% Collapse: 0% Attrition: 0% MLB: 0% *Comparables: Jaime Barria, Bryse Wilson, Raul Alcantara*

The Report: Rodriguez ticks almost every box on the "first-round-Texas-prep-arm" checklist. He lags behind the standard a bit in projectability, but that's only because he's already a very large human. He has the requisite big fastball, sitting around 95 and touching the upper-90s at times. He has a potential plus secondary in the arsenal as well, a power slider with good late tilt.

The rest of the four-pitch mix is below-average—which, granted, is also one of the boxes here. Rodriguez works in a loopy curve and a developing change to round out his repertoire. The mechanics don't scream "slam-dunk-starter" either, as he is very upright and stiff, without much leg drive, and he relies on his arm speed and late torque to hit 98. The arm action is inconsistent and high-effort as well. Still, there are worse building blocks for a pitching prospect than a well-developed 6-foot-5 frame and a potential plus fastball/slider combo.

The Risks: High. He's a prep arm in the complex who needs to develop his secondaries and he has relatively high reliever risk.

Ben Carsley's Fantasy Take: Too long a lead time, too low of a fantasy ceiling and too much an Oriole. Check back next year.

5 Ryan McKenna OF   OFP: 55   Likely: 45   ETA: Early 2020

Born: 02/14/97 Age: 22 Bats: R Throws: R Height: 5'11" Weight: 185 Origin: Round 4, 2015 Draft (#133 overall)

YEAR	TEAM	LVL	AGE	PA	R	2B	3B	HR	RBI	BB	K	SB	CS	AVG/OBP/SLG	DRC+	VORP	BABIP	BRR	FRAA	WARP	PF
2016	ABE	A-	19	252	29	10	1	1	26	22	59	17	6	.241/.320/.309	103	8.0	.319	1.5	CF(57) 0.5	0.4	97
2017	DEL	A	20	530	62	33	2	7	42	43	128	20	2	.256/.331/.380	116	29.0	.336	-0.2	CF(124) -7.6	0.9	92
2018	FRD	A+	21	301	60	18	2	8	37	37	45	5	6	.377/.467/.556	210	46.2	.436	2.5	CF(64) -6.2, LF(2) -0.2	3.4	105
2018	BOW	AA	21	250	35	8	2	3	16	29	56	4	1	.239/.341/.338	91	10.6	.312	2.6	CF(55) 3.4, RF(3) 2.1	0.9	100
2019	*BAL*	*MLB*	*22*	*252*	*26*	*8*	*1*	*6*	*22*	*17*	*69*	*2*	*1*	*.200/.260/.318*	*54*	*-4.5*	*.254*	*-0.2*	*CF -1, LF 0*	*-0.6*	*108*

Breakout: 17% Improve: 44% Collapse: 0% Attrition: 18% MLB: 47% *Comparables: Delino DeShields, Ryan Kalish, Andrew McCutchen*

The Report: A major-league average (50) tool grade doesn't get much effusive praise around these parts. There are some selection bias issues here. The players who make these lists generally have a standout tool or two to fill out the 200-word count for our blurbs. McKenna offers no such easy narrative. He does everything averagely well. That is major-league average though. And it's easy to forget how impressive average major-league talent is. His hit tool—yes, it's a five—presents as short to the ball with above-average barrel control. It's more of a line drive swing, but there's enough leverage that he will get to most of his 50 raw power in play. He's an average center fielder with an average arm. While he's a plus runner at present, he figures to slow down into the average to solid-average range in the majors. It's not quite the five-tool center fielder we tend to rave about—the game power will likely play below-average with some pull-side pop against lefties—but McKenna has turned himself into a quality major-league prospect. It's coincidental that he slots in at #5 in the system, but it does create a nice bit of rankinative determinism.

The Risks: Medium. McKenna hasn't aced Double-A yet and may lack a carrying a tool. Sometimes the average-across-the-board guys play up, other times we find out they aren't actually average-across-the-board. If you want to look for positive risk, he is a cold weather prep bat who just had a bit of a breakout season, which can be a positive marker for additional growth.

Ben Carsley's Fantasy Take: Given the balanced overall skill set, his proximity to the majors and the fact that he could play in a very favorable home park, it's safe to say McKenna is a better fantasy prospect than an IRL one. The risk is that his tweener profile pushes him out of everyday playing time, but given the dearth of talent on the O's roster at present, hopefully he can stave off such a future. McKenna doesn't profile as a guy who'll win you any leagues, but could he be well-rounded enough to push his way to OF4 or OF5 status in deeper formats? Sure. He probably won't make the top-101, but he might make a top-150.

6 Dillon Tate RHP   OFP: 55   Likely: 45   ETA: 2019

Born: 05/01/94 Age: 25 Bats: R Throws: R Height: 6'2" Weight: 195 Origin: Round 1, 2015 Draft (#4 overall)

YEAR	TEAM	LVL	AGE	W	L	SV	G	GS	IP	H	HR	BB/9	K/9	K	GB%	BABIP	WHIP	ERA	DRA	WARP	PF
2016	HIC	A	22	3	3	0	17	16	65	78	5	3.7	7.6	55	44%	.376	1.62	5.12	3.36	1.2	96
2016	CSC	A	22	1	0	0	7	0	17^{1}	21	1	3.1	7.8	15	57%	.351	1.56	3.12	4.77	0.0	100
2017	TAM	A+	23	6	0	0	9	9	58^{1}	48	4	2.3	7.1	46	61%	.262	1.08	2.62	3.97	0.9	102
2017	TRN	AA	23	1	2	0	4	4	25	23	3	3.2	6.1	17	56%	.270	1.28	3.24	5.19	0.0	96
2018	TRN	AA	24	5	2	0	15	15	82^{2}	67	7	2.7	8.2	75	48%	.263	1.11	3.38	3.18	2.1	88
2018	BOW	AA	24	2	3	0	7	7	40^{2}	48	3	2.0	4.6	21	63%	.324	1.40	5.75	4.28	0.5	101
2019	*BAL*	*MLB*	*25*	*1*	*1*	*0*	*14*	*3*	*26^{2}*	*30*	*4*	*3.6*	*6.2*	*19*	*48%*	*.304*	*1.52*	*5.38*	*5.26*	*0.0*	*108*

Breakout: 10% Improve: 15% Collapse: 13% Attrition: 23% MLB: 33% *Comparables: Alex Wilson, Sam Howard, Myles Jaye*

The Report: Put aside his draft status as the fourth overall pick three-and-a-half years ago and what you have is a 95-and-a-slider guy with terribly inconsistent performance due to command that comes and goes. The fastball is pretty straight. He doesn't always hold his velocity well. It's a plus-flashing slider, but one of the things that's changed in baseball over the last decade is that a whole lot of pitchers have a plus-flashing slider now. The changeup still isn't quite what you want. The fastball/slider combo can be good enough, and the changeup isn't hopeless. Even coming off a hideous end to the season as a 24-year-old in Double-A, there's still flickering hope for a mid-rotation arm. He's also pitched better at times out of the pen, and the stigma on dumping your top pitching prospects there is dissipating. At some point though, someone's developmental clock ticks long enough that you stop giving him the benefit of the doubt; the guys selected two picks ahead of Tate and three picks behind him were also college draftees of the same age, and both are already established MLB stars.

The Risks: Well, there's a heck of a lot of signs here he's going to end up in the bullpen, aren't there? Strictly speaking we aren't supposed to care about the organizational change when writing him up, but the Orioles pitching development has become an industry punchline, and he was much worse after the trade. There's also a long history of underperformance here, such that he's gotten traded twice now already.

Ben Carsley's Fantasy Take: Well, if you've held on to Tate all this time, I guess you can take the fact that he's somewhat dynasty-relevant again as a good sign. But the real question is: why did you hold on to Tate this long? He's bounced around multiple organizations that would be terrible for his future fantasy value, and the odds that he's just a frustrating reliever in the end are too high. You gotta know when to hold em, know when to fold em, know when to walk away, etc.

7 Keegan Akin LHP   OFP: 50   Likely: 45   ETA: Late 2019

Born: 04/01/95 Age: 24 Bats: L Throws: L Height: 6'0" Weight: 225 Origin: Round 2, 2016 Draft (#54 overall)

YEAR	TEAM	LVL	AGE	W	L	SV	G	GS	IP	H	HR	BB/9	K/9	K	GB%	BABIP	WHIP	ERA	DRA	WARP	PF
2016	ABE	A-	21	0	1	0	9	9	26	15	0	2.4	10.0	29	51%	.231	0.85	1.04	4.46	0.2	93
2017	FRD	A+	22	7	8	0	21	21	100	89	12	4.1	10.0	111	38%	.307	1.35	4.14	5.88	-0.7	109
2018	BOW	AA	23	14	7	0	25	25	137^{2}	114	16	3.8	9.3	142	32%	.278	1.25	3.27	4.07	2.0	102
2019	*BAL*	*MLB*	*24*	*5*	*9*	*0*	*22*	*22*	*106^{1}*	*109*	*21*	*4.2*	*8.5*	*100*	*35%*	*.297*	*1.50*	*5.60*	*5.51*	*0.0*	*108*

Breakout: 6% Improve: 11% Collapse: 5% Attrition: 12% MLB: 19% *Comparables: Caleb Smith, James Houser, Drew Anderson*

The Report: Last year Akin slotted in at seventh in a below-average Orioles system as your typical funky lefty starter with a decent change-up and a fastball around 90. This year he slots in at seven once again, but both he and the system are markedly improved. It's easy to peg the culprit here. Akin's fastball has jumped to 93-95 and touches 97. The plus velo—combined with a hitchy, deceptive delivery, a bit of gloveside run, and above-average command—generated a lot of late swings from Double-A hitters. While Akin never had a frame you would call "projectable," the velocity bump makes his fastball a borderline plus-plus offering at its best. The fastball will need to carry the profile here as the changeup is merely average and the slider below that. The latter is a flat 1-8 offering that breaks enough to keep it off barrels most of the time, but lacks the depth to consistently miss bats. The improved fastball hasn't markedly changed the ceiling here, but it makes Akin more likely to have a substantial major-league career.

The Risks: Low. As a close-to-the-majors lefty with now plus velocity and a bit of funk, Akin is a low-ceiling guy, but likely to get major-league opportunities.

Ben Carsley's Fantasy Take: If you read the DL Hall blurb and thought "I just wish this prospect had less upside," Akin is the guy for you. Also why is every Orioles lefty's name a synonym for being in pain?

8 Austin Hays OF

OFP: 50 Likely: 45 ETA: Debuted in 2017

Born: 07/05/95 Age: 23 Bats: R Throws: R Height: 6'1" Weight: 195 Origin: Round 3, 2016 Draft (#91 overall)

YEAR	TEAM	LVL	AGE	PA	R	2B	3B	HR	RBI	BB	K	SB	CS	AVG/OBP/SLG	DRC+	VORP	BABIP	BRR	FRAA	WARP	PF
2016	ABE	A-	20	153	14	9	2	4	21	11	32	4	3	.336/.386/.514	171	15.7	.410	-0.9	RF(20) 0.3, CF(5) 0.1	1.0	100
2017	FRD	A+	21	280	42	15	3	16	41	12	40	4	6	.328/.364/.592	147	26.0	.337	0.7	CF(57) 8.1, RF(4) -0.6	2.5	109
2017	BOW	AA	21	283	39	17	2	16	54	13	45	1	1	.330/.367/.594	152	31.3	.345	3.2	CF(31) -3.3, RF(29) -0.4	1.7	105
2017	BAL	MLB	21	63	4	3	0	1	8	2	16	0	0	.217/.238/.317	70	-3.2	.273	-0.4	RF(14) -1.6, CF(8) -1.3	-0.4	103
2018	BOW	AA	22	288	34	12	2	12	43	12	59	6	3	.242/.271/.432	89	8.3	.263	0.9	RF(36) 6.7, LF(16) -0.3	0.6	98
2019	*BAL*	*MLB*	*23*	*276*	*29*	*12*	*1*	*11*	*37*	*7*	*67*	*2*	*1*	*.238/.261/.419*	*76*	*-0.3*	*.274*	*-0.3*	*RF 0, LF 0*	*0.0*	*108*

Breakout: 15% Improve: 44% Collapse: 2% Attrition: 22% MLB: 54% *Comparables: Dayan Viciedo, Josh Kroeger, Anthony Santander*

The Report: This feels unfair to Hays who broke out across two levels in 2017 and made the majors that September. While we weren't quite as high on his ultimate ceiling as some of our prospect-ranking counterparts, we did have him comfortably as a Top 101 guy, and the second best prospect in the system. How'd he do in 2018? Well, he was bad and then he was hurt. This ranking may be a bit of an overreaction, but let's zoom out a bit.

Hays had about a half-season of Double-A baseball before his call-up. Now he has about a season and has posted a slugging-heavy .829 OPS at appropriate prospect ages. He had to have offseason ankle surgery to remedy the issue that limited him to a half-season last year. There are mitigating factors all over his 2018, and honestly the ordinal distance between him and Ryan McKenna overstates the gap as prospects. That said, like McKenna he is a "sum of the average tools" guy and doesn't even have McKenna's glove in center. When you get evidence that one of those 50-55 offensive tools might not play to projection, the whole profile becomes far riskier.

The Risks: Low. While we aren't quite as sold on the plus regular ceiling as we were last year, a healthy Hays should be a productive major-league piece in 2019.

Ben Carsley's Fantasy Take: Hays was a guy I liked a lot a year ago, and I'm not ready to jump ship just yet. He's got a clear path to playing time (stop me if you've heard that before) and while he's not the defender McKenna is, his fantasy profile is starkly similar. He might just be a fourth outfielder, sure, but fourth outfielders who play every day because their teams are bad can still have some value.

9 Luis Ortiz RHP

OFP: 50 Likely: 40 ETA: Debuted in 2018

Born: 09/22/95 Age: 23 Bats: R Throws: R Height: 6'3" Weight: 230 Origin: Round 1, 2014 Draft (#30 overall)

YEAR	TEAM	LVL	AGE	W	L	SV	G	GS	IP	H	HR	BB/9	K/9	K	GB%	BABIP	WHIP	ERA	DRA	WARP	PF
2016	HDS	A+	20	3	2	0	7	6	27^{2}	23	4	2.0	9.1	28	51%	.264	1.05	2.60	3.19	0.7	106
2016	FRI	AA	20	1	4	1	9	8	39^{2}	47	3	1.6	7.7	34	47%	.352	1.36	4.08	4.10	0.5	107
2016	BLX	AA	20	2	2	0	6	6	23^{1}	26	2	3.9	6.2	16	33%	.316	1.54	1.93	3.41	0.5	90
2017	BLX	AA	21	4	7	0	22	20	94^{1}	79	12	3.5	7.5	79	36%	.258	1.23	4.01	3.43	1.9	99
2018	BLX	AA	22	3	4	2	16	11	68	63	7	2.4	8.6	65	48%	.289	1.19	3.71	3.49	1.4	98
2018	NOR	AAA	22	2	1	0	6	6	31^{2}	34	4	2.3	6.0	21	40%	.297	1.33	3.69	7.37	-0.6	94
2018	BAL	MLB	22	0	1	0	2	1	2^{1}	7	0	11.6	0.0	0	53%	.467	4.29	15.43	7.94	-0.1	104
2019	*BAL*	*MLB*	*23*	*2*	*2*	*0*	*16*	*5*	38^{1}	*41*	*6*	*3.3*	*7.3*	*31*	*41%*	*.304*	*1.45*	*5.13*	*5.01*	*0.1*	*108*

Breakout: 11% Improve: 15% Collapse: 13% Attrition: 28% MLB: 34% *Comparables: Taylor Guerrieri, Alex Cobb, Ronald Herrera*

The Report: It feels like we have been writing about Ortiz forever. You know the cliff notes by now—hefty righty, plus fastball, oft-injured, traded twice. Well, the fastball isn't quite plus anymore, whether due to his litany of maladies or just normal pitching prospect attrition. His fastball sits more in the low-90s now, touching 95. It still features good run and sink when it's down in the zone, but it's very hittable when elevated, and his velocity can tick down into the upper-80s later in starts. The movement keeps the pitch above-average and covers at times for average command. Ortiz fills out his repertoire with an average change that works off the fastball well with similar movement in the low-80s; an average, mid-80s slider with short, late tilt; and a fringy curve he steals strikes with now and again. He's no longer a Top 101 candidate, and he still has durability issues: He missed a month early in the year and left his first big-league start with a pulled hamstring. But he's reached the majors and is now with an organization that will have, uh, let's say "starting pitching opportunities" in the short-to-medium term.

The Risks: Medium. Ortiz got a cup of coffee in the majors, but he didn't exactly look great, and has still never thrown 100 innings in a season.

Ben Carsley's Fantasy Take: Well, if innings pitched is your league's only pitching category, Ortiz might end up being decent. If you care about scary things like ERA, WHIP and W, however, Ortiz is best left to the waiver wire.

10 Jean Carlos Encarnacion 3B

OFP: 50 Likely: 45 ETA: 2021

Born: 01/17/98 Age: 21 Bats: R Throws: R Height: 6'3" Weight: 195 Origin: International Free Agent, 2016

YEAR	TEAM	LVL	AGE	PA	R	2B	3B	HR	RBI	BB	K	SB	CS	AVG/OBP/SLG	DRC+	VORP	BABIP	BRR	FRAA	WARP	PF
2016	DBR	RK	18	156	19	3	3	0	16	11	30	4	0	.264/.340/.329	100	6.5	.336	1.4	3B(19) -2.0, SS(16) 0.0	0.3	114
2017	BRA	RK	19	107	16	8	4	2	16	4	22	4	2	.350/.374/.563	149	10.6	.430	0.3	3B(15) -1.9, 1B(14) 1.0	0.3	103
2017	DNV	RK	19	98	14	3	0	1	6	3	21	3	5	.290/.316/.355	105	6.2	.361	0.9	3B(23) 4.1	0.6	91
2018	ROM	A	20	379	45	23	5	10	57	13	100	5	5	.288/.314/.463	105	24.8	.370	-0.2	3B(92) 5.0	1.2	98
2018	DEL	A	20	104	10	4	2	2	7	3	34	0	0	.218/.240/.356	106	2.6	.308	2.2	3B(21) 2.0	0.6	87
2019	*BAL*	*MLB*	*21*	*252*	*16*	*3*	*0*	*6*	*23*	*1*	*82*	*0*	*0*	*.170/.173/.258*	*6*	*-22.9*	*.223*	*-0.4*	*3B 2*	*-2.2*	*108*

Breakout: 5% Improve: 8% Collapse: 0% Attrition: 8% MLB: 8% *Comparables: Josh Bell, Nick Castellanos, Neftali Soto*

The Report: Encarnacion was one of the most polarizing reports in the South Atlantic League. Reports varied considerably depending on when the evaluator saw him. The easy tools to nail down are his raw power, which will end up at least plus, and an above-average arm that plays at third. He has the swing to tap into this power, with big lift and extension out front. How much he gets to in games is the question.

Encarnacion is susceptible to basic sequencing, and his lengthy cut suggests that there will likely be plenty of swing and miss long-term. His swing will look different from one at-bat to the next, and between that and his lack of discipline, he projects as a below-average hitter. Encarnacion's glove is equally iffy. He has smooth actions at times, but he'll take plays off and goes to the backhand too often. He needs to make strides to stick at third, but he has the athleticism to stick there as a fringe-average defender. Ultimately, Encarnacion's tools suggest a high-ceiling corner-infield slugger with huge projection, but the gap between his present and potential abilities is massive, and will require time and patience.

The Risks: Very High. The gap between Encarnacion's present and potential is huge. A lackadaisical approach at times doesn't help, but athletic actions and size are in his favor.

Ben Carsley's Fantasy Take: Encarnacion is a good one for your watch list, but the risk/reward mix isn't favorable enough to make him a truly meaningfully dynasty asset yet. Keep an eye on him though, and pick him up in deeper leagues if the power plays at High-A.

The Next Five:

11 Bruce Zimmermann LHP

Born: 02/09/95 Age: 24 Bats: L Throws: L Height: 6'2" Weight: 215 Origin: Round 5, 2017 Draft (#140 overall)

YEAR	TEAM	LVL	AGE	W	L	SV	G	GS	IP	H	HR	BB/9	K/9	K	GB%	BABIP	WHIP	ERA	DRA	WARP	PF
2017	DNV	RK	22	0	1	0	11	11	23^{1}	21	0	3.5	10.8	28	58%	.350	1.29	3.09	3.10	0.7	91
2018	ROM	A	23	7	3	0	14	14	84^{2}	74	5	1.9	10.5	99	48%	.319	1.09	2.76	3.12	2.1	97
2018	MIS	AA	23	2	1	0	6	6	28^{2}	25	3	6.0	8.2	26	41%	.286	1.53	3.14	4.95	0.1	92
2018	BOW	AA	23	2	3	0	5	5	21^{1}	25	2	3.0	6.8	16	30%	.324	1.50	5.06	7.19	-0.5	99
2019	*BAL*	*MLB*	*24*	*4*	*8*	*0*	*20*	*20*	*91*	*98*	*16*	*4.4*	*8.1*	*81*	*44%*	*.309*	*1.57*	*5.55*	*5.44*	*0.0*	*108*

Breakout: 7% Improve: 13% Collapse: 4% Attrition: 9% MLB: 17% *Comparables: Dinelson Lamet, Matt Hall, Alex Wilson*

Zimmermann is an advanced left-hander with the command to carve up the minor leagues and the stuff of an up-and-down guy or long reliever. His fringy fastball doesn't have much life or movement, but it sits in the low-90s and plays up because of his command. The better secondary varies from start to start, but his changeup has greater potential at solid-average with fade and arm speed. The breaker should settle at fringe-average with moderate bite and depth. Zimmermann is maxed out physically and he has a durable frame conducive to eating innings. Players like this tend to produce in the minors before big-league hitters expose the limitations of a pitchability arm without a dominant secondary.

12 Adam Hall SS

Born: 05/22/99 Age: 20 Bats: R Throws: R Height: 6'0" Weight: 170 Origin: Round 2, 2017 Draft (#60 overall)

YEAR	TEAM	LVL	AGE	PA	R	2B	3B	HR	RBI	BB	K	SB	CS	AVG/OBP/SLG	DRC+	VORP	BABIP	BRR	FRAA	WARP	PF
2018	ABE	A-	19	256	35	9	3	1	24	17	58	22	5	.293/.368/.374	134	24.9	.386	2.6	SS(59) -3.0, 2B(4) 0.4	1.0	92
2019	*BAL*	*MLB*	*20*	*252*	*26*	*3*	*1*	*5*	*18*	*4*	*81*	*7*	*2*	*.179/.209/.266*	*21*	*-13.4*	*.244*	*1.1*	*SS -1, 2B 0*	*-1.6*	*108*

Breakout: 5% Improve: 5% Collapse: 0% Attrition: 1% MLB: 5% *Comparables: Tyler Wade, Amed Rosario, Tim Beckham*

A second-round pick out of a Canadian high school, Hall has good instincts at short and covers a lot of ground at the six. He's less physical than most other prospects in his draft orbit. He looks shorter than his listed height—six feet on the dot in the media guide—and he's not especially toolsy. He does make plenty of contact and he's a disciplined hitter, so he's not a total black hole at the plate. Ultimately though, Hall's more of a reliable defender with an adequate bat than any kind of building block.

13 Zac Lowther LHP

Born: 04/30/96 Age: 23 Bats: L Throws: L Height: 6'2" Weight: 235 Origin: Round 2, 2017 Draft (#74 overall)

YEAR	TEAM	LVL	AGE	W	L	SV	G	GS	IP	H	HR	BB/9	K/9	K	GB%	BABIP	WHIP	ERA	DRA	WARP	PF
2017	ABE	A-	21	2	2	0	12	11	54¹	35	1	1.8	12.4	75	47%	.283	0.85	1.66	2.59	1.7	101
2018	DEL	A	22	3	1	0	6	6	31	12	2	2.6	14.8	51	33%	.192	0.68	1.16	2.38	1.0	94
2018	FRD	A+	22	5	3	0	17	16	92²	74	6	2.5	9.7	100	40%	.288	1.08	2.53	3.88	1.5	105
2019	*BAL*	*MLB*	*23*	*4*	*7*	*0*	*17*	*17*	*87¹*	*85*	*14*	*3.4*	*9.3*	*90*	*37%*	*.301*	*1.35*	*4.67*	*4.53*	*0.9*	*108*

Breakout: 3% Improve: 6% Collapse: 15% Attrition: 17% MLB: 25% *Comparables: Aaron Blair, Jon Gray, Dylan Bundy*

Lowther lacks a blazing fastball, true out pitch, or elite command, but he still pitched well across two levels in 2018. The southpaw's success stems from his deceptive motion. He works from a low three-quarters arm slot, and uses a long stride to get his arm over the front of his body. Hitters don't see the ball well and that helps his pedestrian velocity play up. Lowther also has an above-average curveball with depth; his slider and changeup are both fringy. He works both sides of the plate well, and his plus command could allow him to stick as a No. 5 starter.

14 Alex Wells LHP

Born: 02/27/97 Age: 22 Bats: L Throws: L Height: 6'1" Weight: 190 Origin: International Free Agent, 2015

YEAR	TEAM	LVL	AGE	W	L	SV	G	GS	IP	H	HR	BB/9	K/9	K	GB%	BABIP	WHIP	ERA	DRA	WARP	PF
2016	ABE	A-	19	4	5	0	13	13	62²	48	1	1.3	7.2	50	46%	.269	0.91	2.15	3.32	1.4	97
2017	DEL	A	20	11	5	0	25	25	140	118	16	0.6	7.3	113	43%	.251	0.91	2.38	3.76	2.5	92
2018	FRD	A+	21	7	8	0	24	24	135	142	19	2.2	6.7	101	36%	.301	1.30	3.47	4.49	1.3	105
2019	*BAL*	*MLB*	*22*	*4*	*10*	*0*	*20*	*20*	*109*	*129*	*25*	*2.9*	*5.8*	*71*	*36%*	*.297*	*1.51*	*6.17*	*6.08*	*-0.8*	*108*

Breakout: 4% Improve: 6% Collapse: 7% Attrition: 10% MLB: 18% *Comparables: Zach Eflin, Jen-Ho Tseng, Gabriel Ynoa*

Alex Wells is the same sort of funky-lefty-with-a-change as Keegan Akin. If you really, really prefer fastball command to fastball velocity you could even get Wells ahead of Akin…I suppose. I won't be going there. Wells' fastball is pinned around 90, and while his command and change are probably a half-grade better than Akin's, the breaker is similarly a show-me pitch. Wells just has far less margin for error at 89-91, so he's more likely to land at the swingman end of his outcome range.

15 Cadyn Grenier SS

Born: 10/31/96 Age: 22 Bats: R Throws: R Height: 5'11" Weight: 188 Origin: Round 1, 2018 Draft (#37 overall)

YEAR	TEAM	LVL	AGE	PA	R	2B	3B	HR	RBI	BB	K	SB	CS	AVG/OBP/SLG	DRC+	VORP	BABIP	BRR	FRAA	WARP	PF
2018	DEL	A	21	183	23	12	2	1	13	17	53	3	2	.216/.297/.333	85	9.9	.312	-0.5	SS(39) 2.7	0.3	87
2019	*BAL*	*MLB*	*22*	*252*	*20*	*10*	*1*	*5*	*19*	*10*	*92*	*1*	*0*	*.149/.181/.257*	*13*	*-17.5*	*.211*	*-0.3*	*SS 2*	*-1.7*	*108*

Breakout: 4% Improve: 7% Collapse: 0% Attrition: 6% MLB: 8% *Comparables: Pete Kozma, Ian Desmond, Argenis Diaz*

Grenier got plenty of amateur scouting coverage this year as Nick Madrigal's double play partner at Oregon State, and the Orioles popped him with the 37th overall pick. While the White Sox are trying to slide Madrigal to the left side, Grenier is likely to stay at 6 for a while at least. It's not a frame you usually associate with shortstop, but Grenier is an above-average runner who moves well in the field. The arm is perhaps a bit light for the left side, and if his frame continues to mature, he might be forced to slide to second base. The offensive question marks loom larger, as the swing is a little stiff (although he'll show decent feel with the barrel head) and there's more swing-and-miss than you'd prefer in your comp-round college bat. Grenier is likely a fifth infielder, although there's a chance the profile coalesces into a second-division type if he sticks at short or the bat improves with pro reps.

Others of note:

Brett Cumberland, C, Double-A Bowie

Cumberland has enough bat to reach the major leagues in a backup or up-and-down role, but any defensive value at all would lift that projection. Right now, he's a bat-first guy with above-average power and advanced plate discipline: He'll never hit for average, but the home runs and walks will carry the profile at the plate. His defensive future is still in question, but to his credit, he's made strides behind the plate. Even so, fringy athleticism and slow feet limit his ceiling back there. Without a clear defensive home, he may get the dreaded Quad-A label. He fits best on an American League team, and getting dealt from Atlanta can only help his career.

D.J. Stewart, OF, Baltimore Orioles

We wrote last year that Stewart would need to keep hitting to keep his Top Ten Orioles prospect status (the lowest tier of Starwood Preferred Member). While the system improved around him, Stewart's performance with the bat was more mixed. Most of the power surge from 2017 remained, but overall Stewart didn't mash as much as you'd like in Triple-A. He did reach Baltimore in September and did hit there, but the profile remains a tough sell. He's a fringy corner outfielder and has never hit as much as you'd like to overcome the profile issues. It's hard to project more than 4 hit/5 pop here, and it doesn't help that the Orioles have other fringy corner outfielders, but Stewart is going to end up higher on the Roster Resource depth chart than you'd think.

Dean Kremer, RHP, Double-A Bowie

The Dodgers moved Kremer from relief to starting this year at Rancho. Usually scuffling college arms go in the opposite direction, but Kremer popped in longer stints despite his previous mid-90s fastball in the pen sitting in the low-90s when stretched out. The heater plays up due to Kremer's extension and slight crossfire, which makes it sneak up on hitters. He has a full four-pitch arsenal with both breaking balls ahead of the change. The curve shows good 12-6 action, and Kremer can spot it or get chases down and away. The slider has been his out pitch and he can manipulate it as well. The change is the clear fourth pitch here and the lack of an armside option against lefties might make Kremer more of a multi-inning reliever or swingman than backend starter. This isn't significantly different from most of the arms above, and you could go a lot of different ways with a pref list after the top five in this improving but still shallow Orioles system.

Zach Pop, RHP, Double-A Bowie

Pop is your prototypical, fastball/slider relief prospect. He's already on the express track to the majors, having blitzed three minor league levels in 2018 on the back of his mid-90s fastball and potential plus slider. Despite his tall and lanky frame, Pop keeps everything pretty compact and throws strikes consistently. His fastball features good tail from his low-three-quarters slot, and he's grown more comfortable manipulating the slider in his first full pro season. It's not a consistently plus pitch yet, but he'll throw a hard backfoot one to righties often enough to project it getting there, and soon. Pop could be 7th or 8th inning help for the Orioles in 2019, and given the state of the O's bullpen, he might even be up before soft-shell crab season starts.

Michael Baumann, RHP, Advanced-A Frederick

Despite a successful season across two A-ball levels, this Michael Baumann still can't top his own Google search results. Maybe he needs to tweet about Rod Sex to drive those page hits on his baseball-reference page. Now major-league b-ref pages tend to show up atop dudes writing about college baseball and Hulu originals, and this Michael Baumann certainly has a shot to earn one on the strength of his big fastball. The mid-90s heater flashes good life up, although it can run a bit true below the letters. Baumann has two fringy breakers, and the curve and slider can bleed together a bit. He has the frame to log innings, but the stuff is more middle relief. And while the high hard one missed bats in the Sally, Carolina League hitters were fooled far less. Still, if he does make the show, maybe the other Baumann will finally buy some non-Gamecock baseball gear.

Hunter Harvey, RHP, Double-A Bowie

Hunter Harvey is hurt again and didn't throw at instructs. He did pitch 32 innings in 2018, which is the most he's thrown since 2014. Harvey also got a major league call-up back in April, but didn't get into a game. Given what happened after, it might be a Moonlight Graham type of scenario, although Graham didn't have Harvey's pure stuff. There are plenty of pitchers who have put together careers where they were either "very good or unavailable." Harvey might end up one of them, but the ratio has skewed way too much towards "unavailable" thus far during his pro career.

Top Talents 25 and Under (born 4/1/93 or later):

1. Yusniel Diaz
2. Ryan Mountcastle
3. Cedric Mullins
4. DL Hall
5. Grayson Rodriguez
6. Chance Sisco
7. Ryan McKenna
8. Dillon Tate
9. Keegan Akin
10. Austin Hays

Cedric Mullins is just barely ineligible for the prospect list, having taken over duties in center late in the season. With Adam Jones gone, he seems to have a clear shot at the job. As has been the case virtually throughout the minors, he was completely hopeless batting right-handed, and we're well past the point of openly wondering why he's still switch-hitting. He profiles as a nifty platoon center fielder, which in this organization qualifies as a huge developmental success.

Chance Sisco, on the other hand, has not developed much at all lately. He's stuck at catcher, which is good, because his bat won't support a corner position at this point. Catchers often develop oddly and late, and there's absolutely a latent hit tool somewhere down there, but the dude couldn't even shove aside Caleb Joseph and Austin Wynns to claim more playing time on a team that went 47-115.

The Orioles have a half-dozen or so more guys that aren't prospect-eligible but are eligible here. They just aren't better than Austin Hays moving forward. (Trust us, we wanted to get Gabriel Ynoa in here somewhere.) It's going to be a long rebuild.

Boston Red Sox

The State of the System:

In hindsight, I should have ended this five month slog of research and writing with a better system, like... well... any of the other ones really.

The Top Ten:

1 Bobby Dalbec 3B

OFP: 55 Likely: 45 ETA: 2020

Born: 06/29/95 Age: 24 Bats: R Throws: R Height: 6'4" Weight: 225 Origin: Round 4, 2016 Draft (#118 overall)

YEAR	TEAM	LVL	AGE	PA	R	2B	3B	HR	RBI	BB	K	SB	CS	AVG/OBP/SLG	DRC+	VORP	BABIP	BRR	FRAA	WARP	PF
2016	LOW	A-	21	143	25	13	2	7	33	9	33	2	2	.386/.427/.674	213	19.0	.473	1.3	3B(22) 2.5	1.9	115
2017	GRN	A	22	329	48	15	0	13	39	36	123	4	5	.246/.345/.437	112	12.9	.383	-2.0	3B(67) -2.3	0.4	105
2018	SLM	A+	23	419	59	27	2	26	85	60	130	3	1	.256/.372/.573	160	44.2	.318	0.9	3B(91) 5.2, SS(1) 0.0	3.8	102
2018	PME	AA	23	124	14	8	1	6	24	6	46	0	0	.261/.323/.514	96	7.1	.377	-0.1	3B(18) -3.9, 1B(2) -0.3	-0.4	104
2019	*BOS*	*MLB*	*24*	*252*	*25*	*10*	*0*	*11*	*33*	*15*	*99*	*0*	*0*	*.193/.248/.377*	*66*	*-4.9*	*.274*	*-0.6*	*3B 0, 1B 0*	*-0.6*	*107*

Breakout: 12% Improve: 30% Collapse: 12% Attrition: 26% MLB: 52% *Comparables: Matt Chapman, J.D. Davis, Dylan Cozens*

The Report: Two years ago, we ranked Dalbec as an other of note with the epithet "Possibly a better pitching prospect." Last year he slotted into the next ten and I made a strained milkshake duck joke about his swing and miss tendencies. This year he's the number one prospect in the system. I don't feel great about this, but I don't feel great about the Red Sox system generally. Dalbec achieved this ranking in part by becoming even more Bobby Dalbec than he was before. He just leaned into the whole profile, striking out, walking, or homering in over half of his plate appearances. He's Rob Manfred's worst nightmare.

Dalbec offers 70 raw power but it's unlikely to end up playing to full grade in the majors. In short, he's gonna strike out a lot. He has bat speed to spare, but the swing is grooved and he's vulnerable to hard stuff up sequenced with spin down. That's something major-league pitchers have in their locker. Dalbec is still taking the vast majority of his reps at third, and he's improved enough there to be passably averageish. As long as he continues to hit around .240-.250 and get those big bombs into games though, you won't care if he's a first baseman either.

The Risks: Medium. With this much swing-and-miss in play, it's just never gonna be low. Even if he hits in the upper minors this year.

Ben Carsley's Fantasy Take: I understand why Dalbec can be considered the best IRL prospect in this system, but he's a borderline top-150 dynasty prospect at best. I personally don't love his chances of bringing his prodigious power into games, and even if I'm wrong it's still a shade below the Joey Gallo brand of 40-plus homer potential. If you really love him, you're closing your eyes and hoping for something like the prime Mike Moustakas years offensively. That'd make Dalbec a useful but hardly irreplaceable fantasy piece, and again, that's his ceiling.

2 Michael Chavis 3B   OFP: 55   Likely: 45   ETA: 2019

Born: 08/11/95 Age: 23 Bats: R Throws: R Height: 5'10" Weight: 216 Origin: Round 1, 2014 Draft (#26 overall)

YEAR	TEAM	LVL	AGE	PA	R	2B	3B	HR	RBI	BB	K	SB	CS	AVG/OBP/SLG	DRC+	VORP	BABIP	BRR	FRAA	WARP	PF
2016	GRN	A	20	312	30	11	3	8	35	22	74	3	1	.244/.321/.391	98	13.2	.303	1.3	3B(68) -0.4	0.4	100
2016	SLM	A+	20	27	5	0	0	0	1	2	7	1	0	.160/.222/.160	40	-0.8	.222	1.1	3B(2) -0.7	-0.1	99
2017	SLM	A+	21	250	50	17	2	17	55	19	57	1	0	.318/.388/.641	170	28.8	.360	1.3	3B(24) -1.6	1.9	103
2017	PME	AA	21	274	39	18	0	14	39	20	56	1	0	.250/.310/.492	104	12.0	.265	0.1	3B(39) -0.5, SS(1) 0.0	0.2	105
2018	PME	AA	22	139	23	7	0	6	17	13	35	3	1	.303/.388/.508	145	13.3	.383	0.5	3B(18) 1.5, 1B(11) -0.5	1.0	102
2018	PAW	AAA	22	34	8	3	0	2	7	1	12	0	0	.273/.294/.545	91	4.7	.368	0.2	3B(4) -1.2, 1B(1) 0.0	-0.1	95
2019	*BOS*	*MLB*	*23*	*34*	*3*	*1*	*0*	*1*	*4*	*2*	*10*	*0*	*0*	*.207/.254/.379*	*42*	*-1.6*	*.256*	*0.0*	*3B 0*	*-0.2*	*107*

Breakout: 12% Improve: 27% Collapse: 5% Attrition: 14% MLB: 44% *Comparables: Alex Liddi, J.D. Davis, Paul DeJong*

The Report: After serving an 80-game suspension for testing positive for a banned substance, Chavis picked up where he left off in 2017 as a three-true-outcomes slugger. Chavis has 70 raw pop derived from plus bat speed and a big uppercut, but the swing can get long and only really has one gear. Chavis knows balls and strikes well enough, but he has a prominent hole up in the zone which major-league arms may exploit. How much of his power he gets into games will ultimately shape his major-league role, as the hit tool will likely play fringe at best, and he's a below-average third baseman.

Chavis moves well enough at the hot corner, and he's sneaky athletic despite a bit of a beer-keg physique, but the arm is fringy and he especially struggles throwing on the move. He started to play more first base in 2018, and the power might carry the profile even on the right side of the infield. Still, an R/R first base profile is a tough sell unless there's clear plus regular upside.

The Risks: Moderate, which is higher than you'd like from a corner bat profile in the upper minors. Chavis doesn't offer a ton outside of the light tower power, so if he can't get it into games consistently, or stick at third base, he's a tough fit on a modern roster.

Ben Carsley's Fantasy Take: I fully understand why Chavis isn't the best IRL prospect in this system, but he *is* the best dynasty prospect in the system. That being said, he was still only in the 90s in our Top 101. You'd usually list a future in Boston as a positive with a hitting prospect, but Chavis' best bet at fantasy relevancy may be as a second-division starter on a worse team. If he gets to 500 or so PA, he could challenge for 30 homers a year, hopefully while retaining 3B eligibility throughout his 20s. If he stays on the Red Sox, he may end up as a short-side platoon bat, and it's tough to care about those guys in mixed leagues no matter how much power they have.

3 Triston Casas 1B   OFP: 55   Likely: 45   ETA: 2022

Born: 01/15/00 Age: 19 Bats: L Throws: R Height: 6'4" Weight: 238 Origin: Round 1, 2018 Draft (#26 overall)

The Report: It's almost like the Red Sox have a type. Casas is another corner slugger—this one of the more hulking variety—albeit one a fair bit further from the majors than Dalbec or Chavis. He also suffered a season-ending thumb injury in his second pro game. When you are drafting a prep first baseman in the first round, you naturally expect game-changing power in the tool shed, and it's not hard to see where Casas gets his prodigious raw pop. The swing has length and uppercut and he's a big, strong kid.

The long term question—as it always is for this profile—is how much of that raw power will get into games. It's not the world's most athletic swing, and the bat speed is only solid-average, so he's gonna be riskier than Dalbec and Chavis even irrespective of the distance from the majors. Casas played third base in high school, and his one pro game for the Sox was at the hot corner, but it's unlikely they'll roll him out there forever. His long term home will be first base.

The Risks: High.

Ben Carsley's Fantasy Take: Bret ranked Casas at 21 on his Top 50 2019 signees list, and that seems fair to me. Casas is almost certainly a first baseman, which isn't great, but he has more fantasy upside than, say, Pavin Smith did a year ago. He's probably a top 200 dynasty prospect right now, though closer to the end of that list than the front half.

4 Tanner Houck RHP

OFP: 55 Likely: 45 ETA: 2020

Born: 06/29/96 Age: 23 Bats: R Throws: R Height: 6'5" Weight: 210 Origin: Round 1, 2017 Draft (#24 overall)

YEAR	TEAM	LVL	AGE	W	L	SV	G	GS	IP	H	HR	BB/9	K/9	K	GB%	BABIP	WHIP	ERA	DRA	WARP	PF
2017	LOW	A-	21	0	3	0	10	10	22^1	21	0	3.2	10.1	25	49%	.333	1.30	3.63	3.32	0.5	104
2018	SLM	A+	22	7	11	0	23	23	119	110	11	4.5	8.4	111	50%	.298	1.43	4.24	5.61	-0.4	103
2019	*BOS*	*MLB*	*23*	*5*	*6*	*0*	*19*	*19*	83^2	*87*	*11*	*4.9*	*7.5*	*69*	*43%*	*.302*	*1.58*	*5.13*	*5.42*	*0.1*	*107*

Breakout: 5% Improve: 11% Collapse: 5% Attrition: 11% MLB: 16%

Comparables: Max Fried, Jimmy Barthmaier, Mike Hinckley

The Report: Houck didn't exactly hold up his end of the bargain as the kind of quick-moving first-round college arm the Sox probably thought they popped in 2017. There's several markers here that suggest he will be better suited to the pen long term. The delivery is funky and high effort, with a bit of crossfire and a low-three-quarters slot. He has struggled to develop a third pitch, making him primarily a fastball/slurve guy. The fastball is easy plus though, touching the mid-90s with good run and sink.

Houck struggles to get consistent shape with his breaking ball, which tends to have more sweep than depth and overall slurvy break. He commands the pitch well enough, but it projects more as average or solid-average than a true bat-misser. He has an athletic, projectable frame, and was used about as heavily as any college arm will be in his first pro season, so durability is less of a concern w/r/t starting than... well, everything else. The sinking fastball is potentially good enough that he could be a very effective reliever though, even if he isn't one of the strikeout monsters we normally see in the late innings nowadays.

The Risks: Medium. The sinking fastball is enough to dispatch most of the hitters he will face in the minors, but there are profile risks given the delivery and lack of a third pitch.

Ben Carsley's Fantasy Take: Even if Houck does remain a starter, he lacks the type of strikeout stuff we need to have much interest from a fantasy POV. Honestly, his best odds at being of much use for our purposes will come if he emerges as a closer some day. Sadz.

5 Durbin Feltman RHP

OFP: 55 Likely: 45 ETA: Early 2019

Born: 04/18/97 Age: 22 Bats: R Throws: R Height: 6'0" Weight: 205 Origin: Round 3, 2018 Draft (#100 overall)

YEAR	TEAM	LVL	AGE	W	L	SV	G	GS	IP	H	HR	BB/9	K/9	K	GB%	BABIP	WHIP	ERA	DRA	WARP	PF
2018	GRN	A	21	0	1	3	7	0	7	6	0	1.3	18.0	14	43%	.429	1.00	2.57	1.65	0.3	100
2018	SLM	A+	21	1	0	1	11	0	12^1	12	0	2.9	10.9	15	58%	.364	1.30	2.19	2.64	0.3	100
2019	*BOS*	*MLB*	*22*	*1*	*0*	*0*	*24*	*0*	25^1	*23*	*3*	*4.4*	*9.7*	*27*	*44%*	*.308*	*1.41*	*4.05*	*4.26*	*0.2*	*107*

Breakout: 7% Improve: 10% Collapse: 1% Attrition: 8% MLB: 11%

Comparables: Danny Barnes, Jacob Rhame, Ryan Burr

The Report: Feltman was arguably the best college closer in the country this spring, and in his pro debut he looked like a dude you could drop right into a major-league pen. While not always working with his upper-90s velocity he showed in college, Feltman throws a plus fastball. He changes eye levels well with it. It shows good riding life up, and he can sink it down in the zone from his OTT slot. His power slider is a mid-80s monster that drops off the deck and is already plus. The delivery is very high effort, bordering on violent, but I mean, he's a reliever. It's not closer™ stuff at present, but if he starts touching 99 again, he could get there. Regardless he's about as safe a late-inning relief prospect as you'll find in the minors right now.

The Risks: Low. Feltman is a major-league ready reliever.

Ben Carsley's Fantasy Take: Between the 20-grade name and the fact that he'll only be fantasy-relevant if closing, Feltman is a dude you can avoid.

6 Jay Groome LHP

OFP: 55 Likely: 40 ETA: 2021-22

Born: 08/23/98 Age: 20 Bats: L Throws: L Height: 6'6" Weight: 220 Origin: Round 1, 2016 Draft (#12 overall)

YEAR	TEAM	LVL	AGE	W	L	SV	G	GS	IP	H	HR	BB/9	K/9	K	GB%	BABIP	WHIP	ERA	DRA	WARP	PF
2017	LOW	A-	18	0	2	0	3	3	11	5	0	4.1	11.5	14	58%	.208	0.91	1.64	3.33	0.2	103
2017	GRN	A	18	3	7	0	11	11	44^{1}	44	6	5.1	11.8	58	55%	.355	1.56	6.70	3.80	0.8	105
2019	*BOS*	*MLB*	*20*	*2*	*3*	*0*	*8*	*8*	*32^{1}*	*32*	*4*	*5.7*	*8.7*	*31*	*45%*	*.310*	*1.63*	*4.94*	*5.21*	*0.1*	*107*

Breakout: 0% Improve: 2% Collapse: 1% Attrition: 1% MLB: 3% *Comparables: Timothy Melville, Michael Kopech, Anthony Swarzak*

The Report: On talent, Groome is clearly the best prospect in the system. He spins a potential 80-grade curve. He has a fastball that bumps into the mid-90s. He has an advanced changeup. He has a classic pitcher's frame and motion.

He's also becoming an advertisement for waiting a bit into a guy's pro career before drawing firm conclusions. After an abbreviated post-draft debut in 2016, Groome missed nearly half of 2017 with a lat problem. He did not pitch well when he did get on the mound, with inconsistent velocity and poor command. He didn't even make it to the regular season in 2018, injuring his elbow during spring training and ultimately undergoing Tommy John surgery in mid-May.

It's currently unclear when—or even whether—Groome will get on a mound in 2019. It's even less clear what it's going to look like when he does. Throw in the long-reported makeup concerns that we discussed last year, and it's hard to be terribly optimistic until and unless he gets back and throws well.

The Risks: Extreme, but also with positive risk if he finally gets healthy and gets it together.

Ben Carsley's Fantasy Take: Despite having done nothing but disappoint since being drafted, Groome is pretty clearly the best dynasty pitching prospect in this system. That may say more about the Sox's farm than it does Groome himself, but there's still top-of-the-fantasy rotation upside here. Groome is just very, very unlikely to reach it at this point.

7 Darwinzon Hernandez LHP

OFP: 50 Likely: 40 ETA: 2020

Born: 12/17/96 Age: 22 Bats: L Throws: L Height: 6'2" Weight: 245 Origin: International Free Agent, 2013

YEAR	TEAM	LVL	AGE	W	L	SV	G	GS	IP	H	HR	BB/9	K/9	K	GB%	BABIP	WHIP	ERA	DRA	WARP	PF
2016	LOW	A-	19	3	5	0	14	14	48^{1}	39	1	6.7	10.8	58	51%	.304	1.55	4.10	3.71	0.9	111
2017	GRN	A	20	4	5	0	23	23	103^{1}	85	8	4.3	10.1	116	50%	.292	1.30	4.01	3.71	1.9	104
2018	SLM	A+	21	9	5	0	23	23	101	80	1	5.3	11.0	124	46%	.326	1.39	3.56	4.91	0.5	101
2018	PME	AA	21	0	0	0	5	0	6	6	0	9.0	15.0	10	36%	.429	2.00	3.00	2.35	0.2	100
2019	*BOS*	*MLB*	*22*	*1*	*1*	*0*	*2*	*2*	*10*	*10*	*1*	*7.3*	*9.6*	*11*	*42%*	*.308*	*1.76*	*5.52*	*5.83*	*0.0*	*107*

Breakout: 7% Improve: 8% Collapse: 3% Attrition: 11% MLB: 12% *Comparables: Jimmy Barthmaier, Jose Cisnero, Dellin Betances*

The Report: Hernandez is a lefty who sits around 95, so there's a pretty good chance he pitches in the bigs at some point. I would definitely lobby for a soccer-style use of the first name on the back of his jersey, as there were seven Hernandezes in the majors last year but only one Darwinzon knocking on the door. The 70-grade name here is better than any of his pitches, but the stuff is major-league-quality as well.

In addition to a plus fastball, Hernandez has an above-average, low-80s slider that tunnels well off the heater despite lacking big two-plane break. There's a slower curve as well for a different look (although it's far less consistent at present than the slider) and a changeup that flashes average as well. Hernandez has a compact arm action, but he has struggled to repeat it or throw strikes consistently throughout his pro career. The fastball/slider combo is enough to be a major league reliever—perhaps even in the late innings if his fastball bumps in short bursts—but even in that role he will have to find the plate more consistently to get past "frustrating middle-inning arm," even if the stuff should make him far better than that.

The Risks: Medium. It's mid-90s velocity from the left side. He's going to get chances.

Ben Carsley's Fantasy Take: If it seemed more likely that Hernandez could start, he'd be a potential top-150 dynasty prospect thanks to his strikeout potential. Unfortunately, Hernandez probably isn't a starter, so…

8 Bryan Mata RHP OFP: 50 Likely: 40 ETA: 2021

Born: 05/03/99 Age: 20 Bats: R Throws: R Height: 6'3" Weight: 160 Origin: International Free Agent, 2016

YEAR	TEAM	LVL	AGE	W	L	SV	G	GS	IP	H	HR	BB/9	K/9	K	GB%	BABIP	WHIP	ERA	DRA	WARP	PF
2016	DRX	RK	17	4	4	0	14	14	61	54	2	2.8	9.0	61	51%	.319	1.20	2.80	2.25	2.3	89
2017	GRN	A	18	5	6	0	17	17	77	75	3	3.0	8.6	74	53%	.333	1.31	3.74	5.45	-0.1	106
2018	SLM	A+	19	6	3	0	17	17	72	58	1	7.2	7.6	61	59%	.292	1.61	3.50	5.01	0.3	103
2019	*BOS*	*MLB*	*20*	*3*	*5*	*0*	*13*	*13*	*59*	*62*	*7*	*6.5*	*7.1*	*47*	*49%*	*.306*	*1.78*	*5.71*	*6.03*	*-0.4*	*107*

Breakout: 0% Improve: 0% Collapse: 0% Attrition: 0% MLB: 0% *Comparables: Kohl Stewart, Duane Underwood, Tyler Matzek*

The Report: Last year for Mata we wrote that "[he] can lose his release point and overthrow. He'll just lose the zone completely at times." 'At times' in 2017, became 'way too much of the time' in 2018. His release point got even more scattershot in 2018, although it was mostly of the alternating miss "armside and up and then down and away" variety. When Mata did find the zone, he touched 95 more consistently with some armside run from his three-quarters slot, a potentially average curveball, and an improving changeup. He just wasn't in the zone enough and had his season cut short by six weeks or so due to back stiffness. While I wouldn't go so far as to call it a lost year, it's certainly one he'll want to forget. The raw stuff is still there for a mid-rotation arm, and Mata doesn't turn 20 until a month into the season, but that projection seems further away now than it did a year ago.

The Risks: High. He walked seven per nine in A-ball and had back issues.

Ben Carsley's Fantasy Take: You think this is painful for you? I'm a Red Sox fan…

9 Michael Shawaryn RHP OFP: 50 Likely: 40 ETA: 2019

Born: 09/17/94 Age: 24 Bats: R Throws: R Height: 6'2" Weight: 200 Origin: Round 5, 2016 Draft (#148 overall)

YEAR	TEAM	LVL	AGE	W	L	SV	G	GS	IP	H	HR	BB/9	K/9	K	GB%	BABIP	WHIP	ERA	DRA	WARP	PF
2017	GRN	A	22	3	2	0	10	10	53^1	44	5	2.2	13.2	78	42%	.331	1.07	3.88	2.34	1.8	102
2017	SLM	A+	22	5	5	0	16	16	81^1	71	10	3.9	10.1	91	34%	.289	1.30	3.76	3.76	1.4	105
2018	PME	AA	23	6	8	0	19	19	112^2	100	7	2.2	7.9	99	40%	.287	1.13	3.28	4.12	1.6	102
2018	PAW	AAA	23	3	2	0	7	6	36^2	30	6	2.7	8.1	33	34%	.247	1.12	3.93	3.21	1.0	91
2019	*BOS*	*MLB*	*24*	*1*	*1*	*0*	*2*	*2*	*10*	*10*	*2*	*3.3*	*8.4*	*9*	*36%*	*.295*	*1.38*	*4.97*	*5.25*	*0.0*	*107*

Breakout: 13% Improve: 27% Collapse: 18% Attrition: 31% MLB: 55% *Comparables: Yefrey Ramirez, Thomas Pannone, Adam Plutko*

The Report: Shawaryn's stuff won't pop off the page here, but he's a bulldog who goes after hitters and is a particularly tough at-bat for righties due to his funk and low armslot. He'll touch 95 with the fastball, but generally sits in the low-90s. The pitch is sneaky fast due to the deception in his delivery, and there's some natural gloveside run from his slot. The command and control are fringy, and he has trouble hitting his spots east-west.

Shawaryn shows a full four-pitch mix, but only the slider is worth writing home about. He gets better depth on it than you'd expect given his low-three-quarters slot, and he manipulates the shape and speed of the offering well. It will flash plus, but projects as average. Shawaryn will use a slower curve to steal a strike now and again, but it lacks a distinct shape and may just be further slider manipulation. The change lacks ideal velocity separation. It's generally too firm in the upper-80s, although it will flash enough fade at times for you to project it to at least have some major-league utility keeping lefties honest. There's a fair bit of effort in Shawaryn's delivery and the stuff will back up later in games, making a reliever outcome likely here.

The Risks: Medium. The stuff just might not play against major-league bats, but Shawaryn has little left to prove in the minors.

Ben Carsley's Fantasy Take: A back-end starter or reliever prospect who'll call Fenway home? Sorry, but most of these guys don't turn into Derek Lowe.

10 Nick Decker OF OFP: 50 Likely: 40 ETA: 2023

Born: 10/02/99 Age: 19 Bats: L Throws: L Height: 6'0" Weight: 200 Origin: Round 2, 2018 Draft (#64 overall)

The Report: Decker is the cold weather prep outfielder version of Dalbec, Chavis, and Casas. Okay, that's a bit of an unfair oversimplification. Decker has potential plus raw power due to his natural strength—dude looks good in the uniform—plus bat speed, and loft in the swing. The barrel control at present is a little loose, and it's gonna be a slow burn on the hit tool.

The stick is going to need to get to average though, as Decker is likely to slide to right field in his twenties due to fringy range on the grass. A wrist injury limited him to just two games in the complex this summer, but this was going to take a while regardless.

The Risks: Extreme. Cold weather prep bat with only a complex league resume, and barely one at that. Tweener/positional questions.

Ben Carsley's Fantasy Take: Watch List City. At least he's not a budding middle reliever!

Others of note:

Josh Ockimey, 1B, Triple-A Pawtucket

One more corner slugger for the road perhaps? Ockimey is certainly one possible future for Triston Casas if the hit tool doesn't develop. He's not that far off the Dalbec and Chavis types either, except he is definitely a first baseman—and not a particularly good one—and has actualized less of his ample raw power in games. He's less athletic than any of the top three bats in the system and despite being the closest to the majors, ranks much further below them—although the distance here overstates the gap; this is a mushy system past the first five names or so.

The culprit here is a long swing and average bat speed. The swing and miss has gone up at every stop, and Ockimey struggles with same-side pitching and spin generally. He does have the long side of the platoon 1B/DH at least, but his bat is going to have to conquer Triple-A first, and as you will probably gather from the other 29 lists, this profile is disappearing from major-league benches.

Travis Lakins, RHP, Triple-A Pawtucket

One of the advantages of publishing the Boston list last on the website is we have a pretty good idea what their offseason has looked like. It makes those potential "Factors on the Farm" a bit more obvious. Well, Roster Resource currently lists their closer as a Rule of Two of Ryan Brasier and Matt Barnes. The only reliever they have added so far is Jenrry Mejia. So yeah, they could probably use some bullpen help.

Lakins might be exactly what they need. He took off after a conversion to the pen in 2018, riding a plus fastball/cutter combination to a late-season promotion to Pawtucket. He continued to miss bats in Triple-A, and there isn't really anything stopping him from staking a claim at a 2019 bullpen slot.

Top Talents 25 and Under (born 4/1/93 or later):

1. Andrew Benintendi
2. Eduardo Rodriguez
3. Rafael Devers
4. Bobby Dalbec
5. Michael Chavis
6. Triston Casas
7. Tanner Houck
8. Durbin Feltman
9. Jay Groome
10. Darwinzon Hernandez

There weren't many difficult calls here. The trio of Red Sox veterans are unambiguously ahead of the farmhands, whose ranks were noticeably thinned in an effort to bolster the big-league team in recent years; this is how a U25 list usually looks after a championship.

Benintendi has quietly developed into one of the league's best outfielders. Now, it's strange to use "quiet" here: we're talking about a former top prospect who just helped lead his team to a championship—in Boston no less. But the Arkansas product's well-rounded game, stoic demeanor, and linear big-league development path have pushed him further below the radar than other young stars of similar caliber. That shouldn't obscure Benintendi's emergence as a great player in his own right. He's an impact contributor on both sides of the ball, as capable of swaying a game at the plate as in the field. He'll be a perennial 20/20 threat well into the next decade, and I wouldn't bet against him winning a batting title or two, either.

By all measures, Rodriguez has pitched well for the Red Sox. He's been considerably above-average on a rate basis over the last two seasons, and he posted a tidy 3.77 DRA (84.2 DRA-) in 2018. Per traditional scouting convention, that makes him a low No. 2 or very good No. 3 starter.

Rodriguez is a man of his time though, and like many pitchers of his generation, he hasn't been pushed particularly hard: He's never started more than 24 games in his four big-league seasons, nor has he topped 140 innings. You can't really be a Role 70 player with that kind of workload—not with an ERA in the high 3's, anyway. Barring a significant acceleration in roster trends and innings management, "starting pitchers" aren't going away any time soon. But more and more of the good ones will have usage patterns that resemble how the Red Sox have handled Rodriguez.

Given that, you could argue Devers should slot second and I wouldn't put up much of a fight. We ranked him as our fifth best prospect in the midseason 2017 list, just three weeks before the Red Sox summoned him to Boston. He played well down the stretch that summer and appeared on the cusp of stardom.

Stardom may yet lie in Devers' future, but he didn't get any closer to reaching it in 2018. After a decent start, his bat cooled down in mid-May and never really got going again. He missed a few weeks on both sides of mid-August and was yanked in and out of the lineup against lefties (against whom he hit just .229/.272/347). That, along with a few notably bad throwing errors, gives me pause. Devers still projects as an impact hitter, and if a seer told me tomorrow that one of he and Rodriguez was about to post a 5-WARP campaign in 2019, I'd assume it was the former. For now though, the southpaw seems more likely to be a good player this season.

Only two other big leaguers were considered here. Sam Travis hit his first big-league dinger last September, but he doesn't project as a regular and has little chance of finding consistent playing time in Boston. Tzu-Wei Lin hit his first homer in the same game as Travis, and his positional flexibility gives him a decent chance to be a Swiss Army knife off the bench. Both just missed the list; perhaps their World Series rings will help alleviate some of the disappointment.

Chicago Cubs

The State of the System:

It's better at the top than it was last year, but calling the Cubs system "improved" overall is a stretch.

The Top Ten:

1 Nico Hoerner SS   OFP: 60   Likely: 50   ETA: Late 2020

Born: 05/13/97 Age: 22 Bats: R Throws: R Height: 6'1" Weight: 200 Origin: Round 1, 2018 Draft (#24 overall)

YEAR	TEAM	LVL	AGE	PA	R	2B	3B	HR	RBI	BB	K	SB	CS	AVG/OBP/SLG	DRC+	VORP	BABIP	BRR	FRAA	WARP	PF
2018	EUG	A-	21	28	6	0	1	1	2	5	3	4	1	.318/.464/.545	170	4.1	.333	-0.5	SS(5) -0.4	0.1	91
2019	*CHN*	*MLB*	*22*	*252*	*24*	*2*	*1*	*7*	*24*	*22*	*64*	*4*	*1*	*.152/.229/.267*	*33*	*-10.5*	*.171*	*0.5*	*SS 0, 2B 0*	*-1.1*	*101*

Breakout: 13% Improve: 18% Collapse: 0% Attrition: 17% MLB: 25% *Comparables: Yamaico Navarro, Rosell Herrera, Marcus Semien*

The Report: Most years there is a late first-round pick or two who pops the summer after signing, and this year it was a... Stanford infielder? Not the usual type, but Hoerner looked like he should have been one of the best college bats in the draft before an elbow injury ended his season in July. Then he went to the AFL and shockingly the #HornyforHoerner hashtag still failed to catch on despite him raking for a month in the desert, flashing advanced bat-to-ball skills, and the usual strong approach we expect from Cubs draft picks.

Hoerner may not stick at shortstop per se, but he's athletic enough to play there, and he's in the right org to make use of his potential positional versatility. The ultimate ceiling here is going to be dependent on his turning some of his present gap power into the over-the-fence variety. But this level of polish, combined with a potential plus hit tool, a good approach, and the ability to at least stand at short makes Hoerner a high-probability major-leaguer, one who both should move fast and bring decent upside to the table.

The Risks: Medium. He's a polished, athletic college bat, so this is probably closer to low than medium, but we will round up until he has a full healthy pro season.

Bret Sayre's Fantasy Take: The last 20 years of music history has led us to sink the 90s into one giant mashup of mood lighting and dark lyrics. How many people actually remember that The Verve and The Verve Pipe were actually different bands? It's true, it's just a thing that sounds made up now that we're so far removed from it. You're also probably wondering what the hell this has to do with Hoerner.

Well, those two bands were different in one major way. While they each had one hit, The Verve's album was actually quite good and underrated. On the other hand, The Verve Pipe's album was trash... Just truly unlistenable. Unfortunately for Cubs fans (and, well, me) their farm system is basically Villans incarnate. Hoerner can flat out hit and despite not having extreme utility in either homers or steals (he's a poor bet to reach 20 of either regularly), he checks in as a borderline top 101 prospect for me in dynasty formats and a second-round pick among "The Freshmen" entering pro ball this year. These other guys, though? Not so much.

2 Miguel Amaya C OFP: 60 Likely: 50 ETA: 2022

Born: 03/09/99 Age: 20 Bats: R Throws: R Height: 6'1" Weight: 185 Origin: International Free Agent, 2015

YEAR	TEAM	LVL	AGE	PA	R	2B	3B	HR	RBI	BB	K	SB	CS	AVG/OBP/SLG	DRC+	VORP	BABIP	BRR	FRAA	WARP	PF
2016	DCH	RK	17	242	29	12	0	1	22	21	27	9	3	.245/.344/.317	120	15.3	.276	2.4	C(33) -0.1, 1B(16) 3.0	1.4	94
2017	EUG	A-	18	244	21	14	1	3	26	11	49	1	0	.228/.266/.338	67	1.6	.274	-1.5	C(43) -0.5, 1B(8) -0.4	-1.0	92
2018	SBN	A	19	479	54	21	2	12	52	50	91	1	0	.256/.349/.403	118	31.5	.298	0.6	C(95) 2.5, 1B(9) -0.7	2.5	98
2019	*CHN*	*MLB*	*20*	*252*	*18*	*7*	*0*	*7*	*24*	*9*	*67*	*0*	*0*	*.146/.181/.259*	*16*	*-15.4*	*.168*	*-0.5*	*C 0, 1B 0*	*-1.6*	*101*

Breakout: 6% Improve: 8% Collapse: 0% Attrition: 5% MLB: 8% *Comparables: Carson Kelly, Jake Bauers, Freddie Freeman*

The Report: A breakout and bright spot in a very shallow farm system, Amaya is a potential above-average two-way catching prospect. The two standout tools at present are above-average arm strength and above-average raw power. Those are two good building blocks for an everyday catcher, but both have their caveats. The arm comes with an efficient transfer, but inconsistent throwing mechanics. The receiving isn't as good as the arm, although there are positive markers for improvement given Amaya's athleticism and quick hands.

The raw power comes from natural lift and strength from the swing, and there is enough barrel control and hand/eye to project most of it getting into games. But Amaya's swing lacks lower-half engagement and he can get off-balance and out in front when he falls in love with his pull side power. He does show the makings of a strong approach, so with even an average hit tool, Amaya should offer enough on-base and pop to be at least a solid everyday catcher.

The Risks: High. He's an A-ball catcher who needs significant refinement both at and behind the plate. And as always, catchers are weird.

Bret Sayre's Fantasy Take: "Cup of Tea" as in not quite my. How many times do we need to go over this about catching prospects? If you think Amaya is going to be the one to break through and become a top-five catcher, you might not ultimately be wrong, but there are so many things that can go haywire along the way. Waiting 3-4 years for a .260/20-homer catcher is just a bad idea when you can always get someone like Welington Castillo for basically free.

3 Alex Lange RHP OFP: 55 Likely: 45 ETA: 2020

Born: 10/02/95 Age: 23 Bats: R Throws: R Height: 6'3" Weight: 197 Origin: Round 1, 2017 Draft (#30 overall)

YEAR	TEAM	LVL	AGE	W	L	SV	G	GS	IP	H	HR	BB/9	K/9	K	GB%	BABIP	WHIP	ERA	DRA	WARP	PF
2017	EUG	A-	21	0	1	0	4	4	9^{1}	9	0	2.9	12.5	13	42%	.375	1.29	4.82	2.90	0.3	92
2018	MYR	A+	22	6	8	0	23	23	120^{1}	104	6	2.8	7.6	101	45%	.287	1.18	3.74	3.78	2.2	99
2019	*CHN*	*MLB*	*23*	*5*	*6*	*0*	*17*	*17*	*83*	*83*	*13*	*3.8*	*7.8*	*72*	*39%*	*.304*	*1.43*	*4.94*	*5.46*	*-0.1*	*101*

Breakout: 4% Improve: 8% Collapse: 5% Attrition: 8% MLB: 17% *Comparables: Jonathan Holder, Daniel Mengden, Sam Howard*

The Report: The first thing you notice with Lange is his potential plus curveball. When on, it has tight spin and sharp break. However, he simply throws it too much and has shown a tendency to hang it in the zone a bit just due to the sheer amount of times it leaves his hand. The fastball clocks in around 90-92 and has some movement, but he needs to incorporate it more with his curve and improve his changeup, which is clearly his third option.

There were plenty of flashes of the good Lange this season. While his somewhat quirky motion reveals the ball a bit too much before release, his curve—if paired better with his fastball—could carry him to a mid-rotation future. Keep in mind though, he is 23 and has yet to reach Double-A. While it may simply be a product of his four-year career as a college player, he needs a strong showing next season in the upper minors to make noise in this depleted system.

The Risks: High. A two-pitch pitcher at the moment, Lange needs to rely less on his curveball (despite its effectiveness) as he rises through the ranks. There is obvious potential here, but clear inconsistency with his fastball and overall control.

Bret Sayre's Fantasy Take: Mid-rotation prospects like Lange are the "Villans" of dynasty rosters everywhere unless you roster 250 farmhands or more. There's not enough swing-and-miss here for us to be super interested in a fantasy sense as he projects to be closer to an SP5 than anything else.

4 Adbert Alzolay RHP OFP: 55 Likely: 45 ETA: 2019

Born: 03/01/95 Age: 24 Bats: R Throws: R Height: 6'0" Weight: 179 Origin: International Free Agent, 2012

YEAR	TEAM	LVL	AGE	W	L	SV	G	GS	IP	H	HR	BB/9	K/9	K	GB%	BABIP	WHIP	ERA	DRA	WARP	PF
2016	SBN	A	21	9	4	0	22	20	120^1	119	9	2.1	6.1	81	44%	.292	1.22	4.34	3.62	2.0	101
2017	MYR	A+	22	7	1	0	15	15	81^2	65	8	2.4	8.6	78	39%	.263	1.07	2.98	3.56	1.6	96
2017	TEN	AA	22	0	3	0	7	7	32^2	27	0	3.3	8.3	30	36%	.297	1.19	3.03	4.08	0.4	99
2018	IOW	AAA	23	2	4	0	8	8	39^2	43	4	2.9	6.1	27	37%	.307	1.41	4.76	4.19	0.6	90
2019	*CHN*	*MLB*	*24*	*1*	*0*	*0*	*15*	*0*	*15^1*	*16*	*3*	*3.2*	*7.2*	*12*	*38%*	*.300*	*1.41*	*5.25*	*5.80*	*-0.6*	*101*

Breakout: 3% Improve: 3% Collapse: 7% Attrition: 8% MLB: 14% *Comparables: Jason Adam, Myles Jaye, Ryan Sherriff*

The Report: Before a lat strain ended his season around Memorial Day, Alzolay seemed well on his way to some sort of major-league role with the big club. The lack of progression with his command and changeup are concerning, but it's difficult to read into eight starts, of course. The fastball and slider combo is still plus, although he didn't always have his usual mid-90s heat as a starter. The mid-80s slider looks like a true out pitch, most of the time. It will still get slurvy when he tries to spot it, and it's more effective as a chase pitch gloveside and down. Alzolay's athleticism on the mound is notable and between that and good arm speed on the change you can project further growth with the pitch. Given the crowded nature of the Cubs rotation though, the org might first fashion him as a fastball/slider pen arm.

The Risks: Medium. Alzolay's lat strain was ill-timed in 2018, but it shouldn't have lingering effects into 2019. However, the changeup and command will need to tighten up this season to forestall a move to the bullpen.

Bret Sayre's Fantasy Take: The starting pitcher future for Alzolay is merely a "Veneer" on the reliever material that lies underneath. On the bright side, he's likely to be in the majors this year and could contribute in ratios and strikeouts decently for a middle reliever. On the other hand, he's a reliever who is extremely unlikely to get saves.

5 Aramis Ademan SS OFP: 55 Likely: 45 ETA: 2021

Born: 09/13/98 Age: 20 Bats: L Throws: R Height: 5'11" Weight: 160 Origin: International Free Agent, 2015

YEAR	TEAM	LVL	AGE	PA	R	2B	3B	HR	RBI	BB	K	SB	CS	AVG/OBP/SLG	DRC+	VORP	BABIP	BRR	FRAA	WARP	PF
2016	DCH	RK	17	248	37	5	4	0	16	34	28	17	9	.254/.366/.316	125	12.4	.293	1.1	SS(52) -1.6	1.2	94
2017	EUG	A-	18	183	23	9	4	4	27	14	30	10	6	.286/.365/.466	128	19.4	.331	-3.5	SS(38) -1.0	0.1	90
2017	SBN	A	18	134	13	6	1	3	15	4	24	4	2	.244/.269/.378	72	3.0	.275	0.1	SS(29) -5.0	-0.6	103
2018	MYR	A+	19	452	49	11	3	3	38	38	95	9	5	.207/.291/.273	68	1.1	.264	0.0	SS(112) -8.9	-1.5	98
2019	*CHN*	*MLB*	*20*	*252*	*23*	*4*	*0*	*6*	*18*	*10*	*63*	*2*	*1*	*.151/.193/.240*	*11*	*-17.7*	*.177*	*-0.1*	*SS -4*	*-2.3*	*101*

Breakout: 5% Improve: 5% Collapse: 0% Attrition: 1% MLB: 5% *Comparables: Amed Rosario, Ruben Tejada, Wilfredo Tovar*

The Report: Just 20 years old, Ademan already has a quick bat that allows him to drive the ball to all fields. He didn't show that much in High-A last year, but while his results were more than a bit concerning, there's still plenty of talent under the hood.

Ademan is just 160 pounds and he looks it, but when he is able to fully extend his hands through the zone, his bat has a nice whip to it. His athleticism is obvious, as he is able to get to balls a bit beyond the range of your average High-A shortstop. His hands and actions remain a work in progress. He has room to grow, and with an open stance and clean swing, Ademan has the potential to be a serviceable MLB shortstop. That bodes well given Chicago's track record of development for middle infielders (Baez, Russell, Torres) in recent years.

The Risks: High. The tools are good, but he was pretty bad in High-A last year.

Bret Sayre's Fantasy Take: There may be more upside than hinted at during his brutal 2018 season from a fantasy standpoint as well, but shy of a potential .280 average, the rest of his fantasy ceiling is sure to "Drive You Mild."

6 Justin Steele LHP

OFP: 55 Likely: 45 ETA: 2019 as a reliever, 2020 as a starter.

Born: 07/11/95 Age: 23 Bats: L Throws: L Height: 6'2" Weight: 195 Origin: Round 5, 2014 Draft (#139 overall)

YEAR	TEAM	LVL	AGE	W	L	SV	G	GS	IP	H	HR	BB/9	K/9	K	GB%	BABIP	WHIP	ERA	DRA	WARP	PF
2016	SBN	A	20	5	7	0	19	19	77^{1}	93	3	4.5	8.8	76	46%	.385	1.71	5.00	5.34	-0.3	100
2017	MYR	A+	21	6	7	0	20	20	98^{2}	100	6	3.3	7.5	82	50%	.315	1.38	2.92	4.18	1.2	92
2018	CUB	RK	22	0	0	0	5	5	18^{1}	9	1	2.0	13.3	27	43%	.222	0.71	1.47	1.42	0.9	96
2018	MYR	A+	22	2	1	0	4	4	18^{1}	12	0	2.9	9.3	19	41%	.261	0.98	2.45	4.03	0.3	96
2018	TEN	AA	22	0	1	0	2	2	10	8	1	2.7	6.3	7	32%	.233	1.10	3.60	3.68	0.2	89
2019	*CHN*	*MLB*	*23*	*3*	*3*	*0*	*10*	*10*	*45^{1}*	*45*	*6*	*4.3*	*8.7*	*44*	*41%*	*.320*	*1.48*	*4.61*	*5.10*	*0.1*	*101*

Breakout: 1% Improve: 4% Collapse: 3% Attrition: 4% MLB: 10%

Comparables: Heath Fillmyer, Dylan Covey, Ty Taubenheim

The Report: Toeing a professional mound a mere 11 months after undergoing Tommy John surgery, Steele quickly reestablished himself as one of the top arms in the Cubs system. The snarkier among you may regard that as damning with faint praise, but I'll always have kind words for a lefty with mid-90s heat and a potential plus curve. Steele could move quickly as a reliever, and the third pitch and command issues may dictate that role change eventually anyway, but I'd expect him to continue as a starter for the extra post-TJ reps if nothing else.

The power relief arsenal from the left side would tempt me, though. While the fastball doesn't move a ton, he pounds the zone with plus velocity. The curve is a tight, 1-7 breaker that he can manipulate to spot or bury. He's comfortable going backdoor or back foot with it, which covers for the lack of a real armside weapon against righties at present.

The Risks: Medium. There's still some post-TJ risks, although he looked fine in his brief 2018 appearance, and somewhat more substantial reliever risk.

Bret Sayre's Fantasy Take: I don't want to sound too much like an "Ominous Man" (though the quality of these prospects isn't helping) and yet there's little reason to believe that Steele can end up as a starting pitcher who sits above the waiver wire line in mixed leagues.

7 Brailyn Marquez LHP

OFP: 50 Likely: 40 ETA: 2022

Born: 01/30/99 Age: 20 Bats: L Throws: L Height: 6'4" Weight: 185 Origin: International Free Agent, 2015

YEAR	TEAM	LVL	AGE	W	L	SV	G	GS	IP	H	HR	BB/9	K/9	K	GB%	BABIP	WHIP	ERA	DRA	WARP	PF
2016	DCU	RK	17	4	2	0	12	12	54^{2}	44	1	3.8	7.9	48	60%	.287	1.23	1.48	3.04	1.6	99
2017	CUB	RK	18	2	1	0	11	9	44	50	3	2.5	10.6	52	52%	.367	1.41	5.52	3.33	1.2	104
2018	EUG	A-	19	1	4	0	10	10	47^{2}	46	5	2.6	9.8	52	52%	.333	1.26	3.21	3.05	1.2	88
2018	SBN	A	19	0	0	0	2	2	7	7	0	2.6	9.0	7	33%	.333	1.29	2.57	3.54	0.1	93
2019	*CHN*	*MLB*	*20*	*2*	*4*	*0*	*10*	*10*	*43^{1}*	*46*	*7*	*4.8*	*7.9*	*38*	*46%*	*.316*	*1.59*	*5.47*	*6.06*	*-0.4*	*101*

Breakout: 0% Improve: 0% Collapse: 0% Attrition: 0% MLB: 0%

Comparables: Yohander Mendez, Luis Severino, Jayson Aquino

The Report: If you are going to wager on any prospect outside of, oh let's say the top 200 or so, to have a significant major league career, you won't go broke betting on the lefty sitting 96-98. Absent anything else, southpaws with that kind of velocity get chances. Marquez has a bit more to recommend than just the fastball, but just a bit. It's a plus-plus fastball though, with only command issues and velocity bleed keeping it from being a top-of-the-scale offering. Lefties facing it would be forgiven if they flinched a bit given that it comes from a low-three-quarters armslot with some funk in the delivery. The change and breaking ball are both well-below-average at present, and Marquez's delivery doesn't exactly scream "average command/control projection" either. There's effort in the arm action, and it's a bit stiff overall, but the ball does come absolutely screaming out of his left hand. And that's not nothing.

The Risks: High. This profile is mostly an arm strength bet, but man it's a lot of arm strength from the left side.

Bret Sayre's Fantasy Take: His velocity is very "Real," but his fantasy value is very not real. He doesn't need to be owned in any dynasty formats.

8 Cole Roederer OF

OFP: 50 Likely: 40 ETA: 2023

Born: 09/24/99 Age: 19 Bats: L Throws: L Height: 6'0" Weight: 175 Origin: Round 2C, 2018 Draft (#77 overall)

YEAR	TEAM	LVL	AGE	PA	R	2B	3B	HR	RBI	BB	K	SB	CS	AVG/OBP/SLG	DRC+	VORP	BABIP	BRR	FRAA	WARP	PF
2018	CUT	RK	18	161	30	4	4	5	24	18	37	13	4	.275/.354/.465	124	13.6	.337	2.1	CF(29) -1.3, RF(4) -1.1	0.3	102
2019	*CHN*	*MLB*	*19*	*252*	*21*	*3*	*2*	*7*	*23*	*7*	*92*	*4*	*2*	*.134/.155/.252*	*1*	*-19.5*	*.172*	*1.3*	*CF 0, RF 0*	*-2.1*	*101*

Breakout: 5% Improve: 7% Collapse: 0% Attrition: 3% MLB: 9% *Comparables: Engel Beltre, Carlos Tocci, Nomar Mazara*

The Report: Roederer is your typical "athletic Cali prep outfielder without quite loud enough tools to go in round one." Yeah, it's not as unusual a taxonomy as you might think. He has above-average bat speed, but his swing plane—especially as an amateur—was not geared for much in the way of power. The problem is that he may slow down enough to force a slide over to left field (his below-average arm won't play in the other corner). He flashed more power in the complex, but let's wait and see if he shows it against better arms before we get too excited.

The Risks: High. Roederer has only a complex league resume and may end up in a corner outfield spot.

Bret Sayre's Fantasy Take: Herding prospects in a dynasty draft without the requisite fantasy upside we're looking is like herding "Cattle" in that there's safety in numbers when it comes to deeper formats. There are always a handful of guys like Roederer every year who don't look like they have a notable fantasy future but take an unforeseen step forward in pro ball. You just can't roster all of them.

9 Brennen Davis OF

OFP: 50 Likely: 40 ETA: 2024

Born: 11/02/99 Age: 19 Bats: R Throws: R Height: 6'4" Weight: 175 Origin: Round 2, 2018 Draft (#62 overall)

YEAR	TEAM	LVL	AGE	PA	R	2B	3B	HR	RBI	BB	K	SB	CS	AVG/OBP/SLG	DRC+	VORP	BABIP	BRR	FRAA	WARP	PF
2018	CUT	RK	18	72	9	2	0	0	3	10	12	6	1	.298/.431/.333	160	4.4	.370	0.0	CF(10) 0.6, RF(4) -0.6	0.3	102
2019	*CHN*	*MLB*	*19*	*252*	*19*	*3*	*0*	*4*	*19*	*16*	*80*	*3*	*1*	*.147/.209/.211*	*16*	*-17.1*	*.201*	*-0.1*	*CF 0, RF 0*	*-1.8*	*101*

Breakout: 5% Improve: 7% Collapse: 0% Attrition: 3% MLB: 9% *Comparables: Carlos Tocci, Engel Beltre, Nomar Mazara*

The Report: Davis has louder tools than Roederer, but significantly more rawness in his game as well. He looks every bit the basketball player he was for much of high school, and his frame is extremely projectable—which is to say, he's skinny. The frame and swing portend significant raw power, but everything is very mechanical at present, and he doesn't really have the strength to drive the ball without yoking up for it yet. He's a plus runner with a strong arm, so if he can stick in center, you could be cooking with gas here in a half decade or so, but the lead time here is likely to be significant. I do have a weird thing about ex-basketball-players though (Amir Garrett and Monte Harrison jump to mind…welp), so I can't help but like Davis, even if we could share jeans at this point.

The Risks: This is closer to extreme than high, so let's just go very high. He's raw even by prep outfielder standards and has only briefly focused full-time on baseball. There's a fair bit of positive variance here too given his inexperience and projectability.

Bret Sayre's Fantasy Take: If Davis were a "Photograph," he'd take so long to develop that the photo store you brought the film into would have closed down, turned into a dry cleaner, then the dry cleaner would have gone out of business and been replaced by a store that fixes electronics but has such a terrible and kitschy name that you couldn't imagine going in there without feeling shame.

10 Alec Mills RHP

OFP: 45 Likely: 40 ETA: Debuted in 2016

Born: 11/30/91 Age: 27 Bats: R Throws: R Height: 6'4" Weight: 190 Origin: Round 22, 2012 Draft (#673 overall)

YEAR	TEAM	LVL	AGE	W	L	SV	G	GS	IP	H	HR	BB/9	K/9	K	GB%	BABIP	WHIP	ERA	DRA	WARP	PF
2016	NWA	AA	24	1	2	0	12	12	67^{2}	57	2	1.6	9.0	68	44%	.314	1.02	2.39	3.73	1.1	97
2016	OMA	AAA	24	4	3	0	12	11	58	62	8	2.9	8.4	54	47%	.323	1.40	4.19	3.97	0.9	99
2016	KCA	MLB	24	0	0	0	3	0	3^{1}	3	0	13.5	10.8	4	44%	.333	2.40	13.50	7.15	-0.1	102
2017	IOW	AAA	25	2	0	0	3	3	14	12	0	1.9	4.5	7	47%	.255	1.07	3.21	5.61	0.0	102
2018	IOW	AAA	26	5	12	0	23	23	124^{2}	121	10	3.0	7.8	108	42%	.303	1.30	4.84	3.78	2.5	91
2018	CHN	MLB	26	0	1	0	7	2	18	11	1	3.5	11.5	23	51%	.250	1.00	4.00	2.42	0.6	101
2019	*CHN*	*MLB*	*27*	*2*	*2*	*0*	*20*	*5*	*42*	*42*	*6*	*3.2*	*7.9*	*37*	*43%*	*.309*	*1.35*	*4.49*	*4.95*	*0.1*	*101*

Breakout: 5% Improve: 11% Collapse: 32% Attrition: 30% MLB: 51% *Comparables: Luke Farrell, Edwar Cabrera, Tyler Pill*

The Report: I have a soft spot for Mills, even though he stretches the definition of "prospect" as far as anyone on any list. A bone bruise on his pitching arm cost him most of the 2017 season, or else he would have likely already established himself as a useful Swiss Army knife for the Cubs pitching staff. If you need him to start, he has four pitches at the offer. Granted, the curve is a slow strike-stealer with a bit of 12-6 depth, and the slider is inconsistent and can back up at times, but it's improved enough to be a useful, perhaps even average major-league offering.

Mills can also come in out of the pen and give you a couple innings, leaning more on his low-90s fastball and change. The two-seam version of the heater shows sink and run and he spots it down in the zone well. The change works well off the heater with 10 mph of velocity separation and late sink. The total package here is on the fringy side—and given the profile, you'd like to see a longer track record of throwing strikes—but he had his moments both as a starter and reliever late last season in Chicago. Mills is a useful piece for your pitching staff that I've always liked more than most (and perhaps more than I should).

The Risks: Low. Doesn't get much more finished product than a 27-year-old who debuted in 2016.

Bret Sayre's Fantasy Take: "Barely (If At All)". Sometimes when these things work, they really work. The Brewers' list is going to be better. I promise.

Others of note:

Brendon Little, LHP, Low-A South Bend

Little struggled last year during his first minor-league season. The command was inconsistent and his fastball velocity was down from what was reported last year. The fastball actually looked quite pedestrian, sitting in the low-90s with little movement. A serviceable third pitch also never developed, and instead Little relied solely on his fastball and curve.

There is some optimism for a rebound in 2019. Little's strength is the curveball, which features 12-6 shape and sharp break. He's confident enough to throw it in any count and will bury it to get batters to chase. The Cubs hope some minor mechanical changes will solve the troubles that plagued him at South Bend. Lacking an effective third pitch, the profile looks like it's destined for a bullpen role.

Jhonny Pereda, C, High-A Myrtle Beach

Overshadowed by Amaya, Pereda quietly had a solid season as Myrtle Beach's backstop. He doesn't have Amaya's loud offensive tools but he's worked diligently with Chicago's minor league staff to become a legitimate catching prospect. He's athletic and agile behind the plate with one of the best arms in the organization. Offensively, he has a solid approach and some sneaky pull-side power. He looks like a glove-first backup, but with continued development at the plate, Pereda could become the Cubs' next breakout catching prospect.

Jose Albertos, RHP, Low-A South Bend

Man, I thought for sure I would have been writing about Albertos much further up this list and even on the 101. Pitchers are notoriously risky, but if you were gonna bet on it going bad for Albertos it would have been injury-related, not suddenly walking 20 per nine. His calling card had been polish and advanced fastball command in 2017, but that was nowhere to be found in 2018. And this wasn't just generic wildness: this was "often not in the same zip code as the strike zone" wildness.

There have been arm concerns with Albertos before, but this doesn't appear to be that. The yips aren't insurmountable, but there's a better chance I skip this section entirely next year than spend time trying to fit Albertos onto the back end of 2020's Top 101.

Top Talents 25 and Under (born 4/1/93 or later):

1. Ian Happ
2. Albert Almora
3. Addison Russell
4. Miguel Amaya
5. David Bote
6. Victor Caratini
7. Alex Lange
8. Adbert Alzolay
9. Aramis Ademan
10. Justin Steele
11. ~~Addison Russell~~

These past few years, writers on this list have had things pretty easy. Reserve the top six or seven spots for core big-leaguers, sprinkle in some intriguing low-level guys, and call it a day. It's become a little more complicated this year, with the last World Series starters aging off and a farm system that has been depleted by trades. There are still a few guys at the top who will get major-league at-bats this year, but the talent drops off fast.

Since losing Dexter Fowler, the Cubs have struggled to replace his bat at the top of the order. The opportunity was ripe for either Ian Happ or Albert Almora to fill the void and cement their place as part of Chicago's core. But neither completely gained Joe Maddon's trust.

Happ's rookie campaign was solid, with a 111 DRC+ and the defensive versatility that the Cubs love. His sophomore season was less so, as his strikeouts skyrocketed and the power faded. The hope in Chicago is that 2018 was an aberration and that the bat will return to form.

Almora appeared to be having a breakout 2018 season, slashing .319/.357/.438 and playing exceptional centerfield defense. However, an extended July slump and a rejuvenated Zobrist cut into his playing time down the stretch. Again, there's plenty of hope: his bat is solid and he plays a mean centerfield.

David Bote spent seven years in Chicago's minor-league system as an unheralded prospect before reworking his swing and finding his way onto the 40-man roster. He filled in nicely for the injured Kris Bryant and even provided one of the best highlights of the year with his walk off grand slam against Washington. Like many rookies, he hit a wall when scouts figured out his weaknesses, and he'll need to make adjustments to thrive. It's unlikely that he will ever have a positional home given the stars in Chicago's infield, but he's versatile enough to fill in almost anywhere on the field and provide some pop at the plate.

On a team with a deeper farm system, backup catcher Victor Caratini probably doesn't make this list. There's not a lot of upside remaining in his game but he does provide value as a switch-hitting catcher who can fill in at a corner infield spot when needed.

Chicago White Sox

The State of the System:

The prospects have arrived. There's more to come. And yet, and yet… well, this isn't a state of the "organization" I guess. The system is still good.

The Top Ten:

1 **Eloy Jimenez OF** OFP: 70 Likely: 60 ETA: 2019, likely shortly after the clawback date
Born: 11/27/96 Age: 22 Bats: R Throws: R Height: 6'4" Weight: 205 Origin: International Free Agent, 2013

YEAR	TEAM	LVL	AGE	PA	R	2B	3B	HR	RBI	BB	K	SB	CS	AVG/OBP/SLG	DRC+	VORP	BABIP	BRR	FRAA	WARP	PF
2016	SBN	A	19	464	65	40	3	14	81	25	94	8	3	.329/.369/.532	160	35.7	.391	-0.3	LF(86) -4.6, RF(11) 0.4	2.9	101
2017	MYR	A+	20	174	23	6	2	8	32	18	35	0	0	.271/.351/.490	155	10.1	.304	-0.3	LF(13) 0.3, RF(6) -0.1	1.0	93
2017	WNS	A+	20	122	20	11	1	8	26	12	21	0	2	.345/.410/.682	155	14.1	.370	0.4	RF(19) -0.6	0.7	102
2017	BIR	AA	20	73	11	5	0	3	7	5	16	1	1	.353/.397/.559	160	9.0	.429	0.1	RF(15) -1.1	0.4	93
2018	BIR	AA	21	228	36	15	2	10	42	18	39	0	0	.317/.368/.556	158	23.9	.344	-1.3	LF(30) -3.6, RF(13) -1.8	0.7	95
2018	CHR	AAA	21	228	28	13	1	12	33	14	30	0	1	.355/.399/.597	170	19.9	.371	-1.8	LF(41) -0.2, RF(6) 0.0	1.8	104
2019	*CHA*	*MLB*	*22*	*465*	*56*	*23*	*2*	*19*	*64*	*25*	*91*	*0*	*0*	*.281/.324/.476*	*116*	*21.2*	*.315*	*-0.8*	*LF -1, RF 0*	*2.1*	*103*

Breakout: 17% Improve: 51% Collapse: 1% Attrition: 14% MLB: 63% *Comparables: Oswaldo Arcia, Austin Hays, Joel Guzman*

The Report: The only things that could slow Jimenez down in 2018 were minor pectoral and hip injuries. When he was on the field he mashed. While never a hitter that needed to sell out to get his 80-grade raw power into games, the assumption was that Jimenez would start to have the usual power hitter swing-and-miss issues in the upper minors. That did not happen. While it doesn't radically alter the projection—we postulated he could be a plus hitter the last two seasons—it does make us a bit more confident that he'll reach the upper bounds of his OFP. He's not going to win a batting title, but he's shown enough with the bat now to make us think he could win a home run crown.

Jimenez looks like a left fielder at the highest level—and not an asset there—so as we've intoned before, he will have to hit. But the only thing keeping him from proving it in the majors was Chicago's ~~attempts at service time manipulation~~ insistence that he needed further work on his outfield defense. We don't think it's getting all that much better. We also don't think it will matter much in the end.

The Risks: Low. He's hit in the upper minors. The top-of-the-scale raw is making its way into games. He probably should have been up already, but that's now one for the courts to decide, maybe.

Ben Carsley's Fantasy Take: Hey now, this is what ya came for. Jimenez is on the short list of best fantasy prospects in the game. Worst case, Jimenez figures to be a top-25 outfielder in the mold of a modern day Justin Upton who hits 30-plus bombs with a tolerable average. If he really clicks, we could be talking about more of a top-10 outfielder who mashes .280-plus with closer to 40 bombs, a la vintage Nelson Cruz. Either way, you'll be happy you own him for years to come.

2 Nick Madrigal IF

OFP: 70 Likely: 60 ETA: Late 2019 if the White Sox push him. Probably 2020.

Born: 03/05/97 Age: 22 Bats: R Throws: R Height: 5'7" Weight: 165 Origin: Round 1, 2018 Draft (#4 overall)

YEAR	TEAM	LVL	AGE	PA	R	2B	3B	HR	RBI	BB	K	SB	CS	AVG/OBP/SLG	DRC+	VORP	BABIP	BRR	FRAA	WARP	PF
2018	KAN	A	21	49	9	3	0	0	6	1	0	2	2	.341/.347/.409	143	5.3	.319	1.1	2B(12) 0.9	0.5	97
2018	WNS	A+	21	107	14	4	0	0	9	5	5	6	3	.306/.355/.347	120	2.7	.319	0.0	2B(25) -1.8	0.1	103
2019	*CHA*	*MLB*	*22*	*252*	*24*	*7*	*0*	*5*	*23*	*6*	*37*	*6*	*3*	*.232/.258/.319*	*54*	*-5.5*	*.256*	*-0.2*	*2B -2, SS 0*	*-0.8*	*103*

Breakout: 17% Improve: 25% Collapse: 0% Attrition: 19% MLB: 26% *Comparables: Breyvic Valera, Alexi Amarista, Yolmer Sanchez*

The Report: If you are reading this blurb, you are the type of high-info fan who doesn't need me to tell you that Nick Madrigal was the best pure hitter in the 2018 draft class. So let's pose a question: Is Nick Madrigal an 8 hit? Granted, the connotation is more "should you give Nick Madrigal an 8 hit?" The scale only works if you use all of it, as KG used to write, but I'm more comfortable giving an 8 OFP than an 8 hit. You can't replicate major-league stuff, scouting, and sequencing in the minors, and you certainly won't do it in the Pac-12.

However, you can see Madrigal's elite barrel control. You might notice he struck out five times in 173 pro plate appearances coming off a full college season where he struck out seven times in 201 PA. It's not a metal bat swing, and there's present 4 raw power here despite his frame. He'll sting baseballs in the gap, and you'd think all that raw would get into play eventually. The White Sox are enthusiastic about moving him to shortstop, and he may have the hands and range for the 6—he's a plus-plus runner—but his arm likely won't allow him to make all the throws you want from a major-league shortstop. A plus second base glove isn't a bad fallback though, nor are "the lesser Altuve seasons" as a reasonable projection. I guess I never really answered the question I asked at the outset, did I?

The Risks: Low. There may not be enough power in the profile to be an impact bat in the end—famous last words nowadays—but Madrigal was the safest bet to hit major-league pitching in his draft class and immediately became one of the safest bets in the minors as well. David Lee likened him to "a major leaguer on rehab" when he saw him in A-ball this summer.

Ben Carsley's Fantasy Take: Aren't you just so, so tired of every short middle infielder getting compared to Dustin Pedroia? I mean, Pedroia isn't even the game's preeminent short middle infielder at this point! It's so annoying. Anyway, uhh, Pedroia hit .305/.372/.457 with an average of 16 bombs and 20 steals per season from 2007-2013. Add a few more steals, and that's likely what we're looking at in Madrigal, who's already got a pretty solid case as a top-15 dynasty league prospect.

3 Michael Kopech RHP

OFP: 70 Likely: 55 ETA: Debuted in 2018

Born: 04/30/96 Age: 23 Bats: R Throws: R Height: 6'3" Weight: 205 Origin: Round 1, 2014 Draft (#33 overall)

YEAR	TEAM	LVL	AGE	W	L	SV	G	GS	IP	H	HR	BB/9	K/9	K	GB%	BABIP	WHIP	ERA	DRA	WARP	PF
2016	SLM	A+	20	4	1	0	11	11	52	25	1	5.0	14.2	82	45%	.273	1.04	2.25	2.78	1.6	104
2017	BIR	AA	21	8	7	0	22	22	119^{1}	77	6	4.5	11.7	155	42%	.272	1.15	2.87	3.29	2.7	95
2017	CHR	AAA	21	1	1	0	3	3	15	15	0	3.0	10.2	17	35%	.375	1.33	3.00	3.90	0.3	96
2018	CHR	AAA	22	7	7	0	24	24	126^{1}	101	9	4.3	12.1	170	40%	.316	1.27	3.70	5.03	0.7	104
2018	CHA	MLB	22	1	1	0	4	4	14^{1}	20	4	1.3	9.4	15	28%	.381	1.53	5.02	6.84	-0.3	102
2019	*CHA*	*MLB*	*23*	*6*	*8*	*0*	*24*	*24*	118^{2}	*97*	*13*	*5.0*	*11.4*	*151*	*39%*	*.297*	*1.36*	*4.15*	*4.34*	*1.5*	*103*

Breakout: 20% Improve: 31% Collapse: 12% Attrition: 29% MLB: 51% *Comparables: Trevor May, Zack Wheeler, Tyler Thornburg*

The Report: Kopech had another frustrating season, although for slightly different reasons than we're used to with him. At the end of 2017 there was a #narrative that Kopech was taking a little off of his triple-digit fastball to improve his command, prompting speculation that that adjustment explained his dominant second half. Kopech didn't carry it over into 2018 though, and was back to his Wild Thing ways until August, when he posted a 36:1 K:BB ratio and was called up to Chicago.

Then came the torn UCL. 2019 will be a lost season for Kopech, his most frustrating yet. That's all plot, but the story hasn't changed significantly. Kopech still has an elite fastball flanked by a potential plus-plus slider that has led to video game minor league K-rates. His change may actually have gone from "improving" to "improved," although it still isn't a significant part of his repertoire. The problem here is that he's just never showed the ability to throw enough strikes to hit his lofty ceiling for more than one- or two-month bursts. That's better than never doing it at all, but it still leaves us with the same control/command questions on top of the new Tommy John recovery questions. The TJ might accelerate a move to the pen for Kopech, but 18 months can change many things in baseball. For now, all we'll do is bump his risk factor.

The Risks: High. The "not everyone comes back 100% from Tommy John" caveat aside, Kopech does not have much of a track record of throwing enough strikes or enough good strikes to be a front-of-the-rotation starter. Check back in 2020.

Ben Carsley's Fantasy Take: I stood my ground on Kopech last year, holding firm to the notion that he was a top-5 dynasty league pitching prospect even when the going got rough. Unfortunately, there's no real way for me to make that argument now that Kopech is likely 18 months away from any sort of meaningful fantasy contribution. It's still reasonable to hope that Kopech blossoms into a high-WHIP, high-strikeout fantasy starter a la Chris Archer, but there are quite a few red flags at this point. Hold on to him if you've got him, but don't look to aggressively trade for him either.

4 **Dylan Cease RHP** OFP: 70 Likely: 55 ETA: Mid-to-late 2019

Born: 12/28/95 Age: 23 Bats: R Throws: R Height: 6'2" Weight: 190 Origin: Round 6, 2014 Draft (#169 overall)

YEAR	TEAM	LVL	AGE	W	L	SV	G	GS	IP	H	HR	BB/9	K/9	K	GB%	BABIP	WHIP	ERA	DRA	WARP	PF
2016	EUG	A-	20	2	0	0	12	12	44^2	27	1	5.0	13.3	66	55%	.295	1.16	2.22	3.00	1.2	90
2017	SBN	A	21	1	2	0	13	13	51^2	39	2	4.5	12.9	74	46%	.339	1.26	2.79	3.50	1.1	99
2017	KAN	A	21	0	8	0	9	9	41^2	35	1	3.9	11.2	52	43%	.330	1.27	3.89	3.00	1.1	99
2018	WNS	A+	22	9	2	0	13	13	71^2	52	5	3.5	10.3	82	50%	.273	1.12	2.89	2.90	2.0	105
2018	BIR	AA	22	3	0	0	10	10	52^1	30	3	3.8	13.4	78	50%	.273	0.99	1.72	2.77	1.6	92
2019	*CHA*	*MLB*	*23*	*3*	*3*	*0*	*23*	*8*	56^1	*48*	*6*	*5.3*	*10.9*	*68*	*43%*	*.298*	*1.44*	*4.31*	*4.51*	*0.4*	*103*

Breakout: 12% Improve: 20% Collapse: 17% Attrition: 25% MLB: 42% *Comparables: Zack Wheeler, Stephen Gonsalves, Carl Edwards Jr.*

The Report: It feels like we've been waiting a very long time to witness the firepower of this fully armed and operational battle station. After years of caution from both sides of Chi-Town, the White Sox unleashed Cease in the spring, letting him throw full starts on a fairly regular rest cycle. He responded brilliantly, showing off his full arsenal, including an improved slider and change to go along with a fastball and curve combo that both rank among the better pitches in the minors.

The Risks: High—similar to Kopech's, actually. Cease's health record is spotty at best: Tommy John around draft time, some shoulder soreness here, arm fatigue there. His 23 starts and 124 innings in 2018 both represent career-highs, and that's still a good pace off an MLB starter's workload in his fourth full pro season. He might end up being more of a good candidate for the Josh Hader high-leverage multi-inning reliever role than a starter's role, even in a higher-end outcome.

Ben Carsley's Fantasy Take: The Spiderman pointing at himself meme works here with "A healthy Michael Kopech as a dynasty prospect" on one Spidey and "A healthy Dylan Cease as a dynasty prospect" on the other.

5 **Luis Robert OF** OFP: 60 Likely: 50 ETA: 2020, give or take a year

Born: 08/03/97 Age: 21 Bats: R Throws: R Height: 6'3" Weight: 185 Origin: International Free Agent, 2017

YEAR	TEAM	LVL	AGE	PA	R	2B	3B	HR	RBI	BB	K	SB	CS	AVG/OBP/SLG	DRC+	VORP	BABIP	BRR	FRAA	WARP	PF
2017	DWS	RK	19	114	17	8	1	3	14	22	23	12	3	.310/.491/.536	206	21.7	.397	2.5	CF(19) -0.5	1.5	97
2018	KAN	A	20	50	5	3	1	0	4	4	12	4	2	.289/.360/.400	105	3.0	.394	-0.2	CF(10) 0.0	0.0	96
2018	WNS	A+	20	140	21	6	1	0	11	8	37	8	2	.244/.317/.309	84	2.7	.341	0.5	CF(27) 3.1, RF(4) -0.4	0.2	103
2019	*CHA*	*MLB*	*21*	*252*	*29*	*11*	*0*	*5*	*19*	*18*	*81*	*8*	*2*	*.182/.255/.292*	*48*	*-6.2*	*.257*	*0.5*	*CF 2, RF 0*	*-0.4*	*103*

Breakout: 1% Improve: 1% Collapse: 0% Attrition: 1% MLB: 1% *Comparables: Joe Benson, Xavier Avery, Abraham Almonte*

The Report: The international man of mystery… wasn't really healthy enough to solve much of the mystery, was he? Limited by thumb and knee problems, he never made it out of A-ball and didn't hit much when he was on the field. Sent to the Arizona Fall League to make up for lost reps, he promptly pulled his hamstring. When healthy, he's shown off the high-end speed and hit potential that prompted the White Sox to give him so much money in the first place. Despite uncertainty about the shape of his future performance, there's enough bat speed and control here to give him a real shot to hit for average. He's flashed significant raw power too, but that aspect hasn't quite made it to 7 PM yet. He should comfortably stick in center, perhaps even excelling there.

The Risks: He's a speed guy who keeps hurting his legs. Like last year, we still suspect the underlying tools are there for him to shoot up our lists, but we'll continue to hedge until he puts together a sustained run of health and offensive performance.

Ben Carsley's Fantasy Take: If Robert's injury history prevents him from running a ton or keeps him off the field, obviously that's a big fantasy issue. But people tend to discount just how much rope stealing bases gives a fantasy player: Only 11 players swiped more than 30 bags last season, and only another 17 swiped 20-plus. Let's assume a healthy Robert's floor is something like Ender Inciarte 2018: .265 with 10 bombs and 28 steals with 83 runs scored. That was still enough to qualify as the 21st best outfielder in 5×5 leagues, per ESPN's player rater. Robert is still super valuable, is what we're saying. Be patient.

6 Dane Dunning RHP

OFP: 60 Likely: 50 ETA: Assuming no further arm issues, late 2019.

Born: 12/20/94 Age: 24 Bats: R Throws: R Height: 6'4" Weight: 200 Origin: Round 1, 2016 Draft (#29 overall)

YEAR	TEAM	LVL	AGE	W	L	SV	G	GS	IP	H	HR	BB/9	K/9	K	GB%	BABIP	WHIP	ERA	DRA	WARP	PF
2016	AUB	A-	21	3	2	0	7	7	33^2	26	1	1.9	7.8	29	65%	.263	0.98	2.14	3.92	0.5	91
2017	KAN	A	22	2	0	0	4	4	26	13	0	0.7	11.4	33	64%	.224	0.58	0.35	3.10	0.7	107
2017	WNS	A+	22	6	8	0	22	22	118	114	15	2.7	10.3	135	52%	.316	1.27	3.51	4.05	1.7	106
2018	WNS	A+	23	1	1	0	4	4	24^1	20	2	1.1	11.5	31	61%	.300	0.95	2.59	3.51	0.5	103
2018	BIR	AA	23	5	2	0	11	11	62	57	0	3.3	10.0	69	49%	.343	1.29	2.76	3.58	1.3	93
2019	*CHA*	*MLB*	*24*	*4*	*6*	*0*	*15*	*15*	80^1	*79*	*11*	*3.3*	*8.8*	*79*	*48%*	*.304*	*1.36*	*4.38*	*4.58*	*0.8*	*103*

Breakout: 13% Improve: 26% Collapse: 14% Attrition: 30% MLB: 45% *Comparables: Jordan Montgomery, Sean Nolin, Cody Martin*

The Report: I'll grouse a lot in these column inches about needing new ways to describe mid-rotation projections. Regardless, Dunning might just be the template for this profile. His body is built to log innings—"eyes of doe and thighs of stallion" as Los Campesinos! sing—with an easy delivery and relatively compact arm action that portends at least average command of four at least average pitches. His fastball is a low-90s heavy sinker with wicked armside run. Dunning spots it to both sides, and when he's locating well armside he might as well be playing catch. The movement and command make the velocity play up, and you could call it a potential plus fastball without raising my hackles.

The secondaries all settle in between average and solid-average. Dunning offers two different breaking ball looks: An 11-5 big breaking curve that shows a bit early, but that he commands well, and a shorter mid-80s slider that almost looks cutterish at times. His feel for the change can come and go, but it flashes plus with good sink and fade when he gets it in to lefties. There's no clear major-league bat misser, but everything works, and everything works well off each other. Everything was humming along for Dunning in 2018, and he might have even seen big-league time in September if not for a sprained elbow that put him on the shelf for the entire second half of the season. Pitchers, man.

The Risks: Medium. Dunning is throwing again with no issues, but "elbow sprain" is always going to make me dramatically tug at my collar in a Vaudevillian way. Beyond that, this profile is carried at least in part by pitch mix and command, and that doesn't always get fully sussed out until major-league bats get involved.

Ben Carsley's Fantasy Take: Dunning has proximity on his side, but upside and that elbow sprain are two pretty big strikes against him. Do I prefer him to many of the other dozen-plus mid-rotation starters who could be pitching by July? Yes. Does that make him a lock for the top-101? No, but if he misses it won't be by much.

7 Luis Alexander Basabe OF

OFP: 50 Likely: 40 ETA: 2020

Born: 08/26/96 Age: 22 Bats: B Throws: R Height: 6'0" Weight: 160 Origin: International Free Agent, 2012

YEAR	TEAM	LVL	AGE	PA	R	2B	3B	HR	RBI	BB	K	SB	CS	AVG/OBP/SLG	DRC+	VORP	BABIP	BRR	FRAA	WARP	PF
2016	GRN	A	19	451	61	24	8	12	52	40	116	25	5	.258/.325/.447	113	26.3	.330	2.7	CF(98) 11.6	2.6	101
2017	WNS	A+	20	435	52	12	5	5	36	49	104	17	6	.221/.320/.320	86	10.3	.292	4.4	CF(78) 0.1, RF(10) -0.4	0.2	102
2018	WNS	A+	21	245	36	12	5	9	30	34	64	7	8	.266/.370/.502	141	19.7	.341	-2.0	CF(28) 2.2, LF(16) 1.5	1.4	103
2018	BIR	AA	21	270	41	9	3	6	26	30	76	9	4	.251/.340/.394	106	13.3	.344	2.1	CF(42) -1.9, RF(15) 0.3	0.5	92
2019	*CHA*	*MLB*	*22*	*252*	*28*	*7*	*2*	*7*	*22*	*18*	*78*	*5*	*2*	*.179/.241/.312*	*51*	*-5.7*	*.230*	*0.3*	*CF 2, LF 0*	*-0.3*	*103*

Breakout: 6% Improve: 26% Collapse: 0% Attrition: 14% MLB: 31% *Comparables: Austin Jackson, Michael Saunders, Ryan Kalish*

The Report: Basabe began 2018 where he ended 2017, in High-A Winston-Salem. In his first go-around, the athletic outfielder didn't display much power and scuffled through an injury-laden campaign that finally ended when he got surgery to repair his left meniscus. 2018 was a different story, as a healthy Basabe looked more comfortable and showed a much better approach.

At the plate, Basabe uses a moderate leg kick to create plenty of torque from his lower half, and that's something that just wasn't there the year before. It's a sweet pull-happy swing from the left side, and there's above-average raw power in the bat from that side of the dish. He was listed at just 160 pounds last year, so he has room to add weight.

Basabe's ultimate value will be shaped by his defensive home, and I'm fairly optimistic he'll be able to stick in center. He tracks the ball well and takes a good first step, though his routes could use a little work. The arm is above-average and would play up in a corner spot, but he'll have every opportunity to make it work in center. While he didn't have the same kind of offensive performance in Double-A as he did in Winston-Salem, he looked healthy again and it was a positive season overall.

The Risks: High. The swing can get a little long, with a mild bat wrap that sometimes hinders his ability to get the stick through the zone. If he can't play center, he loses value and perhaps winds up in a reserve role.

Ben Carsley's Fantasy Take: Basabe is a better IRL prospect than a fantasy one, but he's not without his uses in our world. The hope is he ends up as a solid all-around contributor and fantasy OF4/5 once he grows into a little more power. The fear is that he becomes the type of generic 20-homer threat who's only interesting if he's playing every day. Still, if you held on to him after his miserable 2017, his stock is trending up.

8 Blake Rutherford OF

OFP: 50 Likely: 40 ETA: Late 2020

Born: 05/02/97 Age: 22 Bats: L Throws: R Height: 6'3" Weight: 195 Origin: Round 1, 2016 Draft (#18 overall)

YEAR	TEAM	LVL	AGE	PA	R	2B	3B	HR	RBI	BB	K	SB	CS	AVG/OBP/SLG	DRC+	VORP	BABIP	BRR	FRAA	WARP	PF
2016	YAT	RK	19	30	3	1	0	1	3	4	6	0	0	.240/.333/.400	108	2.8	.263	0.0	CF(6) -1.1	-0.1	94
2016	PUL	RK	19	100	13	7	4	2	9	9	24	0	2	.382/.440/.618	178	14.7	.500	0.0	CF(14) -1.7, LF(2) -0.2	0.4	96
2017	CSC	A	20	304	41	20	2	2	30	25	55	9	4	.281/.342/.391	99	11.0	.341	-2.6	CF(39) -5.6, LF(13) -0.5	-0.8	95
2017	KAN	A	20	136	11	5	0	0	5	13	21	1	0	.213/.289/.254	98	-4.8	.257	-0.1	CF(13) -1.3, LF(10) -0.3	-0.1	102
2018	WNS	A+	21	487	67	25	9	7	78	34	90	15	8	.293/.345/.436	120	18.7	.351	1.1	RF(74) -2.5, LF(15) -2.7	0.4	104
2019	*CHA*	*MLB*	*22*	*252*	*20*	*8*	*1*	*5*	*24*	*9*	*69*	*2*	*1*	*.193/.220/.304*	*35*	*-12.3*	*.243*	*0.0*	*RF 0, LF -1*	*-1.5*	*103*

Breakout: 4% Improve: 7% Collapse: 0% Attrition: 6% MLB: 8% *Comparables: Jorge Bonifacio, Destin Hood, Rymer Liriano*

The Report: Rutherford makes fairly consistent contact from the left side of the plate, with quick hands and a fluid swing without a lot of pre-pitch noise. He's always had an advanced feel at the plate, and he's able to get ahead in counts and drive the ball into the gaps. For now, power isn't a huge part of his game. He's still young and still learning his body, and you'd naturally expect him to add some weight as he matures. If he can incorporate more lift in the swing it would be easier to project him as a future 20-homer guy.

It's also worth mentioning that Rutherford has struggled with southpaws throughout his minor league career. While he saw time at all three outfield spots last season, the majority of it was in right field. A corner spot may suit him best, as his average arm and solid-average speed are perhaps a bit short of requirements in center, particularly if he gets bigger.

The Risks: High. As Rutherford grows into his body, he's less likely to stay in center. Could a team put him there? Sure. But he's going to be better suited as a corner outfielder, and if his power doesn't develop, he's going to be a tweener. Factor in the concerns against left-handed pitching, and there are an awful lot of variables in the profile.

Ben Carsley's Fantasy Take: Basically you're hoping for Stephen Piscotty as a best-case outcome here. That gives Rutherford a pretty modest ceiling, but I like his odds of hitting it more than most. A potential very back-end of the top-101 guy for me, though it's likely he falls short in favor of higher upside dudes. Still, if you held on for his rough 2017 second-half, good job.

9 Alec Hansen RHP

OFP: 50 Likely: 40 ETA: Over/under is around early-2020.

Born: 10/10/94 Age: 24 Bats: R Throws: R Height: 6'7" Weight: 235 Origin: Round 2, 2016 Draft (#49 overall)

YEAR	TEAM	LVL	AGE	W	L	SV	G	GS	IP	H	HR	BB/9	K/9	K	GB%	BABIP	WHIP	ERA	DRA	WARP	PF
2016	WSX	RK	21	0	0	0	3	3	7	1	0	5.1	14.1	11	70%	.100	0.71	0.00	2.03	0.3	101
2016	GRF	RK	21	2	0	0	7	7	36^{2}	12	3	2.9	14.5	59	52%	.161	0.65	1.23	1.92	1.5	95
2016	KAN	A	21	0	1	0	2	2	11	11	0	3.3	9.0	11	53%	.344	1.36	2.45	2.40	0.4	91
2017	KAN	A	22	7	3	0	13	13	72^{2}	57	3	2.8	11.4	92	32%	.292	1.10	2.48	2.80	2.1	100
2017	WNS	A+	22	4	5	0	11	11	58^{1}	42	5	3.9	12.7	82	38%	.296	1.15	2.93	3.42	1.3	100
2017	BIR	AA	22	0	0	0	2	2	10^{1}	15	0	2.6	14.8	17	36%	.536	1.74	4.35	2.95	0.3	90
2018	BIR	AA	23	0	4	0	9	9	35^{2}	30	3	10.6	8.8	35	33%	.293	2.02	6.56	5.96	-0.3	91
2018	WNS	A+	23	0	1	0	5	5	15^{2}	14	0	9.8	11.5	20	27%	.378	1.98	5.74	4.53	0.1	106
2019	*CHA*	*MLB*	*24*	*3*	*5*	*0*	*12*	*12*	56^{1}	*54*	*9*	*7.1*	*10.1*	*63*	*38%*	*.304*	*1.75*	*5.71*	*6.02*	*-0.4*	*103*

Breakout: 6% Improve: 9% Collapse: 7% Attrition: 13% MLB: 19% *Comparables: Humberto Sanchez, Josh Collmenter, Austin Brice*

The Report: Oof. There's a player development maxim that once a player shows a particular ability, he can always rediscover it. This might run the other way for Hansen, in that his 2016 implosion in college shows that it can all fall apart for him at any time. Hansen came down with the dreaded forearm tightness in spring training, didn't show up on a field until June, and was beyond terrible upon his return. He struggled mightily to throw strikes, and after consecutive starts of six, nine, and seven walks in Double-A, he was demoted back to High-A. He wasn't much better there, failing to make it to the fifth inning in any of his five starts and walking more than he struck out. We're still ranking him because there's still a big fastball and breaking ball kicking around somewhere in there, and he has an injury excuse. But he's gotta get back on track.

The Risks: Extreme. Well, if he keeps on the present track with the whole balls and strikes thing he's never going to reach the majors. Forearm stuff generally isn't great for a pitcher. There was lots of reliever risk here anyway, and it would not surprise me at all if he gets it together in the pen and even becomes dominant, a la Dellin Betances. Both the positive and negative risk probably aren't quite captured in the OFP/likely scale.

Ben Carsley's Fantasy Take: I'd rather roll the dice on someone like Hansen than on any of the myriad back-end starter types who appear at this junction on lists for lesser farm systems. That's a bit of a false choice though, and while Hansen should be owned if your league rosters 150-plus prospects, he's really just a lottery ticket. For our purposes, his best odds at sustained success may come as a closer.

10 Micker Adolfo OF

OFP: 50 Likely: 40 ETA: 2021

Born: 09/11/96 Age: 22 Bats: R Throws: R Height: 6'3" Weight: 200 Origin: International Free Agent, 2013

YEAR	TEAM	LVL	AGE	PA	R	2B	3B	HR	RBI	BB	K	SB	CS	AVG/OBP/SLG	DRC+	VORP	BABIP	BRR	FRAA	WARP	PF
2016	KAN	A	19	265	30	13	1	5	21	14	88	0	1	.219/.269/.340	69	0.7	.318	0.0	RF(61) 8.9, CF(2) -0.2	0.1	95
2017	KAN	A	20	473	60	28	2	16	68	31	149	2	0	.264/.331/.453	116	17.5	.366	-4.1	RF(102) -12.1	-0.8	99
2018	WNS	A+	21	336	48	18	1	11	50	34	92	2	1	.282/.369/.464	137	14.6	.372	-1.5		0.8	104
2019	*CHA*	*MLB*	*22*	*252*	*22*	*8*	*0*	*9*	*28*	*10*	*92*	*0*	*0*	*.175/.220/.319*	*43*	*-14.2*	*.239*	*-0.6*		*-1.5*	*103*

Breakout: 2% Improve: 9% Collapse: 0% Attrition: 7% MLB: 10% *Comparables: Chris Parmelee, Ryan O'Hearn, Lars Anderson*

The Report: Adolfo's injury log is staggeringly long for a 22-year-old position player. Ankle and hand issues bothered him in 2015 and 2016, and then his 2017 was cut short after he punched a wall and fractured his hand. Last year, he labored through a torn flexor muscle and strained UCL until July, when the White Sox shut him down so he could undergo Tommy John surgery. His 2018 maladies kept him away from the outfield and limited him to DH duties.

Adolfo has plus raw power, and between the loft in the swing and his considerable upper-body strength, he gets to it pretty often in games. He doesn't have a great feel for contact and there will be some swing and miss in his game, but his eye is improving and he's chasing fewer pitches out of the zone these days. He'll have to continue to make adjustments to pick up off-speed stuff, but damn it, he'll hit mistakes and he's got a cannon for an arm; there are usable tools in the shed.

The Risks: Very High. The injury bug has bit Adolfo in some way in each of the last four years. While he finished the year at High-A, he's also going to be 23 in September of 2019, so you'd like to see some sort of progress next season. It's unclear when he'll be ready to return from Tommy John, but when he does, he needs to stay in the lineup.

Ben Carsley's Fantasy Take: He could be interesting if he ends up getting regular playing time, but that's a pretty big if at this point. Frankly, it's not too difficult to find guys like this on the waiver wire even in super deep leagues. You can pass.

The Next Six:

11 Zack Collins C

Born: 02/06/95 Age: 24 Bats: L Throws: R Height: 6'3" Weight: 220 Origin: Round 1, 2016 Draft (#10 overall)

YEAR	TEAM	LVL	AGE	PA	R	2B	3B	HR	RBI	BB	K	SB	CS	AVG/OBP/SLG	DRC+	VORP	BABIP	BRR	FRAA	WARP	PF
2016	WNS	A+	21	153	24	7	0	6	18	33	39	0	0	.258/.418/.467	155	10.8	.333	-0.4	C(18) -0.6	0.8	101
2017	WNS	A+	22	426	63	18	3	17	48	76	118	0	2	.223/.365/.443	119	22.9	.282	-2.6	C(63) 1.5	1.5	102
2017	BIR	AA	22	45	7	2	0	2	5	11	11	0	0	.235/.422/.471	156	4.8	.286	-0.1	C(11) -2.4	0.1	93
2018	BIR	AA	23	531	58	24	1	15	68	101	158	5	0	.234/.382/.404	124	33.7	.329	-3.2	C(74) -14.4	0.3	94
2019	*CHA*	*MLB*	*24*	*29*	*3*	*1*	*0*	*1*	*3*	*4*	*10*	*0*	*0*	*.180/.304/.351*	*66*	*0.0*	*.242*	*-0.1*	*C -2*	*-0.2*	*103*

Breakout: 10% Improve: 14% Collapse: 2% Attrition: 17% MLB: 34% *Comparables: Carlos Santana, Derek Norris, Travis Shaw*

I got a chat question this summer about Collins 2018 season so far, and described it as "holding serve." The combination of his long, leveraged swing and good eye at the plate has kept him on the three true outcome slugger path, which would make him an easy top ten guy in this system if we thought he was even passable at catcher. But Collins still struggles with his receiving and spent a significant amount of time in Birmingham as a DH (FWIW, our advanced catching metrics had him as one of the worst framers in Double-A). Collins has a strong arm, but there is a lot of bulk to get going, and his throwing mechanics aren't always clean. Teams are far less willing to play this type of profile behind the plate these days, and it's possible that Collins just isn't playable in the majors as a backstop. The bat won't be quite good enough to carry first base, so while strictly speaking he's a 5/4 type profile, the actual variance here is much larger.

12 Luis Gonzalez OF

Born: 09/10/95 Age: 23 Bats: L Throws: L Height: 6'1" Weight: 185 Origin: Round 3, 2017 Draft (#87 overall)

YEAR	TEAM	LVL	AGE	PA	R	2B	3B	HR	RBI	BB	K	SB	CS	AVG/OBP/SLG	DRC+	VORP	BABIP	BRR	FRAA	WARP	PF
2017	KAN	A	21	277	26	13	4	2	12	38	50	2	3	.245/.356/.361	115	11.3	.302	-0.2	CF(31) -2.9, LF(18) -0.1	0.3	100
2018	KAN	A	22	255	35	16	2	8	26	21	57	7	2	.300/.358/.491	145	19.8	.365	-0.6	CF(39) -1.0, RF(13) -1.9	1.1	96
2018	WNS	A+	22	288	50	24	3	6	45	27	46	3	5	.313/.376/.504	145	26.8	.354	5.8	CF(31) 3.9, LF(14) 0.2	2.5	104
2019	*CHA*	*MLB*	*23*	*252*	*25*	*8*	*1*	*6*	*22*	*16*	*62*	*1*	*1*	*.188/.241/.311*	*49*	*-7.2*	*.223*	*-0.4*	*CF 1, RF 0*	*-0.7*	*103*

Breakout: 5% Improve: 22% Collapse: 1% Attrition: 10% MLB: 28% *Comparables: Jake Cave, Johnny Field, Michael Hermosillo*

Gonzalez has perceived makeup concerns—which may partially explain why he fell to the third round in the 2017 draft—but his on-field performance in 2018 offers little to quibble with. He has one of those sweet lefty swings and hits line drives line to line. There's enough loft in the swing to project average game pop, and Gonzalez stays in well against lefties. He's splitting time between center and the corners at present, and to be honest he doesn't exactly have a lower half that screams "up the middle" player. Gonzalez also mashed at levels you'd expect a college bat to mash at. The offensive profile still may be good enough to carry an everyday corner outfield spot, but we'll know more when the polished New Mexico product gets his first taste of Double-A next season.

13 Ian Hamilton RHP

Born: 06/16/95 Age: 24 Bats: R Throws: R Height: 6'0" Weight: 200 Origin: Round 11, 2016 Draft (#326 overall)

YEAR	TEAM	LVL	AGE	W	L	SV	G	GS	IP	H	HR	BB/9	K/9	K	GB%	BABIP	WHIP	ERA	DRA	WARP	PF
2016	KAN	A	21	1	1	8	21	0	31^{2}	22	3	4.0	7.7	27	49%	.235	1.14	3.69	3.04	0.6	100
2017	BIR	AA	22	1	3	1	14	0	19	26	0	3.8	10.4	22	52%	.419	1.79	5.21	4.95	0.0	100
2017	WNS	A+	22	3	3	6	30	0	52^{2}	33	1	1.4	8.9	52	46%	.241	0.78	1.71	2.82	1.3	100
2018	BIR	AA	23	2	1	12	21	0	25^{1}	20	0	4.3	12.1	34	47%	.323	1.26	1.78	3.45	0.4	100
2018	CHR	AAA	23	1	1	10	22	0	26^{1}	18	2	1.4	9.6	28	49%	.254	0.84	1.71	3.47	0.5	100
2018	CHA	MLB	23	1	2	0	10	0	8	6	2	2.2	5.6	5	48%	.174	1.00	4.50	3.37	0.1	104
2019	*CHA*	*MLB*	*24*	*2*	*1*	*0*	*36*	*0*	38^{1}	*34*	*5*	*4.4*	*9.8*	*42*	*44%*	*.292*	*1.37*	*4.34*	*4.54*	*0.3*	*103*

Breakout: 10% Improve: 13% Collapse: 8% Attrition: 17% MLB: 23% *Comparables: Heath Hembree, Abel De Los Santos, Diego Moreno*

14 Ryan Burr RHP

Born: 05/28/94 Age: 25 Bats: R Throws: R Height: 6'4" Weight: 225 Origin: Round 5, 2015 Draft (#136 overall)

YEAR	TEAM	LVL	AGE	W	L	SV	G	GS	IP	H	HR	BB/9	K/9	K	GB%	BABIP	WHIP	ERA	DRA	WARP	PF
2016	KNC	A	22	1	2	0	14	0	21	22	0	3.9	7.7	18	43%	.328	1.48	3.86	4.98	-0.1	100
2017	KNC	A	23	1	2	4	22	0	32	29	3	4.2	12.9	46	48%	.361	1.38	2.81	3.17	0.7	100
2017	VIS	A+	23	1	0	1	17	0	25	13	0	2.2	10.4	29	74%	.245	0.76	0.72	3.68	0.4	100
2017	WNS	A+	23	0	0	1	6	0	8^{1}	5	0	5.4	14.0	13	47%	.333	1.20	0.00	5.20	0.0	100
2018	BIR	AA	24	4	2	2	30	0	43	30	3	4.8	9.0	43	51%	.248	1.23	2.72	3.48	0.7	100
2018	CHR	AAA	24	0	1	0	7	0	8^{1}	4	0	2.2	8.6	8	80%	.200	0.72	1.08	3.42	0.2	100
2018	CHA	MLB	24	0	0	0	8	0	9^{2}	12	3	5.6	5.6	6	39%	.321	1.86	7.45	6.33	-0.2	103
2019	*CHA*	*MLB*	*25*	*1*	*0*	*0*	*26*	*0*	27^{1}	*25*	*4*	*5.3*	*9.1*	*28*	*45%*	*.294*	*1.51*	*4.88*	*5.12*	*0.0*	*103*

Breakout: 4% Improve: 8% Collapse: 9% Attrition: 14% MLB: 18% *Comparables: Kevin McCarthy, Jose Ortega, Angel Nesbitt*

HAMILTON: Pardon me, are you relief pitcher Ryan Burr, sir?
I'm Ian Hamilton, flamethrowing reliever at your service, sir
God, I wish we put up more WAR
Then we could prove we're worth more than we're collectively bargained for
BURR: Fastball less, slider more

Okay, so usually I run out of ways to describe fastball/slider college closers much later in the offseason. Hamilton is the slightly harder-throwing one, and Burr is the taller one. They're close friends and remarkably similar prospects on the whole. Both blew us all away in Double-A and Triple-A this year, and both came up in August and struggled a bit in the majors. Usual caveats about command and functionality of third pitch from this profile also apply if they're going to stay in the room where it happens. The Hahn administration has built a lot of potential high-end reliever stock, so it remains to be seen whether the White Sox bullpen is wide enough for both. And yes, they're in on the joke.

15 Jake Burger 3B

Born: 04/10/96 Age: 23 Bats: R Throws: R Height: 6'2" Weight: 210 Origin: Round 1, 2017 Draft (#11 overall)

YEAR	TEAM	LVL	AGE	PA	R	2B	3B	HR	RBI	BB	K	SB	CS	AVG/OBP/SLG	DRC+	VORP	BABIP	BRR	FRAA	WARP	PF
2017	KAN	A	21	200	21	9	2	4	27	13	28	0	1	.271/.335/.409	120	9.6	.300	-0.2	3B(42) -0.8	0.6	100

The Double Stack took a double thwack to his 2018 season. Two Achilles ruptures, the first in spring training, the second while rehabbing, cost him an entire year of development. Burger was already a large adult son—check that nickname again—and likely bound for the cold corner in the medium term, but the injuries will certainly accelerate that process. There's enough uncertainty in his pro career in general now that you could argue for dropping him off the list entirely, but... well, we really like the bat.

16 Seby Zavala C

Born: 08/28/93 Age: 25 Bats: R Throws: R Height: 5'11" Weight: 215 Origin: Round 12, 2015 Draft (#352 overall)

YEAR	TEAM	LVL	AGE	PA	R	2B	3B	HR	RBI	BB	K	SB	CS	AVG/OBP/SLG	DRC+	VORP	BABIP	BRR	FRAA	WARP	PF
2016	KAN	A	22	404	40	19	3	7	49	35	108	1	1	.253/.330/.381	105	17.9	.341	-1.3	C(92) -1.3	1.0	97
2017	KAN	A	23	207	32	8	0	13	34	13	52	0	0	.259/.327/.514	131	17.6	.289	0.9	C(43) -1.5	1.2	99
2017	WNS	A+	23	228	31	13	0	8	38	24	52	1	0	.302/.376/.485	139	20.6	.373	3.0	C(31) 0.9	1.7	106
2018	BIR	AA	24	232	32	7	0	11	31	27	65	0	0	.271/.358/.472	133	18.4	.339	0.0	C(31) 4.0	1.5	95
2018	CHR	AAA	24	191	18	15	0	2	20	6	44	0	2	.243/.267/.359	81	-2.5	.304	-1.2	C(35) -3.0	-0.4	103
2019	*CHA*	*MLB*	*25*	*58*	*6*	*3*	*0*	*2*	*7*	*3*	*17*	*0*	*0*	*.221/.267/.376*	*70*	*0.5*	*.284*	*-0.1*	*C -1*	*-0.1*	*103*

Breakout: 5% Improve: 19% Collapse: 0% Attrition: 18% MLB: 29% *Comparables: Luke Montz, Andrew Knapp, Johnny Monell*

While BP's website wants to autocorrect this guy's name to "Sexy Zavala," there is nothing in the profile here that suggests such nominative determinism. Zavala is... well, "Zack-Collins-lite" isn't precisely correct. He's a superior defender to Collins—one of the reasons he was bumped to the International League first—but not so good that you'd want him as your first choice backstop. The bat isn't quite as loud as Collins, and backup backstops nowadays don't fit the "medium-power, fringy glove" profile that was all the rage in the 2000s; where have you gone, Henry Blanco? Zavala also isn't athletic enough to be a "jack-of-all-trades-and-also-a-catcher," which is en vogue on the north side of town. So we're left with a bit of a square peg prospect, although at a quick glance he might appear like many of the fringy catching prospects in most teams' 11-20.

Others of note:

Bernardo Flores, LHP, Double-A Birmingham

Flores is an uptempo southpaw with a high leg kick and hand break that sends his lean limbs in a bunch of different directions. It looks gangly but it's deceptive, he repeats well, and there isn't pronounced effort at any point. His fastball only sits low-90s, but Flores puts it where he wants and can change eye levels effectively. As you might have deduced from the lead-in, the changeup has above-average projection. He sells it well and can get it in to righties with sink and fade. He has two breaking balls—a slow, inconsistent curve that rolls across the plate and a slurvy slider—and both are below average. Flores doesn't really have a consistent bat-missing option, but there's enough command and change he could soak up some innings as a 5th starter/swingman/middle reliever.

Gavin Sheets, 1B, Advanced-A Winston Salem

Last year Sheets clocked in the Next Ten as a college first baseman with plus raw, not much of a pro track record, and a positional future that would put a lot of pressure on the bat. These are almost as common as polished lefties with an above-average change. As much as we love Big Boy SZN here at the BP Prospect Team, it's not as aesthetically pleasing as those crafty lefties, and in 2018 Sheets couldn't even offer much in the way of majestic dingers. Despite a leveraged swing and only average bat speed, he also didn't strike out all that much. He did, however, take 52 walks. Given his pedigree, he should have smashed the Carolina League, but after a weird season, for now we can just say there is still a lot of pressure on the bat.

Zack Burdi, RHP, complex-league AZL

Burdi has fallen behind the other power relief arms in the White Sox org while he sat on the sidelines rehabbing his 2017 Tommy John surgery. But there is a reason he went in the first round as a relief-only college arm. Burdi offers triple-digit heat, a wipeout slider, and he was essentially major-league-ready when his UCL blew. His few weeks of rehab in the AZL were uneven, as you'd expect, and he's getting some extra reps in Fall Ball as well. We'll have to wait to see him in camp next spring before confirming the closer stuff is still there, but if so he could walk into the White Sox Opening Day bullpen. Yep, that's all I got. I've never seen Hamilton.

Top Talents 25 and Under (born 4/1/93 or later):

1. Eloy Jimenez
2. Tim Anderson
3. Yoan Moncada
4. Nick Madrigal
5. Michael Kopech
6. Dylan Cease
7. Luis Robert
8. Reynaldo Lopez
9. Dane Dunning
10. Luis Alexander Basabe

The top three are already major league contributors or very close to it. Jimenez's superstar potential far outweighs the already productive if not quite finished products that are Anderson and Moncada.

Anderson over Moncada was a tough call, but the placement says more about the strides the former made in 2018 than the latter's perceived struggles. Anderson's essentially league-average offense in 2017 made him… well, essentially a league-average player, especially given how well his glove has come along at short. He paired a sterling defensive season with essentially the same offensive production as ever, albeit with a considerable leap in the power department. As a sure-handed defender at a key position with adequate offense and solid power, he gets the edge.

Moncada hasn't yet matured into the type of player many expected when he was a top prospect. Still, his league-leading strikeout total obscures some growth at the plate, particularly in eschewing pitches outside of the strike zone (18th best among qualified hitters). Even with his contact issues last year, he still showed enough of the tools people once raved about to portend a career as a very good regular, even if he doesn't look like a superstar.

Kopech likely would have ranked No. 2 on this list if he hadn't torn his UCL, which will keep him out until 2020. He slots in right behind Madrigal, the White Sox top pick in the 2018 draft. Madrigal more than held his own in High-A in the few months we saw of him following the draft. Kopech still has the higher ceiling, but arm injuries to pitchers are… well, you know.

The back five falls right in line with the prospect rankings above, with Lopez sandwiched in the middle. Lopez was just about the only young White Sox pitcher to not suffer any significant setback in 2018. He outpitched his peripherals for most of the season and showed enough durability to suggest he can stick in the rotation. He likely settles in as something of a backend starter, which limits his ceiling to the point where I'm comfortable putting talented but volatile prospects like Cease and Robert ahead of him. Still, his raw stuff—even if it winds up in the bullpen—is good enough to outweigh the high floor/low ceiling types like Dunning (who also missed time with an injury) and Basabe.

Cincinnati Reds

The State of the System:

It's more of a fun system than a great system. But it's also a good system, even if you have no confidence that they will ever develop a pitcher.

The Top Ten:

1 Nick Senzel IF   OFP: 70   Likely: 60   ETA: Let's try 2019 this time

Born: 06/29/95 Age: 24 Bats: R Throws: R Height: 6'1" Weight: 205 Origin: Round 1, 2016 Draft (#2 overall)

YEAR	TEAM	LVL	AGE	PA	R	2B	3B	HR	RBI	BB	K	SB	CS	AVG/OBP/SLG	DRC+	VORP	BABIP	BRR	FRAA	WARP	PF
2016	BIL	RK	21	41	3	1	0	0	4	6	5	3	0	.152/.293/.182	50	-1.5	.172	0.1	3B(10) 1.0	0.0	97
2016	DYT	A	21	251	38	23	3	7	36	32	49	15	7	.329/.415/.567	181	34.0	.392	1.6	3B(56) 3.2	3.2	104
2017	DAY	A+	22	272	41	26	2	4	31	23	54	9	2	.305/.371/.476	152	24.5	.378	1.3	3B(60) 5.1	2.4	106
2017	PEN	AA	22	235	40	14	1	10	34	26	43	5	4	.340/.413/.560	169	26.5	.391	-0.5	3B(56) 1.7	2.2	99
2018	LOU	AAA	23	193	23	12	2	6	25	19	39	8	2	.310/.378/.509	150	19.5	.367	1.9	2B(28) -0.8, 3B(14) 0.8	1.6	94
2019	*CIN*	*MLB*	*24*	*434*	*56*	*22*	*1*	*16*	*54*	*36*	*102*	*9*	*4*	*.264/.327/.448*	*109*	*20.0*	*.316*	*0.0*		*2.3*	*101*

Breakout: 12% Improve: 38% Collapse: 8% Attrition: 26% MLB: 63% *Comparables: Vince Belnome, Ryan Rua, Rob Refsnyder*

The Report: Coming into the year, Senzel was considered one of the safest prospect bets in baseball. Perhaps he lacked the superstar upside of some of the big names ranked around him on the 101, but he was a moneyline favorite to be an above-average regular at the hot corner. Well, I like to say that a year is an eternity in the life of a prospect, and boy did Senzel have a year. After a Eugenio Suarez breakout in 2017, the Reds decided to experiment with Senzel at second base (and even a little at short). Next, a torn finger tendon and then elbow surgery cost him most of the season. Now, the Reds are trying him in the outfield.

But when he was on the field in 2018, he was pretty much Nick Senzel—a polished plus prospect who might make a few All-Star games. Outfield might be a bit of an adventure, but he's likely fine at second, and I imagine he can still handle third. Wherever Senzel stands, the bat should play. He is a potential .300 hitter with solid-average raw power that should play to 20+ home runs given his approach, bat control, and home park. He's still a top ten prospect in baseball, just a year older now. Run it back again.

The Risks: Medium. His injury record is a bit troubling now, but there's nothing too traumatic or tools-sapping here. He's been basically major league-ready since last spring, although I'd be a little concerned about how he might take to being moved around the field this much.

Bret Sayre's Fantasy Take: You don't get too many instances where the circumstances around a top prospect make them an actual buy-low candidate, but we may have stumbled into one here. Take advantage of the slight prospect fatigue and questions about where Senzel will ultimately play, and make sure he's valued as the certain top-10 dynasty prospect he is. A potential .290 hitter with 25 homers and 15-20 steals is plenty valuable at any position.

2 Taylor Trammell OF

OFP: 70 Likely: 60 ETA: Mid-to-late 2020

Born: 09/13/97 Age: 21 Bats: L Throws: L Height: 6'2" Weight: 195 Origin: Round 1, 2016 Draft (#35 overall)

YEAR	TEAM	LVL	AGE	PA	R	2B	3B	HR	RBI	BB	K	SB	CS	AVG/OBP/SLG	DRC+	VORP	BABIP	BRR	FRAA	WARP	PF
2016	BIL	RK	18	254	39	9	6	2	34	23	57	24	7	.303/.374/.421	92	15.1	.396	2.7	LF(39) 0.5, CF(11) 2.1	0.2	102
2017	DYT	A	19	571	80	24	10	13	77	71	123	41	12	.281/.368/.450	126	41.6	.345	3.1	LF(104) -3.7, CF(17) -0.9	2.0	103
2018	DAY	A+	20	461	71	19	4	8	41	58	105	25	10	.277/.375/.406	126	26.4	.358	-0.8	CF(60) -1.7, LF(29) 4.5	1.7	103
2019	*CIN*	*MLB*	*21*	*252*	*25*	*5*	*1*	*6*	*24*	*17*	*75*	*7*	*2*	*.180/.235/.296*	*38*	*-9.6*	*.231*	*0.7*	*CF 0, LF 1*	*-0.9*	*101*

Breakout: 14% Improve: 28% Collapse: 1% Attrition: 13% MLB: 29% *Comparables: Anthony Gose, Jake Marisnick, Victor Robles*

The Report: You could argue there were two different versions of Trammell on display in 2018. There was the steady but unspectacular performer in Daytona, whose tools only flashed. And then there was the Futures Game version. So let's tease them out.

The Florida State League version: Trammell remained who we thought he was, which is an athletic, still raw player who still struggles at times on the defensive side. His 2018 didn't answer as many questions in the profile as we'd like. He still has work to do to develop his hit tool and get his power into games. Trammell still takes some curious routes to balls in the outfield and has not shown enough arm to get to average for center.

The Futures Game version: HARDWARE. Incredibly athletic frame, dumping balls second tank in BP. Looks the part. This is the exact kind of profile I want to bet on despite his only okay top line numbers in the minors. Plus tools profile, can likely stick in center. Why exactly hasn't he hit in the minors again?

So how do we remedy this? Showcases are dangerous, but it isn't like what Trammell showed hasn't flashed at other times. Having your national prospect coming out party in front of literally every prospect writer may put a bit of a finger on the scale, but now everyone knows what is in there.

The Risks: Medium. The foundation of tools is solid enough to almost guarantee a major-league future. We just need to see how much power, arm, and defense are going to develop.

Bret Sayre's Fantasy Take: I'm very bullish on Trammell's dynasty value. His plate discipline remained intact as he moved up a level, and there's little reason to think it will disintegrate upon reaching the upper minors. The approach will help him tap into 20-homer power and hit for a reasonable average (think .260-.270, with upside to boot). The big selling point is the speed, though. While he probably won't be efficient enough to really run up the score in the category, 30-35 steals is achievable. In this environment, that would make him a borderline OF1/OF2, and it's a big reason why he's an easy top-20 dynasty prospect.

3 Jonathan India 3B

OFP: 60 Likely: 55 ETA: 2020

Born: 12/15/96 Age: 22 Bats: R Throws: R Height: 6'1" Weight: 200 Origin: Round 1, 2018 Draft (#5 overall)

YEAR	TEAM	LVL	AGE	PA	R	2B	3B	HR	RBI	BB	K	SB	CS	AVG/OBP/SLG	DRC+	VORP	BABIP	BRR	FRAA	WARP	PF
2018	GRV	RK	21	62	11	2	1	3	12	15	12	1	0	.261/.452/.543	161	6.2	.290	0.6	3B(12) -0.6, SS(2) -0.2	0.4	101
2018	DYT	A	21	112	17	7	0	3	11	13	28	5	0	.229/.339/.396	104	7.0	.292	1.5	3B(21) 2.4, SS(4) -0.1	0.6	101
2019	*CIN*	*MLB*	*22*	*252*	*22*	*8*	*0*	*7*	*25*	*18*	*83*	*2*	*1*	*.148/.212/.280*	*29*	*-14.9*	*.188*	*-0.1*	*3B 0, SS 0*	*-1.6*	*101*

Breakout: 9% Improve: 11% Collapse: 0% Attrition: 10% MLB: 11% *Comparables: Jesus Guzman, Kyle Kubitza, Steven Souza*

The Report: India is the roasted salmon of the world of top prospects; it's likely quite good, but it's not going to be what I order in your *Michelin*-starred restaurant. At the plate, India is an intelligent and adaptable hitter who won't be fooled by the same pitch twice in a row. Enough raw power gets into games to punish misplaced offerings, and he should hit a lot of doubles while chipping in 15-20 homers. His defense is nothing to write home about, but third will remain his long-term home. I spoke to a few National League scouts who weren't overly impressed with him, and I understand why. India is not as exciting as it feels like the No. 5 overall pick should be. That said, he had the best present package of skills I saw in the Midwest League in 2018.

The Risks: Low. He's more likely to end up at the low end of the spectrum but there's very little delta between India's floor and ceiling. I'll be interested to see how he handles premium velocity. Assuming he can catch up to it and that he doesn't stall out with injuries, he's a major leaguer.

Probably.

Prospects, man.

Bret Sayre's Fantasy Take: There's a fair amount of hype in dynasty circles on India, who was drafted highly by a team with a strong home park after a dynamic college season. That said, the fantasy upside with India isn't all that high. He doesn't have impact power or speed, and he'll be challenged to hit for a high average despite doing so in college this year. There's definitely a place for an infielder with all-around skills in leagues of all size—just ask those who relied on Jurickson Profar in 2018—but his limited overall upside makes him a good, but not great, dynasty prospect.

4 Hunter Greene RHP OFP: 60 Likely: 50 ETA: 2022

Born: 08/06/99 Age: 19 Bats: R Throws: R Height: 6'4" Weight: 215 Origin: Round 1, 2017 Draft (#2 overall)

YEAR	TEAM	LVL	AGE	W	L	SV	G	GS	IP	H	HR	BB/9	K/9	K	GB%	BABIP	WHIP	ERA	DRA	WARP	PF
2018	DYT	A	18	3	7	0	18	18	68^{1}	66	6	3.0	11.7	89	43%	.353	1.30	4.48	3.69	1.2	103
2019	*CIN*	*MLB*	*19*	*3*	*4*	*0*	*13*	*13*	*48^{2}*	*48*	*8*	*4.3*	*9.5*	*52*	*40%*	*.322*	*1.47*	*4.94*	*5.38*	*0.0*	*101*

Breakout: 1% Improve: 1% Collapse: 0% Attrition: 1% MLB: 1% *Comparables: Kolby Allard, Vicente Campos, Roberto Osuna*

The Report: Before he sprained his UCL, Greene looked the part of the typical "pitch-and-a-half" prep arm that dominates A-ball. But the results didn't match the stuff, which is especially weird given that your typical high-pick prep arm doesn't touch 100+ as often as Greene. He's got the premium athleticism you'd expect from a prospect who could have easily been drafted as a shortstop or two-way experiment, with an uptempo delivery and lightning-fast arm. The slider is still a bit slurvy, but he commands it well enough, and—again—dude throws 103. So why didn't Greene *really* dominate the Midwest League?

Well, the heater is very true, the command fringy, and he'll telegraph the slider with his arm speed. Everything's just a bit more hittable than it should be. These aren't fatal flaws by any means, but he doesn't have a well-rounded profile like MacKenzie Gore, Shane Baz, or DL Hall—the other highly-touted prep arms in his draft class. Greene's elbow situation puts his 2019 in doubt, so that could be a year of lost development time. And the risk factor here was already higher than you'd like from just looking at his draft position. You never want to dismiss the plus athlete firing triple-digit bullets, but—and lord do I abhor this phrase—he was more of a thrower than a pitcher in 2018.

The Risks: Extreme. I had some questions about how the profile was gonna develop before the UCL sprain, which just adds additional risk.

Bret Sayre's Fantasy Take: It's not that I don't like prep arms with premium velocity, it's just that there isn't much separation between guys with this pedigree from a dynasty league standpoint. The perceived value here because of his name recognition and especially high radar gun readings is a dangerous vortex to enter, made even more perilous by a right elbow that may as well have a skull-and-crossbones tattoo on it. Yes, it's an SP2 ceiling but there is just so much that can go wrong here, and it leaves Greene as a back-end Top 101 guy (come fight me, Ben).

5 Tony Santillan RHP OFP: 60 Likely: 50 ETA: September 2019

Born: 04/15/97 Age: 22 Bats: R Throws: R Height: 6'3" Weight: 240 Origin: Round 2, 2015 Draft (#49 overall)

YEAR	TEAM	LVL	AGE	W	L	SV	G	GS	IP	H	HR	BB/9	K/9	K	GB%	BABIP	WHIP	ERA	DRA	WARP	PF
2016	BIL	RK	19	1	0	0	8	8	39	32	4	3.7	10.6	46	46%	.292	1.23	3.92	2.36	1.5	97
2016	DYT	A	19	2	3	0	7	7	30^{1}	27	3	7.1	11.3	38	38%	.338	1.68	6.82	3.51	0.6	105
2017	DYT	A	20	9	8	0	25	24	128	104	9	3.9	9.0	128	45%	.281	1.25	3.38	4.17	1.6	101
2018	DAY	A+	21	6	4	0	15	15	86^{2}	81	5	2.3	7.6	73	44%	.298	1.19	2.70	5.03	0.3	102
2018	PEN	AA	21	4	3	0	11	11	62^{1}	65	8	2.3	8.8	61	46%	.315	1.30	3.61	4.19	0.8	97
2019	*CIN*	*MLB*	*22*	*0*	*0*	*0*	*10*	*0*	*10^{2}*	*11*	*2*	*4.6*	*8.8*	*11*	*40%*	*.312*	*1.51*	*5.26*	*5.73*	*0.0*	*101*

Breakout: 12% Improve: 17% Collapse: 8% Attrition: 17% MLB: 33% *Comparables: Jake Thompson, Jayson Aquino, Greg Reynolds*

The Report: Santillan performed across two levels in 2018 and was fine in his first taste of Double-A. His fastball sits in the mid-90s and shows above-average movement. Santillan improved his fastball command this season as well, making the pitch a true plus offering. While his slider can have some inconsistent shape, it's a hard bat-missing offering despite that. The development of a third pitch will be the key here. Santillan's change needs further refinement, but will flash average. More consistency with the secondaries will be the deciding factor between his sticking in the middle of a rotation or being just another 95-and-a-slider reliever.

The Risks: Medium. The development of his third pitch will shape his ultimate role. As is often the case with this profile, the gap in realistic outcomes at this point is pretty wide.

Bret Sayre's Fantasy Take: Santillan is almost the polar opposite of Greene, but were I faced with a decision between the two of them today in a dynasty league, I'd take the former. His 2018 season showed more upside than originally anticipated and he could settle in as a solid SP3 if he can hold the command improvement. He'll likely be someone who stands out more in WHIP than in strikeouts, but he could still run up 175-180 per year.

6 Mike Siani OF   OFP: 55   Likely: 45   ETA: 2022

Born: 07/16/99 Age: 19 Bats: L Throws: L Height: 6'1" Weight: 180 Origin: Round 4, 2018 Draft (#109 overall)

YEAR	TEAM	LVL	AGE	PA	R	2B	3B	HR	RBI	BB	K	SB	CS	AVG/OBP/SLG	DRC+	VORP	BABIP	BRR	FRAA	WARP	PF
2018	GRV	RK	18	205	24	6	3	2	13	16	35	6	4	.288/.351/.386	118	10.7	.342	-0.1	CF(45) 6.5	1.0	104
2019	*CIN*	*MLB*	*19*	*252*	*20*	*3*	*0*	*5*	*18*	*4*	*74*	*1*	*0*	*.166/.176/.241*	*7*	*-18.9*	*.210*	*-0.3*	*CF 2*	*-1.9*	*101*

Breakout: 5% Improve: 7% Collapse: 0% Attrition: 3% MLB: 8% *Comparables: Carlos Tocci, Engel Beltre, Francisco Pena*

The Report: The Reds went well over slot to sign Siani, a Northeast prep bat they popped in the fourth round of last summer's draft. Well, maybe not as a "bat" per se. Siani has plus-plus athletic tools that make him as sure-shot a center fielder as you'll see in a teenager. He's a 70 runner with a near elite arm. There are questions about how much he will hit, and the swing is a tad mechanical at present, although it feels like something he'll grow out of. There's some feel for contact already too, and he was perfectly fine during what you could consider a slightly aggressive first-summer assignment.

Siani is a little bit old for his prep class, if that matters to you. He may grow into some power, though it won't be a huge part of his game. But the defensive tools are so good that he won't have to hit all that much to be a productive major leaguer. It was a little surprising that he lasted as long as he did on the draft board, and while the Reds ended up paying him like a first-round pick, they also got commensurate first-round upside.

The Risks: High. Only a short-season resume so far, questions about the bat. The athletic tools give him a bit of a floor though, if not a major-league one quite yet.

Bret Sayre's Fantasy Take: One of my favorite underrated prospects in dynasty drafts this offseason, Siani isn't your typical fourth-round pick. He's raw and risky, but he's also a potential five-category contributor in the outfield who showed a better approach at the plate than expected in his pro debut. He doesn't need to go inside the top-30 this offseason, but he probably deserves to.

7 Vladimir Gutierrez RHP   OFP: 50   Likely: 45   ETA: Late 2019

Born: 09/18/95 Age: 23 Bats: R Throws: R Height: 6'0" Weight: 190 Origin: International Free Agent, 2016

YEAR	TEAM	LVL	AGE	W	L	SV	G	GS	IP	H	HR	BB/9	K/9	K	GB%	BABIP	WHIP	ERA	DRA	WARP	PF
2017	DAY	A+	21	7	8	0	19	19	103	108	10	1.7	8.2	94	42%	.320	1.23	4.46	4.71	0.7	107
2018	PEN	AA	22	9	10	0	27	27	147	139	18	2.3	8.9	145	46%	.298	1.20	4.35	3.75	2.7	96
2019	*CIN*	*MLB*	*23*	*1*	*0*	*0*	*10*	*0*	*10²*	*10*	*2*	*2.8*	*8.9*	*11*	*41%*	*.312*	*1.28*	*4.25*	*4.59*	*0.0*	*101*

Breakout: 9% Improve: 14% Collapse: 25% Attrition: 34% MLB: 44% *Comparables: Felix Jorge, Chih-Wei Hu, Brett Kennedy*

The Report: There were a couple of positive markers in Gutierrez's 2018 Southern League campaign. For starters, he was mostly fine there, striking out about a batter per inning. Now, we don't scout the statline, but performance matters a bit for this kind of profile in Double-A. His change looks better these days, with more consistent dive now, although it's still used sparingly.

The rest of the profile remains mostly unchanged from when he signed. He sits in the low-90s. The fastball is a bit of a riser, and there's generally enough armside movement to keep it off barrels. Gutierrez manipulates his curveball well. He'll show a slower roller for strikes, and then ramp up the velocity and tightness to entice chases. He doesn't always get consistent 12-5 action on it, but it's a potential above-average offering.

Gutierrez still struggles at times with his fastball command, and the heater can straighten out. He doesn't really have an offering to get grounders, and the stuff isn't good enough to live in the zone. But he has shown enough durability—along with three potentially average-or-better offerings and a bit of pitchability and polish—to project him as a back-end innings-eater type. We'll just gloss over Cincinnati's lack of success in converting this type of prospect into an actual back-end innings eater.

The Risks: Medium. He was fine though not dominant in Double-A. Has been relatively durable. Could use additional command and changeup refinement.

Bret Sayre's Fantasy Take: We started out so well with this system and now we're down to "guy who is durable and might not be a reliever." Gutierrez isn't relevant at this point outside of very deep mixed and NL leagues.

8 Jose Siri OF

OFP: 55 Likely: 40 ETA: 2020

Born: 07/22/95 Age: 23 Bats: R Throws: R Height: 6'2" Weight: 175 Origin: International Free Agent, 2012

YEAR	TEAM	LVL	AGE	PA	R	2B	3B	HR	RBI	BB	K	SB	CS	AVG/OBP/SLG	DRC+	VORP	BABIP	BRR	FRAA	WARP	PF
2016	DYT	A	20	87	5	3	0	0	3	2	34	3	2	.145/.163/.181	8	-8.9	.240	0.6	CF(17) 1.7, RF(9) -0.2	-0.6	104
2016	BIL	RK	20	255	52	12	8	10	35	8	66	17	4	.320/.348/.560	123	25.2	.404	3.9	RF(33) 4.6, CF(21) 5.4	1.9	102
2017	DYT	A	21	552	92	24	11	24	76	33	130	46	12	.293/.341/.530	135	49.1	.349	7.4	CF(103) 15.7, RF(9) 1.5	5.6	103
2018	DAY	A+	22	126	15	9	2	1	9	4	32	9	1	.261/.280/.395	90	2.2	.341	1.1	CF(26) 0.4	0.1	101
2018	PEN	AA	22	283	42	8	9	12	34	24	91	14	5	.229/.300/.474	91	15.0	.301	2.2	CF(59) -3.9	-0.1	97
2019	*CIN*	*MLB*	*23*	*165*	*19*	*4*	*2*	*6*	*18*	*4*	*56*	*5*	*2*	*.190/.208/.365*	*42*	*-3.9*	*.240*	*1.2*	*CF 2*	*-0.2*	*101*

Breakout: 11% Improve: 21% Collapse: 2% Attrition: 12% MLB: 24% *Comparables: Teoscar Hernandez, Franchy Cordero, Kirk Nieuwenhuis*

The Report: Man, I don't know. I think there's a general feeling among the outside onlookers that "Baseball Prospectus" as a prospect-ranking entity overrates this type of player. This has now endured through four different eras of lead prospect writers. We value upside over dudes who can or have actually hit. Is that fair? Man, I don't know. I'm probably gonna have Leody Taveras 50 spots higher than anyone else. So maybe.

Leody Taveras is not Jose Siri, and this is the Reds list not the Rangers. But Siri has big tools: Plus raw, plus run, plus arm, may stick in center field, [insert overly sexual descriptors and/or your favorite #hashtag here].

We often wax philosophically about how the hardest thing to evaluate is whether a prospect will hit major-league pitching. Siri is not one of the prospects that inspires a treatise. The swing gets long in order to tap into that power. He struggles with pitch recognition. Neither of those things stop him from being hyper-aggressive. He struck out 32% of the time in Double-A. This is a known issue. There's a ticket open already. But if it clicks…

Last year Steve Givarz argued that he'd write Siri as a 70/30 if he could. Yeah, that's generally frowned upon in every era of Baseball Prospectus prospect writing, but I get it. I'll go about as wide as I can here, and really this ranking feels like throwing a dart. Honestly it's not a profile I love, except for when I do.

The Risks: Extreme. The swing and miss might eat into everything here. He's older than you think.

Bret Sayre's Fantasy Take: Imagine you're in a bar and you strike up a conversation with a woman. She casually mentions that she plays bass in a local band and you two really hit it off. You go to see her band, expecting to get a Kim Deal vibe that's always gotten you a little more excited than it should. Instead, it's a reggae cover band. You knew the risks. You should have seen it coming when she said the band's name was The Kingston Cops. Now things are just weird and the potential has soured. You can't unhear her doing backup vocals on "Get Up, Stand Up."

Anyway, don't let Siri's power/speed combination get you too excited.

9 Jose Garcia SS

OFP: 50 Likely: 40 ETA: 2021

Born: 04/05/98 Age: 21 Bats: R Throws: R Height: 6'2" Weight: 175 Origin: International Free Agent, 2017

YEAR	TEAM	LVL	AGE	PA	R	2B	3B	HR	RBI	BB	K	SB	CS	AVG/OBP/SLG	DRC+	VORP	BABIP	BRR	FRAA	WARP	PF
2018	DYT	A	20	517	61	22	4	6	53	19	112	13	9	.245/.290/.344	84	10.3	.307	1.8	SS(93) -0.7, 2B(29) -1.8	0.3	102
2019	*CIN*	*MLB*	*21*	*252*	*22*	*5*	*0*	*5*	*19*	*1*	*71*	*2*	*1*	*.173/.187/.261*	*11*	*-17.9*	*.219*	*-0.2*	*SS 0, 2B -1*	*-2.0*	*101*

Breakout: 2% Improve: 2% Collapse: 0% Attrition: 2% MLB: 2% *Comparables: Dawel Lugo, Marwin Gonzalez, Juan Diaz*

The Report: Garcia's first season stateside started poorly. He appeared overmatched at the plate, and he didn't have much of an approach nor any discernible feel for the strike zone. As the year progressed, he quieted his hands and put together better at-bats. Tall and high waisted, his athleticism stands out on the field. It's a projectable frame and he should add good weight as he matures. Blessed with a strong arm, he has the defensive chops to stick at the six. Combine that with some sneaky pop, plus speed, and improving plate discipline, and you have a player poised for a breakout in 2019.

The Risks: High, still adjusting to pro ball, questions about the long term value of the bat.

10 Tyler Stephenson C

OFP: 50 Likely: 40 ETA: 2021

Born: 08/16/96 Age: 22 Bats: R Throws: R Height: 6'4" Weight: 225 Origin: Round 1, 2015 Draft (#11 overall)

YEAR	TEAM	LVL	AGE	PA	R	2B	3B	HR	RBI	BB	K	SB	CS	AVG/OBP/SLG	DRC+	VORP	BABIP	BRR	FRAA	WARP	PF
2016	DYT	A	19	153	17	4	1	3	16	12	45	0	0	.216/.278/.324	72	0.0	.297	0.9	C(27) -1.2	-0.2	105
2017	DYT	A	20	348	39	22	0	6	50	44	58	2	1	.278/.374/.414	138	19.9	.322	-2.6	C(53) -4.0	1.5	101
2018	DAY	A+	21	450	60	20	1	11	59	45	98	1	0	.250/.338/.392	117	24.3	.301	0.2	C(97) -3.3	1.5	104
2019	*CIN*	*MLB*	*22*	*252*	*21*	*7*	*0*	*6*	*25*	*16*	*69*	*0*	*0*	*.179/.234/.293*	*38*	*-8.0*	*.221*	*-0.5*	*C -1*	*-1.0*	*101*

Breakout: 11% Improve: 27% Collapse: 0% Attrition: 24% MLB: 29% *Comparables: Victor Caratini, Christian Vazquez, Lou Marson*

The Report: A series of one-sentence summaries detailing how we've handled, are handling, and project to handle Tyler Stephenson's career trajectory on these lists:

2016: "All prep catchers are inherently a work in progress, but he can hit for power and he's pretty good behind the dish already."

2017: "Well that was a lost year."

2018: "What do you mean '53 games behind the plate are a new career-high?'"

2019: "All prep catchers are inherently a work in progress, and that's reflected in Stephenson's receiving, footwork, and hit tool."

2020: "There was more to dream on back when he wasn't playing, but Stephenson's strong arm, plus raw power, and developing receiving skills portend a future as a backup catcher."

The Risks: High. The track record of health is now marginally less abysmal, but there is still a lot of remaining development required here on both sides of the ball.

The Next Five:

11 T.J. Friedl OF

Born: 08/14/95 Age: 23 Bats: L Throws: L Height: 5'10" Weight: 170 Origin: Undrafted Free Agent, 2016

YEAR	TEAM	LVL	AGE	PA	R	2B	3B	HR	RBI	BB	K	SB	CS	AVG/OBP/SLG	DRC+	VORP	BABIP	BRR	FRAA	WARP	PF
2017	DYT	A	21	292	47	20	6	5	25	29	46	14	8	.284/.378/.472	137	24.7	.328	4.1	RF(22) 0.7, CF(18) -3.0	1.5	102
2017	DAY	A+	21	199	15	6	2	2	13	10	39	2	1	.257/.313/.346	83	3.1	.317	0.0	CF(20) -1.3, RF(18) -2.5	-0.3	102
2018	DAY	A+	22	274	40	10	4	3	35	38	44	11	4	.294/.405/.412	136	23.4	.350	4.7	LF(39) 2.0, CF(19) -1.0	1.8	102
2018	PEN	AA	22	296	47	10	3	2	16	28	56	19	5	.276/.359/.360	111	12.7	.345	3.3	LF(53) 5.1, CF(9) -1.0	1.2	98
2019	*CIN*	*MLB*	*23*	*37*	*4*	*1*	*0*	*1*	*3*	*2*	*9*	*1*	*0*	*.226/.289/.340*	*70*	*0.2*	*.281*	*0.1*	*CF -1*	*-0.1*	*101*

Breakout: 6% Improve: 16% Collapse: 0% Attrition: 11% MLB: 18% *Comparables: Dwight Smith, Jake Smolinski, Phil Ervin*

Friedl was at the center of one of the most glaring draft oversights in recent memory. A second-round talent, the Nevada product went unpicked in 2016 because nobody knew he was eligible. Cincinnati, who was scouting him aggressively that summer anyway, pounced on the mistake. Most draftees had already signed by that point, and the Reds—who had more money remaining in their bonus pool than any other club—gave Friedl $700,000 to sign.

On the field, Friedl is a plus runner who projects as a quality fourth outfielder. He has the speed to play center and just enough arm to handle right if needed. He battles every at bat, can take a walk, and has sufficient gap power to keep pitchers honest. He's a smart baserunner and he could post double-digit steal totals in a part-time role. There's not quite enough pop here to project him as a regular, but even in a tough time for reserve outfielders, he should get a few big-league cracks.

12 Stuart Fairchild OF

Born: 03/17/96 Age: 23 Bats: R Throws: R Height: 6'0" Weight: 190 Origin: Round 2, 2017 Draft (#38 overall)

YEAR	TEAM	LVL	AGE	PA	R	2B	3B	HR	RBI	BB	K	SB	CS	AVG/OBP/SLG	DRC+	VORP	BABIP	BRR	FRAA	WARP	PF
2017	BIL	RK	21	234	36	5	4	3	23	19	35	12	4	.304/.393/.412	107	15.0	.355	1.8	CF(43) -9.4, RF(5) -0.6	-0.3	105
2018	DYT	A	22	276	40	12	5	7	37	31	65	17	4	.277/.377/.460	136	20.2	.352	2.3	CF(30) -2.3, LF(26) -0.4	1.4	104
2018	DAY	A+	22	242	25	14	1	2	20	17	63	6	2	.250/.306/.350	98	-4.2	.335	-4.4	LF(31) 0.1, CF(30) -2.4	-0.6	104
2019	*CIN*	*MLB*	*23*	*252*	*22*	*3*	*1*	*6*	*23*	*10*	*72*	*4*	*1*	*.180/.223/.271*	*36*	*-10.3*	*.231*	*0.6*	*CF -1, LF 0*	*-1.3*	*101*

Breakout: 4% Improve: 5% Collapse: 0% Attrition: 5% MLB: 5% *Comparables: Michael Taylor, Blake Tekotte, Daniel Fields*

A first-rounder back in 2017, Fairchild was a slightly undersized outfielder who destroyed the ACC as Wake Forest's center fielder. Despite lofty power numbers in college, many scouts questioned whether Fairchild's pop was the product of a small ballpark and an all-or-nothing approach that could potentially be exploited by professional arms. A year-and-a-half later, those concerns have grown. He only homered nine times in 130 minor-league games last season, and while the Florida State League isn't a great place to hit, he was far too easy of an out at that level. He's an aggressive hitter who swings and misses often, even against fringy stuff, and he will likely always struggle with quality spin.

There are things to like: Fairchild is athletic, he has a very quick bat, he's an above-average runner, and his arm is strong enough for right if he needs to shift down the defensive spectrum. But there are now legitimate reasons to think he won't hit enough to tap into his power; you might also fairly question whether the power is coming at all. If he doesn't dispel one of those notions, he'll slide off this list come 2019.

13 Jimmy Herget RHP

Born: 09/09/93 Age: 25 Bats: R Throws: R Height: 6'3" Weight: 170 Origin: Round 6, 2015 Draft (#175 overall)

YEAR	TEAM	LVL	AGE	W	L	SV	G	GS	IP	H	HR	BB/9	K/9	K	GB%	BABIP	WHIP	ERA	DRA	WARP	PF
2016	DAY	A+	22	4	4	24	50	0	60^2	47	3	3.3	12.3	83	38%	.310	1.14	1.78	2.42	1.8	100
2017	PEN	AA	23	1	3	16	24	0	29^2	22	1	3.6	13.3	44	32%	.323	1.15	2.73	2.10	1.0	100
2017	LOU	AAA	23	3	1	9	28	0	32^1	30	4	2.5	7.8	28	38%	.283	1.21	3.06	3.93	0.5	100
2018	LOU	AAA	24	1	3	0	50	0	59^2	59	5	3.2	9.8	65	36%	.327	1.34	3.47	3.69	1.0	100
2019	*CIN*	*MLB*	*25*	*2*	*1*	*2*	*49*	*0*	*52^1*	*50*	*8*	*4.0*	*9.6*	*56*	*36%*	*.315*	*1.41*	*4.66*	*5.06*	*-0.1*	*101*

Breakout: 12% Improve: 15% Collapse: 13% Attrition: 23% MLB: 32% *Comparables: Josh Osich, Cody Eppley, Matt Reynolds*

Herget didn't make the majors this year—as we prognosticated on last year's list—but there isn't much left for him to accomplish in the minors. He doesn't have huge stuff. The fastball might touch 95 on occasion, but sits more 90-93, with sink and run from a near sidearm slot. His delivery is funky, uptempo, and a tough look for righties. He commands a low-80s slider well, although there isn't enough depth to consistently miss bats. It's still not really a late-inning arm, but Herget is a major league-ready bullpen piece who has gotten it done at every level.

14 Lyon Richardson RHP

Born: 01/18/00 Age: 19 Bats: B Throws: R Height: 6'2" Weight: 175 Origin: Round 2, 2018 Draft (#47 overall)

YEAR	TEAM	LVL	AGE	W	L	SV	G	GS	IP	H	HR	BB/9	K/9	K	GB%	BABIP	WHIP	ERA	DRA	WARP	PF
2018	GRV	RK	18	0	5	0	11	11	29	37	3	5.0	7.4	24	41%	.362	1.83	7.14	5.20	0.3	104
2019	*CIN*	*MLB*	*19*	*1*	*4*	*0*	*8*	*8*	*30*	*38*	*7*	*8.0*	*5.8*	*19*	*40%*	*.322*	*2.15*	*8.04*	*8.84*	*-1.2*	*101*

Breakout: 0% Improve: 0% Collapse: 0% Attrition: 0% MLB: 0% *Comparables: Antonio Senzatela, Juan Minaya, Duane Underwood*

The Reds other second round arm from 2018, Richardson is a typical advanced Florida prep arm. While he doesn't feature a ton of remaining projection, the fastball sits low-90s and can touch the upper-90s, so it's not like you need to dream on the frame or a velocity bump here. The secondaries are on the raw side with the curveball at least flashing at times, and given his uptempo delivery with some late effort, you might be best off letting him try to more consistently find the plus-or-better velocity in short bursts out of the pen. That decision is a ways down the road at this point though.

15 Tanner Rainey RHP

Born: 12/25/92 Age: 26 Bats: R Throws: R Height: 6'2" Weight: 235 Origin: Round 2, 2015 Draft (#71 overall)

YEAR	TEAM	LVL	AGE	W	L	SV	G	GS	IP	H	HR	BB/9	K/9	K	GB%	BABIP	WHIP	ERA	DRA	WARP	PF
2016	DYT	A	23	5	10	1	29	20	103[1]	109	9	5.7	9.8	113	39%	.353	1.69	5.57	3.93	1.3	105
2017	DAY	A+	24	2	2	9	39	0	45	21	4	4.4	15.4	77	47%	.230	0.96	3.80	1.97	1.5	100
2017	PEN	AA	24	1	1	4	14	0	17	8	2	5.8	14.3	27	62%	.222	1.12	1.59	1.96	0.6	100
2018	CIN	MLB	25	0	0	0	8	0	7	13	4	15.4	9.0	7	31%	.409	3.57	24.43	9.00	-0.3	105
2018	LOU	AAA	25	7	2	3	44	0	51	25	2	6.2	11.5	65	37%	.221	1.18	2.65	3.40	1.0	100
2019	*WAS*	*MLB*	*26*	*1*	*0*	*0*	*19*	*0*	*20[2]*	*17*	*3*	*6.6*	*11.2*	*26*	*38%*	*.305*	*1.55*	*4.73*	*5.39*	*-0.1*	*100*

Breakout: 18% Improve: 31% Collapse: 7% Attrition: 20% MLB: 42% *Comparables: Maikel Cleto, Jose Ramirez, Drew Steckenrider*

The good news for Rainey is that when you throw in the upper-90s with a wipeout slider you usually get opportunities to bring down that 24.43 MLB ERA. While he wasn't exactly painting the corners in the minors, Rainey's stuff was all over the place in the majors, and his delivery suffers from endemic and severe bouts of overthrowing. In the minors, this was less of an issue when he was pumping 99 somewhere in the general vicinity of the bottom of the zone and pairing it with a low-90s slider. That's still uncommon even in la grande liga, but major leaguers see it enough to recognize when it ain't close. Any real refinement here in the control/command could make Rainey a late-inning arm, but either way, upper-90s and a slider gets opps.

Others of note:

Aristides Aquino, OF, Cincinnati Reds

Can I interest you in Jose Siri with fewer tools but more actualized game power? Aquino did a bit better in a repeat engagement in Double-A—slightly more contact, general improvement around the margins. Power is the only real standout tool here though, and while hey, I'm never gonna tell you dingers aren't cool, if Siri looks like this after his age-24 season... well, he'll be down here too, I guess. Aquino did get the briefest of looks in the majors—a function of his being on the 40-man and Joey Votto having a balky knee—but he's not a lock to get back to improve on that 100% K-rate.

Top Talents 25 and Under (born 4/1/93 or later):

1. Nick Senzel
2. Taylor Trammell
3. Jonathan India
4. Jesse Winker
5. Hunter Greene
6. Tony Santillan
7. Jose Peraza
8. Mike Siani
9. Sal Romano

Though the Reds appear intent on moving beyond the rebuilding phase, the bulk of their young talent has not yet reached Cincinnati. Injuries have delayed the arrival of Nick Senzel, the fast-moving college bat™ who turns 24 in June. Senzel might burst out of the gate as the super-advanced hitter he's been billed as, but any slow start will raise questions about whether the club complicated his rise by foisting new defensive positions upon him. It's one thing to plan around Eugenio Suarez, but it doesn't feel like Senzel should be the tail wagged by Scooter Gennett's breakout.

We'll soon see how the Reds approach the development of fellow fast-moving college bat™ Jonathan India, also a third baseman. Trammell represents a welcome diversification of the portfolio. He's not nearly ready for the show yet, but could one day bring electricity to the top of the order.

As for the present-day top of the order, Winker might be a Bizarro Joey Votto who simply isn't allowed to work out. Before losing half his season to a shoulder injury, he showed premium plate discipline, though his slugging percentage was caught in a battle with his (admittedly excellent) OBP. While Winker likely wouldn't rank ahead of the scintillating Greene if the young hurler were fully healthy, he wins points for his steady bat and an eye that anyone can appreciate.

Jose Peraza doesn't inspire such confidence. A long-declining stock, his surface stats hinted at progress in 2018. He lifted and pulled the ball a bit more to post average-ish numbers, yet there was no discernible change in his approach to fuel any optimism going forward. He still chases too much and lacks the exceptional in-zone aggression that works for some of Atlanta's free-swingers, for instance. The result is a limp noodle of a bat that will live and die on BABIP fluctuations and the carry of fly balls down the line. Incoming hitting coach Turner Ward isn't known for any particular strategy, but a new voice in the room probably can't hurt. Regardless of how you feel about him, expect Peraza to get 600 more plate appearances to prove he deserves a role on a team that's trying.

The Reds continue to flail on the mound. Romano's inclusion here may be charitable, and could soon look silly. He gets the nod over Brandon Finnegan, Cody Reed and Lucas Sims though, because his fastball and slider do look good together and, indeed, rate well in BP's tunneling metrics. Though he took his lumps, the combination improved as the season went on. Really only in possession of two good pitches, he might benefit from the shorter outings of a Rays or playoff-Brewers style pitching plan.

Cleveland Indians

The State of the System:

Cleveland's system is bolstered by a strong 2018 draft class and a couple IFA breakouts in the low minors, but that also means limited help for the big club in the near term.

The Top Ten:

1 **Triston McKenzie RHP** OFP: 60 Likely: 55 ETA: Late 2019/Early 2020

Born: 08/02/97 Age: 21 Bats: R Throws: R Height: 6'5" Weight: 165 Origin: Round 1, 2015 Draft (#42 overall)

YEAR	TEAM	LVL	AGE	W	L	SV	G	GS	IP	H	HR	BB/9	K/9	K	GB%	BABIP	WHIP	ERA	DRA	WARP	PF
2016	MHV	A-	18	4	3	0	9	9	49^{1}	31	2	2.9	10.0	55	37%	.248	0.95	0.55	2.92	1.3	100
2016	LKC	A	18	2	2	0	6	6	34	27	2	1.6	13.0	49	40%	.333	0.97	3.18	2.33	1.1	97
2017	LYN	A+	19	12	6	0	25	25	143	105	14	2.8	11.7	186	43%	.283	1.05	3.46	2.60	4.5	91
2018	AKR	AA	20	7	4	0	16	16	90^{2}	63	8	2.8	8.6	87	34%	.234	1.00	2.68	4.03	1.4	87
2019	*CLE*	*MLB*	*21*	*1*	*1*	*0*	*3*	*3*	*15*	*15*	*3*	*3.5*	*8.9*	*15*	*35%*	*.293*	*1.37*	*4.87*	*5.24*	*0.0*	*106*

Breakout: 6% Improve: 17% Collapse: 6% Attrition: 17% MLB: 29% *Comparables: Chris Tillman, Jacob Turner, Julio Teheran*

The Report: This would all be easier if McKenzie were left-handed. It would fit more neatly. It feels like he should be left-handed. Yes, he's still rail-thin so we can all still call him projectable, but the fastball is also still pinned around 90, albeit with good plane and plus command. It's an above-average pitch regardless of stalker readings. There's the same plus mid-70s curve that McKenzie might command even better than the fastball. That's the start of a very nice pitching prospect, but one that is usually a southpaw. I have no idea if that should matter, or if this weirdness is located merely in my head. He throws his changeup sparingly and doesn't have ideal velocity separation, but it's potentially average as well. McKenzie is in Double-A now. He's knocking on the door of the majors. The stuff is fine, better than fine really. He's never had issues getting minor-league hitters out, and the whole profile still feels like a Top 50 prospect. Yet the cognitive dissonance remains.

Oh yeah, McKenzie also missed the first few months with a "forearm," as Al Michaels would say. That's a little more concrete, but maybe not meaningful. We'll see.

The Risks: Medium. He's always been good on the mound, and has been on the mound more often than not. He pitched well in Double-A at 20. Still, McKenzie is rail-thin and missed time this year with an arm injury. We can't write "low."

Bret Sayre's Fantasy Take: McKenzie remains the top fantasy prospect in this system, but it's almost by default and he's getting close to relinquishing that honor. The lack of a high-end ceiling hurts, but his combination of ETA and command helps solidify an SP4 future that could be coming as soon as later this year.

2 Luis Oviedo RHP

OFP: 60 Likely: 50 ETA: 2021

Born: 05/15/99 Age: 20 Bats: R Throws: R Height: 6'4" Weight: 170 Origin: International Free Agent, 2015

YEAR	TEAM	LVL	AGE	W	L	SV	G	GS	IP	H	HR	BB/9	K/9	K	GB%	BABIP	WHIP	ERA	DRA	WARP	PF
2016	DIN	RK	17	2	8	0	14	14	63	67	1	2.4	8.0	56	42%	.349	1.33	4.00	3.52	1.5	100
2017	CLE	RK	18	4	2	0	14	7	51^{2}	62	2	3.8	12.2	70	52%	.411	1.63	7.14	3.76	1.2	107
2018	MHV	A-	19	4	2	0	9	9	48	34	3	1.9	11.4	61	52%	.274	0.92	1.88	3.31	1.1	102
2018	LKC	A	19	1	0	0	2	2	9	5	0	7.0	6.0	6	44%	.217	1.33	3.00	4.44	0.1	93
2019	*CLE*	*MLB*	*20*	*2*	*3*	*0*	*13*	*8*	*43^{2}*	*46*	*7*	*4.4*	*8.4*	*41*	*42%*	*.312*	*1.55*	*5.07*	*5.44*	*0.0*	*106*

Breakout: 0% Improve: 0% Collapse: 0% Attrition: 0% MLB: 0% *Comparables: Gabriel Ynoa, Luis Severino, Parker Bridwell*

The Report: Ah, the fun of signing 16-year-old Dominican arms. Oviedo was a projectable righty sitting in the upper-80s when he signed. He's now got an ideal starting pitcher's frame and often sits in the mid-90s. The fastball can run a little true at times, but there's enough armside wiggle to keep it off barrels and he commands it well gloveside at present—although the control is still ahead of the command generally. His mechanics are fairly clean, and while there is a bit of late torque and twist, I don't see it meaningfully inhibiting his long-term command projection.

Oviedo added a slider in 2017 and this year it looked like a potential monster out-pitch down the line. At its best it had big, late two-plane break that he could locate to the back foot of lefties. His curve offers a different look, although it's a bit on the loopy side when he tries to spot it in the zone, and at others it can be slurvy and bleed into the slider. Still, there's enough feel to project it to average at maturity. The same is true of the change, which is inconsistent and often firm, but flashes good sink.

Despite the control/command blip in Lake County, there really isn't much to dislike with Oviedo's profile. He's a long way from the majors and mostly physically maxed, but the stuff is really good and doesn't require much refinement. He's probably the youngest arm we will throw into our mid-rotation starter or late-inning reliever bucket on the back of the 101, but that undersells both his upside and realistic floor a little.

The Risks: High. There's only a short-season track record here, and he is a pitcher after all. Sometimes pop-up velocity guys give some of it back as they get stretched out in the pros more.

Bret Sayre's Fantasy Take: Can I interest you in trading nearly all of that certainty for a bit of ceiling? Why, of course. Oviedo has the potential to miss a lot of bats, but we've said that about countless other arms with little to no full-season experience. There are enough ways this can break to fill a Choose Your Own Adventure novel, but the 1-in-5 chance that he breaks right and turns into a future SP2 is very alluring if you prefer to deal in quantity when it comes to fantasy pitching prospects.

3 George Valera OF

OFP: 60 Likely: 45 ETA: 2023

Born: 11/13/00 Age: 18 Bats: L Throws: L Height: 5'10" Weight: 160 Origin: International Free Agent, 2017

The Report: Valera was one of the top prospects available in the 2017 IFA class. He got paid accordingly. He got brought stateside immediately, which is a slightly aggressive baseball assignment, if less so an acculturation one as he was born in Queens and spent most of his childhood in New York. He played a grand total of six official pro games before being shut down with a hamate injury. Those are the background deets. Primarily what we are betting on here is a very pretty left-handed swing with plus bat speed. God knows there are far worse things to bet on in, well, life really, but it's going to have to the lion's share of carrying the profile. Valera will likely get reps in all three outfield spots for a while, but he's already filling out so I'll just mention he has the arm for right. He might not have the power for either corner, but we won't know any of this for sure for a half decade, so just roll that beautiful swing footage for now.

The Risks: Extreme. He's a teenager who might not stick up-the-middle, has played exactly six professional games, and will be coming off a hamate injury.

Bret Sayre's Fantasy Take: For my money, short of Wander Franco, there's not a better fantasy prospect who hasn't reached full-season ball than Valera. The swing portends a .300-plus, 25-homer future and while he's a very long way off, I will fight Ben to claw him up as high on the 101 as I can.

4 Nolan Jones 3B

OFP: 55 Likely: 45 ETA: Late 2020/Early 2021

Born: 05/07/98 Age: 21 Bats: L Throws: R Height: 6'4" Weight: 185 Origin: Round 2, 2016 Draft (#55 overall)

YEAR	TEAM	LVL	AGE	PA	R	2B	3B	HR	RBI	BB	K	SB	CS	AVG/OBP/SLG	DRC+	VORP	BABIP	BRR	FRAA	WARP	PF
2016	CLE	RK	18	134	10	5	2	0	9	23	49	3	1	.257/.388/.339	120	7.7	.459	0.2	3B(28) 4.6, SS(5) 0.2	0.7	103
2017	MHV	A-	19	265	41	18	3	4	33	43	60	1	0	.317/.430/.482	171	28.4	.417	1.7	3B(53) 0.0	2.1	104
2018	LKC	A	20	389	46	12	0	16	49	63	97	2	1	.279/.393/.464	151	33.5	.347	-0.9	3B(77) -4.1	2.3	102
2018	LYN	A+	20	130	23	9	0	3	17	26	34	0	0	.298/.438/.471	155	12.7	.418	0.1	3B(28) -0.3	0.9	100
2019	*CLE*	*MLB*	*21*	*252*	*23*	*7*	*0*	*7*	*26*	*27*	*92*	*0*	*0*	*.164/.251/.291*	*49*	*-10.2*	*.232*	*-0.6*	*3B 0*	*-1.1*	*106*

Breakout: 12% Improve: 19% Collapse: 1% Attrition: 9% MLB: 23%

Comparables: Ryan McMahon, Matt Dominguez, Willy Adames

The Report: Jones is a prospect who would fit quite neatly into our old Good/Bad format, so let's give it a spin:

The Good: Jones converted some of his ample raw power into games and did so as a 20-year-old in a difficult hitting environment. The swing has always been geared for plus pull-side power, while he tended to work more gap-to-gap, but Jones managed to marry the two without adding substantial swing-and-miss. He's unlikely to get all of his plus raw into games, as the swing can get long when he goes for it, but both offensive tools look more likely to reach solid-average than they did last year.

The Bad: It's still unclear where Jones' long term defensive home is. Errors are a bad way to measure minor-league defense, but his range and hands don't pass muster yet either. Jones has filled out enough—he looks about 20 pounds or so heavier than the weight above—where a move to left field or first base might be on the offer eventually, putting an awful lot of pressure on his bat.

The Risks: Medium. The bat has taken a big step forward and his performance in A-ball matched it, but there's still significant role/positional risk in the profile.

Bret Sayre's Fantasy Take: The step forward in power is certainly encouraging, but it still doesn't raise his ceiling to a potential top-10 option at the position. The average isn't likely to be a positive contribution, though the approach could lead his on-base percentage to be one, and without big-time power, the entire profile just falls a bit short. He'd certainly make a top-150 at this point, but I don't think he belongs among the top 101.

5 Sam Hentges LHP

OFP: 55 Likely: 45 ETA: Early 2020

Born: 07/18/96 Age: 22 Bats: L Throws: L Height: 6'6" Weight: 245 Origin: Round 4, 2014 Draft (#128 overall)

YEAR	TEAM	LVL	AGE	W	L	SV	G	GS	IP	H	HR	BB/9	K/9	K	GB%	BABIP	WHIP	ERA	DRA	WARP	PF
2016	LKC	A	19	2	4	0	14	14	60^1	71	8	4.3	10.9	73	42%	.375	1.66	6.12	3.37	1.2	100
2017	CLE	RK	20	0	3	0	6	6	13	16	2	2.1	12.5	18	43%	.400	1.46	4.85	3.01	0.4	108
2017	MHV	A-	20	0	1	0	5	5	17^2	5	1	6.1	11.7	23	65%	.121	0.96	2.04	3.99	0.3	103
2018	LYN	A+	21	6	6	0	23	23	118^1	114	4	4.0	9.3	122	41%	.343	1.41	3.27	3.99	1.9	102
2019	*CLE*	*MLB*	*22*	*4*	*7*	*0*	*19*	*19*	*81^2*	*89*	*15*	*5.1*	*8.9*	*81*	*40%*	*.318*	*1.66*	*5.48*	*5.89*	*-0.4*	*106*

Breakout: 1% Improve: 2% Collapse: 0% Attrition: 1% MLB: 2%

Comparables: Tony Sipp, Michael Ynoa, Josh Lindblom

The Report: I may have gotten a bit of feedback from inside baseball for leaving Hentges off our Cleveland list last year. Fair play, they were likely right. Now, he was a fourth-round prep arm coming off Tommy John surgery who had pitched to a 6 ERA in A-ball before going under the knife, but that's a minor quibble, no?

There's no quibbling with Hentges' 2018 season. The big lefty got back on the mound and showed a potential plus fastball/curve combination. The heater routinely touched 95 with armside run, and Hentges commands it well to both sides of the plate. His high-70s curve shows above-average 12-6 break, while the changeup is projectable, but presently below-average. Hentges is still building up arm strength coming off TJ, but is otherwise in the general range of "interesting mid-rotation arm with third pitch concerns." A lefty with a MLB-quality fastball/curve combo always has a relief fall back, but given the frame and relatively clean delivery, Hentges is a solid bet to stick in a rotation, health and continued refinement permitting.

The Risks: Medium. There's a fair bit of polish here, but Hentges has a recent Tommy John on his resume and has yet to pitch in Double-A.

Bret Sayre's Fantasy Take: The road to fantasy purgatory was laid with mid-rotation pitching prospects, yet we still keep pressing on. Mostly because one out of every 10 of these guys turns into Patrick Corbin or Mike Clevinger rather than Franklin Morales or Deolis Guerra. That said, Hentges is one of the better ones to grab in leagues that roster 200 or more prospects given that his cost is likely to be minimal and you won't have to wait much longer than this calendar year to figure out if you should toss him back in order to gamble on a different future SP4.

6 Yu-Cheng Chang IF   OFP: 55   Likely: 45   ETA: 2019, when someone gets hurt

Born: 08/18/95   Age: 23   Bats: R   Throws: R   Height: 6'1"   Weight: 175   Origin: International Free Agent, 2013

YEAR	TEAM	LVL	AGE	PA	R	2B	3B	HR	RBI	BB	K	SB	CS	AVG/OBP/SLG	DRC+	VORP	BABIP	BRR	FRAA	WARP	PF
2016	LYN	A+	20	477	78	30	8	13	70	45	110	11	3	.259/.332/.463	112	35.1	.316	2.9	SS(104) 0.0	1.6	101
2017	AKR	AA	21	508	72	24	5	24	66	52	134	11	4	.220/.312/.461	102	33.8	.254	2.3	SS(119) 20.3	3.7	99
2018	COH	AAA	22	518	56	28	2	13	62	44	144	4	3	.256/.330/.411	103	16.6	.341	-3.3	SS(94) -7.3, 3B(23) -0.7	0.3	99
2019	*CLE*	*MLB*	*23*	*205*	*21*	*9*	*1*	*7*	*24*	*13*	*64*	*1*	*1*	*.202/.265/.365*	*73*	*-1.4*	*.264*	*-0.2*	*3B -3, SS 0*	*-0.4*	*106*

Breakout: 15%   Improve: 26%   Collapse: 4%   Attrition: 11%   MLB: 37%   *Comparables: Todd Frazier, Alex Blandino, Trevor Story*

The Report: Last year's Cleveland list was peppered from top to bottom with three-true-outcome bats, but only Chang really maintained his value proposition in 2018. It helps that he's a passable, if fringy, shortstop. His International League performance was solid, and his scouting report looks similar a year later. The profile remaining more or less the same at a higher level is always good on balance; it's just not the most exciting profile in the world. Chang is probably going to slide over to third in the majors—which won't exactly open additional playing time in Cleveland either—and while he has the raw power for the hot corner, a fringe-average hit tool means it's likely to play down to average in games. Hitting .250 with some pop and the ability to play three infield positions is useful—though again, less so in Cleveland—just not exciting.

The Risks: Medium. There's some risk the hit tool doesn't play at the highest level, more significant risk he has to move off shortstop.

Bret Sayre's Fantasy Take: You're basically closing your eyes and hoping that Chang turns into Aledmys Diaz, and no one wants Aledmys Diaz. Just the mere mention of Aledmys Diaz caused you to move on to the next player on this list. The more open and honest we are about this, the healthier it is for us all.

7 Ethan Hankins RHP   OFP: 55   Likely: 45   ETA: 2023

Born: 05/23/00   Age: 19   Bats: R   Throws: R   Height: 6'6"   Weight: 200   Origin: Round 1C, 2018 Draft (#35 overall)

YEAR	TEAM	LVL	AGE	W	L	SV	G	GS	IP	H	HR	BB/9	K/9	K	GB%	BABIP	WHIP	ERA	DRA	WARP	PF
2019	*CLE*	*MLB*	*19*	*2*	*3*	*0*	*7*	*7*	31^{1}	*34*	*5*	*5.4*	*8.1*	*28*	*40%*	*.313*	*1.68*	*5.81*	*6.24*	*-0.3*	*106*

Breakout: 0%   Improve: 0%   Collapse: 0%   Attrition: 0%   MLB: 0%   *Comparables: Bryse Wilson, Jaime Barria, Jamie Callahan*

The Report: Every year, usually around this time in fact, draftniks start talking themselves into another "Great Right Hope." Yes, this will be the year a prep righty finally goes 1.1. It never happens for a variety of reasons, sometimes injury, other times just remembering that prep righties tend to be among the worst investments you can make in the first round. Hankins was the 2018 Great Right Hope, but a shoulder injury early in the season scuttled any slim chance he had of going first overall.

When he's fully healthy, Hankins offers present mid-90s heat with movement and plenty of projection left as well. He has a remarkably advanced changeup for a prep pitcher, and the curveball will flash. Sure, it wasn't exactly Casey Mize even before the arm issues, but when healthy, Hankins might have more upside than last year's 1:1. There's a chance that the roles below will look hopelessly out of date by the end of April; on the other hand, I did use the phrase "shoulder injury" in this report.

The Risks: High. He's a prep righty who needs a more consistent breaking ball and whose senior season was marred by a shoulder injury. You could certainly argue for "extreme" here if you like.

Bret Sayre's Fantasy Take: If you're going to bet on a prep arm out of the draft, might as well go with one who scraped triple digits before falling into injury purgatory. He's a fine flier in the third round or later, depending on how large your league is, in dynasty formats this winter as he's unlikely to go with a top-30 pick and still carries a fair amount of strikeout upside.

8 Lenny Torres RHP   OFP: 55   Likely: 45   ETA: 2023

Born: 10/15/00   Age: 18   Bats: R   Throws: R   Height: 6'1"   Weight: 190   Origin: Round 1, 2018 Draft (#41 overall)

YEAR	TEAM	LVL	AGE	W	L	SV	G	GS	IP	H	HR	BB/9	K/9	K	GB%	BABIP	WHIP	ERA	DRA	WARP	PF
2018	CLT	RK	17	0	0	0	6	5	15[1]	14	0	2.3	12.9	22	51%	.400	1.17	1.76	2.98	0.5	112
2019	*CLE*	*MLB*	*18*	*2*	*2*	*0*	*12*	*6*	*32*	*34*	*5*	*5.3*	*8.3*	*30*	*46%*	*.313*	*1.64*	*5.35*	*5.74*	*-0.1*	*106*

Breakout: 0%   Improve: 0%   Collapse: 0%   Attrition: 0%   MLB: 0%   *Comparables: Mike Soroka, Roberto Osuna, Martin Perez*

The Report: I don't have particularly strong feelings about the order of Cleveland's top three 2018 picks—you can toss in Rocchio too—but if this was closer to a personal pref list, I would have Torres ahead. There's not a real objective reason I can point to, mind you—that's why they call it a pref list. Hankins looks the part of a high-pick prep starter. He's 6'6", has a projectable frame, and a potential four-pitch mix with two-to-three above-average offerings down the road.

Torres is on the shorter side—although having just turned 18, he might add an inch or two still—and a cold-weather prep arm. The delivery is uptempo, the arm action has some effort. He's primarily fastball/slider, albeit with a potential plus slider and a fastball that popped even more post-draft. The changeup is of course mostly theoretical. Torres is a plus athlete, and I suppose notably, hasn't had a bout of shoulder soreness. Well, not yet anyway; he is a pitcher after all. The reliever risk here is not insubstantial, but what good pitching prospect doesn't carry that burden nowadays?

The Risks: High. Take the Hankins risks, subtract the shoulder woes, add in cold-weather prep arm and less developed secondaries.

Bret Sayre's Fantasy Take: While it's never a bad idea to gamble on the high-velocity guy, it's also never a bad idea to gamble on the "obnoxiously young for his draft class" guy. Torres was the youngest player of note drafted last June and while that's a more meaningful fun fact with hitters than pitchers, it's still notable. I'd take Hankins before Torres in a dynasty draft, but at that point, everyone looks both good and bad simultaneously.

9 Bo Naylor C   OFP: 55   Likely: 45   ETA: 2023

Born: 02/21/00   Age: 19   Bats: L   Throws: R   Height: 6'0"   Weight: 195   Origin: Round 1, 2018 Draft (#29 overall)

YEAR	TEAM	LVL	AGE	PA	R	2B	3B	HR	RBI	BB	K	SB	CS	AVG/OBP/SLG	DRC+	VORP	BABIP	BRR	FRAA	WARP	PF
2018	CLT	RK	18	139	17	3	3	2	17	21	28	5	1	.274/.381/.402	126	12.3	.341	0.3	C(19) -0.4, 3B(5) -0.7	0.3	107
2019	*CLE*	*MLB*	*19*	*252*	*16*	*2*	*1*	*5*	*20*	*17*	*89*	*0*	*0*	*.123/.181/.202*	*1*	*-20.2*	*.168*	*0.1*	*C 0, 3B 0*	*-2.2*	*106*

Breakout: 5%   Improve: 7%   Collapse: 0%   Attrition: 3%   MLB: 9%   *Comparables: Francisco Pena, Franmil Reyes, Nomar Mazara*

The Report: Rumored at various times to be in play for an underslot deal early in the first round, Naylor wound up signing for slightly overslot with Cleveland at the 29th pick. We've long waxed on these web pages about the risks inherent in drafting high school catchers, and Naylor's lower half might remind you a bit too much of his older brother Josh's at that age. Derriere isn't destiny though, and while Naylor is a project behind the plate he has sneaky athleticism for his size and a strong throwing arm. Cleveland got him some reps at third as well, and he could be more of a modern "positionless baseball" backstop where he spends a couple days a week in the field to ease the strain on his body and get his bat into the lineup.

It's a nice bat too. Naylor has plus bat speed with good whip and enough leverage to show off some game power without striking out too often. He is still a cold weather prep bat of course, so there's risk on both the offensive and defensive sides—and a long horizon to major-league utility—but Naylor may end up a very modern draft and development story. Also a very old one: sometimes you just take the guy you think will hit.

The Risks: High. It's the usual prep catcher risks, plus he's less likely to be a long-term every day catcher.

Bret Sayre's Fantasy Take: Of course, I'd take Naylor over both of those pitchers. Short of Valera, Naylor has the best hit tool in this system and while being a catcher should technically disqualify him as an interesting fantasy prospect, there's enough offensive potential and athleticism for him to move off the position. It's a risky profile, for sure, but a .290 average and 20-25 bombs is valuable whether he's still squatting in three years or not.

10 Brayan Rocchio SS

OFP: 55 Likely: 45 ETA: 2024

Born: 01/13/01 Age: 18 Bats: B Throws: R Height: 5'10" Weight: 150 Origin: International Free Agent, 2017

YEAR	TEAM	LVL	AGE	PA	R	2B	3B	HR	RBI	BB	K	SB	CS	AVG/OBP/SLG	DRC+	VORP	BABIP	BRR	FRAA	WARP	PF
2018	DIN	RK	17	111	19	2	3	1	12	5	14	8	5	.323/.391/.434	137	9.7	.369	-1.0	SS(15) -0.2, 2B(8) 0.6	0.6	90
2018	CLT	RK	17	158	21	10	1	1	17	10	17	14	8	.343/.389/.448	166	15.0	.378	1.2	SS(26) 5.2, 3B(8) -1.1	1.5	107
2019	*CLE*	*MLB*	*18*	*252*	*25*	*9*	*0*	*4*	*18*	*1*	*62*	*6*	*3*	*.199/.199/.287*	*23*	*-14.6*	*.241*	*0.0*	*SS 1, 3B 0*	*-1.5*	*106*

Breakout: 0% Improve: 0% Collapse: 0% Attrition: 0% MLB: 0%

Comparables: Adalberto Mondesi, Wilmer Flores, Tommy Brown

The Report: Rocchio has quickly turned into a low-six-figure coup for Cleveland. There's a lot to work with here as far as "shortstop prospects born two months after *Mass Romantic* was released" go. He's a switch hitter with good feel for contact from both sides. He's an above-average runner with a good shot to stick at shortstop. The frame could go in a variety of different ways across the rest of his teenage years and into his early 20s, but the swing is contact over power at present, and Rocchio doesn't have a ton of present physicality. He just turned 18, so the delta in the profile is huge, but he's definitely worth watching.

The Risks: Extreme. I'm writing a 2024 ETA below. I will be 42. I'll be in relaxed fit Dad jeans before he's in the majors. Anyway, he's a complex league shortstop who didn't get a huge bonus.

Bret Sayre's Fantasy Take: It's never easy to tell just how high a fantasy ceiling is when a player hasn't taken a single at-bat as an adult, but the plate discipline junkies will get excited that he barely struck out as a 17-year-old spanning complex leagues in two different countries. Take a flier, why not. Otherwise just shrug and see how 2019 goes. He should be rostered in leagues where 250 prospects are owned just in case he makes the jump.

The Next Five:

11 Nick Sandlin RHP

Born: 01/10/97 Age: 22 Bats: R Throws: R Height: 5'11" Weight: 175 Origin: Round 2, 2018 Draft (#67 overall)

YEAR	TEAM	LVL	AGE	W	L	SV	G	GS	IP	H	HR	BB/9	K/9	K	GB%	BABIP	WHIP	ERA	DRA	WARP	PF
2018	LKC	A	21	0	0	1	10	0	10^{1}	9	0	0.0	13.1	15	52%	.391	0.87	1.74	1.08	0.5	100
2018	LYN	A+	21	1	0	4	7	0	6^{1}	2	0	2.8	14.2	10	50%	.167	0.63	1.42	2.43	0.2	100
2019	*CLE*	*MLB*	*22*	*2*	*1*	*1*	*32*	*0*	33^{2}	*32*	*4*	*4.4*	*9.7*	*36*	*43%*	*.310*	*1.44*	*4.26*	*4.56*	*0.2*	*106*

Breakout: 5% Improve: 8% Collapse: 0% Attrition: 6% MLB: 8%

Comparables: Ryan Burr, Jacob Rhame, Danny Barnes

Sandlin was arguably the most dominant starting pitcher in college this year, posting a 1.06 ERA and striking out nearly 13 per nine for Southern Mississippi. This wouldn't be notable past being, well, notable, except for the fact that Sandlin is (mostly) a sidearmer. He will move his slot around, but mostly everything is coming in low. Cleveland drafted him as a quick-moving pen arm—he was a reliever his first two years of college—and he hasn't disappointed so far. He has more fastball than your typical low-armslot guy, sitting in the low-90s and touching higher. Sandlin leans heavily on his slider, which is already plus, and he uses a slower curve as a change of pace as well. He has advanced control and command of the whole arsenal and could very well be the first 2018 draftee to reach the big leagues.

12 James Karinchak RHP

Born: 09/22/95 Age: 23 Bats: R Throws: R Height: 6'3" Weight: 230 Origin: Round 9, 2017 Draft (#282 overall)

YEAR	TEAM	LVL	AGE	W	L	SV	G	GS	IP	H	HR	BB/9	K/9	K	GB%	BABIP	WHIP	ERA	DRA	WARP	PF
2017	MHV	A-	21	2	2	0	10	6	23^{1}	30	1	3.5	12.0	31	30%	.468	1.67	5.79	4.42	0.2	102
2018	LKC	A	22	3	0	1	7	0	11^{1}	8	0	5.6	15.9	20	55%	.400	1.32	0.79	2.95	0.3	100
2018	LYN	A+	22	1	1	13	25	0	27	14	1	5.7	15.0	45	40%	.295	1.15	1.00	2.85	0.7	100
2018	AKR	AA	22	0	1	0	10	0	10^{1}	7	1	10.5	13.9	16	29%	.300	1.84	2.61	5.46	-0.1	100
2019	*CLE*	*MLB*	*23*	*2*	*1*	*1*	*29*	*2*	35^{2}	*31*	*4*	*5.9*	*11.1*	*44*	*34%*	*.309*	*1.53*	*4.28*	*4.59*	*0.2*	*106*

Breakout: 1% Improve: 2% Collapse: 5% Attrition: 5% MLB: 7%

Comparables: C.D. Pelham, Pedro Araujo, Jeff Beliveau

Karinchak doesn't have the same amateur pedigree as Sandlin—he was a ninth-round pick out of Bryant in 2017—but he has similar upside in the pen. The fastball is borderline elite, sitting 95-97 with deception from his funky mechanics and plane from his high slot. There's enough wiggle to keep it off barrels, and it's a swing-and-miss offering on its own. He pairs it with a plus 12-6 curve that comes out of the hand just like the heater. Karinchak dominated three levels in his first professional season, and it's no-doubt closer stuff when he's in or even around the zone. But the combination of the mechanics and effort in the delivery has led to well-below-average control so far. Iron that out, and Cleveland may have found their next reliever monster.

13 Bobby Bradley 1B

Born: 05/29/96 Age: 23 Bats: L Throws: R Height: 6'1" Weight: 225 Origin: Round 3, 2014 Draft (#97 overall)

YEAR	TEAM	LVL	AGE	PA	R	2B	3B	HR	RBI	BB	K	SB	CS	AVG/OBP/SLG	DRC+	VORP	BABIP	BRR	FRAA	WARP	PF
2016	LYN	A+	20	572	82	23	1	29	102	75	170	3	0	.235/.344/.466	120	23.4	.293	0.2	1B(116) -6.4	-0.4	102
2017	AKR	AA	21	532	66	25	3	23	89	55	122	3	3	.251/.331/.465	119	17.6	.287	-2.6	1B(123) -6.3	-0.3	99
2018	AKR	AA	22	421	49	19	3	24	64	45	105	1	0	.214/.304/.477	107	17.0	.226	-2.3	1B(97) 1.4	0.0	90
2018	COH	AAA	22	128	11	7	2	3	19	11	43	0	0	.254/.323/.430	99	2.8	.377	0.3	1B(29) 1.5	0.2	99
2019	*CLE*	*MLB*	*23*	*176*	*19*	*8*	*1*	*8*	*24*	*13*	*52*	*0*	*0*	*.200/.264/.410*	*81*	*-1.3*	*.234*	*-0.2*	*1B -1*	*-0.2*	*106*

Breakout: 12% Improve: 29% Collapse: 5% Attrition: 17% MLB: 44% *Comparables: Ryan O'Hearn, Paul Goldschmidt, Jerry Sands*

I'm not entirely sure why Cleveland had Bradley repeat Double-A, but he more or less matched his 2017 performance minus 30 points of batting average and plus a few extra bombs. His brief stint in Triple-A was more bust than boom, however. He's still only 22 and projects as the same three-true-outcome slugger he did last year, but Adam Dunn and Joey Gallo—heck, even Jack Cust—beat up the minors a lot more than Bradley did, so you wonder how the swing is gonna fare against the best arms in the sport. But even in our launch-a-ball era, 30 dingers plays, and Bradley has at least that much power in his locker.

14 Will Benson OF

Born: 06/16/98 Age: 21 Bats: L Throws: L Height: 6'5" Weight: 225 Origin: Round 1, 2016 Draft (#14 overall)

YEAR	TEAM	LVL	AGE	PA	R	2B	3B	HR	RBI	BB	K	SB	CS	AVG/OBP/SLG	DRC+	VORP	BABIP	BRR	FRAA	WARP	PF
2016	CLE	RK	18	184	31	10	3	6	27	22	60	10	2	.209/.321/.424	89	9.1	.293	2.5	RF(39) -2.0	-0.5	103
2017	MHV	A-	19	236	29	8	5	10	36	31	80	7	1	.238/.347/.475	107	11.5	.339	0.1	RF(56) -2.5	-0.3	104
2018	LKC	A	20	506	54	11	1	22	58	82	152	12	6	.180/.324/.370	90	5.6	.218	-0.4	RF(113) 5.4, CF(4) -0.2	0.2	102
2019	*CLE*	*MLB*	*21*	*252*	*21*	*4*	*0*	*9*	*25*	*21*	*105*	*1*	*1*	*.096/.170/.237*	*5*	*-21.9*	*.109*	*-0.2*	*RF 0, CF 0*	*-2.4*	*106*

Breakout: 2% Improve: 5% Collapse: 1% Attrition: 3% MLB: 7% *Comparables: Nomar Mazara, Caleb Gindl, Dylan Cozens*

If you want to get a gauge on what 80 grade raw power looks like, watch Benson take batting practice sometime. It's light-tower power and the ball jumps off the bat making that sound. It's generated by his massive strength and a swing that features natural loft. However, since being drafted 14th overall in 2016, Benson hasn't shown the ability to hit any type of secondary pitches. Low-A pitchers feasted when they got ahead in the count, enticing Benson to chase breaking stuff in and out of the zone. Defensively he's an asset, profiling as an above average right fielder with a cannon for an arm. There's star potential here, with elite power and strong defensive tools, but his issues at the plate make that outcome pretty unlikely.

15 Eric Haase C

Born: 12/18/92 Age: 26 Bats: R Throws: R Height: 5'10" Weight: 180 Origin: Round 7, 2011 Draft (#218 overall)

YEAR	TEAM	LVL	AGE	PA	R	2B	3B	HR	RBI	BB	K	SB	CS	AVG/OBP/SLG	DRC+	VORP	BABIP	BRR	FRAA	WARP	PF
2016	AKR	AA	23	246	28	14	1	12	33	17	75	0	2	.208/.265/.438	71	4.6	.250	0.9	C(46) 8.0, 3B(1) 0.0	0.8	104
2017	AKR	AA	24	381	59	17	5	26	59	44	116	4	2	.258/.349/.574	134	42.1	.313	2.2	C(58) 1.7	2.4	99
2018	COH	AAA	25	477	54	24	3	20	71	31	143	3	1	.236/.288/.443	93	17.5	.296	-0.7	C(90) -6.3	0.0	99
2018	CLE	MLB	25	17	0	0	0	0	1	0	6	0	0	.125/.176/.125	67	-2.1	.200	0.0	C(7) 0.2	0.0	106
2019	*CLE*	*MLB*	*26*	*72*	*7*	*3*	*0*	*3*	*10*	*4*	*25*	*0*	*0*	*.188/.237/.385*	*54*	*-0.8*	*.235*	*-0.1*	*C -1*	*-0.2*	*106*

Breakout: 2% Improve: 18% Collapse: 12% Attrition: 32% MLB: 44% *Comparables: Kelly Shoppach, Tom Murphy, Steven Hill*

After a breakout in 2017 while repeating Double-A, Haase fell back to earth some in Columbus last year. We had concerns about the hit tool even when he was mashing in the Eastern League, and Haase struck out 30% of the time in 2018. The swing is stiff and leveraged to get to his plus raw power, and while Haase still got to enough of it to make him a viable backup catcher, you'd like the glove to be a bit better than it is. He has a strong throwing arm, but his receiving is still rough, and

Cleveland brought in Kevin Plawecki to pair with Roberto Perez. That leaves Haase on the outside looking in until his defense improves. But you always need catchers: Plawecki's health track record isn't great and Perez is a career .205 hitter. Haase may get another shot with the big club before long.

Top Talents 25 and Under (born 4/1/93 or later):

1. Francisco Lindor
2. Triston McKenzie
3. Shane Bieber
4. Luis Oviedo
5. Jake Bauers
6. George Valera
7. Nolan Jones
8. Sam Hentges
9. Yu-Cheng Chang
10. Ethan Hankins

Since he debuted on June 14, 2015—which could've been a holiday in Cleveland if not for the Cavaliers losing Game 5 of the NBA Finals that night—Francisco Lindor has taken more plate appearances than any other major-leaguer. This is, of course, to the great joy of Cleveland and baseball fans alike. He's reached base in 35 percent of those 2,590 trips to the plate, and sparked dozens of GIFs with his vibrant smile along the way.

A 2017 swing change unlocked more power, but also an adjustment period where Lindor's OBP temporarily sank while he became perhaps a bit too enamored with fly ball contact. In 2018 it popped right back up: the power improvements stuck, and now you can confidently pencil in 6-WARP as a baseline for Lindor. He might be the betting favorite for third-best player in the game, even if that's in a thin-stretched plurality.

Beyond Mr. Smile and just-graduated star Jose Ramirez, the Indians' ranks of bankable young talent are thin enough to give you a long face. Bradley Zimmer aged off this list without proving his bat can support even elite center-field defense. Francisco Mejia was shipped off for relievers and replaced by catching jetsam. Much of the star-level promise on this list has yet to experience the thrills and spills of High-A.

The young player who emerged as a contributor in Cleveland last year was instead Shane Bieber. His first 114 2/3 innings adequately introduced the schtick: Dude doesn't walk anyone. Got it. But this isn't New Josh Tomlin. His 4.7 percent walk rate ranked only 14th among major leaguers who threw 100 innings; Nathan Eovaldi and Joe Musgrove gave out fewer free passes. The bigger surprise is that they also had lower strikeout rates than Bieber. Can that FIP-tastic combo continue apace? Well… he's living on a ton of called strikes and a 93-mph fastball without much bat-missing potential. In a year or two, he may get us to believe in his Old Zack Greinke skillset, but for now, there's still concern that he'll get walloped.

Picked up from the Rays for Yandy Diaz, Jake Bauers apparently showed enough as a rookie to be traded instead of DFA'd. That's a joke, but despite some prospect pedigree and a present-day position in Cleveland, his first 388 major league plate appearances cut the shape of a replaceable hitter and raised serious questions. See, Bauers—whose high walk and low strikeout rates impressed in the upper minors—swung at only 40 percent of the pitches he saw in the majors. It's an extremely low number in general, but perhaps a harmfully passive one for someone with a low contact rate. Of the 30 big-league hitters (min. 300 PA) who offered less frequently than Bauers, only two (Max Muncy and Jose Bautista) missed as often. That's how he ended up striking out 26.8 percent of the time after barely exceeding the 20 percent mark in Triple-A. Combine it with a propensity to feed the shift, and you wind up with a confounding .201/.316/.384 line.

So, did expectations ride on the back of a smart approach? Or on the control issues of the young and the mediocre? Even while piling up those intriguing BB:K ratios, he didn't really drive the ball. His slugging percentage over a full year at Double-A was .420. In Bauers' full Triple-A season, 2017, he slugged .412. Those numbers are fine, but among fast-tracked prospects they were more akin to middle infielders like then-teammate Willy Adames and J.P. Crawford than corner-occupying mashers. It's reasonable to expect base-reaching patience to come with power-boosting pitch selection, but Bauers really needs to show evidence of the latter to make it at first or in left—and that's not even mentioning his platoon issue.

Jordan Luplow didn't make the list, but he's the next most likely 25-year-old to make an impact in Cleveland this year. The corner outfielder, acquired from Pittsburgh, would sound a bit like Bauers if he were left-handed—good approach, strong numbers in the upper minors, power potential. But as it is, he'll be fighting to escape the short side of a platoon and prove that the pop is worth a boatload of fly balls. They have mostly fallen into gloves in the majors thus far, torpedoing his production. Still, he avoids strikeouts well and may have a crazy 2017 Yonder Alonso season in him somewhere.

Colorado Rockies

The State of the System:

The prospect pipeline to Denver is slowing a bit, but there's still close-to-ready talent for the win-now Rockies. Well, we think they are trying to win now. The Rockies are always quite confusing.

The Top Ten:

1 Brendan Rodgers SS — OFP: 70 — Likely: 55 — ETA: Late 2019

Born: 08/09/96 Age: 22 Bats: R Throws: R Height: 6'0" Weight: 180 Origin: Round 1, 2015 Draft (#3 overall)

YEAR	TEAM	LVL	AGE	PA	R	2B	3B	HR	RBI	BB	K	SB	CS	AVG/OBP/SLG	DRC+	VORP	BABIP	BRR	FRAA	WARP	PF
2016	ASH	A	19	491	73	31	0	19	73	35	98	6	3	.281/.342/.480	113	21.9	.319	-2.5	SS(56) 0.0, 2B(24) 0.9	1.0	115
2017	HFD	AA	20	164	20	5	0	6	17	8	36	0	2	.260/.323/.413	100	6.5	.306	-0.5	SS(15) -1.2, 2B(3) 0.3	0.2	103
2017	LNC	A+	20	236	44	21	3	12	47	6	35	2	1	.387/.407/.671	174	26.5	.413	0.9	SS(47) -5.6, 2B(4) -0.6	1.6	122
2018	HFD	AA	21	402	49	23	2	17	62	30	76	12	3	.275/.342/.493	113	27.4	.301	0.6	SS(58) -6.7, 2B(21) -2.1	0.9	106
2018	ABQ	AAA	21	72	5	4	0	0	5	1	16	0	0	.232/.264/.290	49	-2.8	.302	-0.3	SS(11) -1.8, 3B(4) -0.2	-0.5	121
2019	*COL*	*MLB*	*22*	*35*	*3*	*1*	*0*	*1*	*4*	*1*	*9*	*0*	*0*	*.212/.252/.366*	*60*	*-0.5*	*.250*	*0.0*	*2B 0*	*-0.1*	*108*

Breakout: 19% Improve: 44% Collapse: 2% Attrition: 24% MLB: 52% *Comparables: Nick Franklin, Alen Hanson, Reid Brignac*

The Report: After struggling during a brief Double-A cameo in 2017, Rodgers played more to the five-tool-shortstop scouting report in 2018. While he took full advantage of the friendly confines of Dunkin' Donuts park, Rodgers is a strong kid who generates plus raw power—although it's not easy per se, he has to work for it. And that means the swing can get a little stiff, making him vulnerable to velocity in his kitchen. Rodgers will go fishing against spin at times too, but he makes adjustments within at-bats and controls the barrel well enough to project an average hit tool. That should allow most of the plus raw power to play in games, even before we consider his future home park.

Rodgers is fine at shortstop, although you can tell he's battling the position at times. He has an above-average arm, but he's not as rangy as you'd like, and his actions can be a bit mechanical. The internal clock just seems slow at times in the field. He may have to slide to second if he loses any additional range, although he's an above-average runner at present. Rodgers is a guy I've sorta had to be talked into as a top tier prospect. I get it, but I've just never really seen it.

The Risks: Medium. Man, this feels like it should be 7/6, low. I just can't quite dispel the nagging voice in my head that thinks there's significant risk in the hit tool against major-league arms.

Ben Carsley's Fantasy Take: Once upon a time, Rodgers seemed a decent bet to some day be considered a top-3 dynasty prospect. While that may never come to pass, don't let prospect fatigue push you off of him completely. Rodgers is still an excellent fantasy asset who could routinely push for 25-plus homers from somewhere on the infield, and Coors may inflate his stats further. The real question for me is whether his hit tool will allow him to put up averages closer to .290 or .260, but either way Rodgers is a guy you want to own. We'll just have to wait and see if he ends up a solid cog or a true fantasy cornerstone.

2 Garrett Hampson IF   OFP: 55   Likely: 50   ETA: Debuted in 2018

Born: 10/10/94 Age: 24 Bats: R Throws: R Height: 5'11" Weight: 185 Origin: Round 3, 2016 Draft (#81 overall)

YEAR	TEAM	LVL	AGE	PA	R	2B	3B	HR	RBI	BB	K	SB	CS	AVG/OBP/SLG	DRC+	VORP	BABIP	BRR	FRAA	WARP	PF
2016	BOI	A-	21	312	43	14	8	2	44	48	56	36	4	.301/.404/.441	154	36.7	.366	4.6	SS(64) 8.2, 2B(1) -0.2	2.9	109
2017	LNC	A+	22	603	113	24	12	8	70	56	77	51	14	.326/.387/.462	130	41.6	.364	7.5	2B(71) -0.4, SS(56) 7.3	3.9	121
2018	HFD	AA	23	172	28	8	2	4	15	21	17	19	1	.304/.391/.466	136	18.7	.323	3.5	SS(18) 0.4, 2B(17) 1.7	1.6	107
2018	ABQ	AAA	23	332	53	17	4	6	25	30	58	17	4	.314/.377/.459	110	16.8	.372	0.9	2B(44) -0.1, SS(23) -2.3	1.1	118
2018	COL	MLB	23	48	3	3	1	0	4	7	12	2	0	.275/.396/.400	81	3.5	.393	1.1	SS(8) 0.2, 2B(7) 0.6	0.2	108
2019	*COL*	*MLB*	*24*	*326*	*39*	*13*	*2*	*8*	*35*	*25*	*65*	*16*	*3*	*.255/.316/.394*	*90*	*9.5*	*.299*	*2.0*	*2B 1, SS 0*	*1.1*	*108*

Breakout: 9% Improve: 23% Collapse: 0% Attrition: 23% MLB: 38%   *Comparables: Jose Pirela, Matt Antonelli, Tim Locastro*

The Report: Hampson is a dirty uniform player, the kind who endears himself to scouts quickly. That type of dude generally doesn't move the "top prospect" needle, but calling him a "grinder"—which to be clear, definitely applies—does a bit of a disservice to just how good a baseball player he is. He's a borderline 7 runner and is hyper-aggressive on the basepaths while also picking his spots well. He'll nab 30 steals a year and won't get caught much. Hampson is not a natural shortstop, but he fights the position to a draw. He is rangy with good hands and instincts, and he's smooth around the bag. His arm is just a bit light for an everyday shortstop role, but he should have an above-average glove at second.

The hit tool is solid-average. Hampson is pesky at the plate, fouling stuff off and working counts. He'll take a walk, lean into a pitch running inside. He's a good bunter. The swing does have more moving parts than you'd like though. There's a big leg kick and a bit of a hitch, but he has above-average bat speed and just barrels everything. The one hole in the profile is power. Even in Coors, Hampson is gonna shoot balls gap-to-gap and try and take an extra base or two. He'll probably top out around 10 home runs or so most seasons. It's not a sexy profile and the only endorsement he'll be getting is from Tide, but Hampson will do a job for you, and he'll do it well. This is normally a prospect profile I look slightly askance at, but he endeared himself quickly to me too.

The Risks: Low. He has hit in the upper minors just like he hit in the lower minors and he has a strong case to be the Rockies Opening Day second baseman. I gave up trying to figure out how Colorado will handle young players years ago, though.

Ben Carsley's Fantasy Take: Bret and I (especially Bret) were aggressive in our rankings of Hampson last season, and whatdya know, blind squirrels, nuts, etc. Hampson is comfortably a top-25 dynasty prospect thanks to his proximity to the majors, speed-based upside, and insanely favorable contextual factors. Assuming he gets near-every day playing time, he could genuinely challenge for a top-10 finish at second base as soon as this season. There's definitely some danger that a slow start could see Hampson lose out on playing time, but that's something he'll eventually overcome; he's simply too good to be relegated to utility duty.

3 Ryan Rolison LHP   OFP: 55   Likely: 50   ETA: 2021

Born: 07/11/97 Age: 21 Bats: R Throws: L Height: 6'2" Weight: 195 Origin: Round 1, 2018 Draft (#22 overall)

YEAR	TEAM	LVL	AGE	W	L	SV	G	GS	IP	H	HR	BB/9	K/9	K	GB%	BABIP	WHIP	ERA	DRA	WARP	PF
2018	GJR	RK	20	0	1	0	9	9	29	15	2	2.5	10.6	34	66%	.200	0.79	1.86	3.40	0.8	107
2019	*COL*	*MLB*	*21*	*2*	*2*	*0*	*9*	*9*	*33²*	*36*	*4*	*4.9*	*8.0*	*30*	*56%*	*.331*	*1.60*	*4.63*	*5.07*	*0.1*	*108*

Breakout: 0% Improve: 0% Collapse: 0% Attrition: 0% MLB: 0%   *Comparables: Thyago Vieira, Yency Almonte, Kendry Flores*

The Report: Rolison ticks all the usual suspect boxes for a late first-round left-handed college arm. He hides the ball well and his low-90s fastball will sneak up on you. He can spot it to both sides and cut it occasionally, but the command is just average and his high arm slot produces only fringy wiggle. The party piece here is a potential plus curve that shows good tilt, but can get slurvy on occasion. Rolison's command of the curve outpaces his command of the fastball at times. He's got a sinking change as well, but he slows his arm speed and tends to spike it. The best ones flash average, and his feel for spin gives the pitch some projection despite being presently well below-average.

Rolison throws strikes and attacks hitters and is left-handed. The stuff is only average to solid-average, but he is polished and left-handed. He's not the most exciting member of the 2018 draft class, but he's one of the more likely ones to be a major-leaguer. Also, he's left-handed.

The Risks: Medium. He's a polished college lefty, albeit one with a very short pro track record.

Ben Carsley's Fantasy Take: From a dynasty perspective there is juuuuuust a little bit of a drop off from the top two names on this list to the third. In a neutral setting, Rolison would likely get lost in the glut of mid-rotation prospects we advise you not to invest heavily in every season. Add in that he's a Rockie and there's basically no need for you to pay him any mind. That may sound harsh, but it's got more to do with Rolison's circumstances than anything he's done himself. Kyle Freeland is the exception, not the rule.

4 Peter Lambert RHP

OFP: 55 Likely: 50 ETA: Late 2019

Born: 04/18/97 Age: 22 Bats: R Throws: R Height: 6'2" Weight: 185 Origin: Round 2, 2015 Draft (#44 overall)

YEAR	TEAM	LVL	AGE	W	L	SV	G	GS	IP	H	HR	BB/9	K/9	K	GB%	BABIP	WHIP	ERA	DRA	WARP	PF
2016	ASH	A	19	5	8	0	26	26	126	125	7	2.4	7.7	108	47%	.324	1.25	3.93	6.30	-2.0	117
2017	LNC	A+	20	9	8	0	26	26	142[1]	147	18	1.9	8.3	131	43%	.321	1.24	4.17	3.92	2.2	119
2018	HFD	AA	21	8	2	0	15	15	92[2]	80	6	1.2	7.3	75	50%	.282	0.99	2.23	4.53	0.9	105
2018	ABQ	AAA	21	2	5	0	11	11	55[1]	72	5	2.4	5.0	31	52%	.345	1.57	5.04	4.62	0.6	118
2019	*COL*	*MLB*	*22*	*1*	*1*	*0*	*3*	*3*	*15*	*17*	*2*	*2.7*	*6.8*	*11*	*43%*	*.320*	*1.41*	*4.76*	*5.18*	*0.0*	*108*

Breakout: 15% Improve: 23% Collapse: 8% Attrition: 22% MLB: 41% *Comparables: Ariel Jurado, Enyel De Los Santos, Will Smith*

The Report: Lambert is a command and pitchability righty. This is usually the type of prospect profile that forces me to stifle an involuntary yawn, but most command righties don't dominate Double-A the way the 21-year-old Lambert did. He's not a soft tosser, touching as high as 96 for me this year, but generally working 91-94. He'll cut it at times and there's enough movement and deception to keep it off the fat part of the barrel, but the pitch's efficacy is command over movement. Lambert throws the fastball to all four quadrants and is particularly effective changing eye levels.

The changeup is his best secondary, and it plays off the fastball well. It only features 5-6 mph of velocity separation, but the firmness makes it look like the fastball right up until it tumbles off the deck, and it flashes plus. Lambert also throws a slider and a curve. The curve is better at present, showing consistent 11-5 shape, but it's more of a spot than chase pitch at present, and can get a bit humpy at the lower end of it's 76-81 velo band. The slider is used occasionally for a different breaking ball look right-on-right, but functions more as a cutter. Lambert is a plus athlete, repeats well, throws strikes with everything, and fields his position well. There's a bit of projection left in his frame as well.

The Risks: Medium. Lambert is a righty command dude with an averagish fastball. He may not have a true major league out pitch, and uh, he's gonna pitch in a place that will punish that.

Ben Carsley's Fantasy Take: See Rolison, Ryan, but now imagine him as a righty.

5 Colton Welker 3B

OFP: 55 Likely: 50 ETA: 2020

Born: 10/09/97 Age: 21 Bats: R Throws: R Height: 6'2" Weight: 195 Origin: Round 4, 2016 Draft (#110 overall)

YEAR	TEAM	LVL	AGE	PA	R	2B	3B	HR	RBI	BB	K	SB	CS	AVG/OBP/SLG	DRC+	VORP	BABIP	BRR	FRAA	WARP	PF
2016	GJR	RK	18	227	38	15	2	5	36	13	28	6	4	.329/.366/.490	138	20.3	.356	-0.4	3B(48) -5.8	0.3	105
2017	ASH	A	19	279	32	18	1	6	33	18	42	5	7	.350/.401/.500	153	19.6	.399	-1.6	3B(52) -7.3	1.0	109
2018	LNC	A+	20	509	74	32	0	13	82	42	103	5	1	.333/.383/.489	139	30.0	.395	1.1	3B(92) -9.3, 1B(6) -0.7	1.2	117
2019	*COL*	*MLB*	*21*	*252*	*22*	*10*	*0*	*7*	*28*	*7*	*60*	*0*	*0*	*.234/.256/.360*	*66*	*-5.1*	*.281*	*-0.6*	*3B -6, 1B 0*	*-1.3*	*108*

Breakout: 7% Improve: 13% Collapse: 0% Attrition: 12% MLB: 14% *Comparables: Cheslor Cuthbert, Jeimer Candelario, Wilmer Flores*

The Report: Welker's hitting-count rips are a sight to behold, with a long, majestic bat path and the bat speed for the barrel to traverse it with impressive haste. It's all a bit of an illusion at present, however, as the approach into the zone is steeper and he leverages his attack angle less often than most young power hitters. High-end hand-eye and an intelligent, all-fields approach underlie an impressive hit tool that may push plus when all's said and done—minor-league statistical salt grains and all, but he's sitting on a .337 professional average in more than 900 at-bats now. Above-average game power will come with maturity, but for now he's a drill-it-on-a-line kinda guy, and that's a-ok.

Welker's thick frame and heavy legs aren't masking any hidden speed above his present 30 grade, but he's got the quickness and short-range agility to play a better third base than you'd expect. He gets down well on balls in reach, and a powerful crossover extends the range just enough. Above-average arm strength ties off a workable, solid-average defensive profile at the hot corner.

The Risks: Relatively low: This level-a-year prep bat has hit the ball consistently hard through each of his first three levels. The frame's on the bulkier side, but he showed strong work ethic all year and the physicality should work. The foundational hitting talent is strong enough that he's on a pretty straight path toward an everyday role at the highest level.

Ben Carsley's Fantasy Take: I actually like Welker a bit more than the write-up above suggests I should. I've long been a believer in his bat-to-ball ability, and even if the power hasn't shown up big time yet, a) it still could b) it almost definitely will in Coors. Of course the big risk here is that Welker won't get to enjoy such friendly confines given that there are about a half-dozen talented infielders ahead of him on the current depth chart. But even if Welker does change organizations, he's a potential top-15 fantasy third baseman in a neutral setting, and could fight his way into top-10 or -12 if he stays in Colorado. He's a top-101 guy for me, if only by a little.

6 Riley Pint RHP [this space left intentionally blank]

Born: 11/06/97 Age: 21 Bats: R Throws: R Height: 6'4" Weight: 195 Origin: Round 1, 2016 Draft (#4 overall)

YEAR	TEAM	LVL	AGE	W	L	SV	G	GS	IP	H	HR	BB/9	K/9	K	GB%	BABIP	WHIP	ERA	DRA	WARP	PF
2016	GJR	RK	18	1	5	0	11	11	37	43	2	5.6	8.8	36	60%	.383	1.78	5.35	4.48	0.5	106
2017	ASH	A	19	2	11	0	22	22	93	96	3	5.7	7.6	79	60%	.325	1.67	5.42	4.58	0.8	111
2018	BOI	A-	20	0	2	0	3	3	8	4	0	10.1	9.0	8	47%	.235	1.62	1.12	4.88	0.0	112
2019	*COL*	*MLB*	*21*	*2*	*3*	*0*	*8*	*8*	*31^{1}*	*34*	*4*	*7.8*	*7.3*	*25*	*46%*	*.330*	*1.98*	*6.13*	*6.74*	*-0.5*	*108*

Breakout: 1% Improve: 1% Collapse: 0% Attrition: 2% MLB: 2% *Comparables: Elvin Ramirez, Greg Reynolds, James Houser*

The Report: Ordinal team lists—really ordinal prospect rankings at all—to a certain extent are always going to be exercises in false precision. But some prospects are going to be more dart throws than others—Tommy John recoveries, third-round prep picks with upside, complex league guys (who might also be third-round prep picks with upside). Then there's Riley Pint. He was limited to just eight innings in 2018 due to a forearm injury. This followed a 2017 that was developmentally weird at best. The potential talent here is undeniable, but eventually the potential has to actualize. I can tell you that the Rockies are still saying all the right things publicly here, because of course they are. I can tell you there's still an elite fastball lurking in the profile. But we've now gone beyond unknown unknowns with Pint.

Now strictly speaking, Riley Pint is probably not the sixth best prospect in the Rockies system. He's maybe second or perhaps not on the list; there's your one standard deviation. But this feels close enough, nestled in a tier of his own between the safer major-league bets and the relievers and fourth outfielders. Prospect lists are a snapshot in time as my predecessor used to say. This report is an underdeveloped polaroid.

The Risks: Extreme. That one I can answer.

Ben Carsley's Fantasy Take: He's the arm I'd be most willing to gamble on in this system, but sometimes it's smarter to just walk away from the table.

7 Yency Almonte RHP OFP: 55 Likely: 45 ETA: Debuted in 2018

Born: 06/04/94 Age: 25 Bats: B Throws: R Height: 6'3" Weight: 205 Origin: Round 17, 2012 Draft (#537 overall)

YEAR	TEAM	LVL	AGE	W	L	SV	G	GS	IP	H	HR	BB/9	K/9	K	GB%	BABIP	WHIP	ERA	DRA	WARP	PF
2016	MOD	A+	22	8	9	0	22	22	138^{1}	124	14	2.5	8.7	134	47%	.285	1.18	3.71	3.36	3.3	91
2016	NBR	AAX	22	3	1	0	5	5	30	22	4	4.8	6.6	22	37%	.212	1.27	3.00			101
2017	HFD	AA	23	5	3	0	14	14	76^{1}	58	4	3.7	8.4	71	45%	.267	1.17	2.00	4.74	0.4	100
2017	ABQ	AAA	23	3	1	0	8	7	35	41	7	5.4	5.7	22	50%	.321	1.77	4.89	6.51	-0.3	114
2018	ABQ	AAA	24	3	5	1	18	10	43^{2}	44	8	2.9	7.0	34	45%	.283	1.33	5.56	4.43	0.5	119
2018	COL	MLB	24	0	0	0	14	0	14^{2}	15	1	2.5	8.6	14	48%	.341	1.30	1.84	4.37	0.1	120
2019	*COL*	*MLB*	*25*	*2*	*2*	*0*	*15*	*5*	*35^{2}*	*35*	*5*	*3.5*	*8.2*	*33*	*43%*	*.308*	*1.37*	*4.56*	*4.98*	*0.1*	*108*

Breakout: 20% Improve: 27% Collapse: 14% Attrition: 34% MLB: 54% *Comparables: Tyler Wagner, Tyler Anderson, Andrew Chafin*

The Report: I've always had a soft spot for Almonte. When I saw him in Hartford, he worked quickly, threw strikes, flashed a plus slider, and did a good job measuring out his stuff across his outings. He was usually good for keeping the game time under 2:45 so I could get down the road to the cocktail bar at a reasonable hour. So yeah, he was easy to like. I did think he was a reliever long term because of intermittent shoulder issues and the lack of an average changeup. The Rockies transitioned him to the pen full-time after a June call-up, and the early results were quite good.

As you'd expect with this kind of conversion, Almonte's velocity ticked up into the mid-90s, and he leaned more heavily on his mid-80s plus slider. Almonte manipulates the slider well and he's comfortable enough throwing it to the backfoot against lefties to make it a crossover weapon. The change is still below-average. It's very firm but flashes average run and sink. It's enough to keep it in the back of hitters' minds at least, but not much more than that. Health permitting, Almonte is a major-league-ready late-inning reliever, although a part of me wishes they gave him a little more time in the rotation outside of the launching pad in Albuquerque.

The Risks: Low. Almonte got a fair bit of major-league time, has two present above-average major league offerings, and has a chance to break camp in the Rockies bullpen.

Ben Carsley's Fantasy Take: I'm a bit bummed that the Rockies have transitioned Almonte to the pen, as I liked him a bit as a starter prospect. Alas, it's tough for us to get excited about *any* reliever prospects, nevermind ones who'll be pitching in Coors. Sadly, you can pass, though Almonte may be worthy of your watch list in super-deep formats or leagues with holds as a category.

8 Tyler Nevin 1B

OFP: 55 Likely: 45 ETA: 2020

Born: 05/29/97 Age: 22 Bats: R Throws: R Height: 6'4" Weight: 200 Origin: Round 1, 2015 Draft (#38 overall)

YEAR	TEAM	LVL	AGE	PA	R	2B	3B	HR	RBI	BB	K	SB	CS	AVG/OBP/SLG	DRC+	VORP	BABIP	BRR	FRAA	WARP	PF
2017	BOI	A-	20	30	4	3	0	1	5	0	9	0	1	.233/.233/.433	53	0.1	.300	0.1	3B(3) 0.0, 1B(2) -0.2	-0.2	110
2017	ASH	A	20	335	45	18	3	7	47	27	56	10	5	.305/.364/.456	131	18.8	.349	1.3	1B(32) 1.6, 3B(23) -2.5	1.2	108
2018	LNC	A+	21	417	59	25	1	13	62	34	77	4	3	.328/.386/.503	140	15.0	.383	-4.4	1B(67) -0.7, 3B(17) 1.0	0.8	116
2019	*COL*	*MLB*	*22*	*252*	*23*	*8*	*0*	*7*	*28*	*11*	*62*	*1*	*0*	*.217/.254/.343*	*59*	*-7.8*	*.259*	*-0.5*	*1B 0, 3B -1*	*-0.9*	*108*

Breakout: 16% Improve: 25% Collapse: 1% Attrition: 20% MLB: 25% *Comparables: Nick Evans, Jose Osuna, Dominic Smith*

The Report: Health has been a limiting factor for Nevin since he was knee-high to a baseball-playing grasshopper. But he finally showed flashes of what he's capable of with the bat last season. He wears the standard Lancaster caveat for last year's when-healthy production, but he attacks hittable pitches in the zone well and he can hit balls that'll get out of any stadium. He's built long, square, and powerful, and the swing stays fluid off a long stride into the attack. He sprayed balls all over the place in Arizona in a rousing fall campaign, and has at least enough physicality and arm strength to keep giving him reps at third base.

The Risks: They're high physically until they're not. His medical file's long and storied, though despite a couple short stints in the tent last season he did log 117 games. As it is for so many guys, Double-A presents a significant test here.

Ben Carsley's Fantasy Take: Nevin is a platoon guy/corner bench bat through and through for me. If he remains a Rockie, he's unlikely to play everyday. If he gets traded he could be a second-division starter, but then, well, he's not a Rockie. His offensive upside and proximity may be enough to sneak him on a top-200, but any rosier outlook right now relies too heavily on bloodlines.

9 Yonathan Daza OF

OFP: 50 Likely: 40 ETA: Late 2019

Born: 02/28/94 Age: 25 Bats: R Throws: R Height: 6'2" Weight: 190 Origin: International Free Agent, 2010

YEAR	TEAM	LVL	AGE	PA	R	2B	3B	HR	RBI	BB	K	SB	CS	AVG/OBP/SLG	DRC+	VORP	BABIP	BRR	FRAA	WARP	PF
2016	ASH	A	22	516	63	35	2	3	58	23	78	2	7	.307/.341/.408	107	18.3	.361	5.2	RF(81) 3.3, CF(31) 5.0	2.1	114
2016	MOD	A+	22	36	1	2	0	0	3	1	7	1	1	.242/.306/.303	61	-0.5	.308	-0.5	RF(4) 0.2, LF(3) -0.4	-0.2	88
2017	LNC	A+	23	569	93	34	11	3	87	30	88	31	8	.341/.376/.466	124	37.2	.397	7.8	CF(75) 2.9, RF(46) 5.4	3.2	122
2018	HFD	AA	24	228	27	18	2	4	29	7	24	4	5	.306/.330/.461	118	7.3	.330	-0.6	CF(30) 1.3, RF(16) 4.2	1.1	106
2019	*COL*	*MLB*	*25*	*252*	*22*	*11*	*1*	*5*	*25*	*4*	*50*	*4*	*2*	*.243/.255/.362*	*62*	*-2.7*	*.280*	*-0.1*	*CF 2, RF 0*	*-0.1*	*108*

Breakout: 7% Improve: 9% Collapse: 2% Attrition: 12% MLB: 13% *Comparables: Nick Buss, Noel Cuevas, Juan Perez*

The Report: Daza was limited to just 54 games in Hartford this year because of a hamstring injury. Despite the rawness in his game, he acquitted himself well in his first taste of Double-A. He's a quick-twitch athlete, a plus runner who's a steady defender in center field, and he shows enough arm for right. His bat needs to take a step forward to get him over the hump from fourth outfielder to starter, though.

Daza's swing is loose—in a good way—with quick wrists. It's bat speed over barrel control at present. He has the raw physical tools for average hit, but struggles with spin and his general aggressiveness at the plate looks ripe for exploitation by major-league arms. There's enough strength and loft—he'll put a charge in a mistake—to project average power, but you wonder how much of that he will get into games against elite pitching. Daza turns 25 in February and seems ticketed for a return engagement with the Eastern League, so the clock is ticking on his development, and the Rockies already have a very crowded outfield picture.

The Risks: High. He's overaged, hasn't fully conquered Double-A, and there are hit tool questions.

Ben Carsley's Fantasy Take: There are worse bets than a toolsy outfielder who could challenge for playing time in Colorado this season, but Daza has enough red flags in his profile that I'm wary of going all-in here. Between the health issues, his age relative to competition and the glut of outfielders in front of him, Daza seems destined for a future as a fourth outfielder. Could he be of use for us if he ends up getting more playing time? Sure. But the odds of him starting everyday for the Rox seem pretty slim.

10 Ryan Vilade SS

OFP: 50 Likely: 40 ETA: 2021

Born: 02/18/99 Age: 20 Bats: R Throws: R Height: 6'2" Weight: 194 Origin: Round 2, 2017 Draft (#48 overall)

YEAR	TEAM	LVL	AGE	PA	R	2B	3B	HR	RBI	BB	K	SB	CS	AVG/OBP/SLG	DRC+	VORP	BABIP	BRR	FRAA	WARP	PF
2017	GJR	RK	18	146	23	3	2	5	21	27	31	5	5	.308/.438/.496	130	13.9	.378	0.4	SS(30) -2.1	0.6	120
2018	ASH	A	19	533	77	20	4	5	44	49	96	17	13	.274/.353/.368	113	25.8	.333	-1.9	SS(116) -6.3	1.1	107
2019	*COL*	*MLB*	*20*	*252*	*25*	*3*	*0*	*6*	*20*	*16*	*72*	*3*	*2*	*.176/.225/.267*	*31*	*-12.0*	*.219*	*-0.3*	*SS -2*	*-1.5*	*108*

Breakout: 9% Improve: 9% Collapse: 0% Attrition: 1% MLB: 9% *Comparables: Ruben Tejada, Tyler Wade, Orlando Arcia*

The Report: The Rockies second-round prep pick in 2017, Vilade drew a somewhat aggressive A-ball assignment in his first full pro season. He held his own against generally older competition—albeit while playing his home games in one of the better hitter's parks in the minors. Drafted as a power over hit third baseman, Vilade played every game in the field this year at shortstop. He's "okay" there, but likely will slide back to third at some point in his pro career where the range and actions will play better. The arm is fine for either spot on the left side though.

At the plate, Vilade has plus bat speed, but works with an upper-body heavy swing that doesn't always keep him in balance or allow him to tap into his plus raw power. He's got enough hand-eye to make consistent contact at this level, but without further refinement both the quality and amount of contact might go down by the upper minors. He's athletic, projectable, and you usually can't teach this kind of bat speed. Ultimately, there's a foundation worth betting on here. even if the upside might not be much beyond "major-league starter" unless the power takes a big step forward.

The Risks: High. May have to shift off shortstop and only an A-ball track record.

Ben Carsley's Fantasy Take: I think it's fair to say that Vilade's upside appears much lower today than it did when he was drafted. Does an average-ish third baseman who plays half of his games in Coors Field have fantasy value? You betcha. But considering that's Vilade's upside, he'd likely be toward the end of a top-200 list and nothing more.

The Next Five:

11 Grant Lavigne 1B

Born: 08/27/99 Age: 19 Bats: L Throws: R Height: 6'4" Weight: 220 Origin: Round 1, 2018 Draft (#42 overall)

YEAR	TEAM	LVL	AGE	PA	R	2B	3B	HR	RBI	BB	K	SB	CS	AVG/OBP/SLG	DRC+	VORP	BABIP	BRR	FRAA	WARP	PF
2018	GJR	RK	18	258	45	13	2	6	38	45	40	12	7	.350/.477/.519	190	27.3	.410	-0.6	1B(53) -6.8	1.1	109
2019	*COL*	*MLB*	*19*	*252*	*24*	*7*	*0*	*7*	*26*	*26*	*70*	*2*	*1*	*.193/.275/.315*	*58*	*-8.5*	*.242*	*-0.5*	*1B -2*	*-1.1*	*108*

Breakout: 7% Improve: 9% Collapse: 0% Attrition: 4% MLB: 12% *Comparables: Franmil Reyes, Nomar Mazara, Gleyber Torres*

Our image of the prep first baseman usually fits in one of two molds. (1) The advanced hitters with fringe athleticism who may or may not add enough game power as they move up the totem pole (Dominic Smith or Nick Pratto). (2) The leveraged slugger with even fringier athleticism and usually significant hit tool questions (Josh Ockimey or Bobby Bradley). Lavigne threads the needle here. He's a strong kid with a reasonably athletic frame that doesn't need to get too long or too leveraged to tap into his substantial raw power. There's the beginnings of a quality approach here as well, with more polish than you'd expect from a cold-weather high school bat.

The main quibble is that, well, he's still a first baseman. Lavigne may not be your *average* prep first base pick, but the bar for major-league performance is still as high as every other cold corner prospect. And the hit or pop alone might not be a carrying tool, so he will still have to prove it level-by-level.

12 Justin Lawrence RHP

Born: 11/25/94 Age: 24 Bats: R Throws: R Height: 6'3" Weight: 220 Origin: Round 12, 2015 Draft (#347 overall)

YEAR	TEAM	LVL	AGE	W	L	SV	G	GS	IP	H	HR	BB/9	K/9	K	GB%	BABIP	WHIP	ERA	DRA	WARP	PF
2016	ASH	A	21	2	5	0	26	0	36^1	48	4	3.5	5.7	23	60%	.352	1.71	7.18	4.77	-0.1	100
2016	BOI	A-	21	2	1	8	23	0	28^2	27	0	1.9	12.6	40	68%	.380	1.15	2.20	1.94	1.0	100
2017	ASH	A	22	0	2	6	16	0	16^1	10	1	2.2	11.0	20	76%	.243	0.86	1.65	4.19	0.1	100
2018	LNC	A+	23	0	2	11	55	0	54^1	36	2	4.5	10.3	62	63%	.264	1.16	2.65	3.41	1.0	100
2019	*COL*	*MLB*	*24*	*1*	*0*	*0*	*10*	*0*	*10^2*	*10*	*1*	*4.5*	*9.0*	*11*	*54%*	*.322*	*1.45*	*4.14*	*4.52*	*0.1*	*108*

Breakout: 4% Improve: 4% Collapse: 1% Attrition: 2% MLB: 5% *Comparables: Preston Claiborne, Barret Browning, Kyle McClellan*

Lawrence got beat in a couple high-profile prospect showcases and ran out of steam a bit by Arizona, but he was absolutely disgusting for most of the year. At his peak he threw a nice stretch of innings in the Antelope Valley summertime elements. He sits in the high-90s with a darting, two-plane slider a dozen mph slower, all out of a twisting, slingshotting delivery that creates a real tough pick-up for righties and a pretty difficult one for lefties too. It was unclear to the naked eye why he never graduated to Hartford last season, but if he brings that stuff with him when he does, he'll force his way into Colorado's bullpen development plan this season.

13 Ben Bowden LHP

Born: 10/21/94 Age: 24 Bats: L Throws: L Height: 6'4" Weight: 235 Origin: Round 2, 2016 Draft (#45 overall)

YEAR	TEAM	LVL	AGE	W	L	SV	G	GS	IP	H	HR	BB/9	K/9	K	GB%	BABIP	WHIP	ERA	DRA	WARP	PF
2016	ASH	A	21	0	1	0	26	0	23^2	23	1	5.7	11.0	29	43%	.373	1.61	3.04	3.99	0.2	100
2018	ASH	A	23	3	0	0	15	0	15^1	17	2	2.9	14.7	25	43%	.429	1.43	3.52	3.21	0.3	100
2018	LNC	A+	23	4	2	0	34	0	36^2	35	6	3.7	13.0	53	35%	.337	1.36	4.17	4.64	0.1	100
2019	*COL*	*MLB*	*24*	*2*	*1*	*1*	*35*	*0*	*36^2*	*36*	*5*	*5.3*	*10.1*	*41*	*37%*	*.332*	*1.56*	*4.71*	*5.16*	*-0.1*	*108*

Breakout: 0% Improve: 0% Collapse: 2% Attrition: 2% MLB: 2% *Comparables: Brian Schlitter, Neil Wagner, Josh Fields*

14 Robert Tyler RHP

Born: 06/18/95 Age: 24 Bats: R Throws: R Height: 6'4" Weight: 226 Origin: Round 1, 2016 Draft (#38 overall)

YEAR	TEAM	LVL	AGE	W	L	SV	G	GS	IP	H	HR	BB/9	K/9	K	GB%	BABIP	WHIP	ERA	DRA	WARP	PF
2016	BOI	A-	21	0	2	0	5	5	7	2	0	20.6	6.4	5	53%	.105	2.57	6.43	4.84	0.0	96
2018	ASH	A	23	4	2	8	34	0	38^1	37	5	1.6	12.2	52	62%	.323	1.15	3.99	2.85	0.9	100
2018	LNC	A+	23	0	1	0	12	0	9^1	17	2	4.8	4.8	5	46%	.429	2.36	9.64	5.52	-0.1	100
2019	*COL*	*MLB*	*24*	*1*	*1*	*1*	*27*	*1*	*31^2*	*33*	*4*	*8.1*	*8.7*	*30*	*46%*	*.330*	*1.93*	*5.90*	*6.50*	*-0.5*	*108*

Breakout: 1% Improve: 1% Collapse: 1% Attrition: 3% MLB: 3% *Comparables: Andrew Triggs, Reyes Moronta, Bobby Wahl*

These two are a package deal. They've travelled a bizarrely exact path—they were drafted seven picks apart, both missed 2017 recuperating from Tommy John, and they've climbed Colorado's minor league ladder nearly in lockstep—and each should get their chances at Double-A this year. Both have fast-track potential if they show well when they do. Tyler was gassed at the end of the season, while Bowden held up better and flashed a slightly higher-end ceiling. Tyler throws a bit harder and Bowden offers a quality pitch mix from the left side. Neither looks like a budding relief ace but they could both wind up as valuable bullpen contributors.

15 Rico Garcia RHP

Born: 01/10/94 Age: 25 Bats: R Throws: R Height: 5'11" Weight: 190 Origin: Round 30, 2016 Draft (#890 overall)

YEAR	TEAM	LVL	AGE	W	L	SV	G	GS	IP	H	HR	BB/9	K/9	K	GB%	BABIP	WHIP	ERA	DRA	WARP	PF
2016	BOI	A-	22	0	4	0	16	8	35^{1}	50	1	4.3	8.9	35	47%	.422	1.90	6.37	3.46	0.7	112
2017	BOI	A-	23	0	4	0	8	8	41	50	2	2.4	7.7	35	45%	.369	1.49	3.95	4.93	0.2	116
2017	ASH	A	23	2	2	0	8	4	28	27	2	2.2	9.6	30	49%	.316	1.21	2.57	3.83	0.4	114
2018	LNC	A+	24	7	7	0	16	15	100	99	12	2.0	9.1	101	46%	.315	1.21	3.42	4.28	1.2	108
2018	HFD	AA	24	6	2	0	11	11	67	54	8	2.7	8.2	61	44%	.264	1.10	2.28	4.18	0.9	105
2019	*COL*	*MLB*	*25*	*7*	*8*	*0*	*23*	*23*	120^{1}	*129*	*20*	*3.7*	*7.7*	*103*	*40%*	*.319*	*1.49*	*4.97*	*5.42*	*-0.1*	*108*

Breakout: 7% Improve: 11% Collapse: 14% Attrition: 24% MLB: 35% *Comparables: Brad Peacock, Sam Howard, J.R. Graham*

Garcia reached Double-A in 2018, closing out a very productive season for the Hawaii product. There is minimal projection left for Garcia, but he's effective filling up the zone with three averageish offerings. The fastball sits low-90s (although he has flashed higher at times) and features some sink and run from his high-three-quarters slot. His slider is pinned around 80. While it lacks consistent shape, the best are solid-average with late, tight bite. The changeup is on the fringier side of average and is a clear third pitch. Garcia is a shorter, overaged righty, but the present stuff is good enough for a backend starter or swing projection, with a middle relief fallback if he finds more velo in shorter bursts.

Others of note:

Sam Hilliard, OF, Double-A Hartford

Hilliard falls along the Tauchmann/Patterson continuum of fringy Rockies corner prospects. He's not a precise fit for this type. He's sneaky athletic, an average runner who's a good glove/plus arm in right and could probably even stand in center for you once a week. It is still a corner outfield profile though, and the bat may not carry it.

The power is on point. It's plus raw and Hilliard will absolutely punish mistakes, but the stiffness in his swing and pitch recognition issues limited how much of that raw got into games against Double-A arms. Hilliard also has platoon issues, and it's fair to mention that he benefited from Hartford's short porch in right. He will be 25 before Opening Day. He straddles the bench outfielder/org guy line for now, but I always liked Jordan Patterson more than most too.

Ryan Castellani, OF, Double-A Hartford

Castellani entered the 2018 season as the fifth best prospect in the Colorado system and a long-list 101 guy. I ended up seeing him four times in 2017 the way the schedule shook out and saw a slightly different dude each time. He was extremely young for Double-A though. You could easily imagine a scenario where he put it together in a second look at the Eastern League and beat a path to the majors as another homegrown arm in a suddenly rich Rockies pipeline. Instead, his age-22 season in Double-A went far worse than his age-21 campaign.

The vagaries of the schedule meant I didn't catch Castellani until the last couple weeks of the season, but he again looked like a different pitcher, in not in a good way. His slot was higher, his arm action more rigid. Gone was the athletic delivery that garnered physical comps to Max Scherzer. There was more effort to sit 89-91, the slider was slurvier, and he just didn't look right. You'd catch glimpses of the 2017 top prospect—a fastball that bored in under a lefty's hands, a mid-80s slider with late tilt, but if you only saw him last year, you wouldn't be filing him as an acquire. Twenty-three in Double-A, even as a double repeater, isn't a prospect death sentence. But pitchers, man.

Top Talents 25 and Under (born 4/1/93 or later):

1. German Marquez
2. Kyle Freeland
3. Brendan Rodgers
4. David Dahl
5. Garrett Hampson
6. Ryan McMahon
7. Raimel Tapia
8. Trevor Story
9. Ryan Rolison
10. Antonio Senzatela
11. Peter Lambert

Trevor Story aged off of this list just in the nick of time to avoid launching the whole exercise into the sun, and yet even with that kind of heavyweight graduation, this is still one of the best batches of young talent this franchise has ever accumulated.

The dual emergence of Marquez and Freeland last year was a sight for the sorest of pitching-shriveled eyes, especially as former staple of this list Jon Gray staggered throughout the year. Marquez really honed his raw talent quickly over the last year, developing one of the filthiest Kershaw mixes since, well, Kershaw. Freeland threw the ball well all year, then added a couple ticks to his cutter and took his game to the next level down the stretch. The Rockies have never started a season with as much reason for optimism about their starting pitching, and both guys are under club control for the next four years.

Dahl just balled once he got rolling in Coors. His raw talent has long been obvious, but he's missed so much time and spent so much recovery effort on the shelf over the years that he's long been a bit of a wild card. There were a few ugly indicators about his approach all year, but he just kept right on crushing the ball. He's always been a talented player; here's hoping we see what it looks like for a full season.

McMahon's hit well in a bunch of runs against Triple-A pitching now, and the club gave him 200 trips between two demotions to show them what he could do in Denver last year. Then he ended up riding pine for nearly all of September and Rocktober. The Daniel Murphy signing clouds his short-term outlook all the more, but he is currently a talented, versatile young infielder with some potential.

Tapia put up a modestly above-average offensive season when controlled for Albuquerque's shenanigans, but it was chock-full of the kind of doubles and triples with eyes he should be able to spray all around Coors Field. He'll be 25 on Opening Day and really needs to get some at-bats.

Senzatela was able to work pretty effectively last year off a fastball-slider-curve three-piece, then brought in the ol' number four wiggle down the stretch, coaxing a nice boost in whiff rate when he did. He'll have an interesting multi-inning swing profile for as long as the fastball holds.

Detroit Tigers

The State of the System:

Dave Dombrowksi may be celebrating a World Series back east, but the rebuilding Tigers still have a whole bunch of right-handed pitching prospects.

The Top Ten:

1 **Casey Mize RHP** OFP: 60 Likely: 55 ETA: Late 2019
Born: 05/01/97 Age: 22 Bats: R Throws: R Height: 6'3" Weight: 220 Origin: Round 1, 2018 Draft (#1 overall)

YEAR	TEAM	LVL	AGE	W	L	SV	G	GS	IP	H	HR	BB/9	K/9	K	GB%	BABIP	WHIP	ERA	DRA	WARP	PF
2018	LAK	A+	21	0	1	0	4	4	11^2	13	2	1.5	7.7	10	44%	.344	1.29	4.63	4.44	0.1	95
2019	*DET*	*MLB*	*22*	*2*	*3*	*0*	*8*	*8*	*33^2*	*35*	*5*	*3.6*	*7.5*	*28*	*42%*	*.301*	*1.44*	*5.03*	*5.28*	*0.1*	*104*

Breakout: 2% Improve: 3% Collapse: 0% Attrition: 2% MLB: 3% *Comparables: Jace Fry, Michael Ynoa, Chi Chi Gonzalez*

The Report: Mize is the first college arm to go 1.1 since Mark Appel. Like Appel, he is more of a surety over upside pick. That's not to poo-poo the stuff here. Mize has three potential plus pitches in his fastball/slider/split combo. The fastball sits comfortably mid-90s and Mize attacks the zone with it to set up his power slider and split-change. The slider has mid-80s velocity and good two-plane break, and his split has big velo separation and plenty of tumble. The Tigers have taken a fairly conservative path with him so far—he had some injury issues his sophomore year—but he could debut next year and I'd expect him to start in the Eastern League. There is some effort in his delivery to note. The mechanics are extremely arm-heavy and he will whack and recoil at times. It remains to be seen whether that will work across a starter's workload in the pros. Regardless, he's essentially major-league-ready now, which was the argument for him as the first overall pick as opposed to a huge projection or ceiling.

The Risks: Medium. Mize could probably be dropped into a rotation Opening Day and be at least average. That won't happen for the obvious reasons. He has had arm issues in college and is a pitching prospect so there's always that.

Ben Carsley's Fantasy Take: It's not Mize's fault that he went 1.1, but because of his draft slot he's nearly guaranteed to be overrated in dynasty circles. Reading up on Mize above, he profiles similarly to how Kyle Wright did coming into 2018, whom we ranked at 81 on our top-101 before last season. Such a ranking for Mize might seem harsh, but is more indicative of the risk-to-reward ratio that comes with any mid-rotation starting pitching prospect than any real flaw on Mize's part.

2 Matt Manning RHP OFP: 60 Likely: 50 ETA: 2020

Born: 01/28/98 Age: 21 Bats: R Throws: R Height: 6'6" Weight: 190 Origin: Round 1, 2016 Draft (#9 overall)

YEAR	TEAM	LVL	AGE	W	L	SV	G	GS	IP	H	HR	BB/9	K/9	K	GB%	BABIP	WHIP	ERA	DRA	WARP	PF
2016	TGW	RK	18	0	2	0	10	10	29^{1}	27	2	2.1	14.1	46	38%	.379	1.16	3.99	2.54	1.0	104
2017	ONE	A-	19	2	2	0	9	9	33^{1}	27	0	3.8	9.7	36	31%	.310	1.23	1.89	3.75	0.6	96
2017	WMI	A	19	2	0	0	5	5	17^{2}	14	0	5.6	13.2	26	49%	.341	1.42	5.60	3.43	0.4	97
2018	WMI	A	20	3	3	0	11	11	55^{2}	47	3	4.5	12.3	76	43%	.344	1.35	3.40	3.23	1.3	96
2018	LAK	A+	20	4	4	0	9	9	51^{1}	32	4	3.3	11.4	65	47%	.241	0.99	2.98	3.69	1.0	98
2018	ERI	AA	20	0	1	0	2	2	10^{2}	11	0	3.4	11.0	13	46%	.393	1.41	4.22	3.06	0.3	105
2019	*DET*	*MLB*	*21*	*5*	*7*	*0*	*20*	*20*	*86*	*80*	*11*	*4.4*	*9.5*	*91*	*38%*	*.301*	*1.43*	*4.55*	*4.75*	*0.7*	*104*

Breakout: 5% Improve: 9% Collapse: 2% Attrition: 7% MLB: 15% *Comparables: Sean Reid-Foley, Michael Kopech, Mike Montgomery*

The Report: Manning looked more like the ninth overall pick in 2018. He's now sitting in the mid-90s and sawing off hitters with the heater's natural cutter-like action. His curveball is getting sharper, too. It isn't consistently plus, but he's flashing the best version of it more and more. Manning still has quite a few flaws in his profile, though. He's cleaned up his mechanics somewhat, and his command has improved accordingly, but he doesn't take full advantage of his size. His back knee collapses as he begins his stride, which limits the plane his 6-foot-6 frame can provide. More importantly, he hasn't settled on a changeup that works for him. Detroit has him working with a fosh for now, but that may change. There's still plenty of time for Manning to reach his high ceiling and he'll likely spend 2019 in Double-A as a 21-year old. It isn't difficult to envision him as one of the top prospects in the game a year from now, but...

The Risks: ...it could also quickly go the other way. You don't have to squint very hard to see why people get squirmy projecting him as a starter. Despite tinkering with several grips, he has yet to find a consistently usable changeup. Pair that with spotty command and you've got reliever risk written all over him.

Ben Carsley's Fantasy Take: If you subscribe to the theory that the only thing that matters with pitching prospects is upside, you may actually prefer Manning to Mize. I won't go that far given all the red flags, but I am intrigued by Manning's ceiling as a high-K fantasy SP4/5. That his floor appears to be as a bullpen arm matters, though, and it will be tough for Manning to crack the back of the top-101 dynasty list despite his proximity to the majors.

3 Isaac Paredes IF OFP: 55 Likely: 50 ETA: Early 2020

Born: 02/18/99 Age: 20 Bats: R Throws: R Height: 5'11" Weight: 225 Origin: International Free Agent, 2015

YEAR	TEAM	LVL	AGE	PA	R	2B	3B	HR	RBI	BB	K	SB	CS	AVG/OBP/SLG	DRC+	VORP	BABIP	BRR	FRAA	WARP	PF
2016	CUB	RK	17	185	23	14	3	1	26	13	20	4	0	.305/.359/.443	149	15.6	.338	-0.3	SS(45) 6.6	1.5	99
2017	SBN	A	18	384	49	25	0	7	49	29	54	2	1	.264/.343/.401	111	17.4	.294	-1.0	SS(70) -2.7, 3B(7) 2.5	1.2	100
2017	WMI	A	18	133	16	3	0	4	21	13	13	0	0	.217/.323/.348	110	0.2	.214	-0.5	SS(22) -2.4, 3B(5) 1.4	0.4	99
2018	LAK	A+	19	347	50	19	2	12	48	32	54	1	0	.259/.338/.455	127	24.2	.274	0.3	SS(59) 3.2, 2B(22) 0.5	2.0	96
2018	ERI	AA	19	155	20	9	0	3	22	19	22	1	0	.321/.406/.458	141	13.7	.358	0.3	3B(18) 0.6, SS(15) 0.9	1.2	102
2019	*DET*	*MLB*	*20*	*252*	*21*	*10*	*0*	*7*	*27*	*11*	*53*	*0*	*0*	*.187/.235/.317*	*50*	*-6.8*	*.211*	*-0.5*	*SS 0, 2B 0*	*-0.6*	*104*

Breakout: 17% Improve: 27% Collapse: 0% Attrition: 6% MLB: 27% *Comparables: Jurickson Profar, Carlos Correa, J.P. Crawford*

The Report: Performance-wise Paredes' season was an unqualified success: He reached Double-A as a 19-year-old and had the best overall offensive season of his career. We mostly exist to qualify here though. Although Paredes was the youngest player at his levels, he's not exactly projectable at this point—see the listed height/weight above for one—and those thighs portend a below-average runner in his twenties. He's an aggressive hitter with some length to his swing, but his bat speed/control are sufficient to smooth the edges enough to project at least an average hit tool.

The fire hydrant physique belies above-average raw power, and Paredes should get to enough of it to be a 15-20 home run guy. He's not gonna be rangey enough for shortstop or perhaps even second, but he has plenty of arm for third and the hands and actions to be at least average there. He may retain enough defensive flexibility to play three spots in the infield if you want to spot someone once a week as well. Paredes' profile lacks upside on the scouting sheet—averagish tools across the board and a corner infield projection—but this is also the type of profile (and physique) that seems to pop (so to speak) in the majors these days.

The Risks: Medium. It's more of an all-around profile than a standout, toolsy one, and he's only played a handful of games in the upper minors.

Ben Carsley's Fantasy Take: I feel personally attacked by the description of Paredes' thighs. Anyway, Eduardo Escobar just hit .272 with 23 homers and decent R/RBI stats, and that well-roundedness was enough to make him a top-20 third baseman, per ESPN's player rater. That's the dream with Paredes, who I don't think is on a lot of dynasty radars right now and who could very well be available in your league.

4 Daz Cameron OF

OFP: 55 Likely: 50 ETA: Late 2019

Born: 01/15/97 Age: 22 Bats: R Throws: R Height: 6'2" Weight: 195 Origin: Round 1, 2015 Draft (#37 overall)

YEAR	TEAM	LVL	AGE	PA	R	2B	3B	HR	RBI	BB	K	SB	CS	AVG/OBP/SLG	DRC+	VORP	BABIP	BRR	FRAA	WARP	PF
2016	QUD	A	19	87	5	2	2	0	6	8	33	4	3	.143/.221/.221	40	-5.6	.244	0.1	CF(10) -0.6, LF(6) -0.3	-0.6	103
2016	TCV	A-	19	89	13	3	1	2	14	6	26	8	2	.278/.352/.418	111	4.7	.392	0.0	CF(15) 0.0, LF(2) -0.3	0.1	113
2017	QUD	A	20	511	79	29	8	14	73	45	108	32	12	.271/.349/.466	132	38.4	.323	3.1	CF(110) 1.8, RF(4) 0.1	3.2	102
2018	LAK	A+	21	246	35	9	3	3	20	25	69	10	4	.259/.346/.370	117	9.9	.366	2.5	CF(38) 1.9, RF(18) 0.9	1.2	95
2018	ERI	AA	21	226	32	12	5	5	35	25	53	12	5	.285/.367/.470	124	11.4	.366	3.4	CF(34) -7.0, RF(16) 1.5	0.7	102
2018	TOL	AAA	21	62	8	4	1	0	6	2	15	2	2	.211/.246/.316	55	-1.1	.279	0.7	CF(14) 0.3, RF(1) 0.0	-0.1	94
2019	*DET*	*MLB*	*22*	*252*	*29*	*8*	*2*	*6*	*21*	*15*	*77*	*7*	*3*	*.185/.237/.315*	*49*	*-5.9*	*.242*	*0.6*	*CF -1, RF 0*	*-0.6*	*104*

Breakout: 4% Improve: 14% Collapse: 0% Attrition: 10% MLB: 20% *Comparables: Kirk Nieuwenhuis, Ryan Kalish, Michael Saunders*

The Report: Cameron is a tricky guy to project, and Jeff begged off the blurb because he said that it was "breaking his brain." I can see why. Cameron is constantly evolving, which makes it difficult to get a bead on him. With an athletic build and plenty of tools, he checked all the boxes but never performed to potential in Houston's system. A year-and-a-half later, he looks like a major leaguer. He's an above-average hitter with average raw power, but the gap between those two could narrow sooner rather than later. He's a plus runner on the bases and in the field. Cameron is built for center field, but he has enough of an arm that he could play right if that becomes necessary. In the end, his role will be determined by how his bat plays against major-league arms. It won't take much more polish to turn him into a glove-first fourth outfielder, but with a little more power and consistency of contact, he'll be a well-rounded, every day guy.

The Risks: Low. He's close to the majors, handled a halfish season of Double-A well, and has a fairly safe floor as a bench outfielder due to the glove, speed, and arm. Like Paredes there is some positive variance here too if more power comes.

Ben Carsley's Fantasy Take: Cameron is one of the toughest guys in the minors to project from a dynasty standpoint, too. His floor seems to be a faster version of Jackie Bradley Jr., and we've seen JBJ serve as an OF4/5 during his best years. But it's always scary when the hit tool is the biggest question mark with any prospect with this profile. I think Cameron's upside and proximity should push him into top-101 territory, but odds are I won't feel great about the placement. I also wouldn't feel great about leaving him off. Ugh, my brain is broken as well.

5 Beau Burrows RHP

OFP: 55 Likely: 50 ETA: Late 2019

Born: 09/18/96 Age: 22 Bats: R Throws: R Height: 6'2" Weight: 200 Origin: Round 1, 2015 Draft (#22 overall)

YEAR	TEAM	LVL	AGE	W	L	SV	G	GS	IP	H	HR	BB/9	K/9	K	GB%	BABIP	WHIP	ERA	DRA	WARP	PF
2016	WMI	A	19	6	4	0	21	20	97	87	2	2.8	6.2	67	42%	.283	1.21	3.15	3.87	1.3	102
2017	LAK	A+	20	4	3	0	11	11	58^{2}	45	3	1.7	9.5	62	45%	.298	0.95	1.23	3.14	1.5	87
2017	ERI	AA	20	6	4	0	15	15	76^{1}	79	5	3.9	8.8	75	40%	.339	1.47	4.72	4.38	0.7	105
2018	ERI	AA	21	10	9	0	26	26	134	126	12	3.8	8.5	127	32%	.310	1.36	4.10	6.93	-2.5	99
2019	*DET*	*MLB*	*22*	*6*	*9*	*0*	*23*	*23*	*111*	*113*	*18*	*3.7*	*8.1*	*100*	*35%*	*.298*	*1.44*	*5.08*	*5.32*	*0.2*	*104*

Breakout: 5% Improve: 9% Collapse: 7% Attrition: 10% MLB: 20% *Comparables: Reynaldo Lopez, Joe Ross, Chris Flexen*

The Report: Burrows followed up his successful 2017 campaign with a full season in Double-A that ultimately raised more questions than answers. The plus heater was a couple ticks down all year, sitting 91-94 instead of the 93-96. His changeup is still his most advanced secondary, and the excellent velo separation and arm speed are enough to project it as an above-average future offering despite average movement. His 12-6 curve flashes plus too, but the inconsistency in its movement and an overall lack of command causes it to play half a grade down.

Three above-average future offerings is all good and well, but Burrows has yet to make the necessary command refinements in order to get the most out of his stuff. He struck out less than a batter per inning and walked almost four per nine this season. His mechanics are clean and he repeats well though, so the command may just be what it is at this point. The quality of his pitch mix will always leave you wanting more, but this is still a 21-year-old former first rounder who just spent the season in Double-A. Burrows may never develop into the mid-rotation arm many thought he would, but he projects as a solid fourth starter who should begin 2019 in Triple-A.

The Risks: Moderate. Burrows does throw baseballs for a living but unless the command regresses at the big-league level, he's a probable rotation piece with the upside for more.

Ben Carsley's Fantasy Take: Burrows just doesn't miss enough bats for us to get particularly excited about his fantasy future, especially in an era when strikeouts are at an all-time high. Burrows figures to have his uses in uber-deep leagues or AL-only formats, but for those of you who play in standard keeper/dynasty leagues with 100-150ish prospects owned, he's an afterthought at present.

6 Franklin Perez RHP

OFP: 60 Likely: 45 ETA: 2020

Born: 12/06/97 Age: 21 Bats: R Throws: R Height: 6'3" Weight: 197 Origin: International Free Agent, 2014

YEAR	TEAM	LVL	AGE	W	L	SV	G	GS	IP	H	HR	BB/9	K/9	K	GB%	BABIP	WHIP	ERA	DRA	WARP	PF
2016	QUD	A	18	3	3	1	15	10	66^{2}	63	1	2.6	10.1	75	39%	.344	1.23	2.84	3.40	1.2	102
2017	BCA	A+	19	4	2	2	12	10	54^{1}	38	4	2.7	8.8	53	38%	.236	0.99	2.98	3.49	1.1	98
2017	CCH	AA	19	2	1	1	7	6	32	33	2	3.1	7.0	25	35%	.316	1.38	3.09	3.51	0.6	101
2018	LAK	A+	20	0	1	0	4	4	11^{1}	15	2	6.4	7.1	9	43%	.371	2.03	7.94	5.38	0.0	99
2019	*DET*	*MLB*	*21*	*2*	*2*	*0*	*13*	*6*	*33*	*36*	*5*	*3.9*	*6.6*	*24*	*37%*	*.301*	*1.54*	*5.34*	*5.62*	*-0.2*	*104*

Breakout: 1% Improve: 3% Collapse: 0% Attrition: 5% MLB: 7% *Comparables: Jake Odorizzi, Matt Magill, Homer Bailey*

The Report: The 2018 report on Perez is actually an HMO explanation of benefits. A lat strain last spring cost him the first half of the season, and shoulder irritation shut him down in the second half after ~20 mostly ineffective innings. This comes a year after a knee issue that kept him under 100 innings in 2017. We know what he is capable of when healthy—a heavy fastball that touches 96, a potential plus curve and change—but we are going to need to see it for a full season on the mound... at some point. On the one hand he is still 21 for a few more weeks, on the other—well, the phrase "shoulder irritation" basically.

The Risks: High. Perez has never thrown more than 86 1/3 innings in a season due to a variety of maladies. He's only made seven starts above A-ball, and 2018 was a lost developmental year. We have no idea if he can handle a real workload.

Ben Carsley's Fantasy Take: Despite the massive risks, I prefer Perez to Burrows from a fantasy perspective. Sure, he's got greater odds of flaming out or moving to the pen, but if he does stay on the mound for significant periods of time, he's likely to miss plenty of bats while doing so. He's one for the watch list if he's been dropped in your league, as there's SP5/6 upside here.

7 Alex Faedo RHP

OFP: 55 Likely: 45 ETA: 2020

Born: 11/12/95 Age: 23 Bats: R Throws: R Height: 6'5" Weight: 230 Origin: Round 1, 2017 Draft (#18 overall)

YEAR	TEAM	LVL	AGE	W	L	SV	G	GS	IP	H	HR	BB/9	K/9	K	GB%	BABIP	WHIP	ERA	DRA	WARP	PF
2018	LAK	A+	22	2	4	0	12	12	61	49	3	1.9	7.5	51	33%	.263	1.02	3.10	3.19	1.5	94
2018	ERI	AA	22	3	6	0	12	12	60	54	15	3.3	8.9	59	28%	.250	1.27	4.95	4.38	0.7	102
2019	*DET*	*MLB*	*23*	*4*	*7*	*0*	*16*	*16*	*81*	*84*	*16*	*3.2*	*7.5*	*67*	*30%*	*.285*	*1.39*	*5.45*	*5.73*	*-0.2*	*104*

Breakout: 2% Improve: 6% Collapse: 16% Attrition: 19% MLB: 28% *Comparables: Wes Parsons, Jon Gray, Brett Kennedy*

The Report: Faedo is not exactly the same pitcher who was a 1.1 candidate going into the 2017 season. He's lost a few ticks off the fastball now and works either side of 90. The slider is still potentially a plus offering, but now comes in only a bit slower than the fastball. Faedo also features an average change with sink and fade in the low-80s. It's now an averageish repertoire tied together by plus command. Faedo has a solid frame and efficient delivery, but the stuff is now more back-of-the-rotation.

The Risks: Medium. Despite the stuff not popping like it did at U of F, Faedo has had pro success due to his command and secondaries. Although unlikely at this point, there's also some positive variance in play if the mid-90s velo returns.

Ben Carsley's Fantasy Take: Faedo was a popular sleeper pick among newly eligible dynasty league prospects last offseason, but the velo drop and corresponding drop in ceiling are big deals for us. If you look at the report and not the name value/draft position, there's little that distinguishes Faedo from lots of guys with similar profiles. He's like a riskier Burrows who's also another year away.

8 Jake Rogers C

OFP: 50 Likely: 45 ETA: Late 2019

Born: 04/18/95 Age: 24 Bats: R Throws: R Height: 6'1" Weight: 190 Origin: Round 3, 2016 Draft (#97 overall)

YEAR	TEAM	LVL	AGE	PA	R	2B	3B	HR	RBI	BB	K	SB	CS	AVG/OBP/SLG	DRC+	VORP	BABIP	BRR	FRAA	WARP	PF
2016	TCV	A-	21	104	11	7	1	2	12	13	18	0	2	.253/.369/.425	127	4.3	.299	-2.0	C(24) 0.1	0.3	113
2016	QUD	A	21	82	7	3	1	1	4	8	25	1	0	.208/.305/.319	81	1.6	.304	-0.7	C(19) -0.1	0.0	101
2017	QUD	A	22	116	17	7	1	6	15	9	28	1	0	.255/.336/.520	129	10.2	.290	0.3	C(21) 0.9	0.8	103
2017	BCA	A+	22	367	43	18	3	12	55	44	72	13	8	.265/.357/.457	133	30.2	.302	-0.8	C(24) 1.4	2.0	92
2018	ERI	AA	23	408	57	15	1	17	56	41	112	7	1	.219/.305/.412	88	20.8	.261	2.7	C(98) 29.4, 1B(1) 0.0	4.2	101
2019	*DET*	*MLB*	*24*	*69*	*7*	*2*	*0*	*2*	*8*	*5*	*21*	*1*	*0*	*.171/.236/.326*	*41*	*-1.8*	*.207*	*0.0*	*C 2*	*0.1*	*104*

Breakout: 6% Improve: 11% Collapse: 0% Attrition: 12% MLB: 18% *Comparables: Andrew Knapp, Michael McKenry, Josh Donaldson*

The Report: You aren't going to find a better defensive catching prospect than Rogers. Nimble and athletic behind the dish, he's a fantastic receiver with a plus arm that plays even better due to one of the quickest releases you'll ever see. His defense has been big-league ready for several years now and Rogers clubbed 17 homers for Double-A Erie this season, practically ensuring he'll reach the majors in some capacity.

So, what's the catch? Well, Rogers has extreme bat-to-ball issues and he struck out in 27.5% of his plate appearances last year. The Tigers have been working with him to tame his leg kick, but the swing is still a bit of a mess. His timing is all over the place and isn't helped in the slightest by his poor breaking ball recognition. His bat control is well below-average too, and pitchers often exploit him on the outside part of the plate. Rogers does work the count and he walked in more than 10 percent of his plate appearances for the third season running. Still, quality arms won't be afraid to challenge him in the zone. There's average raw power here, yet it's becoming increasingly unlikely that Rogers can fully realize it in games. Essentially, he's a three true outcomes hitter with below-average game power.

The Risks: Moderate. Usually when a prospect is facing major questions with the stick he's exclusively of the high-risk variety. The defensive package is too good to keep Rogers from a major-league role though, so we'll go with "moderate" here. He's either going to hit enough dongs to profile as a regular or he'll carve out a decade-long career as a defensive-oriented backup.

Ben Carsley's Fantasy Take: Rogers is a great prospect for those of you in 30-team, two-catcher AL Central-only formats.

9 Kyle Funkhouser RHP

OFP: 50 Likely: 40 ETA: Late 2019, health permitting

Born: 03/16/94 Age: 25 Bats: R Throws: R Height: 6'2" Weight: 220 Origin: Round 4, 2016 Draft (#115 overall)

YEAR	TEAM	LVL	AGE	W	L	SV	G	GS	IP	H	HR	BB/9	K/9	K	GB%	BABIP	WHIP	ERA	DRA	WARP	PF
2016	ONE	A-	22	0	2	0	13	13	37^{1}	34	0	1.9	8.2	34	53%	.324	1.12	2.65	3.04	1.0	98
2017	WMI	A	23	4	1	0	7	7	31^{1}	30	3	3.7	14.1	49	56%	.403	1.37	3.16	3.18	0.8	95
2017	LAK	A+	23	1	1	0	5	5	31^{1}	23	1	1.7	9.8	34	57%	.275	0.93	1.72	2.97	0.8	81
2018	ERI	AA	24	4	5	0	17	17	89	88	10	3.9	9.0	89	44%	.326	1.43	3.74	4.01	1.4	101
2018	TOL	AAA	24	0	2	0	2	2	8^{2}	8	0	10.4	7.3	7	54%	.333	2.08	6.23	3.71	0.2	90
2019	*DET*	*MLB*	*25*	*4*	*6*	*0*	*17*	*17*	*77*	*78*	*11*	*3.7*	*8.2*	*71*	*44%*	*.305*	*1.43*	*4.69*	*4.91*	*0.5*	*104*

Breakout: 11% Improve: 19% Collapse: 12% Attrition: 30% MLB: 38% *Comparables: Matt Maloney, George Kontos, Jeff Niemann*

The Report: In 2018 Funkhouser continued to flash better stuff than he had his senior year and first pro summer, but again he had trouble staying healthy. This year it was a broken foot instead of vague arm issues, which is an improvement of sorts one supposes. Still, Funkhouser will be 25 in March and has yet to complete a full healthy pro season. More maddening is that the stuff remains inconsistent. He'll show mid-90s heat at times, but often works a few ticks lower. He struggles to command the fastball armside, and his control is fringy generally. He'll flash occasional wiggle to back it over the plate gloveside, but the pitch is a bit straight otherwise.

Funkhouser will flash a plus slider with good depth, but the pitch can get a bit lazy/slurvy. His curve rides high too often and doesn't really show good 12-6 action. The change is used sparingly but has a chance to be average. There's some effort in the delivery despite compact arm action. He might be best deployed as a fastball/slider reliever. There's enough here to keep chasing that first round pick people saw his junior season at Louisville, but I haven't really seen it in the pros.

The Risks: Medium. He's been old for his levels and rarely as durable or efficient as you'd like, but the stuff is mostly major-league-ready.

Ben Carsley's Fantasy Take: As a card-carrying member of Weird-Ass Baseball Name Twitter I'm rooting for Funkhouser to succeed. As a dynasty leaguer, I'm staying away.

10 Carlos Guzman RHP

OFP: 50 Likely: 40 ETA: 2022

Born: 05/16/98 Age: 21 Bats: R Throws: R Height: 6'1" Weight: 170 Origin: International Free Agent, 2015

YEAR	TEAM	LVL	AGE	W	L	SV	G	GS	IP	H	HR	BB/9	K/9	K	GB%	BABIP	WHIP	ERA	DRA	WARP	PF
2017	TGR	RK	19	1	1	4	11	0	20	12	0	2.7	8.1	18	45%	.245	0.90	0.45	2.77	0.6	100
2018	ONE	A-	20	3	4	0	12	12	51^{1}	45	5	2.5	9.1	52	50%	.288	1.15	3.86	3.38	1.1	89
2019	*DET*	*MLB*	*21*	*2*	*2*	*0*	*18*	*5*	*36^{2}*	*40*	*6*	*4.2*	*6.9*	*28*	*41%*	*.305*	*1.57*	*5.53*	*5.82*	*-0.3*	*104*

Breakout: 0% Improve: 0% Collapse: 0% Attrition: 0% MLB: 0% *Comparables: Cesar Vargas, Wily Peralta, Abel De Los Santos*

The Report: Guzman spent his first two professional seasons as an infielder before converting to the mound in 2017. Given his lack of pitching experience, the present arsenal is impressive. His low-90s fastball comes out easy and features wicked armside run that you can't teach. His velocity was inconsistent this season. He touched 95 at times, but also had starts where he sat 89-92. There's projection left in his frame though, and his mechanics are free and easy, so I wouldn't be shocked if he's a 92-95 guy with more reps and physical development.

The change is his best secondary currently, which is unusual for a position player convert. It flashes plus in the low-80s with fade and sink. Guzman is confident enough to throw it at any time and to both righties and lefties, although again, it could be an inconsistent offering. The breaking ball, a slurvy high-70s slider, lags behind; he tends to guide the pitch and snap it off. This ranking is very much a projection bet based on Guzman's frame, present stuff, and general athleticism, but the present stuff is better than you'd expect given his background.

The Risks: Extreme. He's a recent pitching convert with only a short-season resume and questions about his durability and breaking ball.

Ben Carsley's Fantasy Take: You know the look I'm giving you.

The Next Five:

11 Christin Stewart OF

Born: 12/10/93 Age: 25 Bats: L Throws: R Height: 6'0" Weight: 205 Origin: Round 1, 2015 Draft (#34 overall)

YEAR	TEAM	LVL	AGE	PA	R	2B	3B	HR	RBI	BB	K	SB	CS	AVG/OBP/SLG	DRC+	VORP	BABIP	BRR	FRAA	WARP	PF
2016	LAK	A+	22	442	60	22	1	24	68	74	105	3	1	.264/.403/.534	169	32.4	.306	-6.6	LF(94) -15.2	0.8	107
2016	ERI	AA	22	100	17	2	0	6	19	12	26	0	0	.218/.310/.448	128	4.1	.232	0.7	LF(22) 1.0	0.5	109
2017	ERI	AA	23	555	67	29	3	28	86	56	138	3	0	.256/.335/.501	116	31.3	.294	-0.8	LF(120) -10.6	-0.1	105
2018	TOL	AAA	24	522	69	21	3	23	77	67	108	0	0	.264/.364/.480	136	36.1	.296	0.8	LF(97) 9.8, RF(12) -0.7	3.5	93
2018	DET	MLB	24	72	7	1	1	2	10	10	13	0	0	.267/.375/.417	107	3.4	.304	-0.3	LF(15) -0.9	0.1	103
2019	*DET*	*MLB*	*25*	*512*	*65*	*18*	*2*	*23*	*63*	*48*	*133*	*0*	*0*	*.211/.290/.406*	*90*	*8.5*	*.242*	*-0.6*	*LF -1*	*0.9*	*104*

Breakout: 14% Improve: 44% Collapse: 4% Attrition: 33% MLB: 73% *Comparables: Khris Davis, Jerry Sands, Matt LaPorta*

Stewart cut down on the whiffs in 2018, but gave back a bit of his prodigious pop to do it. The overall profile hasn't changed much. He's better suited to DH than play corner OF—fortunately the Tigers have an opening there for 2019—and the bat might end up less than ideal for your designated masher. Still, a guy who hits .260 with 25 bombs has his uses on a second division team, which the Tigers look to be for a bit, and he can occasionally rotate out to 1B or LF and not kill. You may need to platoon him, and if the swing-and-miss issues creep back in against major-league pitching, the bottom drops out of this profile quickly.

12 Parker Meadows OF

Born: 11/02/99 Age: 19 Bats: L Throws: R Height: 6'5" Weight: 185 Origin: Round 2, 2018 Draft (#44 overall)

YEAR	TEAM	LVL	AGE	PA	R	2B	3B	HR	RBI	BB	K	SB	CS	AVG/OBP/SLG	DRC+	VORP	BABIP	BRR	FRAA	WARP	PF
2018	TGW	RK	18	85	16	2	1	4	8	8	25	3	1	.284/.376/.500	126	6.1	.378	0.0	CF(20) -3.1	-0.1	98
2019	*DET*	*MLB*	*19*	*252*	*18*	*3*	*0*	*8*	*25*	*4*	*103*	*1*	*0*	*.144/.157/.253*	*4*	*-20.0*	*.200*	*-0.4*	*CF -1*	*-2.2*	*104*

Breakout: 5% Improve: 7% Collapse: 0% Attrition: 3% MLB: 9% *Comparables: Engel Beltre, Nomar Mazara, Carlos Tocci*

The Tigers used their savings at 1.1 to go significantly overslot for Meadows, younger brother of Austin. Parker is even longer and leaner than his older sibling. He's a borderline plus-plus runner and a good bet to stick in center field even as the frame fills out. The offensive profile will require a bit more projection. More power may come in time, as Meadows is currently short to the ball without much in the way of lift. Well, short to the ball once he starts to swing. There's a hand dip which could affect his timing against better velocity. There's clearly the starter kit for a major-league center fielder here, but it may take a while, and a fourth outfielder projection always lurks in the shadows of these profiles.

13 Elvin Rodriguez RHP

Born: 03/31/98 Age: 21 Bats: R Throws: R Height: 6'3" Weight: 160 Origin: International Free Agent, 2014

YEAR	TEAM	LVL	AGE	W	L	SV	G	GS	IP	H	HR	BB/9	K/9	K	GB%	BABIP	WHIP	ERA	DRA	WARP	PF
2016	DAN	RK	18	2	0	0	7	6	30	14	2	2.4	10.2	34	49%	.185	0.73	1.50	1.72	1.3	107
2016	ANG	RK	18	2	2	2	7	5	28^{2}	18	1	1.9	7.2	23	40%	.215	0.84	1.57	4.44	0.4	98
2017	ORM	RK	19	5	1	0	11	11	54	45	5	1.8	8.2	49	43%	.272	1.04	2.50	4.26	1.0	115
2017	BUR	A	19	0	2	0	3	3	14	20	2	1.9	7.7	12	40%	.400	1.64	4.50	4.13	0.2	102
2018	WMI	A	20	8	7	0	21	21	113^{1}	108	9	2.5	8.7	109	37%	.320	1.24	3.34	4.93	0.4	99
2019	*DET*	*MLB*	*21*	*3*	*8*	*0*	*17*	*17*	*81^{2}*	*94*	*18*	*3.9*	*7.0*	*63*	*37%*	*.303*	*1.58*	*6.18*	*6.51*	*-1.0*	*104*

Breakout: 0% Improve: 0% Collapse: 0% Attrition: 1% MLB: 1% *Comparables: Eric Hurley, Jacob Faria, Jayson Aquino*

The Tigers took on a long-term project when they acquired this skinny righty from the Angels. Rodriguez's three-pitch mix won't blow anyone away, but his consistently solid performances have earned him a spot on the radar. His fastball, which comes in at 89-93, is effective in every part of the zone when he has his best command. It's reasonable to believe that the heater will get a tick better as he matures and adds muscle to his thin frame. Rodriguez also throws a curveball, his most consistently above-average pitch. He does a good job of keeping it low in the zone and preventing solid contact. His changeup is also projectable and he has more confidence in it than many minor leaguers do. He maintains his arm speed on the pitch and it looks like a fastball before fading below the zone. All three pitches flash above-average. They aren't quite there yet, though, and that puts extra pressure on his command. There's little margin for error here, but Rodriguez could be a backend starter when all is said and done.

14 Wenceel Perez SS

Born: 10/30/99 Age: 19 Bats: B Throws: R Height: 5'11" Weight: 170 Origin: International Free Agent, 2016

YEAR	TEAM	LVL	AGE	PA	R	2B	3B	HR	RBI	BB	K	SB	CS	AVG/OBP/SLG	DRC+	VORP	BABIP	BRR	FRAA	WARP	PF
2017	DTI	RK	17	258	31	8	1	0	22	27	21	16	6	.314/.387/.358	118	16.0	.343	2.6	SS(50) -6.8, 2B(11) 2.4	1.0	100
2018	TGW	RK	18	93	20	7	0	2	14	12	14	2	1	.383/.462/.543	211	14.4	.446	0.6	SS(19) 1.0	1.2	98
2018	ONE	A-	18	87	8	2	0	1	8	5	12	.7	3	.244/.287/.305	124	2.0	.275	0.3	SS(21) -2.9	0.0	90
2018	WMI	A	18	71	8	3	3	0	9	2	8	4	1	.309/.324/.441	104	4.8	.344	0.1	SS(14) -0.6	0.2	96
2019	*DET*	*MLB*	*19*	*252*	*24*	*4*	*1*	*5*	*18*	*7*	*57*	*5*	*2*	*.175/.195/.259*	*18*	*-15.1*	*.204*	*0.4*	*SS -3*	*-1.9*	*104*

Breakout: 4% Improve: 5% Collapse: 0% Attrition: 3% MLB: 6% *Comparables: Carlos Triunfel, Wilmer Flores, Gleyber Torres*

Perez has bat-to-ball ability that rivals any player in the low minors. He has a knack for contact and he'll likely add strength as he matures. A little extra power could excuse some of his poorer choices when it comes to pitch selection, an area he could stand to improve. That said, he's a bat-first middle infielder with the tools to play everyday if all goes well. His defense is less impressive. He doesn't react as quickly as one would hope and his actions are stiff at times. While his future is on the dirt, he may need to move to second base, which would put more stress on the bat. In any case, it'll be years before we find out.

15 Willi Castro SS

Born: 04/24/97 Age: 22 Bats: B Throws: R Height: 6'1" Weight: 165 Origin: International Free Agent, 2013

YEAR	TEAM	LVL	AGE	PA	R	2B	3B	HR	RBI	BB	K	SB	CS	AVG/OBP/SLG	DRC+	VORP	BABIP	BRR	FRAA	WARP	PF
2016	LKC	A	19	548	68	21	8	7	49	19	96	16	11	.259/.286/.371	84	11.5	.302	-1.8	SS(119) -1.7	0.1	101
2017	LYN	A+	20	510	69	24	3	11	58	28	90	19	9	.290/.337/.424	118	35.3	.336	1.6	SS(116) 5.0	2.8	93
2018	AKR	AA	21	410	55	20	2	5	39	28	84	13	4	.245/.303/.350	96	17.4	.304	1.3	SS(96) 7.5	1.9	90
2018	ERI	AA	21	114	12	9	2	4	13	6	25	4	1	.324/.366/.562	95	10.0	.395	-0.8	SS(10) 0.7, 2B(9) -0.2	0.1	101
2019	*DET*	*MLB*	*22*	*252*	*27*	*8*	*1*	*7*	*23*	*6*	*60*	*4*	*2*	*.210/.230/.338*	*49*	*-5.7*	*.246*	*0.3*	*SS 1, 2B 0*	*-0.5*	*104*

Breakout: 18% Improve: 23% Collapse: 1% Attrition: 15% MLB: 27% *Comparables: Yairo Munoz, Chris Nelson, Trevor Plouffe*

I was half-tempted to do the Spiderman-pointing-at-himself meme here with Dixon Machado and Willi Castro's faces photoshopped on the webcrawlers', but of course Ben Carsley already beat me to the gag. That's also a bit unfair to Castro—there's a range of outcomes here from Dixon Machado to, like, Jose Iglesias. Castro is a sure-shot shortstop, a switch-hitter with potentially fringy pop. That makes for a very useful utility infielder even if his aggressive approach gets exploited in the majors.

Others of note:

Kody Clemens, IF, High-A Lakeland

Clemens is a high effort player and an offensively-minded middle infielder. His defensive actions are a bit choppy but his gritty, all-out play compensates for that somewhat. At the plate, Clemens was far more polished than your average Midwest League player. He's poised in the box and has an efficient swing path, strong pitch selection, and enough power to punish misplaced offerings. If things go sour at the keystone, he may still hit enough to make a transition to left a viable option. Impressing in the MWL didn't move the needle much in his favor, though—he only did what he was supposed to do. A full season against better pitchers will provide a better litmus test as to how he'll fare going forward. If he hits next year, he'll be in legitimate contention for a top ten spot, even as the Tigers system continues to improve.

Tarik Skubal, LHP, Full-season-A West Michigan

Just on the stuff Skubal should be up there with the ordinal dudes, arguably even in the Top Ten. Of course, just on the stuff he should never have lasted to the ninth round and should have signed for far more than $350,000. You can probably guess the hanging thread here. Skubal had Tommy John surgery in college, and then struggled some to throw strikes in the WAC this past spring in his first season back. He'll also turn 22 next week. How much does this matter? Well, it makes it more likely he's a reliever, despite potentially having three major-league pitches in his locker. It matters less when he's pumping mid-90s heat down in the zone from the left side, when the breaker has two-plane bite, when the change is showing average tumble and fade. Also, he might just be a really good reliever, and that was always in the cards given the effort in his arm action and the funk in the mechanics. Regardless, I think he's a safe bet to be a 2020 Top Ten Tigers prospect. But of course, he's also not safe at all.

Wilkel Hernandez, RHP, Full-season-A West Michigan

Hernandez was the other live arm the Tigers got in 2017 for Ian Kinsler. I can report that the arm is still very much live in 2018. There's mid-90s heat with good life up, and he can touch higher. It's easy velocity from a classically projectable frame. Hernandez shows some feel for spin and the requisite crude change-up. Hernandez is athletic, though not always enough to keep his long limbs and herky-jerky mechanics all under control. He's probably a reliever long term. He may never manage to throw enough strikes to get out of A-ball, but it could also come together next year and we'll see him near the top of our 2020 Tigers Prospect List.

Top Talents 25 and Under (born 4/1/93 or later):

1. Casey Mize
2. Matt Manning
3. Isaac Paredes
4. Daz Cameron
5. Jeimer Candelario
6. Beau Burrows
7. Franklin Perez
8. Joe Jimenez
9. Alex Faedo
10. Jake Rogers

Those of you familiar with the state of the Tiger's 25U list will note that Michael Fulmer has finally aged out of it. In his place lies Mize, the No. 1 overall draft pick who should be a fair replacement holder for fans' hopes and dreams. He throws right-handed too so if you miss Fulmer too much, go ahead and just scribble a bushy beard on him in your head.

Candelario's spot was determined with no small amount of hand wringing. Given the variance in defensive metrics, and which ones you choose to place your faith in, he could conceivably slide up or down a spot or two. He probably won't be much more than the competent regular he was last year, but competence is an often underrated skill, and one the Tigers could certainly use more of.

The rest of the big-league squad is much older than a team that just lost 98 games for the second straight season has any sense being. Nick Castellanos is too old for our purposes, and while Daniel Norris continues to exist, he does so only just. Joe Jimenez is an easy punchline, as giving a team's sole All-Star spot to a setup reliever should be a jailable offense, though that's no fault of his. He's a perfectly fine, if non-elite, relief arm with a powerful arsenal and now a full year of major-league success.

After that, this list takes a strong turn for the minors, and you can find plenty of insight on all of these players through the magic of scrolling upwards. Overall, the Tigers are preparing to enter year three of the inevitable dark period that comes from spending to the hilt and leveraging your farm for big-league upgrades at every opportunity. While the best players in this group don't appear to have the superstar ceiling of other organizations, the Tigers are starting to see the results of a commitment to development with a large cache of projectable talent, particularly among their right-handed pitchers. With the addition of last year's 1.1 pick, expect to see Detroit rise in the farm system rankings and, if all goes to plan, the big-league standings come 2020.

Houston Astros

The State of the System:

The Astros system is on the rise again due to improvements across the board from their deep well of pitching prospects.

The Top Ten:

1 **Forrest Whitley RHP** OFP: 70 Likely: 60 ETA: Should be on the opening day squad for 2019.

Born: 09/15/97 Age: 21 Bats: R Throws: R Height: 6'7" Weight: 195 Origin: Round 1, 2016 Draft (#17 overall)

YEAR	TEAM	LVL	AGE	W	L	SV	G	GS	IP	H	HR	BB/9	K/9	K	GB%	BABIP	WHIP	ERA	DRA	WARP	PF
2016	AST	RK	18	1	1	0	4	2	7^1	8	0	3.7	16.0	13	29%	.471	1.50	7.36	1.53	0.3	89
2016	GRV	RK	18	0	1	0	4	4	11^1	11	0	2.4	10.3	13	53%	.344	1.24	3.18	2.34	0.4	92
2017	QUD	A	19	2	3	0	12	10	46^1	42	2	4.1	13.0	67	37%	.388	1.36	2.91	3.10	1.2	101
2017	BCA	A+	19	3	1	0	7	6	31^1	28	2	2.6	14.4	50	40%	.394	1.18	3.16	2.06	1.2	95
2017	CCH	AA	19	0	0	0	4	2	14^2	8	1	2.5	16.0	26	48%	.292	0.82	1.84	2.15	0.5	107
2018	CCH	AA	20	0	2	0	8	8	26^1	15	2	3.8	11.6	34	39%	.220	0.99	3.76	3.49	0.6	100
2019	*HOU*	*MLB*	*21*	*5*	*4*	*0*	*18*	*13*	*74^1*	*62*	*9*	*4.3*	*10.8*	*89*	*39%*	*.292*	*1.32*	*4.22*	*4.50*	*0.8*	*97*

Breakout: 9% Improve: 15% Collapse: 8% Attrition: 14% MLB: 27% *Comparables: Jake McGee, Robert Stephenson, Trevor May*

The Report: How many times do we need to say that Forrest Whitley is good? I guess one more time before he dons an Astros jersey and never looks back won't hurt.

Whitley is a plus athlete with excellent quick twitch, body control, and strength. The days where his body was described as soft are gone, and he's now impressively filled out with a towering frame on the mound.

The right-hander works 94-97 with the fastball with some arm-side life on it. It can be hard to pick up, as Whitley comes from over the top and releases out in front with good extension. Whitley has two distinct plus breaking balls, one at 80-81 with traditional curveball spin and break, one 85-87 with sharp dive. Whitley throws a plus changeup with deceptive arm speed and plus tumble and fade. He occasionally mixes in a 91-93 above-average cutter that he likes to break off the plate against righties to get whiffs later after they've gotten a few looks at his regular fastball.

If there's one place to look for weakness in the profile, it's the command. Whitley has pretty consistent feel for all of his offerings, but he can struggle to locate at any given time. His fastball location in particular is spotty and he's prone to falling behind early in counts.

Overall though, Whitley is the best pitching prospect in baseball. He has five above-average or better offerings, giving him a tremendous ceiling and high floor despite the command concerns. He's one of the few pitchers in the sport with elite upside, and he can get there if his command ticks up a grade.

The Risks: Low. The arsenal is so deep, it's just hard to see him not being an effective MLB starter even with some command issues. Pitches in an org that will let him pitch backwards if he needs to lean away from fastball.

Ben Carsley's Fantasy Take: Thanks to his strikeout upside and proximity to the majors, we ranked Whitley as the best pitching prospect in baseball on our Dynasty Top 101 list. That doesn't necessarily mean he'll reach true fantasy SP1 status, but we think he has a chance to do so in his peak years. Be happy to "settle" for more of a fantasy SP2/3 performance in the mold of what Mike Foltynewicz did last season, and treat anything else as the gravy on top. He's great.

2 Kyle Tucker OF   OFP: 70   Likely: 60   ETA: Debuted in 2018

Born: 01/17/97 Age: 22 Bats: L Throws: R Height: 6'4" Weight: 190 Origin: Round 1, 2015 Draft (#5 overall)

YEAR	TEAM	LVL	AGE	PA	R	2B	3B	HR	RBI	BB	K	SB	CS	AVG/OBP/SLG	DRC+	VORP	BABIP	BRR	FRAA	WARP	PF
2016	QUD	A	19	428	43	19	5	6	56	40	75	31	9	.276/.348/.402	127	20.9	.322	1.3	CF(61) -5.2, LF(17) -0.3	1.3	101
2016	LNC	A+	19	69	13	6	2	3	13	10	6	1	3	.339/.435/.661	178	8.0	.340	0.2	RF(6) -0.1, LF(4) 0.2	0.5	115
2017	BCA	A+	20	206	31	12	4	9	43	24	45	13	5	.288/.379/.554	144	21.3	.336	-3.1	RF(16) -1.8, CF(7) 1.2	0.6	97
2017	CCH	AA	20	318	39	21	1	16	47	22	64	8	4	.265/.325/.512	132	19.6	.286	1.2	CF(37) -5.3, RF(18) -1.4	0.6	100
2018	FRE	AAA	21	465	86	27	3	24	93	48	84	20	4	.332/.400/.590	160	52.8	.364	1.7	RF(54) 0.3, LF(32) -0.4	3.6	103
2018	HOU	MLB	21	72	10	2	1	0	4	6	13	1	1	.141/.236/.203	73	-5.7	.176	-0.4	LF(20) -2.1, RF(3) 0.2	-0.3	96
2019	*HOU*	*MLB*	*22*	*292*	*41*	*17*	*1*	*13*	*40*	*23*	*63*	*8*	*3*	*.272/.335/.487*	*120*	*15.9*	*.312*	*0.4*	*LF -4, RF 0*	*1.2*	*97*

Breakout: 18% Improve: 55% Collapse: 1% Attrition: 15% MLB: 62% *Comparables: Oswaldo Arcia, Tyler Austin, Joc Pederson*

The Report: Kyle Tucker's profile doesn't jump off the board at first glance. His 6'4'' frame looks more lanky than lean, he has a laid back demeanor, and he lacks flashy foot speed.

But Tucker gets the barrel on the ball as well as anyone. His quickness, plus bat speed, and barrel control allow him to make consistently hard contact. He has plus raw power and he's made the kind of adjustments in his swing that suggest he'll get to all of it in games. Tucker's pitch recognition is subpar, but he made tremendous strides last year to both improve his selectiveness and recognize spin. Overall, Tucker projects as a 70 bat. Between that, improving walk rates, and his raw power, he could develop into an offensive force.

His defense in the corner outfield is considerably less exciting. He has below-average speed, and despite decent instincts, that translates into below-average range. He makes good reads, takes efficient routes, and has a strong arm, so he isn't a complete disaster in a corner. He should be average or just a bit worse in right or left. Regardless, Tucker's work at the plate will get him in the lineup. If his plate discipline takes a step forward, he could be a perennial all-star.

The Risks: Low: Unlike many who have concerns about the profile after a sluggish start, I've seen Tucker make adjustments over a season or two. I'm not concerned about him, and expect him to settle into a big-league lineup as soon as he gets a consistent opportunity.

Ben Carsley's Fantasy Take: We ranked Tucker as a top-10 overall dynasty prospect on the strength of his hit tool, speed, power and proximity to the majors. He is perhaps the safest bet of anyone in the minors to at least become a fantasy OF3, and there's borderline fantasy OF1 upside here for those seasons in which it all clicks. Although they're quite different physically, Tucker comps fairly well to Andrew Benintendi from a fantasy POV, with an even higher ceiling. He should be a mainstay for our purposes by June.

3 Josh James RHP   OFP: 60   Likely: 50   ETA: Debuted in 2018

Born: 03/08/93 Age: 26 Bats: R Throws: R Height: 6'3" Weight: 206 Origin: Round 34, 2014 Draft (#1006 overall)

YEAR	TEAM	LVL	AGE	W	L	SV	G	GS	IP	H	HR	BB/9	K/9	K	GB%	BABIP	WHIP	ERA	DRA	WARP	PF
2016	LNC	A+	23	9	5	1	23	19	110^1	120	11	3.3	9.9	121	48%	.350	1.45	4.81	4.46	1.2	113
2017	CCH	AA	24	4	8	3	21	11	76	79	1	3.8	8.5	72	53%	.338	1.46	4.38	3.59	1.3	98
2018	CCH	AA	25	0	0	1	6	4	21^2	17	1	4.2	15.8	38	58%	.364	1.25	2.49	1.73	0.9	95
2018	FRE	AAA	25	6	4	0	17	17	92^2	62	8	3.8	12.9	133	41%	.278	1.09	3.40	2.35	3.3	95
2018	HOU	MLB	25	2	0	0	6	3	23	15	3	2.7	11.3	29	42%	.240	0.96	2.35	3.20	0.5	99
2019	*HOU*	*MLB*	*26*	*7*	*5*	*0*	*29*	*19*	*106*	*85*	*11*	*3.7*	*10.7*	*126*	*44%*	*.287*	*1.22*	*3.67*	*3.89*	*2.1*	*97*

Breakout: 17% Improve: 34% Collapse: 17% Attrition: 33% MLB: 62% *Comparables: Tom Mastny, Adam Conley, D.J. Snelten*

The Report: Here's the most improbable prospect rise of 2018. After getting treatment for sleep apnea and improving his health, James spiked his stuff by about 10 MPH and in the process went from an organizational player to a mid-tier 101 prospect. Now we just have to figure out where he settles in.

James now throws a 96-98 mph fastball with some arm-side life, especially when working that side of the plate, and he touched 101 in the majors in September. His best secondary is a hard slider at 85-87 mph. It flashes plus with plus horizontal break and spin, and with a little depth too. His 87-89 mph changeup also flashes plus. At present, James has below-average command and it's hard to project definite improvement there, given his high-maintenance delivery.

The raw stuff and velocity from James is strong enough to overcome the command issues he will likely carry into his MLB career. A high-90's fastball and two pitches that project as plus secondaries suggest a future in the rotation, but even if he isn't a starter, he should transition well into a high-leverage relief role.

The Risks: Low, since he's already an MLB arm. Even if his command plays down more than I expect in the starting rotation, he has an excellent bullpen repertoire and should seamlessly shift into that role.

Ben Carsley's Fantasy Take: One of the more intriguing pop-up prospects from 2018, James is ready to contribute now, and indeed looks like he should compete for a spot in Houston's starting rotation. If he wins one, he could emerge as an excellent all-around fantasy SP3 in the Mike Clevinger mold. If not, James has closer upside but is perhaps more likely to settle in as a setup man, which would give us a serious sadz. Let's hope Houston gives him every chance to succeed as a starter.

4 Yordan Alvarez 1B OFP: 60 Likely: 50 ETA: September 2019

Born: 06/27/97 Age: 22 Bats: L Throws: R Height: 6'5" Weight: 225 Origin: International Free Agent, 2016

YEAR	TEAM	LVL	AGE	PA	R	2B	3B	HR	RBI	BB	K	SB	CS	AVG/OBP/SLG	DRC+	VORP	BABIP	BRR	FRAA	WARP	PF
2016	DAR	ROK	19	57	7	2	1	1	4	12	7	2	1	.341/.474/.500	174	8.1	.378	0.1		0.4	95
2017	QUD	A	20	139	26	6	0	9	33	23	36	2	0	.360/.468/.658	189	18.2	.449	-1.6	LF(13) -1.5, 1B(7) 0.0	1.1	104
2017	BCA	A+	20	252	19	11	3	3	36	19	41	6	1	.277/.329/.393	116	7.2	.316	-0.2	1B(9) -0.4, LF(6) 2.6	0.5	91
2018	CCH	AA	21	190	39	13	0	12	46	19	45	5	2	.325/.389/.615	164	21.5	.377	0.2	LF(31) 3.6, 1B(5) -0.1	1.6	101
2018	FRE	AAA	21	189	24	8	0	8	28	23	47	1	0	.259/.349/.452	110	5.3	.315	-2.0	LF(34) -6.3	-0.5	96
2019	*HOU*	*MLB*	*22*	*63*	*8*	*3*	*0*	*3*	*9*	*5*	*18*	*0*	*0*	*.233/.299/.443*	*102*	*1.2*	*.283*	*-0.1*	*1B 0*	*0.1*	*97*

Breakout: 16% Improve: 45% Collapse: 1% Attrition: 13% MLB: 52% *Comparables: Thomas Neal, Clint Frazier, Jesse Winker*

The Report: Alvarez is long and strong with more athleticism than meets the eye. He posts surprisingly solid home-to-first-times, and he's twitchy with impressive body control. Even if he adds a couple more pounds in the next few years, they might come without a corresponding reduction in mobility.

Alvarez has plus barrel control and bat speed, which allows him to mostly compensate for a long swing. He still can get beat on velocity inside and up if he's caught off guard, but he tends to fight the pitch off pretty well most of the time. He's patient and isn't afraid to let close pitches go by; if anything, a bit more aggressiveness would be appropriate. He struggles somewhat with breaking stuff and offspeed, but showed an aptitude for making adjustments both over a season and in games. Alvarez doesn't tap fully into his double-plus raw power, as a great deal of his hardest contact comes on line drives, but he should provide plus power regardless.

Alvarez has the hands and reactions to be an above-average first baseman and the foot speed to be fringy in a corner outfield spot. First is his long-term home though, and Alvarez's bat and approach should allow him to provide above-average value there.

The Risks: Medium. Yordan has good offensive tools, makes adjustments, and has a good approach. The main concern is how much MLB pitchers will be able to take advantage of the small holes in the swing.

Ben Carsley's Fantasy Take: Alvarez is a good fantasy prospect—we ranked him at no. 25 overall in our Top 101—but that's largely because we think he's safe and will be ready to hit soon. I don't see any star upside with Alvarez, but I do think he could be a more athletic 2017 Josh Bell-like player who hits .275 with 25-plus bombs, and who hopefully retains dual 1B/OF eligibility throughout his early career. That may not sound super exciting, but let a player with those underlying skills hit in Houston's lineup and at Minute Maid and you've got the makings of a four-category fantasy force.

5 J.B. Bukauskas RHP OFP: 60 Likely: 50 ETA: Late 2019

Born: 10/11/96 Age: 22 Bats: R Throws: R Height: 6'0" Weight: 196 Origin: Round 1, 2017 Draft (#15 overall)

YEAR	TEAM	LVL	AGE	W	L	SV	G	GS	IP	H	HR	BB/9	K/9	K	GB%	BABIP	WHIP	ERA	DRA	WARP	PF
2017	TCV	A-	20	0	0	0	2	2	6	4	0	6.0	9.0	6	53%	.267	1.33	4.50	3.27	0.1	103
2018	TCV	A-	21	0	0	0	3	3	8^1	8	0	2.2	9.7	9	46%	.364	1.20	0.00	2.48	0.3	98
2018	QUD	A	21	1	2	0	4	4	15	15	0	4.2	12.6	21	55%	.395	1.47	4.20	1.62	0.6	104
2018	BCA	A+	21	3	0	0	5	5	28	13	1	4.2	10.0	31	59%	.194	0.93	1.61	3.13	0.7	89
2018	CCH	AA	21	0	0	0	1	1	6	1	0	3.0	12.0	8	60%	.100	0.50	0.00	3.18	0.2	93
2019	*HOU*	*MLB*	*22*	*3*	*3*	*0*	*9*	*9*	*39^2*	*35*	*5*	*4.9*	*8.9*	*40*	*45%*	*.284*	*1.41*	*4.59*	*4.90*	*0.3*	*97*

Breakout: 16% Improve: 23% Collapse: 5% Attrition: 16% MLB: 33% *Comparables: Carl Edwards Jr., Matt Moore, Trevor May*

The Report: The party piece here is a plus-plus slider, one of the best non-fastball pitches in the entire minors. It falls off the table in a way that is difficult for hitters to read, and it comes in hard at 86-88. He pairs that with a diving fastball that sat 95-98 in the Arizona Fall League, and a hard, cutting changeup that is more than just a show-me type pitch. It's a strong pitch mix, and more than good enough for rotation work.

Despite that, the major question here is whether JBB can start. He missed most of the 2018 regular season due to back injuries suffered in a spring car accident, and he wasn't really right until the end of the year and in the AFL. Bukauskas is short and doesn't generate a lot of plane, and his delivery has enough jerky violence to make one pause on visual inspection. He might just fit best blowing folks away with the fastball and slider for 20 pitches or so.

As a creative team open to amorphous pitching roles, Houston is well-positioned to find a role in which he can thrive and stay healthy—if they keep him. We learned after the season from The Athletic's Ken Rosenthal that Houston nearly traded JBB at the deadline to borrow Bryce Harper's services for the stretch, a deal nixed by ownership in Washington.

The Risks: Medium because of health and difficulty in projecting a role. On skill the floor is high, because we think he could pitch well in an MLB bullpen tomorrow.

Ben Carsley's Fantasy Take: If you think Bukauskas can start, he's a top-60ish dynasty prospect who you will likely prefer over safer guys with less upside like Kyle Wright, Adrian Morejon and Chris Paddack. Unfortunately, I believe Bukauskas' future lies in the bullpen, which is why I did not push to rank him on our list. I'd love to be proven wrong, because this is a live, fun arm, and one definitely still worth gambling on if you roster 150-or-so prospects in your league.

6 Corbin Martin RHP

OFP: 55 Likely: 50 ETA: September 2019

Born: 12/28/95 Age: 23 Bats: R Throws: R Height: 6'2" Weight: 200 Origin: Round 2, 2017 Draft (#56 overall)

YEAR	TEAM	LVL	AGE	W	L	SV	G	GS	IP	H	HR	BB/9	K/9	K	GB%	BABIP	WHIP	ERA	DRA	WARP	PF
2017	TCV	A-	21	0	1	1	8	3	27²	20	1	2.6	12.4	38	63%	.297	1.01	2.60	2.54	0.8	99
2018	BCA	A+	22	2	0	1	4	3	19	4	0	3.3	12.3	26	64%	.111	0.58	0.00	3.10	0.5	91
2018	CCH	AA	22	7	2	0	21	18	103	84	7	2.4	8.4	96	48%	.277	1.09	2.97	3.41	2.3	104
2019	*HOU*	*MLB*	*23*	*3*	*2*	*0*	*8*	*8*	*40*	*34*	*5*	*3.5*	*9.0*	*40*	*47%*	*.273*	*1.23*	*4.27*	*4.56*	*0.4*	*97*

Breakout: 17% Improve: 24% Collapse: 21% Attrition: 38% MLB: 58% *Comparables: Matt Magill, Giovanni Soto, Nestor Cortes*

The Report: Martin fits the mould of a mid-rotation arm to a tee. He has an athletic build with a high waist and strong core. He's a quality athlete, and throws three strong, if not overpowering, pitches from a clean arm and delivery.

Martin sits 91-94 with his four-seamer. Most of the time, he has average command of his fastball and mixes in the other two offerings off of it, but sometimes he'll pitch backwards and use it high in the zone later in counts. Martin mixes in an almost vertical 83-85 slider with plus dive and a changeup that flashes above-average with deceptive arm speed and some tumble and fade.

Pitchibility is Martin's bread and butter. He's comfortable mixing speeds, using the same tunnel for the slider and changeup, and throwing first-pitch strikes with his fastball or slider. When he loses his release point, he's comfortable pitching backwards and turning to his secondaries. All three pitches are above-average or better. He projects as a quality No. 4 starter, perhaps a tick more if he refines his command.

The Risks: Low. Already has the pitch mix and showed much improved command in 2018.

Ben Carsley's Fantasy Take: Martin has proximity on his side, but upside... not so much. He is adrift amidst the sea of IRL no. 4 and fantasy no. 6/7 starters who'd probably occupy about 40 percent of a theoretical Top 101-through-201 list. At least we should have a pretty good idea as to who he is and what he can do sooner rather than later.

7 Freudis Nova SS

OFP: 60 Likely: 45 ETA: 2023

Born: 01/12/00 Age: 19 Bats: R Throws: R Height: 6'1" Weight: 180 Origin: International Free Agent, 2016

YEAR	TEAM	LVL	AGE	PA	R	2B	3B	HR	RBI	BB	K	SB	CS	AVG/OBP/SLG	DRC+	VORP	BABIP	BRR	FRAA	WARP	PF
2017	DAR	ROK	17	190	30	6	0	4	16	15	33	8	3	.247/.342/.355	108	10.6	.287	-2.1		0.2	88
2018	AST	RK	18	157	21	3	1	6	28	6	21	9	5	.308/.331/.466	126	9.8	.317	0.4	SS(24) -0.8, 2B(9) 0.0	0.4	102
2019	*HOU*	*MLB*	*19*	*252*	*23*	*4*	*0*	*7*	*21*	*1*	*67*	*3*	*1*	*.165/.172/.266*	*10*	*-18.5*	*.192*	*-0.2*	*SS -1, 2B 0*	*-2.0*	*97*

Breakout: 4% Improve: 5% Collapse: 0% Attrition: 3% MLB: 6% *Comparables: Gleyber Torres, Adalberto Mondesi, Wilmer Flores*

The Report: If Nova's namesake was a prospect writer he might have instead written: "Complex-league shortstops have no obvious use; nor is there any clear cultural necessity for them. Yet prospect lists could not do without them." Nova fell into the Astros lap after a reported failed drug test scuttled his deal with the Marlins, and he's been a steady performer as a pro so far. The horizon to major-league contribution is long here, and he's not super likely to be a big breakout guy. While he has good tools, they're more moderately loud, average-to-above across the board. He already shows plus bat speed and loud contact and there's plenty of reason to believe he will grow into above-average power as he matures. Nova is another for the "maybe" bucket at shortstop and he's already gotten reps at second and third as a pro. The bat may be good enough to carry any of the infield spots, but it's human nature to try and overfit narrative stories to even the fuzziest of dreams.

The Risks: Extreme. Complex league resume only here.

Ben Carsley's Fantasy Take: Nova remains an intriguing prospect who had a strong 2018 season in the GCL. He's yet to be truly challenged, but could be a sneaky top-101 candidate next season if he repeats his performance against more advanced arms. Guys like this tend to get forgotten in favor of the shinier/newer J2 and draft classes; they shouldn't be.

8 Seth Beer 1B OFP: 55 Likely: 50 ETA: 2020

Born: 09/18/96 Age: 22 Bats: L Throws: R Height: 6'3" Weight: 195 Origin: Round 1, 2018 Draft (#28 overall)

YEAR	TEAM	LVL	AGE	PA	R	2B	3B	HR	RBI	BB	K	SB	CS	AVG/OBP/SLG	DRC+	VORP	BABIP	BRR	FRAA	WARP	PF
2018	TCV	A-	21	51	9	3	0	4	7	6	10	0	0	.293/.431/.659	178	7.7	.296	-0.8	LF(7) -1.0, 1B(4) -0.1	0.1	93
2018	QUD	A	21	132	15	7	0	3	16	15	17	1	0	.348/.443/.491	161	11.6	.391	-1.2	RF(10) -0.9, LF(9) -1.1	0.6	102
2018	BCA	A+	21	114	15	4	0	5	19	4	22	0	1	.262/.307/.439	107	1.1	.288	-2.2	LF(13) -1.4, 1B(6) -0.2	-0.4	94
2019	*HOU*	*MLB*	*22*	*252*	*27*	*7*	*0*	*9*	*26*	*10*	*62*	*0*	*0*	*.206/.247/.346*	*62*	*-5.6*	*.241*	*-0.5*	*LF -1, 1B 0*	*-0.8*	*97*

Breakout: 7% Improve: 25% Collapse: 1% Attrition: 16% MLB: 27% *Comparables: Austin Dean, Andrew Lambo, Anthony Santander*

The Report: Beer was the most ballyhooed freshman ballplayer in recent memory after his .369/.535/.700 performance in 2016 for Clemson. He was still a fine, fine player for the Tigers after that, but he never quite lived up to the first impression, and ultimately fell quite a bit from the early predictions that had him going 1.1 in 2018.

If you liked watching various members of the Giambi family play the big-league version of beer-league softball (pun intended) back in the day, this is your dude. Beer combines rare patience for his age with plus-plus power that he brings into games. There's some disagreement over the hit tool projection. If you like him, you can point to a smooth swing with good bat speed. If you don't, you can point to more swing-and-miss than you'd like given the rest of the offensive profile. For the time being, we're going to split the difference and acknowledge the validity in both arguments. He's probably going to hit a lot.

We have Beer listed as primarily a first baseman here, even though he played more left than first after signing. He's not an outfielder in any real sense, and he might not even be a first baseman. The Astros play in the DH league, and we do think he's going to hit, but don't be surprised if the positional appellation switches to designated hitter pretty soon. It might even be before he graduates.

The Risks: Low. There's profile risk in that the bat is going to really have to carry the mail here, but this is about as low risk of a hitting profile as you can get out of the draft. He should move quickly—through the system, that is; he's not much of a runner.

Ben Carsley's Fantasy Take: I really hope he reaches his full potential for the fantasy team name pun potential alone. Realistically it's tough for these DH-types to matter much—that's a lesson I'm trying very hard to take away from The Dan Vogelbach Experience. But if Beer does end up hitting nearly every day, he could bash 35-plus bombs with a fine average. That'd make him rosterable in any league format, but just beware that that's his ceiling, and there's a very low platoon/bench bat floor here too.

9 Cionel Perez LHP OFP: 50 Likely: 45 ETA: Debuted in 2018

Born: 04/21/96 Age: 23 Bats: L Throws: L Height: 5'11" Weight: 170 Origin: International Free Agent, 2016

YEAR	TEAM	LVL	AGE	W	L	SV	G	GS	IP	H	HR	BB/9	K/9	K	GB%	BABIP	WHIP	ERA	DRA	WARP	PF
2017	QUD	A	21	4	3	2	12	9	55^1	52	2	2.8	8.9	55	51%	.331	1.25	4.39	3.65	1.0	103
2017	BCA	A+	21	2	1	0	5	4	25^1	27	1	1.8	6.4	18	46%	.325	1.26	2.84	3.58	0.5	100
2017	CCH	AA	21	0	0	0	4	3	13	15	1	3.5	6.9	10	33%	.341	1.54	5.54	3.51	0.2	93
2018	CCH	AA	22	6	1	1	16	11	68^1	54	3	2.9	10.9	83	47%	.304	1.11	1.98	3.08	1.7	101
2018	HOU	MLB	22	0	0	0	8	0	11^1	6	3	5.6	9.5	12	58%	.130	1.15	3.97	4.58	0.0	96
2019	*HOU*	*MLB*	*23*	*3*	*2*	*0*	*36*	*5*	57^2	*49*	*6*	*3.5*	*9.5*	*61*	*44%*	*.286*	*1.24*	*3.91*	*4.16*	*1.0*	*97*

Breakout: 10% Improve: 14% Collapse: 7% Attrition: 14% MLB: 29% *Comparables: Matt Bowman, Buddy Baumann, Gio Gonzalez*

The Report: Cionel Perez is a small guy with a lanky build, and he still hasn't really filled out. Despite that, he's a solid athlete who can control a fairly noisy delivery and arm action from the left side better than you'd expect.

Perez sits around 94 with the fastball that comes from a tricky slot on the left side. He likes to work toward the arm-side of the plate and tends to have better command of the pitch there as well. He doesn't miss the zone much, but when he tries to go in on righties he leaves the pitch over the plate fairly often.

Perez mixes in two breaking balls, an above-average 83-84 slider with two-plane movement and a fringy 12-6 curveball in the upper-70s that floats when left up in the zone. He throws a fringe-average changeup that has some fade, but hitters can usually recognize it well enough to fight it off even when he locates well.

Perez's control is well ahead of his command at this point: he doesn't struggle to throw strikes, but he's not terribly precise. His delivery is loud enough that it's hard to see it improving down the road and it will likely keep him out of a starting rotation long term.

Perez has the tools and the repertoire to be an effective one-time-through-the-order or low-setup pitcher in an MLB bullpen. The fastball-slider combo will be tough on lefties, but he doesn't have a lot to neutralize righties with. Ultimately, there are a lot of productive directions his career can go, even if most of them are in a relief role of some sort.

The Risks: Medium. The command and curveball consistency leaves two important pieces to be cleaned up before breaking into the big leagues. His fastball isn't overpowering enough to leave as much middle/middle as he does, especially given the lack of secondaries to compensate with against righties.

Ben Carsley's Fantasy Take: Get this Present Day Martin Perez-ass dynasty prospect out of my face, please.

10 Framber Valdez LHP

OFP: 50 Likely: 45 ETA: Debuted in 2018

Born: 11/19/93 Age: 25 Bats: L Throws: L Height: 5'11" Weight: 170 Origin: International Free Agent, 2015

YEAR	TEAM	LVL	AGE	W	L	SV	G	GS	IP	H	HR	BB/9	K/9	K	GB%	BABIP	WHIP	ERA	DRA	WARP	PF
2016	GRV	RK	22	1	0	0	2	2	10^2	7	0	2.5	12.7	15	79%	.292	0.94	1.69	1.41	0.5	92
2016	TCV	A-	22	2	1	0	5	2	21^2	22	0	2.9	11.6	28	78%	.379	1.34	3.74	2.99	0.5	112
2016	QUD	A	22	1	3	0	6	6	35^1	31	1	2.8	8.9	35	65%	.316	1.19	3.06	4.40	0.3	98
2017	BCA	A+	23	2	3	1	13	9	61^1	41	3	4.3	10.7	73	57%	.257	1.14	2.79	3.54	1.2	99
2017	CCH	AA	23	5	5	0	12	9	49	60	4	4.2	9.7	53	60%	.394	1.69	5.88	4.12	0.6	98
2018	CCH	AA	24	4	5	1	20	13	94^1	92	7	2.8	11.4	120	58%	.363	1.28	4.10	3.58	1.8	100
2018	FRE	AAA	24	2	0	0	2	1	8^2	8	0	3.1	9.3	9	48%	.348	1.27	4.15	4.16	0.1	91
2018	HOU	MLB	24	4	1	0	8	5	37	22	3	5.8	8.3	34	71%	.213	1.24	2.19	6.12	-0.4	94
2019	*HOU*	*MLB*	*25*	*3*	*2*	*0*	*39*	*3*	53^1	*46*	*5*	*3.9*	*9.5*	*56*	*54%*	*.296*	*1.29*	*3.85*	*4.08*	*1.3*	*97*

Breakout: 18% Improve: 34% Collapse: 24% Attrition: 34% MLB: 68%

Comparables: Jeremy Jeffress, Luke Jackson, Enny Romero

The Report: Our reports and rankings exist in a vacuum. So we don't consider that Brendan Rodgers will be playing his home game in Coors or that DL Hall is in a system that hasn't developed a starting pitching prospect since Mike Mussina. The only context is the prospect and what they can do. That said, Framber Valdez is in the right organization to get the most out of spamming an advanced curveball, as is his wont.

It's a potential plus curveball as well. While not the biggest breaker, the 1-7 action is tight and late and Valdez commands it well. He's not a soft tosser either, touching 95 from the left side with some sink when he's down in the zone. The delivery is a bit on the stiff side, the frame is a bit on the thick side, and his age is a bit on the old side. And we do need to consider this context: As an Astros pitching prospect he tends to see shorter outings, so even if there weren't already some bullpen markers here, we'd have no idea if he can hold up under a full starter's workload. Houston does seem to get a lot out of this general profile though [gestures wildly up and down the rest of this list], and it is a very nice curveball.

The Risks: Low. Valdez pitched well in the upper minors and while there's significant relief risk, the fastball/curve combo is just about ready for the Houston metroplex.

Ben Carsley's Fantasy Take: How many times do I need to tell you not to invest in back-end starter prospects?

The Next Five:

11 Rogelio Armenteros RHP

Born: 06/30/94 Age: 25 Bats: R Throws: R Height: 6'1" Weight: 215 Origin: International Free Agent, 2014

YEAR	TEAM	LVL	AGE	W	L	SV	G	GS	IP	H	HR	BB/9	K/9	K	GB%	BABIP	WHIP	ERA	DRA	WARP	PF
2016	QUD	A	22	0	2	0	4	3	18^{2}	12	0	1.4	9.6	20	67%	.245	0.80	1.93	3.02	0.4	98
2016	LNC	A+	22	6	4	1	19	16	90^{1}	87	13	3.7	10.7	107	39%	.323	1.37	4.18	5.06	0.4	113
2016	CCH	AA	22	2	0	0	3	3	18^{1}	17	1	2.0	6.4	13	36%	.308	1.15	1.96	3.71	0.3	96
2017	CCH	AA	23	2	3	1	14	10	65^{1}	49	3	2.6	10.2	74	42%	.284	1.04	1.93	2.93	1.7	100
2017	FRE	AAA	23	8	1	0	10	10	58^{1}	42	5	2.9	11.1	72	50%	.276	1.05	2.16	1.97	2.4	103
2018	FRE	AAA	24	8	1	1	22	21	118	106	15	3.7	10.2	134	38%	.301	1.31	3.74	3.59	2.6	100
2019	*HOU*	*MLB*	*25*	*3*	*2*	*0*	*21*	*6*	*46^{1}*	*39*	*6*	*3.6*	*9.7*	*50*	*39%*	*.275*	*1.23*	*4.20*	*4.48*	*0.3*	*97*

Breakout: 10% Improve: 29% Collapse: 22% Attrition: 25% MLB: 62% *Comparables: Brian Johnson, Austin Voth, Nick Tropeano*

Rogelio takes a bit of a tumble down the list, but that's more due to the system strengthening around him than any potholes along his development path. It's also probably for the best that Jarrett had lead on this list as I'd perhaps be inclined to over-rank Armenteros due to the #aesthetics here, which are extremely Yusmeiro Petitish. As I like to say, "it's not a pref list, except when it's a pref list." Rogelio is a hefty righty as well with an easy delivery, averageish fastball and breaker, and a potential plus change. Frankly, that's more prospect-Petit than major-leaguer-Petit, but that only helps with the aesthetics. He hits the glove without issue and misses more bats than you'd think, but the profile is always going to have fine margins as a FB/CH righty with only an average heater. Yusmeiro Petit's career is maybe more like a 40th percentile outcome here, as we still think Rogelio has a chance to be a back-end starter. But hey, that below-median outcome came with eight-figure income and a World Series ring last time.

12 Luis Santana 2B

Born: 07/20/99 Age: 19 Bats: R Throws: R Height: 5'8" Weight: 175 Origin: International Free Agent, 2016

YEAR	TEAM	LVL	AGE	PA	R	2B	3B	HR	RBI	BB	K	SB	CS	AVG/OBP/SLG	DRC+	VORP	BABIP	BRR	FRAA	WARP	PF
2016	MET	RK	16	73	2	4	2	0	10	3	6	0	1	.284/.342/.403	133	0.7	.311	-1.8	2B(10) 1.3	0.2	94
2017	MET	RK	17	287	47	12	8	3	52	34	22	16	4	.325/.430/.481	168	28.3	.346	2.4	2B(61) 1.0, SS(4) 0.4	2.7	102
2018	KNG	RK	18	242	34	13	0	4	35	27	23	8	3	.348/.446/.471	185	26.6	.376	-0.4	2B(51) -1.5, 3B(1) -0.1	1.6	106
2019	*HOU*	*MLB*	*19*	*252*	*20*	*7*	*0*	*6*	*24*	*11*	*55*	*1*	*0*	*.188/.233/.287*	*39*	*-10.2*	*.220*	*-0.5*	*2B 0, 3B 0*	*-1.0*	*97*

Breakout: 6% Improve: 8% Collapse: 0% Attrition: 4% MLB: 10% *Comparables: Rougned Odor, Gleyber Torres, Adalberto Mondesi*

Santana is the first of two prospects on this list acquired recently from the Mets in the J.D. Davis trade. He will go as far as his hit tool takes him, and in that way, Santana is reminiscent of another R/R second baseman from his former organization, T.J. Rivera. Rivera—an undrafted free agent who was significantly overage at every minor league stop—has almost nothing else in common with Santana, but the former's unlikely path to the majors offers a roadmap for the latter. Let's cover the issues with the profile first. Santana is not 5-foot-8 for starters; he's more likely a stocky 5-foot-6. He's a fringy runner with below-average power. He's good enough at second base, but his arm strength is below-average and his throws can get casual.

He also hit .350 in the Appy League and didn't turn 19 until a month into the season. He barrels everything he sees. At a glance, it sure looks like a potential plus hit tool. But Santana's swing is... noisy. His hands are in constant motion pre-swing, and while he ends up short to the ball, I wonder how that bat path will work as he sees more dudes throwing 95. It's a very tough profile, but a plus hit tool will paper over a lot of faults. And for Santana it might be enough to make him an average regular in the majors.

13 Ross Adolph OF

Born: 12/17/96 Age: 22 Bats: L Throws: R Height: 6'1" Weight: 203 Origin: Round 12, 2018 Draft (#350 overall)

YEAR	TEAM	LVL	AGE	PA	R	2B	3B	HR	RBI	BB	K	SB	CS	AVG/OBP/SLG	DRC+	VORP	BABIP	BRR	FRAA	WARP	PF
2018	BRO	A-	21	264	47	9	12	7	35	21	52	14	3	.276/.348/.509	146	26.3	.322	4.4	CF(27) 1.2, LF(18) -0.5	1.4	94
2019	*HOU*	*MLB*	*22*	*252*	*26*	*4*	*6*	*8*	*24*	*8*	*73*	*3*	*1*	*.162/.196/.326*	*38*	*-9.0*	*.192*	*1.6*	*CF 0, LF 0*	*-0.9*	*97*

Breakout: 3% Improve: 5% Collapse: 0% Attrition: 4% MLB: 5% *Comparables: Michael Taylor, Darrell Ceciliani, Aaron Altherr*

The second player acquired for Davis lies just below him on this list, just as he did on the Mets list. The Mets popped Adolph—a first team All-MAC player—in the 12th round in 2018 and gave him full pool. I was prepared to be unimpressed; however, he won me over almost immediately, showing average tools across the board. Despite a stocky physique, he's an above-average runner with a high motor who can go get it in center field. He's short to the ball with sneaky pop that plays pull side and oppo gap. He stays in well against lefties. There's no plus tool here, and the profile screams 'tweener,' but Adolph projects as a quality fourth outfielder who might surprise you (and me) and end up a second-division type.

14 Jonathan Arauz SS

Born: 08/03/98 Age: 20 Bats: B Throws: R Height: 6'0" Weight: 150 Origin: International Free Agent, 2014

YEAR	TEAM	LVL	AGE	PA	R	2B	3B	HR	RBI	BB	K	SB	CS	AVG/OBP/SLG	DRC+	VORP	BABIP	BRR	FRAA	WARP	PF
2016	GRV	RK	17	229	26	10	1	2	18	19	45	1	3	.249/.323/.338	87	8.6	.308	0.5	SS(35) 0.6, 2B(18) 0.6	0.1	98
2017	QUD	A	18	149	23	3	2	0	4	20	18	0	1	.220/.331/.276	91	2.9	.257	-0.3	SS(32) -1.3, 2B(4) -0.4	0.0	103
2017	TCV	A-	18	135	16	7	1	1	11	12	29	1	0	.264/.341/.364	133	7.0	.341	0.2	SS(28) -3.1, 3B(5) -0.4	0.3	101
2018	QUD	A	19	237	31	11	6	4	29	30	38	7	6	.299/.392/.471	147	22.0	.350	0.4	SS(33) 0.6, 2B(17) 0.4	1.9	100
2018	BCA	A+	19	253	25	10	3	4	18	16	36	1	2	.167/.223/.288	39	-1.6	.180	-2.6	SS(70) -5.5, 2B(1) -0.1	-2.0	94
2019	*HOU*	*MLB*	*20*	*252*	*21*	*5*	*1*	*6*	*19*	*12*	*63*	*1*	*1*	*.149/.188/.251*	*9*	*-18.4*	*.173*	*-0.1*	*SS -2, 2B 0*	*-2.2*	*97*

Breakout: 12% Improve: 13% Collapse: 0% Attrition: 2% MLB: 13% *Comparables: Ruben Tejada, Orlando Arcia, Francisco Lindor*

It was a tale of two seasons for Arauz. In the first half, the 19-year-old was one of the better players in the Midwest League. In the second, sandwiched around his 20th birthday, he was one of the worst players in the Carolina League. It was an aggressive promotion, and he's too good to give up on. We were concerned about his propensity to make weak contact last year, and that certainly actualized some, but a .180 BABIP in High-A is ridiculous even by that standard. Arauz has already been exposed to second and third, and carries with him a decent bundle of secondary hitting skills, but he's going to have to start driving the ball with more authority to beat the "utility dude" projection.

15 Abraham Toro-Hernandez 3B

Born: 12/20/96 Age: 22 Bats: B Throws: R Height: 6'1" Weight: 190 Origin: Round 5, 2016 Draft (#157 overall)

YEAR	TEAM	LVL	AGE	PA	R	2B	3B	HR	RBI	BB	K	SB	CS	AVG/OBP/SLG	DRC+	VORP	BABIP	BRR	FRAA	WARP	PF
2016	GRV	RK	19	193	20	6	3	0	19	10	31	2	1	.254/.301/.322	74	0.1	.302	-3.3	3B(41) -3.7	-1.1	98
2017	TCV	A-	20	128	21	8	0	6	16	19	21	1	3	.292/.414/.538	178	14.1	.316	-2.1	3B(25) -2.5, C(6) -0.1	0.6	100
2017	QUD	A	20	158	25	3	2	9	17	21	30	2	0	.209/.323/.463	112	11.2	.198	1.1	3B(17) 0.8, C(9) -0.2	0.6	102
2018	BCA	A+	21	349	54	20	1	14	56	45	62	5	1	.257/.361/.473	152	31.1	.278	1.7	3B(81) 3.4	2.9	95
2018	CCH	AA	21	202	16	15	2	2	22	17	46	3	3	.230/.317/.371	87	1.1	.298	-2.6	3B(43) -0.7	-0.5	103
2019	*HOU*	*MLB*	*22*	*252*	*22*	*9*	*1*	*7*	*26*	*13*	*67*	*1*	*1*	*.171/.223/.309*	*42*	*-12.1*	*.203*	*-0.3*	*3B 0*	*-1.2*	*97*

Breakout: 18% Improve: 39% Collapse: 1% Attrition: 26% MLB: 41% *Comparables: Taylor Green, Lonnie Chisenhall, Matt Dominguez*

Two decades ago, a Montreal-area native by way of Seminole State College in Oklahoma exploded on the prospect scene. Eric Gagne would go on to become one of baseball's rare Cy Young closers, a monster of a reliever until he got hurt. Toro-Hernandez followed the same path, from a Montreal high school to Seminole State to the Astros. He's not quite on Gagne's level as a prospect and stands little chance to get there, but he's a nifty player in his own right.

The former fifth-rounder combines average pop with a good feel for the bat. He has a solid understanding of the strike zone, and played well in last year's AFL. He should stick at third base, and he even dabbled a little with catching in 2017, enough that he should be fine to handle a third catcher role in the majors. He's not likely to be a star, and cracking the Astros lineup with this skill set isn't going to be easy, but he has a shot to be someone's regular third baseman for awhile.

Others of note:

Alex McKenna, OF Short-season Tri-City

The Astros popped McKenna in 2018's fourth round and, oddly for a college junior in that part of the draft, he got slightly over slot value to sign. McKenna was a star hitter at Cal Poly for most of his college career, winning the Big West Player of the Year award in 2018, and he also performed well in 2017 with wood bats on the Cape. He's a solid all-around hitter with some athleticism, versatility between the outfield slots, and sneaky power. More interestingly, he looked to be adding some loft to his swing as a pro. There's a lot of similarity here between McKenna and Adolph, both college-performer outfielders who torched the New York-Penn League in their pro debuts. The Astros do have a type.

Jairo Solis, RHP Low-A Quad Cities

The Astros tend to exercise more caution with their pitchers than most teams, and they've done very well with pitcher development in general. In that vein, Solis was one of the most lightly used "starters" in the minors. He was held back in extended until late-May, frequently went on extra rest, and never once pierced 100 pitches or went past the sixth inning. All that care... and it didn't matter anyway, as he went down with Tommy John surgery after being shut down in August. He'll miss the entire 2019 season. Before the surgery, Solis was a low-to-mid-90s righty with a potentially plus curve and average or better change. He did pitch decently as an 18-year-old in full-season ball, so he won't be far behind developmentally when he returns in 2020; it still stinks.

Top Talents 25 and Under (born 4/1/93 or later):

1. Carlos Correa
2. Forrest Whitley
3. Kyle Tucker
4. Josh James
5. Roberto Osuna
6. Yordan Alvarez
7. Francis Martes
8. J.B. Bukauskas
9. Corbin Martin
10. Freudis Nova

Don't worry about the Astros. Sure, the first homegrown rebuild crop doesn't quite have the green shoots of youth anymore: George Springer turns 30 this year, Altuve will be 29, and of course the 34-year-old Yuli Gurriel came over with plenty of Cuban League wear-and-tear. But the Astros will keep the line moving, as Whitley, Tucker, and James are set to add a timely infusion of fresh arms and bats.

March 30th birthday boy Alex Bregman misses this list by roughly 48 hours, otherwise he might—given last season's growth—have nosed out Correa for top honors here. As it is, Correa is the clear headliner, injury worries aside. 2019 will be a pivotal season for the former first-overall pick. If healthy, he'll be expected to pick up his interrupted trajectory toward superstardom, forming an infield left-side whose only competition for supremacy would be the Ramirez-Lindor pairing in Cleveland. The fact that Correa is still on this list, even with more than 2,000 major-league plate appearances under his belt, prompts a degree of optimism for his full recovery. We won't dwell on darker, Tulowitzkian timelines in this space.

Osuna comes in halfway through this list. He is still a hard-throwing closer with a devastating slider, but closers are commodities with a limited shelf life and a sharp decrease in his strikeout rate bears watching. In an unjust irony, his 75-game suspension for a domestic assault incident in May gave some rest to an arm that had been used for nearly 260 high-leverage innings over the previous three years.

Francis Martes, BP's #28 prospect heading into 2017, spent significant time that summer in the Astros bullpen, striking out plenty but walking far too many. Soon after the 2018 season began, a rough start in Triple-A spiraled into a blown UCL and Tommy John surgery. He probably won't pitch much in 2019, but the promise of future health, plus the recent memory of the lights-out prospect he was before his elbow revolted, puts him in a holding pattern on this list for the time being.

Folks, the Astros are still great. Folding the prospects near the top of this list into the current late-twenties core will keep them at short odds for championship hardware well into the next decade—assuming there's still baseball to care about then.

Kansas City Royals

The State of the System:

The Royals system is improving but still top-heavy. A loaded 2018 draft class could help the organization take the next step forward.

The Top Ten:

1 Seuly Matias OF

OFP: 60 Likely: 50 ETA: 2022

Born: 09/04/98 Age: 20 Bats: R Throws: R Height: 6'3" Weight: 200 Origin: International Free Agent, 2015

YEAR	TEAM	LVL	AGE	PA	R	2B	3B	HR	RBI	BB	K	SB	CS	AVG/OBP/SLG	DRC+	VORP	BABIP	BRR	FRAA	WARP	PF
2016	DRY	RK	17	27	2	1	0	0	2	2	13	0	0	.125/.222/.167	21	-1.4	.273	0.0	CF(7) 0.6	-0.1	94
2016	ROY	RK	17	198	32	11	2	8	29	22	73	2	4	.250/.348/.477	101	9.9	.385	0.0	CF(23) -1.6, RF(19) 0.6	-0.3	105
2017	BNC	RK	18	246	27	13	3	7	36	16	72	2	1	.243/.297/.423	81	7.0	.318	0.7	RF(52) 9.0	0.3	95
2018	LEX	A	19	376	62	13	1	31	63	24	131	6	0	.231/.303/.550	96	18.8	.264	0.7	RF(75) -2.1	-0.4	113
2019	*KCA*	*MLB*	*20*	*252*	*18*	*6*	*0*	*10*	*28*	*4*	*113*	*0*	*0*	*.122/.135/.274*	*-2*	*-24.4*	*.157*	*-0.5*	*RF -1*	*-2.7*	*102*

Breakout: 20% Improve: 24% Collapse: 0% Attrition: 4% MLB: 24% *Comparables: Giancarlo Stanton, Domingo Santana, Cody Bellinger*

The Report: Scouts will often talk about how it "sounds different" when an elite prospect makes contact. Matias may not be an elite prospect yet, but it sounds like an M-80 when he squares one up. Not coincidentally, that's also the grade on his raw power projection. Matias has plus bat speed and gets easy extension. The power plays line-to-line when he connects—just ask Justus Sheffield—but he needs to make more contact. His swing isn't super stiff or overly leveraged and Matias' pitch recognition is pretty decent for a 19-year-old facing mostly older arms, but he swings hard and he'll come up empty fairly often. Lucky for him, a 35% strikeout rate isn't a deal breaker in today's game.

In the field Matias is an average runner at present and should be an average glove in a corner. He has plenty of arm for right, which is another plus-plus tool in his locker. He projects as your prototypical right field slugger. Matias may only hit .250, but it could come with a shiny OBP and 35 bombs.

The Risks: High. It's top of the scale power, but he will have to get most of it into games to carry the corner outfield profile and early returns on the hit tool are mixed.

Ben Carsley's Fantasy Take: This isn't my favorite profile for fantasy prospects, but it's hard not to drool when you hear about Matias' power potential. Assuming the rest of the profile holds up, Matias could end up as a slightly less prodigious version of Khris Davis, who was a top-15 outfielder in standard 5×5 formats this season. That being said, Matias could also end up going the Joey Gallo route, and that risk is enough to keep him from entering the upper echelon of dynasty outfield prospects. He's still a good one, though.

2 Khalil Lee OF OFP: 60 Likely: 50 ETA: 2021

Born: 06/26/98 Age: 21 Bats: L Throws: L Height: 5'10" Weight: 170 Origin: Round 3, 2016 Draft (#103 overall)

YEAR	TEAM	LVL	AGE	PA	R	2B	3B	HR	RBI	BB	K	SB	CS	AVG/OBP/SLG	DRC+	VORP	BABIP	BRR	FRAA	WARP	PF
2016	ROY	RK	18	222	43	9	6	6	29	33	57	8	4	.269/.396/.484	131	18.6	.358	-0.4	CF(23) -2.5, RF(15) -2.5	-0.3	105
2017	LEX	A	19	532	71	24	6	17	61	65	171	20	18	.237/.344/.430	109	20.1	.338	-2.2	CF(67) -6.2, RF(52) 4.3	0.6	105
2018	WIL	A+	20	301	42	13	4	4	41	48	75	14	3	.270/.402/.406	140	26.4	.371	2.2	CF(57) 3.8, RF(9) 0.3	2.2	99
2018	NWA	AA	20	118	15	5	0	2	10	11	28	2	2	.245/.330/.353	82	1.2	.319	0.6	CF(17) 0.3, LF(9) 0.7	0.0	105
2019	*KCA*	*MLB*	*21*	*252*	*23*	*6*	*1*	*7*	*23*	*19*	*90*	*4*	*2*	*.150/.222/.271*	*30*	*-12.2*	*.206*	*0.0*	*CF -2, RF 0*	*-1.6*	*102*

Breakout: 4% Improve: 9% Collapse: 0% Attrition: 5% MLB: 9% *Comparables: Clint Frazier, Daniel Fields, Brandon Nimmo*

The Report: Overall, Lee is still raw at the plate, but he showed an advanced approach and strong feel for the strike zone while cutting down on his strikeouts in 2018. A 15.9% walk rate at High-A is nothing to scoff at, and though he struggled at Double-A, there's little question about his athleticism or ability to make adjustments. The raw power is above-average at present, and when he turns on a fastball, it's a sight to see.

Lee's lightning-fast hands allow him to get the bat through the zone quickly, and he's got plus bat speed and above-average control of the barrel. He should also be an above-average runner at full maturity. In center field, Lee is still learning. He'll take a bad route to a ball every now and again, but he fields his position competently. He'd be a plus defender at a corner spot, but there's plenty of time to let him develop up the middle. The tools are all there for Lee to be a productive player. His ultimate role will be shaped by how much of his power he can get to in games.

The Risks: High. There are times when Lee's mild bat wrap and short stride falls apart a bit at the plate, and the swing can get a little long when he rushes. If the above-average raw power doesn't show up in games, Lee's a solid table-setting top of the order guy. But if that power develops, you could see him in an All-Star Game or two.

Ben Carsley's Fantasy Take: I may be in the minority, but from a dynasty perspective I like Lee as the best prospect in this system. His speed is more valuable than Matias' power within the confines of fantasy, and I like his more well-rounded approach and multiple paths to value. I'm expecting to be the high guy on Lee all offseason, so take everything I'm saying here with a grain of salt, but he's already a borderline top-50 dynasty prospect for me.

3 MJ Melendez C OFP: 60 Likely: 50 ETA: 2022

Born: 11/29/98 Age: 20 Bats: L Throws: R Height: 6'1" Weight: 185 Origin: Round 2, 2017 Draft (#52 overall)

YEAR	TEAM	LVL	AGE	PA	R	2B	3B	HR	RBI	BB	K	SB	CS	AVG/OBP/SLG	DRC+	VORP	BABIP	BRR	FRAA	WARP	PF
2017	ROY	RK	18	198	25	8	3	4	30	26	60	4	2	.262/.374/.417	117	11.4	.385	0.1	C(28) 0.5	0.2	102
2018	LEX	A	19	472	52	26	9	19	73	43	143	4	6	.251/.322/.492	103	24.5	.327	-1.7	C(73) 1.4	0.8	109
2019	*KCA*	*MLB*	*20*	*252*	*18*	*6*	*2*	*8*	*25*	*11*	*101*	*0*	*0*	*.130/.166/.265*	*11*	*-16.6*	*.174*	*0.0*	*C 0*	*-1.8*	*102*

Breakout: 5% Improve: 7% Collapse: 0% Attrition: 4% MLB: 7% *Comparables: Gary Sanchez, Matt Olson, Tommy Joseph*

The Report: Melendez is fighting against 15 years of demographics. The last early-round prep catcher to turn into a reliable above-average regular was Brian McCann in 2002. "Catchers are weird" as we say around these parts, but we could also say "Prep catchers are usually first basemen." That's less of a concern with Melendez, who projects as an above-average defender due to his innate athleticism and plus throwing arm. The power is plus as well.

The lingering question with Melendez is that pesky ol' hit tool. His swing can get out of sync, and even when he's locked in there's length, loft, and issues with lefties. The bar for catcher offense is so low that even an Austin Hedgish bat would make Melendez a viable major leaguer, but there's still a lot of variance in the profile. That's normal for a 19-year-old prep catcher in the Sally, but it makes him risky enough to slot him third on this list, even if the ultimate ceiling here may be higher than the two outfielders ranked ahead of him.

The Risks: High. Prep catchers in A-ball are always going to check in at the upper end of our risk range, and Melendez has additional questions about how the hit tool will play at upper levels.

Ben Carsley's Fantasy Take: Melendez may be a good fantasy catching prospect, but fantasy catching prospects stink. Given the long lead time, the risk and the good-but-not-great Wilson Ramos-esque ceiling here, Melendez is a prospect I'm likely going to lose out on to people who value the position more. At this point I think the attrition rate for catchers is just too high to put them on the top-101, but we'll see how I feel once I've written up 300-plus other guys.

Brady Singer RHP   OFP: 60   Likely: 50   ETA: 2020

Born: 08/04/96 Age: 22 Bats: R Throws: R Height: 6'5" Weight: 210 Origin: Round 1, 2018 Draft (#18 overall)

The Report: The Royals leveraged the largest draft pool in the league to go nearly a million over slot to nab Singer, who tumbled on draft day due to his bonus demands. The Gators Friday night starter dominated the SEC on the strength of his plus fastball/slider combo. The fastball reaches the mid-90s, and the slider shows hard, late tilt. But there is more reliever risk here then you'd expect/hope for from the second-best college arm in the draft. Singer's slot is a tick below three-quarters, and there is significant effort in his arm action. His changeup needs refinement to give him an armside weapon against lefties given the lower slot, and the Royals might be best off letting him air it out in 1-2 inning bursts. Ultimately, we have here a classic mid-rotation starter or late-inning reliever profile.

The Risks: Medium. No pro track record to speak of—although you could argue Friday night starter in the SEC is basically A-ball—and there's legitimate relief risk.

Ben Carsley's Fantasy Take: Singer is likely to be overvalued in dynasty drafts this offseason, as his draft slot/name recognition/SEC track record are going to fool some into thinking he's a potential future ace. He's not, and between the reliever risk and the fact that his ceiling appears to be something of a fantasy SP4/5, Singer should be valued as more of a fringe top-101 guy than a true fantasy stud in the making.

5 Jackson Kowar RHP   OFP: 55   Likely: 50   ETA: 2020

Born: 10/04/96 Age: 22 Bats: R Throws: R Height: 6'5" Weight: 180 Origin: Round 1C, 2018 Draft (#33 overall)

YEAR	TEAM	LVL	AGE	W	L	SV	G	GS	IP	H	HR	BB/9	K/9	K	GB%	BABIP	WHIP	ERA	DRA	WARP	PF
2018	LEX	A	21	0	1	0	9	9	26^1	19	2	4.1	7.5	22	59%	.239	1.18	3.42	3.90	0.4	108
2019	*KCA*	*MLB*	*22*	*2*	*3*	*0*	*9*	*9*	32^2	*36*	*4*	*5.0*	*6.6*	*24*	*48%*	*.308*	*1.65*	*5.25*	*5.54*	*0.0*	*102*

Breakout: 2% Improve: 2% Collapse: 0% Attrition: 1% MLB: 2% *Comparables: Chi Chi Gonzalez, Seranthony Dominguez, Michael Ynoa*

The Report: As usual, the Florida Gators rotation was an embarrassment of prospect riches, and Kowar joined his college teammate in the Royals system after getting popped in the Comp A round. Kowar doesn't have Singer's raw stuff, but his delivery looks the part of a major-league starter and his mid-90s fastball is nothing to sneeze at. The big heater showed up less in his first pro summer—sitting more 93-94 in A-ball—and it can run a bit true, but Kowar shows above-average command of the pitch. A pitcher's first professional summer can be a tricky time to evaluate them, though some guys never throw harder than they did in college. If the consistent plus velocity comes back, it will round out an arsenal with two potential above-average secondaries. Kowar's changeup is more advanced at present, while his power curveball requires a bit more projection. Right now, its shape is inconsistent but flashes plus with hard biting action.

The Risks: Medium. Obviously there isn't much professional track record, and also less swing-and-miss stuff than you'd like from a highly-ranked college arm. But Kowar is fairly polished and he should encounter few speed bumps in the minors beyond the usual pitcher health concerns.

Ben Carsley's Fantasy Take: Kowar may be a safer bet to return at least *some* fantasy value than Singer is, but ultimately he's shaping up to be a pretty replaceable fantasy asset. He might be worthy of a stash once he's closer to the majors, but you can keep the dime-a-dozen back-end starter prospects on waivers when they're this far from the show.

6 Nicky Lopez IF   OFP: 55   Likely: 45   ETA: 2019

Born: 03/13/95 Age: 24 Bats: L Throws: R Height: 5'11" Weight: 175 Origin: Round 5, 2016 Draft (#163 overall)

YEAR	TEAM	LVL	AGE	PA	R	2B	3B	HR	RBI	BB	K	SB	CS	AVG/OBP/SLG	DRC+	VORP	BABIP	BRR	FRAA	WARP	PF
2016	BNC	RK	21	283	54	6	5	6	29	35	30	24	4	.281/.393/.429	151	34.1	.296	5.4	SS(62) 7.8	2.9	95
2017	WIL	A+	22	324	42	12	7	2	27	36	23	14	8	.295/.376/.407	126	26.0	.315	0.8	SS(58) 4.4	2.1	94
2017	NWA	AA	22	253	26	6	1	0	11	16	29	7	4	.259/.312/.293	74	4.5	.296	2.2	SS(33) -2.9, 2B(25) 2.5	-0.2	102
2018	NWA	AA	23	325	42	8	5	2	27	33	23	9	4	.331/.397/.416	124	25.9	.351	2.8	SS(58) -4.8, 2B(14) 0.4	1.2	108
2018	OMA	AAA	23	256	33	6	2	7	26	27	29	6	2	.278/.364/.417	120	19.5	.294	0.0	SS(36) -1.0, 2B(18) 1.7	1.3	91
2019	*KCA*	*MLB*	*24*	*106*	*11*	*2*	*1*	*3*	*11*	*7*	*15*	*2*	*1*	*.250/.304/.367*	*89*	*2.2*	*.267*	*0.1*	*SS 0, 3B 0*	*0.3*	*102*

Breakout: 16% Improve: 28% Collapse: 1% Attrition: 24% MLB: 43% *Comparables: Kevin Newman, Tony Kemp, Greg Garcia*

The Report: Fans of The Grinder—the short-lived Fred Savage/Rob Lowe FOX comedy vehicle—take heart: Nicky Lopez may be coming to a baseball park near you in time for the 2019 upfronts. Is he actually 5-foot-11? Probably not. Can he really play shortstop? He'll give you all he's got. Is he a pest at the plate? You betcha. He'll choke up, foul off, and draw walks. He's a fringy runner, but he'll grab the extra base where he can. He's short to the ball, contact-oriented, and his uniform is gonna be dirty by the time the mascot race rolls around. This profile is always tricky, because it lacks a carrying tool, and a well-below-average power projection means that major-league pitchers are going to be able to challenge him. Lopez will have to prove he can hit at every level, but at least now there is only one level left to go.

The Risks: Medium. You could call Lopez low risk given his approach, bat control, and defensive flexibility, but sometimes these profiles get the bat knocked out of their hands at the highest level.

Ben Carsley's Fantasy Take: With all due respect to Brock Holt, do you really want to roster the prospect version of Brock Holt?

7 Nick Pratto 1B

OFP: 55 Likely: 45 ETA: 2021

Born: 10/06/98 Age: 20 Bats: L Throws: L Height: 6'1" Weight: 195 Origin: Round 1, 2017 Draft (#14 overall)

YEAR	TEAM	LVL	AGE	PA	R	2B	3B	HR	RBI	BB	K	SB	CS	AVG/OBP/SLG	DRC+	VORP	BABIP	BRR	FRAA	WARP	PF
2017	ROY	RK	18	230	25	15	3	4	34	24	58	10	4	.247/.330/.414	111	4.7	.319	-0.8	1B(48) 5.2	-0.1	102
2018	LEX	A	19	537	79	33	2	14	62	45	150	22	5	.280/.343/.443	111	14.4	.375	1.4	1B(125) -0.6	0.3	110
2019	*KCA*	*MLB*	*20*	*252*	*20*	*10*	*0*	*6*	*24*	*8*	*90*	*3*	*1*	*.158/.184/.277*	*13*	*-21.6*	*.214*	*0.0*	*1B 1*	*-2.2*	*102*

Breakout: 3% Improve: 5% Collapse: 0% Attrition: 3% MLB: 5% *Comparables: Jose Osuna, Chris Marrero, Dominic Smith*

The Report: Pratto does not have your typical first-base profile. Most first-base prospects are big, power-first bats playing other positions in the minor leagues. Pratto breaks that mold a bit as an undersized hit-first lefty. His hit tool is the most impressive of the bunch, but he was able to tap into a bit of power this season. While he doesn't have prototypical first-base size, Pratto is strong throughout, with plenty of wrist and forearm strength. He may never hit 30 bombs in a season, but you can expect plenty of doubles.

Pratto has an advanced approach. He rarely has bad at-bats and sees the ball really well. He's balanced at the plate, and his quick hips let him get to velocity and anything on the inner-half. Pratto is also capable of hitting the ball to all fields. No one is going to call him "fast" but you can expect healthy steal totals from a really smart, Goldschmidt-esque runner. He should also wind up one of the better defenders at his position. You won't get to see it often, but Pratto throws well, and some considered him a two-way prospect as an amateur

The Risks: High. There is no room for error when it comes to first basemen. If the bat don't play, you don't play.

Ben Carsley's Fantasy Take: You need to be a really good hitter or really potent slugger to be a worthwhile fantasy first baseman. Guys who sort of fall just short of either distinction—your Yonder Alonsos, Brandon Belts, and Eric Hosmers, etc—generally end up ranking somewhere between the 20th and 35th best options at the position. That's what we're likely going to see from Pratto, which makes him worth rostering in deep leagues and an afterthought in shallower formats.

8 Daniel Lynch LHP

OFP: 55 Likely: 45 ETA: As a reliever in 2019. 2020 is more likely.

Born: 11/17/96 Age: 22 Bats: L Throws: L Height: 6'6" Weight: 190 Origin: Round 1C, 2018 Draft (#34 overall)

YEAR	TEAM	LVL	AGE	W	L	SV	G	GS	IP	H	HR	BB/9	K/9	K	GB%	BABIP	WHIP	ERA	DRA	WARP	PF
2018	BNC	RK	21	0	0	0	3	3	11^1	9	0	1.6	11.1	14	59%	.310	0.97	1.59	3.28	0.3	95
2018	LEX	A	21	5	1	0	9	9	40	35	1	1.4	10.6	47	51%	.343	1.02	1.58	3.57	0.8	105
2019	*KCA*	*MLB*	*22*	*2*	*2*	*0*	*8*	*8*	34^2	*35*	*4*	*3.2*	*8.3*	*32*	*45%*	*.314*	*1.37*	*4.15*	*4.36*	*0.4*	*102*

Breakout: 4% Improve: 7% Collapse: 4% Attrition: 7% MLB: 12% *Comparables: Carson Fulmer, Nik Turley, Frankie Montas*

The Report: The pre-draft reports all had Lynch as a projectable lefty currently pinned around 90 mph. Well, in a bit of TV cooking show magic, the rib roast goes in the oven and one clock wipe later he's touching 97 in the pros. The velocity range is still wide here, but Lynch will sit 93-95 with good boring action in on righties. He's able to reach back for plus-plus velo late in outings and he elevates the pitch effectively.

The secondaries are more forgettable side dishes at present. Lynch's slider can flatten out, and he struggles to get it down in the zone consistently, but it flashes 55 with big tilt. The breaking ball also comes in from a tough angle for fellow lefties. The change doesn't always turnover for him, and it can be too firm, but he'll show a hard sinking version at times that bumps average. There should be enough cambio for him to crossover at least.

The mechanics might force him to the pen, as it's a slingy arm action thrown across his body with some effort. Control is well ahead of command at present, and he'll have tall pitcher issues with regard to repeating his delivery. It's not quite "set it, and forget it" yet, but Lynch won't need sous vide cooking times to impact the majors.

The Risks: Medium. Lynch dominated levels you'd expect him too, and the command issues won't come to a head until the upper minors, but as a lefty with a plus fastball, a decent slider, and some funk, there's a major-league role here, health permitting.

Ben Carsley's Fantasy Take: How many non-closing relievers were rostered in your league last year? Yeah...

9 Kris Bubic LHP

OFP: 50 Likely: 40 ETA: 2021

Born: 08/19/97 Age: 21 Bats: L Throws: L Height: 6'3" Weight: 220 Origin: Round 1, 2018 Draft (#40 overall)

YEAR	TEAM	LVL	AGE	W	L	SV	G	GS	IP	H	HR	BB/9	K/9	K	GB%	BABIP	WHIP	ERA	DRA	WARP	PF
2018	IDA	RK	20	2	3	0	10	10	38	38	2	4.5	12.6	53	47%	.379	1.50	4.03	2.95	1.3	100
2019	*KCA*	*MLB*	*21*	*1*	*3*	*0*	*7*	*7*	*30²*	*33*	*4*	*7.4*	*8.1*	*28*	*44%*	*.317*	*1.89*	*5.91*	*6.23*	*-0.3*	*102*

Breakout: 0% Improve: 0% Collapse: 0% Attrition: 0% MLB: 0% *Comparables: Thyago Vieira, Bryan Mitchell, Kendry Flores*

The Report: Hey, it's another polished lefty with a deceptive delivery and a potential plus changeup! Bubic was a dominant starter for Stanford this past spring on the strength of his change and he continued to miss bats with it in the pros. He sells the pitch well, and while it doesn't feature huge fade, the 10-15 mph gap between the cambio and his fastball gets guys to swing through, Bugs Bunny-style. The fastball can sit in the low-90s, but sometimes only touches 90. He still gets late swings on it due to his hitchy, uphill delivery and some gloveside run.

Bubic's unorthodox mechanics tend to impact his control and command of the fastball though. His path can wander during his long arm action, and he doesn't always get on top of his release. There's a tradeoff here obviously, but it remains to be seen if he can throw enough quality strikes with the fastball at the upper levels to set up his change. The breaking ball is a slurvy curveball that flashes average, but is even more inconsistent than Kowar's. It's fine as a show-me pitch to lefties, but lacks the depth to be a bat-misser at present. Bubic has a mature frame with a thick lower half, so while he lacks physical projection, it's also a starting-pitching-ready body. His upside as a starter is limited though, without command or breaking ball improvement.

The Risks: Medium. Bubic is polished enough that he should breeze through the minors, but lefties with fringy heaters and breaking balls often bump the ceiling hard in the majors.

Ben Carsley's Fantasy Take: Too far away and too low a ceiling. No thank you.

10 Kyle Isbel OF

OFP: 50 Likely: 40 ETA: 2021

Born: 03/03/97 Age: 22 Bats: L Throws: R Height: 5'11" Weight: 183 Origin: Round 3, 2018 Draft (#94 overall)

YEAR	TEAM	LVL	AGE	PA	R	2B	3B	HR	RBI	BB	K	SB	CS	AVG/OBP/SLG	DRC+	VORP	BABIP	BRR	FRAA	WARP	PF
2018	IDA	RK	21	119	27	10	1	4	18	14	17	12	3	.381/.454/.610	195	18.0	.429	-0.8	CF(19) 4.5, RF(2) 1.1	1.6	105
2018	LEX	A	21	174	30	12	1	3	14	12	43	12	3	.289/.345/.434	110	7.0	.377	2.8	CF(27) 0.8, LF(11) -0.5	0.7	109
2019	*KCA*	*MLB*	*22*	*252*	*27*	*12*	*0*	*6*	*21*	*7*	*77*	*7*	*2*	*.191/.210/.315*	*33*	*-10.5*	*.247*	*0.7*	*CF 2, LF 0*	*-0.9*	*102*

Breakout: 4% Improve: 4% Collapse: 0% Attrition: 4% MLB: 5% *Comparables: Darrell Ceciliani, Roger Bernadina, Xavier Avery*

The Report: Isbel is a smart player who will earn the "gritty" label soon enough. As you might expect, he plays hard, looks the part, and takes a patient approach at the dish. Isbel's quick hands cover the inner-half of the plate well, though his swing can lengthen at times. The power may end up a tick below average, but four tools could get to 50, and he's a plus runner. Isbel can handle center field and would be an above average defender in either corner spot. He played some infield at UNLV and there may be a world where Kansas City turns him into a utility type.

The Risks: Medium. Isbel will likely be worthy of an MLB roster spot, but if the bat doesn't develop, it's impossible to see an everyday or even a platoon role.

Ben Carsley's Fantasy Take: Isbel's speed could make him somewhat interesting if he finds himself with regular playing time, but the upside here is very, very modest. You don't need to pay attention until he's on an MLB roster.

The Next Five:

11 Carlos Hernandez RHP

Born: 03/11/97 Age: 22 Bats: R Throws: R Height: 6'4" Weight: 175 Origin: International Free Agent, 2014

YEAR	TEAM	LVL	AGE	W	L	SV	G	GS	IP	H	HR	BB/9	K/9	K	GB%	BABIP	WHIP	ERA	DRA	WARP	PF
2017	BNC	RK	20	1	4	0	12	11	62^1	64	6	3.9	9.0	62	44%	.322	1.46	5.49	4.36	1.1	100
2018	LEX	A	21	6	5	0	15	15	79^1	71	7	2.6	9.3	82	44%	.298	1.18	3.29	6.02	-0.8	108
2019	*KCA*	*MLB*	*22*	*3*	*5*	*0*	*12*	*12*	*60*	*68*	*11*	*4.6*	*7.3*	*49*	*39%*	*.310*	*1.64*	*5.83*	*6.15*	*-0.5*	*102*

Breakout: 4% Improve: 8% Collapse: 0% Attrition: 4% MLB: 8% *Comparables: Scott Barlow, Ricky Romero, Max Povse*

Hernandez was signed at 19, which is practically AARP age for international free agents. Usually when one of these guys hits, you've managed to find a polished arm who had a late-teenage velocity jump. Usually you pencil these guys in as relievers long term, but Hernandez has major-league starter upside. He's certainly got the frame, as he looks to be significantly heavier than his listed 175, and his delivery doesn't have any notable red flags. While his fastball works in an average velo band (91-94) he can show more in short bursts, and he commands the pitch well to both sides. There is some giddy up when he tries to elevate for strikeouts as well.

Hernandez's breaker is a bit of a slurve. It can get humpy when he wants to drop it in, but there's a tighter 11-5 version which he can start in the zone and get chases or spot gloveside. The change is the clear third pitch, and Hernandez lacks consistent feel for it at present. If the breaking ball and change improve he'll project as a fourth starter although, sure, you could pencil him in as a reliever long-term.

12 Kelvin Gutierrez 3B

Born: 08/28/94 Age: 24 Bats: R Throws: R Height: 6'3" Weight: 215 Origin: International Free Agent, 2013

YEAR	TEAM	LVL	AGE	PA	R	2B	3B	HR	RBI	BB	K	SB	CS	AVG/OBP/SLG	DRC+	VORP	BABIP	BRR	FRAA	WARP	PF
2016	AUB	A-	21	35	5	3	0	0	6	3	5	4	0	.323/.371/.419	128	2.9	.370	0.3	3B(8) 0.4	0.2	92
2016	HAG	A	21	417	58	19	6	3	48	29	65	19	7	.300/.349/.406	129	22.3	.349	0.2	3B(95) 3.3	2.2	100
2016	POT	A+	21	44	7	1	0	1	2	3	5	2	2	.237/.326/.342	93	1.9	.250	0.7	3B(9) -0.1	0.1	102
2017	POT	A+	22	245	34	10	6	2	16	19	59	3	0	.288/.347/.414	120	12.6	.380	2.0	3B(54) 6.4	1.7	98
2017	NAT	RK	22	37	6	3	1	0	1	4	7	2	0	.212/.297/.364	65	0.5	.269	0.8	3B(8) -1.1	-0.2	103
2018	HAR	AA	23	249	36	6	3	5	26	16	62	10	1	.274/.321/.391	96	9.2	.352	1.0	3B(56) 12.7, SS(1) 0.1	1.8	102
2018	NWA	AA	23	264	29	8	3	6	40	20	46	10	3	.277/.337/.409	104	9.8	.321	1.3	3B(62) -0.7, SS(2) -0.2	0.4	109
2019	*KCA*	*MLB*	*24*	*141*	*13*	*3*	*1*	*3*	*14*	*6*	*38*	*3*	*1*	*.225/.256/.340*	*54*	*-3.6*	*.287*	*0.4*	*3B 1, SS 0*	*-0.3*	*102*

Breakout: 6% Improve: 13% Collapse: 0% Attrition: 11% MLB: 15% *Comparables: Patrick Kivlehan, Jordy Mercer, Jefry Marte*

The glove-first third base profile will not be the most exciting one we'll catalog across our other 29 lists, but catalog it we shall. Gutierrez moves well at third, and he has good instincts and hands. He has an accurate plus-plus arm and projects as an above-average defender at the hot corner. He struggles with right-on-right spin, but will flash acceptable power, even if he sometimes elongates his swing to tap into it. Overall his swing plane is fairly flat, and Gutierrez sees the ball much better from lefties, making a short-side platoon outcome a distinct possibility. If he manages to show an average hit tool and fringy game power in the majors, the glove will be enough to support a fringe everyday role. Look, we warned you it wasn't that exciting.

13 Yefri Del Rosario RHP

Born: 09/23/99 Age: 19 Bats: R Throws: R Height: 6'2" Weight: 180 Origin: International Free Agent, 2017

YEAR	TEAM	LVL	AGE	W	L	SV	G	GS	IP	H	HR	BB/9	K/9	K	GB%	BABIP	WHIP	ERA	DRA	WARP	PF
2017	BRA	RK	17	1	1	0	11	6	32^{1}	37	1	2.8	8.1	29	48%	.343	1.45	3.90	3.15	0.9	103
2018	LEX	A	18	6	5	0	15	15	79	69	10	3.3	8.2	72	40%	.263	1.24	3.19	4.95	0.2	113
2019	*KCA*	*MLB*	*19*	*2*	*5*	*0*	*18*	*11*	*56^{1}*	*65*	*12*	*5.0*	*6.5*	*41*	*39%*	*.303*	*1.71*	*6.43*	*6.80*	*-1.0*	*102*

Breakout: 0% Improve: 0% Collapse: 0% Attrition: 0% MLB: 0% *Comparables: Luiz Gohara, Deolis Guerra, Jake McGee*

del Rosario grew up idolizing Yordano Ventura. There are reports on the kids of Mike Cameron, Vlad Guerrero, and Fernando Tatis elsewhere in this publication, but that is the sentence that's made me feel the oldest so far in this gig. Anywho, it shouldn't be a huge surprise then that del Rosario signed with the Royals after being granted free agency as part of the punishment for the Braves CBA violations in Latin America. Unlike his idol though, del Rosario isn't particularly likely to stick in a major-league rotation. There's some projection left in his 6-foot-2 frame, and I'd expect him to sit more consistently in the mid-90s as he matures (he works more in the low-90s now, although he'll touch 95 or higher). The fastball is a lively pitch with some natural cut, and del Rosario pairs it with a very projectable curveball for an 18-year-old. The velocity and shape can be wildly inconsistent, but he'll show a tight downer in the upper-70s. The change is firm, but occasionally flashes split action.

While del Rosario might develop three pitches in time, his mechanics may limit him to the pen. It's arm speed and torque over leg drive, and his halves tend to get out of sync. The arm action requires some effort as well, and while he generally throws strikes, he tends to be wild within the zone. del Rosario is athletic enough to keep it all mostly together, but if you need to project two pitches and a command jump, you can usually also project a move to the bullpen.

14 Blake Perkins OF

Born: 09/10/96 Age: 22 Bats: B Throws: R Height: 6'1" Weight: 165 Origin: Round 2, 2015 Draft (#69 overall)

YEAR	TEAM	LVL	AGE	PA	R	2B	3B	HR	RBI	BB	K	SB	CS	AVG/OBP/SLG	DRC+	VORP	BABIP	BRR	FRAA	WARP	PF
2016	AUB	A-	19	241	31	5	1	1	16	25	39	10	3	.233/.318/.281	109	12.5	.279	1.5	CF(49) 9.0, LF(2) -0.1	1.4	93
2016	HAG	A	19	33	4	0	0	0	2	5	6	0	1	.200/.333/.200	80	-1.2	.263	-1.4	CF(7) -1.2	-0.3	112
2017	HAG	A	20	572	105	27	4	8	48	72	118	31	8	.255/.354/.378	118	35.7	.318	7.4	CF(118) 8.4, LF(10) 0.9	3.7	99
2018	POT	A+	21	305	39	11	0	1	21	42	67	12	5	.234/.344/.290	101	7.9	.307	2.7	CF(62) -6.6, LF(1) 0.1	0.0	101
2018	WIL	A+	21	291	48	11	1	2	18	50	67	17	4	.240/.381/.322	100	11.3	.329	0.4	CF(61) 11.9, LF(1) -0.1	1.6	97
2019	*KCA*	*MLB*	*22*	*252*	*26*	*4*	*0*	*5*	*18*	*22*	*68*	*5*	*2*	*.162/.236/.245*	*32*	*-10.8*	*.201*	*0.1*	*CF 1, LF 0*	*-1.0*	*102*

Breakout: 7% Improve: 13% Collapse: 0% Attrition: 9% MLB: 16% *Comparables: Aaron Hicks, Che-Hsuan Lin, Mallex Smith*

Part of the Kelvin Herrera trade in June, the switch-hitting Perkins ended up being That Guy You Saw Too Much Of. And that's certainly not a bad thing; Perkins could become a fun player to watch at the top of a lineup. As the year went on, there was a bit more fight in his bat, and he'd work the count well enough and draw walks. But he doesn't hit for much power, and he's often trying to go the other way and slap a ball through the infield. He also seems much more comfortable from the right side of the plate at the moment. Defensively, he can handle center field: He's a sound route runner, and he'll wow you with his ability to reach balls in the gaps. His arm isn't much to write home about, but his instincts make him a sure bet to stick in center.

15 Meibrys Viloria C

Born: 02/15/97 Age: 22 Bats: L Throws: R Height: 5'11" Weight: 220 Origin: International Free Agent, 2013

YEAR	TEAM	LVL	AGE	PA	R	2B	3B	HR	RBI	BB	K	SB	CS	AVG/OBP/SLG	DRC+	VORP	BABIP	BRR	FRAA	WARP	PF
2016	IDA	RK	19	259	54	28	3	6	55	20	36	1	1	.376/.436/.606	174	39.5	.418	2.3	C(50) -0.8	2.3	109
2017	LEX	A	20	398	42	25	0	8	52	25	79	4	3	.259/.313/.394	104	8.5	.310	-0.4	C(92) -0.4	1.2	106
2018	WIL	A+	21	407	34	16	1	6	44	40	75	2	1	.260/.342/.360	107	11.0	.313	-2.8	C(88) 2.8	1.3	98
2018	KCA	MLB	21	29	4	2	0	0	4	1	9	0	0	.259/.286/.333	74	0.2	.389	0.1	C(10) -1.0	0.0	101
2019	*KCA*	*MLB*	*22*	*35*	*3*	*2*	*0*	*1*	*4*	*1*	*9*	*0*	*0*	*.203/.235/.337*	*48*	*-0.7*	*.245*	*-0.1*	*C -1*	*-0.2*	*102*

Breakout: 9% Improve: 23% Collapse: 0% Attrition: 18% MLB: 26% *Comparables: Austin Hedges, Blake Swihart, John Ryan Murphy*

Viloria might have been the most unlikely big-league call-up this past season. With his year winding down with High-A Wilmington, Viloria was expected to wrap things up and get a break before heading to the AFL. Surprise! Injuries and a roster shuffle pushed Viloria from Wilmington all the way to Kansas City in September, and his advanced approach at the plate and arm prevented him from looking too helpless out there. He posted pop times around 1.93-1.95 and he's got an accurate arm, but he still needs a lot of work behind the plate. He doesn't have the softest hands, and he'll clank a few balls here and there. As he fills out, he could develop into a 15-homer guy and average game-caller with a plus arm. But first, a return to the minors awaits.

Others of note:

Daniel Tillo, LHP, High-A Wilmingon

Another large lefty in a system full of sizeable southpaws, the 6-foot-5 Tillo doesn't have Lynch's fastball or Bubic's change, but his tall-and-fall delivery and slingy, three-quarters slot makes for a tough AB for same-side sluggers. The fastball comes in around 90, but it offers solid plane and bores in on righties. Tillo will guide the change a bit, but there's good sink at times, and he is comfortable throwing it behind in counts. He also mixes in a short slider as well. The results weren't great for a 22-year-old college arm in A-ball, but there's enough rawness left that you can dream on a bit of projection being left in the profile. Barring that, you can always wring a LOOGY out of this.

Josh Staumont, RHP, Triple-A Omaha

Richard Lovelady, LHP, Triple-A Omaha

Two relief prospects coming from opposite ends of Royals prospect lists and meeting in Others of Note in 2019.

Staumont finally got his long-assumed conversion to relief in 2018. But there wasn't much room for the stuff to bump, and he still struggled to throw strikes in shorter bursts. As many bats as his power fastball/curve combo may miss when he's running good, he'll issue almost as many walks. The culprit is still an uptempo—bordering on violent—delivery, combined with a long arm action to get to his overhand slot. The over the top angle makes his stuff even harder to square, but until he proves he can be more effectively wild—or preferably just less wild—it's hard to see a late inning major-league pen role in the near-term. He'll get chances though; guys with high-90s heat and a curve that flashes plus-plus always will. And hey, it kept him in the top ten a year longer than it maybe should have.

Richard Lovelady first came to wider prominence due to an... unfortunate bit of character saving on twitter dot com. But he also has power stuff, and he commands it far better than Staumont at present. Lovelady's fastball is a couple ticks shy of Staumont's but he changes levels well, and it also comes from a tricky angle due to his crossfire delivery and low-three-quarters slot. He pairs it with a plus slider that shows good, late depth. He's been a next ten stalwart for two years running now, but may make an impact in the Royals bullpen before Staumont. Lovelady may not have the same upside, but you don't have to wishcast nearly as much to see a lefty setup arm here.

Michael Gigliotti, OF, Low-A Lexington

Gigliotti rounded out our top ten last year, but a knee injury ended his 2018 season after just a week. An ACL issue is not what you want for any prospect, but it will have an even more profound effect on Gigliotti, who generates much of his value from his plus-plus speed in center field. Until we see him back on the field and running down balls in the gap with similar aplomb, he's back to sleeperdom in an improving Royals system.

Top Talents 25 and Under (born 4/1/93 or later):

1. Adalberto Mondesi
2. Seuly Matias
3. Khalil Lee
4. MJ Melendez
5. Brady Singer
6. Jackson Kowar
7. Brad Keller
8. Ryan O'Hearn
9. Brett Phillips
10. Nicky Lopez

Last year's edition of this list was (let's be honest) really, really bad. This year's list is still bad but at least it's interesting bad—and that may be the first sign that Dayton Moore is slowly beginning to turn the creaking frame of the organizational ship toward the friendlier waters of a legitimate rebuild.

Same person, different name: last year's #1 Raul has become this year's #1 Adalberto. But after a superlative late-season run, a straight ordinal ranking cannot capture the distance between Mondesi and numbers two through ten on this list. The power production arrived unexpectedly while he fully actualized his speed at the major-league level. All that being said, a sober assessment has to note that the breakout came in both a small sample and with a continuation of some worrying peripherals, most obviously his aversion to taking walks (3.8 BB%), which, barring a significant change of approach, hard-caps his on-base potential around .300. Additionally, with a 19.7 HR/FB% almost certain to regress, you'd be optimistic to expect more than 15-20 homers in a full season. None of this cold water means Mondesi isn't a talent: Even if his approach might make for a bumpy ride, the defense is strong, and the speed is elite. It all makes for a package that is immensely fun to watch.

After the great tranche of prospects come two out-of-the blue major-league producers from 2018. Well, the second half of 2018, anyway. Keller, a Rule 5 pick from the Diamondbacks in 2017, was the most consistent Royals starter all season (something something land of the blind, one-eyed man, king). Even looking charitably at a strong final two months, where he cut his walks and started missing a few bats, Keller is a fairly standard-issue pitch-to-contact groundballer, which tightens the upside-floor bar between a No. 3 and No. 4 starter. Just behind Keller lies O'Hearn, who displayed a sudden power spike that only seems bizarre these days because the lefty-hitting first baseman didn't alter his swing plane at all. O'Hearn was slugging .391 in 406 PA at Triple-A before shredding major-league arms to the tune of a .262/.353/.597 line over the final two months. His exit velocities suggest legit power, and he also brings double-digit walk rates, but he was helpless against lefties after his call-up. Suffice to say, there's a sizable scoop of interest here, but it comes dolloped with heaping toppings of uncertainty.

Phillips, the major piece in the Mike Moustakas trade, earns a back-end spot over fellow outfielder Jorge Bonifacio based on the fact that he has the defensive chops for centerfield (oh, that right arm!) and hopes of developing an offensive profile that could yield everyday work. Bonifacio, by contrast, had a league-average 422 major-league plate appearances, got slapped with an 80-game PED suspension, then came back to have 270 below-average plate appearances. In particular, the disappearance of his power bodes poorly. If you've got a ceiling of an everyday centerfielder with league-average offense and a corner outfielder who will likely impress with neither on-base nor power abilities, you take the former all day, every day (even if it means more airtime for his inimitable donkey-pterodactyl laugh).

Even if it isn't yet reflected in this list, the Royals—aided significantly by the infusion of college pitching arms at the top of the draft—are beginning those slow, painful steps toward a rebuild. There's not much short-term hope at the major-league level, but at least the pipeline has something more than rust, cobwebs, and the musty stench of despair in it.

Los Angeles Angels

The State of the System:

It's not the deepest system in the world, but we are on two straight years now of it being an okay system, and man does that feel weird to type.

The Top Ten:

1 **Jo Adell OF** OFP: 70 Likely: 60 ETA: 2020

Born: 04/08/99 Age: 20 Bats: R Throws: R Height: 6'3" Weight: 208 Origin: Round 1, 2017 Draft (#10 overall)

YEAR	TEAM	LVL	AGE	PA	R	2B	3B	HR	RBI	BB	K	SB	CS	AVG/OBP/SLG	DRC+	VORP	BABIP	BRR	FRAA	WARP	PF
2017	ANG	RK	18	132	18	6	6	4	21	10	32	5	0	.288/.351/.542	122	13.2	.361	1.9		0.0	98
2017	ORM	RK	18	90	25	5	2	1	9	4	17	3	2	.376/.411/.518	133	7.2	.463	0.4		0.3	119
2018	BUR	A	19	108	23	7	1	6	29	11	26	4	1	.326/.398/.611	161	12.4	.391	1.2	CF(16) -0.4, RF(3) -0.9	0.9	107
2018	INL	A+	19	262	46	19	3	12	42	15	63	9	2	.290/.345/.546	142	21.8	.345	2.0	CF(36) -5.6, RF(8) -1.1	0.7	101
2018	MOB	AA	19	71	14	6	0	2	6	6	22	2	0	.238/.324/.429	99	4.5	.333	-0.3	CF(17) -1.9	-0.1	100
2019	*ANA*	*MLB*	*20*	*252*	*26*	*8*	*2*	*9*	*25*	*9*	*85*	*3*	*1*	*.165/.196/.320*	*34*	*-10.7*	*.208*	*0.4*	*CF -4, RF -1*	*-1.6*	*99*

Breakout: 15% Improve: 21% Collapse: 0% Attrition: 6% MLB: 21% *Comparables: Ronald Acuna, Byron Buxton, Domingo Santana*

The Report: I've been doing this for eight seasons now. I've watched and evaluated and ranked a lot of prospects. I've got a feel for my strengths and weaknesses, my predilections and preferences. But I haven't quite figured out the secret sauce for how and why I go gonzo over a prospect. This isn't just about being a "good" prospect, a high upside guy, big stuff. I enjoyed my time watching Andrew Benintendi in Double-A. I ranked him as the third best prospect in baseball because I thought it was appropriate. It was dispassionate, academic.

Jo Adell will rank in that general area on our 2019 Top 101. Nothing that follows will be nearly as antiseptic as above.

He's built like an NFL wideout. The ball jumps off his bat. It makes *that* sound. Then it makes another sound. You can't hear it—perhaps because sound doesn't travel in the vacuum of space—but I can only assume it's the secondary thrusters going off. It. Just. Looks. Right. He's 4.2 down the line at a level of effort that would get angry diatribes written by men with graying goatees about Manny Machado. His batting practice sessions justify every watery, obviously shaken Manhattan I've had in an Appy League hotel bar. Watching Jo Adell play baseball is like watching a true virtuoso handle Tchaikovsky's Piano Concerto #1. All the movements look simple enough, familiar enough, but somehow foreign, impossible. Just remember that there is no cheering in the press box. He is not the best prospect I've ever seen, but that doesn't really matter to me. He's a very, very good one. Jo Adell is an argument for style points, for the Russian judge on presentation, and yes *sigh* even for #rig.

"The answer is dreams. Dreaming on and on. Entering the world of dreams and never coming out. Living in dreams for the rest of time." — Haruki Murakami, Sputnik Sweetheart

The Risks: Medium. Well, he struggled a little at Double-A at 19 while battling minor injuries. Past that…

Ben Carsley's Fantasy Take: You can stop asking us who the next Ronald Acuna or Juan Soto is; it's Adell, who's got such obvious upside that even the most consistent prospect doubters among us can't quibble with it. All the ingredients are here for a true, five-tool, eff-you OF1 who routinely challenges for 20/20 and maybe even 30/30 in his best years. It's always tricky throwing fantasy comps on guys like this—maybe 85% of Mookie Betts, or prime Grady Sizemore, or George Springer with 15 more steals?—because in the end, they're all special, unique fantasy unicorns. He'll likely be the top dynasty prospect in the game a year from now, and if he's not it'll more likely be because he exhausted eligibility than because anyone passed him. Craig was right.

2 Griffin Canning RHP

OFP: 60 Likely: 50 ETA: 2019

Born: 05/11/96 Age: 23 Bats: R Throws: R Height: 6'1" Weight: 170 Origin: Round 2, 2017 Draft (#47 overall)

YEAR	TEAM	LVL	AGE	W	L	SV	G	GS	IP	H	HR	BB/9	K/9	K	GB%	BABIP	WHIP	ERA	DRA	WARP	PF
2018	INL	A+	22	0	0	0	2	2	8^{2}	4	0	3.1	12.5	12	56%	.222	0.81	0.00	0.79	0.5	91
2018	MOB	AA	22	1	0	0	10	10	45^{2}	27	2	3.7	9.7	49	48%	.229	1.01	1.97	3.86	0.8	101
2018	SLC	AAA	22	3	3	0	13	13	59	68	6	3.4	9.8	64	42%	.376	1.53	5.49	3.95	1.1	119
2019	*ANA*	*MLB*	*23*	*2*	*1*	*0*	*5*	*5*	*25*	*21*	*3*	*3.6*	*9.3*	*26*	*42%*	*.283*	*1.26*	*4.20*	*4.24*	*0.4*	*99*

Breakout: 18% Improve: 27% Collapse: 16% Attrition: 29% MLB: 52% *Comparables: Zack Wheeler, Stephen Gonsalves, Chad Bettis*

The Report: Canning brushed aside most of the concerns about the health of his arm in 2018, blitzing through three levels of the minors and leaving a trail of Ks in his wake. He might bear a passing resemblance to the cavalcade of averagish-stuff starters we have discussed so far this year, but he's a rarer avis—the above-averagish-stuff starter. Canning is wildly advanced with four present average or better offerings. He's comfortable throwing any of them for strikes at any time, in any count.

The fastball features only average velocity but his plus command of the pitch makes it play up. He has a big 12-6 curve from his hitchy, overhead slot that has consistent shape and deception. It plays well off a tighter, shorter slider that comes out like the fastball but with sharp late tilt. The change only has average fade but he sells it well. Canning is a more-than-the-sum-of-his-parts arm, but all those parts are also above-average.

I wrote that Canning brushed aside most of the concerns about his health. His workload was tightly monitored in 2018, and he only threw ~100 innings across 25 starts. So whether or not he can handle a full starter's workload is still an open question. It's the last one here though.

The Risks: Medium. The stuff is ready; we'll see if the arm is too.

Ben Carsley's Fantasy Take: See all that stuff about how Canning has more upside than the majority of starters we've covered to this point? That means you should go all in. It feels to me as though the Dynasty Prospect Industrial Complex does not fully appreciate Canning yet; in fact, in shallower leagues that roster only 100-or-so prospects, I'd say there's a good chance he's not even owned. You should fix that, as Canning has all the ingredients of a fantasy SP4 or 5, especially playing in that cavernous park. Yes, he might get hurt, but you could also get hit by a meteor tomorrow, so let's not dwell on the bad things that could happen.

3 Jahmai Jones 2B

OFP: 60 Likely: 50 ETA: 2020

Born: 08/04/97 Age: 21 Bats: R Throws: R Height: 6'0" Weight: 215 Origin: Round 2, 2015 Draft (#70 overall)

YEAR	TEAM	LVL	AGE	PA	R	2B	3B	HR	RBI	BB	K	SB	CS	AVG/OBP/SLG	DRC+	VORP	BABIP	BRR	FRAA	WARP	PF
2016	ORM	RK	18	226	49	12	3	3	20	21	29	19	6	.321/.404/.459	145	23.1	.364	1.3	CF(41) -4.2, RF(4) -0.5	0.8	106
2016	BUR	A	18	70	8	1	0	1	10	5	13	1	0	.242/.294/.306	85	-1.3	.286	0.2	CF(8) -0.7, LF(4) -0.1	0.1	102
2017	BUR	A	19	387	54	18	4	9	30	32	63	18	7	.272/.338/.425	115	27.2	.309	5.7	CF(65) -3.4, LF(16) 0.5	1.5	102
2017	INL	A+	19	191	32	11	3	5	17	13	43	9	6	.302/.368/.488	125	17.7	.379	2.0	CF(37) -9.7, LF(3) -0.5	-0.3	103
2018	INL	A+	20	347	47	10	5	8	35	43	63	13	3	.235/.338/.383	112	12.5	.272	1.5	2B(70) -6.9	-0.1	101
2018	MOB	AA	20	212	33	10	4	2	20	24	51	11	1	.245/.335/.375	104	5.7	.323	-1.5	2B(45) -1.7	-0.1	101
2019	*ANA*	*MLB*	*21*	*252*	*28*	*7*	*1*	*6*	*22*	*15*	*64*	*6*	*2*	*.196/.246/.321*	*48*	*-6.4*	*.237*	*0.7*	*2B -2, CF 0*	*-0.9*	*99*

Breakout: 20% Improve: 22% Collapse: 0% Attrition: 14% MLB: 22% *Comparables: Jonathan Schoop, Adrian Cardenas, Delino DeShields*

The Report: Absolutely nothing has changed for Jones in terms of the physicality, work ethic, or underlying tools over the past year. He was and is an impressive specimen, with present and projectable strength throughout his frame. It's a powerful swing, though it'll still get stiff at launch and fall into rotational movement when he gets vertical and stuck on his back side. He transfers compact and short into the zone, and impressive wrist strength tracks a quick bat to the point of contact. The barrel delivery can be uneven, but it projects to become better, and he has solid-average power that's there for the gettin' to. The defensive conversion from center to second has gone okay. Not great and immediate, but steady and progressive. He's got plenty of body control and quickness to pull it off, and the arm is accurate and strong enough to work up the middle or on the turn.

The Risks: The defensive change pushed his development back a bit, and there were times in the first half where the offense looked to suffer for the split attention. He's a higher-probability prospect than most, and he still shows outstanding effort and focus on the field. The tools speak for themselves. There might be a smidge more uncertainty to the outcome than there was a year ago, but not much.

Ben Carsley's Fantasy Take: I'm in the camp that doesn't see any fantasy star upside with Jones, but that doesn't mean he can't be useful for our purposes. For example, consider that D.J. LeMahieu hit .276 with 15 homers and 6 steals last season and was a top-20 fantasy option at the position, per ESPN's player rater. That type of contribution would seem to be Jones' floor once he's established (and likely undersells his speed), and he could end up with more of a Cesar Hernandez-esque top-15 finish as a .270 hitter who can challenge for 15 bombs and steals each. His probability and ETA are good enough to keep Jones on the 101.

4 Brandon Marsh OF

OFP: 60 Likely: 50 ETA: 2020

Born: 12/18/97 Age: 21 Bats: L Throws: R Height: 6'4" Weight: 210 Origin: Round 2, 2016 Draft (#60 overall)

YEAR	TEAM	LVL	AGE	PA	R	2B	3B	HR	RBI	BB	K	SB	CS	AVG/OBP/SLG	DRC+	VORP	BABIP	BRR	FRAA	WARP	PF
2017	ORM	RK	19	192	47	13	5	4	44	9	35	10	2	.350/.396/.548	120	18.1	.417	3.2	RF(26) -1.9, CF(11) 1.5	0.7	118
2018	BUR	A	20	154	26	12	1	3	24	21	40	4	0	.295/.390/.470	137	12.2	.400	2.9	CF(14) 1.2, RF(13) -1.3	1.2	110
2018	INL	A+	20	426	59	15	6	7	46	52	118	10	4	.256/.348/.385	108	21.2	.356	4.3	CF(50) -0.8, RF(33) 3.0	1.1	99
2019	*ANA*	*MLB*	*21*	*252*	*25*	*10*	*1*	*6*	*23*	*15*	*80*	*2*	*0*	*.203/.247/.332*	*54*	*-5.4*	*.275*	*-0.1*	*CF 0, RF 0*	*-0.5*	*99*

Breakout: 1% Improve: 5% Collapse: 0% Attrition: 2% MLB: 5% *Comparables: Michael Saunders, Daniel Fields, Domonic Brown*

The Report: When the 20-year-old Marsh arrived at Inland Empire mid-summer, his load generally looked mechanical and uncertain, which led to imbalanced swings that lacked extension. From there though, he made adjustments to incorporate his lower half better and control the outer part of the plate, and things started to click. His approach is patient but appropriately aggressive in context, he hangs in pretty well against lefties, and he creates good torque to bring plenty of natural strength into his swings. There's plus power in the tank, but the game version'll probably top out at average without a significant mechanical overhaul.

Marsh is an excellent athlete with advanced control of his Jim Mackey-framed levers, and there's plus speed that should stay at least above-average through maturity. He leverages plus arm strength with high-effort throws that track well and hold line. He goes and gets it in center as well as anyone the system has produced in recent years, but can hold down right just as easily, thanks to a strong arm and good reads off the bat.

The Risks: Moderate. He's been pushed quickly, and the combination of raw offensive skills and aggressive promotions means we're projecting more development than usual for a High-A guy. The high-end strength and athleticism gives him a lot to work with, however, and his demonstrated ability to make in-season adjustments points to a higher-likelihood prospect.

Ben Carsley's Fantasy Take: I think Marsh often gets oversold as a super high-upside fantasy outfielder because of his natural raw power. That's likely a mistake—there is no future OF1 upside here—but Marsh could be plenty useful as a fantasy OF3/4 who's more of a pure OF3 in OBP leagues. Overall, I see some Aaron Hicks potential in Marsh's future as a guy who does enough in the power and speed categories to mitigate a mediocre (but certainly tolerable) average. We'll just hope that, unlike with Hicks, it doesn't take Marsh like five years to reach that modest but meaningful ceiling.

5 Jordyn Adams OF

OFP: 60 Likely: 50 ETA: 2022

Born: 10/18/99 Age: 19 Bats: R Throws: R Height: 6'2" Weight: 180 Origin: Round 1, 2018 Draft (#17 overall)

YEAR	TEAM	LVL	AGE	PA	R	2B	3B	HR	RBI	BB	K	SB	CS	AVG/OBP/SLG	DRC+	VORP	BABIP	BRR	FRAA	WARP	PF
2018	ANG	RK	18	82	8	2	2	0	5	10	23	5	2	.243/.354/.329	83	2.3	.362	0.9	CF(14) -4.2, RF(1) 0.0	-0.5	100
2018	ORM	RK	18	40	5	4	1	0	8	4	7	0	1	.314/.375/.486	113	1.3	.379	-0.8	CF(8) 3.1	0.3	115
2019	*ANA*	*MLB*	*19*	*252*	*18*	*2*	*1*	*4*	*14*	*8*	*103*	*2*	*1*	*.110/.137/.177*	*-22*	*-27.0*	*.165*	*0.7*	*CF -1, RF 0*	*-3.0*	*99*

Breakout: 5% Improve: 7% Collapse: 0% Attrition: 3% MLB: 9% *Comparables: Carlos Tocci, Engel Beltre, Franmil Reyes*

The Report: You can't really blame the Angels for trying their luck again with a toolsy outfielder named Jordy(o)n, given how the last one worked out. There are some differences though, and it's not just the preferred spelling. While I wrote above that Jordon Adell is built like a wideout, Adams actually was a wide receiver, and a highly-rated college recruit as well. While still raw at the plate, he has the quick-twitch wrists to portend a good hit tool although the ultimate power projection is an open question. The athletic tools should allow him to stick in center field and he could be an asset there. This is not something that normally comes into play in our projections but the Angels have done quite well developing these kind of athletic outfield types in recent years, and Adams gives them ideal clay to work with.

The Risks: High. He's still quite raw at the plate, so this is an athleticism bet. It's a whole lotta athleticism at least.

Ben Carsley's Fantasy Take: Are the Angels the new Rangers or something? Adams is one of the more exciting, higher-upside additions to the dynasty player pool. He's likely to be a slow burn type of dude, but if you don't get in on the ground floor now you're likely to miss out altogether. He's a top-101 guy for me already, albeit probably close to the bottom of said list.

6 Matt Thaiss 1B

OFP: 55 Likely: 50 ETA: 2019. The Angels have a bit of a DH/1B glut through 2021 or so.

Born: 05/06/95 Age: 24 Bats: L Throws: R Height: 6'0" Weight: 195 Origin: Round 1, 2016 Draft (#16 overall)

YEAR	TEAM	LVL	AGE	PA	R	2B	3B	HR	RBI	BB	K	SB	CS	AVG/OBP/SLG	DRC+	VORP	BABIP	BRR	FRAA	WARP	PF
2016	ORM	RK	21	71	16	7	1	2	12	4	4	2	4	.338/.394/.569	110	4.7	.339	-1.0	1B(15) 0.7	-0.1	107
2016	BUR	A	21	226	24	12	3	4	31	22	28	1	0	.276/.351/.427	131	5.2	.302	-3.6	1B(43) 5.5	0.9	107
2017	INL	A+	22	385	46	13	4	8	48	40	59	4	3	.265/.353/.399	121	13.4	.299	0.5	1B(78) 2.8	0.6	101
2017	MOB	AA	22	221	29	14	0	1	25	37	50	4	3	.292/.412/.388	151	12.2	.389	-1.2	1B(46) -1.5	0.7	95
2018	MOB	AA	23	176	24	10	2	6	25	16	35	2	1	.287/.352/.490	123	9.0	.331	-1.1	1B(36) 2.6	0.5	99
2018	SLC	AAA	23	400	54	24	6	10	51	28	68	6	3	.277/.328/.457	94	-0.6	.314	0.2	1B(77) 5.4	0.3	120
2019	*ANA*	*MLB*	*24*	*100*	*11*	*5*	*1*	*3*	*11*	*7*	*23*	*1*	*0*	*.230/.287/.395*	*69*	*-2.0*	*.272*	*-0.1*	*1B 1*	*-0.1*	*99*

Breakout: 3% Improve: 14% Collapse: 0% Attrition: 14% MLB: 17% *Comparables: O'Koyea Dickson, David Cooper, Chad Wallach*

The Report: We usually toss around the term "prospect fatigue" with big name prospects, top 101 guys: J.P. Crawfords, Lewis Brinsons or Nick Gordon. It doesn't feel to me like Matt Thaiss was only drafted two years ago, but the record books say he was; you may remember that Thaiss was one of the two big college catchers in that draft, along with Zack Collins. He immediately shifted to first base, which made him much less interesting as a prospect, but he's hung around an improving Angels Top 10 year-over-year because he's just kept hitting. Some additional power showed up in 2018, although that happens to many 23-year-olds in the PCL. Couple that with a plus hit tool, strong approach, and above-average defense at first and you have... well, there's a reason we've already run out of interesting things to say about him.

The Risks: Low. It's all profile risk here, the bat isn't particularly high variance, although he could use some positive variance in the power column.

Ben Carsley's Fantasy Take: Matt Thaiss has become a bit of a punching bag in the BP dynasty circle—I specifically highlighted my (eventually successful) attempts to sell high on him last year in TDGX—but he's a reasonable asset in deeper leagues. First base isn't quite as flush of a fantasy position as it used to be; Jose Abreu was a top-20 guy last year despite hitting just .265 with 22 homers. Thaiss is capable of matching that output, which will make him a reasonable if unexciting fantasy MI once he's playing every day.

7 Jose Suarez LHP

OFP: 55 Likely: 50 ETA: 2019

Born: 01/03/98 Age: 21 Bats: L Throws: L Height: 5'10" Weight: 170 Origin: International Free Agent, 2014

YEAR	TEAM	LVL	AGE	W	L	SV	G	GS	IP	H	HR	BB/9	K/9	K	GB%	BABIP	WHIP	ERA	DRA	WARP	PF
2016	ANG	RK	18	1	3	0	11	5	40^{1}	48	1	2.9	10.3	46	42%	.395	1.51	5.36	2.91	1.2	98
2017	ANG	RK	19	1	0	0	3	3	14	10	1	2.6	12.2	19	40%	.310	1.00	1.93	2.02	0.6	101
2017	BUR	A	19	5	1	0	12	12	54^{2}	49	7	3.0	11.7	71	48%	.333	1.23	3.62	2.85	1.6	102
2018	INL	A+	20	0	1	0	2	2	9	6	0	1.0	18.0	18	67%	.400	0.78	2.00	0.89	0.5	103
2018	MOB	AA	20	2	1	0	7	7	29^{2}	34	0	2.4	15.5	51	37%	.500	1.42	3.03	2.56	1.0	99
2018	SLC	AAA	20	1	4	0	17	17	78^{1}	81	5	4.0	8.4	73	48%	.336	1.48	4.48	4.44	1.0	122
2019	*ANA*	*MLB*	*21*	*1*	*1*	*0*	*14*	*3*	26^{1}	*24*	*4*	*4.2*	*9.9*	*29*	*42%*	*.300*	*1.39*	*4.70*	*4.79*	*0.1*	*99*

Breakout: 15% Improve: 20% Collapse: 9% Attrition: 22% MLB: 33% *Comparables: Shelby Miller, Jake McGee, Robert Stephenson*

The Report: It took Orange County three tries to find an appropriate level for Suarez last year, who embarrassed first High-A, then Double-A hitters in the season's early months. A velocity spike presaged Suarez's coming-out party, as he'll now wander into the mid-90s consistently enough to make a plus-on-its-merits straight change play up all the more. He's aggressive within the zone, moving his fastball around and attacking the hands at will with late life that helps him bust into kitchens and avoid barrels. Occasional issues spotting the pitch periodically landed him in trouble in Triple-A, but he repeats well and projects to have above-average command. His curveball will flash above-average with bat-missing two-plane finishing action at its best, though it is his least consistent pitch at present.

The Risks: The frame is pretty maxed out, and there'll be some conditioning and maintenance concerns as he matures further. There isn't much good projection left here, and the mechanics are already pretty on-brand with his physical signature, so another jump in stuff is unlikely. What he's got already is plenty good, though, which reduces risk considerably. Ongoing development of his hook will go a long way toward determining where in the rotation he lands.

Ben Carsley's Fantasy Take: Suarez is one of my favorite pop-up prospect targets for deep leaguers. There's some Eduardo Rodriguez potential here in terms of the strikeout potential, the lack of consistency, and the potential conditioning issues, but hey now let's get back to those strikeouts. Better yet, Suarez will be ready soon, so he's a good "fail fast" prospect and not a guy you'll need to sit on for three years to figure out who he is. Buy, buy, buy.

8 D'Shawn Knowles OF

OFP: 55 Likely: 45 ETA: 2023

Born: 01/16/01 Age: 18 Bats: B Throws: R Height: 6'0" Weight: 165 Origin: International Free Agent, 2017

YEAR	TEAM	LVL	AGE	PA	R	2B	3B	HR	RBI	BB	K	SB	CS	AVG/OBP/SLG	DRC+	VORP	BABIP	BRR	FRAA	WARP	PF
2018	ANG	RK	17	130	19	4	1	1	14	15	27	7	4	.301/.385/.381	134	9.6	.384	1.1	LF(13) -3.1, CF(9) -0.5	0.0	100
2018	ORM	RK	17	123	27	9	2	4	15	13	38	2	3	.321/.398/.550	123	8.6	.463	0.3	CF(17) -1.2, RF(9) 1.8	0.4	112
2019	*ANA*	*MLB*	*18*	*252*	*17*	*3*	*0*	*4*	*20*	*9*	*84*	*2*	*1*	*.157/.185/.225*	*3*	*-21.5*	*.215*	*-0.5*	*CF 0, RF 0*	*-2.4*	*99*

Breakout: 0% Improve: 0% Collapse: 0% Attrition: 0% MLB: 0% *Comparables: Adalberto Mondesi, Wilmer Flores, Tommy Brown*

The Report: We keep hammering this point, but the Bahamas are a rapidly emerging market for international talent. Along with Kristian Robinson in the Diamondbacks system, Knowles is at the forefront of the next wave of Bahaman ballplayers. He's an athletic, well-rounded outfield prospect who is reasonably polished for his level of experience. As you can see above, he's hit the ground running in LA's system, getting a stateside assignment at just 17 and continuing to hit when promoted outside the complex.

Knowles is on the smaller, skinnier side—his listed height might be generous but his weight probably isn't. He runs well and projects to stay in center, although we'll always note that players this young and projectable can easily grow out of the middle of the field. It's a sweet swing with some bat speed, and occasionally surprising pop. This all constitutes the makings of a really cool prospect, and he could fly up our lists next year.

The Risks: High, mostly because he was born in 2001 and hasn't played above rookie ball. You can be both high risk and less risky than most of your cohort, I suppose.

Ben Carsley's Fantasy Take: Just a watch-list guy for us, but a fun one! In fact, I'd argue Knowles is a better bet than some of the Rule 4 draft guys you'll start popping in the third or fourth rounds of your new player entry drafts. Especially if those other guys are pitchers.

9 Michael Hermosillo OF

OFP: 50 Likely: 45 ETA: Debuted in 2018

Born: 01/17/95 Age: 24 Bats: R Throws: R Height: 5'11" Weight: 190 Origin: Round 28, 2013 Draft (#847 overall)

YEAR	TEAM	LVL	AGE	PA	R	2B	3B	HR	RBI	BB	K	SB	CS	AVG/OBP/SLG	DRC+	VORP	BABIP	BRR	FRAA	WARP	PF
2016	BUR	A	21	160	22	8	1	2	22	18	22	4	3	.326/.411/.442	151	10.4	.377	0.2	CF(20) -4.9, LF(11) -0.6	0.4	105
2016	INL	A+	21	174	36	7	4	4	17	16	30	6	7	.309/.393/.490	149	22.5	.359	2.5	CF(25) -3.3, RF(8) -0.7	0.6	97
2017	INL	A+	22	64	5	6	0	0	2	9	15	5	2	.321/.438/.434	161	4.2	.447	-1.3	CF(9) -2.3, LF(3) -0.3	0.0	98
2017	MOB	AA	22	340	40	13	2	4	26	40	73	21	9	.248/.361/.353	116	15.4	.316	-2.0	CF(52) -2.3, RF(13) 2.3	0.7	93
2017	SLC	AAA	22	129	20	6	1	5	16	7	28	9	2	.287/.341/.487	90	5.3	.337	0.3	LF(14) -0.1, CF(10) 0.6	0.2	106
2018	SLC	AAA	23	323	43	14	4	12	46	30	87	10	5	.267/.357/.480	90	11.6	.341	-0.4	CF(36) 5.5, RF(19) 0.3	1.0	121
2018	ANA	MLB	23	62	7	4	0	1	1	3	17	0	1	.211/.274/.333	61	-1.2	.282	-0.5	CF(12) 1.5, RF(12) 0.7	0.1	99
2019	*ANA*	*MLB*	*24*	*233*	*28*	*8*	*1*	*7*	*24*	*19*	*66*	*7*	*3*	*.205/.289/.352*	*75*	*0.8*	*.263*	*0.1*	*CF 0, LF -1*	*0.1*	*99*

Breakout: 11% Improve: 33% Collapse: 4% Attrition: 19% MLB: 49% *Comparables: Brian Goodwin, Brandon Nimmo, Brian Anderson*

The Report: A veteran of much crappier Angels prospect lists, Hermosillo finally percolated up to the big leagues in 2018. He even earned semi-regular playing time for a few weeks early in the summer and a few more towards the end of September.

A former Illinois running back commit—who subtweeted noted member of the human race Skip Bayless for suggesting Kyler Murray would only be happy on the gridiron—Hermosillo has the general toolsiness and athleticism that you'd expect from someone FBS schools were after to carry the rock. He runs well, throws well, plays the outfield well, and has a reasonable power projection. We do worry about his hit tool playing down due to approach, and he rose through the system very fast and might need some consolidation time at Triple-A.

The Risks: Medium. He might not hit and he's probably not playing much center field in Los Angeles of Anaheim anytime soon. You may have heard of the guy the Angels have out there already.

Ben Carsley's Fantasy Take: Hermosillo could be of interest if he gets regular playing time because of his speed, but until then he is... super not of interest. Please continue to read Baseball Prospectus for our expert dynasty league analysis.

10 Luis Rengifo IF

OFP: 50 Likely: 45 ETA: 2019

Born: 02/26/97 Age: 22 Bats: B Throws: R Height: 5'10" Weight: 165 Origin: International Free Agent, 2013

YEAR	TEAM	LVL	AGE	PA	R	2B	3B	HR	RBI	BB	K	SB	CS	AVG/OBP/SLG	DRC+	VORP	BABIP	BRR	FRAA	WARP	PF
2016	MRN	RK	19	124	16	7	2	1	9	13	31	22	3	.239/.325/.367	92	7.1	.325	3.3	3B(12) -0.5, 2B(10) 2.9	0.3	98
2017	CLN	A	20	450	65	24	4	11	44	33	80	29	14	.250/.318/.413	108	22.0	.285	4.3	SS(31) -2.8, 2B(25) 2.8	1.7	99
2017	BGR	A	20	104	14	3	1	1	8	8	17	5	3	.250/.308/.333	109	6.0	.295	0.4	SS(23) -1.5	0.3	104
2018	INL	A+	21	190	36	11	3	2	16	27	22	22	8	.323/.426/.466	174	28.1	.365	2.5	SS(36) 3.9, 2B(2) 0.0	2.3	98
2018	MOB	AA	21	181	37	10	5	2	21	23	22	13	2	.305/.420/.477	143	14.2	.346	-1.0	SS(30) -3.4, 2B(9) -0.8	0.7	101
2018	SLC	AAA	21	219	36	9	5	3	27	25	31	6	6	.274/.358/.421	112	12.0	.310	3.3	2B(31) -1.5, SS(16) 0.1	1.0	116
2019	*ANA*	*MLB*	*22*	*133*	*17*	*5*	*2*	*3*	*13*	*13*	*25*	*5*	*2*	*.239/.321/.390*	*99*	*4.8*	*.278*	*0.4*	*SS -1, 3B 0*	*0.4*	*99*

Breakout: 18% Improve: 38% Collapse: 0% Attrition: 23% MLB: 42% *Comparables: Ivan De Jesus, Daniel Robertson, J.P. Crawford*

The Report: Kudos to the scout(s) who saw it coming; the Halos snagged Rengifo from Tampa in March to complete their trade of C.J. Cron, and all he did was hit, and run, and hit some more, and then run some more. His is a dense frame, packed to the gills with compact muscle and outsized strength, but he retains quick-twitch athleticism in his lower half. The speed is only solid-average, maybe a true 55, but he's nimble in and out of breaks, and his advanced instincts help the speed play up on the bases.

At the dish, he's a switch-hitter with compact actions from both sides. There's comparatively more loft to the right-handed swing, but he's pretty direct and short in both directions. He'll take a lot of pitches, including some he'd probably be better served to attack. But he works himself into good counts on the regular, and coupled with an all-fields approach, he does well to create positive hitting situations and translate them into quality at-bats. There's sneaky average power, but the game utility is geared much more toward the gaps than the fences.

His quickness manifests in impressive lateral agility up the middle, and he has a strong feel for the six with an accurate internal clock and good body control to set up his transfers and throws. The arm strength is okay for the left side, above-average for the keystone, and he has the tools to hold down either position, with above-average leather at the latter.

The Risks: Moderate; the approach can get passive and may be exploited by big-league arms if he doesn't try to drive the ball more. The baserunning value may also continue to dip a little lower against the best batteries, and he's not quite as dynamic a defender as you'd ideally like for that utility role.

Ben Carsley's Fantasy Take: Oh God, it's a fast middle infielder. I can't be trusted with this profile. I... I suggest buying.

The Next Five:

11 Patrick Sandoval LHP

Born: 10/18/96 Age: 22 Bats: L Throws: L Height: 6'3" Weight: 190 Origin: Round 11, 2015 Draft (#319 overall)

YEAR	TEAM	LVL	AGE	W	L	SV	G	GS	IP	H	HR	BB/9	K/9	K	GB%	BABIP	WHIP	ERA	DRA	WARP	PF
2016	GRV	RK	19	2	3	0	13	8	52^2	53	4	4.3	8.7	51	48%	.331	1.48	5.30	3.53	1.2	96
2017	TCV	A-	20	1	1	0	4	4	19	19	0	2.8	13.3	28	47%	.404	1.32	3.79	2.83	0.5	98
2017	QUD	A	20	2	2	1	9	7	40	38	1	3.6	10.8	48	48%	.333	1.35	3.83	3.29	0.9	102
2018	QUD	A	21	7	1	1	14	10	65	58	4	1.5	9.8	71	48%	.305	1.06	2.49	3.25	1.4	99
2018	BCA	A+	21	2	0	1	5	3	23	12	1	1.6	10.2	26	46%	.216	0.70	2.74	2.78	0.7	86
2018	INL	A+	21	1	0	0	3	3	14^2	6	0	3.7	12.9	21	47%	.200	0.82	0.00	2.59	0.5	92
2018	MOB	AA	21	1	0	0	4	4	19^2	12	0	3.7	12.4	27	40%	.286	1.02	1.37	2.48	0.7	101
2019	*ANA*	*MLB*	*22*	*5*	*5*	*1*	*31*	*14*	*87^1*	*81*	*13*	*4.5*	*9.1*	*88*	*42%*	*.290*	*1.42*	*4.89*	*4.99*	*0.4*	*99*

Breakout: 19% Improve: 27% Collapse: 6% Attrition: 16% MLB: 38% *Comparables: Jay Jackson, Anibal Sanchez, Gerrit Cole*

A $900,000 overslot prep once upon a time, Sandoval is still a big, live-armed lefty who got picked up from the Astros at the deadline in the Martin Maldonado trade. He's a bit of a hidden breakout guy because his lines are very split up between promotions and the trade, but he had a brilliant season all-in-all, with midseason promotions from Low-A up to Double-A and plenty of strikeouts to go around. Violence in the delivery points toward a bullpen future. He's a low-90s dude with feel for a curve and the makings of other secondaries, so you'd want him to stay in the rotation, and while there's a lot of reliever risk here, it's not so extreme that it's a fait accompli. Regardless of role, Sandoval will end up being a high price to pay for a half-season of an okay catcher.

12 Ty Buttrey RHP

Born: 03/31/93 Age: 26 Bats: L Throws: R Height: 6'6" Weight: 230 Origin: Round 4, 2012 Draft (#151 overall)

YEAR	TEAM	LVL	AGE	W	L	SV	G	GS	IP	H	HR	BB/9	K/9	K	GB%	BABIP	WHIP	ERA	DRA	WARP	PF
2016	PME	AA	23	1	9	0	33	9	79	80	6	5.2	5.9	52	52%	.292	1.59	4.44	4.41	0.5	107
2017	PAW	AAA	24	1	1	0	10	0	17^2	21	2	5.1	9.2	18	53%	.358	1.75	7.64	3.41	0.4	100
2017	PME	AA	24	1	4	4	30	0	46	39	1	4.5	11.0	56	50%	.339	1.35	3.72	3.56	0.7	100
2018	PAW	AAA	25	1	1	1	32	0	44	36	4	2.9	13.1	64	45%	.320	1.14	2.25	2.65	1.2	100
2018	ANA	MLB	25	0	1	4	16	0	16^1	15	0	2.8	11.0	20	58%	.333	1.22	3.31	2.90	0.4	99
2019	*ANA*	*MLB*	*26*	*3*	*1*	*6*	*54*	*0*	*57*	*49*	*6*	*4.4*	*10.1*	*64*	*47%*	*.296*	*1.34*	*4.09*	*4.13*	*0.8*	*99*

Breakout: 15% Improve: 29% Collapse: 7% Attrition: 20% MLB: 45% *Comparables: Tom Mastny, Davis Romero, Patrick Light*

Buttrey is your classic "Failed starter Day 2 prep arm turned good reliever." He bounced around Red Sox affiliates for five seasons before finally putting it together in the bullpen in 2017. He's taxonomically a "95-and-a-slider" guy, but really more of a "97-and-a-slider guy," and it's a plus slider with good two plane break. He even has enough of a changeup to at least keep it in the back of the batter's mind. It's more eighth inning stuff than closer stuff, but he also might already be the Angels eighth inning guy. There is value in surety, although relievers are rarely a place to find surety, I suppose.

13 Trent Deveaux OF

Born: 05/04/00 Age: 19 Bats: R Throws: R Height: 6'0" Weight: 160 Origin: International Free Agent, 2017

YEAR	TEAM	LVL	AGE	PA	R	2B	3B	HR	RBI	BB	K	SB	CS	AVG/OBP/SLG	DRC+	VORP	BABIP	BRR	FRAA	WARP	PF
2018	ANG	RK	18	194	20	5	0	1	11	24	68	7	4	.199/.309/.247	65	-1.4	.327	1.4	CF(26) -6.1, RF(14) -0.3	-1.0	100
2019	*ANA*	*MLB*	*19*	*252*	*17*	*2*	*0*	*4*	*14*	*9*	*118*	*1*	*1*	*.098/.131/.156*	*-29*	*-30.9*	*.161*	*-0.3*	*CF -1, RF 0*	*-3.4*	*99*

Breakout: 6% Improve: 8% Collapse: 0% Attrition: 3% MLB: 10% *Comparables: Carlos Tocci, Engel Beltre, Nomar Mazara*

The 2017 Bahamian class also brought the Angels this fellow, a $1.2 million signee. His pro debut didn't quite go as smoothly as Knowles', as Deveaux was under the Mendoza line in complex league ball. It's questionable whether we should even be keeping stats in that league, let alone paying particularly close attention to them, and a stateside assignment as a first-year pro is, itself, actually somewhat promising. We did repeatedly hear good things about his athleticism and speed—you have probably discerned by now that the Angels have a type here—and it's a projectable body. We just don't know whether he's going to hit quite yet.

14 Chris Rodriguez RHP

Born: 07/20/98 Age: 20 Bats: R Throws: R Height: 6'2" Weight: 185 Origin: Round 4, 2016 Draft (#126 overall)

YEAR	TEAM	LVL	AGE	W	L	SV	G	GS	IP	H	HR	BB/9	K/9	K	GB%	BABIP	WHIP	ERA	DRA	WARP	PF
2016	ANG	RK	17	0	0	0	7	5	11^{1}	6	0	2.4	13.5	17	68%	.273	0.79	1.59	1.65	0.5	98
2017	ORM	RK	18	4	1	0	8	8	32^{1}	35	1	1.9	8.9	32	46%	.343	1.30	6.40	3.61	0.9	115
2017	BUR	A	18	1	2	0	6	6	24^{2}	32	1	2.6	8.8	24	54%	.403	1.58	5.84	3.34	0.6	100
2019	*ANA*	*MLB*	*20*	*2*	*3*	*0*	*9*	*9*	33^{2}	*32*	*4*	*4.7*	*8.6*	*32*	*50%*	*.298*	*1.47*	*4.86*	*4.95*	*0.2*	*99*

Breakout: 1% Improve: 4% Collapse: 1% Attrition: 1% MLB: 4% *Comparables: Tyrell Jenkins, Randall Delgado, Jake Thompson*

Rodriguez missed all of 2018 with a back injury. I'm familiar enough with the level of hushed tones required for various arm injuries, but back issues leave me a bit nonplussed. The most recent good pitching prospects with back issues I can think of are Kolby Allard, AJ Puk, and Thomas Szapucki. One of them lost a bunch of velocity—although not immediately—and the other two are currently rehabbing from Tommy John. Hardly a significant sample, and hardly enough information on Rodriguez to feel confident in any sort of 2019 projection. What I do know was I expected him to be up with the Top 101 types in the top five by this point, and while the injury injects a fair bit of uncertainty, I don't know that it dings the upside as much.

15 Livan Soto SS

Born: 06/22/00 Age: 19 Bats: L Throws: R Height: 6'0" Weight: 160 Origin: International Free Agent, 2017

YEAR	TEAM	LVL	AGE	PA	R	2B	3B	HR	RBI	BB	K	SB	CS	AVG/OBP/SLG	DRC+	VORP	BABIP	BRR	FRAA	WARP	PF
2017	BRA	RK	17	208	24	5	0	0	14	27	26	7	3	.225/.332/.254	101	5.9	.260	1.2	SS(44) -3.1, 2B(3) -0.9	0.0	104
2018	ORM	RK	18	200	31	10	0	0	11	24	24	9	3	.291/.385/.349	110	8.3	.336	1.6	SS(28) 2.7, 2B(18) -1.1	0.8	111
2019	*ANA*	*MLB*	*19*	*252*	*19*	*3*	*0*	*4*	*16*	*13*	*62*	*1*	*0*	*.136/.179/.198*	*1*	*-21.1*	*.163*	*-0.4*	*SS 0, 2B 0*	*-2.3*	*99*

Breakout: 5% Improve: 7% Collapse: 0% Attrition: 4% MLB: 9% *Comparables: Gleyber Torres, Carlos Triunfel, Adalberto Mondesi*

The other guy the Angels signed out of the Braves international prospect scandal might now be the best prospect. Soto got $850,000 from the Angels late in 2017 to pair with his $1,000,000 from the Braves. He's not a particularly physical player—there's literally no present power here and not a ton of projection, and he's not speedy either. He does have contact skills and precocious control of the strike zone given his age, and he has good defensive ability. The question is whether his lack of impact athleticism and potential physical growth might push him off the 6. He was already playing a fair amount of second at Orem.

Others of note:

Kevin Maitan, 3B/SS, Short-Season Orem

For years, Maitan was considered the best player in the world in his age group. The Braves locked him up early in the 2016 pool—far, far earlier than they were allowed—for $4.25 million, and then he got another $2.2 million from the Angels when the league made him a free agent. The problem is that, in the period between when Atlanta locked him up and when he actually started playing professionally, it sure seems like his baseball skills deteriorated a lot. He's gotten big and slow, and he hasn't hit much either. There's still bat speed and some latent interesting hitting ability, but it's a long swing and it's already getting exploited by low-level pitchers. It's too early to give up—he did get that $2.2 million just a year ago—but we're officially worried now.

Top Talents 25 and Under (born 4/1/93 or later):

1. Shohei Ohtani
2. Jo Adell
3. Griffin Canning
4. Jahmai Jones
5. Brandon Marsh
6. Jordyn Adams
7. David Fletcher
8. Jaime Barria
9. Matt Thaiss
10. Jose Suarez

Tommy John surgery is just a bummer, straight-up. It sucks when it robs us of the opportunity to watch special pitchers do special things, and it sucks when it blunts burgeoning careers before they can become special. Luckily for us all, at least Shohei Ohtani can hit really well, too. For all the gnashing of teeth about holes awaiting exposure by big-league stuff last spring, the young phenom more than held his own in his first taste of the world's best pitching, to the tune of a 122 DRC+ and one of the best barrel rates in baseball. He's not going to throw many more pitches while still eligible for this list, but that doesn't stop him from holding some of the highest 25U value in the game, both on the field and off.

It's difficult to believe we're here and admitting as much, but I think we're still undervaluing David Fletcher. In his first taste of The Show he sparkplugged a whole heap of defensive value all over the dirt, his wheels and aggressiveness played well on the bases, and he held his own against big-league arms. That's a recipe for a long career, and at least the earliest returns indicate that he deserves a bit more love.

Pressed into urgent service earlier than expected, Jaime Barria responded with acceptable topline production across nearly 130 innings, even as the DRA warning light flashed with furious urgency throughout. The overperformance to underlying metrics isn't especially surprising given the profile, and the stuff played basically as advertised. It's an archetype that tends to garner more doubt than benefit thereof, as middling velocity and 90th-percentile results in launch angles and batted ball distances allowed tends to be an awfully tough mix to sustain. Barria's deception and strong command affords more optimism than usual, but the ceiling remains fairly well-defined.

The rest of this list reiterates just how far Anaheim's system has come in a relatively short time. This is a franchise, after all, that just two winters ago sat 29th on our organizational rankings with a single, solitary BP101er. That guy's still going to feature on this year's list, along with at least three organization mates, and with swells of interesting, tooled-up youngin's at the complex level it's now a system capable of adding more high-end volume to the ranks right quick.

Los Angeles Dodgers

The State of the System:

The Dodgers system is coming towards a dip in their org cycle, but still has some very cool high end talent at the top.

The Top Ten:

1 **Alex Verdugo OF** OFP: 70 Likely: 60 ETA: Debuted in 2017

Born: 05/15/96 Age: 23 Bats: L Throws: L Height: 6'0" Weight: 205 Origin: Round 2, 2014 Draft (#62 overall)

YEAR	TEAM	LVL	AGE	PA	R	2B	3B	HR	RBI	BB	K	SB	CS	AVG/OBP/SLG	DRC+	VORP	BABIP	BRR	FRAA	WARP	PF
2016	TUL	AA	20	529	58	23	1	13	63	44	67	2	6	.273/.336/.407	119	20.8	.292	-1.2	CF(91) -1.0, RF(30) -0.1	1.2	97
2017	OKL	AAA	21	495	67	27	4	6	62	52	50	9	3	.314/.389/.436	114	32.4	.340	3.1	CF(59) -5.5, RF(46) 3.1	1.7	103
2017	LAN	MLB	21	25	1	0	0	1	1	2	4	0	1	.174/.240/.304	86	-1.2	.167	-0.1	CF(6) -0.7, RF(3) 0.0	0.0	88
2018	OKL	AAA	22	379	44	19	0	10	44	34	47	8	2	.329/.391/.472	130	24.0	.359	-0.5	CF(45) 2.0, RF(31) 2.4	2.2	96
2018	LAN	MLB	22	86	11	6	0	1	4	8	14	0	0	.260/.329/.377	85	3.2	.306	1.5	RF(16) -0.1, LF(12) 0.2	0.1	99
2019	*LAN*	*MLB*	*23*	*455*	*50*	*19*	*1*	*12*	*50*	*34*	*73*	*3*	*2*	*.254/.315/.394*	*94*	*9.3*	*.280*	*-0.6*	*RF 1, LF 1*	*1.2*	*97*

Breakout: 14% Improve: 50% Collapse: 0% Attrition: 19% MLB: 60% *Comparables: L.J. Hoes, Michael Brantley, Desmond Jennings*

The Report: There's little to say about Verdugo that hasn't been said a hundred times. He parlays an excellent approach at the plate with double-plus contact ability into a high OBP offensive profile where any power is a bonus. Verdugo's power started to appear more in Triple-A last year and he's ready to see if he can translate that success to the highest level.

Defensively, he doesn't look like he can play center at this point, due to fringy range for the position. Good instincts and a plus arm still should allow him to be an above-average corner outfielder. Overall, Verdugo profiles as a low-risk corner outfielder with upside if he can tap into more of the raw power that he's shown in BPs for years.

The Risks: Very Low. Verdugo is ready to learn and adjust at the MLB level. A high OBP/contact combo make him an extremely low flameout risk and the power is cooking along nicely.

Ben Carsley's Fantasy Take: Verdugo is a fairly boring fantasy prospect, but that doesn't make him an inherently bad one. There's no OF1 ceiling here, but Verdugo could develop into a well-rounded fantasy OF3 in deeper leagues. Perhaps a fantasy OF 4/5 outfielder outcome is more likely, but Verdugo is among the safest bets in the minors to provide value in some capacity. That's good enough to make him a top-50 dude despite the low-ish ceiling.

2 **Dustin May RHP** OFP: 70 Likely: 60 ETA: 2020

Born: 09/06/97 Age: 21 Bats: R Throws: R Height: 6'6" Weight: 180 Origin: Round 3, 2016 Draft (#101 overall)

YEAR	TEAM	LVL	AGE	W	L	SV	G	GS	IP	H	HR	BB/9	K/9	K	GB%	BABIP	WHIP	ERA	DRA	WARP	PF
2016	DOD	RK	18	0	1	1	10	6	30^{1}	37	0	1.2	10.1	34	57%	.394	1.35	3.86	4.29	0.4	107
2017	GRL	A	19	9	6	0	23	23	123	121	8	1.9	8.3	113	52%	.306	1.20	3.88	4.81	0.7	98
2017	RCU	A+	19	0	0	0	2	1	11	6	0	0.8	12.3	15	60%	.240	0.64	0.82	3.57	0.2	108
2018	RCU	A+	20	7	3	0	17	17	98^{1}	91	9	1.6	8.6	94	58%	.294	1.10	3.29	4.47	1.0	108
2018	TUL	AA	20	2	2	0	6	6	34^{1}	27	0	3.1	7.3	28	54%	.267	1.14	3.67	4.38	0.4	106
2019	*LAN*	*MLB*	*21*	*7*	*7*	*0*	*22*	*22*	115^{1}	*108*	*15*	*2.8*	*7.9*	*101*	*50%*	*.294*	*1.24*	*4.23*	*4.71*	*0.8*	*97*

Breakout: 4% Improve: 10% Collapse: 4% Attrition: 12% MLB: 16% *Comparables: Brad Keller, Antonio Senzatela, Jhoulys Chacin*

The Report: Dustin May is fun. He is a 6'6" lanky athlete with surprising body control given the length of his frame. He is a good athlete with quick twitch and a fun demeanor on the mound. He generates plus arm speed and good spin rates.

May has a plus fastball that sits in the mid-90's with heavy sink. He also throws a plus breaking ball with good depth and high spin and has advanced feel for the pitch. He'll also show an average mid-80s changeup with good arm speed and average tumble. His feel for the changeup will need to improve, but the three-pitch mix gives May weapons to use deep into a game, and he can always fall back on his plus sinker to generate weak contact.

In addition to the quality repertoire, May has above-average command due to his body control and athleticism. He locates well low in the zone with the sinker and can throw his breaking ball for strikes or break it off the plate at will. Overall, his pitch mix and command should allow him to develop into a No. 3 starter with upside from there if he can improve his command and changeup consistency.

The Risks: Medium. May is a pitcher and that automatically comes with some risk, but he has good pitchability and a quality three-pitch mix. He just needs to improve the consistency of command before he's ready.

Ben Carsley's Fantasy Take: A clear-cut top-101 arm, May will likely fall somewhere in the middle third of the list in the top-half of the glut of good-not-great fantasy arms who'll be ready soonish. The upside here isn't crazy, but May shouldn't hurt you in any one category while contributing solidly across the board. I expect him to develop into a very solid fantasy SP4 who occasionally teases more upside.

3 Keibert Ruiz C

OFP: 70 Likely: 55 ETA: 2020

Born: 07/20/98 Age: 20 Bats: B Throws: R Height: 6'0" Weight: 200 Origin: International Free Agent, 2015

YEAR	TEAM	LVL	AGE	PA	R	2B	3B	HR	RBI	BB	K	SB	CS	AVG/OBP/SLG	DRC+	VORP	BABIP	BRR	FRAA	WARP	PF
2016	DOD	RK	17	39	5	4	1	0	15	3	4	0	0	.485/.513/.667	231	7.4	.516	-0.8	C(7) -0.1	0.3	100
2016	OGD	RK	17	206	28	18	2	2	33	12	23	0	0	.354/.393/.503	140	17.0	.389	-1.6	C(35) -1.2	0.7	103
2017	GRL	A	18	251	34	16	1	2	24	18	30	0	0	.317/.372/.423	127	15.7	.355	-3.2	C(49) -0.9	0.9	97
2017	RCU	A+	18	160	24	7	1	6	27	7	23	0	0	.315/.344/.497	129	13.2	.333	0.0	C(37) -0.3	0.8	106
2018	TUL	AA	19	415	44	14	0	12	47	26	33	0	1	.268/.328/.401	92	8.3	.266	-3.8	C(86) 3.5	0.5	109
2019	*LAN*	*MLB*	*20*	*252*	*22*	*9*	*0*	*7*	*28*	*6*	*45*	*0*	*0*	*.218/.247/.347*	*46*	*-5.8*	*.240*	*-0.5*	*C -2*	*-0.9*	*97*

Breakout: 14% Improve: 18% Collapse: 0% Attrition: 6% MLB: 18%

Comparables: Carson Kelly, Jake Bauers, Freddie Freeman

The Report: The switch-hitting Ruiz is one of the most impressive young prospects in the game, thanks to a combination of polish, elite coordination, and quickness. Even better, he's proven adept at making in-season adjustments and improvements.

Ruiz uses his elite bat-to-ball ability to make consistent, quality contact from a compact swing. He's able to adjust his swing to location and understands how to put the ball on a line to all fields. He has above-average raw power, and although the swing doesn't tap fully into it yet, he can put a charge into the ball, especially when he gets out in front. The one downside to his offensive profile is that he can get over-aggressive, which often leads to weak contact.

Ruiz's framing is a work in progress, but improved over the course of the season. He often stabs at balls low in the zone, which can make it hard to get the call. Overall though, he's still an average receiver, due to his soft hands. He has an average arm, but his lightning quick transitions and excellent footwork allow him to effectively control the run game.

Ruiz has significant offensive upside and should be an average defensive catcher. His contact abilities and raw power should make him one of the better catchers in the league, and if he's able to improve his patience at the plate, he could be one of the best offensive backstops in baseball.

The Risks: Medium. Ruiz has shown both a polish and ability to quickly adjust well beyond his years. His ability to handle a pitching staff and excellent coordination give him a high floor at the plate and behind it.

Ben Carsley's Fantasy Take: Ruiz is pretty obviously the second-best dynasty catching prospect in the game (behind Francisco Mejia), and he's a lock to make our dynasty top-101. At the risk of repeating myself, please remember that Ruiz's MLB eta and fantasy impact ETA are likely quite different. That being said, Ruiz has all the tools necessary to develop into a consistent top-7 option at the position. This is a bad position, but he's a good one.

4 Will Smith C

OFP: 60 Likely: 50 ETA: Late 2019

Born: 03/28/95 Age: 24 Bats: R Throws: R Height: 6'0" Weight: 192 Origin: Round 1, 2016 Draft (#32 overall)

YEAR	TEAM	LVL	AGE	PA	R	2B	3B	HR	RBI	BB	K	SB	CS	AVG/OBP/SLG	DRC+	VORP	BABIP	BRR	FRAA	WARP	PF
2016	OGD	RK	21	33	4	0	0	1	5	4	1	0	0	.321/.394/.429	166	3.2	.296	0.4	C(5) -0.1, 2B(1) 0.0	0.3	100
2016	GRL	A	21	97	12	1	0	1	7	11	18	2	1	.256/.371/.305	113	6.3	.317	2.0	C(18) 0.0, 2B(3) -0.2	0.6	95
2016	RCU	A+	21	115	13	4	0	2	12	14	31	1	0	.216/.330/.320	74	1.8	.292	-1.3	C(16) 0.4, 3B(6) 0.9	-0.1	100
2017	RCU	A+	22	305	38	15	3	11	43	37	71	6	2	.232/.355/.448	102	16.8	.273	-2.0	C(55) 2.7, 3B(6) -1.0	0.5	108
2018	TUL	AA	23	307	48	14	0	19	53	36	75	4	0	.264/.358/.532	131	25.5	.295	-1.8	C(33) 7.4, 3B(33) -1.3	2.0	111
2018	OKL	AAA	23	98	9	4	0	1	6	7	37	1	0	.138/.206/.218	7	-3.8	.216	1.4	C(16) 1.4, 3B(10) 0.3	-0.4	104
2019	*LAN*	*MLB*	*24*	*68*	*7*	*2*	*0*	*3*	*8*	*5*	*23*	*0*	*0*	*.190/.258/.363*	*38*	*-2.1*	*.245*	*-0.1*	*C 2*	*-0.1*	*97*

Breakout: 9% Improve: 15% Collapse: 0% Attrition: 15% MLB: 30% *Comparables: Andrew Knapp, Michael McKenry, Josh Donaldson*

The Report: The Dodgers are flush with potentially impact catchers. Smith is another advanced receiver who has a real shot to become a force at the plate. Smith combines good feel for barrel with an excellent approach that helps his offensive tools play up significantly. The swing can get long, but it allows him to tap into more of his above-average raw power. Smith struggles with quality breaking stuff, but his other tools mitigate that to an extent.

Smith is an above-average receiver with a good understanding of how to handle counts and the pitcher. He has a plus arm and good footwork that will allow him to control the running game effectively. The combination of a solid offensive profile on top of an above-average defensive projection portend a future as a regular behind the plate. There's also room for more if his pitch recognition takes a step forward.

The Risks: Medium. Contact is the one concern with Smith, and it makes him a riskier bet. Other than that, the profile is fairly low risk, as he's a quality defensive catcher with good coordination and polish.

Ben Carsley's Fantasy Take: While I love Ruiz as a dynasty prospect I'm considerably less enthused by Smith. Sure, he's got solid upside as someone with potential catcher eligibility who can hit for power. But I don't fully trust his hit tool, and lots of these tweener positional guys tend to get lost in the shuffle: for every Russell Martin, there are many an Austin Barnes or Blake Swihart, etc. Smith is a top-150 guy due to the upside and proximity, but he won't be on my personal top-101.

5 Gavin Lux SS

OFP: 55 Likely: 50 ETA: 2020

Born: 11/23/97 Age: 21 Bats: L Throws: R Height: 6'2" Weight: 190 Origin: Round 1, 2016 Draft (#20 overall)

YEAR	TEAM	LVL	AGE	PA	R	2B	3B	HR	RBI	BB	K	SB	CS	AVG/OBP/SLG	DRC+	VORP	BABIP	BRR	FRAA	WARP	PF
2016	DOD	RK	18	219	34	10	5	0	18	25	43	1	0	.281/.365/.385	138	16.6	.360	1.1	SS(43) -7.9	0.0	103
2016	OGD	RK	18	34	7	3	0	0	3	3	8	1	0	.387/.441/.484	159	4.1	.522	0.0	SS(8) -1.3	0.1	104
2017	GRL	A	19	501	68	14	8	7	39	56	88	27	10	.244/.331/.362	97	19.5	.288	3.4	SS(65) 3.8, 2B(43) 4.0	2.1	98
2018	RCU	A+	20	404	64	23	7	11	48	43	68	11	7	.324/.396/.520	145	34.3	.374	-1.8	SS(66) -0.6, 2B(17) 0.8	2.2	110
2018	TUL	AA	20	120	21	4	1	4	9	14	20	2	2	.324/.408/.495	150	11.6	.370	1.3	SS(26) -0.6	0.9	107
2019	*LAN*	*MLB*	*21*	*252*	*26*	*5*	*2*	*6*	*22*	*15*	*65*	*3*	*2*	*.184/.232/.303*	*41*	*-8.2*	*.220*	*0.3*	*SS 0, 2B 0*	*-0.9*	*97*

Breakout: 22% Improve: 28% Collapse: 1% Attrition: 11% MLB: 29% *Comparables: Francisco Lindor, Daniel Robertson, Jorge Polanco*

The Report: Lux had about as good and complete a season as a prospect can have, both statistically and developmentally. On the latter he performed at a consistently high level throughout his ~four months at Rancho, and then again after a promotion to Double-A. More impressively though, he earned the numbers. His patient approach facilitated in-zone aggressiveness without sacrificing his command of the zone along the way. He added plane and loft gradually to increase pull and lift balls without compromising outer-third coverage. He managed to improve his reactions, lateral agility, and quickness while growing into a larger, rapidly maturing frame.

His raw reads in the field and digs out of the blocks on stolen base attempts could use refinement, but these are minor nits to pick. His above-average speed and demonstrated work ethic suggests potential for improvement on the bases, and despite its limitations, the arm plays up a bit with consistent accuracy and body positioning on his throws. He should be good enough to stay at the six for at least a few years.

The Risks: Low. He's got talent, pedigree, and impressive demonstrated growth all working on his side. This is a significantly higher-probability 21-year-old than most.

Ben Carsley's Fantasy Take: Generally when we talk about "pop-up" prospects, we're referring to guys with big upside who finally saw their tools click. That's not the case with Lux—his upside is fairly low, but his ceiling is quite high as a dude who should be able to play nearly every day for a contending team. Is there some risk that Lux becomes just a super-utility dude in what will be a crowded Dodgers infield? Sure. But if we zoom out, Lux will likely be a starter at second or short for the majority of his career, at which point he'll be an unexciting but very reasonable MI option in deeper leagues. The probability and proximity here are enough to make Lux a top-101 guy, albeit on the back-half of the list.

6 Dennis Santana RHP   OFP: 55   Likely: 50   ETA: Debuted in 2018

Born: 04/12/96 Age: 23 Bats: R Throws: R Height: 6'2" Weight: 160 Origin: International Free Agent, 2013

YEAR	TEAM	LVL	AGE	W	L	SV	G	GS	IP	H	HR	BB/9	K/9	K	GB%	BABIP	WHIP	ERA	DRA	WARP	PF
2016	GRL	A	20	5	9	0	25	14	111^1	84	2	4.5	10.0	124	56%	.290	1.26	3.07	3.56	1.8	95
2017	RCU	A+	21	5	6	0	17	14	85^2	87	5	2.3	9.7	92	50%	.340	1.27	3.57	3.54	1.7	113
2017	TUL	AA	21	3	1	0	7	7	32^2	32	2	6.3	10.2	37	52%	.337	1.68	5.51	3.48	0.7	106
2018	TUL	AA	22	0	2	0	8	8	38^2	26	3	3.3	11.9	51	56%	.258	1.03	2.56	2.72	1.2	111
2018	OKL	AAA	22	1	1	0	2	2	11	10	0	1.6	11.5	14	45%	.345	1.09	2.45	2.58	0.4	91
2018	LAN	MLB	22	1	0	0	1	0	3^2	6	0	2.5	9.8	4	31%	.462	1.91	12.27	3.78	0.0	126
2019	*LAN*	*MLB*	*23*	*2*	*1*	*0*	*5*	*5*	*25*	*21*	*3*	*3.9*	*10.4*	*29*	*48%*	*.304*	*1.26*	*3.74*	*4.17*	*0.3*	*97*

Breakout: 10% Improve: 13% Collapse: 9% Attrition: 21% MLB: 27%   *Comparables: Chris Reed, Max Scherzer, Garrett Richards*

The Report: Santana's conversion from gangly shortstop to fireballing hurler took another big step forward, culminating in a welcome-to-the-show-kid debut at Coors Field before a shoulder strain cut the festivities short in early June. Prior to the injury, he continued refining a delivery that had improved significantly over the past couple seasons.

Working out of a proper windup, he's still fairly closed-off into his turn down hill. He's a lot straighter down that hill than he used to be, though there's enough cross-fire and sneaky arm speed that he still generates some deception to help the stuff play up. He'll run the gas up to 97 with huge sink and some run, and he's coaxed along his changeup to a point where the pitch tunnels pretty well and holds the heater's line with decent velocity separation. The slider has quickly evolved into a knockout pitch, with hard vertical action and swing-and-miss potential.

Between all of the pitch movement and standard timing stuff that'll crop up in his delivery, the command and control still aren't great, but he has improved it considerably. Between that and honing the third pitch, he's got a better shot at hanging on to a starting role now than it looked like he'd have at this time last year.

The Risks: High. The shoulder injury is a red flag, and while a 180-inning projection's not the prerequisite it once was for a starting pitching prospect, it'd still be helpful to see how he holds up past 120—a number he hasn't yet hit.

Ben Carsley's Fantasy Take: Santana is a reliever through and through for me. The stuff may be exciting, but add in the injury history and he's a player I'm staying away from in all but the very deepest of formats.

7 Tony Gonsolin RHP   OFP: 50   Likely: 45   ETA: Health permitting 2019

Born: 05/14/94 Age: 25 Bats: R Throws: R Height: 6'2" Weight: 180 Origin: Round 9, 2016 Draft (#281 overall)

YEAR	TEAM	LVL	AGE	W	L	SV	G	GS	IP	H	HR	BB/9	K/9	K	GB%	BABIP	WHIP	ERA	DRA	WARP	PF
2016	OGD	RK	22	1	0	2	10	0	17^1	12	1	2.6	7.8	15	47%	.239	0.98	2.60	3.99	0.3	100
2016	GRL	A	22	0	2	2	9	0	13^2	17	0	2.0	6.6	10	35%	.370	1.46	5.27	3.12	0.3	100
2017	GRL	A	23	0	1	1	3	0	8	8	2	0.0	13.5	12	38%	.316	1.00	3.38	1.51	0.3	100
2017	RCU	A+	23	7	5	5	39	0	62	61	5	2.6	10.6	73	43%	.344	1.27	3.92	3.22	1.2	100
2018	RCU	A+	24	4	2	0	17	17	83^2	72	5	2.8	11.4	106	38%	.319	1.17	2.69	4.03	1.3	110
2018	TUL	AA	24	6	0	0	9	9	44^1	32	3	3.2	9.9	49	39%	.261	1.08	2.44	3.45	1.0	108
2019	*LAN*	*MLB*	*25*	*0*	*0*	*0*	*10*	*0*	*10^1*	*9*	*2*	*3.7*	*9.5*	*11*	*38%*	*.299*	*1.32*	*4.48*	*5.01*	*0.0*	*97*

Breakout: 13% Improve: 15% Collapse: 10% Attrition: 22% MLB: 27%   *Comparables: Osmel Morales, Glenn Sparkman, Luis Santos*

The Report: Gonsolin hopped onto the radar when he added a metric ton of in-season velocity out of the 'pen in 2017, and he remains there after keeping most of it upon returning to the rotation in 2018. He cleaned up a significant spine tilt and smoothed out his progressions to a high three-quarter release, leading to a nice bump in utility for his four-pitch arsenal. The delivery is still on the bumpier side, with some exertion that joggles his command and limits its projection. The gas sat mid-90s and touched 98 in the rotation, and while it's a relatively flat pitch with some homerun vulnerability, it holds plane and he works it effectively north and south.

A tight curveball is his best bat-misser. He also punched up a couple more miles an hour on the hook, and it's now a hard spiker with quality depth and above-average utility when he's on top of it. He'll mix in a slider that flashes average as well, though it's less consistent and lacks great bite and finish. A hard trap-door change rounds things out in the mid-80s, and he made strides in better holding his arm speed to sell and locate the pitch more consistently. If he can continue to refine the feel, it plays well enough off his four-seam line that it, too, has potential to grow into an average pitch.

The Risks: High. The fine command profile's sketchy enough that the reliever risk remains significant, though his arsenal is deep and effective enough that he projects to add value out of the 'pen if it comes to that.

Ben Carsley's Fantasy Take: Gonsolin is maybe worth spot-starting if he forces his way into the Dodgers rotation, but that seems pretty unlikely. Even if he does start, his upside is very limited. You can pass.

8 DJ Peters OF OFP: 55 Likely: 45 ETA: 2020

Born: 12/12/95 Age: 23 Bats: R Throws: R Height: 6'6" Weight: 225 Origin: Round 4, 2016 Draft (#131 overall)

YEAR	TEAM	LVL	AGE	PA	R	2B	3B	HR	RBI	BB	K	SB	CS	AVG/OBP/SLG	DRC+	VORP	BABIP	BRR	FRAA	WARP	PF
2016	OGD	RK	20	302	63	24	3	13	48	35	66	5	3	.351/.437/.615	200	46.4	.432	0.5	CF(31) 4.5, RF(28) -3.6	2.7	103
2017	RCU	A+	21	587	91	29	5	27	82	64	189	3	3	.276/.372/.514	118	43.2	.385	0.9	CF(80) -3.5, LF(18) -1.0	0.7	107
2018	TUL	AA	22	559	79	23	3	29	60	45	192	1	2	.236/.320/.473	95	20.6	.316	-3.6	CF(96) -3.1, RF(29) 1.4	-0.4	110
2019	*LAN*	*MLB*	*23*	*252*	*26*	*10*	*1*	*11*	*33*	*14*	*98*	*0*	*0*	*.199/.262/.387*	*79*	*2.5*	*.290*	*-0.4*	*CF -1, RF 0*	*0.2*	*97*

Breakout: 9% Improve: 29% Collapse: 5% Attrition: 22% MLB: 52% *Comparables: Greg Halman, Joe Benson, Derek Fisher*

The Report: DJ Peters is one of the most physically impressive players on a baseball field. He is tall, high-waisted with a perfect athlete's build. He looks like he could immediately step onto football field as a premier NFL linebacker. He is also a quick-twitch athlete who moves well for his size and shows quality coordination.

The offensive profile is all power. Peters generates extreme swing velocity with a vicious long stroke that generates double-plus raw. He has quality feel for the barrel and he's quick enough to get around on velocity. Unfortunately, Peters struggles to recognize even below-average breaking stuff or offspeed. This—in addition to his longer levers—means that he has low contact rates, which hinders his ability to tap into that raw pop. Despite the K-rates, Peters isn't an overly aggressive swinger on pitches he does recognize and is more than willing to take a walk, which boosts his overall offensive profile.

Defensively, Peters has fair instincts in the outfield and average foot speed, which translates into average range in right field. That along with a plus arm should let allow him to be an above-average fielder in either corner and an occasional fill-in in center field. The extreme offensive profile and the defensive versatility in the outfield fits the mold of a platoon power bat who can provide pop off the bench in favorable matchups.

The Risks: High. He swings and misses quite a bit, even by 2019 standards. The swing is long and he doesn't recognize spin well.

Ben Carsley's Fantasy Take: Sure, Peters has upside, but between his long swing and pitch-recognition issues he's got a slim chance of reaching it. He's a top-200 guy thanks to the power ceiling, but he's definitely not one of my personal favorites.

9 Mitch White RHP OFP: 50 Likely: 45 ETA: 2021

Born: 12/28/94 Age: 24 Bats: R Throws: R Height: 6'4" Weight: 207 Origin: Round 2, 2016 Draft (#65 overall)

YEAR	TEAM	LVL	AGE	W	L	SV	G	GS	IP	H	HR	BB/9	K/9	K	GB%	BABIP	WHIP	ERA	DRA	WARP	PF
2016	GRL	A	21	0	0	0	8	4	16	3	0	3.4	11.2	20	72%	.094	0.56	0.00	3.32	0.3	96
2017	RCU	A+	22	2	1	0	9	9	38^{2}	26	0	3.7	11.4	49	64%	.286	1.09	3.72	2.78	1.1	108
2017	TUL	AA	22	1	1	0	7	7	28	17	2	4.2	10.0	31	51%	.217	1.07	2.57	3.08	0.7	106
2018	TUL	AA	23	6	7	0	22	22	105^{1}	114	12	2.9	7.5	88	49%	.317	1.41	4.53	5.32	0.0	107
2019	*LAN*	*MLB*	*24*	*6*	*6*	*0*	*21*	*21*	87^{2}	*79*	*12*	*3.6*	*8.4*	*82*	*49%*	*.291*	*1.30*	*4.46*	*4.98*	*0.3*	*97*

Breakout: 11% Improve: 20% Collapse: 11% Attrition: 25% MLB: 41% *Comparables: Kyle Weiland, Blake Wood, Scott Barlow*

The Report: White is coming off of another season where he missed a good chunk of time due to rehab from injury. When he was on the field, he didn't look quite like the guy we've pumped more aggressively in the past.

White sat in the low 90's with a flat fastball. His cutter flashed above average, but was inconsistent. His upper-70s breaking ball flashed above-average with traditional curveball break, but again the quality was inconsistent and hitters often took advantage. White also threw a below average mid-80s change that he showed consistent feel for, though it lacked quality tumble.

Athleticism is the hardest thing to find again after injury and it plays an important part with pitchers. The velocity, arm speed, and body control play vital roles in pitch quality and command. If White can stay healthy and regain some of the athleticism that the injuries have sapped, it's possible that his breaking ball and cutter could tick up. Until then the profile looks much more like a middle reliever mix where his velocity and arm speed could play up in short stints.

The Risks: High. Injuries and inconsistent mechanics have taken a bite out of White's stuff. His final Double-A appearances were kinda ugly, and he never quite looked like the pitcher who evaluators saw earlier in his career.

Ben Carsley's Fantasy Take: White had some prospect helium a year or two ago. If someone in your league hasn't been paying attention and wants to pay for him based on name value, take advantage. Otherwise you can pass.

10 Josiah Gray RHP

OFP: 50 Likely: 45 ETA: 2021

Born: 12/21/97 Age: 21 Bats: R Throws: R Height: 6'1" Weight: 190 Origin: Round 2, 2018 Draft (#72 overall)

YEAR	TEAM	LVL	AGE	W	L	SV	G	GS	IP	H	HR	BB/9	K/9	K	GB%	BABIP	WHIP	ERA	DRA	WARP	PF
2018	GRV	RK	20	2	2	0	12	12	52[1]	29	1	2.9	10.1	59	38%	.219	0.88	2.58	2.98	1.7	102
2019	*LAN*	*MLB*	*21*	*2*	*3*	*0*	*7*	*7*	*34*	*34*	*6*	*5.1*	*8.3*	*31*	*38%*	*.307*	*1.56*	*5.39*	*6.05*	*-0.3*	*97*

Breakout: 0% Improve: 0% Collapse: 0% Attrition: 0% MLB: 0% *Comparables: Thyago Vieira, John Gant, Vincent Velasquez*

The Report: Gray has the rawness you'd expect from a cold-weather, young-for-his-class college arm who converted from shortstop. The raw arm strength is there. He sat in the low-90s his last year in college, but in the pros Gray found a bit more velocity as a starter in the Appy, if not quite as much as he showed on the Cape in 2017. He gets good sink on the pitch as well, despite his height and a slot a tick below three-quarters. His best secondary is an advanced low-80s slider that shows plus tilt with late tail, while the changeup is going to need significant refinement. Gray is a premium athlete with big arm speed, but there is effort in his mechanics and he throws across his body a bit. Given the slot, present change, and the better velocity he's shown in relief, Gray might be best-suited for the late innings. For now, he needs starter's reps more than a quicker track to the majors.

The Risks: High. Cold-weather arm, significant reliever risk, only a short season track record.

Bret Sayre's Fantasy Take: If you're looking for an arm to gamble on 50 picks into a dynasty draft this offseason, Gray's not a bad name to keep in mind. That said, the better advice might be to not take a pitcher at all.

The Next Five:

11 Jeren Kendall OF

Born: 02/04/96 Age: 23 Bats: L Throws: R Height: 6'0" Weight: 190 Origin: Round 1, 2017 Draft (#23 overall)

YEAR	TEAM	LVL	AGE	PA	R	2B	3B	HR	RBI	BB	K	SB	CS	AVG/OBP/SLG	DRC+	VORP	BABIP	BRR	FRAA	WARP	PF
2017	GRL	A	21	155	21	5	7	2	18	13	42	5	8	.221/.290/.400	79	2.0	.299	-0.6	CF(24) 3.5, RF(5) -0.4	0.1	99
2018	RCU	A+	22	494	68	20	3	12	42	52	158	37	14	.215/.300/.356	66	6.6	.305	2.5	CF(92) 1.1, RF(8) 0.8	-1.0	108
2019	*LAN*	*MLB*	*23*	*252*	*25*	*5*	*2*	*6*	*21*	*15*	*91*	*8*	*4*	*.139/.190/.259*	*17*	*-14.7*	*.188*	*1.2*	*CF 0, RF 0*	*-1.5*	*97*

Breakout: 3% Improve: 4% Collapse: 0% Attrition: 4% MLB: 4% *Comparables: Keon Broxton, Adam Engel, Drew Stubbs*

You'd have to look real hard and far for a prospect who had a poorer showing in 2018 than Kendall. His obvious physicality and raw tools remain intact, as Kendall boasts twitchy athleticism and excellent speed in space. While he's still developing his instincts in center, he's fairly quick in his reads and his burst catapults him into hot pursuit of balls in any direction. It's an above-average glove up the middle, with plenty of arm to go with it. There's impressive wiry strength on his frame, too; when he squares a ball in BP the raw power'll flirt with plus.

The swing and approach are just... well, they're awful. His setup is unworkable, with low, stiff hands and no rhythm at all into his load. The weight transfer is wildly inconsistent, the swing length is all over the place, and he has no recourse to alter or cut off a swing once initiated. He doesn't see left-handers at all, he shows below-average recognition of breaking stuff below the zone from either hand, and he'll swing through fat in-zone fastballs from righties with the best of 'em. Most problematically, he demonstrated no ability to buy in to, or really even attempt, necessary adjustments at any point during a full season in High-A. This placement is conditional, to the degree that the tools remain quite loud and in line with the 1:1 potential he once held. But he needs to make a whole bunch of progress with the bat pretty quickly to keep pace, and it currently looks less likely than ever that he one day approaches his lofty ceiling.

12 Jeter Downs SS

Born: 07/27/98 Age: 20 Bats: R Throws: R Height: 5'11" Weight: 180 Origin: Round 1, 2017 Draft (#32 overall)

YEAR	TEAM	LVL	AGE	PA	R	2B	3B	HR	RBI	BB	K	SB	CS	AVG/OBP/SLG	DRC+	VORP	BABIP	BRR	FRAA	WARP	PF
2017	BIL	RK	18	209	31	3	3	6	29	27	32	8	5	.267/.370/.424	97	12.9	.288	-1.5	SS(50) -4.5	-0.1	104
2018	DYT	A	19	524	63	23	2	13	47	52	103	37	10	.257/.351/.402	122	23.2	.306	-1.6	2B(73) -2.9, SS(43) -9.3	0.8	102
2019	*LAN*	*MLB*	*20*	*252*	*29*	*2*	*0*	*8*	*21*	*15*	*67*	*8*	*2*	*.158/.213/.265*	*31*	*-11.4*	*.181*	*0.6*	*2B -1, SS -2*	*-1.5*	*97*

Breakout: 15% Improve: 17% Collapse: 0% Attrition: 7% MLB: 17% *Comparables: Delino DeShields, Dilson Herrera, Jorge Polanco*

Downs, the Reds' CBA pick from 2017, found his defensive home this season at second base. Stretched at short, his athleticism allowed for a smooth transition to the keystone. Falling down the defensive hierarchy puts more pressure on his bat, which projects to fringe-average. The good news is that Downs' power continues to develop beyond what scouts projected on draft day. He's not a big guy, but he has above-average bat speed and a swing that generates loft. All the tools grade out close to average, which suggests a career as a second-division starter or solid utilityman.

13 Edwin Rios IF

Born: 04/21/94 Age: 25 Bats: L Throws: R Height: 6'3" Weight: 220 Origin: Round 6, 2015 Draft (#192 overall)

YEAR	TEAM	LVL	AGE	PA	R	2B	3B	HR	RBI	BB	K	SB	CS	AVG/OBP/SLG	DRC+	VORP	BABIP	BRR	FRAA	WARP	PF
2016	GRL	A	22	128	17	8	1	6	13	8	44	3	1	.252/.305/.487	110	7.6	.348	0.0	3B(20) -0.1, 1B(9) 0.6	0.3	94
2016	RCU	A+	22	188	37	11	1	16	46	8	35	0	0	.367/.394/.712	188	30.3	.383	1.0	3B(20) 1.1, 1B(18) 0.9	1.9	95
2016	TUL	AA	22	135	14	7	0	5	17	8	31	0	0	.254/.304/.434	103	5.3	.292	0.1	3B(28) 0.8, 1B(4) 0.2	0.3	101
2017	TUL	AA	23	332	47	21	0	15	62	17	69	1	1	.317/.358/.533	139	23.7	.363	0.9	3B(38) -4.1, 1B(28) 1.8	1.1	107
2017	OKL	AAA	23	190	23	13	0	9	29	18	42	0	1	.296/.368/.533	122	9.0	.345	-2.6	1B(33) 0.6, 3B(9) -1.0	0.3	103
2018	OKL	AAA	24	341	45	25	0	10	55	23	110	0	1	.304/.355/.482	116	16.5	.433	-2.4	3B(38) -4.2, 1B(28) -1.3	0.1	97
2019	*LAN*	*MLB*	*25*	*34*	*4*	*2*	*0*	*1*	*4*	*2*	*10*	*0*	*0*	*.244/.289/.424*	*86*	*0.3*	*.318*	*-0.1*	*LF 0*	*0.1*	*97*

Breakout: 12% Improve: 32% Collapse: 9% Attrition: 41% MLB: 61% *Comparables: J.D. Davis, Russ Canzler, Neftali Soto*

Look, it's an ugly profile. You know it, we know it, everyone knows it. Rios is graceful, but in a big-bodied, lumbering kind of way that just doesn't really cut it quickness-wise at his most frequent position to date, third base. He saw some time in left last year, but bottom-of-the-scale speed really limits the utility out there, too. He's smooth and steady-handed at first, and that helps offset some of the range limitations. Still, the glove's not really an asset there either.

At the dish his approach is aggressive in the zone, as he'll consistently offer at early-count strikes. He works with a long, majestic, flowing swing that relies on exceptional timing and hand-eye to work, and that's usually problematic against high-level pitching. There's a "but," though, and that's why he's here. He'll show the right kind of timing and hand-eye on the regular, and he has continued to hit at every stop along the way. He's strong enough to muscle balls to vacant patches of grass, and he's smart enough to go with balls where they're pitched. The power is the light-tower kind. He's carried an above-average offensive profile all the way to the doorstep of the big leagues, as his type is asked to do, and the skills are there for him to take it to the highest level when the opportunity arises.

14 Connor Wong C

Born: 05/19/96 Age: 23 Bats: R Throws: R Height: 6'1" Weight: 181 Origin: Round 3, 2017 Draft (#100 overall)

YEAR	TEAM	LVL	AGE	PA	R	2B	3B	HR	RBI	BB	K	SB	CS	AVG/OBP/SLG	DRC+	VORP	BABIP	BRR	FRAA	WARP	PF
2017	GRL	A	21	107	19	6	0	5	18	7	26	1	1	.278/.336/.495	125	7.2	.328	0.0	C(27) 0.2	0.7	101
2018	RCU	A+	22	431	64	20	2	19	60	38	138	6	2	.269/.350/.480	114	27.8	.372	0.9	C(71) 0.7, 2B(11) -0.5	1.2	108
2019	*LAN*	*MLB*	*23*	*252*	*24*	*9*	*0*	*10*	*31*	*12*	*89*	*0*	*0*	*.189/.233/.354*	*57*	*-3.0*	*.249*	*-0.5*	*C 0, 2B 0*	*-0.3*	*97*

Breakout: 7% Improve: 15% Collapse: 1% Attrition: 9% MLB: 17% *Comparables: Eric Haase, Jacob Nottingham, Peter O'Brien*

The Dodgers draft athletic catchers will multi-position utility as often as they breathe these days, and the club's third-rounder in 2017 fits the mold to a T. He shows decent receiving chops already, with a strong glove hand that'll hold true around the margins of the zone, though he'll lose focus on the endeavor from time to time and muff balls off the webbing. His blocking technique is similarly inconsistent. There's plenty of agility and body control to suggest (potentially rapid) development, however, and he did indeed show better as the season progressed. The story's the same on his catch-and-throw, as he'll need to tighten up his pop in order to keep an average arm playing acceptably. The good news is that he has the physical tools to do all of these things.

At the plate, his right-handed swing is relatively compact, with surprising strength and situational loft. His AB's aren't always pretty, as he'll get coaxed into expanding the zone and swinging non-competitively on his share of pitches. But he also demonstrates an ability to make quick adjustments within at-bats and come right back to barrel something up a pitch or two later. The hit tool's likely to remain on the fringier side, but there's enough pop and baseline athleticism—he's also a solid-average runner with a frame to hold speed—that the sum of the parts can round into a useful player with passable skills behind the dish and additional versatility around the infield dirt. Double-A will test him, and it may take a bit of time for everything to come together, but there's nice raw material here.

15 Jordan Sheffield RHP

Born: 06/01/95 Age: 24 Bats: R Throws: R Height: 5'10" Weight: 190 Origin: Round 1, 2016 Draft (#36 overall)

YEAR	TEAM	LVL	AGE	W	L	SV	G	GS	IP	H	HR	BB/9	K/9	K	GB%	BABIP	WHIP	ERA	DRA	WARP	PF
2016	GRL	A	21	0	1	0	7	7	11	11	2	4.9	10.6	13	43%	.346	1.55	4.09	3.25	0.2	95
2017	GRL	A	22	3	7	0	20	20	89¹	86	9	4.2	9.2	91	43%	.320	1.43	4.03	4.08	1.3	100
2017	RCU	A+	22	0	2	0	5	4	18	23	2	7.5	9.0	18	40%	.375	2.11	8.00	4.84	0.1	103
2018	RCU	A+	23	1	3	0	14	7	34	39	8	5.3	10.6	40	44%	.337	1.74	6.88	4.83	0.2	115
2019	*LAN*	*MLB*	*24*	*3*	*3*	*0*	*16*	*11*	*46*	*44*	*7*	*4.8*	*8.7*	*44*	*40%*	*.308*	*1.50*	*4.94*	*5.54*	*-0.1*	*97*

Breakout: 7% Improve: 9% Collapse: 3% Attrition: 12% MLB: 15% *Comparables: Matt Marksberry, Chris Narveson, Jon Huber*

Sheffield battled a forearm strain that cost him half the year and jettisoned him to the bullpen upon return, and he never really looked quite right on either end of the layoff, even as the bullpen role appeared to suit him better. A smaller-sized righty, Sheffield's delivery at present lacks the kind of cohesion and simplicity to suit his frame, and the result is a command profile that flutters at best and dips precipitously from there. The bet here is on the raw stuff, and it is among the system's best. He'll sit mid-90s and hump it up to 98, and while the pitch lacks consistent movement, it'll flash ride and finish consistently enough to dream on. He draws out tight, late break on a slider he'll toggle down into a lower velocity band to land in the zone, and it can miss bats when he takes it down below. There's a changeup that projects for occasional utility, too. Similar to his Quakes (and former Vanderbilt) teammate Kendall, there's too much talent to write him off just yet. The shadows are creeping up right quick, though.

Others of note:

Yadier Alvarez, RHP

On raw stuff, Alvarez remains at or near the top of the system. The problem is that he still only possesses raw stuff, and has not yet demonstrated a sustained interest in putting in the work to refine it. Throwing high-90s comes as natural to Alvarez as breathing; the delivery is beautifully efficient and it should be relatively low-maintenance. It's not, though. He consistently runs into subtle timing issues along the way, leading to poor command in the zone and control around it. It's still easy enough to see the on-paper justification for the $12 million the Dodgers paid him a couple years back, but that outlay (and its matching luxury tax penalty) increasingly looks like a sunk cost. The club flirted with bringing him out of the bullpen at points last season, and that seems the likeliest route ahead. If things ever come together, it's a high-leverage ceiling.

Top Talents 25 and Under (born 4/1/93 or later):

1. Corey Seager
2. Walker Buehler
3. Cody Bellinger
4. Alex Verdugo
5. Dustin May
6. Julio Urias
7. Keibert Ruiz
8. Caleb Ferguson
9. Will Smith
10. Gavin Lux

The top three on this list still includes the same names that headlined last year's tour, though a full season of healthy domination by Walker Buehler and some sophomore exposure for Bellinger's bat sparked a mild rejiggering in our long-term valuation. Seager's lost season should not in any way, shape, or form dampen expectations for another monster season ahead as he returns to the fold fully healed.

Buehler emerged as a true heir of the Ace mantle in LA, which is no light claim for a team still featuring the greatest pitcher of his generation. The young fireballer matured considerably in his pitch design and execution through his first full-time run in the rotation, differentiating a cutter and slider to gain pitchability and increase his early-count, off-barrel contact. And he simultaneously added bat-missing utility in the process. Quite the trick.

For his part, Bellinger provided valuable versatility between first base and center. While pitchers were able to adjust and beat him to his blind spots more regularly, his offensive drop-off still yielded a solidly above-average effort amidst a three-win season. He'll still be just 23 for most of 2019, and there's a reasonable case that he should have retained the second spot on this list. Ordinal quibbles aside, this remains one of the best young troikas under any club's control league-wide.

It's been a many-day's journey through the darkest of nights for former (and really still current) wunderkind Julio Urias. Despite just turning 22 last August, he's already worked his way back from a torn anterior capsule, and that he returned to the bump to sit just a tick-plus shy of his pre-injury velocity already is pretty dang incredible. It's a wildcard of an injury in longer terms, insofar as the list of comparables to survive and thrive off this particular surgery is not real long. But if the stuff and panache he showed once activated turns out to be his new normal, the Dodgers will take it in a heartbeat.

Caleb Ferguson's just a damn good young arm. After debuting in his standard starting role in early June he quickly emerged as a trusted option in Dave Roberts' bullpen during the dog days. The role suits his tough fastball and hard hook from the left side, and while big-league hitters rarely had the pleasure, there's enough changeup and utility against right-handers to suggest a higher ceiling still.

It all adds up to a nice annual reminder of just how well-positioned the Dodgers are to sustain their recent run of success into the foreseeable future. And while the minor-league system has thinned some, the top of it offers promise of a further-still extension of cost-controlled core talent well into the next decade.

Miami Marlins

The State of the System:

When you trade for a lot of high-variance players to rebuild your farm system, well... you don't always get the good end of the variance.

The Top Ten:

1 **Victor Victor Mesa** **OF** OFP: 60 Likely: 50 ETA: Could be as soon as 2019. Or it could not be.
Born: 07/20/96 Age: 22 Bats: R Throws: R Height: 6'0" Weight: 185 Origin: International Free Agent, 2018

The Report: I think everyone in baseball has made the Albert Almora comp by now, publicly and privately. We hate comps here at Baseball Prospectus, but this one makes sense. Like Almora, Victor Victor is a right-handed, defensively-minded center fielder who can hit, though not for much power. They're similarly built and they take a similar-looking swing.

It's not a perfect comparison, of course. We think Mesa will run more: He stole 40 bases in just 70 games in his last full season in Serie Nacional, and scuttlebutt had him putting up 60-yard-dash times in his private workout that would give him a couple grades of speed on Almora. And although there's broad agreement that Mesa will stick in center and can handle the bat, it remains to be seen whether he has Almora's keen overall baseball instincts. It's also probably worth noting when throwing this comp out that Almora would be playing more if the embarrassment of riches in the Cubs outfield didn't permit them to deploy him in a somewhat sheltered role. But if you're doing broad strokes, sure, it's an Albert Almora sort of profile.

The Risks: High. He hasn't played competitive baseball in a year. If he falls just a bit short of Almora's 2018 he might not be a regular. There's more disagreement on his power and speed projections than you'd like there to be. The quality of Serie Nacional has deteriorated enough that even the guys who have dominated there have needed to adjust to American pitching, and Mesa didn't always dominate there. There are all kinds of cultural and social challenges facing high-profile Cuban players coming over.

Bret Sayre's Fantasy Take: I'm a fan. Mesa is likely to make his strongest contributions in average and runs, as he should hit and hit at the top of the Marlins lineup in the not-to-distant future. He also has the speed to steal 30 bags if he so chooses, which only exacerbates the profile. If it all works, Mesa's upside probably looks pretty similar to 2018 Lorenzo Cain, who was a top-10 outfielder—which makes him a top-25 dynasty prospect and a strong candidate for the first pick in dynasty drafts this offseason.

2 Sandy Alcantara RHP OFP: 60 Likely: 50 ETA: Debuted in 2017

Born: 09/07/95 Age: 23 Bats: R Throws: R Height: 6'4" Weight: 170 Origin: International Free Agent, 2013

YEAR	TEAM	LVL	AGE	W	L	SV	G	GS	IP	H	HR	BB/9	K/9	K	GB%	BABIP	WHIP	ERA	DRA	WARP	PF
2016	PEO	A	20	5	7	0	17	17	90^1	78	4	4.5	11.9	119	46%	.333	1.36	4.08	3.09	2.1	99
2016	PMB	A+	20	0	4	0	6	6	32^1	25	0	3.9	9.5	34	52%	.294	1.21	3.62	2.78	1.0	87
2017	SFD	AA	21	7	5	0	25	22	125^1	125	13	3.9	7.6	106	46%	.305	1.43	4.31	4.95	0.3	103
2017	SLN	MLB	21	0	0	0	8	0	8^1	9	2	6.5	10.8	10	26%	.333	1.80	4.32	6.58	-0.1	94
2018	JUP	A+	22	0	0	0	3	3	11^1	10	0	4.0	6.4	8	62%	.294	1.32	3.97	6.50	-0.2	84
2018	NWO	AAA	22	6	3	0	19	19	115^2	107	10	3.0	6.8	88	50%	.283	1.25	3.89	4.08	1.9	90
2018	MIA	MLB	22	2	3	0	6	6	34	25	3	6.1	7.9	30	50%	.250	1.41	3.44	5.57	-0.1	84
2019	*MIA*	*MLB*	*23*	*4*	*5*	*0*	*13*	*13*	*69*	*61*	*8*	*4.0*	*8.4*	*64*	*45%*	*.291*	*1.33*	*4.27*	*5.03*	*0.2*	*90*

Breakout: 17% Improve: 26% Collapse: 15% Attrition: 36% MLB: 57% *Comparables: Jake Thompson, Archie Bradley, Scott Barnes*

The Report: Eligible by only eight innings, Alcantara has one of the most electric arms we'll cover this list cycle. His fastball sits in the mid-90s, can touch triple digits, and moves with wiffle-ball run and sink. Alcantara also features a power slider in the upper-80s that falls off the deck with late tilt. His changeup can be too firm, low-90s and just a bit of a runner, but it will flash good sink when he has feel for it. There's also a show-me curve he uses sparingly.

The stuff all comes free and easy from a fairly compact delivery. For a batter, an inning, sometimes even a start, Alcantara can look like a true front-of-the-rotation arm, but he struggles to command his stuff consistently. In part, that's because everything moves so much. The fastball can miss armside just because of the sheer amount of run. It's also not entirely clear that he knows where everything is going. Sometimes that means it's center cut at 96, and other times it means he's walking guys on four pitches. The command and third pitch issues might be mitigated some in the pen—that's always been a strong possibility for the profile—but the Marlins have every reason to let Alcantara figure it out in the rotation over the next couple seasons. The fallback late-inning role will still be there, and the rewards in the rotation could be significant.

The Risks: Low. He might not be a starter long term, but Alcantara has major-league stuff and should spend all of 2019 somewhere on the Marlins staff.

Bret Sayre's Fantasy Take: It's a tale as old as time. Probable starter with great stuff seeks consistent command. You know what to expect by now. There's about a 20 percent change Alcantara harnesses the stuff enough to be a strong SP3. There's about a 40 percent chance he's a starting pitcher who gets streamed at home in shallower leagues. There's about a 20 percent chance he's a closer, and, well, you don't care about the rest, really. Best realistic scenario is a 3.50 ERA with a strikeout per inning and a WHIP slightly better than shade-your-eyes level.

3 Monte Harrison OF OFP: 60 Likely: 50 ETA: 2020

Born: 08/10/95 Age: 23 Bats: R Throws: R Height: 6'3" Weight: 220 Origin: Round 2, 2014 Draft (#50 overall)

YEAR	TEAM	LVL	AGE	PA	R	2B	3B	HR	RBI	BB	K	SB	CS	AVG/OBP/SLG	DRC+	VORP	BABIP	BRR	FRAA	WARP	PF
2016	WIS	A	20	298	34	11	1	6	37	20	97	8	3	.221/.294/.337	78	0.4	.321	1.0	CF(48) -0.7, RF(14) 1.0	-0.2	107
2017	WIS	A	21	261	32	12	1	11	32	29	70	11	3	.265/.359/.475	132	21.9	.333	1.3	CF(62) 1.6	1.7	102
2017	CAR	A+	21	252	41	16	1	10	35	14	69	16	1	.278/.341/.487	126	21.4	.358	3.3	CF(27) -1.8, RF(18) 2.1	1.3	100
2018	JAX	AA	22	583	85	20	3	19	48	44	215	28	9	.240/.316/.399	96	28.5	.368	3.6	CF(121) -8.0, RF(14) 0.4	0.1	95
2019	*MIA*	*MLB*	*23*	*35*	*4*	*1*	*0*	*1*	*4*	*1*	*13*	*1*	*0*	*.185/.232/.332*	*57*	*-0.7*	*.265*	*0.1*	*LF 0*	*-0.1*	*90*

Breakout: 9% Improve: 19% Collapse: 4% Attrition: 15% MLB: 29% *Comparables: Trayce Thompson, Joe Benson, Franchy Cordero*

The Report: Double-A was always going to be a tough test for Harrison after his breakout 2017 season. The premium athleticism is still present, but less of a carrying tool in the upper minors. Not that it hurts mind you; Harrison is a plus runner with a plus arm and he can still outrun any mistakes he might make with routes and reads in center. His raw power bumps the top of the scale now that he's filled out, and he has the kind of baseball body that makes our dear, departed Craig Goldstein mutter "hardware" involuntarily. All good so far, very good even.

The stat line above isn't egregiously bad for a still little-bit-raw prospect in his first season in Double-A. But here's the thing: Harrison struck out 215 times last season. That's… a lot. We've become a little inured to high K-rates in this era, and when you hit the ball as hard as Harrison does, a 30% K-rate might be manageable. Or, it would in the majors; this is 37% in the minors. A lot of it stems from timing issues, as Harrison tends to drift forward early in his swing and get out of sync. He also has issues recognizing quality spin as well. The athletic tools give him a floor, but if you want a picture of how it might go bad at the highest level, look no further than a guy he was traded with, Lewis Brinson. I'm going to float Harrison for another year because the tools are so loud (and I tend to be enamored with this profile like with, uh, Lewis Brinson), but the bust risk is real.

The Risks: High. On the one hand, Harrison has a broad base of athletic skills and he'll be an above-average defensive center fielder. With that as a baseline, he won't have to hit that much to have some sort of major league career. On the other hand, he struck out 215 times in the Southern League.

Bret Sayre's Fantasy Take: Congrats to those of you who traded Harrison away after his breakout 2017 season. Condolences to those of you who didn't. The speed is still the selling point, and Harrison has long had the baserunning acumen to match, which could help him push 25-30 steals in the majors. The power will be dampened a little by his home park, but not nearly as much as the wind power he generates at the plate. If he's a 20/20 guy with a .220 average, that's likely a borderline top-40 outfielder, and makes Harrison a very borderline top-101 dynasty prospect.

4 Isan Diaz 2B

OFP: 60 Likely: 50 ETA: Late 2019

Born: 05/27/96 Age: 23 Bats: L Throws: R Height: 5'10" Weight: 185 Origin: Round 2, 2014 Draft (#70 overall)

YEAR	TEAM	LVL	AGE	PA	R	2B	3B	HR	RBI	BB	K	SB	CS	AVG/OBP/SLG	DRC+	VORP	BABIP	BRR	FRAA	WARP	PF
2016	WIS	A	20	587	71	34	5	20	75	72	148	11	8	.264/.358/.469	141	37.7	.332	2.5	SS(90) -0.1, 2B(41) 1.0	4.3	107
2017	CAR	A+	21	455	59	20	0	13	54	62	121	9	3	.222/.334/.376	105	14.8	.283	0.1	2B(58) -1.9, SS(32) -4.8	0.0	103
2018	JAX	AA	22	356	44	19	1	10	42	53	95	10	3	.245/.365/.418	122	22.5	.325	0.0	2B(82) 2.1	1.4	94
2018	NWO	AAA	22	155	19	4	4	3	14	15	45	4	0	.204/.281/.358	65	-2.0	.278	0.8	2B(35) -1.6	-0.4	95
2019	*MIA*	*MLB*	*23*	*35*	*4*	*1*	*0*	*1*	*4*	*4*	*11*	*0*	*0*	*.200/.286/.360*	*64*	*-0.3*	*.269*	*0.0*	*2B 0*	*0.0*	*90*

Breakout: 7% Improve: 14% Collapse: 2% Attrition: 7% MLB: 17% *Comparables: Carlos Asuaje, Brandon Lowe, Travis Denker*

The Report: The package the Marlins got back for Christian Yelich was "high-variance" as top prospect packages go, and the Fish generally got the short end of the production projection in 2018. Diaz arguably had the best overall performance with the stick, but he also has the least defensive value—average second baseman—while both Brinson and Harrison could be plus center fielders. So there will be more pressure generally on Diaz's bat, and there was actually plenty to like this year, even if the top line numbers won't wow you.

Diaz offers plus raw power from a relatively compact swing. There's enough muscle and lift to it that he can get beat in the zone, but he has a decent approach at the plate and better bat control than you'd think. He's strong enough to dump hits into the outfield off his mistakes, and while he's likely to be Three-True-Outcomish, there's a decent shot at a solid-average hit tool due to the quality of his contact. In the field, Diaz gets it done. He isn't the slickest fielder in the world, but the actions and arm are fine for the keystone.

The Risks: High. Upper minors arms didn't show much mercy for this Diaz brother, and the swing-and-miss might never allow enough of the raw power into games to carry a starting role.

Bret Sayre's Fantasy Take: Diaz's time as a fantasy-relevant prospect has outlasted the TINO Podcast, on which Mauricio Rubio fawned over him on multiple occasions as a teenager. Now older and seemingly less interesting, just like the rest of us, Diaz is on the cusp of being lineup ready. Don't let the prospect fatigue get to you. For my money, Diaz is the second-best fantasy prospect in this system and has the power/speed potential of Harrison on the infield and without the extreme strikeout rate.

5 Nick Neidert RHP   OFP: 55   Likely: 50   ETA: Late 2019

Born: 11/20/96 Age: 22 Bats: R Throws: R Height: 6'1" Weight: 180 Origin: Round 2, 2015 Draft (#60 overall)

YEAR	TEAM	LVL	AGE	W	L	SV	G	GS	IP	H	HR	BB/9	K/9	K	GB%	BABIP	WHIP	ERA	DRA	WARP	PF
2016	CLN	A	19	7	3	0	19	19	91	75	7	1.3	6.8	69	41%	.262	0.97	2.57	3.67	1.5	97
2017	MOD	A+	20	10	3	0	19	19	104^{1}	95	7	1.5	9.4	109	43%	.318	1.07	2.76	3.16	2.6	98
2017	ARK	AA	20	1	3	0	6	6	23^{1}	33	4	1.9	5.0	13	47%	.341	1.63	6.56	4.19	0.3	97
2018	JAX	AA	21	12	7	0	26	26	152^{2}	142	17	1.8	9.1	154	47%	.309	1.13	3.24	3.79	2.8	96
2019	*MIA*	*MLB*	*22*	*7*	*8*	*0*	*25*	*25*	123^{1}	*113*	*14*	*2.3*	*7.9*	*108*	*41%*	*.294*	*1.17*	*3.84*	*4.54*	*1.1*	*90*

Breakout: 16% Improve: 29% Collapse: 13% Attrition: 27% MLB: 54%   *Comparables: Alex White, Erasmo Ramirez, Aaron Poreda*

The Report: Welcome to the "pitchability righty" portion of the list. Neidert has a bit of funk and deception in his delivery, and it looks almost like he's throwing darts up there. He's no baz on the mound though, as Neidert has above-average command of his low-90s fastball. It's a heavy fastball and there is some tail and riding life when he elevates it. His best secondary is an above-average change that fades and sinks, and it plays to grade in part because he maintains his armspeed on the pitch.

Neidert's slider has improved this year and gives him a swing-and-miss option against righties. It can get a little slurvy, but there's good two-plane action when he stays on top of it and gets it down and out of the zone. He can also backdoor it to lefties. Neidert's curve is below-average, a humpy 12-6 that tends to show a bit early, but gives him another look to steal a strike with here and there. Despite the unorthodox delivery, he is a strike thrower, although the best pitch here is a 55, and he will have fine margins with his command against the best hitters in the world.

The Risks: Low. While Neidert may not offer the most potential impact of the arms on this list, he's pitched well in the upper minors. These profiles aren't safe per se—sometimes the pitchability dudes without a clear plus offering get Aaron Blair'd—but Neidert is major-league-ready and can get you out in a few different ways.

Bret Sayre's Fantasy Take: Welcome to five years of fantasy experts telling you that Neidert is a great matchups guy against crappy teams at home. They'll also spell his name "N-i-e-d-e-r-t" at least 20 percent of the time.

6 Connor Scott OF   OFP: 55   Likely: 45   ETA: 2022

Born: 10/08/99 Age: 19 Bats: L Throws: L Height: 6'4" Weight: 180 Origin: Round 1, 2018 Draft (#13 overall)

YEAR	TEAM	LVL	AGE	PA	R	2B	3B	HR	RBI	BB	K	SB	CS	AVG/OBP/SLG	DRC+	VORP	BABIP	BRR	FRAA	WARP	PF
2018	MRL	RK	18	119	15	1	4	0	8	14	29	8	5	.223/.319/.311	89	0.5	.307	-1.2	CF(22) -1.6	-0.4	104
2018	GRB	A	18	89	4	2	0	1	5	10	27	1	3	.211/.295/.276	58	-2.5	.300	-1.9	CF(22) -3.0	-0.8	104
2019	*MIA*	*MLB*	*19*	*252*	*20*	*1*	*0*	*5*	*16*	*11*	*93*	*2*	*2*	*.121/.159/.193*	*-14*	*-25.0*	*.166*	*0.0*	*CF -3*	*-3.0*	*90*

Breakout: 6% Improve: 8% Collapse: 0% Attrition: 3% MLB: 10%   *Comparables: Carlos Tocci, Engel Beltre, Nomar Mazara*

The Report: I get Mickey Moniak vibes from Scott, which makes for an interesting comp. It doesn't reallllllllly fit the profile, mind you. Scott is taller, much more physical, more projectable, less likely to stick in center field, much less polished with the stick. There are some similarities with the swing though: They both bail out at times and get a little long and hitchy with the hand path. They are both plus runners, although Scott is more likely to fill out and slow down and he's looked lost in center field at times.

We at the BP Prospect Team have always contended that the problem with Moniak the prospect—well other than the lack of production or projection so far—was that he went 1.1. If he had gone, say, 13th overall like Scott, the conversation around him would be different. But the "1.1 prep outfielder" has a connotation. Scott even looks that part more, one could argue. It's a classic projectable frame with some plus tools. He'll flash really loud contact at times. The swing is more geared for power too. The rawness against A-ball arms is more acceptable for the 13th overall pick.

In each case, the underlying problem is the same: Both just need to hit more. Scott didn't have the plus-plus projection on the hit tool coming out of the showcase circuit, which makes his production thus far seem less dire. Before this turns into "What we talk about when we talk about prep outfielders," Scott isn't the same prospect Moniak was post-draft, but they may both end up fourth outfielders in the end. Only one will be considered a true draft disappointment when that happens.

The Risks: Extreme. Scott is a polarizing prospect with variance way beyond his written OFP/Likely here. He may not hit at all (and hasn't so far). He may end up in a corner. He may grow into a plus regular. We likely won't know for a while.

Bret Sayre's Fantasy Take: It's far easier for dynasty owners to take the risk on prospects like Scott because there are always more coming. In a deep 2018 dynasty draft class, Scott has the tools of someone who should be taken in the back of the first round, and while the (very) early returns weren't super encouraging, he'll be 19 for all of the 2019 season and will get to grow into full-season ball. There's five-tool potential here and an OF2 ceiling to boot.

7 Zac Gallen RHP

OFP: 55 Likely: 45 ETA: 2019

Born: 08/03/95 Age: 23 Bats: R Throws: R Height: 6'2" Weight: 191 Origin: Round 3, 2016 Draft (#106 overall)

YEAR	TEAM	LVL	AGE	W	L	SV	G	GS	IP	H	HR	BB/9	K/9	K	GB%	BABIP	WHIP	ERA	DRA	WARP	PF
2016	CRD	RK	20	0	0	1	6	3	9^{2}	7	0	0.0	14.0	15	48%	.333	0.72	1.86	1.29	0.5	88
2017	PMB	A+	21	5	2	0	9	9	55^{2}	44	1	1.6	9.1	56	48%	.283	0.97	1.62	3.39	1.2	92
2017	SFD	AA	21	4	5	0	13	13	71^{1}	76	8	2.4	5.3	42	42%	.292	1.33	3.79	4.08	0.9	105
2017	MEM	AAA	21	1	1	0	4	4	20^{2}	18	2	2.6	10.0	23	47%	.314	1.16	3.48	4.02	0.4	101
2018	NWO	AAA	22	8	9	0	25	25	133^{1}	148	14	3.2	9.2	136	41%	.351	1.47	3.64	3.95	2.4	94
2019	*MIA*	*MLB*	*23*	*6*	*8*	*0*	*22*	*22*	118^{2}	*110*	*16*	*3.2*	*8.8*	*116*	*42%*	*.302*	*1.27*	*4.14*	*4.88*	*0.6*	*90*

Breakout: 11% Improve: 15% Collapse: 9% Attrition: 21% MLB: 27% *Comparables: Taylor Guerrieri, Alex Cobb, Brady Rodgers*

The Report: I'd be tempted to cut-and-paste the Neidert report here, but there are a few subtle differences in the profiles. Gallen works primarily off a fastball/cutter combo that sit either side of 90 mph. The lean righty is a good athlete who repeats his delivery well. His upright landing and near-OTT slot gives the fastball some plane, and you'll occasionally see some armside wiggle as well.

Gallen has above-average command of both the fastball and cutter and is quite effective when working down in the zone. The fastball can be a bit hittable up, where it tends to flatten out. The cutter works well off the fastball and features late, tight tilt. He rounds out his arsenal with a fringy change and curve. Four offerings either side of average and above-average command is not the most exciting profile, but Gallen has had success all the way up the ladder, and the cutter should miss enough bats to make him an effective backend starter.

The Risks: Low. While Gallen may not offer the most potential impact of the arms on this list, he's pitched well in the upper minors. These profiles aren't safe per se—sometimes the pitchability dudes without a clear plus offering get Aaron Blair'd—but Gallen is major-league-ready and can get you out in a few different ways.

Bret Sayre's Fantasy Take: There have been pitchers like this who have turned into mixed-league types, but odds are Gallen simply ends up as a solid NL-only starter, who is just slightly outpacing the stronger setup relievers in fantasy value. The short-term opportunity is there in Miami as well. Also, just like Aaron Blair, Gallen will always be a lefty to me.

8 Jorge Guzman RHP

OFP: 55 Likely: 45 ETA: 2020; could move quickly with spring pen conversion.

Born: 01/28/96 Age: 23 Bats: R Throws: R Height: 6'2" Weight: 182 Origin: International Free Agent, 2014

YEAR	TEAM	LVL	AGE	W	L	SV	G	GS	IP	H	HR	BB/9	K/9	K	GB%	BABIP	WHIP	ERA	DRA	WARP	PF
2016	AST	RK	20	1	1	0	7	4	17^{1}	4	0	5.2	13.0	25	77%	.129	0.81	3.12	3.03	0.5	90
2016	GRV	RK	20	2	3	0	6	4	22^{2}	25	1	2.8	11.5	29	56%	.387	1.41	4.76	2.29	0.8	94
2017	STA	A-	21	5	3	0	13	13	66^{2}	51	4	2.4	11.9	88	55%	.311	1.03	2.30	2.14	2.4	89
2018	JUP	A+	22	0	9	0	21	21	96	84	7	6.0	9.5	101	40%	.303	1.54	4.03	4.95	0.4	91
2019	*MIA*	*MLB*	*23*	*4*	*7*	*0*	*18*	*18*	78^{1}	*72*	*12*	*5.8*	*9.1*	*79*	*44%*	*.301*	*1.56*	*5.15*	*6.05*	*-0.7*	*90*

Breakout: 2% Improve: 2% Collapse: 2% Attrition: 2% MLB: 4% *Comparables: Steve Johnson, J.A. Happ, Josh Outman*

The Report: Guzman was the main piece in the Giancarlo Stanton trade last winter, and his first year in full-season ball likely wasn't good enough to dissuade people that it was a salary dump on the Marlins part. But if you catch Guzman on the right day, you'll wonder how anyone squares him up (and on the wrong day, you'll wonder why anyone swings at all). The elite velocity is still there, as Guzman sat in the upper-90s as a starter and routinely touched triple digits. Despite the easy cheese, his command and movement are both below-average. His arm action is compact and quick, but the fastball comes out with all the accuracy of a toddler holding a firehose.

Guzman's best secondary is a power breaker in the mid-80s that flashes plus, but the feel and shape will come and go. He offers a firm change that touches 90 as well. This is a standard power right-handed relief arsenal, but we don't know yet if the control will play better in short bursts. He'll be 23 in 2019 and hasn't pitched in the upper minors yet, so there's more uncertainty than you'd want in this profile.

The Risks: High. Given Guzman's stuff and age you'd expect him to have been more dominant in the Florida State League, and he's a high probability reliever where 100 mph isn't as special as it once was.

Bret Sayre's Fantasy Take: There's way more name recognition with Guzman than actual dynasty value, so if you can get something useful for him, I'd advise it. The odds of him surviving into the majors as a half-decent starter are low.

9 Jordan Yamamoto RHP   OFP: 55   Likely: 45   ETA: 2020

Born: 05/11/96   Age: 23   Bats: R   Throws: R   Height: 6'0"   Weight: 185   Origin: Round 12, 2014 Draft (#356 overall)

YEAR	TEAM	LVL	AGE	W	L	SV	G	GS	IP	H	HR	BB/9	K/9	K	GB%	BABIP	WHIP	ERA	DRA	WARP	PF
2016	WIS	A	20	7	8	0	27	18	134^1	130	6	2.1	10.2	152	48%	.343	1.20	3.82	2.99	3.2	106
2017	CAR	A+	21	9	4	1	22	18	111	91	8	2.4	9.2	113	40%	.286	1.09	2.51	3.59	2.1	102
2018	JUP	A+	22	4	1	0	7	7	40^2	26	0	1.8	10.4	47	44%	.268	0.84	1.55	2.89	1.2	89
2018	MRL	RK	22	1	0	0	3	3	11	5	1	1.6	12.3	15	64%	.190	0.64	2.45	1.77	0.5	98
2018	JAX	AA	22	1	0	0	3	3	17	12	1	2.1	12.2	23	45%	.282	0.94	2.12	4.05	0.3	91
2019	*MIA*	*MLB*	*23*	*2*	*1*	*0*	*19*	*3*	32^1	*27*	*3*	*3.0*	*9.4*	*34*	*41%*	*.300*	*1.18*	*3.53*	*4.18*	*0.6*	*90*

Breakout: 6%   Improve: 9%   Collapse: 15%   Attrition: 20%   MLB: 33%   *Comparables: Austin Gomber, Jharel Cotton, Miguel Almonte*

The Report: Back to the low-90s we go with Yamamoto, although he posted a better K-rate than Guzman in 2018 with his array of average-to-solid-average stuff. Yamamoto is adept at spotting his fastball armside and there is a bit of wiggle that way as well. He'll work all four quadrants with the pitch, but it's a bit more hittable than you'd like if he isn't painting the corners.

You could make a case for the slider or change as his best secondary. The slider is more heavily-used and will flash plus, but it doesn't always invite chases gloveside due to his inconsistent command of it. It won't always show ideal depth either given his lower slot. Yamamoto often has good feel for the change, and there's a bit of fade to it, but it's not a true "pull the string" offering yet. He also throws a big, loopy curve which can dip into the upper-60s. It gives a different eye line and velo band for the hitters, but he has trouble manipulating its shape and location.

Yamamoto doesn't have an obvious bat-misser here, but he'll throw anything in any count. You can ding him for his height as well; the track record for short righties throwing in the low-90s is neither long nor inspiring, but he's another "greater-than-the-sum-of-his-parts" dude in this system. You'd bet on one of them working out at least?

The Risks: Medium. Yamamoto is a polished righty in the mold of Neidert and Gallen, but he has a longer injury history and a shorter track record of success in the upper minors.

Bret Sayre's Fantasy Take: There's some buzz around Yamamoto from his strong performance in the AFL, but he's still a poor bet to be more than an SP5 at peak, even with Marlins Park backing him. If he has a few seasons along the lines of the one Marco Gonzales just put up (don't laugh, Gonzales was a top-50 starter), it'll be a highly successful outcome.

10 Braxton Garrett LHP   OFP: 55   Likely: 45   ETA: 2022

Born: 08/05/97   Age: 21   Bats: L   Throws: L   Height: 6'3"   Weight: 190   Origin: Round 1, 2016 Draft (#7 overall)

YEAR	TEAM	LVL	AGE	W	L	SV	G	GS	IP	H	HR	BB/9	K/9	K	GB%	BABIP	WHIP	ERA	DRA	WARP	PF
2017	GRB	A	19	1	0	0	4	4	15^1	13	3	3.5	9.4	16	49%	.250	1.24	2.93	2.87	0.4	107
2019	*MIA*	*MLB*	*21*	*2*	*3*	*0*	*8*	*8*	35^1	*34*	*5*	*4.2*	*8.0*	*31*	*42%*	*.300*	*1.42*	*4.77*	*5.61*	*-0.1*	*90*

Breakout: 1%   Improve: 2%   Collapse: 1%   Attrition: 3%   MLB: 5%   *Comparables: Tyrell Jenkins, Elvis Araujo, Keury Mella*

The Report: "This space left intentionally blank" is not really going to fly in this format, but we don't have anything new to add to the Garrett report after he missed all of 2018 recovering from Tommy John surgery. He was one of my favorite arms in the 2016 draft, but that was two years ago, and he's made exactly four professional starts. The fastball wasn't overwhelming before the surgery, and his plus command projection may take awhile to come back after the surgery. There was a potential plus-plus curve that got him drafted in the top ten. Will it come back? We'll have a better idea next year. All of this is to say that I'm basically blindfolded and throwing a dart for rankings/role purposes here. Perhaps there is some merit to John Sickels throwing a C+ on all these TJ guys until they are back on a mound. Regardless, we seem to be writing more and more of them lately.

The Risks: Extreme. He still hasn't thrown a pitch in a live game since the Tommy John surgery, so the stuff/projection is still an open-ended question until 2019.

Bret Sayre's Fantasy Take: Garrett is an interesting name to keep an eye on in deep formats (think 250-300 prospects deep), as a return to form post-TJ could shoot him back up to a top-150-or-so dynasty prospect at this time next year. Just don't waste the roster spot yet.

The Next Five:

11 Trevor Rogers LHP

Born: 11/13/97 Age: 21 Bats: L Throws: L Height: 6'6" Weight: 185 Origin: Round 1, 2017 Draft (#13 overall)

YEAR	TEAM	LVL	AGE	W	L	SV	G	GS	IP	H	HR	BB/9	K/9	K	GB%	BABIP	WHIP	ERA	DRA	WARP	PF
2018	GRB	A	20	2	7	0	17	17	72²	86	4	3.3	10.5	85	48%	.394	1.56	5.82	4.46	0.6	102
2019	*MIA*	*MLB*	*21*	*3*	*4*	*0*	*12*	*12*	*54¹*	*53*	*7*	*3.9*	*8.5*	*51*	*41%*	*.312*	*1.40*	*4.31*	*5.08*	*0.1*	*90*

Breakout: 0% Improve: 0% Collapse: 0% Attrition: 0% MLB: 0% *Comparables: Robbie Ross, John Gant, Christian Friedrich*

The Marlins went back to the lefty prep pitcher well in the 2017 draft. Unlike Garrett, Rogers did pitch in 2018, but his results were poor. Is it fair to penalize bad performance more than no performance? Perhaps not, but Rogers confirmed a lot of the concerns I had about him as an amateur. Despite being a lefty projection bet, he's already 20 and still won't consistently show plus fastball velocity. Both secondaries—a change and a slurvy slider—remain below average, and it will take some squinting and a fair bit of projection to get them to 5s. "Tall pitcher" command issues remain. Rogers is still a project with some upside, but there's been little progress on the deliverables so far.

12 Brian Miller OF

Born: 08/20/95 Age: 23 Bats: L Throws: R Height: 6'1" Weight: 186 Origin: Round 1, 2017 Draft (#36 overall)

YEAR	TEAM	LVL	AGE	PA	R	2B	3B	HR	RBI	BB	K	SB	CS	AVG/OBP/SLG	DRC+	VORP	BABIP	BRR	FRAA	WARP	PF
2017	GRB	A	21	258	42	17	1	1	28	23	35	21	6	.322/.384/.416	146	15.7	.374	0.9	CF(35) 1.9, RF(13) -0.4	1.9	101
2018	JUP	A+	22	276	28	13	3	0	29	14	27	19	6	.324/.358/.398	124	17.0	.358	0.7	CF(33) -1.5, LF(19) 0.2	0.8	91
2018	JAX	AA	22	287	29	8	2	0	14	18	39	21	7	.267/.319/.313	88	4.1	.314	0.8	LF(49) 0.1, RF(12) 0.0	-0.3	96
2019	*MIA*	*MLB*	*23*	*252*	*29*	*8*	*1*	*4*	*19*	*8*	*45*	*11*	*3*	*.240/.264/.334*	*58*	*-3.5*	*.275*	*1.0*	*LF 1, CF 0*	*-0.2*	*90*

Breakout: 6% Improve: 10% Collapse: 0% Attrition: 7% MLB: 11% *Comparables: Ben Gamel, Alex Romero, Whit Merrifield*

There will be a lot of speedy, no-pop center field blurbs in the coming months. It's a continuum from 101 guys (The Manuel Margots and Magneuris Sierras) to the bench outfielders; I need to pad some of these lesser systems out to 6,000 words or so.

The underlying skill set won't change much. There will be below-average power (Miller has one home run in 185 career games). There will be above-average run times, plus centerfield glove projections, and then the question will be "how much will he actually hit?" We are not always great at divining this (see… uh, Manuel Margot and Magneuris Sierra), and this is not merely an excuse to spout one of my favorite mantras: "The hardest thing to project is the major-league hit tool." Okay, it's a little bit that, but this profile is specifically tricky due to the complete lack of power.

Miller has a very high contact rate now, but how good is that contact against premium stuff? If he's a .250 hitter, he's an up and down guy. If he's a .300 hitter, maybe he's Ben Revere. That's a hit a week, as Bull Durham taught us, "one groundball with eyes." Miller has the kind of inside-out, oppo-geared swing endemic to this profile, and you worry about the bat getting knocked out of his hands in the majors. The production already took a bit of a dip in Double-A. Sometimes you are just Zack Granite (sigh, I should probably double check his list eligibility).

13 Will Banfield C

Born: 11/18/99 Age: 19 Bats: R Throws: R Height: 6'0" Weight: 200 Origin: Round 2, 2018 Draft (#69 overall)

YEAR	TEAM	LVL	AGE	PA	R	2B	3B	HR	RBI	BB	K	SB	CS	AVG/OBP/SLG	DRC+	VORP	BABIP	BRR	FRAA	WARP	PF
2018	MRL	RK	18	94	7	8	1	0	14	7	28	0	1	.256/.330/.378	81	1.8	.375	-0.9	C(22) 1.2	0.0	105
2018	GRB	A	18	52	5	0	0	3	4	4	15	0	0	.208/.269/.396	77	0.7	.233	0.1	C(14) 0.1	0.0	105
2019	*MIA*	*MLB*	*19*	*252*	*16*	*5*	*0*	*6*	*22*	*6*	*94*	*0*	*0*	*.133/.154/.232*	*-6*	*-21.6*	*.179*	*-0.5*	*C 0*	*-2.3*	*90*

Breakout: 6% Improve: 8% Collapse: 0% Attrition: 4% MLB: 11% *Comparables: Francisco Pena, Nomar Mazara, Gleyber Torres*

A nice get in the second round of this year's draft, Banfield was regarded by some as the best prep catcher in the 2018 draft. You probably know how I feel about that general profile by now, but I will just mention that I have already made several unsuccessful attempts at repurposing boygenius lyrics for a player blurb ("Prep catcher in the rear view mirror / hasn't caught a thing yet / Batting practice souvenirs / Anything's worth trying").

Banfield breaks the usual mold a bit here due to his advanced defensive skills. He has plus arm strength, good footwork, a quick transfer, and polished receiving skills for his experience level. Although he's on the slender side for the position at present, there's the outline of the catcher body here—mostly in the butt. Instead the questions here are about the bat. Banfield has some pop—his first three hits in the Sally league were all bombs, but there's length and leverage to get it. There is substantial swing-and-miss risk here, but both the bat and glove have plenty of time to develop since you won't see Banfield in the majors until about the time the third boygenius album drops (one can hope).

14 Bryson Brigman SS

Born: 06/19/95 Age: 24 Bats: R Throws: R Height: 5'11" Weight: 180 Origin: Round 3, 2016 Draft (#87 overall)

YEAR	TEAM	LVL	AGE	PA	R	2B	3B	HR	RBI	BB	K	SB	CS	AVG/OBP/SLG	DRC+	VORP	BABIP	BRR	FRAA	WARP	PF
2016	EVE	A-	21	318	51	6	1	0	19	41	43	17	12	.260/.369/.291	121	11.0	.308	0.8	SS(51) -1.3, 2B(15) -0.2	0.6	108
2017	CLN	A	22	518	55	14	4	2	36	44	74	16	8	.235/.306/.296	78	3.9	.274	4.0	2B(80) 1.5, SS(35) -0.3	0.2	100
2018	MOD	A+	23	425	47	13	7	2	38	37	58	15	6	.304/.373/.391	129	36.2	.354	4.3	SS(83) -0.3, 2B(7) 1.2	2.4	96
2018	JUP	A+	23	77	9	4	0	0	5	3	13	4	0	.338/.368/.394	124	5.0	.407	-0.2	SS(16) 3.0	0.6	95
2018	JAX	AA	23	46	1	2	0	1	6	2	6	2	0	.310/.348/.429	105	1.6	.333	-0.2	2B(10) 0.0, SS(2) -0.1	0.0	100
2019	*MIA*	*MLB*	*24*	*252*	*24*	*2*	*1*	*5*	*18*	*14*	*52*	*3*	*1*	*.184/.229/.263*	*32*	*-10.9*	*.212*	*0.6*	*SS 1, 2B 0*	*-1.0*	*90*

Breakout: 30% Improve: 35% Collapse: 0% Attrition: 31% MLB: 37% *Comparables: Blake Trahan, James Beresford, Justin Sellers*

Having multiple ex-Mariners prospects dotting this list may speak to how far the Marlins still have to go with this rebuild, but Brigman started to show a bit with the stick to go with his slick glove. Acquired from Seattle as part of the Cameron Maybin deal, Brigman is an above-average defender with good range and enough arm to make most of the throws at the 6. He's more grinder than quick-twitch, but he has a good enough first step, above-average speed, and gets it done on the dirt.

Brigman finally started to hit for average this year as a 23-year-old in High-A, which might raise an eyebrow or two, but the profile at the plate supports it. He's a pesky type that prioritizes line-drive contact over power. He works oppo primarily, but can sting a ball pull-side now and again. Brigman profiles best as a fifth infielder due to the lack of game power and lingering questions about his bat against better pitching, but there's a non-zero chance he can be a table-setting middle infielder for a second-division team... like, say, the Marlins.

15 Jose Devers SS

Born: 12/07/99 Age: 19 Bats: L Throws: R Height: 6'0" Weight: 155 Origin: International Free Agent, 2016

YEAR	TEAM	LVL	AGE	PA	R	2B	3B	HR	RBI	BB	K	SB	CS	AVG/OBP/SLG	DRC+	VORP	BABIP	BRR	FRAA	WARP	PF
2017	DYA	RK	17	47	4	2	1	0	7	0	16	1	0	.239/.255/.326	55	-2.5	.367	-0.7	SS(7) 0.2, 2B(3) -0.1	-0.2	113
2017	YAN	RK	17	169	17	7	2	1	9	18	21	15	3	.246/.359/.348	123	10.4	.277	-2.9	SS(39) -0.4	0.2	92
2018	GRB	A	18	362	46	12	4	0	24	15	49	13	6	.273/.313/.332	92	4.0	.318	-2.6	SS(59) 2.2, 2B(15) 0.0	0.2	104
2019	*MIA*	*MLB*	*19*	*252*	*20*	*4*	*1*	*4*	*17*	*1*	*69*	*3*	*1*	*.166/.170/.237*	*5*	*-19.6*	*.208*	*0.2*	*SS -1, 2B 0*	*-2.1*	*90*

Breakout: 4% Improve: 6% Collapse: 0% Attrition: 3% MLB: 7% *Comparables: Carlos Triunfel, Alcides Escobar, Elvis Andrus*

Brigman and Devers make a neatly matched pair at the end of our ordinal rankings as glove-first middle infielders. Devers is a better defender—a clear everyday shortstop with the leather. He's a better runner as well, but the bat is less advanced and he's shown even less raw power than Brigman. Devers has also been young for his levels, so if you want to try and squint and see some projection in the bat through your age-relative-to-league colored glasses, we won't stop you. There's even a bit of physical projection left, although he's likely to always be on the skinny side; Rafael got all the Big Boy SZN genes in the family. You'd be forgiven for thinking that Jose fell off the Cesar Izturis family tree.

Others of note:

Tristan Pompey, OF, Advanced-A Jupiter

On the other hand, the Marlins third round pick—and Dalton's brother—didn't fall far from the family tree. A switch-hitting, quick twitch outfielder with fringe power projection, the younger Pompey handled his fairly aggressive A-ball assignments without issue. While a small sample, it was still a positive signpost after his poor showing with wood on the Cape the previous summer. He's susceptible to spin, and there's swing and miss issues generally, but if he can stay healthier than Dalton, he should slot into a bench outfielder role fairly quickly.

Joe Dunand, SS, Low-A Greensboro

Falling even in the same zip code as the A-Rod family tree would be a boon to any baseball prospect, though Dunand—Rodriguez's nephew—is more Brian-Anderson-lite than Alex-Rodriguez-lite. He's a shortstop for now, though his frame and limited range will shift him over to third base where the arm and glove will play as solid-average. Dunand struggled badly in his first taste of Double-A, but if he can get to enough of his plus raw power in games he could be a fringy third base option or corner infield bench bat.

Victor Mesa, OF, Did not play

Opportunities to see the 17-year-old play have been limited even by Cuban mystery player standards. I can tell you that he has a projectable body and a nice swing from the left side, but this has the look of an obvious package deal, with Victor Jr. along for the ride with Victor Victor (even though those are supposed to be banned). As we wrote when the Mesas signed, it's not even clear just yet whether the Marlins are going to have Victor Jr. hit from both sides or just the left. Truth be told, we wouldn't be writing him up here if he hadn't signed at the same time as his more regarded brother. He'll probably play in a complex league and we're likely a year or two away from even knowing if he's a few years away.

Top Talents 25 and Under (born 4/1/93 or later):

1. Victor Victor Mesa
2. Sandy Alcantara
3. Lewis Brinson
4. Brian Anderson
5. Trevor Richards
6. Monte Harrison
7. Isan Diaz
8. Nick Neidert
9. Magneuris Sierra
10. Connor Scott

I'll be honest and say that I don't have the slightest idea what to do with Lewis Brinson here; I can make the case for virtually any spot in the top ten. We've ranked him as a top 20 prospect in baseball for the last three years, but because of his swing length and pitch recognition issues there was always an unusually high delta in the hit tool for his ranks and levels. More than we'd have liked, there was some risk that he wouldn't hit.

Here today, it really, really looks like Brinson just can't hit major-league pitching; he has nearly a full season of combined playing time in the majors where he's hit .189 with 24 walks to 137 strikeouts. I can't even tell you that he's looked any better than that, because he hasn't. The other four tools still show up enough, but you can't steal first base. He's needed adjustment time before and came out the other side, and a summer hip problem is just enough of an injury excuse to give him a chance to re-run it all, so I'm hesitant to declare all hope lost and send him spiraling down quite as far as I sent Sierra. But I sure wouldn't make him the centerpiece of a Christian Yelich trade again, either.

Brian Anderson entered 2018 as a defense-first third baseman with raw power but questions about his overall hitting. He proceeded to spend much of the season in right field to accommodate, uh, Martin Prado and Miguel Rojas, and he put together an above-average offensive campaign that, in a down year for newcomers, might have won him the Rookie of the Year Award. The Marlins finally let Anderson settle in at third in August, and you'd think they'd just roll him out there for the next couple years. Alas, Prado is probably going to be back in 2019; sometimes paychecks drive decisions over player development. Anderson is already 25 and 2018 might be his peak if the power never spikes, but he's already a pretty nifty player.

We never put Trevor Richards on a prospect list here at Baseball Prospectus. He pitched four years at Division II Drury University, and even though any vaguely promising senior now gets popped for a small bonus in the draft for bonus manipulation these days, he went undrafted multiple times. Before entering organized baseball, he spent parts of two seasons in the independent Frontier League. He signed with the Marlins in the middle of 2016, initially to fill a bullpen spot in the short-season New York-Penn League. Just a season-and-a-half later, he won the Marlins fifth starter job out of camp, held it for most of the season, and struck out more than a batter per inning working off a dominant changeup. His fastball and breaking ball both remain fringy, but it's a hell of a change, and DRA thinks he was even better in 2018 than the traditional rates do. So we'll take our last best chance to plug him to the world on a list before he graduates with Anderson.

Magneuris Sierra had a nightmare season. There's no way to sugarcoat how bad he was: he compiled the fifth-worst position player WARP in the majors in just 156 plate appearances, and he didn't hit in Triple-A at all either. It was his age-22 season, so there's some time to recover, and he has enough secondary skills with his defensive prowess and speed to provide some reserve value even if the offense never rebounds. Yet he's in even more danger than Brinson of being lapped on the organizational depth chart.

With Brinson, Harrison, Sierra, and Guzman all running into roadblocks on the path to success, and nobody particularly making a leap in the other direction, we'd be remiss not to point out that the return on the Jeter-led firesale of Miami's incumbent MLB stars looks far worse today than it did last winter. Then again, accumulating talent was never the point there, was it?

Milwaukee Brewers

The State of the System:

While the Brew Crew did edge out the Cubs in the NL Central last year, they are going to fall just short of them in our org rankings. We don't think they'll mind.

The Top Ten:

1 **Keston Hiura 2B** OFP: 70 Likely: 60 ETA: Late 2019
Born: 08/02/96 Age: 22 Bats: R Throws: R Height: 5'11" Weight: 190 Origin: Round 1, 2017 Draft (#9 overall)

YEAR	TEAM	LVL	AGE	PA	R	2B	3B	HR	RBI	BB	K	SB	CS	AVG/OBP/SLG	DRC+	VORP	BABIP	BRR	FRAA	WARP	PF
2017	BRR	RK	20	72	18	3	5	4	18	6	13	0	2	.435/.500/.839	262	17.1	.500	0.5		0.7	104
2017	WIS	A	20	115	14	11	2	0	15	7	24	2	0	.333/.374/.476	138	10.3	.422	1.1	2B(3) -0.4	0.5	100
2018	CAR	A+	21	228	38	16	3	7	23	14	47	4	6	.320/.382/.529	159	20.8	.386	0.6	2B(15) 0.6	1.5	102
2018	BLX	AA	21	307	36	18	2	6	20	22	56	11	5	.272/.339/.416	116	13.9	.323	0.6	2B(64) -3.5	0.5	97
2019	*MIL*	*MLB*	*22*	*160*	*17*	*8*	*1*	*5*	*17*	*7*	*39*	*2*	*1*	*.234/.277/.390*	*84*	*2.4*	*.288*	*-0.1*	*2B -2*	*0.1*	*95*

Breakout: 17% Improve: 41% Collapse: 1% Attrition: 21% MLB: 45% *Comparables: Jonathan Schoop, Arismendy Alcantara, Ryan Brett*

The Report: Hiura started his season 1-16 with five strikeouts and by my second chat of the year, people were clearly concerned. There's a song for that. Over the rest of the season, Hiura mashed. He then mashed in Fall Ball. And he's going to continue to mash. Although it doesn't usually draw superlatives for its aesthetic qualities, Hiura has a nearly perfect swing. Yes, there is a fairly significant leg kick for timing purposes, but the swing has Swiss-pocket-watch precision once he starts. Oh, and there's the matter of the plus bat speed married to a remarkably advanced approach. There's more raw power here than you might expect too. It's average, maybe even a smidge above, and you'd expect Hiura to get to almost all of it.

The bat will carry the profile here, but we have heard far fewer concerns about Hiura staying at the keystone lately. He's unlikely to be much more than average there, but he should be average there. The real show here is in the batter's box anyway, where he could be a perennial .300 hitter with a few 20-home-run seasons mixed in to boot.

The Risks: Medium. There's little to quibble with here, but you'd like to see Hiura more thoroughly mash upper minors pitching at the outset of the 2019 season, and the defensive side of his game—while we are far more confident he's a long term second baseman than this time last year—still bears watching.

Bret Sayre's Fantasy Take:

reads comments above

takes deep exhale Yeeaaaaaaah that's the stuff.

Hiura is just a hitter through and through. If all goes according to plan, he should be able to approximate the fantasy stats of Anthony Rendon—and do it from a middle infield spot.

2 Tristen Lutz OF OFP: 60 Likely: 50 ETA: 2021

Born: 08/22/98 Age: 20 Bats: R Throws: R Height: 6'3" Weight: 210 Origin: Round 1, 2017 Draft (#34 overall)

YEAR	TEAM	LVL	AGE	PA	R	2B	3B	HR	RBI	BB	K	SB	CS	AVG/OBP/SLG	DRC+	VORP	BABIP	BRR	FRAA	WARP	PF
2017	HEL	RK	18	111	23	1	1	6	16	12	21	2	4	.333/.432/.559	141	11.5	.373	-1.1	CF(22) -1.7	0.3	110
2017	BRR	RK	18	76	12	4	3	3	11	4	21	1	0	.279/.347/.559	119	3.9	.364	0.1	CF(11) 0.5, LF(4) -1.2	0.0	104
2018	WIS	A	19	503	63	33	3	13	63	46	139	9	3	.245/.321/.421	115	13.1	.322	-0.9	RF(68) -11.4, LF(29) 1.9	-0.2	103
2019	*MIL*	*MLB*	*20*	*252*	*22*	*8*	*1*	*8*	*23*	*7*	*91*	*0*	*0*	*.147/.171/.286*	*16*	*-18.1*	*.190*	*-0.2*	*RF -3, LF -1*	*-2.4*	*95*

Breakout: 4% Improve: 4% Collapse: 0% Attrition: 2% MLB: 4% *Comparables: Chris Parmelee, Caleb Gindl, Nomar Mazara*

The Report: Athletic and strong, Lutz has the loudest tools of anyone on this list. Plus raw power and a strong throwing arm give him the profile of a future right fielder. At the plate he's got a quick, violent swing that has a swing path ideal for getting the ball in the air. He had trouble recognizing and adjusting to secondary pitches early on last year, but looked more comfortable as the season wore on.

Lutz is an exceptional athlete who can handle centerfield, but his future lies in right. He moves well for a big man, showing good instincts and range. The arm is strong and accurate and will be more than enough for any outfield spot. He's an above-average runner now but will probably slip to fringe-average as he matures physically. On the bases, he's not a burner but is aggressive enough to put pressure on defenders. The overall skill set is good with no tool projected to be below-average. It's the power potential that gives Lutz such a high ceiling, one that makes him stand out in a shallow Brewers' system.

The Risks: High. He's got a good base of skills but there are still some questions with bat and has yet to face advanced pitching.

Bret Sayre's Fantasy Take: If you're into a risk/reward profile, Lutz is for you. The thunder is real, but there are real questions as to how much of it he'll get to at peak, which would leave him more in the range of a .250 hitter with 30 homers. With a little speed to boot, Lutz is certainly a top-150 fantasy prospect right now and could easily make a notable jump in 2019 if he can make strides in his approach in High-A.

3 Zack Brown RHP OFP: 55 Likely: 45 ETA: 2019

Born: 12/15/94 Age: 24 Bats: R Throws: R Height: 6'1" Weight: 180 Origin: Round 5, 2016 Draft (#141 overall)

YEAR	TEAM	LVL	AGE	W	L	SV	G	GS	IP	H	HR	BB/9	K/9	K	GB%	BABIP	WHIP	ERA	DRA	WARP	PF
2016	WIS	A	21	1	2	1	9	4	33	29	3	1.4	7.9	29	45%	.257	1.03	3.00	5.40	-0.2	102
2017	WIS	A	22	4	5	0	18	13	85	78	7	3.6	8.9	84	47%	.316	1.32	3.39	4.78	0.4	100
2017	CAR	A+	22	3	0	0	4	4	25	24	1	0.7	8.3	23	56%	.319	1.04	2.16	3.35	0.6	99
2018	BLX	AA	23	9	1	0	22	21	125[2]	95	8	2.6	8.3	116	57%	.257	1.04	2.44	3.42	2.8	97
2019	*MIL*	*MLB*	*24*	*6*	*6*	*1*	*32*	*17*	*102[2]*	*91*	*13*	*3.2*	*8.2*	*94*	*46%*	*.289*	*1.25*	*4.13*	*4.74*	*0.7*	*95*

Breakout: 16% Improve: 23% Collapse: 16% Attrition: 35% MLB: 48% *Comparables: Eric Jokisch, Steven Brault, Nick Kingham*

The Report: Brown had a breakout year in 2018, although granted, the organization did help clear a path for him. He's a shorter, slight right-hander with some effort in his arm action, but it does spit out low-90s heat with some sink and run that he effectively spots down more often than not. Brown will flash an above-average curveball and changeup as well. The curve can show with inconsistent shape or command, but at it's best it's a power 11-6 breaker. The change works well off the fastball with similar fade and depth and he sells the pitch well.

There's nothing overpowering here. Brown's command may never be much past average and his fastball is hittable up in the zone. Still, he's a polished three-pitch arm with some upper minors success under his belt. It'd be a breakout in better systems too.

The Risks: Medium. We're always gonna feel a little weird when projecting a short righty with some effort as a starter, but Brown has been relatively durable as a minor-league starter, and already has three advanced offerings. It's not huge upside, but he's a useful pitcher who should be ready this season. And he doesn't even have to pitch in Colorado Springs first.

Bret Sayre's Fantasy Take: Deeper leagues and certainly NL-only formats are places where Brown, and his ilk, can be most valuable. In mixed leagues, his brand of "SP5 in a poor ballpark" is one that can be replicated many times over for free during a given season. He's only worth worrying about at this point if your league rosters more than 200 prospects.

4 Corey Ray OF

OFP: 55 Likely: 45 ETA: Late 2019/Early 2020

Born: 09/22/94 Age: 24 Bats: L Throws: L Height: 6'0" Weight: 195 Origin: Round 1, 2016 Draft (#5 overall)

YEAR	TEAM	LVL	AGE	PA	R	2B	3B	HR	RBI	BB	K	SB	CS	AVG/OBP/SLG	DRC+	VORP	BABIP	BRR	FRAA	WARP	PF
2016	BRV	A+	21	254	24	13	2	5	17	20	54	9	5	.247/.307/.385	88	2.4	.299	-1.9	CF(40) -3.3	-0.7	100
2017	CAR	A+	22	503	56	29	4	7	48	48	156	24	10	.238/.311/.367	97	8.0	.346	-2.5	CF(69) 5.5, RF(21) 0.9	0.6	101
2018	BLX	AA	23	600	86	32	7	27	74	60	176	37	7	.239/.323/.477	118	35.8	.303	0.5	CF(126) 1.8, LF(6) 1.4	2.4	97
2019	*MIL*	*MLB*	*24*	*252*	*33*	*11*	*2*	*9*	*26*	*16*	*82*	*9*	*2*	*.193/.248/.372*	*64*	*-0.1*	*.249*	*1.2*	*CF 1, LF 0*	*0.1*	*95*

Breakout: 13% Improve: 18% Collapse: 2% Attrition: 11% MLB: 24% *Comparables: Trayce Thompson, Melky Mesa, Matt Den Dekker*

The Report: The series of unfortunate events that seemed to plague Ray since he was a top-five draft pick finally came to an end in 2018. Well, sort of. Ray played a full, healthy season and did more than just flash the power/speed combo that made him a top amateur prospect in the first place. He's added some loft to his swing and his well-documented raw power turned into significant game power. The speed is back from knee surgery and he has a shot to be an every day center fielder.

Ray always drew a wide range of projections, even dating back to his time in college. Last season was the first time he hit at all as a pro—as a 23-year-old in Double-A. That performance also came saddled with a ~30% K-rate and a swing long enough to preclude any significant future swing-and-miss improvement in its current form. His below-average hit tool may also limit how much of his plus raw power gets into games. Ultimately, Ray kept the flicker of an athletic 20/20 center fielder dream alive in 2018, but the three true outcome Double-A mashers aren't always great bets to maintain that performance in the majors.

The Risks: High. Ray has always been a risky one, and despite some performance gains in 2018, there's still significant hit tool/tweener risk.

Bret Sayre's Fantasy Take: I should really want to jump back in on Ray. We're talking about a former high-end draft pick who just hit nearly 30 homers and stole nearly 40 bases in Double-A two years after entering pro ball. We should all be excited, yet we're not. The hit tool is just too unlikely to allow the homers or the steals to matter. I'm not saying you should give up on him, but he's not a Top 101 fantasy prospect for me.

5 Brice Turang SS

OFP: 55 Likely: 45 ETA: 2022

Born: 11/21/99 Age: 19 Bats: L Throws: R Height: 6'1" Weight: 165 Origin: Round 1, 2018 Draft (#21 overall)

YEAR	TEAM	LVL	AGE	PA	R	2B	3B	HR	RBI	BB	K	SB	CS	AVG/OBP/SLG	DRC+	VORP	BABIP	BRR	FRAA	WARP	PF
2018	BRR	RK	18	57	11	2	0	0	7	9	6	8	1	.319/.421/.362	157	4.5	.357	0.0	SS(12) 2.0	0.5	99
2018	HEL	RK	18	135	26	4	1	1	11	22	28	6	1	.268/.385/.348	119	9.7	.345	1.7	SS(23) -0.1, 2B(5) -0.1	0.6	105
2019	*MIL*	*MLB*	*19*	*252*	*22*	*4*	*0*	*4*	*16*	*14*	*68*	*3*	*1*	*.154/.200/.225*	*12*	*-17.5*	*.192*	*0.0*	*SS 0, 2B 0*	*-1.9*	*95*

Breakout: 5% Improve: 7% Collapse: 0% Attrition: 4% MLB: 9% *Comparables: Gleyber Torres, Adalberto Mondesi, Elvis Andrus*

The Report: Turang slid down draft boards before the Brewers popped him with the 21st overall pick last June. A prep shortstop who is likely to stick at shortstop is never going to fall all that far, and Turang has the tools to be solid or better at the 6. Turang is an above-average runner who moves well in the field, and he shows good infield actions and enough arm for the left side of the dirt. He's not a surefire can't miss shortstop glove, but he's near the top of the "maybe" bucket.

The glove may have to be the carrying tool here, because it is tougher to see one at the plate. Turang steps in the bucket a bit, and his swing emphasizes contact with a slashy approach. None of this lends itself to consistently driving the ball. That—coupled with his smaller build—also limits any power projection, so he's going to have to find infield holes enough to hit .280 or so to be an above-average regular. Not impossible, but we are a long way off from that at present.

The Risks: High. Short-season resume with questions about how the bat will play at higher levels. Probably a shortstop isn't "a shortstop."

Bret Sayre's Fantasy Take: Sometimes when players fall in the draft, it's because of defensive questions. That's unfortunately not the case here. Turang may have somewhat limited upside from a fantasy standpoint, but he does have the contact ability to hit for a good average and steal 25-30 bases. There's also not zero power. It's basically a Jose Peraza profile with a little less speed. There's enough there to make him a solid third-round pick in dynasty drafts this year.

6 Mauricio Dubon IF OFP: 50 Likely: 45 ETA: 2019

Born: 07/19/94 Age: 24 Bats: R Throws: R Height: 6'0" Weight: 160 Origin: Round 26, 2013 Draft (#773 overall)

YEAR	TEAM	LVL	AGE	PA	R	2B	3B	HR	RBI	BB	K	SB	CS	AVG/OBP/SLG	DRC+	VORP	BABIP	BRR	FRAA	WARP	PF
2016	SLM	A+	21	279	53	11	3	0	29	33	25	24	4	.306/.387/.379	138	25.6	.338	5.5	SS(61) -11.6	0.8	104
2016	PME	AA	21	270	48	20	6	6	40	11	36	6	3	.339/.371/.538	143	25.7	.374	4.1	SS(62) -5.7	1.7	110
2017	BLX	AA	22	304	34	14	0	2	24	25	42	31	9	.276/.338/.351	101	6.7	.319	0.3	SS(53) 5.4, 2B(20) 3.0	1.6	100
2017	CSP	AAA	22	244	40	15	0	6	33	14	34	7	6	.272/.320/.420	74	0.3	.297	-0.4	SS(30) -1.0, 2B(27) 3.5	0.2	122
2018	CSP	AAA	23	114	18	9	2	4	18	2	19	6	3	.343/.348/.574	107	10.6	.379	1.5	SS(23) 0.3, 2B(4) 0.6	0.7	114
2019	*MIL*	*MLB*	*24*	*67*	*8*	*3*	*0*	*2*	*7*	*2*	*13*	*3*	*1*	*.244/.274/.390*	*65*	*-0.2*	*.273*	*0.2*	*SS 0, 2B 1*	*0.0*	*95*

Breakout: 19% Improve: 37% Collapse: 2% Attrition: 31% MLB: 54% *Comparables: Eduardo Nunez, Kevin Newman, Trevor Plouffe*

The Report: Would a healthy Dubon have stopped the Brewers from needing to go out and trade for every infielder available at the 2018 deadline? Well, that's a bit hyperbolic, but he at least would have provided useful depth. Dubon has never quite recaptured the magic of that summer in Portland when he slugged .538, but he's stayed on pace to be a good fifth infielder/second-division starter type all along. A speedy middle infield type with experience at three infield spots—and even a brief center field run in the 2016 Arizona Fall League—Dubon is a nifty reserve in this era of small benches. He's never going to be much of a power hitter, and his bat control has covered for issues with spin at times, but assuming he returns more or less fit from his knee injury, Dubon should be a useful cog during Milwaukee's next playoff run.

The Risks: Low, but not actually low. Dubon was major-league-ready when he tore his ACL and he's a fairly low variance "good utility type," but that lack of risk was predicated on him being a speedy middle infielder type. Now he's one that just blew out his knee, so...

Bret Sayre's Fantasy Take: Mixed leaguers can pass here, as much as Matt Collins might object to me saying that. Dubon looks like a utility guy through and through, leaving him as a pretty valuable NL-only play, but a wanting one everywhere else.

7 Troy Stokes OF OFP: 50 Likely: 40 ETA: Late 2019/Early 2020

Born: 02/02/96 Age: 23 Bats: R Throws: R Height: 5'8" Weight: 182 Origin: Round 4, 2014 Draft (#116 overall)

YEAR	TEAM	LVL	AGE	PA	R	2B	3B	HR	RBI	BB	K	SB	CS	AVG/OBP/SLG	DRC+	VORP	BABIP	BRR	FRAA	WARP	PF
2016	WIS	A	20	366	50	20	4	4	29	36	62	20	4	.268/.358/.395	126	11.3	.319	-1.2	LF(59) -2.3, CF(10) -0.3	1.1	106
2017	CAR	A+	21	426	60	19	5	14	56	47	77	21	9	.250/.344/.445	118	21.5	.278	0.5	LF(73) 5.5	1.5	102
2017	BLX	AA	21	153	19	9	0	6	18	16	34	9	3	.252/.333/.452	119	5.9	.292	-0.3	LF(34) 1.0, CF(1) 0.0	0.4	100
2018	BLX	AA	22	551	74	23	6	19	58	65	147	19	2	.233/.343/.430	117	28.5	.295	-1.5	LF(114) 4.1, CF(9) -1.5	1.4	97
2019	*MIL*	*MLB*	*23*	*252*	*32*	*9*	*2*	*9*	*26*	*20*	*71*	*6*	*1*	*.194/.269/.362*	*73*	*0.1*	*.238*	*0.7*	*LF 3, CF 0*	*0.3*	*95*

Breakout: 10% Improve: 23% Collapse: 2% Attrition: 13% MLB: 27% *Comparables: Chad Huffman, Jordan Luplow, Thomas Neal*

The Report: In some ways the outfield version of Dubon—plus a couple grades of pop to be fair—Stokes is another in the long line of Brewers speed/power outfield prospects with hit tool questions. You could also call him stocky Corey Ray I suppose, although he lacks Ray's premium athleticism. Stokes does offer a broad base of defensive skills, enough to play all three outfield spots, along with some sneaky pull power. He can get into pull mode a bit too much, and the present issues with spin suggest a below-average hit tool long term, but he projects as a useful MLB bench piece.

The Risks: Medium. There's a chance the hit tool just doesn't get there and he's more of an up-and-down type.

Bret Sayre's Fantasy Take: This is just not a profile that ends well in dynasty leagues. Use the roster spot someone else. Anyone else will do.

8 Joe Gray OF

OFP: 50 Likely: 40 ETA: 2023

Born: 03/12/00 Age: 19 Bats: R Throws: R Height: 6'1" Weight: 195 Origin: Round 2, 2018 Draft (#60 overall)

YEAR	TEAM	LVL	AGE	PA	R	2B	3B	HR	RBI	BB	K	SB	CS	AVG/OBP/SLG	DRC+	VORP	BABIP	BRR	FRAA	WARP	PF
2018	BRR	RK	18	98	14	5	0	2	9	18	25	6	0	.182/.347/.325	109	3.6	.235	2.0	CF(18) -1.0, LF(4) 0.4	0.2	101
2019	*MIL*	*MLB*	*19*	*252*	*21*	*6*	*0*	*6*	*17*	*20*	*94*	*2*	*0*	*.088/.160/.193*	*-5*	*-22.9*	*.107*	*-0.1*	*CF 0, LF 0*	*-2.4*	*95*

Breakout: 5% Improve: 8% Collapse: 0% Attrition: 3% MLB: 10% *Comparables: Carlos Tocci, Engel Beltre, Nomar Mazara*

The Report: Gray is a projection pick with a right fielder's arm and raw power. The height and weight listed above are probably a fair bit light on both accounts already, and he's still got plenty of room to fill out and add strength. The overall profile at the plate is quite raw at present and the swing can get tentative and mechanical outside of batting practice. He's playing center for now, but he's probably a right fielder at the end of the day. Still, there are five potential tools here, and Gray provides a much needed shot of upside in a shallow system.

The Risks: High. Gray is a projection bet with only a complex-league resume and hit tool questions.

Bret Sayre's Fantasy Take: Gray barely registered on my top 50 signees from 2018, but the fact that he showed up at all means he's a worthy 4th or 5th round flier. It's far more tools than anything else, as you'd expect, but with the specter of above-average power and speed to at least match that, there are far worse profiles to gamble on.

9 Mario Feliciano C

OFP: 50 Likely: 40 ETA: 2021

Born: 11/20/98 Age: 20 Bats: R Throws: R Height: 6'1" Weight: 195 Origin: Round 2, 2016 Draft (#75 overall)

YEAR	TEAM	LVL	AGE	PA	R	2B	3B	HR	RBI	BB	K	SB	CS	AVG/OBP/SLG	DRC+	VORP	BABIP	BRR	FRAA	WARP	PF
2016	BRR	RK	17	127	16	5	3	0	16	7	19	2	2	.265/.307/.359	99	4.7	.310	-0.3	C(20) -0.6	-0.1	103
2017	WIS	A	18	446	47	16	2	4	36	34	72	10	2	.251/.320/.331	89	11.0	.297	1.4	C(78) -2.8	0.3	102
2018	CAR	A+	19	165	20	7	1	3	12	13	59	2	0	.205/.282/.329	53	0.4	.318	0.5	C(25) -0.6	-0.5	103
2019	*MIL*	*MLB*	*20*	*252*	*17*	*5*	*0*	*5*	*22*	*8*	*78*	*0*	*0*	*.148/.179/.238*	*6*	*-18.5*	*.190*	*-0.4*	*C -1*	*-2.1*	*95*

Breakout: 3% Improve: 3% Collapse: 0% Attrition: 1% MLB: 3% *Comparables: Carson Kelly, Francisco Pena, Dominic Smith*

The Report: Last year we ranked Feliciano in the next ten and wrote "Do expect him to occupy the space further up this list in the coming years." Well, we were right, but not for the right reasons. He missed most of 2018 with arm issues that eventually required offseason shoulder surgery. It was all but a lost season for the 19-year-old, who struggled even when on the field. The lost reps are concerning given the work Feliciano still needs to do on the defensive end, but he remains an athletic, potential bat-first backstop with time on his side... for now.

The Risks: High. Catchers are weird. Prep catchers are weirder. And this prep catcher might not hit.

Bret Sayre's Fantasy Take: Man, if you think I'm hard on catching prospects who have somewhat of a track record, just wait until you see how hard I am on ones who don't.

10 Lucas Erceg 3B

OFP: 50 Likely: 40 ETA: 2020

Born: 05/01/95 Age: 24 Bats: L Throws: R Height: 6'3" Weight: 210 Origin: Round 2, 2016 Draft (#46 overall)

YEAR	TEAM	LVL	AGE	PA	R	2B	3B	HR	RBI	BB	K	SB	CS	AVG/OBP/SLG	DRC+	VORP	BABIP	BRR	FRAA	WARP	PF
2016	HEL	RK	21	115	17	8	1	2	22	8	16	8	1	.400/.452/.552	168	14.0	.460	0.6	3B(20) 0.3	0.8	104
2016	WIS	A	21	180	17	9	3	7	29	12	38	1	3	.281/.328/.497	126	10.1	.325	-0.8	3B(37) -0.6	0.7	107
2017	CAR	A+	22	538	66	33	1	15	81	35	95	2	3	.256/.307/.417	100	12.6	.287	-1.6	3B(85) -0.6	0.2	102
2018	BLX	AA	23	508	52	21	1	13	51	37	82	3	1	.248/.306/.382	96	8.5	.274	-0.4	3B(117) -0.7	0.4	97
2019	*MIL*	*MLB*	*24*	*252*	*21*	*9*	*0*	*8*	*28*	*9*	*58*	*0*	*0*	*.206/.236/.343*	*49*	*-9.9*	*.237*	*-0.5*	*3B -1*	*-1.2*	*95*

Breakout: 5% Improve: 12% Collapse: 0% Attrition: 10% MLB: 13% *Comparables: Carlos Rivero, Luis Jimenez, Jordy Mercer*

The Report: We liked Erceg a fair bit coming out of the draft, but his OFP has dropped precipitously as he's struggled to bring his plus raw power into games. Now he's a 23-year-old coming off a Double-A season where he posted an OPS under .700. Life comes at you fast and all that.

The culprit here isn't too tricky to identify. Erceg's swing is a bit long and a bit awkward coming from a closed off stance. He has enough control of the barrel to avoid big strikeout issues, but the quality of his contact has suffered, and he's always had an aggressive approach at the plate. He's a solid defensive third baseman with a big arm, but you have to hit at that corner infield spot too.

The Risks: High. Would you be surprised to learn this is another Brewers prospect with hit tool questions?

Bret Sayre's Fantasy Take: I'm completely out here. Erceg just doesn't have the offensive potential to be a top-250 prospect anymore. I'd rather gamble on about 50 complex league guys hoping to catch lightning in a bottle.

Other of note:

Drew Rasmussen, RHP, Did not pitch

Rasmussen was a first-round pick in 2017, but failed to come to an agreement with the Rays, and a fall Tommy John surgery—his second—has kept him on the shelf since. The Brewers took a flyer on him in the sixth round of this year's draft, and he showed a potential plus fastball along with two average secondaries at Oregon State when healthy. He hasn't been healthy in a very long while though, but in a system this shallow, he's a mere season away from a place on the Top 10's. That's a, uh, significant ask though, so check back this time next year.

Top Talents 25 and Under (born 4/1/93 or later):

1. Keston Hiura
2. Josh Hader
3. Corbin Burnes
4. Orlando Arcia
5. Brandon Woodruff
6. Tristen Lutz
7. Freddy Peralta
8. Zack Brown
9. Corey Ray
10. Brice Turang

Not 400 days ago, the Brewers looked like a team of the future. Now, they're living in the present, as recent success and this under-25 list will affirm. A club with less urgency wouldn't have dealt away high-variance, high-potential youngsters like Lewis Brinson, Monte Harrison and Isan Diaz. That club also wouldn't have nabbed blossoming NL MVP Christian Yelich, who just turned 27. So this thin list doesn't give a full picture of the organization's overall health, but does hint at where to watch for movement.

Hader and Burnes were pushed into relief roles to fill pressing holes on the big-league roster. Hader couldn't have been more suited for the role, while Burnes looked very "getting some reps and biding his time before trying the rotation." That's not a negative, either. Burnes' profile won't blow you away with upside, but could solid command and a more nuanced, versatile slider fuel him to No. 3 starter status? Sure!

Everyone just saw Hader's peak. If that wasn't the best he'll ever be, it was darn close—ideally he approximates that a few more times, and is a very good bullpen piece in seasons where his control falters. Both pitchers are important parts of the Brewers' core, but neither matches the potential impact of Hiura, who projects as a premier player at an up-the-middle position. No shame in that.

Orlando Arcia remains in a bit of a holding pattern. If he can summon even half of his postseason hitting ability, he's ranked too low here. That's not a statement made lightly—he's an impact shortstop defensively. The bat really needs to return to 2017 form, though, and it's anyone's guess on whether that'll be in the cards. If his feeble 2018 numbers prove to be the norm, he'll probably get lapped on this list by 2020.

Brandon Woodruff and Freddy Peralta live in a similar space. Of the two, Woodruff had loftier billing as a prospect, and he's proven he can miss bats and eat innings at the highest level. Peralta had some impressive moments of his own during his maiden big-league voyage, but he's almost entirely reliant on a magic fastball. It sits 90-92 and somehow still evades hitters in heavy, heavy doses. It would almost be more of a surprise if his schtick did hold up through multiple spins around the league. For now, proof of concept keeps him above Zack Brown's more diverse starter's repertoire.

Minnesota Twins

The State of the System:

The Twins have once again assembled a very good, very deep farm system. Perhaps it will work out better for the big club this time.

The Top Ten:

1 Royce Lewis SS OFP: 70 Likely: 60 ETA: 2020

Born: 06/05/99 Age: 20 Bats: R Throws: R Height: 6'2" Weight: 188 Origin: Round 1, 2017 Draft (#1 overall)

YEAR	TEAM	LVL	AGE	PA	R	2B	3B	HR	RBI	BB	K	SB	CS	AVG/OBP/SLG	DRC+	VORP	BABIP	BRR	FRAA	WARP	PF
2017	TWI	RK	18	159	38	6	2	3	17	19	17	15	2	.271/.390/.414	158	17.3	.292	4.6	SS(32) -0.9	1.2	106
2017	CDR	A	18	80	16	2	1	1	10	6	16	3	1	.296/.363/.394	110	6.5	.364	1.0	SS(17) 1.9	0.6	103
2018	CDR	A	19	327	50	23	0	9	53	24	49	22	4	.315/.368/.485	152	31.3	.349	3.7	SS(67) 0.8	3.2	105
2018	FTM	A+	19	208	33	6	3	5	21	19	35	6	4	.255/.327/.399	106	11.6	.291	1.7	SS(45) -4.8	0.3	97
2019	*MIN*	*MLB*	*20*	*252*	*28*	*5*	*0*	*7*	*22*	*11*	*60*	*5*	*2*	*.188/.228/.299*	*40*	*-8.6*	*.219*	*0.3*	*SS -1*	*-1.0*	*105*

Breakout: 20% Improve: 23% Collapse: 0% Attrition: 5% MLB: 23% *Comparables: Alen Hanson, Carlos Correa, J.P. Crawford*

The Report: Lewis was perhaps a slight surprise first overall pick in 2017, but his 2018 season made it seem silly that the Twins considered anyone else (okay, Keston Hiura should still be in this hypothetical mix, but allow me some rhetorical flourish). Lewis is a potential five-tool shortstop, and these ain't 50s and 55s. He was one of the best overall bats in the Midwest League and was 18 for almost his entire tenure in Cedar Rapids. He's got bat speed and barrel control to spare, and enough potential physical development left to project an above-average power tool to go with plus (or better) hit. Lewis will show you more loft and raw pop in batting practice as well, so he might only be a tweak or two away from finding even more thump.

He doesn't really need much more bat given his athletic tools at shortstop. We idly speculated last year that Lewis might grow off shortstop and end up in center field, but the early returns on his glove suggest he can not only stick at the 6, but be above-average there. His range, hands, and arm are all solid-or-better, and he has some room to fill out without losing his premium athleticism. Lewis is one of the best prospects in baseball now, combining projection with present performance at a premium defensive spot. What's not to like?

The Risks: Medium. Lewis doesn't have an upper minors track record yet, but the tools here are so robust, he can fall short in one or two of the five and still be a productive major-leaguer.

Bret Sayre's Fantasy Take: A power/speed middle infielder with a potential plus hit tool? That's fantasy gold right there. Lewis is likely not being talked about as a top-10 dynasty prospect yet, but there's an argument to be made that he's already there. Ultimately, I don't think he'll be elite in any fantasy category, but his all-around game could carry him toward a future as a potential top-five fantasy shortstop. Think about Lewis the way we all dreamed of Jurickson Profar.

2 Brusdar Graterol RHP   OFP: 70   Likely: 55   ETA: Late 2020

Born: 08/26/98   Age: 20   Bats: R   Throws: R   Height: 6'1"   Weight: 180   Origin: International Free Agent, 2014

YEAR	TEAM	LVL	AGE	W	L	SV	G	GS	IP	H	HR	BB/9	K/9	K	GB%	BABIP	WHIP	ERA	DRA	WARP	PF
2017	TWI	RK	18	2	0	0	5	2	19^1	10	1	1.9	9.8	21	58%	.205	0.72	1.40	2.83	0.6	113
2017	ELZ	RK	18	2	1	0	5	5	20^2	16	1	3.9	10.5	24	59%	.300	1.21	3.92	3.76	0.5	106
2018	CDR	A	19	3	2	0	8	8	41^1	30	3	2.0	11.1	51	64%	.270	0.94	2.18	3.57	0.8	103
2018	FTM	A+	19	5	2	0	11	11	60^2	59	0	2.8	8.3	56	49%	.343	1.29	3.12	4.21	0.8	99
2019	*MIN*	*MLB*	*20*	*4*	*5*	*0*	*15*	*15*	71^1	*73*	*10*	*4.3*	*8.3*	*65*	*50%*	*.308*	*1.50*	*4.91*	*5.16*	*0.3*	*105*

Breakout: 4%   Improve: 5%   Collapse: 1%   Attrition: 3%   MLB: 6%   *Comparables: Brad Keller, Will Smith, Jenrry Mejia*

The Report: This is my least favorite blurb to write this year, because I have to admit that Craig Goldstein was right about something. All season he was in my ear about our being too low on Graterol, clashing with my general wariness about short, stocky right-handers. I like my hitting prospects to look like Jo Adell and my pitching prospects to look like... eh, to hell with it, they should look like Jo Adell too. Graterol looks like a fire hydrant. But this fire hydrant touches 101 with sink and run, and he pairs the fastball with a potential plus-plus power slider that he can front-door or run off the gloveside part of the plate with tight, late tilt. At its best, it will remind you of the Dan Warthen slider tree guys, and Graterol already has advanced command of the pitch.

Graterol's curve is a short, tight, 11-5 breaker that gives hitters a distinct look from his slider. He also tosses a very firm change in the low-90s with some sink but limited fade. The delivery is a bit stiff, and he doesn't always keep his arm speed under control, but he's generally been able to throw strikes and you don't need super-fine command at 101. Graterol is actually a bit more effective at 97-98 when he gets better movement and flashes above-average command armside. When he overthrows at the top end of his velo band, he can lose the plate or flatten out the heater. Given his size and delivery, there are reliever red flags all over the profile, but (1) he'd be a really, really good reliever with this two-pitch combo, and (2) he's shown enough present feel for spin/pitching in general that I wouldn't bet against him putting everything together with his change and command to stick in a rotation. He may look like a fireplug, but he could also look like Jose Berrios.

The Risks: High. He's a short righty who needs a more consistent third pitch and he hasn't reached the upper minors yet. Insert bullpen alarm emoji here.

Bret Sayre's Fantasy Take: There's still time before Graterol is properly appreciated in dynasty circles, which is great because once low-minors pitching prospects are, they stop being fun targets. The fireballer has the raw ingredients to be a high-upside SP2 with bushels of strikeouts, but we just need to remember that those ingredients are still pretty raw, and the Twins take a casual approach to advancing their prospects. So long as you can wait a couple more years (he probably won't realize his fantasy impact until 2022), this borderline top-50 overall dynasty prospect is worth the investment.

3 Alex Kirilloff OF   OFP: 60   Likely: 55   ETA: 2020

Born: 11/09/97   Age: 21   Bats: L   Throws: L   Height: 6'2"   Weight: 195   Origin: Round 1, 2016 Draft (#15 overall)

YEAR	TEAM	LVL	AGE	PA	R	2B	3B	HR	RBI	BB	K	SB	CS	AVG/OBP/SLG	DRC+	VORP	BABIP	BRR	FRAA	WARP	PF
2016	ELZ	RK	18	232	33	9	1	7	33	11	32	0	1	.306/.341/.454	111	8.6	.328	0.8	RF(39) 5.2, CF(12) -2.7	0.3	107
2018	CDR	A	20	281	36	20	5	13	56	24	47	1	1	.333/.391/.607	163	27.2	.364	-0.8	RF(53) -4.0, CF(1) 0.0	1.5	104
2018	FTM	A+	20	280	39	24	2	7	45	14	39	3	2	.362/.393/.550	163	26.9	.399	-0.8	RF(51) 0.4, CF(3) 0.3	1.7	99
2019	*MIN*	*MLB*	*21*	*252*	*20*	*9*	*1*	*8*	*29*	*4*	*60*	*0*	*0*	*.197/.208/.340*	*40*	*-11.3*	*.222*	*-0.4*	*RF -2, CF 0*	*-1.4*	*105*

Breakout: 15%   Improve: 25%   Collapse: 1%   Attrition: 15%   MLB: 28%   *Comparables: Nomar Mazara, Jorge Bonifacio, Caleb Gindl*

The Report: Kirilloff showed no signs of rust from a 2017 season lost to Tommy John surgery. In fact, he came back looking even stronger than he did as a recent draftee in the Appy League. The bat is a rare combination of power and contact. He's a big strong kid who uses that strength well, getting leverage and barrelling up pitches. Kirilloff also shows an advanced approach, taking outside pitches to the opposite field rather than trying to pull everything. Pair that approach with an athletic frame that can handle more weight, and you can project power that will play to all fields. Defensively, he lacks the foot speed and lateral quickness for anything other than a corner position, and he may slide down the spectrum from there. Ultimately, we mostly care about the bat. It has a chance to be very good and Kirilloff should eventually find his way to the heart of Minnesota's lineup.

The Risks: High. We love the bat but, he's limited defensively, a year removed from major surgery, and yet to face advanced pitching in the upper minors.

Bret Sayre's Fantasy Take: Well, that's one way to re-introduce yourself to the fantasy community. One of my favorite bats from the 2016 draft, Kirilloff quickly worked his way back into dynasty leaguers' hearts by destroying A-ball arms and reestablishing a ceiling of 30 dingers and a respectable average. I want to see it against upper-minors arms before going all-in and declaring him a top-25 dynasty prospect, but he's on the verge and there's a good chance he'll get there by this time next year.

4 Trevor Larnach OF

OFP: 60 Likely: 50 ETA: Late 2020

Born: 02/26/97 Age: 22 Bats: L Throws: R Height: 6'4" Weight: 210 Origin: Round 1, 2018 Draft (#20 overall)

YEAR	TEAM	LVL	AGE	PA	R	2B	3B	HR	RBI	BB	K	SB	CS	AVG/OBP/SLG	DRC+	VORP	BABIP	BRR	FRAA	WARP	PF
2018	ELZ	RK	21	75	10	5	0	2	16	10	11	2	0	.311/.413/.492	168	5.4	.340	-1.5	RF(14) 3.8	0.6	99
2018	CDR	A	21	102	17	8	1	3	10	11	17	1	0	.297/.373/.505	150	8.8	.338	0.7	RF(17) -1.5	0.5	101
2019	*MIN*	*MLB*	*22*	*252*	*22*	*12*	*0*	*7*	*28*	*14*	*60*	*0*	*0*	*.197/.240/.345*	*53*	*-7.7*	*.228*	*-0.4*	*RF 0*	*-0.8*	*105*

Breakout: 2% Improve: 6% Collapse: 1% Attrition: 4% MLB: 6% *Comparables: Jorge Bonifacio, Destin Hood, Billy McKinney*

The Report: Larnach isn't the easiest blurb to write this offseason (that would be Vladitio), but it's in the bottom quintile of difficulty. He's a big ol' lad who can really hit and he's going to be a right fielder… so he will need to really hit. Mashing in the Appy and Midwest League doesn't tell us much more than his 1.115 OPS as a junior at Oregon State did. Those levels were not going to be a challenge for him.

Larnach doesn't have a long track record of hitting for right-field-profile power, but again, he's a big ol' lad who hits the ball hard. He doesn't have ideal lift at present for big over-the-fence pop, but it's a pretty swing coupled with good bat speed and a strong approach. That works for Jesse Winker. Like Winker, Larnach isn't exactly going to break Statcast with spectacular plays in the outfield, but he moves well out there and has more than enough arm for right. I wouldn't expect the Florida State League to be much more of a challenge for him, and he could be one of the first college bats from his class to reach the majors.

The Risks: Medium. It's a corner profile all the way, which might limit the upside unless he can tap more into his raw power with wood bats. But he's also an extremely advanced hitter who should move quickly.

Bret Sayre's Fantasy Take: There aren't too many other bats with the combination of average and power available in dynasty drafts this offseason, making him a prime candidate for a top-five selection. Ultimately his profile isn't too dissimilar in a 5×5 roto sense from the player he has a decent chance of playing alongside in the Twins outfield soon: Eddie Rosario. Of course, if you're in an OBP league, you'll surely notice a huge difference, as Larnach could be more of a .360-.370 on-base guy in his prime.

5 Nick Gordon IF

OFP: 55 Likely: 45 ETA: Possibly 2019

Born: 10/24/95 Age: 23 Bats: L Throws: R Height: 6'0" Weight: 160 Origin: Round 1, 2014 Draft (#5 overall)

YEAR	TEAM	LVL	AGE	PA	R	2B	3B	HR	RBI	BB	K	SB	CS	AVG/OBP/SLG	DRC+	VORP	BABIP	BRR	FRAA	WARP	PF
2016	FTM	A+	20	494	56	23	6	3	52	23	87	19	13	.291/.335/.386	113	25.2	.353	-2.9	SS(103) 4.1, 2B(2) -0.1	1.7	97
2017	CHT	AA	21	578	80	29	8	9	66	53	134	13	7	.270/.341/.408	116	34.0	.347	1.1	SS(104) 0.4, 2B(14) 0.4	2.4	99
2018	CHT	AA	22	181	22	10	3	5	20	11	27	7	2	.333/.381/.525	139	13.8	.366	-1.4	SS(34) 2.4, 2B(6) -0.3	1.2	106
2018	ROC	AAA	22	410	40	13	4	2	29	23	82	13	3	.212/.262/.283	53	-7.1	.264	2.8	SS(69) 2.6, 2B(30) 4.1	-0.1	93
2019	*MIN*	*MLB*	*23*	*69*	*6*	*3*	*0*	*1*	*7*	*3*	*17*	*1*	*0*	*.213/.254/.335*	*38*	*-2.5*	*.265*	*0.1*	*SS 0, 2B 1*	*-0.2*	*105*

Breakout: 28% Improve: 41% Collapse: 1% Attrition: 33% MLB: 44% *Comparables: Orlando Calixte, Yairo Munoz, Tim Beckham*

The Report: The streak is over. Gordon made marginal improvements for four years running, slightly rising up the lists and staying on track for a relatively high-end outcome. He started the 2018 season along the same path, with a nice spring repeating Double-A. It was a conservative, though reasonable assignment after a successful 2017 campaign there. After his Triple-A promotion, it quickly became clear why the Twins sent him back to Chattanooga to begin with.

The competent, well-rounded Role 55 player type requires everything to stay in place. You need to keep an average-or-better hit tool; you can't hit .212 with a collapsing walk rate and no power. But that's what Gordon did at Triple-A, and it's not like the reports on him out of the International League were much better than the line above. It was an ugly summer. The defensive consensus is largely the same as it ever was—we think he has the physical ability to play shortstop, but he could really excel at second base.

Although it's a big half-grade for global rankings, we're only bumping Gordon down a half-grade for now because the broad base of skills he showed in his first four calendar years in pro ball are generally not skills you lose forever this quickly. It was a terrible three months, but it was only three months, and we're not giving up. Yet.

The Risks: Mixed. It's high variance for whether he's a good regular because he may not hit. It's low variance for a significant MLB career because there's probably enough defensive utility, speed, and name value for a utility run even if he hovers around the Mendoza Line.

Bret Sayre's Fantasy Take: Usually when we talk about prospect fatigue, we're talking about more exciting players than Gordon from a dynasty perspective. And yet here we are. Of course, when we usually talk about prospect fatigue, it's Ben or myself coaxing you through it and telling you it's all going to be okay; that your patience is about to be rewarded if you just wait a touch longer. That's not happening here. I'm out. Middle infield is not the desert it once was, and Gordon is much more blur than oasis.

6 Brent Rooker OF

OFP: 55 Likely: 45 ETA: Late 2019

Born: 11/01/94 Age: 24 Bats: R Throws: R Height: 6'3" Weight: 215 Origin: Round 1, 2017 Draft (#35 overall)

YEAR	TEAM	LVL	AGE	PA	R	2B	3B	HR	RBI	BB	K	SB	CS	AVG/OBP/SLG	DRC+	VORP	BABIP	BRR	FRAA	WARP	PF
2017	ELZ	RK	22	99	19	5	0	7	17	11	21	2	2	.282/.364/.588	140	10.0	.288	0.6	LF(17) 0.4	0.4	98
2017	FTM	A+	22	162	23	6	0	11	35	16	47	0	0	.280/.364/.552	160	12.9	.341	-1.5	LF(16) -2.6, 1B(11) -0.4	0.4	102
2018	CHT	AA	23	568	72	32	4	22	79	56	150	6	1	.254/.333/.465	116	13.2	.316	-4.7	1B(47) -5.7, LF(44) -8.2	-1.2	103
2019	*MIN*	*MLB*	*24*	*252*	*30*	*10*	*1*	*11*	*30*	*17*	*80*	*1*	*0*	*.200/.258/.393*	*72*	*-3.0*	*.250*	*-0.2*	*1B -2, LF -3*	*-0.9*	*105*

Breakout: 18% Improve: 31% Collapse: 5% Attrition: 31% MLB: 53% *Comparables: Chris Shaw, Scott Schebler, Corey Dickerson*

The Report: Yet another bat-first corner prospect, Rooker started horribly in 2018. This raised red flags. He was already an older prospect, reliant on the bat to carry the entire profile. I'm not one to overreact to a couple bad months—see every chat answer I gave about Francisco Mejia in April and May—but for a prospect who needs to mash, when you stop mashing, I'm gonna be a little concerned. The rest of the way Brent Rooker looked more or less like Brent Rooker (much like Mejia looked more or less like Mejia to continue this weirdo comp). That post-Memorial-Day Rooker is a passable R/R first base option, but the Mike Hessman lurking within should give you pause. The upside here is a TTO corner guy with some positional flexibility, if you include designated hitter as a position, who could bash 30 home runs and get on base enough to be an above-average regular.

The Risks: Medium. There's high profile risk, low bat risk, split the difference.

Bret Sayre's Fantasy Take: I usually like this profile more than I should, but the combination of Rooker's age and contact issues make me wary. It's Cron city, baby.

7 Akil Baddoo OF

OFP: 55 Likely: 45 ETA: 2021

Born: 08/16/98 Age: 20 Bats: L Throws: L Height: 5'11" Weight: 195 Origin: Round 2, 2016 Draft (#74 overall)

YEAR	TEAM	LVL	AGE	PA	R	2B	3B	HR	RBI	BB	K	SB	CS	AVG/OBP/SLG	DRC+	VORP	BABIP	BRR	FRAA	WARP	PF
2016	TWI	RK	17	128	15	0	2	2	15	18	36	8	1	.178/.299/.271	74	-0.6	.243	0.2	RF(23) -0.5, CF(11) -3.2	-0.8	92
2017	TWI	RK	18	86	18	4	3	1	10	9	13	4	0	.267/.360/.440	143	4.4	.311	0.9	CF(8) -0.7	0.2	107
2017	ELZ	RK	18	157	39	15	2	3	19	27	19	5	4	.357/.478/.579	212	26.4	.400	0.8	CF(28) -4.2	1.2	104
2018	CDR	A	19	517	83	22	11	11	40	74	124	24	5	.243/.351/.419	116	30.7	.311	4.7	CF(97) -12.1, LF(3) 0.1	1.0	104
2019	*MIN*	*MLB*	*20*	*252*	*25*	*8*	*1*	*6*	*20*	*22*	*78*	*4*	*1*	*.139/.212/.267*	*24*	*-13.2*	*.173*	*0.5*	*CF -4, LF 0*	*-1.9*	*105*

Breakout: 7% Improve: 9% Collapse: 0% Attrition: 5% MLB: 9% *Comparables: Kyle Tucker, Billy McKinney, Victor Robles*

The Report: After crushing the rookie-ball leagues last year, we pegged Baddoo as one to watch in 2018, but his full-season debut was uneven at best. He's bulked up a bit and his surprising 2017 pop is less surprising in 2018. He's still a plus runner who projects well in center field. However, more advanced arms and spin gave him trouble in 2018. He's still got an intriguing power/speed combo in center—although the power is unlikely to play more than fringy in games—but his struggles against better arms are a scary harbinger for the profile. Baddoo played most of the 2018 season as a 19-year-old, so there's no need for too much panic yet, and his overall the performance wasn't even that bad. Still, the breakers don't get any easier from here on out.

The Risks: High. His adjustment to full-season pitching was rough and while he spent most of the season as a 19-year-old there are reasons to worry about the long term offensive projection.

Bret Sayre's Fantasy Take: There's more to like with Baddoo if you're in an OBP league than an AVG one, but there's potential for an OF4 future with the ability to near 20/20 in his strong seasons. Whether there's upside beyond that depends on whether he can hit .270 or not. He's likely to struggle in the Florida State League, but he'll be extremely young, and you should hang on to him if and when that happens.

8 Jhoan Duran RHP OFP: 55 Likely: 45 ETA: 2021

Born: 01/08/98 Age: 21 Bats: R Throws: R Height: 6'5" Weight: 175 Origin: International Free Agent, 2014

YEAR	TEAM	LVL	AGE	W	L	SV	G	GS	IP	H	HR	BB/9	K/9	K	GB%	BABIP	WHIP	ERA	DRA	WARP	PF
2016	DIA	RK	18	1	2	0	4	4	20	24	1	2.2	5.8	13	55%	.354	1.45	5.85	4.33	0.3	106
2016	MSO	RK	18	0	1	0	3	3	12^2	14	1	3.6	6.4	9	49%	.283	1.50	3.55	9.57	-0.5	111
2017	DIA	RK	19	0	2	0	3	3	11^1	19	0	3.2	10.3	13	64%	.452	2.03	7.15	5.61	0.1	94
2017	YAK	A-	19	6	3	0	11	11	51	44	5	3.0	6.4	36	54%	.253	1.20	4.24	4.32	0.6	94
2018	KNC	A	20	5	4	0	15	15	64^2	69	6	3.9	9.9	71	52%	.346	1.50	4.73	3.51	1.3	106
2018	CDR	A	20	2	1	0	6	6	36	19	2	2.5	11.0	44	66%	.218	0.81	2.00	2.51	1.1	101
2019	*MIN*	*MLB*	*21*	*4*	*6*	*0*	*16*	*16*	75^1	*81*	*10*	*4.6*	*7.6*	*63*	*47%*	*.308*	*1.58*	*5.07*	*5.34*	*0.1*	*105*

Breakout: 5% Improve: 9% Collapse: 3% Attrition: 10% MLB: 14% *Comparables: Jarrod Parker, Patrick Corbin, Jarred Cosart*

The Report: The Twins did pretty well in their return for Eduardo Escobar, getting two prospects with an interesting collection of tools in Duran and Gabriel Maciel. Duran's fastball jumps off the scouting sheet here. It's mid-90s heat—with upper-90s in reserve—and power sink and run. It's a heavy pitch that drew swings and misses on its own in the Midwest League. Duran does spray it a bit at present, as there's a fair bit of effort in his mechanics when he wants to ramp up his arm speed, but the velocity and movement compensate for his well-below-average command of the pitch.

Duran has a power slurve that, at it's best, shows downer 11-6 break, but it's inconsistent in shape and command. The best ones show plus potential, the worst ones get spiked. There's a firm change with good tumble/split action at times as well, but it's more of a work in progress. Duran has a tall, lean, projectable frame and he should add enough bulk to start. The mechanics and stuff might not cooperate with the whole starting pitching thing, however. He's a power arm worth keeping tabs on either way, and there's impact potential as a late-inning reliever.

The Risks: High. Command and third pitch need grade jumps, no upper minors track record, might just be a late inning arm.

Bret Sayre's Fantasy Take: Welcome to the Mid-Rotation Starter Emporium. We've got secondaries with potential! We've got command issues that might get better one day! And if you spend $25 today, we'll even throw in Moderate Bullpen Risk*! Come and bring home your future SP4/5 who might be an SP3 if you ignore important pieces of the scouting report above today!

**Moderate Bullpen Risk not available in Tampa Bay, San Diego or Toronto.*

9 Lewis Thorpe LHP OFP: 55 Likely: 45 ETA: 2019

Born: 11/23/95 Age: 23 Bats: R Throws: L Height: 6'1" Weight: 160 Origin: International Free Agent, 2012

YEAR	TEAM	LVL	AGE	W	L	SV	G	GS	IP	H	HR	BB/9	K/9	K	GB%	BABIP	WHIP	ERA	DRA	WARP	PF
2017	CHT	AA	21	1	0	0	1	1	6	5	2	3.0	10.5	7	19%	.214	1.17	6.00	3.45	0.1	94
2017	FTM	A+	21	3	4	0	16	15	77	62	3	3.6	9.8	84	39%	.304	1.21	2.69	3.59	1.5	102
2018	CHT	AA	22	8	4	0	22	21	108	105	13	2.5	10.9	131	38%	.327	1.25	3.58	3.89	1.8	105
2018	ROC	AAA	22	0	3	0	4	4	21^2	20	3	2.5	10.8	26	45%	.321	1.20	3.32	3.69	0.5	95
2019	*MIN*	*MLB*	*23*	*1*	*0*	*0*	*22*	*0*	*23*	*22*	*3*	*3.5*	*9.9*	*25*	*37%*	*.307*	*1.33*	*4.11*	*4.30*	*0.0*	*105*

Breakout: 12% Improve: 17% Collapse: 10% Attrition: 23% MLB: 36% *Comparables: John Gant, Jake McGee, Austin Voth*

The Report: Thorpe threw 130 innings in the upper minors after missing all of 2015 and 2016 due to Tommy John surgery and then mono. A Top 101 prospect in the Hawk Trap Guy era of prospect coverage, Thorpe's stuff has come most of the way back now and you can't quibble with the 2018 performance. I will quibble a bit with the upside in a minute here, though.

Thorpe works in the low-90s, touching 95 with some deceptive giddy-up to his mechanics and a slingy, three-quarters slot. It's a fastball-heavy approach and he commands the pitch well to both sides. It's a tricky angle for lefties and his ball has some natural cut.

Thorpe's full secondary repertoire grades out around average. There's a big slow curve that's more effective as a spot pitch than a chase offering. He mixes in a slider/cutter for a different, tighter breaking ball look and also has the requisite average change with some fade. As weird as it is to say for a dude who struck out 10 per nine in the upper minors, I'm not entirely sure what the true swing-and-miss offering is, although that hasn't been an issue so far. In the end, Thorpe checks every "Role 5 arm" box for me with a bit more uncertainty baked in because of the injuries.

The Risks: Medium. Thorpe is knocking on the door to the majors, but he might lack an out pitch and the medical history here is suboptimal.

Bret Sayre's Fantasy Take: Even being on the verge of the majors, Thorpe flirts with the fringes of dynasty relevance in leagues that roster only 200 prospects—that's not to say he shouldn't be owned in leagues of this size, but he's probably one of the first players you're looking to improve upon on your farm team. There's long-term SP4/5 upside, and AL-only relevance in the short-term, but he's unlikely to come up and take the world by storm.

10 Gilberto Celestino OF

OFP: 55 Likely: 45 ETA: 2022

Born: 02/13/99 Age: 20 Bats: R Throws: L Height: 6'0" Weight: 170 Origin: International Free Agent, 2015

YEAR	TEAM	LVL	AGE	PA	R	2B	3B	HR	RBI	BB	K	SB	CS	AVG/OBP/SLG	DRC+	VORP	BABIP	BRR	FRAA	WARP	PF
2016	DAR	ROK	17	165	22	9	3	2	17	25	23	9	2	.279/.388/.434	151	12.6	.316	-0.8		1.1	96
2016	AST	RK	17	65	7	3	1	0	2	8	16	6	1	.200/.308/.291	63	0.5	.275	-0.2	CF(16) -4.0	-0.7	95
2017	GRV	RK	18	261	38	10	2	4	24	22	59	10	2	.268/.331/.379	102	13.6	.339	5.3	CF(43) 2.6, RF(8) 0.1	0.8	98
2018	TCV	A-	19	142	18	8	0	4	21	10	25	14	0	.323/.387/.480	168	15.2	.374	1.6	CF(16) 0.9, RF(12) 2.6	1.2	97
2018	ELZ	RK	19	117	13	4	1	1	13	6	16	8	2	.266/.308/.349	87	-0.8	.301	1.1	CF(23) -1.0	-0.1	101
2019	*MIN*	*MLB*	*20*	*252*	*24*	*6*	*0*	*6*	*19*	*9*	*74*	*4*	*1*	*.159/.187/.258*	*17*	*-16.0*	*.196*	*0.3*	*CF 0, RF 0*	*-1.7*	*105*

Breakout: 1% Improve: 1% Collapse: 0% Attrition: 0% MLB: 1% *Comparables: Engel Beltre, Carlos Tocci, Cedric Hunter*

The Report: Celestino is your typical teenaged toolsy center field type. He certainly looks the part in uniform, with a lean, athletic frame and a bit of physical projection left. He looks the part in the field as well. Celestino can really go get it on the grass with excellent instincts and plus closing speed. He has an above-average throwing arm as well. At the plate, he sprays line drives from a flat swing plane, although he's capable of making hard contact gap-to-gap. Celestino won't be a teenager for much longer though, and it remains to be seen how the bat will adjust to full-season ball or how much power is on the way; the teenaged toolsy center fielders sometimes end up twenty-something fourth outfielders.

The Risks: High. Yes, the speed and glove give him two major-league quality center field tools, but sometimes these dudes don't hit, and we don't know if he can hit yet.

Bret Sayre's Fantasy Take: The speed is nice, but the lack of other substantive tools and the ETA keeps Celestino as more of a name to watch unless your league rosters 250 prospects or more. If you really, really squint you could see an Ender Inciarte type here, but Inciarte himself was readily available on waiver wires in most leagues and didn't require you to hold a farm spot for three-plus years.

What the heck do we do with this guy?

?? Willians Astudillo C

Born: 10/14/91 Age: 27 Bats: R Throws: R Height: 5'9" Weight: 225 Origin: International Free Agent, 2008

YEAR	TEAM	LVL	AGE	PA	R	2B	3B	HR	RBI	BB	K	SB	CS	AVG/OBP/SLG	DRC+	VORP	BABIP	BRR	FRAA	WARP	PF
2016	MIS	AA	24	342	24	9	0	4	30	5	11	1	1	.267/.293/.332	78	3.7	.263	-1.5	C(75) 12.0, 1B(8) -0.7	1.1	90
2017	RNO	AAA	25	128	22	14	0	4	22	4	5	0	1	.342/.370/.558	127	7.8	.330	-1.4	C(19) 0.9, 3B(14) 0.0	0.8	118
2018	ROC	AAA	26	307	30	17	1	12	38	10	14	7	4	.276/.314/.469	110	16.0	.255	-1.4	C(39) 2.5, 3B(28) 0.6	1.3	93
2018	MIN	MLB	26	97	9	4	1	3	21	2	3	0	0	.355/.371/.516	129	8.5	.341	0.4	C(16) 2.1, 3B(6) 0.0	1.0	103
2019	*MIN*	*MLB*	*27*	*192*	*22*	*12*	*1*	*6*	*24*	*7*	*20*	*1*	*1*	*.263/.302/.441*	*97*	*5.8*	*.268*	*-0.3*	*C 1, 3B -1*	*0.6*	*105*

Breakout: 7% Improve: 39% Collapse: 4% Attrition: 37% MLB: 66% *Comparables: Jose Morales, Tomas Telis, Steve Clevenger*

In 2014, a very short, portly man showed up as Lakewood's part-time catcher and first baseman. That was and is the closest park to me, so I saw this fellow a lot. He had a hilarious skill set, like something you'd make in Road To The Show for fun. He never struck out, but never walked and never elevated the ball. He didn't look like he could throw well enough to catch, and his frame looked awkward at first. I don't know that I ever technically wrote him up, but I made a note to follow his career.

We realized during the process of this that five years later Willians Astudillo is still, somehow, eligible for this list, which means we have to deal with him. In the intervening time since that summer, he's become an even more extreme version of himself, putting up contact numbers that make no sense at all—at press time, he'd struck out just once in 189 Dominican Winter League plate appearances. But as you saw in a host of GIFs late in the season, it all just sort of works. DRC+ suggests that his underlying offensive skills are mostly real. FRAA likes his catching defense now, and he's even picked up the ability to stand at positions like second base and center field that should be physical impossibilities for him.

I have no idea what Astudillo's prospect value is in any conventional sense, so we're not ranking him per se, just sticking him down here as an interesting player to talk about. Maybe this is a plus or plus-plus hit and everything plays because of that. Maybe he hits an empty .240 in the first half of 2019 and never has a career. He's a unicorn, and that means he's probably headed down a unique career path. Enjoy it however long it lasts.

The Next Five:

11 Wander Javier SS

Born: 12/29/98 Age: 20 Bats: R Throws: R Height: 6'1" Weight: 165 Origin: International Free Agent, 2015

YEAR	TEAM	LVL	AGE	PA	R	2B	3B	HR	RBI	BB	K	SB	CS	AVG/OBP/SLG	DRC+	VORP	BABIP	BRR	FRAA	WARP	PF
2016	DTW	RK	17	30	7	3	0	2	6	4	5	0	0	.308/.400/.654	131	4.0	.316	-1.0	SS(8) -0.4	0.0	104
2017	ELZ	RK	18	180	34	13	1	4	22	19	49	4	3	.299/.383/.471	132	16.6	.410	1.9	SS(36) -6.5	0.3	103

Jeffrey (Connecticut): Wander Javier's upside is a plus regular on the left side of the infield. This should cover all your Wander Javier questions for another year

12 Stephen Gonsalves LHP

Born: 07/08/94 Age: 24 Bats: L Throws: L Height: 6'5" Weight: 213 Origin: Round 4, 2013 Draft (#110 overall)

YEAR	TEAM	LVL	AGE	W	L	SV	G	GS	IP	H	HR	BB/9	K/9	K	GB%	BABIP	WHIP	ERA	DRA	WARP	PF
2016	FTM	A+	21	5	4	0	11	11	65^{2}	43	2	2.7	9.0	66	48%	.248	0.96	2.33	3.02	1.8	96
2016	CHT	AA	21	8	1	0	13	13	74^{1}	43	1	4.5	10.8	89	38%	.255	1.08	1.82	3.31	1.6	101
2017	CHT	AA	22	8	3	0	15	15	87^{1}	67	7	2.4	9.9	96	35%	.270	1.03	2.68	3.07	2.2	97
2017	ROC	AAA	22	1	2	0	5	4	22^{2}	27	4	3.2	8.7	22	34%	.343	1.54	5.56	4.13	0.4	101
2018	CHT	AA	23	3	0	0	4	4	20^{1}	11	2	4.4	11.1	25	51%	.231	1.03	1.77	3.84	0.4	106
2018	ROC	AAA	23	9	3	0	19	18	100^{1}	65	6	4.9	8.5	95	40%	.237	1.20	2.96	4.72	0.9	94
2018	MIN	MLB	23	2	2	0	7	4	24^{2}	28	2	8.0	5.8	16	40%	.321	2.03	6.57	8.22	-0.9	106
2019	*MIN*	*MLB*	*24*	*2*	*2*	*0*	*6*	*6*	*30*	*27*	*4*	*4.4*	*8.9*	*30*	*39%*	*.284*	*1.39*	*4.57*	*4.81*	*0.2*	*105*

Breakout: 14% Improve: 27% Collapse: 32% Attrition: 39% MLB: 72% *Comparables: Keyvius Sampson, Henry Owens, Aaron Blair*

Gonsalves' profile was always one that would garner the "fine margins" tag. A deceptive lefty who works with a 90 mph fastball and a potential plus change, he managed to stay on the right side of those margins throughout his minor league career. His delivery has some funk and he always enticed just enough whiffs to mitigate the traffic he'd put on base. That stopped working in the majors where the margins get finer, and he walked more than he struck out in his late-season cup of coffee.

There's enough here to make a backend starter profile work. He can dial up to 93-94 when need be. His mid-80s cutter/slider thing is an effective enough gloveside weapon—particularly tough on lefties—and the change has good tumble. But the profile overall is fringy and he'll need to get more comfortable challenging major-league hitters and hope there's still enough funk and enough whiffs.

13 Luis Rijo RHP

Born: 09/06/98 Age: 20 Bats: R Throws: R Height: 6'1" Weight: 200 Origin: International Free Agent, 2015

YEAR	TEAM	LVL	AGE	W	L	SV	G	GS	IP	H	HR	BB/9	K/9	K	GB%	BABIP	WHIP	ERA	DRA	WARP	PF
2016	DYN	RK	17	1	2	0	9	6	32^{1}	30	2	0.6	8.4	30	46%	.298	0.99	1.67	2.44	1.1	110
2017	YAN	RK	18	4	3	0	11	7	54	51	2	1.5	9.2	55	46%	.329	1.11	3.50	2.48	2.0	94
2018	PUL	RK	19	3	1	0	5	3	27	28	0	0.3	8.7	26	59%	.329	1.07	2.67	4.05	0.6	101
2018	TAM	A+	19	1	0	0	1	1	6	6	0	0.0	4.5	3	33%	.286	1.00	3.00	4.69	0.0	105
2018	STA	A-	19	0	0	0	1	1	6	8	0	3.0	4.5	3	41%	.364	1.67	3.00	5.53	0.0	118
2018	ELZ	RK	19	2	0	0	5	5	21^{1}	15	1	1.7	7.2	17	52%	.237	0.89	1.27	3.98	0.5	101
2019	*MIN*	*MLB*	*20*	*2*	*3*	*0*	*18*	*7*	*45^{2}*	*55*	*8*	*3.4*	*5.9*	*30*	*46%*	*.312*	*1.59*	*5.61*	*5.91*	*-0.5*	*105*

Breakout: 0% Improve: 0% Collapse: 0% Attrition: 0% MLB: 0% *Comparables: Jose Alvarez, Andrew Bellatti, Gabriel Ynoa*

Luis Rijo is a typical low-level Yankees pitching prospect. This checks out since he was dealt from the Yanks to the Twins at the deadline for Lance Lynn. Rijo is an athletic righty who repeats well and shows feel for four pitches. He's probably the fastest worker in baseball, a human pace-of-play initiative. The fastball sits low-90s at present but it flashes some gloveside slide and giddy-up when elevated. The curve is the best present secondary, mid-70s with tight 11-5 action. Rijo doesn't have as much upside as his fellow Luises in the Pulaski rotation—which is likely why he was the piece New York moved—but he has a backend starter projection and maybe a bit more lurking within.

14 LaMonte Wade OF

Born: 01/01/94 Age: 25 Bats: L Throws: L Height: 6'1" Weight: 189 Origin: Round 9, 2015 Draft (#260 overall)

YEAR	TEAM	LVL	AGE	PA	R	2B	3B	HR	RBI	BB	K	SB	CS	AVG/OBP/SLG	DRC+	VORP	BABIP	BRR	FRAA	WARP	PF
2016	CDR	A	22	261	32	6	3	4	27	44	27	5	3	.280/.410/.396	145	20.1	.298	2.0	CF(31) -0.8, LF(21) 2.0	1.9	104
2016	FTM	A+	22	127	17	8	1	4	24	10	17	1	1	.318/.386/.518	155	14.9	.337	-0.2	CF(18) -0.7, LF(6) 0.2	0.7	96
2017	CHT	AA	23	519	74	22	3	7	67	76	71	9	2	.292/.397/.408	147	35.5	.328	-0.1	LF(57) 7.1, CF(31) 1.2	3.8	99
2018	CHT	AA	24	201	30	2	1	7	27	26	20	5	2	.298/.393/.444	142	11.9	.301	1.5	LF(25) 1.1, CF(10) 1.1	1.3	106
2018	ROC	AAA	24	294	24	9	3	4	21	38	54	5	1	.229/.337/.336	98	2.0	.277	0.2	LF(58) 2.8, RF(16) 0.5	0.5	93
2019	*MIN*	*MLB*	*25*	*75*	*9*	*2*	*0*	*2*	*7*	*8*	*15*	*1*	*0*	*.230/.316/.360*	*89*	*1.2*	*.266*	*0.0*	*LF 1, RF 0*	*0.2*	*105*

Breakout: 8% Improve: 26% Collapse: 0% Attrition: 24% MLB: 42% *Comparables: Jake Smolinski, Alex Hassan, Joey Rickard*

LaMonte Wade feels like an extremely 2005 prospect crush. He's got that sexy, sexy walk rate, and he combines good knowledge of the strike zone with a short swing and plus barrel control to grind out at-bats. He's a corner outfielder, but above-average there. He could stand in center for you once a week. He has enough arm for right. He does not have enough power for either corner though. Wade "looks" like he should have more, which can almost be a harbinger of a home run spike in this day and age. He checks all the boxes for the kind of prospects we think find more power in the majors, but he's already 24… and not in the majors. He wasn't too good in Triple-A either. So for now he remains an overaged corner outfield prospect with below-average power. And in 2018, that's not #MCM material.

15 Blayne Enlow RHP

Born: 03/21/99 Age: 20 Bats: R Throws: R Height: 6'3" Weight: 170 Origin: Round 3, 2017 Draft (#76 overall)

YEAR	TEAM	LVL	AGE	W	L	SV	G	GS	IP	H	HR	BB/9	K/9	K	GB%	BABIP	WHIP	ERA	DRA	WARP	PF
2017	TWI	RK	18	3	0	0	6	1	20^{1}	10	1	1.8	8.4	19	56%	.176	0.69	1.33	2.53	0.7	101
2018	CDR	A	19	3	5	1	20	17	94	94	4	3.4	6.8	71	47%	.315	1.37	3.26	4.36	0.9	104
2019	*MIN*	*MLB*	*20*	*3*	*4*	*0*	*25*	*10*	*63*	*76*	*13*	*4.9*	*6.1*	*43*	*44%*	*.309*	*1.74*	*6.42*	*6.79*	*-1.5*	*105*

Breakout: 0% Improve: 0% Collapse: 0% Attrition: 0% MLB: 0% *Comparables: Robert Gsellman, James Parr, Raul Alcantara*

Expectations are a funny thing. Enlow was about what you'd expect in 2018. He was 19—a third-round prep pick in 2017—taking on a full-season assignment. The results were solid across a tightly managed workload, as you'd expect. The stuff was as advertised. Low-90s fastball that was effective down in the zone, improving cutter, a curve that flashed at times.

But the concerns evaluators had about the profile post-draft played out in Enlow's first full pro season. There wasn't really a bat-misser in the profile, even in A-ball. The command wasn't as fine as you'd like considering that lack of an out pitch. The fastball was hittable up, the curve could get loopy. Nothing's really changed from last year's list. I can handwave some of the drop with "the system is improving." But it's hard to feel as excited about Enlow as I did last season, even if he still projects as the same No. 4 starter type.

Others of note:

Ryan Jeffers, C, Low-A Cedar Rapids

The Twins second-round selection makes an easy pick for this superlative in a deep system. He's a bat-first catcher who went from a small conference to the Appalachian League to the Midwest League and raked the whole way. Jeffers projects for average hit and power tools, which if he sticks behind the plate would be (thumbs up emoji). There are questions about his ability to handle the defensive rigors of catching though, and he doesn't have a traditional catcher's frame, as he's a relatively lean 6-foot-4. Also, if we were more sure he'd even be fringy with the glove, well, he'd be up in one of the above sections. The bat might also be ready before the glove which might force the Twins hand a bit, but the bat's good enough that Jeffers is... well, worth a follow.

Ricky De La Torre, SS, Short-Season Elizabethton

De La Torre formed an intriguing double play partnership with Yunior Severino in the Appalachian League. Severino in the bigger name as one of Atlanta's free agent prospects but I think I prefer De La Torre at present. He has plus shortstop tools, can pick it, makes strong accurate throws on the run, and has good defensive instincts. He's an above-average runner and is aggressive on the bases.

De La Torre is a bit rougher at the plate. He'll muscle up and get long or try to rip it and lose control of the barrel, but when he's working with a more controlled line drive approach he covers the plate well. There's probably not enough bat in here to be a starter, but the future is very much unwritten for the 18-year-old and I like the athletic toolset at the 6, so he's one to keep an eye on.

Top Talents 25 and Under (born 4/1/93 or later):

1. Royce Lewis
2. Jose Berrios
3. Brusdar Graterol
4. Alex Kirilloff
5. Byron Buxton
6. Fernando Romero
7. Miguel Sano
8. Jorge Polanco
9. Trevor Larnach
10. Nick Gordon

Max Kepler is the only member of last year's 25-and-under list to age out, but last year's no. 1 (Byron Buxton) and no. 3 (Miguel Sano) young talents had miserable 2018 seasons that saw them demoted to the minors. That makes ranking this year's 25-and-under options tricky, which is similar to trying to figure out where the Twins stand in general right now. They still have plenty of young major-league talent, with plenty of long-term upside, but the current crop has failed to establish itself as a winning core and it's hard not to turn your attention to the next wave.

Royce Lewis is a top 10 global prospect, the gem of a vastly improved farm system, and the base around which the next title-contending Twins team could be built. That those same things were said about Buxton, and to a lesser extent Sano, just a couple years ago is a reminder that not every prospect build is structurally sound. That both Buxton and Sano still qualify for this list, and might still be potential building blocks for the Twins when Lewis arrives this year or next, is also a reminder that a wave of talent can hit the same beach more than once.

Jose Berrios is the only member of the current young core to fully live up to the hype, or at least to do so without incident. Still only 24, he's coming off his first All-Star season and is the anchor of the staff. Fernando Romero lost his "prospect" status by five innings, but he won't be 24 until later this month and ended 2018 at Triple-A. Whether you consider him a prospect or a young major-leaguer, and whether you view him as a future starter or reliever, long term he's probably still closer to Brusdar Graterol as the Twins' best non-Berrios pitching hope than many think.

Buxton is impossible to rank definitively, especially compared to Alex Kirilloff, who's yet to reach Double-A. Last year, Kirilloff topping Buxton would've seemed absurd, yet it's reasonable now and if anything Kirilloff has the stronger case to be higher. Buxton is 25. He's an amazing center fielder and runner, but he's also a .230/.285/.387 hitter who generally looks lost at the plate. Similarly, how do you compare Miguel Sano, with his various flaws now exposed, to Trevor Larnach or even Brent Rooker, for whom a positive outcome might look like... Sano?

There's still a timeline where Buxton and Sano get back on track, rejoining Berrios as building blocks, and the Lewis-led next wave turns the Twins into contenders. It's not even that difficult to picture. Lewis, Sano, Jorge Polanco, Nick Gordon, and Rooker in the infield. Buxton flanked by Kirilloff, Kepler, and Larnach in the outfield. Berrios, Graterol, and Romero atop the rotation. But there's also a timeline where this wave dissipates further, leaving only one or two long-term pieces, and Twins fans pin their new hopes on Lewis/Graterol/Kirilloff instead of Buxton/Berrios/Sano.

New York Mets

The State of the System:

What if I told you there was an entire prospect list made out of our low minors sleepers superlative?

The Top Ten:

1 Andres Gimenez SS

OFP: 60 Likely: 55 ETA: September 2019 or earlier

Born: 09/04/98 Age: 20 Bats: L Throws: R Height: 5'11" Weight: 161 Origin: International Free Agent, 2015

YEAR	TEAM	LVL	AGE	PA	R	2B	3B	HR	RBI	BB	K	SB	CS	AVG/OBP/SLG	DRC+	VORP	BABIP	BRR	FRAA	WARP	PF
2016	MET	RK	17	141	24	10	4	1	17	21	13	7	1	.360/.461/.544	192	28.1	.388	2.1	SS(29) 7.1	2.4	90
2016	DME	RK	17	134	28	10	0	2	21	25	9	6	7	.340/.478/.500	191	20.0	.344	-0.9	SS(19) -2.9, 2B(12) -1.1	1.0	102
2017	COL	A	18	399	50	9	4	4	31	28	61	14	8	.265/.346/.349	110	22.5	.310	0.7	SS(89) 6.6	2.2	91
2018	SLU	A+	19	351	43	20	4	6	30	22	70	28	11	.282/.348/.432	112	24.9	.343	3.4	SS(83) 14.2, 2B(2) -0.1	3.1	97
2018	BIN	AA	19	153	19	9	1	0	16	9	22	10	3	.277/.344/.358	101	8.4	.330	1.2	SS(36) -1.3, 2B(1) 0.2	0.4	100
2019	*NYN*	*MLB*	*20*	*252*	*29*	*7*	*1*	*5*	*19*	*11*	*56*	*9*	*3*	*.189/.245/.293*	*45*	*-6.6*	*.225*	*0.6*	*SS 3, 2B 0*	*-0.4*	*90*

Breakout: 18% Improve: 19% Collapse: 0% Attrition: 4% MLB: 19% *Comparables: J.P. Crawford, Francisco Lindor, Elvis Andrus*

The Report: Gimenez showed up this spring in better shape, shed some baby fat, and added athleticism to his polished up-the-middle profile. The 19-year-old hit at both High-A and Double-A, and his plus hit tool projection backs up the statline. Gimenez has exceptional bat control, his path keeps the lumber in the zone a long time, and he can adjust in-swing to offspeed. He very well could have seasons where he hits .300. The power at present plays mostly gap-to-gap. The raw is 40 at present, potentially average at physical maturity if he adds good weight to his frame. He has high-end 6 speed and is a smart, aggressive baserunner who could be good for 30 steals a season.

The plus speed plays in the field as well, giving Gimenez above-average range that plays up further due to a good first step. While we previously had concerns about him sticking at the 6, his defense has improved and he checks every box for a potential plus shortstop—good instincts, hands, and actions; smooth around the bag; plus throwing arm. The lack of power projection and his occasional over aggression against offspeed limits the ceiling a bit, but he's as good a bet as any prospect in baseball to have an eight-year major league career of some variety.

The Risks: Low. While the profile lacks superstar upside at present, Gimenez inherits the "safe middle infield prospect" mantle from predecessors Willy Adames and Ozzie Albies. He doesn't have the power upside they've shown, but he's a plus athlete with a good hit tool. If you want to bet on a "high-floor" profile at the 6, that's the one.

Bret Sayre's Fantasy Take: In some ways, this is a test to see if we've learned anything from the army of smaller, hit-tool-first prospects who have reached higher upsides than we would have ever comfortably projected. Gimenez has everything you want, except for the power, but if he can grow into even 15-homer pop, we're looking at someone who could approximate Jean Segura's fantasy value and maintain top-10 shortstop status even if he never really competes with the Lindors or Machados of the world.

2 Peter Alonso 1B OFP: 60 Likely: 55 ETA: July 2018

Born: 12/07/94 Age: 24 Bats: R Throws: R Height: 6'3" Weight: 245 Origin: Round 2, 2016 Draft (#64 overall)

YEAR	TEAM	LVL	AGE	PA	R	2B	3B	HR	RBI	BB	K	SB	CS	AVG/OBP/SLG	DRC+	VORP	BABIP	BRR	FRAA	WARP	PF
2016	BRO	A-	21	123	20	12	1	5	21	11	22	0	1	.321/.382/.587	179	14.1	.357	-0.5	1B(27) 2.3	0.9	95
2017	SLU	A+	22	346	45	23	0	16	58	25	64	3	4	.286/.361/.516	158	11.8	.314	-5.8	1B(78) 3.2	1.4	107
2017	BIN	AA	22	47	7	4	1	2	5	2	7	0	0	.311/.340/.578	104	3.3	.333	-0.1	1B(5) 0.1	0.0	101
2018	BIN	AA	23	273	42	12	0	15	52	43	50	0	2	.314/.440/.573	177	30.5	.344	-1.6	1B(51) 1.8	2.2	101
2018	LVG	AAA	23	301	50	19	1	21	67	33	78	0	1	.260/.355/.585	122	14.6	.284	1.2	1B(59) 5.0	1.4	116
2019	*NYN*	*MLB*	*24*	*344*	*44*	*17*	*1*	*17*	*50*	*36*	*94*	*0*	*0*	*.220/.316/.454*	*110*	*10.2*	*.259*	*-0.7*	*1B 2*	*1.3*	*90*

Breakout: 25% Improve: 43% Collapse: 9% Attrition: 25% MLB: 69% *Comparables: Rhys Hoskins, Chris Carter, A.J. Reed*

The Report: Listen, we hate this profile as a rule. This is a R/R college first baseman who is a cover model for the BIG BOY SZN catalog and he doesn't play great or even particularly good defense. You will go absolutely broke betting on players of this type to make it. But some do, and we think Peter Alonso is going to be one of the exceptions.

We said last year that 2018 would be a big year for Alonso. He killed Double-A for the first half of the season, did the same in Triple-A from mid-July on after a slow first month, and impressed in the Arizona Fall League. We said he projected for plus game power with a chance for more. Thirty-six homers in the high-minors later, the chance got there, and he now projects for 80 game power. We said Dom Smith might establish himself in the majors first and cloud up Alonso's profile and, well, pretty much the exact opposite of that happened. He's got power, he's got patience, he's got bat speed, he can turn on velocity, he's got better feel for contact than you usually see in these types of players.

It's not all roses, obviously; he'd be ahead of Gimenez if it was. Outside of the Vladitos of the world, you don't know when a guy is going to be able to hit major league sliders until you know, and we don't know yet. The Mets left him in the minors all year, whether because of service time or 40-man considerations or a veteran fetish, robbing us of the chance to know. He's still, generously, a work-in-progress with the glove at first base, although he ranges and throws well enough. We believe that he's "playable bad" there instead of "needs to be traded to the American League," but there are scouts who project the latter.

The Risks: Low-to-medium, depending on how you look at it. There's low risk in the tools, he's about as fully-formed as a prospect can be, in part because he shouldn't be prospect-eligible. There's still substantial risk in the profile until we see how good he is at getting on base against MLB pitching. There isn't a ton separating Rhys Hoskins and C.J. Cron in profile or skills, but that slight gap is the difference between a star and a waiver claim. Mets fans might also cringe at the exit velocity hype after The Eric Campbell Experience.

Bret Sayre's Fantasy Take: Frankly, I'm shocked Brendan let me write this. It's not that my favorite player growing up was Howard Johnson, or that I can still remember exactly where I was when Todd Pratt hit the walkoff homer that sent the Mets to the NLCS in 1999 (the percussion building of the old Sam Ash in midtown Manhattan.) It's that I've been subscribing to BIG BOY SZN for over a decade now. I own a Dan Vogelbach Cubs shirsey unironically. This profile weakens me, and although guidance counselors and career advisors alike will tell you to identify your weaknesses so that you can overcome them, that implies you want to overcome them. So yes I'm on board with Alonso as a top-10 dynasty prospect, and yes I'm on board with Alonso as a 40-homer bat, and yes I'm on board with Alonso being a top-200 pick in redraft formats this season. The average isn't going to be special, but he could run it up to .280, which could leave him with an OBP approaching .400.

3 Ronny Mauricio SS OFP: 60 Likely: 50 ETA: 2022 if things go pretty well.

Born: 04/04/01 Age: 18 Bats: B Throws: R Height: 6'3" Weight: 166 Origin: International Free Agent, 2017

YEAR	TEAM	LVL	AGE	PA	R	2B	3B	HR	RBI	BB	K	SB	CS	AVG/OBP/SLG	DRC+	VORP	BABIP	BRR	FRAA	WARP	PF
2018	MTS	RK	17	212	26	13	3	3	31	10	31	1	6	.279/.307/.421	124	10.1	.310	-0.3	SS(45) 0.3	0.7	107
2018	KNG	RK	17	35	6	3	0	0	4	3	9	1	0	.233/.286/.333	74	1.9	.304	0.5	SS(8) -0.1	0.0	111
2019	*NYN*	*MLB*	*18*	*252*	*13*	*9*	*0*	*4*	*20*	*7*	*88*	*0*	*0*	*.121/.144/.212*	*-15*	*-26.2*	*.162*	*-0.6*	*SS 1*	*-2.7*	*90*

Breakout: 0% Improve: 0% Collapse: 0% Attrition: 0% MLB: 0% *Comparables: Adalberto Mondesi, Wilmer Flores, Tommy Brown*

The Report: Here's an example of both sides of the coin for ranking J2s. Last year, Jeffrey conceded that Mauricio and Adrian Hernandez—two recently-signed, seven-figure Dominican IFAs with great reports—might both be among the ten best prospects in the system, but we lacked enough information to rank them with any precision, or write anything interesting about them. Mauricio then got nothing but buzz in the spring, earned a stateside assignment, reached the Appy League by the end of the season, and is under consideration for the 101. Hernandez was left in the Dominican complex and played okay in the Dominican Summer League. He's still a prospect too, and he could show up on any Mets list between now and 2025 without surprising us, but this is the last time you'll be reading about him on this particular installment.

As the Seattle trade unfolded, there was a lot made of Jarred Kelenic having the highest upside in this system, but for me, Mauricio is a bigger upside play by more than a little—if less likely to hit it. The body is as projectable as they come. There's plus power potential. There's plus hit tool potential as a switch-hitter. He even might stick at shortstop. In two or three years he could absolutely be a bigger, more physical Andres Gimenez, and that's the makings of a tippy-top global guy. We can dream big right now.

Of course, extreme projectability is as much of a curse as it is a compliment, because it implies considerable rawness. These abilities we're gushing about only come across in flashes and bursts right now. Wilmer Flores had this kind of profile once upon a time, very similar actually, and he turned out pretty well, all things considered. Flores still didn't become a full-time regular in his original org, and didn't make it through his arbitration years without being released.

The Risks: He's played eight games in his career outside of a complex. The body can go in a lot of different directions. Projecting hit tools on players like this is more like talking about Delta Airlines than normal baseball prospect delta. There's star potential, Double-A slugger potential, and every potential in between.

Bret Sayre's Fantasy Take: And just like that we've already hit the flier section of this list. I'm probably going to be one of the higher folks on Mauricio this offseason, mostly because the power projection is a lot of fun, but even I can't squint enough to put him in the discussion for the Top 101 at this point. He should be owned in leagues that roster 200 or more prospects, however.

4 Shervyen Newton IF

OFP: 60 Likely: 45 ETA: 2022

Born: 04/24/99 Age: 20 Bats: B Throws: R Height: 6'4" Weight: 180 Origin: International Free Agent, 2015

YEAR	TEAM	LVL	AGE	PA	R	2B	3B	HR	RBI	BB	K	SB	CS	AVG/OBP/SLG	DRC+	VORP	BABIP	BRR	FRAA	WARP	PF
2016	MET	RK	17	150	18	5	1	0	5	22	32	0	5	.169/.347/.229	97	3.6	.233	-1.2	SS(18) -0.5, 3B(11) -0.4	0.1	91
2017	MET	RK	18	303	51	11	9	1	31	50	57	10	4	.311/.433/.444	163	33.9	.398	-2.0	SS(60) 7.7, 3B(5) 0.8	3.3	102
2018	KNG	RK	19	266	50	16	2	5	41	46	84	4	0	.280/.408/.449	130	24.4	.421	2.2	SS(49) 10.8, 2B(3) 0.3	2.3	105
2019	*NYN*	*MLB*	*20*	*252*	*21*	*6*	*1*	*5*	*17*	*23*	*91*	*0*	*0*	*.120/.198/.214*	*13*	*-17.4*	*.165*	*-0.3*	*SS 3, 2B 0*	*-1.5*	*90*

Breakout: 3% Improve: 3% Collapse: 0% Attrition: 1% MLB: 3%

Comparables: Tyler Wade, Tim Beckham, Amed Rosario

The Report: Newton oozes tools and athleticism. He's 6-foot-4 and lean with a high waist. While only an average runner, he eats up ground with long strides and shows a good second gear. There's at least plus raw power at present and he projects for more down the road. He's a better shortstop than you'd think given the frame. Newton's actions are fluid, his arm's plus, and he has great instincts. He is already a captain of the infield as well. He might simply grow off the position, but he'd be a fine third baseman.

Newton is extremely raw at the plate, but there are positive markers for future development with the bat. He shows plus bat speed with loft, and while he can struggle with spin, especially if you back door it for a strike, he's a pesky hitter who stays in against offspeed and will foul stuff off and work deep counts. He does tend to get pull and lift happy which means he will get beat down in the zone, but there's a potential average hit tool in here with plus game power to go with it. That's a borderline star at shortstop. He also might never hit enough to be more than an up-and-down bench piece. It's rookie ball, man.

The Risks: Extreme. Newton led the Appy League in strikeouts. I'm projecting an average hit tool here, but if he doesn't get there, the profile falls apart a bit. Ditto if he grows off of short. There's a few different ways this can go badly, and they all end with him topping out in Double-A.

Bret Sayre's Fantasy Take: You could basically just copy-and-paste Mauricio's comment here, as Newton carries similar upside and risk with the bat. As alluded to above, there's certainly a path to a .250 average and 30-plus homers by the time the next midterms shake out, with the potential for a more notable value in OBP leagues due to his 2.5-true-outcomes approach at this point in his development. Stay tuned, but stay interested, and make sure he's owned if your league rosters 200 prospects.

5 Mark Vientos 3B

OFP: 55 Likely: 45 ETA: 2022

Born: 12/11/99 Age: 19 Bats: R Throws: R Height: 6'4" Weight: 185 Origin: Round 2, 2017 Draft (#59 overall)

YEAR	TEAM	LVL	AGE	PA	R	2B	3B	HR	RBI	BB	K	SB	CS	AVG/OBP/SLG	DRC+	VORP	BABIP	BRR	FRAA	WARP	PF
2017	MTS	RK	17	193	22	12	0	4	24	14	42	0	2	.259/.316/.397	108	8.2	.313	0.8	SS(19) -1.6, 3B(14) 0.1	0.0	99
2018	KNG	RK	18	262	32	12	0	11	52	37	43	1	0	.287/.389/.489	149	17.4	.312	-3.0	3B(54) -1.7	0.7	106
2019	*NYN*	*MLB*	*19*	*252*	*22*	*6*	*0*	*9*	*28*	*18*	*73*	*0*	*0*	*.148/.208/.295*	*32*	*-15.4*	*.165*	*-0.6*	*3B -1*	*-1.7*	*90*

Breakout: 5% Improve: 7% Collapse: 0% Attrition: 3% MLB: 10% *Comparables: Rafael Devers, Gleyber Torres, Nomar Mazara*

The Report: Vientos was in play for the Mets first pick in the 2017 draft, so they were quite pleased when he was still on the board for their second. Still a few days from turning 19 at publication, Vientos has as much upside in his bat as any prospect in this system due to a plus-plus raw power projection. It's a bit of a length and strength approach at the best of times, and he'll add more length with an occasional hitch in his swing path, but this is the kind of thing that can get smoothed out with time—and something the Mets have had particular success with developmentally. At present though there are swing-and-miss issues, especially on the outer half.

The hit tool is more projectable than you'd think. Vientos shows pretty good feel for contact and has an idea at the plate. He shortens up against better velo and doesn't try to lift and pull everything. In the field he's a bit rough at third base, better on the reaction play than the ones where he has time. The arm is above-average but not a cannon, and he may grow off third base and end up in left field or at first. That would put a lot of pressure on the potential 25+ home run power to actualize.

The Risks: High. Short-season hitter with hit tool and positional questions.

Bret Sayre's Fantasy Take: How many of these same comments are we going to suggest copying and pasting? Vientos could be a 30-homer bat down the road, but he's approximately as far away from the majors as Mauricio and Newton. On the other hand, he showed the best approach of the group, which could lead to more success in full-season ball and a quicker path to the majors. If I had to choose one of these three to run with in a dynasty league right now, it'd be Vientos (though it's close).

6 David Peterson LHP

OFP: 55 Likely: 45 ETA: 2020

Born: 09/03/95 Age: 23 Bats: L Throws: L Height: 6'6" Weight: 240 Origin: Round 1, 2017 Draft (#20 overall)

YEAR	TEAM	LVL	AGE	W	L	SV	G	GS	IP	H	HR	BB/9	K/9	K	GB%	BABIP	WHIP	ERA	DRA	WARP	PF
2018	COL	A	22	1	4	0	9	9	59¹	46	1	1.7	8.6	57	68%	.283	0.96	1.82	3.50	1.2	90
2018	SLU	A+	22	6	6	0	13	13	68²	74	1	2.5	7.6	58	64%	.335	1.35	4.33	3.99	1.1	96
2019	*NYN*	*MLB*	*23*	*6*	*6*	*0*	*17*	*17*	*91¹*	*86*	*10*	*3.2*	*8.0*	*82*	*52%*	*.304*	*1.30*	*4.05*	*4.70*	*0.6*	*90*

Breakout: 7% Improve: 18% Collapse: 12% Attrition: 20% MLB: 36% *Comparables: Sal Romano, Brian Flynn, Fernando Romero*

The Report: The Mets were conservative with Peterson in 2018 after a pair of minor injuries in spring training. Despite being a polished college lefty, he finished the season in High-A (we'll return to this theme in a bit). Arguably Peterson's stuff should have overpowered A-ball hitters more than it did. His low-90s fastball comes from a tough angle given his height and slingy, low-three-quarters slot. He pairs it with a very advanced, potential plus slider and commands both offerings well.

The changeup is the clear third pitch at present, and he could use a better armside weapon against righties. Peterson is a massive human, and although there are no real red flags in the delivery past a bit of the usual lefty funk, his body might require some monitoring. Double-A will tell us a lot more about the ultimate profile here, but for now he remains on pace to be a middle or back-end starter, although perhaps not as quickly as you'd have thought when he was drafted.

The Risks: Medium. It's probably low, but I'm hesitant to throw that on any pitching prospect who hasn't seen Double-A yet. Without a changeup grade jump he might fit better in the pen due to platoon issues.

Bret Sayre's Fantasy Take: If you looked up the definition of nondescript potential SP5 in a dictionary—first of all, send me a copy of that dictionary—a picture of Peterson would be right there for all to see. Pitchers like Peterson come off the waiver wire for spells of usefulness upwards of 20 times per season in medium-sized mixed leagues, so use that roster spot on a high-risk hitter who could be a 101 candidate at this time next year.

7 Franklyn Kilome RHP

OFP: 55 Likely: 40 ETA: Late 2019

Born: 06/25/95 Age: 24 Bats: R Throws: R Height: 6'6" Weight: 175 Origin: International Free Agent, 2013

YEAR	TEAM	LVL	AGE	W	L	SV	G	GS	IP	H	HR	BB/9	K/9	K	GB%	BABIP	WHIP	ERA	DRA	WARP	PF
2016	LWD	A	21	5	8	0	23	23	114^2	113	6	3.9	10.2	130	49%	.346	1.42	3.85	3.14	2.6	91
2017	CLR	A+	22	6	4	0	19	19	97^1	96	5	3.4	7.7	83	48%	.325	1.37	2.59	4.55	0.8	96
2017	REA	AA	22	1	3	0	5	5	29^2	25	2	4.6	6.1	20	43%	.267	1.35	3.64	4.00	0.4	105
2018	REA	AA	23	4	6	0	19	19	102	96	7	4.5	7.3	83	46%	.305	1.44	4.24	4.65	0.8	105
2018	BIN	AA	23	0	3	0	7	7	38	31	3	2.4	9.9	42	41%	.289	1.08	4.03	4.50	0.4	101
2019	*NYN*	*MLB*	*24*	*7*	*8*	*0*	*22*	*22*	*115^1*	*107*	*15*	*4.2*	*8.8*	*112*	*42%*	*.305*	*1.40*	*4.55*	*5.28*	*0.0*	*90*

Breakout: 4% Improve: 5% Collapse: 6% Attrition: 12% MLB: 17% *Comparables: Scott Barlow, Caleb Smith, James Houser*

The Report: It gets harder to handwave Kilome's consistency issues now that he's in the upper minors, but on balance his 2018 regular season was at worst a net neutral for his profile. You know the story by now. An easy mid-90s fastball with life up in the zone and heavy down in it. It will flash gloveside cut as well. But sometimes it will just be 90-92, overthrown gloveside for a batter. Sometimes it will be more 92-95 for a start. His curve is a hammer, flashing plus-plus in the low-80s. Kilome sells it like a fastball until it's too late for the batter to do anything other than look foolish.

The search for a third pitch rolls on. The Phillies attempted to teach him a slider for a while, and it still hasn't really taken. It bleeds into the curve too much, just a slurvier version of his 11-6 wipeout downer. Occasionally you'll see one around 85 that is sharp in on lefties, which is a useful different look. A changeup shows itself... occasionally. Kilome has done a better job keeping his mechanics on line since the trade, but there are still a lot of moving parts in both his upper and lower halves, and they can get out of sync, limiting the command projection here to average at best. Then there is the matter of his postseason Tommy John Surgery that will cost him all of 2019. At this point, Kilome might be best served with a move to the pen in 2020.

The Risks: High. This was 6/5 and borderline Top 101 before the UCL tear because we really like the profile, but that was with heavy reliever risk baked in, which is only going up. He will be 25 shortly after he starts throwing meaningful pro innings again, and again, he was riskier than you'd like before he went under the knife.

Bret Sayre's Fantasy Take: I've been along for the ride the last three years, but surgery and a likely reliever future is enough to get me off the bandwagon. Even if the stuff returns, his realistic ceiling at this point is a really good setup option in front of newly-acquired closer Edwin Diaz.

8 Thomas Szapucki LHP

OFP: 55 Likely: 40 ETA: 2020-2021

Born: 06/12/96 Age: 23 Bats: R Throws: L Height: 6'2" Weight: 181 Origin: Round 5, 2015 Draft (#149 overall)

YEAR	TEAM	LVL	AGE	W	L	SV	G	GS	IP	H	HR	BB/9	K/9	K	GB%	BABIP	WHIP	ERA	DRA	WARP	PF
2016	KNG	RK	20	2	1	0	5	5	29	16	2	2.8	14.6	47	46%	.255	0.86	0.62	1.04	1.5	97
2016	BRO	A-	20	2	2	0	4	4	23	10	0	4.3	15.3	39	46%	.256	0.91	2.35	1.89	0.9	100
2017	COL	A	21	1	2	0	6	6	29	24	0	3.1	8.4	27	44%	.304	1.17	2.79	3.38	0.6	89
2019	*NYN*	*MLB*	*23*	*2*	*2*	*0*	*7*	*7*	*35^1*	*31*	*4*	*4.5*	*9.6*	*38*	*40%*	*.306*	*1.38*	*4.30*	*4.98*	*0.1*	*90*

Breakout: 5% Improve: 5% Collapse: 0% Attrition: 3% MLB: 6% *Comparables: Bryan Mitchell, A.J. Morris, Juan Nicasio*

The Report: I really considered recycling last year's report here in full. After Tommy John surgery in summer 2017, Szapucki spent the entire 2018 season rehabbing in the complex.

When healthy, Szapucki has shown a lively fastball in the mid-90s, touching higher, and a big, already-plus hook. He's also flashed a useful change. That's a big, big stuff profile for a lefty. The command profile and repeatability are good for his level of rawness, but he looked pretty raw when he last pitched. Things like fielding, holding runners, and throwing to bases were all issues, and his delivery is unorthodox; this is, conveniently, the type of stuff you can work on while rehabbing. So is changeup consistency.

This profile is fairly similar to Marcos Molina's from several years ago. Molina's stuff just never came even most of the way back from a late-2015 Tommy John, even though the Mets gave him several extra years on the 40-man to get it together. He was ultimately released this past summer. Not all rehabs are alike, and not all rehabs are successful. We might not fully know where Szapucki is at until he steps back on a pro mound (hopefully) this spring. By this time next year, he could've reestablished No. 2 starter upside, or he could be a footnote.

The Risks: He hasn't thrown a competitive pitch since July 2017. In four pro seasons he's thrown 83⅓ innings, and only 29 in full-season ball. He's blown out his elbow already. He's had back problems already. He's had shoulder problems already. There's a lot going on here.

Bret Sayre's Fantasy Take: If you're going to gamble on a pitcher trying to return from an extended absence due to Tommy John, you at least want to bet on upside, and Szapucki still fits the bill here. The risk is sky-high, but a possible SP3 payoff with the ability to run up strikeouts still makes the southpaw worth holding onto in leagues that roster 250 prospects or more.

9 Anthony Kay LHP

OFP: 50 Likely: 45 ETA: 2020

Born: 03/21/95 Age: 24 Bats: L Throws: L Height: 6'0" Weight: 218 Origin: Round 1, 2016 Draft (#31 overall)

YEAR	TEAM	LVL	AGE	W	L	SV	G	GS	IP	H	HR	BB/9	K/9	K	GB%	BABIP	WHIP	ERA	DRA	WARP	PF
2018	COL	A	23	4	4	0	13	13	69^{1}	73	6	2.9	10.1	78	45%	.356	1.37	4.54	4.00	1.0	95
2018	SLU	A+	23	3	7	0	10	10	53^{1}	51	1	4.6	7.6	45	41%	.321	1.46	3.88	4.21	0.7	94
2019	*NYN*	*MLB*	*24*	*5*	*6*	*0*	*16*	*16*	*87*	*87*	*12*	*4.1*	*8.2*	*80*	*39%*	*.310*	*1.45*	*4.79*	*5.55*	*-0.2*	*90*

Breakout: 7% Improve: 8% Collapse: 0% Attrition: 6% MLB: 8% *Comparables: Armando Galarraga, Matt Purke, Chris Narveson*

The Report: Kay was picked in the supplemental round in 2016 as a polished, quick to the majors, but relatively low-ceiling lefty. A UCL tear discovered shortly after the draft cost him six figures off his bonus and the 2017 season. The Mets—being the Mets—took it slowly with Kay in 2018, leaving him in the two full-season A-ball levels all year. The top line performance is fine and the stuff is most of the way back, and he still projects as a back-of-the-rotation three-pitch lefty.

The fastball sits in the low-90s from a tough angle with run and sink, and Kay will reach back for 95 on occasion. His breaking ball is an upper-70s curve that flashes tight 1-7 action, but he doesn't have consistent feel for it. The change was his party piece at UCONN, a potential plus offering, but it was too firm too often in his minor league debut. The hope is the stuff and command will tighten up a bit as he gets further removed from Tommy John surgery, but the whole moving fast thing hasn't happened, and Kay will be 24 in the spring.

The Risks: Medium. Kay was drafted as a fast-moving pitching prospect, but he's developmentally behind now and still hasn't seen the upper minors. We also don't know what the stuff will look like post-TJ.

Bret Sayre's Fantasy Take: A low-upside starting pitcher still recovering from a torn UCL? Sign me up.

10 Simeon Woods-Richardson RHP

OFP: 55 Likely: 40 ETA: 2023

Born: 09/27/00 Age: 18 Bats: R Throws: R Height: 6'3" Weight: 210 Origin: Round 2, 2018 Draft (#48 overall)

YEAR	TEAM	LVL	AGE	W	L	SV	G	GS	IP	H	HR	BB/9	K/9	K	GB%	BABIP	WHIP	ERA	DRA	WARP	PF
2018	MTS	RK	17	1	0	1	5	2	11^{1}	9	0	3.2	11.9	15	50%	.321	1.15	0.00	3.39	0.3	101
2018	KNG	RK	17	0	0	0	2	2	6	6	1	0.0	16.5	11	38%	.417	1.00	4.50	3.92	0.1	114
2019	*NYN*	*MLB*	*18*	*2*	*2*	*0*	*16*	*6*	34^{2}	*33*	*5*	*4.6*	*8.9*	*34*	*44%*	*.308*	*1.46*	*4.92*	*5.70*	*-0.2*	*90*

Breakout: 0% Improve: 0% Collapse: 0% Attrition: 0% MLB: 0% *Comparables: Mike Soroka, Roberto Osuna, Pedro Araujo*

The Report: One of my favorite 2018 draft stories—and an extremely Mets story—was that Simeon Woods-Richardson himself wasn't even expecting to get picked Day One. His velocity popped right before the draft though, and the Mets went overslot to buy him out of his commitment to the Longhorns.

Woods-Richardson dialed it up into the upper-90s in his pro debut after sitting more low-90s for most of high school, with a potential above-average breaker, and a delivery that has relief markers. He was young for his prep class, but is not particularly projectable by Texas prep arm standards. So for now he's an arm strength guy worth keeping an eye on, but he's already more intriguing than that pre-draft Day Two projection.

The Risks: Extreme. Eighteen-year-old arm strength and development bet. This can go several different ways.

Bret Sayre's Fantasy Take: Pro debuts deserve life-sized grains of salt, but SWR (let's save some space here, shall we) impressed enough prior to his 18th birthday to make him a reasonable late-round flier in dynasty drafts this offseason. That said, he's forever away, he's a pitcher, and the ceiling isn't obnoxiously high.

The Next Five:

11 Jordan Humphreys RHP

Born: 06/11/96 Age: 23 Bats: R Throws: R Height: 6'2" Weight: 223 Origin: Round 18, 2015 Draft (#539 overall)

YEAR	TEAM	LVL	AGE	W	L	SV	G	GS	IP	H	HR	BB/9	K/9	K	GB%	BABIP	WHIP	ERA	DRA	WARP	PF
2016	KNG	RK	20	3	5	0	12	12	69^{1}	65	3	1.9	9.9	76	51%	.328	1.15	3.76	2.98	2.1	103
2016	BRO	A-	20	0	1	0	1	1	6	7	0	1.5	13.5	9	20%	.467	1.33	1.50	-2.52	0.5	94
2017	COL	A	21	10	1	0	11	11	69^{2}	41	2	1.2	10.3	80	40%	.241	0.72	1.42	2.57	2.2	87
2017	SLU	A+	21	0	0	0	2	2	11	17	1	2.5	2.5	3	30%	.348	1.82	4.09	5.09	0.0	115
2019	*NYN*	*MLB*	*23*	*2*	*2*	*0*	*6*	*6*	36^{1}	*34*	*5*	*3.1*	*8.6*	*35*	*41%*	*.301*	*1.28*	*4.30*	*4.99*	*0.1*	*90*

Breakout: 2% Improve: 6% Collapse: 3% Attrition: 5% MLB: 10% *Comparables: A.J. Achter, Frank Garces, David Rollins*

Go back and read the Thomas Szapucki blurb, then mentally adjust it to a righty with a slightly worse breaking ball. Humphreys was one of early-2017's best breakout pitchers, suddenly showing three above-average pitches with command. Far too often, a bump in stuff like this is immediately followed by a blown elbow, and sure enough, Humphreys went down that summer. Like Szapucki, he was conservatively held back for the entire 2018 season and we aren't going to know much here until we see him in a competitive game environment again. If healthy, he has mid-rotation upside and could move fast.

12 Tomas Nido C

Born: 04/12/94 Age: 25 Bats: R Throws: R Height: 6'0" Weight: 210 Origin: Round 8, 2012 Draft (#260 overall)

YEAR	TEAM	LVL	AGE	PA	R	2B	3B	HR	RBI	BB	K	SB	CS	AVG/OBP/SLG	DRC+	VORP	BABIP	BRR	FRAA	WARP	PF
2016	SLU	A+	22	370	38	23	2	7	46	19	42	0	1	.320/.357/.459	142	27.8	.344	-2.4	C(88) 4.8	2.7	98
2017	BIN	AA	23	404	41	19	1	8	60	30	63	0	0	.232/.287/.354	70	4.5	.255	2.4	C(82) 28.4	2.9	99
2017	NYN	MLB	23	10	0	1	0	0	3	0	2	0	0	.300/.300/.400	89	0.2	.375	-0.1	C(3) 0.3	0.1	94
2018	BIN	AA	24	228	23	18	1	5	30	7	36	0	0	.274/.298/.437	111	6.1	.303	-2.0	C(48) 8.5	1.6	98
2018	NYN	MLB	24	90	10	3	0	1	9	4	27	0	0	.167/.200/.238	58	-3.7	.224	0.2	C(30) 3.4	0.3	89
2019	*NYN*	*MLB*	*25*	*67*	*7*	*3*	*0*	*2*	*8*	*5*	*16*	*0*	*0*	*.232/.299/.374*	*85*	*1.7*	*.284*	*-0.1*	*C 3*	*0.5*	*90*

Breakout: 17% Improve: 33% Collapse: 1% Attrition: 22% MLB: 40% *Comparables: Tony Cruz, James McCann, Kyle Farmer*

Last year, we thought Nido's defense and bat control would carry the day, despite weak offensive production at Double-A. After a 2018 repeat only went marginally better for the former Florida State League batting champion, Nido's bat now looks more like a backup's than a guy you want to give 400 plate appearances. He'll play anyway, because there's an extreme paucity of decent catching floating around these days. I suppose if you want to be kind, you can say he's likely to be above useless with the stick. But he appears on course to be the umpteenth straight promising Mets catching prospect who tops out well below his projection. Catchers are weird, man.

13 Junior Santos RHP

Born: 08/16/01 Age: 17 Bats: R Throws: R Height: 6'8" Weight: 218 Origin: International Free Agent, 2018

YEAR	TEAM	LVL	AGE	W	L	SV	G	GS	IP	H	HR	BB/9	K/9	K	GB%	BABIP	WHIP	ERA	DRA	WARP	PF
2018	DME	RK	16	1	1	0	11	10	45	35	1	1.2	7.2	36	48%	.270	0.91	2.80	3.19	1.4	89
2019	*NYN*	*MLB*	*17*	*2*	*2*	*0*	*13*	*6*	34^{1}	*38*	*7*	*3.4*	*6.4*	*24*	*45%*	*.304*	*1.48*	*5.76*	*6.68*	*-0.6*	*90*

Breakout: 0% Improve: 0% Collapse: 0% Attrition: 0% MLB: 0% *Comparables: Mike Soroka, Roberto Osuna, Martin Perez*

I'll confess that I am more comfortable making strange calls on the Mets list than most others. This is a particularly good year to do it since functionally this system is now 11 guys and then a Choose Your Own Adventure novel. Sometimes picking the 17-year-old projection bet sets you up to fall in an active volcano, but Santos has advanced stuff and control for a dude who spent most of the 2018 season only eligible for a learner's permit (and ineligible to pitch stateside). He'll flash three pitches, will touch 95, and is a—let's say—very projectable 6-foot-8. The Mets have generally done well with these low six-figures arms with some present feel for pitching. Santos might be nowhere near this list next year, or he might be near the top of it. I'd rather take a chance here than write another bland report on a major-league-ready reliever or Day 2 college pick.

14 Eric Hanhold RHP

Born: 11/01/93 Age: 25 Bats: R Throws: R Height: 6'5" Weight: 220 Origin: Round 6, 2015 Draft (#181 overall)

YEAR	TEAM	LVL	AGE	W	L	SV	G	GS	IP	H	HR	BB/9	K/9	K	GB%	BABIP	WHIP	ERA	DRA	WARP	PF
2016	BRV	A+	22	2	12	0	19	19	101	120	12	2.9	5.7	64	54%	.327	1.51	4.81	5.55	-0.1	99
2017	CAR	A+	23	8	3	2	30	3	64	71	3	3.0	8.4	60	60%	.364	1.44	3.94	4.03	0.7	106
2018	BIN	AA	24	3	1	8	17	0	25^{1}	21	1	3.2	11.4	32	60%	.323	1.18	2.84	2.89	0.6	100
2018	LVG	AAA	24	2	2	0	14	0	19	25	1	3.3	9.5	20	49%	.429	1.68	7.11	3.24	0.4	100
2018	NYN	MLB	24	0	0	0	3	0	2^{1}	4	0	3.9	7.7	2	33%	.444	2.14	7.71	8.70	-0.1	88
2019	*NYN*	*MLB*	*25*	*1*	*0*	*0*	*15*	*0*	16^{1}	*15*	*2*	*3.8*	*9.3*	*17*	*50%*	*.319*	*1.36*	*4.06*	*4.71*	*0.1*	*90*

Breakout: 5% Improve: 8% Collapse: 6% Attrition: 12% MLB: 16% *Comparables: Jeremy Horst, Ryan O'Rourke, Dan Meyer*

Hanhold could be Drew Smith, or Walter Lockett, or Kyle Dowdy, or any other fringy, swingy, middle relievery right-handed arm the Mets have acquired through various means (mostly 2017 deadline deals) to plug an inventory hole in their upper minors bullpens over the last two seasons. You should be developing these kinds of arms internally and in bulk, but the Mets have not. They've already started to weed their way through the new stock, DFAing Jamie Callahan, shipping Gerson Bautista to the Mariners, and sending Bobby Wahl out to Milwaukee. Hanhold is the best of the remaining bunch on the combination of merit and proximity. He has a little major league service time. He has premium fastball velocity and an above-average breaking ball. The variance on these profiles is so high, maybe it's Dowdy breaking out and soaking up middle innings in Citi by May, maybe it's none of them. And it's a problem for the organization that I am mentioning any of them on this prospect list, even if they'd be behind the teenaged bats below on my personal pref list.

15 Desmond Lindsay OF

Born: 01/15/97 Age: 22 Bats: R Throws: R Height: 6'0" Weight: 200 Origin: Round 2, 2015 Draft (#53 overall)

YEAR	TEAM	LVL	AGE	PA	R	2B	3B	HR	RBI	BB	K	SB	CS	AVG/OBP/SLG	DRC+	VORP	BABIP	BRR	FRAA	WARP	PF
2016	BRO	A-	19	134	18	5	0	4	17	20	26	3	1	.297/.418/.450	167	15.3	.358	-0.1	CF(29) -3.8	0.5	98
2017	COL	A	20	251	40	10	1	8	30	33	77	4	2	.220/.327/.388	110	11.2	.298	2.2	CF(62) 2.2	1.1	89
2018	SLU	A+	21	335	27	11	5	3	30	37	89	7	7	.218/.310/.320	86	0.3	.300	-0.7	CF(75) 6.0	0.4	97
2019	*NYN*	*MLB*	*22*	*252*	*22*	*5*	*1*	*7*	*25*	*19*	*82*	*2*	*1*	*.162/.224/.285*	*36*	*-10.0*	*.210*	*-0.1*	*CF 1*	*-1.0*	*90*

Breakout: 2% Improve: 6% Collapse: 0% Attrition: 4% MLB: 9% *Comparables: Daniel Fields, Aaron Hicks, Michael Saunders*

The Mets 2015 second round pick has struggled with injuries throughout his pro career. It used to be that whenever he was on the field, the everyday centerfielder tools would pop and you could talk yourself into him for one more year. All he needed was to stay healthy and get reps. Lower body injuries aren't always chronic, right? His 90 games in 2018 were a professional best, but the tools look more muted now. A swing tweak led to positive reviews in the Arizona Fall League, but what can you really project as the end product now for a 22-year-old that struggles with swing-and-miss and has trouble staying on the field? Short-side platoon outfielder? Normally I'd add here that if I really was completely out on Lindsay—I've long been an advocate—he wouldn't even have slid on to the back of this list. But… well, he didn't until the Mets traded away four prospects. That said, the system is so shallow right now that if Lindsay does come out in 2019 and show an average hit/power combo and the ability to play center again, well, there's a *Godfather 3* quote about that.

Others of note:

Hansel Moreno, IF, Low-A Columbia

To be frank, most of this list could broadly be categorized as "low minors sleepers" given the dearth of upper minors prospects, but we'll add a couple more. Moreno is a toolsy guy with present rawness, but he's already 22-years-old and only in A-ball. The aforementioned tools may not play on the dirt. He's filling out and slowing down, and the hands and arm at shortstop are more solid-average than plus. The Mets tried him all over in the South Atlantic League, and he might fit best in center field. There's potential above-average power in the profile, and he's already tapping into some of it pull side. Moreno's approach is raw enough—and he's old enough—that he might not be more than emergency depth, but he's also weirdly still projectable given his cohort. In conclusion, Hansel Moreno is a land of contrasts.

Stanley Consuegra, OF, GCL Mets

Now if I wanted to make a different weird call at #15, it could have easily been Consuegra on a different day or in a different mood. He's the more traditional 17-year-old complex league hero bet. The Mets gave him $500,000 as part of their 2017 July 2nd class, and he has center field tools and big exit velos, if you are into that sort of thing. He's a premium athlete with a lot of physical projection left, so this is more like the first page of a Choose Your Own Adventure book. The risk of falling into the volcano at the end is still very high.

Jaylen Palmer, IF, GCL Mets

When the Mets aren't spending Day Three popping low-ceiling college performers, they like to mix in the odd overslot local prep. It doesn't get much more locavore than Palmer, whose high school is a ten minute jaunt up I-678 from Citi Field. The Mets have had about as much luck with these prep flyers as the Day Three college bats, but Palmer might be a hidden gem. He had a huge growth spurt in high school and now garners Shervyen Newton comps. He's less likely to stick on the dirt than Newton, profiling best in a corner outfield spot, but he may also have the tools to carry that profile. Check back in four years to see if Gary Cohen will be making references to Flushing's own Jaylen Palmer or if that will be the purview of Tim Heiman.

Top Talents 25 and Under (born 4/1/93 or later):

1. Amed Rosario
2. Edwin Diaz
3. Andres Gimenez
4. Peter Alonso
5. Ronny Mauricio
6. Robert Gsellman
7. Shervyen Newton
8. Mark Vientos
9. David Peterson
10. Dominic Smith

Rosario is, for the time being, still a Met. His performance in the majors has been more mediocre than great, but sometimes we forget that he's only a year-and-a-half off being our no. 2 prospect in baseball on the 2017 midseason top 50. The low bar at shortstop means that even with his weak DRC+ and FRAA numbers, he was still about three-quarters of a win above replacement last year. He's been rumored to be available in trade, because he'll return a superstar and Gimenez is coming quickly; Gimenez might be a better long-term fit at shortstop if not quite a better player overall. That reality also could also push Rosario off shortstop to center field or third base within the next season or two if he remains a Met.

Diaz ahead of the top prospects feels hot takey, but it's also pretty clear that he has more value than Gimenez or Alonso. You'd trade either of those guys for him straight up in a heartbeat, no? Put it another way—Diaz is a role 7, and that's higher than either Gimenez or Alonso's OFP. He's among the small handful of the best relievers in baseball, he doesn't turn 25 until nearly Opening Day, and he's got a pretty clean pro health record. It's okay to question whether the Mets were in a position to be trading for an elite closer, but he's a hell of a pitcher.

Mickey Callaway spent a lot of the spring and summer using Gsellman like he was an Andrew Miller-style durable relief ace. It went better than it did in 2017—his fastball and slider played up in short bursts as we expected they might, and he should be at least a good MLB reliever moving forward. But he looked gassed at various points in the season when used too heavily. Diaz's acquisition should push him into a more traditional setup role, and hopefully he'll be supplemented by further acquisitions in the pen to take some of the load off.

The unceremonious salary dump of Jay Bruce slightly reopens the window for Smith to re-establish himself as a regular. 2018 was rough, with mediocre performance at both the majors and Triple-A followed by a short and difficult stint in winter ball. Somewhat bizarrely, he spent 39 games puttering around in the outfield in a fashion all too familiar to those who remember the escapades of Lucas Duda. There's playing time available at first base until the Mets end the service time charade and call Alonso up, but even there Smith's path has roadblocks. The current situation with four MLB infielders currently projected to split 2B/SS/3B could easily spill over into first base too. Time is becoming Smith's enemy.

Several circumstances conspired to make this list fairly easy. Michael Conforto and Brandon Nimmo are both ineligible by less than a month, and Jeff McNeil was a couple weeks more of missed playing time away from the rare "on the Top Ten but not on the 25U" exacta. Gsellman vs. Justin Dunn would've been a difficult call down here, but Dunn was gone before we had to make that choice. Drew Smith and Tyler Bashlor might've made a top 15, but they're clearly a cut below Kilome and Szapucki.

For the record, Jarred Kelenic would've ranked fourth before the trade, between Alonso and Mauricio. Dunn would've ranked fifth out of the prospects, between Mauricio and Newton. We'll have their full write-ups in the Seattle list, so long as the Mariners actually keep them.

New York Yankees

The State of the System:

The top guys have graduated, leaving a lot of upside and a lot of risk.

The Top Ten:

1 Jonathan Loaisiga RHP OFP: 60 Likely: 50 ETA: Debuted in 2018

Born: 11/02/94 Age: 24 Bats: R Throws: R Height: 5'11" Weight: 165 Origin: International Free Agent, 2012

YEAR	TEAM	LVL	AGE	W	L	SV	G	GS	IP	H	HR	BB/9	K/9	K	GB%	BABIP	WHIP	ERA	DRA	WARP	PF
2017	YAN	RK	22	0	1	0	6	6	13^{2}	10	1	1.3	9.9	15	58%	.257	0.88	2.63	2.59	0.5	84
2017	STA	A-	22	1	0	0	4	4	17	7	0	0.5	9.5	18	51%	.171	0.47	0.53	2.82	0.5	101
2018	TAM	A+	23	3	0	0	4	4	20	19	0	0.4	11.7	26	54%	.365	1.00	1.35	3.60	0.4	103
2018	TRN	AA	23	3	1	0	9	9	34^{1}	37	6	1.6	10.5	40	39%	.356	1.25	3.93	3.08	0.9	88
2018	NYA	MLB	23	2	0	0	9	4	24^{2}	26	3	4.4	12.0	33	52%	.383	1.54	5.11	3.29	0.5	108
2019	*NYA*	*MLB*	*24*	*3*	*4*	*0*	*11*	*11*	*55*	*56*	*9*	*3.6*	*9.1*	*56*	*42%*	*.312*	*1.42*	*4.71*	*4.72*	*0.5*	*109*

Breakout: 27% Improve: 47% Collapse: 13% Attrition: 25% MLB: 75% *Comparables: David Paulino, Daniel Norris, Gio Gonzalez*

The Report: We thought we were being super aggressive by ranking Loaisiga—at the time a 23-year-old who had one start in full-season ball—as our low-minors sleeper last year. The blurb said he might jump into the "next ten" section of our Yankees list; instead he leapt to the top of the system and into the 101, with a few stops in the majors along the way.

Loaisiga has one of the oddest stories in the minors. He was signed out of Nicaragua by the Giants in 2012, never made it stateside while battling shoulder problems, and was released out of extended spring in 2015. He spent the next year puttering around the fringes of baseball, pitching in his home country's league and for various flavors of the Nicaraguan national team. Yankees scout Ricardo Finol saw him pitch in an international competition and signed Loaisiga early in 2016, just before he was about to depart for a stint in the Italian Baseball League. He finally made his United States debut with a spot start for Low-A Charleston in June 2016, only to immediately suffer an elbow injury that required Tommy John surgery.

Loaisiga popped back up in the late-summer of 2017 like a new man, throwing 95-98 with life and command. The out pitch is a two-plane power breaking ball that usually gets labeled a curve. "Slurve" can sometimes be a pejorative, but not always, and here it's more that he throws a breaking ball with slider velocity and curve movement, which is good. The changeup flashes average and functions as a useful third pitch.

The Risks: Medium, overall. There's high health and relief risk—Loaisiga was hampered in the second half of 2018 by shoulder problems, and with his size and medical history he might be more likely to end up in the bullpen than the rotation. But we think he's reasonably likely to be a Dude in some role.

Bret Sayre's Fantasy Take: It's very tempting to look past Loaisiga, given his health problems and lack of track record. And yet, his command is very intriguing and he showed notable ability to miss bats in the majors during his brief 2018 stint. The contextual factors are always going to be against him, but he was a near miss for me on the Dynasty 101 and a potential SP4 even in that park/division—he just needs to be able to throw the requisite innings.

2 Estevan Florial OF

OFP: 60 Likely: 50 ETA: Late 2020

Born: 11/25/97 Age: 21 Bats: L Throws: R Height: 6'1" Weight: 185 Origin: International Free Agent, 2015

YEAR	TEAM	LVL	AGE	PA	R	2B	3B	HR	RBI	BB	K	SB	CS	AVG/OBP/SLG	DRC+	VORP	BABIP	BRR	FRAA	WARP	PF
2016	PUL	RK	18	268	36	10	1	7	25	28	78	10	2	.225/.315/.364	75	5.1	.305	0.0	CF(43) 0.1, LF(6) -0.8	-0.8	98
2017	CSC	A	19	389	64	21	5	11	43	41	124	17	7	.297/.373/.483	131	31.8	.431	-0.7	CF(62) -2.1, LF(13) 2.9	1.8	96
2017	TAM	A+	19	87	13	2	2	2	14	9	24	6	1	.303/.368/.461	121	7.4	.404	0.7	CF(18) 0.4	0.4	102
2018	TAM	A+	20	339	45	16	3	3	27	44	87	11	10	.255/.354/.361	103	10.5	.353	-0.9	CF(59) 1.8, RF(6) -0.2	0.4	103
2019	*NYA*	*MLB*	*21*	*252*	*25*	*6*	*0*	*6*	*20*	*16*	*92*	*4*	*2*	*.154/.206/.264*	*23*	*-14.4*	*.216*	*-0.1*	*CF 1, LF 0*	*-1.5*	*109*

Breakout: 6% Improve: 17% Collapse: 0% Attrition: 9% MLB: 17% *Comparables: Clint Frazier, Anthony Gose, Christian Yelich*

The Report: Florial is the kind of prospect we love to love. He has all the tools, including plus speed, raw power and arm. The only question is whether he'll hit enough for everything to play.

Seeing him several times this past season, I occasionally got bit of a Byron Buxton vibe. When it all works, things fall in place and it's easy to see the player he can be. When it doesn't, it seems that he struggles to translate any of the tools into consistent production. He did miss about two months in 2018 after surgery on his hamate bone and there was an adjustment period when he returned.

Florial made some changes to his bat path to try to get to more of his power, but he has not yet found the right formula. He knows the strike zone, but he struggles with pitch recognition, which leads to bouts of inconsistency and a good bit of swing and miss. He has also not yet translated his speed into base stealing prowess, as he swiped only 11 bases in 21 attempts last year. While he's no finished product, Florial will only be 21 next year, and players with his raw ability often find a way to make everything work.

The Risks: High. As you might expect, there is more variance with Florial than with most other players in the 101.

Bret Sayre's Fantasy Take: There's no question that Florial is the best dynasty prospect in this system, and the tools still make him someone to value highly. He won't make a repeat appearance as a top-50 fantasy prospect when our list drops later this week, but the upside hasn't gone anywhere—he still can be a .270 hitter with 30-35 bombs if he can tap into that raw talent. He's just a riskier proposition now.

3 Antonio Cabello OF

OFP: 60 Likely: 50 ETA: 2023

Born: 11/01/00 Age: 18 Bats: R Throws: R Height: 5'10" Weight: 160 Origin: International Free Agent, 2017

YEAR	TEAM	LVL	AGE	PA	R	2B	3B	HR	RBI	BB	K	SB	CS	AVG/OBP/SLG	DRC+	VORP	BABIP	BRR	FRAA	WARP	PF
2018	DYA	RK	17	30	5	0	1	0	1	6	6	5	1	.227/.433/.318	119	2.5	.313	0.5	CF(3) 0.1, LF(2) -0.3	0.1	117
2018	YAT	RK	17	162	21	9	4	5	20	21	34	5	5	.321/.426/.555	193	20.0	.398	-1.1	CF(28) 0.3, RF(4) 1.0	1.2	103
2019	*NYA*	*MLB*	*18*	*252*	*21*	*2*	*0*	*4*	*14*	*21*	*85*	*3*	*1*	*.107/.182/.175*	*-6*	*-23.2*	*.142*	*0.1*	*CF 0, LF 0*	*-2.4*	*109*

Breakout: 0% Improve: 0% Collapse: 0% Attrition: 0% MLB: 0% *Comparables: Adalberto Mondesi, Wilmer Flores, Tommy Brown*

The Report: The Yankees spent a boatload in the IFA market for the 2014 J2 class. Almost five years later, the organization's top five prospects are all IFAs, but only Florial—who signed late for a small bonus because of birth certificate issues—was a big ticket signing.

Cabello was signed as a catcher out of Venezuela, and he has the frame of a backstop. That belies his athleticism though and the Yanks quickly moved him out from behind the plate. He's an above-average runner with a chance to stick in center field—despite the rather squat physique—but he may slide over to right.

The bat may very well carry a corner outfield spot though. Cabello has a remarkably advanced hit tool and approach for a 17-year-old. He flashes exceptional barrel control and the ability to drive the ball to the opposite field already, and there's potentially above-average raw power down the line as well. It's very early days for the profile, but Cabello arguably has the most upside in this Yankees system.

The Risks: Extreme. Teenage complex bat learning a new position on the job. Lots of risk here.

Bret Sayre's Fantasy Take: Another tough cut from the 101, Cabello is a player I'll be watching very closely in 2019 to see how his power plays in full-season ball (assuming he gets there). The batting average (and on-base percentage) are the driving forces right now, but it's whether the power/speed can be more than just supplementary that decides Cabello's fantasy fate. If he can ring that future up to 20 apiece, he could slide up into the top 50 fantasy prospects by this time next year.

4 Deivi Garcia RHP

OFP: 60 Likely: 45 ETA: Late 2019 or 2020

Born: 05/19/99 Age: 20 Bats: R Throws: R Height: 5'10" Weight: 163 Origin: International Free Agent, 2015

YEAR	TEAM	LVL	AGE	W	L	SV	G	GS	IP	H	HR	BB/9	K/9	K	GB%	BABIP	WHIP	ERA	DRA	WARP	PF
2016	DYN	RK	17	1	5	0	12	12	48^{1}	23	1	6.0	11.4	61	63%	.237	1.14	2.61	3.50	1.2	115
2017	DYA	RK	18	1	1	0	3	3	15^{1}	10	1	1.2	10.6	18	58%	.281	0.78	1.17	3.08	0.5	113
2017	YAT	RK	18	3	0	0	4	2	16^{2}	9	3	2.2	13.0	24	32%	.194	0.78	3.24	1.68	0.8	106
2017	PUL	RK	18	2	1	0	6	5	28	23	3	4.2	13.8	43	32%	.370	1.29	4.50	3.33	0.8	100
2018	CSC	A	19	2	4	0	8	8	40^{2}	31	5	2.2	13.9	63	31%	.302	1.01	3.76	2.40	1.4	85
2018	TAM	A+	19	2	0	0	5	5	28^{1}	19	0	2.5	11.1	35	37%	.292	0.95	1.27	3.18	0.7	99
2019	*NYA*	*MLB*	*20*	*3*	*4*	*0*	*11*	*11*	*52^{1}*	*51*	*11*	*6.3*	*10.6*	*62*	*40%*	*.300*	*1.66*	*6.02*	*6.13*	*-0.4*	*109*

Breakout: 5% Improve: 8% Collapse: 2% Attrition: 7% MLB: 13% *Comparables: Lucas Giolito, Jose Fernandez, Manny Banuelos*

The Report: There's a lot going on here. Garcia made his Double-A debut just three months after his 19th birthday, after buzzing through A-ball with ease. He throws in the low-to-mid-90s, and the party piece is one of the better curveballs in the minors. We can say here what we can't always say publicly elsewhere: Garcia has an extremely high spin rate, and we can confirm that on the record because the Yankees have said it themselves.

What to make of that as evaluators is something we struggle with right now—teams have much greater access to spin rate data than we do, and they have a fuller data set to contextualize it; we get ours anecdotally and less reliably. Garcia's curveball would rank towards the top of the MLB spin rate chart, and that is generally a good thing. But we also don't need that data to project it as a potential plus-plus pitch, either: it's a sharp swing-and-miss breaker that he commands well, which is obvious in any viewing of him.

Our major concern here is that Garcia has never thrown more than the 74 innings he tossed in 2018. He's short and slight of frame, and the Yankees held him back until June in extended spring training. It's a tough projection right now to get him to a MLB starting workload. Not impossible, but tough.

The Risks: High on durability, low on talent.

Bret Sayre's Fantasy Take: It really is a shame that the highest-upside arm in this system is such a bad bet to pitch enough innings to capitalize on that talent. A better frame would make him a top-101 arm, but the reliever risk here makes him both a potential SP3 and barely a top-150 fantasy prospect.

5 Everson Pereira OF

OFP: 55 Likely: 45 ETA: 2022-23

Born: 04/10/01 Age: 18 Bats: R Throws: R Height: 6'0" Weight: 191 Origin: International Free Agent, 2017

YEAR	TEAM	LVL	AGE	PA	R	2B	3B	HR	RBI	BB	K	SB	CS	AVG/OBP/SLG	DRC+	VORP	BABIP	BRR	FRAA	WARP	PF
2018	PUL	RK	17	183	21	8	2	3	26	15	60	3	2	.263/.322/.389	68	3.0	.390	-1.7	CF(36) 5.6	-0.1	100
2019	*NYA*	*MLB*	*18*	*252*	*14*	*5*	*0*	*5*	*21*	*2*	*108*	*0*	*0*	*.129/.136/.213*	*-17*	*-26.6*	*.194*	*-0.5*	*CF 2*	*-2.7*	*109*

Breakout: 0% Improve: 0% Collapse: 0% Attrition: 0% MLB: 0% *Comparables: Adalberto Mondesi, Wilmer Flores, Tommy Brown*

The Report: We're usually somewhat conservative with recent international signings, until they've established themselves outside of a complex. Pereira jumped the complex league level completely and made his pro debut at the tender age of 17 in the Appalachian League. He's even *younger* than Wander Franco, who did the same thing to much greater fanfare.

Pereira isn't quite Franco in terms of impact tools, and he was more fine-to-good in the Appy than great. It's a solid profile—good natural hitting ability, plus runner, goes and gets it in center field—without screaming superstar potential. There's projectability in the body, and he might yet grow into some real power, although it isn't there yet and there's a lot of weight on "might" there. But having a decent season stateside at that age is a huge accomplishment, worthy of substantial praise in and of itself.

The Risks: Medium-to-high. There are enough secondary skills here that we think he's got a strong shot to make it as 17-year-old short-season players go, but the shape of it all is still very uncertain.

Bret Sayre's Fantasy Take: It's still too early to go too far in on Pereira, but he's a great name to keep an eye on in 2019 as a potential riser. Right now it's more of a speed-based OF3 profile, but it is still awfully early. He should be owned if your league rosters 200 prospects.

6 Luis Gil RHP OFP: 55 Likely: 45 ETA: 2022

Born: 06/03/98 Age: 21 Bats: R Throws: R Height: 6'3" Weight: 176 Origin: International Free Agent, 2015

YEAR	TEAM	LVL	AGE	W	L	SV	G	GS	IP	H	HR	BB/9	K/9	K	GB%	BABIP	WHIP	ERA	DRA	WARP	PF
2017	DTW	RK	19	0	2	0	14	14	41^2	31	2	4.3	10.6	49	54%	.287	1.22	2.59	3.45	1.2	126
2018	PUL	RK	20	2	1	0	10	10	39^1	21	1	5.7	13.3	58	35%	.256	1.17	1.37	3.34	1.2	98
2018	STA	A-	20	0	2	0	2	2	6^2	11	1	8.1	13.5	10	39%	.455	2.55	5.40	3.40	0.1	87
2019	*NYA*	*MLB*	*21*	*2*	*3*	*0*	*14*	*7*	*33^2*	*35*	*6*	*9.2*	*9.0*	*34*	*41%*	*.309*	*2.06*	*6.83*	*6.97*	*-0.6*	*109*

Breakout: 0% Improve: 0% Collapse: 0% Attrition: 0% MLB: 0% *Comparables: Nestor Cortes, Domingo German, Rafael Montero*

The Report: We like Jake Cave at Baseball Prospectus. He's a nifty fourth outfielder who might've added enough pop to be a platoon guy or even a regular now. But he was once Rule 5'd, and the Yankees pretty much had to move him last spring in a roster crunch. In return for Cave, the Yanks got Gil, a tall drink of water right out of the Twins' Dominican complex. He throws in the mid-to-upper-90s with ease, along with a potentially useful curveball and a fringy changeup. The command isn't there yet, but he was one of the more impressive pitchers in the Appy League, and has a chance to be an impact arm in three or four years. The Yankees have repeatedly stolen unheralded players out of the low levels of other systems. These moves are a testament to both their scouting and player development operations, which power a strong farm system that never gets to add premium talent in the draft.

The Risks: Extreme, and this is one of those guys I'd write as a 70/30 if it was sensible to do so. Gil has never even thrown as many as 50 innings in a season, is extremely wild, and missed the entire 2017 season with arm problems. There's durability risk, relief risk, injury risk, performance risk, all of it.

Bret Sayre's Fantasy Take: If you're in a deep league and want to bet on arm strength, he's a good risk to take, but in most formats you can sit back on players like this until they've got a little more stateside experience. There are just so many short-season arms you can dream of as potential SP2s if everything clicks.

7 Mike King RHP OFP: 55 Likely: 45 ETA: Late 2019

Born: 05/25/95 Age: 24 Bats: R Throws: R Height: 6'3" Weight: 210 Origin: Round 12, 2016 Draft (#353 overall)

YEAR	TEAM	LVL	AGE	W	L	SV	G	GS	IP	H	HR	BB/9	K/9	K	GB%	BABIP	WHIP	ERA	DRA	WARP	PF
2016	BAT	A-	21	2	2	1	10	1	21^1	22	0	2.5	6.3	15	65%	.338	1.31	3.38	4.17	0.2	98
2017	GRB	A	22	11	9	0	26	25	149	141	14	1.3	6.4	106	57%	.285	1.09	3.14	3.80	2.6	103
2018	TAM	A+	23	1	3	0	7	7	40^1	33	1	2.2	10.0	45	61%	.302	1.07	1.79	3.57	0.8	104
2018	TRN	AA	23	6	2	0	12	11	82	65	4	1.4	8.3	76	46%	.276	0.95	2.09	3.27	1.9	93
2018	SWB	AAA	23	4	0	0	6	6	39	20	3	1.4	7.2	31	54%	.167	0.67	1.15	3.66	0.8	99
2019	*NYA*	*MLB*	*24*	*7*	*8*	*0*	*20*	*20*	*122*	*128*	*20*	*3.3*	*6.7*	*91*	*48%*	*.289*	*1.41*	*5.13*	*5.15*	*0.5*	*109*

Breakout: 16% Improve: 26% Collapse: 23% Attrition: 39% MLB: 57% *Comparables: Steven Brault, Tim Cooney, Nick Kingham*

The Report: King is another great example of the organization's scouting strength. While certainly serviceable in Miami's system, King grew tremendously in his first season with the Yankees, moving through three levels and finding success throughout. The foundation for that success is both physical and mental. He has a plus sinker that he throws at 91-93 with good movement. He uses that offering to generate ground balls. King adds plus command and control to that and he has also shown an ability to read hitters and make adjustments from pitch to pitch.

The biggest shortcoming to this point has been an inability to come up with another plus secondary offering or two to pair with the two-seamer. He made progress this season with his slider, but it's not reliably a swing-and-miss pitch yet. He is also working to add a four-seam fastball and a changeup. Both pitches are slightly behind the slider.

King doesn't hurt himself, keeps the ball in the park, and has shown the ability to succeed even as he has been promoted aggressively. In a system bursting with toolsy but volatile prospects, King stands out as a high-probability big-leaguer, even if his ceiling is a bit lower than most of the names surrounding him on this list.

The Risks: Medium. There is always an injury risk with any pitcher, but King's command/control gives him minimal non-injury risk.

Bret Sayre's Fantasy Take: Innings eaters have value to big-league teams, but dynasty owners just have different priorities. There isn't enough ability to miss bats for us to pay much attention here.

8 Roansy Contreras RHP   OFP: 55   Likely: 45   ETA: 2022ish

Born: 11/07/99   Age: 19   Bats: R   Throws: R   Height: 6'0"   Weight: 175   Origin: International Free Agent, 2016

YEAR	TEAM	LVL	AGE	W	L	SV	G	GS	IP	H	HR	BB/9	K/9	K	GB%	BABIP	WHIP	ERA	DRA	WARP	PF
2017	DYA	RK	17	0	3	0	6	6	22	25	2	2.0	7.0	17	57%	.311	1.36	3.68	4.15	0.4	112
2017	YAN	RK	17	4	1	0	8	5	31^2	35	2	3.4	4.8	17	43%	.297	1.48	4.26	3.96	0.7	94
2018	STA	A-	18	0	0	0	5	5	28^2	15	1	2.8	10.0	32	49%	.219	0.84	1.26	3.91	0.4	88
2018	CSC	A	18	0	2	0	7	7	34^2	29	4	3.1	7.3	28	34%	.255	1.18	3.38	4.40	0.3	84
2019	*NYA*	*MLB*	*19*	*2*	*4*	*0*	*10*	*10*	*45^2*	*54*	*11*	*4.7*	*6.5*	*33*	*39%*	*.302*	*1.72*	*6.67*	*6.78*	*-0.7*	*109*

Breakout: 0%   Improve: 0%   Collapse: 0%   Attrition: 0%   MLB: 0%   *Comparables: Deolis Guerra, Kelvin Herrera, Vicente Campos*

The Report: Last year, we wrote up Contreras as a low-90s guy with a chance to reach the mid-90s. Fast forward, and he's already there and looking pretty advanced for a teenager. His changeup flashes plus. The curveball isn't far behind. It's a pretty good arm action with good command for the level. He's got a nice smooth delivery and repeats well. He's a bit on the slight/small side for now, but there's some physical projectability remaining. I hope you aren't sick of reading about this type of arm, because there are like a half-dozen more ahead.

About that last point: we aren't, strictly speaking, supposed to care about organizational development track records and that sort of thing. On our national products and grades, we generally treat a Yankees pitching prospect the same as an Orioles one. Yet we can't help but note that the Yankees track record of developing pitchers of this type is as good as anyone else in the game. That already shows up in the system depth. The Yankees are perceived to have a farm system that is "down" right now because they've graduated or traded most of their high-end talent, but the arms at this end of the list are awfully good for the back of a Top Ten.

The Risks: High, simply because he's a slight of frame kid who just turned 19 and has made five starts above short-season ball. But on the lower side of high.

Bret Sayre's Fantasy Take: It's very clear at this point the Yankees have a type, and unfortunately it doesn't align with the type that dynasty owners have.

9 Clarke Schmidt RHP   OFP: 55   Likely: 45   ETA: 2020

Born: 02/20/96   Age: 23   Bats: R   Throws: R   Height: 6'1"   Weight: 200   Origin: Round 1, 2017 Draft (#16 overall)

YEAR	TEAM	LVL	AGE	W	L	SV	G	GS	IP	H	HR	BB/9	K/9	K	GB%	BABIP	WHIP	ERA	DRA	WARP	PF
2018	STA	A-	22	0	1	0	2	2	8^1	4	0	2.2	10.8	10	37%	.211	0.72	1.08	3.04	0.2	87
2019	*NYA*	*MLB*	*23*	*2*	*2*	*0*	*11*	*7*	*32^2*	*34*	*5*	*5.0*	*8.0*	*29*	*45%*	*.310*	*1.62*	*5.33*	*5.37*	*0.0*	*109*

Breakout: 2%   Improve: 2%   Collapse: 1%   Attrition: 1%   MLB: 3%   *Comparables: Jonathan Loaisiga, Dillon Peters, Matthew Carasiti*

The Report: I wrote Joe Palumbo up for the Next Year's 101 article under the theory that interesting pitchers often make big jumps the year after returning from Tommy John surgery. One of the other pitchers I strongly considered for that "slot" was Clarke Schmidt. Ultimately, Palumbo had more of a pro track record both before and after surgery, but Schmidt has appeal too: a righty who slings in a heavy fastball in the mid-90s, projects for an easy plus slider, a changeup that also flashes pretty big, and even gives you a show-me curve. And we know the Yankees quite like him, because they drafted Schmidt in the middle of the first round in 2017 even though he'd *already had* surgery earlier that spring.

It takes about two calendar years, give or take, for command and feel to fully return after UCL replacement surgery, and there are often bumps in the road, especially that first year. Schmidt made his pro debut this past June, and was handled extremely carefully, making eight abbreviated starts in the GCL and NYPL. We're going to need to see him make 20-plus starts and throw fuller games before we go crazy here, but early returns were pretty good. He could move quite fast if things fall right, a la Loaisiga.

The Risks: High. We have no idea yet if Schmidt can handle a pro starting workload, although there's probably a fastball/slurve reliever here even if things don't work out. Early signs on his return were promising, but there have been pitchers who haven't made the next step. There's also some positive risk here—the possibility that the injury was hiding his full talent.

Bret Sayre's Fantasy Take: I'd let someone else take the risk here and use the roster spot on someone who's not a pitcher.

10 Chance Adams RHP

OFP: 55 Likely: 45 ETA: Debuted in 2018

Born: 08/10/94 Age: 24 Bats: R Throws: R Height: 6'1" Weight: 220 Origin: Round 5, 2015 Draft (#153 overall)

YEAR	TEAM	LVL	AGE	W	L	SV	G	GS	IP	H	HR	BB/9	K/9	K	GB%	BABIP	WHIP	ERA	DRA	WARP	PF
2016	TAM	A+	21	5	0	0	12	12	57^{2}	41	4	2.3	11.4	73	42%	.276	0.97	2.65	2.39	2.0	103
2016	TRN	AA	21	8	1	0	13	12	69^{2}	35	5	3.1	9.2	71	47%	.181	0.85	2.07	3.15	1.6	98
2017	TRN	AA	22	4	0	0	6	6	35	23	2	3.9	8.2	32	43%	.228	1.09	1.03	3.57	0.7	94
2017	SWB	AAA	22	11	5	0	21	21	115^{1}	81	9	3.4	8.0	103	42%	.236	1.08	2.89	4.14	2.0	98
2018	SWB	AAA	23	4	5	0	27	23	113	101	16	4.6	9.0	113	42%	.282	1.41	4.78	4.15	1.8	98
2018	NYA	MLB	23	0	1	0	3	1	7^{2}	8	3	4.7	4.7	4	38%	.217	1.57	7.04	7.07	-0.2	101
2019	*NYA*	*MLB*	*24*	*3*	*2*	*0*	*30*	*5*	*51*	*45*	*7*	*4.1*	*8.3*	*47*	*41%*	*.268*	*1.32*	*4.68*	*4.70*	*0.4*	*109*

Breakout: 15% Improve: 27% Collapse: 33% Attrition: 38% MLB: 72% *Comparables: Aaron Blair, Keyvius Sampson, Adam Warren*

The Report: Are the days of a fastball up to 98 and a plus-plus slider coming back here? Adams battled elbow problems for much of the season amidst sagging velocity, and was most often 91-94 instead of the 93-96 you'd see at his best. He didn't pitch nearly as well in Triple-A as he'd done in 2017, although he did account fairly well for himself during an emergency start in Fenway in August.

Adams always had significant relief risk; he was a college reliever whom the Yankees converted to starting in 2016. His changeup and curveball are underdeveloped compared to the rest of the profile, and now injuries have taken hold and affected his stuff and command for most of a season. It really is an explosive fastball/slider combo when things are working well, and if the stuff doesn't come all the way back this spring, it might be time to start considering a shift back to the bullpen.

The Risks: High. Health and durability are major concerns at this point.

Bret Sayre's Fantasy Take: You know what we do with likely relievers here. This is the 30th list after all.

The Next Five:

11 Anthony Seigler C

Born: 06/20/99 Age: 20 Bats: B Throws: S Height: 6'0" Weight: 200 Origin: Round 1, 2018 Draft (#23 overall)

YEAR	TEAM	LVL	AGE	PA	R	2B	3B	HR	RBI	BB	K	SB	CS	AVG/OBP/SLG	DRC+	VORP	BABIP	BRR	FRAA	WARP	PF
2018	YAT	RK	19	42	7	2	0	1	4	6	7	0	0	.333/.429/.472	176	4.7	.393	-0.3	C(10) -0.2	0.3	103
2018	PUL	RK	19	53	4	1	0	0	5	8	5	0	0	.209/.340/.233	93	0.4	.231	0.1	C(11) 0.0	0.1	104
2019	*NYA*	*MLB*	*20*	*252*	*19*	*2*	*0*	*4*	*15*	*17*	*64*	*0*	*0*	*.112/.169/.179*	*-11*	*-22.9*	*.128*	*-0.5*	*C 0*	*-2.5*	*109*

Breakout: 1% Improve: 1% Collapse: 0% Attrition: 0% MLB: 1% *Comparables: Francisco Pena, Christian Bethancourt, Brandon Drury*

Pat Venditte has nothing on Anthony Seigler, an athletic switch-hitting catcher with the potential to play other left-spectrum positions. Oh, and he was also a real prospect as a switch-pitcher too.

The Yankees popped the Florida prep in the first round and placed him behind the plate, while noting there might be other possibilities down the line. The bat is fairly advanced, with a sweet-looking, quick swing and a decent idea at the plate. The power projection is another thing still more in the line of possibility than actualization yet. As we frequently note, the history of high school catching prospects is terrible, between the amount of development needed and the pressure put on by the rigor of the position, but Seigler is too interesting not to rank. And hey, putting him eleventh saves us having to come up with a full grade and risk profile for another year.

12 Albert Abreu RHP

Born: 09/26/95 Age: 23 Bats: R Throws: R Height: 6'2" Weight: 175 Origin: International Free Agent, 2013

YEAR	TEAM	LVL	AGE	W	L	SV	G	GS	IP	H	HR	BB/9	K/9	K	GB%	BABIP	WHIP	ERA	DRA	WARP	PF
2016	QUD	A	20	2	8	4	21	14	90	62	5	4.9	10.4	104	49%	.264	1.23	3.50	3.73	1.3	101
2016	LNC	A+	20	1	0	0	3	2	11^2	12	2	6.9	8.5	11	41%	.312	1.80	5.40	4.50	0.1	106
2017	CSC	A	21	1	0	0	3	2	14^2	9	1	1.8	13.5	22	61%	.296	0.82	1.84	2.15	0.5	89
2017	TAM	A+	21	1	3	0	9	9	34^1	33	2	3.9	8.1	31	48%	.316	1.40	4.19	5.20	0.0	100
2018	TAM	A+	22	4	3	0	13	13	62^2	54	9	4.2	9.3	65	45%	.274	1.32	4.16	4.00	1.0	102
2019	*NYA*	*MLB*	*23*	*3*	*4*	*0*	*21*	*11*	*57^1*	*58*	*9*	*5.3*	*8.0*	*51*	*43%*	*.295*	*1.60*	*5.48*	*5.53*	*-0.2*	*109*

Breakout: 7% Improve: 11% Collapse: 4% Attrition: 8% MLB: 16% *Comparables: Scott Barlow, Dean Deetz, Sean Newcomb*

It was a rough year for our former two-time top 101 guy. Abreu missed the first month of the season after having his appendix removed, disappeared for another month later in the season with elbow problems, and didn't pitch well when he toed the rubber. The lost 2018 came after he missed much of 2017 with recurring shoulder problems, so durability is now a major red flag. We needed to see a command jump here if he had much of a chance to stay in the rotation long-term anyway, and that hasn't come yet either. He hasn't fallen quite as much as "101 to off the top ten" suggests, because we're still in the OFP 55 projection range here. The hourglass has started running, but there's still a mid-to-upper-90s fastball and power curve combination to be reckoned with lurking deeper.

13 Luis Medina RHP

Born: 05/03/99 Age: 20 Bats: R Throws: R Height: 6'1" Weight: 175 Origin: International Free Agent, 2015

YEAR	TEAM	LVL	AGE	W	L	SV	G	GS	IP	H	HR	BB/9	K/9	K	GB%	BABIP	WHIP	ERA	DRA	WARP	PF
2017	DYA	RK	18	1	1	0	4	3	15^2	17	0	5.7	9.8	17	61%	.370	1.72	5.74	4.71	0.2	112
2017	PUL	RK	18	1	1	0	6	6	23	14	1	5.5	8.6	22	56%	.217	1.22	5.09	4.66	0.3	101
2018	PUL	RK	19	1	3	0	12	12	36	32	3	11.5	11.8	47	43%	.337	2.17	6.25	5.38	0.3	102
2019	*NYA*	*MLB*	*20*	*1*	*4*	*0*	*7*	*7*	*26*	*28*	*5*	*17.6*	*8.3*	*24*	*47%*	*.310*	*3.03*	*9.85*	*10.16*	*-1.4*	*109*

Breakout: 0% Improve: 0% Collapse: 0% Attrition: 0% MLB: 0% *Comparables: Jamie Callahan, Jefry Rodriguez, Jordan Hicks*

Medina ratchets it up to the upper-90s freely and easily, his curveball projects as a future plus swing-and-miss offering, and his changeup might get to average or fringe-average eventually. We've talked about how deep the system is, sure. Even still, why is he down here in the next five with that kind of raw stuff? Simply put, his command and control are terrible at present, and "terrible" might be generous. Medina walked 46 batters in 36 innings in the Appy League this year, which is genuinely difficult to do when you have that kind of stuff in short-season ball. The arm is special enough that he's going to have a bunch of chances to pull it together in various roles, but there's much to assemble here.

14 Frank German RHP

Born: 09/22/97 Age: 21 Bats: R Throws: R Height: 6'2" Weight: 195 Origin: Round 4, 2018 Draft (#127 overall)

YEAR	TEAM	LVL	AGE	W	L	SV	G	GS	IP	H	HR	BB/9	K/9	K	GB%	BABIP	WHIP	ERA	DRA	WARP	PF
2018	STA	A-	20	1	3	1	10	4	28^1	22	0	1.9	12.1	38	44%	.314	0.99	2.22	1.94	1.0	92
2019	*NYA*	*MLB*	*21*	*2*	*1*	*1*	*21*	*4*	*33^2*	*35*	*6*	*3.9*	*8.7*	*33*	*36%*	*.309*	*1.48*	*4.88*	*4.90*	*0.2*	*109*

Breakout: 0% Improve: 0% Collapse: 0% Attrition: 0% MLB: 0% *Comparables: Brett Kennedy, Tanner Scott, Jose Castillo*

The Yankees have a long history (*gesticulates wildly at the rest of the list*) of developing low-investment arms into significant prospects. One particular type of pitcher they gravitate towards here are southeastern college pitchers. They popped German in the fourth round last year, after a fine career as a starter at the University of North Florida. He came out with a typical fourth-round college starter profile: low-90s fastball, nice breaking ball, decent change, good command; a prospect but not a particularly exciting one. Of course, since it's the Yankees, his velocity almost immediately spiked into the mid-90s and touched 98 as a pro in the Penn League. He was pitching in relatively short stints, up to only four innings and 55 pitches, and he spent the summer of 2017 in relief on the Cape. In other words, he might be a pen guy, which is why we aren't quite going nuts yet, but if he retains these gains in true starting length stints in full-season, he's going to shoot up this list quite fast.

15 Josh Stowers OF

Born: 02/25/97 Age: 22 Bats: R Throws: R Height: 6'1" Weight: 200 Origin: Round 2, 2018 Draft (#54 overall)

YEAR	TEAM	LVL	AGE	PA	R	2B	3B	HR	RBI	BB	K	SB	CS	AVG/OBP/SLG	DRC+	VORP	BABIP	BRR	FRAA	WARP	PF
2018	EVE	A-	21	244	32	15	0	5	28	37	57	20	4	.260/.380/.410	136	12.1	.336	0.5	CF(47) -2.8	0.5	109
2019	*SEA*	*MLB*	*22*	*252*	*25*	*10*	*0*	*7*	*24*	*23*	*78*	*6*	*2*	*.147/.223/.289*	*35*	*-9.8*	*.180*	*0.6*	*CF -2*	*-1.2*	*97*

Breakout: 2% Improve: 2% Collapse: 0% Attrition: 2% MLB: 3% *Comparables: Roger Bernadina, Darrell Ceciliani, Michael Taylor*

Stowers was the Mariners second-round pick this past summer, and the Yankees picked him up in the Sonny Gray/Shed Long three-way deal. We have him rated lower than we rated Shed despite an intriguing power/speed combo and a two-year track record of college performance at Louisville. That part of the deal still makes sense for the Yankees, since Stowers is years away from the 40-man and the Yankees love their athletic outfielders and college performers. Despite present above-average speed, Stowers might end up in a corner—likely left due to a fringy arm. And we don't know how much of that power will get into games against better pitching yet. This is one of those profiles where it may just come down to how many sliders he can lay off, and we didn't learn anything more about that in the Northwest League than we did in the ACC. There's a potential average hit/power every day center fielder there, with a likelier outcome as a bench outfielder.

Others of note:

Josh Breaux, C, Short-season Staten Island

Hall of Fame football coach Bill Parcells had a draft philosophy, which Bill Belichick has copied, where he'd sometimes double-up positions with high picks. This makes intrinsic sense: if you want one really good running back, you have better odds if you draft Butch Woolfork *and* Joe Morris instead of just one of them (the really good one ended up being Joe Morris). This doesn't typically translate to baseball since roles are flexible enough that you don't need to slot guys that tightly at draft time. But catcher is really off to the side on the defensive spectrum, its own little thing with its own little quirks, and the attrition rate is high enough that you're probably going to need to have multiple real prospects donning the tools of ignorance.

Breaux represents that rare double-up, coming in the second round of last year's draft after Seigler went in the first. Like Seigler, he was also a significant prospect on the mound, and there's probably fallback potential there if things don't work out at the plate. There's huge raw power here and thus big upside, but he needs to make significant refinements to his hitting approach if he's going to get there in games, and his defense behind the plate needs work too.

Domingo Acevedo, RHP, Double-A Trenton

Acevedo slipping off the top ten saved us from having to deal with a weird quirk in his ETA—he's been on an MLB roster, called up to serve in an emergency depth role during last season's Subway Series, but he's yet to actually pitch in the majors. He was only intermittently healthy in 2018, missing about six weeks early in the season with blister issues, suffering a concussion while already on the DL, and losing almost a month late in the summer with a bicep strain. He also didn't advance past Double-A, a level he'd already conquered in 2017. With a violent delivery, strong starting system depth, and pre-existing inconsistency, he could be pushed to the bullpen forever any minute now. The fastball and slider are big enough that it still could be a heck of a relief outcome, though.

Trevor Stephan, RHP, Double-A Trenton

Stephan has a weird arm action—he drops late from what looks like a standard overhand or high-3/4 look to a low-3/4 slot. That type of slot isn't always a bullpen profile, but it usually isn't very deceptive to lefties without a strong third pitch to the armside, and Stephan's changeup isn't tracking to get there. He does have a strong two-pitch mix up front with a mid-90's fastball and a frisbee slider, and we wouldn't be shocked if those pop a little more in short relief down the road. If this all sounds like the profile for a righty reliever who mows down same-side hitters, well, you're probably on the right path.

Thairo Estrada, IF

The Yankees have a cast of thousands that we could've written about down here, some of whom might project as bigger prospects than Estrada. He *is* worth talking about on his talent alone, but he also earned a mention for reasons bigger than baseball. Estrada was shot in the hip last offseason during a robbery in his native Venezuela, and he had a brutally complicated recovery that caused him to miss most of the 2018 season. Before the injury, he was a cool hit-tool driven sleeper middle infielder hidden in a deep system. He got back on the field more consistently in the Arizona Fall League, and we'll have a better handle on what he is moving forward in the spring. The Yankees have retained him on the 40-man roster through it all, and it would be a fantastic thing if he can establish himself as a MLB player.

Top Talents 25 and Under (born 4/1/93 or later):

1. Gleyber Torres
2. Miguel Andujar
3. Luis Severino
4. Clint Frazier
5. Jonathan Loaisiga
6. Estevan Florial
7. Antonio Cabello
8. Deivi Garcia
9. Jonathan Holder
10. Tyler Wade

Gleyber Torres came into his full game power right when he hit the majors, and quickly established himself as one of baseball's best young infielders. We use "infielders" instead of "shortstops" because his position isn't quite clear yet over the short-term or the long-term, with a lot of moving parts around New York's infield. He played most of 2018 at second base and excelled there, but he's also fine at shortstop and has experience at third base.

One of those moving pieces ranks just below Torres here. Miguel Andujar had a phenomenal rookie season at the plate, nearly stealing Rookie of the Year honors away from Shohei Ohtani. He wasn't so good in the field at third base, and his poor throwing accuracy had a cascading effect on his all around his game. He could be headed to first base or designated hitter sooner rather than later, possibly as soon as this year.

Luis Severino was just ahead of Torres last year, and would've been at the top of this exercise had we done it in the first half of the season. Even with the terrible second half, he was still one of the better pitchers in the American League overall. He's an ace, albeit one with a touch of risk built in.

You probably don't know what to make of Clint Frazier. I don't either. He's had terrible concussion issues—ones that wrecked his life not just on the baseball field but off it too—and we aren't equipped to project how that impacts him moving forward. Given what he was battling, his 2018 performance at Triple-A is nothing short of remarkable, and the underlying tools here have always been amazing. Let's hope it comes back together for him in 2019.

Sneaking onto the bottom of the list are Jonathan Holder and Tyler Wade. Holder has pretty much solidified himself as a quality setup relief option on skill, who the Yankees will likely continue to use in middle relief because of the depth of their bullpen. Wade's in that weird ineligible for lists/still basically a prospect zone, just 24 and likely headed back to Triple-A for the start of 2019. He hasn't come into the power we thought he had a shot at yet, and he hasn't hit in the majors at all in limited opportunities, but he has retained most of the skills that got him onto the rear of the top 101 two years ago. He deserves a shot to be someone's bench weapon sooner rather than later; the Yankees seem to have blocked him with DJ LeMahieu and Troy Tulowitzki over the short term, unfortunately.

Just as the cherry on top, Aaron Judge, Gary Sanchez, and Greg Bird are all ineligible for this list by less than a year. What a crop of young talent, for the franchise that already has the largest economic advantages in the sport.

Oakland Athletics

The State of the System:

It feels like a better system that it actually is since most of the pitchers are hurt and one of the toolsy outfielders is actually a football player.

The Top Ten:

1 Jesus Luzardo LHP OFP: 70 Likely: 60 ETA: 2019

Born: 09/30/97 Age: 21 Bats: L Throws: L Height: 6'1" Weight: 205 Origin: Round 3, 2016 Draft (#94 overall)

YEAR	TEAM	LVL	AGE	W	L	SV	G	GS	IP	H	HR	BB/9	K/9	K	GB%	BABIP	WHIP	ERA	DRA	WARP	PF
2017	NAT	RK	19	1	0	0	3	3	13^{2}	14	1	0.0	9.9	15	33%	.342	1.02	1.32	2.01	0.6	106
2017	ATH	RK	19	0	1	0	4	3	11^{2}	9	0	0.8	10.0	13	58%	.290	0.86	1.54	2.73	0.4	101
2017	VER	A-	19	1	0	0	5	5	18	12	1	2.0	10.0	20	53%	.250	0.89	2.00	2.56	0.6	105
2018	STO	A+	20	2	1	0	3	3	14^{2}	6	0	3.1	15.3	25	56%	.240	0.75	1.23	1.70	0.6	93
2018	MID	AA	20	7	3	0	16	16	78^{2}	58	5	2.1	9.8	86	46%	.268	0.97	2.29	3.40	1.8	108
2018	NAS	AAA	20	1	1	0	4	4	16	25	2	3.9	10.1	18	51%	.469	2.00	7.31	2.90	0.5	91
2019	*OAK*	*MLB*	*21*	*5*	*5*	*0*	*16*	*16*	*80*	*66*	*10*	*2.9*	*9.4*	*84*	*43%*	*.274*	*1.15*	*3.87*	*4.28*	*1.1*	*96*

Breakout: 9% Improve: 16% Collapse: 8% Attrition: 17% MLB: 30% *Comparables: Henry Owens, Drew Hutchison, Shelby Miller*

The Report: Luzardo is one of the most polished and skilled pitchers you'll see in the minor leagues. He has a relatively short pitcher's frame and doesn't have overly long levers, but is a plus athlete with quality quick twitch and coordination. He has very clean arm action and while his delivery can be a bit rotational, he has no trouble repeating his release point. He sits 93-95 with the four-seam fastball and has average command of the offering. His primary secondary is a plus 85-86 changeup with good arm speed, tumble, and some fade. Luzardo was obviously working on finding consistency with his breaking ball in the two starts I saw him, but the 82-84 curve flashed plus multiple times, with plus depth and spin. The pitch has both vertical and horizontal break when located at the knees or higher, but the bottom drops out when he throws it below the zone.

Luzardo also showed impressive pitchability, as he was comfortable using his breaking ball early in counts to surprise the hitter for an easy strike one. He threw his changeup sparingly and was able to get hitters to whiff just by locating his fastball and breaking ball.

Luzardo profiles as a No. 3 starter on a first division team with a real possibility at being one of the better pitchers in the game if his command develops further.

The Risks: Medium. The risk is about as low as it gets for pitchers who have already had UCL trouble. He has great feel for two of his three plus offerings, and average command. He's ready for the big leagues, and as his body finishes maturing and he gains experience, his command and feel should get even better.

Ben Carsley's Fantasy Take: For my money, Luzardo is the second-best pitching prospect in the game, trailing only Forrest Whitley. In the top-101 I compared him to the best version of James Paxton, and I truly believe that's his upside. Sure, he already has TJ on his resume, but he's far removed from the procedure and clearly hasn't suffered from it. Luzardo is a top-20 overall fantasy prospect and a stud in the making. I expect him to serve as a fantasy SP2/3 for as long as he's healthy.

2 A.J. Puk LHP OFP: 60 Likely: 50 ETA: 2020

Born: 04/25/95 Age: 24 Bats: L Throws: L Height: 6'7" Weight: 220 Origin: Round 1, 2016 Draft (#6 overall)

YEAR	TEAM	LVL	AGE	W	L	SV	G	GS	IP	H	HR	BB/9	K/9	K	GB%	BABIP	WHIP	ERA	DRA	WARP	PF
2016	VER	A-	21	0	4	0	10	10	32^{2}	23	0	3.3	11.0	40	51%	.271	1.07	3.03	2.67	1.0	95
2017	STO	A+	22	4	5	0	14	11	61	44	1	3.4	14.5	98	42%	.336	1.10	3.69	2.11	2.2	106
2017	MID	AA	22	2	5	0	13	13	64	64	2	3.5	12.1	86	48%	.380	1.39	4.36	2.91	1.7	112
2019	*OAK*	*MLB*	*24*	*3*	*3*	*0*	*8*	*8*	*42^{1}*	*36*	*4*	*4.0*	*9.5*	*45*	*41%*	*.287*	*1.29*	*3.92*	*4.34*	*0.6*	*96*

Breakout: 13% Improve: 26% Collapse: 12% Attrition: 24% MLB: 40% *Comparables: Edwar Cabrera, Matt Barnes, Dan Meyer*

The Report: There's an alternate timeline where Puk doesn't blow out his UCL last spring and carves up the minors on the way to a fabulous late-season debut and Wild Card game start. Despite their surprise 2018 playoff run, the A's might have preferred that fork in the multiverse as well, as they enter 2019 with Yusmeiro Petit among their best five starting options. But you can't change the past—even if you have Jose Canseco's time machine—and pitchers of all stripes break. Puk won't be ready for Opening Day 2019, but you should see him sometime in the summer.

Before the injury the stuff was, well, good enough to rank Puk as a top 30 prospect in baseball. He hits the mid-90s—sometimes higher—from the left side with premium extension and deception, a slider that looked like a potential 7 on its good days—and mechanical issues that left him struggling at times to throw enough strikes. The stuff was good enough that it didn't really matter in the minors, but we will have to see how much of it comes back from surgery. (Anecdotally, I tend to be more concerned about the "bad mechanics" dudes coming back, but that's a personal predilection with no real science backing it). There was always a fair bit of reliever risk in the profile, but with that two-pitch combo, Puk would have closer stuff.

The Risks: High. Puk is coming off Tommy John surgery and has missed significant, important development time. We won't really know what he is now until he steps on a mound in Arizona sometime this summer. If you want to look at positive variance this could easily be a 70/50 if you were so inclined.

Ben Carsley's Fantasy Take: As we've preached many, many times, the no. 1 thing dynasty leaguers should be looking for in their pitching prospects is strikeouts. That makes Puk perhaps an even better fantasy prospect than IRL one, as he should routinely strike out more than a batter per inning in whatever capacity he pitches. Is the dream that he morphs into a high-strikeout, tolerable-WHIP pitcher, a la Patrick Corbin? Yes. But even if he as to move to the bullpen, Puk could have Andrew Miller's career. That'd make him ownable in the vast majority of leagues even if he wasn't a closer.

3 Sean Murphy C OFP: 60 Likely: 50 ETA: Late 2019

Born: 10/10/94 Age: 24 Bats: R Throws: R Height: 6'3" Weight: 215 Origin: Round 3, 2016 Draft (#83 overall)

YEAR	TEAM	LVL	AGE	PA	R	2B	3B	HR	RBI	BB	K	SB	CS	AVG/OBP/SLG	DRC+	VORP	BABIP	BRR	FRAA	WARP	PF
2016	VER	A-	21	85	10	1	0	2	7	9	12	1	0	.237/.318/.329	102	3.1	.258	0.4	C(20) 0.4	0.3	96
2017	STO	A+	22	178	22	11	0	9	26	11	33	0	0	.297/.343/.527	132	15.1	.323	0.2	C(40) -0.3	0.9	100
2017	MID	AA	22	217	25	7	0	4	22	21	34	0	0	.209/.288/.309	62	1.8	.232	0.6	C(51) 3.8	0.1	109
2018	MID	AA	23	289	51	26	2	8	43	23	47	3	0	.288/.358/.498	133	22.6	.324	2.1	C(65) 14.5	3.4	111
2019	*OAK*	*MLB*	*24*	*72*	*6*	*2*	*0*	*2*	*8*	*4*	*16*	*0*	*0*	*.184/.232/.323*	*38*	*-2.3*	*.204*	*-0.1*	*C 1*	*-0.1*	*96*

Breakout: 8% Improve: 26% Collapse: 0% Attrition: 23% MLB: 43% *Comparables: Mitch Garver, Jonathan Lucroy, Josh Donaldson*

The Report: Murphy is the best defender among the top tier catching prospects in baseball right now. He flashes a plus-plus arm and is an athletic backstop who draws raves for his receiving and staff management already. There are minor durability concerns, as he's missed time with a broken hamate in both 2016 and 2018, but those tend to be more freakish type things, and he doesn't have a third one to break anyway.

As a potential 70-grade defender behind the plate, Murphy won't have to hit much to be a major-league regular. He has plus raw power in his locker though, and has had some success getting to it in games (it's worth mentioning that he's generally been old for the level at his minor-league stops). The swing is a bit stiff, although that has manifested more in poor quality of contact than swing-and-miss so far. But even with a below-average hit tool and average pop, Murphy's glove is good enough to make him a solid regular. Anything past that, and he could play in a few all-star games.

The Risks: Medium. It would be low, but catchers are weird, and Murphy keeps breaking his hamate bone. The defensive profile should be good enough to keep him employed in the fraternal order of backup catchers for a decade even if he doesn't really hit.

Ben Carsley's Fantasy Take: You should stay away from catching prospects in general in dynasty leagues. Glove-first catching prospects? That's a hard no. Murphy may be of interest in AL-only squads once he starts playing, but he lacks the upside to routinely perform as a top 12-or-so option at the position. And given the state of the position, that's saying something.

4 Kyler Murray OF

OFP: 70 Likely: 60 ETA: NFL - September 2019

Born: 08/07/97 Age: 21 Bats: R Throws: R Height: 5'11" Weight: 195 Origin: Round 1, 2018 Draft (#9 overall)

The Report: Murray originally signed with Texas A&M out of high school as a five-star quarterback recruit, and was widely regarded as the best prep football player in the country. He platooned for the Aggies in 2015 as a true freshman before transferring to Oklahoma where he initially played sparingly behind Baker Mayfield. Murray won a 2018 camp battle to claim Oklahoma's starting role after reaching a deal with the A's to play his redshirt junior football season while under a baseball contract. He proceeded to have one of the best seasons in college football history, usurping Alabama quarterback Tua Tagovailoa for the Heisman Trophy, and leading Oklahoma to the Orange Bowl.

Meanwhile, Murray had a parallel career in baseball. He was also considered a first-round MLB Draft prospect out of high school, but removed his name from the draft pool entirely. He didn't play baseball at all at A&M, but did join the Sooners as a sophomore in 2017. He scuffled badly initially, and scuffled some more in the Cape Cod League that summer. But then he had a brilliant junior campaign, establishing himself once more as a top baseball player for his class as an athletic five-tool center field prospect. This time he was interested in a career on the diamond, and the A's drafted him ninth overall and signed him for $4.66 million, only very slightly below slot value.

Despite his recruiting pedigree, Murray was not considered a particularly great NFL quarterback prospect until this past fall, which was why the A's felt reasonably secure drafting him in the top ten and letting him play an additional season of football. He's small—quarterbacks generally have to be over six feet to be high draft picks—and he just hadn't played enough in college to overcome the height issue perception. But the NFL is changing to a quick passing, dynamic offensive league built around run/pass options and space plays, and Murray is a perfect fit for the new wave of football. Mayfield made a similar late rise in Lincoln Riley's system at Oklahoma, and he exploded on the NFL scene in 2018. Combine all that with a weak quarterback class, and all of a sudden Murray is the talk of the gridiron in a way Oakland couldn't have expected when drafting him.

We're reading tea leaves here, but it seems more likely at this moment in time that he's going to play professional football—and only professional football—moving forward.

The Risks: So yeah, we ranked Kyler Murray as the 101st best prospect in baseball. The list locked for book publication literally the day of the Orange Bowl. At the time, he was still committed to baseball, and we do tend to reserve the 101st spot for the most *interesting* OFP 60 type who didn't make the top 100 proper.

In the month-plus since, Murray has publicly wavered on which sport he'd play, declared for the NFL Draft, failed to come to a new contractual agreement with the Athletics, and is poised to go at or near the top of a second sport's draft. He was already interesting and he's become far more interesting, but not in the way you want if you have a vested interest in seeing him play baseball. He might still play baseball, if not immediately than perhaps down the road. He might even try to play both eventually, and if he was somehow successful at *that*, he'd be the biggest star in sports.

Football jokes aside, we'd rate Murray as a high risk OFP 60/Likely 50 as a baseball prospect. That's akin to Travis Swaggerty, a top 101 guy with a similar toolsy college outfielder profile who went right after him in last summer's draft. He has all the baseball tools you'd expect from a guy who went in the top ten despite all the risk involved, though he's raw due to lack of reps. We're just not convinced he's going to pick baseball anymore, which is a risk so big that it is basically all that's worth talking about.

Ben Carsley's Fantasy Take: He'd be a top-60ish prospect if we knew he was committed to baseball, but it sure seems like he's not committed to baseball. Do with that information what you will.

5 Lazaro Armenteros OF OFP: 60 Likely: 50 ETA: 2021

Born: 05/22/99 Age: 20 Bats: R Throws: R Height: 6'0" Weight: 182 Origin: International Free Agent, 2016

YEAR	TEAM	LVL	AGE	PA	R	2B	3B	HR	RBI	BB	K	SB	CS	AVG/OBP/SLG	DRC+	VORP	BABIP	BRR	FRAA	WARP	PF
2017	DAT	RK	18	26	6	0	0	0	1	3	9	2	2	.167/.385/.167	37	2.0	.300	0.9	CF(6) 1.5	0.2	83
2017	ATH	RK	18	181	24	9	4	4	22	16	48	10	1	.288/.376/.474	112	14.2	.387	2.8	LF(27) 4.2, CF(2) -0.5	0.4	100
2018	BLT	A	19	340	43	8	2	8	39	36	115	8	6	.277/.374/.401	119	21.6	.427	2.1	LF(69) -0.7	1.1	101
2019	*OAK*	*MLB*	*20*	*252*	*24*	*5*	*0*	*7*	*22*	*11*	*102*	*1*	*1*	*.169/.211/.280*	*29*	*-14.7*	*.254*	*-0.4*	*LF 2*	*-1.4*	*96*

Breakout: 4% Improve: 4% Collapse: 0% Attrition: 2% MLB: 4% *Comparables: Clint Frazier, Caleb Gindl, Chris Parmelee*

The Report: Two months into the season, Lazarito looked like a sure shot 2019 Top 101 name. A polished outfielder with potential plus hit and power tools off to a good start in full-season ball at 19? Yes please. Even after a quad injury cost him a month, he made the honorable mentions for the midseason 50.

Lazarito was a mess after coming back from his injury, so we are cooling our jets a little bit. While he didn't quite look one hundred percent in the late summer, we don't foresee any long term effects here. Given that he's a far from a sure shot to stick up the middle, any lower body injuries are going to be a little concerning though, especially since his below-average arm would force him to left.

You're buying the bat here anyway, and despite a toe tap and leg kick for timing, Lazarito has fluid, well-balanced hitting mechanics married to a good approach and above-average barrel control. The plus power is mostly theoretical at this point, but the swing has some loft, and you'd expect him to add strength in his twenties. It wasn't quite the breakout season we expected around Memorial Day, but it's also hard to quibble with the overall performance from a teenager in the Midwest League. So while we aren't firing the afterburners quite yet, we'll keep the engine running.

The Risks: High. He's more polished than toolsy, although the tools aren't bad at all. He's also got half an injury-marred A-ball season under his belt, and he may have to slide to left field.

Ben Carsley's Fantasy Take: Lazarito didn't make it onto our top-101, but he'd be among the next 50 names. A healthy campaign where he holds his own against better competition could see Armenteros make a sizable jump up our rankings, however, and he's a good one to try to buy low on if someone else in your league is out of patience. A future as an OF3 is still in play, albeit perhaps less likely than an OF4/5 outcome.

6 Austin Beck OF OFP: 60 Likely: 45 ETA: 2022

Born: 11/21/98 Age: 20 Bats: R Throws: R Height: 6'1" Weight: 200 Origin: Round 1, 2017 Draft (#6 overall)

YEAR	TEAM	LVL	AGE	PA	R	2B	3B	HR	RBI	BB	K	SB	CS	AVG/OBP/SLG	DRC+	VORP	BABIP	BRR	FRAA	WARP	PF
2017	ATH	RK	18	174	23	7	4	2	28	17	51	7	1	.211/.293/.349	50	2.6	.294	1.8	CF(33) 1.2	-0.5	100
2018	BLT	A	19	534	58	29	4	2	60	30	117	8	6	.296/.335/.383	105	14.9	.377	-4.8	CF(113) 2.0	0.9	101
2019	*OAK*	*MLB*	*20*	*252*	*15*	*5*	*0*	*5*	*21*	*4*	*83*	*0*	*0*	*.159/.171/.242*	*4*	*-20.0*	*.214*	*-0.3*	*CF -1*	*-2.3*	*96*

Breakout: 1% Improve: 1% Collapse: 0% Attrition: 0% MLB: 1% *Comparables: Engel Beltre, Carlos Tocci, Gorkys Hernandez*

The Report: Beck played well in the Midwest League last summer, looking every bit like the toolsy athlete the A's envisioned when they popped him with the sixth overall pick in the 2017 draft. He made great strides at the plate, cleaning up his approach and reducing his strikeout rate. He still tends to chase breaking stuff but he adjusts well and has enough barrel control to project an average hit tool. He's more of a doubles hitter than a true power threat at this point, but his plus raw will eventually play in games. Quick and athletic, he's a plus runner who plays a quality centerfield. His instincts are sound and he's got enough arm for right field if needed.

There's still no guarantee Beck hits upper-level arms, but he's off to a good start. There's plenty of upside remaining too, but to reach his ceiling as a first division centerfielder, he'll need to get more of his raw power into games.

The Risks: High. He's still very raw and has yet to face pitching above Low A.

Ben Carsley's Fantasy Take: I considered Beck toward the end of my personal top-101, and I think it's safe to say he's a top-125-ish prospect at this point. You sort of wish that one out of his ETA, floor, or ceiling was more fantasy-friendly, but at the end of the day there's still the makings of a very solid all-around fantasy OF3 here if it all clicks. If Beck performs well against tougher pitching, it's easy to imagine him being a borderline top-50 guy a year from now.

7 Grant Holmes RHP

OFP: 55 Likely: 40 ETA: Late 2019 or early 2020, health permitting

Born: 03/22/96 Age: 23 Bats: L Throws: R Height: 6'1" Weight: 215 Origin: Round 1, 2014 Draft (#22 overall)

YEAR	TEAM	LVL	AGE	W	L	SV	G	GS	IP	H	HR	BB/9	K/9	K	GB%	BABIP	WHIP	ERA	DRA	WARP	PF
2016	RCU	A+	20	8	4	1	20	18	105^1	103	6	3.7	8.5	100	53%	.316	1.39	4.02	3.64	2.2	97
2016	STO	A+	20	3	3	0	6	5	28^2	44	4	3.1	7.5	24	60%	.408	1.88	6.91	3.52	0.6	93
2017	MID	AA	21	11	12	0	29	24	148^1	149	15	3.7	9.1	150	46%	.328	1.42	4.49	3.75	2.4	109
2018	STO	A+	22	0	0	0	2	2	6	4	1	3.0	12.0	8	47%	.214	1.00	4.50	3.90	0.1	95
2019	*OAK*	*MLB*	*23*	*1*	*1*	*0*	*3*	*3*	*15*	*13*	*1*	*3.9*	*8.7*	*15*	*44%*	*.283*	*1.29*	*4.22*	*4.66*	*0.1*	*96*

Breakout: 18% Improve: 28% Collapse: 9% Attrition: 37% MLB: 48% *Comparables: Justin Wilson, Wily Peralta, Scott Barnes*

The Report: I've been a fan of Holmes since his draft year, and it isn't just the plus-plus flow. He's never quite fully broken out, but looked well on his way to being a useful major-league arm by the close of the 2017 season. And hey, he was 21 and had a year of moderate Double-A success under his belt. Maybe 2018 would be the year he broke out?

Instead, 2018 was the year he broke; pitchers, man. Holmes missed almost the full season with a rotator cuff injury. No one will confuse me with a doctor, but I believe that's connected to the shoulder, and you don't need to be a doctor to know that shoulder injuries for pitchers are, uh, bad. Very bad.

When he did toe the rubber, the stuff looked more or less like it did in 2017: fastball up to 95, potential plus breaker, but six inning samples aren't gonna keep you in a meaningful spot on a team's prospect list. Amazingly though, he's not even the riskiest or the least healthy arm on this list. Pitchers, man.

The Risks: Extreme. The stuff looked fine in his brief post-rotator-cuff-issue appearances, but uh he also missed most of the year with a shoulder injury, so...

Ben Carsley's Fantasy Take: Holmes used to be a bit of a BP Fantasy Team favorite, but at this point there's relatively little that distinguishes him from the myriad backend/spot fantasy starter types who litter these lists... except for a shoulder injury. Unless you roster 200-plus prospects Holmes can be and should already have been dropped.

8 James Kaprielian RHP

OFP: 55 Likely: 40 ETA: 2019, if you feel like gambling he's healthy

Born: 03/02/94 Age: 25 Bats: R Throws: R Height: 6'4" Weight: 200 Origin: Round 1, 2015 Draft (#16 overall)

YEAR	TEAM	LVL	AGE	W	L	SV	G	GS	IP	H	HR	BB/9	K/9	K	GB%	BABIP	WHIP	ERA	DRA	WARP	PF
2016	TAM	A+	22	2	1	0	3	3	18	8	1	1.5	11.0	22	70%	.179	0.61	1.50	2.17	0.7	99
2019	*OAK*	*MLB*	*25*	*2*	*2*	*0*	*8*	*8*	*37*	*30*	*3*	*2.9*	*9.3*	*38*	*56%*	*.281*	*1.13*	*3.21*	*3.55*	*0.8*	*96*

Breakout: 12% Improve: 21% Collapse: 18% Attrition: 34% MLB: 52% *Comparables: Dan Meyer, Boof Bonser, Kevin Hart*

The Report: It's been over 33 months since Kaprielian last took the mound in a regular-season game. He missed most of 2016 with flexor problems, but came back and was fantastically impressive in the Arizona Fall League, with a big velocity spike causing his perceived upside to jump substantially—enough that he climbed into our top 101 that winter. He arrived in camp with the wind at his back and a chance to rocket through New York's farm system and... immediately blew out his UCL.

He was included in the Sonny Gray trade while rehabbing, and was expected to return to game action by midseason as an Oakland farmhand. He didn't return at all, with a troubled rehab plagued by shoulder injuries, although he was throwing during instructs. He's going to (hopefully) return in 2019 as a 25-year-old with 56 1/3 innings, all in the low-minors or the AFL, and all in 2015 and 2016.

The last time we saw Kaprielian toe the rubber regularly, he possessed top-of-the-rotation stuff: four pitches that projected above-average, led with a fastball sitting 94-97 and touching 99. Obviously, we have utterly no idea whether he can recapture that form, or maintain it in any type of regular pitching role. But it was good enough that he landed as the 58th best prospect in baseball back then, despite missing six months with a known Tommy John surgery precursor. It was good enough that he was a key part of a major trade while hurt. It was good enough that two years later, after a troubled rehab and without ever throwing a real pitch in their system, the A's added him to the 40-man roster. And it was good enough that we're still ranking him today.

The Risks: As extreme as anyone in baseball. Our dearly departed leader Craij (RIP Craij) used Kaprielian as the example of players for whom the beta was so high that the role grades undershot the risk last spring, and that was before he missed *another* season. He could be in the majors in a few months if he's healthy; he might also never throw a pitch in the upper-minors.

Ben Carsley's Fantasy Take: I tend not to shy away from injury-prone pitchers if I think they possess big-time upside (hello, Nate Pearson), but Kaprielian is a bridge too far for me. He's a top-200 dude because there just aren't many guys who can match his pure strikeout potential, but he didn't sniff our top-101 and I don't think he'd sniff a theoretical top-150 either. I am too scared.

9 Jorge Mateo SS

OFP: 50 Likely: 40 ETA: Late 2019

Born: 06/23/95 Age: 24 Bats: R Throws: R Height: 6'0" Weight: 190 Origin: International Free Agent, 2012

YEAR	TEAM	LVL	AGE	PA	R	2B	3B	HR	RBI	BB	K	SB	CS	AVG/OBP/SLG	DRC+	VORP	BABIP	BRR	FRAA	WARP	PF
2016	TAM	A+	21	507	65	16	9	8	47	33	108	36	15	.254/.306/.379	95	11.8	.313	3.2	SS(62) -5.1, 2B(40) -0.6	0.2	103
2017	TAM	A+	22	297	39	16	8	4	11	16	79	28	3	.240/.288/.400	89	15.4	.321	7.6	SS(42) 2.9, CF(22) -0.8	1.1	98
2017	TRN	AA	22	140	26	9	3	4	26	15	32	11	7	.300/.381/.525	124	17.0	.372	1.6	SS(16) 1.1, 2B(5) 0.4	0.9	95
2017	MID	AA	22	147	25	5	7	4	20	9	33	13	3	.292/.333/.518	104	14.2	.356	2.2	SS(30) 0.8	0.7	108
2018	NAS	AAA	23	510	50	17	16	3	45	29	139	25	10	.230/.280/.353	58	3.7	.316	1.1	SS(123) -0.8, 2B(4) -0.5	-0.8	91
2019	*OAK*	*MLB*	*24*	*72*	*8*	*3*	*2*	*1*	*7*	*3*	*22*	*3*	*1*	*.213/.256/.366*	*60*	*-0.2*	*.290*	*0.5*	*SS 0*	*0.0*	*96*

Breakout: 13% Improve: 20% Collapse: 0% Attrition: 18% MLB: 23% *Comparables: Grant Green, Erik Gonzalez, Juan Diaz*

The Report: Mateo is one of the fastest players in the minors. He's a premium athlete, full stop. He can play shortstop, center field, and second base, and presumably would be fine at the positions down the defensive spectrum from there. At times, he's shown real flashes of power, and he wound up with 60 extra base hits in the minors in 2017.

At the end of the day though, you can't steal first base. Mateo hit .230 last year, in the PCL of all places. He's not going to put together enough walks or power to make up for that level of bad hitting, and indeed the collapse in hitting ability torpedoed his non-speed secondary offensive skills too. In sum, he had a 58 DRC+ in Triple-A, worse than any regular hitter in the majors except for Chris Davis.

We've had concerns about Mateo's ability to hit for average since basically day one. He has good technical underpinnings in terms of swing plane, bat speed, and bat control, which has led to sporadic bursts of success at the plate. Unfortunately, his plate discipline and pitch recognition often limits him far more than it should. Those concerns were amplified when he spent a year-and-a-half puttering in High-A, and remain significant today.

Mateo is still likely to have a substantial MLB career if things don't work out with the stick, as his speed and defense will give him enough utility to survive in a bench role. But it might not be as a particularly valuable player unless he figures out a way to get to first. We might even suggest the Baltimore chop at this point.

The Risks: Medium, almost all in the overall offensive profile. Speed is a useful tool, but hit is more useful, and Mateo has only consistently shown the former.

Ben Carsley's Fantasy Take: We used to be pretty high on Mateo, but he has proven fairly definitively to us that he can't hit enough for his speed to matter. If you want to call him a top-200 guy because of the pure speed upside that's fine, but I've cut bait pretty much everywhere I held him at this point. If he ends up playing near-every day at some point due to injuries or small steps forward in his bat, then sure, pick him up again. But Mateo looks like a bench piece through and through.

10 Jameson Hannah OF

OFP: 50 Likely: 40 ETA: 2021

Born: 08/10/97 Age: 21 Bats: L Throws: L Height: 5'9" Weight: 185 Origin: Round 2, 2018 Draft (#50 overall)

YEAR	TEAM	LVL	AGE	PA	R	2B	3B	HR	RBI	BB	K	SB	CS	AVG/OBP/SLG	DRC+	VORP	BABIP	BRR	FRAA	WARP	PF
2018	VER	A-	20	95	14	4	1	1	10	9	24	6	0	.279/.347/.384	125	7.6	.377	1.1	CF(18) -2.4	0.0	100
2019	*OAK*	*MLB*	*21*	*252*	*20*	*5*	*0*	*6*	*23*	*11*	*86*	*3*	*1*	*.159/.194/.257*	*18*	*-15.5*	*.214*	*0.1*	*CF -2*	*-1.8*	*96*

Breakout: 1% Improve: 1% Collapse: 0% Attrition: 1% MLB: 1% *Comparables: Abraham Almonte, Trayvon Robinson, Xavier Avery*

The Report: Hannah played on a high-powered offense at Dallas Baptist and was pretty clearly the best player on the team due to his bat and ability in center. He is a plus athlete with good coordination and quick twitch. He has broad shoulders and an athletic build on a short frame that doesn't have much room, if any, to put on weight without losing a step.

Hannah has above-average feel for the barrel and plus bat speed, but his swing generates his hardest contact on low line drives and burners. His average raw power gets left by the wayside in most plate appearances. Hannah is willing to take walks, but struggles with the soft stuff.

Hannah is currently a plus runner and he gets down the line very quickly from the left side. His jumps in center and plus footspeed give him plenty of range, although he will need to clean up his routes and reads to get the most out of his wheels. Hannah's arm is fringy and will likely play best in left or center.

Hannah's athleticism and tools suggest a future as a versatile fourth outfielder who can get on base at a decent clip. If he can tap into more of his raw power without losing a step, he could play himself into regular work in center.

The Risks: Medium: Still far away and although the athleticism, feel for hit, and current approach suggest he will transition well into his first full season of pro ball, he struggled in the Cape against high level pitching.

Ben Carsley's Fantasy Take: Hannah is the type of guy who may end up on the very back of a top-101 the year before he reaches the majors if we think he has a clear path to playing time. But that's his ceiling, and given the likelihood that he ends up more of a good fourth outfielder than a true first division dude, he's just one for the watch list for now.

The Next Five

11 Nick Allen SS

Born: 10/08/98 Age: 20 Bats: R Throws: R Height: 5'9" Weight: 155 Origin: Round 3, 2017 Draft (#81 overall)

YEAR	TEAM	LVL	AGE	PA	R	2B	3B	HR	RBI	BB	K	SB	CS	AVG/OBP/SLG	DRC+	VORP	BABIP	BRR	FRAA	WARP	PF
2017	ATH	RK	18	154	26	3	2	1	14	13	28	7	3	.254/.322/.326	100	6.6	.312	1.1	SS(33) 2.5	0.4	99
2018	BLT	A	19	512	51	17	6	0	34	34	85	24	8	.239/.301/.302	76	15.2	.289	3.7	SS(121) 5.2	1.1	101
2019	*OAK*	*MLB*	*20*	*252*	*21*	*1*	*1*	*4*	*15*	*5*	*66*	*4*	*1*	*.144/.159/.207*	*-9*	*-22.3*	*.174*	*1.4*	*SS 1*	*-2.2*	*96*

Breakout: 5% Improve: 5% Collapse: 0% Attrition: 1% MLB: 5%

Comparables: Freddy Galvis, Wilfredo Tovar, Rey Navarro

12 Kevin Merrell SS

Born: 12/14/95 Age: 23 Bats: L Throws: R Height: 6'1" Weight: 180 Origin: Round 1, 2017 Draft (#33 overall)

YEAR	TEAM	LVL	AGE	PA	R	2B	3B	HR	RBI	BB	K	SB	CS	AVG/OBP/SLG	DRC+	VORP	BABIP	BRR	FRAA	WARP	PF
2017	VER	A-	21	140	27	5	1	2	9	9	22	10	3	.320/.362/.424	154	18.6	.365	4.1	SS(28) 0.4	1.4	98
2018	STO	A+	22	290	38	10	3	0	24	15	66	5	4	.267/.308/.326	88	9.1	.353	1.3	SS(59) -5.3	-0.3	97
2019	*OAK*	*MLB*	*23*	*252*	*24*	*5*	*1*	*5*	*20*	*6*	*67*	*2*	*1*	*.213/.229/.300*	*41*	*-8.8*	*.267*	*-0.2*	*SS -2, 2B 0*	*-1.1*	*96*

Breakout: 18% Improve: 23% Collapse: 4% Attrition: 17% MLB: 27%

Comparables: Anderson Hernandez, Argenis Diaz, Engelb Vielma

About as good a matched pair as you will find back-to-back in any system (although Holmes/Kaprielian aren't far off I suppose).

When the Athletics spent two million bucks in the 2017 draft to buy the diminutive Allen out of his USC commitment, they were purchasing a glove and some speed with the hopes that the bat would develop. He struggled some in an aggressive Midwest League assignment, and it remains hard to see much impact with the bat, but the glove and speed were as advertised. He's strong for his size but this is a gap power profile at best. Allen doesn't have to hit a ton to be a second-division starter type, but the most likely outcome here is speedy utility infielder.

Merrell is the Cal League version of Allen. He's faster by a fair bit, as he'll pop borderline elite run times, but is a bit rougher at the six. He's improved enough that we'll project him as a shortstop though, and he's a more polished hitter—as you'd expect from the college bat versus the prep one. He doesn't offer much in the way of pop either, as he's slight of frame with a relatively flat swing plane and little leg drive. If he slaps enough balls into the alleys and sneaks some extra bases he could play everyday, but again, the most likely outcome here is (very) speedy utility infielder.

13 Jeremy Eierman SS

Born: 09/10/96 Age: 22 Bats: R Throws: R Height: 6'1" Weight: 205 Origin: Round 2, 2018 Draft (#70 overall)

YEAR	TEAM	LVL	AGE	PA	R	2B	3B	HR	RBI	BB	K	SB	CS	AVG/OBP/SLG	DRC+	VORP	BABIP	BRR	FRAA	WARP	PF
2018	VER	A-	21	267	36	8	2	8	26	13	70	10	4	.235/.283/.381	76	5.6	.294	-0.1	SS(56) 0.3, 2B(2) 0.9	-0.3	100
2019	*OAK*	*MLB*	*22*	*252*	*18*	*3*	*0*	*9*	*24*	*2*	*84*	*2*	*1*	*.114/.121/.238*	*-22*	*-27.3*	*.125*	*0.3*	*SS 1, 2B 0*	*-2.9*	*96*

Breakout: 6% Improve: 6% Collapse: 0% Attrition: 6% MLB: 7% *Comparables: Chris Valaika, Yadiel Rivera, Argenis Diaz*

Eierman certainly has more power than the two shortstops ahead of him on this list, but that comes with a price. The swing is long and leveraged, and he tends to take hacks more appropriate for a more stoutly built baseball player. So while he offers plus raw power, how much of it plays in games against better arms is far from determined. He's also less likely to stick at short than Allen or Merrell. I'm happy to write off a poor post-draft performance, even for a polished college performer in the Penn League—it's a long season for those dudes—but it reflects some of the offensive concerns that cropped up his junior year at Missouri State and slid him down everyone's draft board. There's certainly enough power potential here to project a second division starter in the middle infield, but again, the most likely outcome here is utility infielder.

14 Daulton Jefferies RHP

Born: 08/02/95 Age: 23 Bats: L Throws: R Height: 6'0" Weight: 180 Origin: Round 1, 2016 Draft (#37 overall)

YEAR	TEAM	LVL	AGE	W	L	SV	G	GS	IP	H	HR	BB/9	K/9	K	GB%	BABIP	WHIP	ERA	DRA	WARP	PF
2016	ATH	RK	20	0	0	0	5	5	11^1	11	0	1.6	13.5	17	60%	.440	1.15	2.38	1.14	0.6	101
2017	STO	A+	21	0	0	0	2	1	7	7	0	1.3	7.7	6	67%	.292	1.14	2.57	3.01	0.2	102
2019	*OAK*	*MLB*	*23*	*2*	*2*	*0*	*13*	*8*	34^2	*30*	*2*	*4.5*	*7.6*	*29*	*45%*	*.282*	*1.37*	*4.00*	*4.43*	*0.4*	*96*

Breakout: 4% Improve: 4% Collapse: 1% Attrition: 4% MLB: 6% *Comparables: Bryan Mitchell, Chris Devenski, Anthony Lerew*

The last two spots on the top 15 are injury mulligans, which isn't a great sign for your system depth after you had three (arguably three and a half) in your top ten as well. Jefferies is of the more traditional variety, as he spent almost all of 2018 recovering from Tommy John surgery. There were already questions coming out of college about whether his short, slight frame would hold up to the rigors of pro starting, and he has answered exactly none of them two-and-a-half years into his career. He's shown three average-or-better offerings in the past, and Oakland must be getting awfully tempted to turn him loose in the pen. The problem is that Jefferies really needs pro reps. It's easier to get those when you are stretched out, so you might as well give him one more spin as a starter, even if "fastball/slider reliever" looks like his destiny.

15 Greg Deichmann OF

Born: 05/31/95 Age: 24 Bats: L Throws: R Height: 6'2" Weight: 190 Origin: Round 2, 2017 Draft (#43 overall)

YEAR	TEAM	LVL	AGE	PA	R	2B	3B	HR	RBI	BB	K	SB	CS	AVG/OBP/SLG	DRC+	VORP	BABIP	BRR	FRAA	WARP	PF
2017	VER	A-	22	195	31	10	4	8	30	28	40	4	1	.274/.385/.530	160	18.4	.316	0.8	RF(34) 3.1, LF(1) -0.1	1.3	99
2018	ATH	RK	23	43	9	2	2	1	7	5	8	0	0	.289/.372/.526	125	3.3	.345	-0.1	RF(11) -0.4	0.0	104
2018	STO	A+	23	185	18	14	0	6	21	17	63	0	1	.199/.276/.392	66	-0.7	.276	-0.1	RF(28) 0.7, LF(8) -0.8	-0.8	97
2019	*OAK*	*MLB*	*24*	*252*	*20*	*8*	*0*	*9*	*27*	*16*	*89*	*0*	*0*	*.132/.186/.287*	*22*	*-16.8*	*.158*	*-0.5*	*RF 0, LF -1*	*-1.9*	*96*

Breakout: 2% Improve: 3% Collapse: 0% Attrition: 2% MLB: 3% *Comparables: Alex Castellanos, Destin Hood, Jorge Bonifacio*

You can explain away some of Deichmann's struggles this year to the wrist injury that limited him to just 58 games, but you still have to reckon with the fact that a 23-year-old corner outfielder posted a .667 OPS in the Cal League. The tools are there for a power-hitting right fielder, but the wrist injury can't explain away the issues with north-south sequencing or spin. Ultimately, his season was too muddled to write Deichmann off entirely, but it's also a lost year of needed development time and he'll be under a lot of pressure to hit this season.

Top Talents 25 and Under (born 4/1/93 or later)

1. Matt Chapman
2. Jesus Luzardo
3. Matt Olson
4. Ramon Laureano
5. A.J. Puk
6. Sean Murphy
7. Franklin Barreto
8. Dustin Fowler
9. Daniel Mengden
10. Frankie Montas

Well hello there, beautiful. This crew suddenly harkens back to the halcyon days of the early aughts in terms of both quality and quantity of controllable young talent in, or at the cusp of, the big leagues. And it doesn't include recent acquisition and former undisputed champion uber-prospect Jurickson Profar, who aged out of consideration by mere weeks.

Matt Chapman introduced himself to the world last year, bringing his elite leather and game power to bear on American League opponents for a full season. Sure, he'll likely continue to whiff a good bit, and his lack of barrel control may prevent him from becoming a true superstar. But the Fullerton product sure looks like a swell bet to get awfully close and he's set to be one of the game's best players for the next several years.

For his part, Matt Olson followed up a dynamite debut with some expected offensive regression in Year Two. The power is very real though, and the glove looks pretty sweet by cold-corner standards as well. It's certainly not the most dynamic of profiles, and he's never going to win a stolen base title. But a solid two-to-three win first baseman with 30ish bankable dingers remains a very nice thing for a cost-conscious team to be able to bank.

Ramon Laureano introduced himself to the world when he uncorked one of the best throws of the year, but he's looked like a solid all-around ballplayer for much longer than that. A down first half in 2017 took some of the shine off his Lancaster breakout the year before, but he went right on back to hitting at Double-A that summer and hasn't really stopped since. An electric defensive package, strong on-base skills and hard line-drive contact... that's a lot of boxes checked for a potential top-of-the-lineup anchor for years to come.

Barreto made our 101 for four consecutive years from 2015 to 2018, but his stock is down after struggling to make quality contact in his first few big-league cameos. That's not great news for a player whose profile has ostensibly rested on the back of a quality hit tool projection. But he's added a good deal of pop to the package, and the athleticism up the middle remains an asset, albeit on the right side of the second-base bag these days.

Dustin Fowler's gruesome knee injury continues to fade further into the rearview mirror, and while he went the Barreto route and struggled to adapt to life in The Show last year, he raked in Triple-A while also logging the top recorded 90-foot sprint speed in the big leagues. He's a highly aggressive hitter, and that's always going to be a limiting factor for his offensive ceiling. But he's a good enough bat-to-ball guy that it can work, and he profiles as a big-league regular.

Daniel Mengden and Frankie Montas did eerily similar work last season, swinging between the rotation and middle relief to provide wonderfully cheap and useful innings despite not striking anybody out. Neither managed to crack six whiffs per nine, and neither in turn cracked 120 for a DRA-. It's unclear where either finds a next gear, though Mengden's hook and Montas' four-seam heat are both legitimate weapons. The important thing is that both managed to defy their peripherals and establish themselves as legitimate big-league arms.

Philadelphia Phillies

The State of the System:

The system has thinned out significantly through graduations, but the Phillies are ready to contend and still have a fair bit of pitching depth at least.

The Top Ten:

1 Sixto Sanchez RHP OFP: 70 Likely: 55 ETA: Mid-to-late 2019, pending his availability to pitch.

Born: 07/29/98 Age: 20 Bats: R Throws: R Height: 6'0" Weight: 185 Origin: International Free Agent, 2015

YEAR	TEAM	LVL	AGE	W	L	SV	G	GS	IP	H	HR	BB/9	K/9	K	GB%	BABIP	WHIP	ERA	DRA	WARP	PF
2016	PHL	RK	17	5	0	0	11	11	54	33	0	1.3	7.3	44	57%	.236	0.76	0.50	2.61	1.9	97
2017	LWD	A	18	5	3	0	13	13	67^1	46	1	1.2	8.6	64	49%	.251	0.82	2.41	2.93	1.9	81
2017	CLR	A+	18	0	4	0	5	5	27^2	27	1	2.9	6.5	20	42%	.295	1.30	4.55	3.61	0.5	92
2018	CLR	A+	19	4	3	0	8	8	46^2	39	1	2.1	8.7	45	52%	.295	1.07	2.51	3.67	0.9	99
2019	*MIA*	*MLB*	*20*	*3*	*3*	*0*	*9*	*9*	*46^2*	*42*	*5*	*3.0*	*8.0*	*42*	*47%*	*.294*	*1.25*	*4.07*	*4.80*	*0.3*	*90*

Breakout: 4% Improve: 8% Collapse: 5% Attrition: 14% MLB: 17% *Comparables: Jacob Turner, Francis Martes, Ian Krol*

The Report: The official pitching prospect of the BP Prospect Team finally ran into some trouble, but it wasn't on the mound, it was in the doctor's office. Sanchez was chugging right along on his path of destruction when he came down with elbow soreness in early June, and he never returned to game action. He was throwing in fall instructs, and the word around town was that he was just as impressive as always. The Phillies scheduled his comeback for the Arizona Fall League... and then scratched him with collarbone soreness just before that league started.

When healthy, he regularly blasts it into the triple-digits and throws a kitchen sink of pitches that flash above-average to plus-plus. At various points we've seen a four-seamer, a sinker, a cutter, a slider, a slow curve, another breaking ball in between that you could call a slurve, a regular change with circle-type action, and a harder change that moves like a split-change, and they're *all* good. Whether or not these are distinct pitches or flavors and manipulations on a core four-pitch arsenal is sort of irrelevant. We expect him to pick four or five eventually, and he could settle in with a monster repertoire.

Sanchez has frequently been so dominant on the mound as to appear like he isn't being challenged. He will often spend an inning or two, and sometimes even a whole game, working on refining a core offering, as we've also seen from past higher-end Phillies pitching prospects. He's good enough to do this and still pitch effectively, but it does make evaluating his overall deception and sequencing tougher than we'd like. He's also clearly much shorter than listed, which does raise the usual short guy issues like durability and fastball plane.

The Risks: We've heard his name and "potential Tommy John surgery" mentioned far too often together to call it low risk, and we've lowered the likely grade by a half-tick to account for the chance that he can't handle a starting workload. The profile itself is low-to-medium risk. The stuff and command are already there for a fine MLB pitcher, with ace potential, and he might've made the majors in 2018 if healthy.

Ben Carsley's Fantasy Take: It doesn't take a genius to see that the number of 200-plus IP workhorse aces is likely to decrease in the next few years. The few among that class who remain are insanely valuable, yes, but there's also plenty of value to be found in a guy like Sanchez, who may strike out more dudes in 160 innings than, let's say Rick Porcello will in 200. Even if you want to factor in an 18-month layoff at some point for what feels like (but is not actually) the inevitable Tommy John surgery and recovery, Sanchez should be dominating MLB lineups by late 2020 at the latest. He's still a top-three fantasy starting pitching prospect, and he's gonna be insanely fun to watch.

2 Adonis Medina RHP OFP: 60 Likely: 50 ETA: Probably 2020, but 2019 is in play

Born: 12/18/96 Age: 22 Bats: R Throws: R Height: 6'1" Weight: 185 Origin: International Free Agent, 2014

YEAR	TEAM	LVL	AGE	W	L	SV	G	GS	IP	H	HR	BB/9	K/9	K	GB%	BABIP	WHIP	ERA	DRA	WARP	PF
2016	WPT	A-	19	5	3	0	13	13	64^{2}	47	5	3.3	4.7	34	57%	.214	1.10	2.92	3.89	1.0	93
2017	LWD	A	20	4	9	0	22	22	119^{2}	103	7	2.9	10.0	133	49%	.306	1.19	3.01	2.93	3.3	83
2018	CLR	A+	21	10	4	0	22	21	111^{1}	103	11	2.9	9.9	123	51%	.316	1.25	4.12	4.72	0.8	99
2019	*PHI*	*MLB*	*22*	*6*	*6*	*0*	*19*	*19*	*97*	*93*	*13*	*3.9*	*9.0*	*97*	*45%*	*.315*	*1.39*	*4.41*	*4.97*	*0.4*	*96*

Breakout: 3% Improve: 6% Collapse: 5% Attrition: 9% MLB: 13% *Comparables: Anthony Swarzak, Brett Kennedy, John Gant*

The Report: Unlike Sanchez, Medina mostly just kept chugging along in 2018. There wasn't a big step forward, like he had with velocity or the slider in 2017, but there wasn't a big step back or a concerning injury either. He's still pretty consistently in the 91-96 velocity band and he still scrapes a little higher. He still has a smooth, athletic delivery and an advanced feel for pitching. Depending on your descriptive preferences, he's either dropped his so-so loopy curve for a slider, or tightened the curve into a harder slurve. It's semantics, and the important part is that he has a low-80s breaking ball with slidery movement (and we've usually called it a slider) that looks above-average already and projects to get to plus or better. The cambio remains inconsistent.

He didn't put up an overwhelming topline in the Florida State League, although his 2018 strikeout/walk rates are similar to his 2017. The rise in Medina's runs allowed numbers are basically all due to five games where he gave up five or more runs and didn't make it out of the third inning. We'll flag consistency as something to watch for in the future; for now this might just be a quirky statistical oddity.

Medina's stock is pretty much steady from last year, but he's risen three spots on this list. Suffice to say, this system has seen a lot of attrition from graduations, trades, and slowly-developing draft picks recently.

The Risks: Medium. He's going to need a better third pitch to stay in the rotation. He could use more consistent command, while we're at it. We need to see him get high-minors batters out. These are pretty typical risks for a good A-ball pitching prospect, honestly.

Ben Carsley's Fantasy Take: Medina is among my favorite prospects with this fairly standard profile. In general we favor upside over probability, but Medina is close enough to the majors and has just high enough of a ceiling now to probably warrant top-101 inclusion. He won't win you leagues, but he might be your fantasy SP5 for several years. You could do worse!

3 Spencer Howard RHP OFP: 60 Likely: 50 ETA: 2021

Born: 07/28/96 Age: 22 Bats: R Throws: R Height: 6'3" Weight: 205 Origin: Round 2, 2017 Draft (#45 overall)

YEAR	TEAM	LVL	AGE	W	L	SV	G	GS	IP	H	HR	BB/9	K/9	K	GB%	BABIP	WHIP	ERA	DRA	WARP	PF
2017	WPT	A-	20	1	1	0	9	9	28^{1}	22	0	5.7	12.7	40	48%	.349	1.41	4.45	3.41	0.6	100
2018	LWD	A	21	9	8	0	23	23	112	101	6	3.2	11.8	147	40%	.349	1.26	3.78	3.46	2.3	91
2019	*PHI*	*MLB*	*22*	*5*	*6*	*0*	*18*	*18*	*81*	*76*	*13*	*4.7*	*10.3*	*93*	*36%*	*.323*	*1.47*	*4.63*	*5.23*	*0.1*	*96*

Breakout: 4% Improve: 9% Collapse: 3% Attrition: 8% MLB: 12% *Comparables: David Paulino, Alex Wood, Carson Fulmer*

The Report: Remember all of that stuff I just wrote about Adonis Medina? Welcome to part two of the report. Howard sits a free and easy 92-96 with the fastball and regularly touches a tick or two higher, and we've gotten reliable though occasional reports of triple-digits. He blew through the South Atlantic League in a manner that looked a lot like Medina's 2017 campaign. Howard throws the four-pitch starter mix, and there's an above-average slider here along with a useful changeup and curveball. He's a big, durable-looking guy, and just watching him on the mound, you wouldn't expect him to have trouble handling a starter's workload.

Howard ranks below Medina because he's around a year-and-a-half behind on the development curve—Howard's five months older and a level lower, and he only made 14 starts in college before signing as a draft-eligible sophomore. Even considering that, it's still a bit odd that the Phillies left him in Lakewood all season.

The Risks: Medium, and again pretty similar to Medina's. Due to limited experience as a starting pitcher for his age, there's sneaky reliever risk here for a guy with no obvious health, injury, or pitch deficiencies. Then again, is it strictly speaking "risk" if the fastball/slider combo plays up there?

Ben Carsley's Fantasy Take: Maybe I'm just not as up on my Phillies pitching prospects as the rest of my dynasty-playing compatriots, but I was surprised to see such a positive report on Howard. He may not have flashy upside, but I believe he's being pretty undervalued right now if his fantasy comparison is "Medina from a year ago." Players like this often go overlooked in drafts held primarily for new entrants into the dynasty pool. But if you're in round 3 or 4 of one such draft this year and see no inspiring options, maybe check to see if Howard is owned instead.

4 Alec Bohm 3B

OFP: 60 Likely: 50 ETA: Late 2020

Born: 08/03/96 Age: 22 Bats: R Throws: R Height: 6'5" Weight: 225 Origin: Round 1, 2018 Draft (#3 overall)

YEAR	TEAM	LVL	AGE	PA	R	2B	3B	HR	RBI	BB	K	SB	CS	AVG/OBP/SLG	DRC+	VORP	BABIP	BRR	FRAA	WARP	PF
2018	WPT	A-	21	121	9	5	1	0	12	10	19	1	0	.224/.314/.290	90	-0.4	.273	-0.9	3B(20) -2.7	-0.6	95
2019	*PHI*	*MLB*	*22*	*252*	*15*	*5*	*0*	*5*	*21*	*9*	*68*	*0*	*0*	*.122/.161/.210*	*-7*	*-27.2*	*.143*	*-0.4*	*3B -1*	*-3.0*	*96*

Breakout: 1% Improve: 1% Collapse: 0% Attrition: 1% MLB: 1%

Comparables: Ryder Jones, Kaleb Cowart, Mitch Walding

The Report: Bohm was a premium college performer at Wichita State with the best combination of hit and raw power in his draft class. He has a wood bat track record from the Cape in 2017 and was the third overall pick in the draft. He should be higher than this, right? People are going to think we have a vendetta against every Phillies first round pick at this rate.

So, the problems: Bohm is a great hitter but often prioritizes contact and shortness to the ball over fully tapping into his 7 raw. He struggled in his first professional summer—with the reports to match—although his time in short-season was marred by minor injuries. The long-term concern is his ultimate defensive home. It's not a bad body, but it's a big one, and he isn't rangy at the hot corner. Bohm has plenty of arm for the left side, although he can struggle with his accuracy at times. This whole profile could go R/R first base at some point, which means that pop will have to become a priority. We'd also like to see him settle in during 2019 and really mash too.

The Risks: Medium, which I suppose is higher than you'd like for a top-five college bat. He may end up a hit over power third baseman who isn't a great defender there. He also might end up the best overall hitter in his draft class if it all comes together.

Ben Carsley's Fantasy Take: Bohm is pretty clearly the second-best fantasy prospect in this system and one of the better new bats in the dynasty pool. The defensive concerns aren't as pressing for us—he just needs to stay 3B eligible rather than play there every day—and he's got a decent timeline to fantasy relevancy as a college bat. In our midseason top 50 dynasty prospects lists, Bohm slotted in at No. 30 and we compared his upside to Good Eugenio Suarez. That still tracks.

5 Luis Garcia SS

OFP: 60 Likely: 50 ETA: 2023

Born: 10/01/00 Age: 18 Bats: B Throws: R Height: 5'11" Weight: 170 Origin: International Free Agent, 2017

YEAR	TEAM	LVL	AGE	PA	R	2B	3B	HR	RBI	BB	K	SB	CS	AVG/OBP/SLG	DRC+	VORP	BABIP	BRR	FRAA	WARP	PF
2018	PLL	RK	17	187	33	11	3	1	32	15	21	12	8	.369/.433/.488	197	22.6	.418	-0.1	SS(43) -2.1	1.6	99
2019	*PHI*	*MLB*	*18*	*252*	*25*	*8*	*0*	*4*	*19*	*3*	*61*	*5*	*3*	*.224/.231/.309*	*40*	*-8.9*	*.276*	*-0.2*	*SS -1*	*-1.1*	*96*

Breakout: 0% Improve: 0% Collapse: 0% Attrition: 0% MLB: 0%

Comparables: Adalberto Mondesi, Wilmer Flores, Tommy Brown

The Report: Not that Luis Garcia of the Phillies, or that Luis Garcia the shortstop prospect, but he's arguably the best of the Luises Garcia. He's got sure-shot shortstop tools with plus range and arm strength. It's a smaller frame with some projection left but he should maintain his athleticism at 22. Garcia has good barrel control, but lacks physicality and loft in the swing, so power's never going to be a big part of this profile. So we can feel very confident about the glove, and see what the hit tool looks like at… well, 22. If it is a plus hit tool, the Phillies could have a top-of-the-order tablesetter and a Wilson Pickit at the 6. If it doesn't, the glove and speed could still propel Garcia to the majors in a complementary role.

The Risks: Can I use very high? Obviously he is a 17-year-old shortstop in the complex, but the combo of glove and hit seems like it keeps him below extreme.

Ben Carsley's Fantasy Take: Let this serve as proof that I'm not unreasonably high on *every* shortstop prospect named Luis Garcia. That being said, I like the Phillies' version plenty too, and he could be a very fast dynasty riser. Honestly, he's exactly the type of guy Bret and I often put in the back of the top-101 as a flier, and only his ETA (and to a certain extent the lack of pop) keeps him from making the list with ease.

6 Adam Haseley OF

OFP: 55 Likely: 45 ETA: Late-2019/early-2020

Born: 04/12/96 Age: 23 Bats: L Throws: L Height: 6'1" Weight: 195 Origin: Round 1, 2017 Draft (#8 overall)

YEAR	TEAM	LVL	AGE	PA	R	2B	3B	HR	RBI	BB	K	SB	CS	AVG/OBP/SLG	DRC+	VORP	BABIP	BRR	FRAA	WARP	PF
2017	WPT	A-	21	158	18	9	0	2	18	14	28	5	3	.270/.350/.380	129	12.9	.321	2.6	CF(31) 0.1	0.7	101
2017	LWD	A	21	74	15	3	1	1	6	6	13	0	1	.258/.315/.379	108	6.1	.302	1.6	LF(12) 1.3, CF(4) 0.8	0.5	81
2018	CLR	A+	22	354	54	13	5	5	38	19	54	7	3	.300/.343/.415	109	15.2	.346	2.9	LF(39) -2.5, CF(30) -2.2	0.7	101
2018	REA	AA	22	159	23	4	0	6	17	16	19	0	1	.316/.403/.478	133	13.1	.327	-0.5	CF(28) -2.3, LF(5) -0.5	0.4	105
2019	*PHI*	*MLB*	*23*	*252*	*28*	*7*	*1*	*7*	*25*	*13*	*51*	*1*	*0*	*.224/.272/.355*	*69*	*-1.3*	*.254*	*-0.3*	*CF 0, LF 0*	*-0.2*	*96*

Breakout: 8% Improve: 20% Collapse: 0% Attrition: 8% MLB: 23% *Comparables: Matt Szczur, Gary Brown, Logan Schafer*

The Report: Hitters gonna hit. Haseley was drafted based on his advanced hit tool, and he hit .300 in his first full season and made it to Double-A. We're still concerned about how the overall profile plays, because the secondary skills past said hit tool and his arm (he was an early-round prospect as a pitcher too) get worrisome. His future defensive home in the outfield isn't clear, and it would help his stock a lot if he could settle into center field. The power projection is still only fringe-average to average. There's a lot less "wow" here than you'd hope for given his draft position, but he puts the bat on the ball with authority often enough that you can reasonably hope that the hit tool carries it all.

Haseley's 2018 performance feels better than it was because of that shiny .300 marker—if you drop him to .295 at Clearwater it doesn't actually matter, but it would feel like he's a much worse prospect. An ACC batting champion popped in the top ten for his advanced bat and hit tool should hit .300 in A-ball. The Double-A performance is encouraging, and we're a little more optimistic than we were last year. That said, as we have to note every year, Reading is one of the biggest launching pads east of the Rockies.

The Risks: Medium. He might tweener out, and he's already played a lot of corner outfield. We're concerned about the lack of game power. If he's more of a .270 hitter than a .300 hitter, the profile gets tough. He might end up being really duplicative of Nick Williams, and the Phillies might just go sign Bryce Harper to play over both anyway.

Ben Carsley's Fantasy Take: The hope here is that Haseley is able to routinely do something similar to what Corey Dickerson did in 2018: hit .300 with ~15 homers, a handful of steals and respectable RBI/R totals. That well-rounded approach was good enough to help Dickerson be a top-40 outfielder in 5×5 leagues, per ESPN. The problem is that if Haseley comes up short in even one or two of those cats, you're looking at more of a back fantasy OF option in the vein of 2018 Gerardo Parra (.284 with 6 homers and 11 steals, no. 60 OF). That doesn't make him a *bad* fantasy prospect per se, just one who's overvalued based on his draft pedigree.

7 Enyel De Los Santos RHP

OFP: 55 Likely: 45 ETA: Debuted in 2018

Born: 12/25/95 Age: 23 Bats: R Throws: R Height: 6'3" Weight: 170 Origin: International Free Agent, 2014

YEAR	TEAM	LVL	AGE	W	L	SV	G	GS	IP	H	HR	BB/9	K/9	K	GB%	BABIP	WHIP	ERA	DRA	WARP	PF
2016	FTW	A	20	3	2	0	11	7	52^2	38	2	2.4	7.7	45	41%	.242	0.99	2.91	3.50	0.9	102
2016	LEL	A+	20	5	3	0	15	15	68^1	70	11	3.2	6.8	52	38%	.291	1.38	4.35	4.19	1.0	93
2017	SAN	AA	21	10	6	0	26	24	150	131	12	2.9	8.3	138	45%	.290	1.19	3.78	3.25	3.4	94
2018	LEH	AAA	22	10	5	0	22	22	126^2	104	12	3.1	7.8	110	42%	.264	1.16	2.63	3.78	2.5	99
2018	PHI	MLB	22	1	0	0	7	2	19	19	2	3.8	7.1	15	51%	.309	1.42	4.74	4.97	0.0	90
2019	*PHI*	*MLB*	*23*	*2*	*3*	*0*	*8*	*8*	*40*	*37*	*6*	*3.3*	*8.7*	*39*	*40%*	*.296*	*1.28*	*4.43*	*4.98*	*0.2*	*96*

Breakout: 13% Improve: 21% Collapse: 16% Attrition: 34% MLB: 54% *Comparables: Tyler Mahle, Eddie Butler, Jake Thompson*

The Report: De Los Santos has been a bit lost in the shuffle in the Padres and Phillies systems the last two years. You'd think a mid-90s power sinker would garner would more attention, but given the sheer breadth of good pitching prospects his two orgs have had, it takes more than that. His breaking balls bleed together a bit. The slider he's added doesn't always tease out from his curve which is still the more advanced breaker despite being a bit of a short 12-6. Either or both can get slurvy. Both have a chance to be average or a tick above. Neither gets used as much as his advanced change. It can be a bit firm at times and act more like a two-seam fastball, but it will also flash above-average fade. De Los Santos has an ideal frame and a compact arm action and has always thrown strikes, save for his 2018 MLB cameo. Ultimately though, he may lack a true swing-and-miss offering to be more than a backend starter.

The Risks: Low. He might end up a reliever. He might only be the sixth best starter on the 2019 Phillies, but he's close to a finished product.

Ben Carsley's Fantasy Take: It's not just that De Los Santos may not start long-term; it's that even if he does, he's not likely to miss as many bats as you'd need him to. He might be perma-rosterable in his prime or if he ends up in a better home ballpark, but right now he looks like a fantasy spot starter.

8 Mickey Moniak OF   OFP: 55   Likely: 40   ETA: 2022

Born: 05/13/98   Age: 21   Bats: L   Throws: R   Height: 6'2"   Weight: 185   Origin: Round 1, 2016 Draft (#1 overall)

YEAR	TEAM	LVL	AGE	PA	R	2B	3B	HR	RBI	BB	K	SB	CS	AVG/OBP/SLG	DRC+	VORP	BABIP	BRR	FRAA	WARP	PF
2016	PHL	RK	18	194	27	11	4	1	28	11	35	10	4	.284/.340/.409	124	9.0	.345	3.0	CF(30) 4.6, LF(2) 0.1	1.0	98
2017	LWD	A	19	509	53	22	6	5	44	28	109	11	7	.236/.284/.341	85	13.3	.292	-0.1	CF(115) -9.8	-1.1	85
2018	CLR	A+	20	465	50	28	3	5	55	22	100	6	5	.270/.304/.383	85	6.6	.334	-0.1	CF(99) -7.3, LF(9) -0.3	-1.1	100
2019	*PHI*	*MLB*	*21*	*252*	*16*	*7*	*1*	*5*	*22*	*2*	*70*	*1*	*1*	*.164/.172/.259*	*10*	*-18.0*	*.203*	*-0.3*	*CF -3, LF 0*	*-2.2*	*96*

Breakout: 2%   Improve: 2%   Collapse: 0%   Attrition: 2%   MLB: 2%   *Comparables: Abraham Almonte, Xavier Avery, Rafael Ortega*

The Report: Well, it went better than 2017 at least, as Moniak was almost a league-average hitter in the Florida State League. But at the same time, we ranked him last year with some expectation that there could be a big rebound to something closer to his draft status, and instead he's settled in as a medium-upside, high-variance type.

The party piece was supposed to be a plus or plus-plus hit tool, and it just hasn't shown up in pro ball. I think the ultimate underlying force here is an inability to recognize spin, which in turn leads to weak, defensive contact and bad swing habits across the board. That's not entirely unchangeable, and the higher-end bat control is still there, which is why he's sometimes managed league average performance. He's more likely than Haseley to stay in center, and he's a good athlete overall.

We're contractually obligated by Phillies Twitter to tell you that over 2018's last 49 games, Moniak hit .312/.365/.487—the type of performance we envisioned when he was drafted. But the 150 games before the last 49 matter too, and he was dreadfully bad in those. If there's a major change lurking underneath, it hasn't evidenced itself yet, and a hot six weeks on its own is no more important this time than when he had a similar run early in 2017.

The Risks: High. "He might not actually be good at baseball" is a pretty big risk. Expectations remain tremendously and unfairly high on him as a former first-overall pick. He's a prospect, he's just a decent one with a lot of questions instead of a high-probability impact player. It's not what you want from 1.1.

Ben Carsley's Fantasy Take: If you roster 200-plus prospects like in a TDGX-sized format, you're stuck with Moniak unless someone hasn't read the baseball news in two years. You might as well hold on and see if he at least develops into an OF5, or if you can flip him if he has another six-week hot streak. If your league only rosters 100-or-so prospects, he's safe to drop and has been for a while. It's a bummer, but best not to cling to past hopes.

9 JoJo Romero LHP   OFP: 50   Likely: 45   ETA: 2019 in spot duty, 2020 in force

Born: 09/09/96   Age: 22   Bats: L   Throws: L   Height: 6'0"   Weight: 190   Origin: Round 4, 2016 Draft (#107 overall)

YEAR	TEAM	LVL	AGE	W	L	SV	G	GS	IP	H	HR	BB/9	K/9	K	GB%	BABIP	WHIP	ERA	DRA	WARP	PF
2016	WPT	A-	19	2	2	0	10	10	45^{2}	44	2	2.2	6.1	31	58%	.303	1.20	2.56	3.64	0.9	96
2017	LWD	A	20	5	1	0	13	13	76^{2}	61	2	2.5	9.3	79	60%	.299	1.07	2.11	2.95	2.1	89
2017	CLR	A+	20	5	2	0	10	10	52^{1}	43	2	2.6	8.4	49	52%	.289	1.11	2.24	3.28	1.2	99
2018	REA	AA	21	7	6	0	18	18	106^{2}	97	13	3.5	8.4	100	53%	.286	1.29	3.80	4.61	0.9	105
2019	*PHI*	*MLB*	*22*	*1*	*1*	*0*	*3*	*3*	*15*	*14*	*2*	*3.4*	*8.5*	*14*	*48%*	*.305*	*1.31*	*4.17*	*4.68*	*0.1*	*96*

Breakout: 13%   Improve: 18%   Collapse: 12%   Attrition: 22%   MLB: 38%   *Comparables: Scott Barnes, Keyvius Sampson, Jarred Cosart*

The Report: Romero just happens to be sandwiched between the highest variance prospects in the system, but he's a pretty stable commodity himself. He's a fairly standard three-pitch, short, good-command lefty prospect, with all of the positives and negatives that implies.

Romero sits in the high-80s to low-90s with the fastball, although it'll pop higher occasionally. He'll often show an above-average slider and an average changeup, and every now and then you'll get a fourth pitch, a show-me curve. He has very good command and pitchability. He's not ranked aggressively here because he might not have an out pitch, and he's on the short side.

Romero pitched well for much of the season as a 21-year-old in Double-A before going down in mid-July to an oblique injury. It's not sexy and Ben Carsley is about to tell you how these guys don't win you fantasy leagues, but he has the makings of an MLB contributor, and he's on the doorstep of the majors.

The Risks: Low. Romero may not have great upside, but he's as good of a bet as anyone outside of the top two for a significant MLB career.

Ben Carsley's Fantasy Take: Whether you should have any interest in Romero depends entirely on your league size and setup. Deep leagues where average-ish innings eaters count for something? Draft away. Shallow leagues or circuits with innings caps where performance matters more than bulk innings? For sure not.

10 Jhailyn Ortiz OF

OFP: 50 Likely: 40 ETA: 2023

Born: 11/18/98 Age: 20 Bats: R Throws: R Height: 6'3" Weight: 215 Origin: International Free Agent, 2015

YEAR	TEAM	LVL	AGE	PA	R	2B	3B	HR	RBI	BB	K	SB	CS	AVG/OBP/SLG	DRC+	VORP	BABIP	BRR	FRAA	WARP	PF
2017	WPT	A-	18	187	27	15	1	8	30	18	47	5	1	.302/.401/.560	160	17.2	.381	-1.7	RF(42) -5.6	0.2	102
2018	LWD	A	19	454	51	18	2	13	47	35	148	2	2	.225/.297/.375	87	12.5	.313	3.1	RF(96) -4.0	-0.8	90
2019	*PHI*	*MLB*	*20*	*252*	*20*	*10*	*0*	*8*	*28*	*9*	*98*	*0*	*0*	*.163/.203/.311*	*33*	*-13.7*	*.229*	*-0.6*	*RF -4*	*-1.9*	*96*

Breakout: 3% Improve: 3% Collapse: 0% Attrition: 1% MLB: 3% *Comparables: Chris Parmelee, Caleb Gindl, Nomar Mazara*

The Report: Huge dude, huge swing, huge swing-and-miss. We were setting everything up to be on the Ortiz hype train this season, but he fell flat on his face in his full-season debut at Lakewood.

Ortiz shows off plus-plus raw power and extreme bat speed. He also has a long, long swing and gets beat with velocity in the zone and by chasing outside it. He didn't show much barrel control or ability to adjust to full-season pitching, but it's early and he'd shown better on these things previously. A spring shoulder injury provides something of an excuse, and given his powerful stroke and bonus size, he's going to get plenty of chances.

He's athletic for his size, but his size is also enormous (no matter what they're claiming in the program). It's easy to envision a future where he's limited to first base or even DH, and at that point his reasonable upside starts to resemble C.J. Cron. That kind of bat looks a lot better in right field.

The Risks: Extreme. It's not a similar body to Jose Pujols, but it's sort of a similar skill set. If Ortiz gets it together he could be high up the 101 in a year or two's time; he could also stall out in A-ball.

Ben Carsley's Fantasy Take: Sorry, I went into a coma after "the reasonable upside starts to look like C.J. Cron."

The Next Five:

11 Arquimedes Gamboa SS

Born: 09/23/97 Age: 21 Bats: B Throws: R Height: 6'0" Weight: 175 Origin: International Free Agent, 2014

YEAR	TEAM	LVL	AGE	PA	R	2B	3B	HR	RBI	BB	K	SB	CS	AVG/OBP/SLG	DRC+	VORP	BABIP	BRR	FRAA	WARP	PF
2016	WPT	A-	18	147	15	6	0	2	15	9	28	5	1	.200/.254/.292	68	4.9	.235	0.0	SS(35) -0.4	-0.2	96
2017	LWD	A	19	350	44	12	3	6	29	33	52	8	0	.261/.328/.378	109	25.2	.291	2.9	SS(79) -3.3	1.2	87
2018	CLR	A+	20	497	49	14	4	2	37	53	111	6	4	.214/.304/.279	74	2.1	.281	-1.0	SS(109) -2.0	-0.6	99
2019	*PHI*	*MLB*	*21*	*252*	*21*	*4*	*0*	*5*	*19*	*12*	*64*	*0*	*0*	*.149/.190/.237*	*8*	*-19.0*	*.175*	*-0.3*	*SS -1, 3B 0*	*-2.2*	*96*

Breakout: 3% Improve: 4% Collapse: 0% Attrition: 2% MLB: 4% *Comparables: Jose Pirela, Tyler Pastornicky, Ehire Adrianza*

This is why you have to be a bit cautious about Mickey Moniak's big late-season surge. Gamboa was unconscious towards the end of 2017 in Lakewood, driving the ball with authority and looking for all the world like he was breaking out. He even had a narrative explanation in that he finally recovered from a hamstring injury that bothered him for much of the season. Then he went to the Florida State League and his slugging percentage started with a 2; it didn't get much better in the AFL.

The Phillies protected Gamboa from the Rule 5 Draft despite a crowded farm, because he can go get it at shortstop already and would've made an obvious selection for a tanking team. In doing so, they started the clock on how long he has to get his offensive game together. It's a catch-22.

12 Ranger Suarez LHP

Born: 08/26/95 Age: 23 Bats: L Throws: L Height: 6'1" Weight: 180 Origin: International Free Agent, 2012

YEAR	TEAM	LVL	AGE	W	L	SV	G	GS	IP	H	HR	BB/9	K/9	K	GB%	BABIP	WHIP	ERA	DRA	WARP	PF
2016	WPT	A-	20	6	4	0	13	13	73^2	61	4	2.9	6.5	53	53%	.260	1.15	2.81	3.62	1.4	98
2017	LWD	A	21	6	2	0	14	14	85	52	4	2.5	9.5	90	58%	.233	0.89	1.59	3.05	2.2	84
2017	CLR	A+	21	2	4	0	8	8	37^2	43	1	2.6	9.1	38	50%	.382	1.43	3.82	3.76	0.7	93
2018	REA	AA	22	4	3	0	12	12	75	64	2	2.4	6.5	54	51%	.283	1.12	2.76	4.71	0.6	106
2018	LEH	AAA	22	2	0	0	9	9	49^1	48	2	2.7	5.7	31	50%	.297	1.28	2.74	4.02	0.9	94
2018	PHI	MLB	22	1	1	0	4	3	15	21	3	3.6	6.6	11	52%	.367	1.80	5.40	5.73	-0.1	104
2019	*PHI*	*MLB*	*23*	*2*	*2*	*0*	*6*	*6*	*30*	*30*	*5*	*3.5*	*7.6*	*25*	*46%*	*.305*	*1.39*	*4.86*	*5.47*	*-0.1*	*96*

Breakout: 16% Improve: 20% Collapse: 10% Attrition: 27% MLB: 41% *Comparables: Troy Patton, Michael Bowden, Jorge Lopez*

See JoJo Romero. Adjust quality of slider down. Stir in warm water. Rinse. Repeat.

Suarez is pretty similar to Romero overall, except he's more balanced between the slider and changeup and has even less upside. He also made the majors faster—40-man considerations sometimes matter here—although he didn't pitch well in spot start duty. The Phillies don't seem particularly interested in handing him a spot on the staff, so he's probably headed to Triple-A to try to consolidate things and wait for an opportunity to fill in.

13 Francisco Morales RHP

Born: 10/27/99 Age: 19 Bats: R Throws: R Height: 6'4" Weight: 185 Origin: International Free Agent, 2016

YEAR	TEAM	LVL	AGE	W	L	SV	G	GS	IP	H	HR	BB/9	K/9	K	GB%	BABIP	WHIP	ERA	DRA	WARP	PF
2017	PHL	RK	17	3	2	0	10	9	41^1	34	1	4.4	9.6	44	44%	.308	1.31	3.05	3.27	1.2	100
2018	WPT	A-	18	4	5	0	13	13	56^1	54	6	5.3	10.9	68	42%	.324	1.54	5.27	3.82	0.9	93
2019	*PHI*	*MLB*	*19*	*2*	*4*	*0*	*10*	*10*	*45^1*	*47*	*9*	*6.7*	*8.9*	*45*	*37%*	*.318*	*1.77*	*6.20*	*7.02*	*-0.9*	*96*

Breakout: 0% Improve: 0% Collapse: 0% Attrition: 0% MLB: 0% *Comparables: Luiz Gohara, Keury Mella, Adalberto Mejia*

The Phillies have had a lot of luck with five-figure bonus arms in Latin America in recent years. Morales was their first seven-figure one in a while and early returns have been mostly good. He has an athletic, uptempo delivery and will flash mid-90s heat at times. This will vary start-to-start and within starts as well. Sometimes it will be more low-90s and he can dip into the 80s at times too. The slider is potentially plus, a tight two-plane breaker that has more present polish and command than you'd expect in an 18-year-old short-season arm. Morales needs more consistency with the velocity and an actual third pitch at some point, but the upside here is as high as any of the arms in the back half of the top ten.

14 Rafael Marchan C

Born: 02/25/99 Age: 20 Bats: B Throws: R Height: 5'9" Weight: 170 Origin: International Free Agent, 2015

YEAR	TEAM	LVL	AGE	PA	R	2B	3B	HR	RBI	BB	K	SB	CS	AVG/OBP/SLG	DRC+	VORP	BABIP	BRR	FRAA	WARP	PF
2016	DPL	RK	17	192	23	7	1	0	34	16	14	6	0	.333/.380/.386	147	17.6	.352	1.5	C(24) 0.2, 1B(6) -0.1	1.3	83
2017	PHL	RK	18	93	10	5	0	0	10	4	8	1	0	.238/.290/.298	85	0.7	.256	-0.5	C(29) -0.7	-0.1	99
2018	WPT	A-	19	210	28	8	2	0	12	11	18	9	6	.301/.343/.362	135	14.5	.330	0.3	C(47) 2.7	1.2	93
2019	*PHI*	*MLB*	*20*	*252*	*17*	*5*	*0*	*5*	*21*	*1*	*52*	*2*	*1*	*.172/.177/.246*	*7*	*-17.4*	*.196*	*-0.3*	*C 1*	*-1.8*	*96*

Breakout: 3% Improve: 3% Collapse: 0% Attrition: 1% MLB: 3% *Comparables: Christian Bethancourt, Francisco Pena, Carson Kelly*

And here come the catchers! You can have worse player development strategies than to collect as many viable backstops as possible, because, well, catchers are weird. Marchan got $200k from the Phillies. He played some shortstop as an amateur but is very much built like a catcher. He's new to the position and will be a project behind the plate, but he has the raw physical tools to be a solid catcher in time. Marchan has already shown extremely impressive bat-to-ball skills for his age and level, so he may be more a bat-first backstop in the end, unlike...

15 Rodolfo Duran C

Born: 02/19/98 Age: 21 Bats: R Throws: R Height: 5'9" Weight: 181 Origin: International Free Agent, 2015

YEAR	TEAM	LVL	AGE	PA	R	2B	3B	HR	RBI	BB	K	SB	CS	AVG/OBP/SLG	DRC+	VORP	BABIP	BRR	FRAA	WARP	PF
2016	PHL	RK	18	78	14	2	1	3	14	4	14	1	1	.315/.346/.493	138	6.6	.351	0.0	C(32) -0.2	0.3	98
2017	WPT	A-	19	171	14	9	3	0	6	8	36	0	1	.252/.298/.346	91	2.6	.323	-0.2	C(47) 1.4	0.3	102
2018	LWD	A	20	336	44	17	1	18	46	20	75	1	1	.260/.304/.495	125	27.5	.285	-0.2	C(81) 3.7	2.2	91
2019	*PHI*	*MLB*	*21*	*252*	*19*	*6*	*0*	*8*	*25*	*2*	*76*	*0*	*0*	*.160/.165/.284*	*9*	*-16.9*	*.188*	*-0.6*	*C 1*	*-1.7*	*96*

Breakout: 7% Improve: 9% Collapse: 1% Attrition: 7% MLB: 11% *Comparables: Gary Sanchez, Tommy Joseph, Wilson Ramos*

Catchers remain weird. Duran wasn't hugely on the radar coming into the season, and started off sharing time with organizational soldier Gregori Rivero. Very quickly, it became clear that Duran was actually an interesting prospect. He's a short, stout man who looks like a catcher, and he takes a big uppercut out of an open stance. It works for him because there's a lot of power here. He's also potentially a dude behind the plate, with a strong arm and the early signs of decent hands. What isn't there yet is his hit tool—contact is a real problem and he could get eaten alive at higher levels—but a 20-year-old catcher who projects for power and defense is a real prospect.

Others of note:

Deivi Grullon, C, Double-A Reading

The raw power we've long trumpeted showed up in games this year for Grullon—but how much did playing in Reading help? He hit much better overall within the friendly confines of FirstEnergy than he did in the rest of the Eastern League, with 14 of his 21 dingers at home. Grullon has always flashed a lot of arm strength, and he has a simple swing that can make the ball go a long way. Pitch selectivity remains a problem, however, and limits his hit tool. The Phillies left him off the 40-man roster, and catchers who can be MLB backups now but have some upside are Rule 5 staples; there were no takers.

Daniel Brito, 2B, Low-A Lakewood

Brito was also left off the 40-man and exposed to the Rule 5 draft, but he's in no way ready. We've spilled a lot of ink on Brito here at Baseball Prospectus, so let's summarize where he's at now: He's a fine defender at second who has rarely tapped into his above-average raw power, hasn't taken advantage of the sweet lefty swing that makes you think he should have a plus hit tool, and is prone to lapses on the field. He's only 20, he hasn't been that bad in A-ball, he's still quite athletic, and will often do something to keep you believing. He was one of the better prospects available in the last Rule 5 Draft, but like Pedro Gonzalez from Texas, he'd be nearly impossible to keep on a competitive roster.

Mauricio Llovera, RHP, Complex-Level GCL

I'll be honest and say that I didn't really see Mauricio Llovera as a guy entering this season. He yo-yo'd between the rotation and the pen in Lakewood in 2017, and he seemed like every 95-and-a-slider short middle relief prospect you see a half-dozen times in any given series now. Then he went out and threw 121 good innings in the Clearwater rotation with reports of an improved changeup and far greater consistency. The build and recoil still point toward a future relief role, and I'd like to see him pull the act off again in Double-A before I jump in with both feet. But there's more here than I thought at first glance.

Kyle Dohy, LHP, High-A Clearwater

You can find them everywhere now. Kyle Dohy was a 16th round pick in 2017 who was a terrible college starter and a terrible short-season reliever after the draft. Then he spent last offseason working with agent-slash-pitching guru-slash-former prospect Caleb Cotham, completely reworking his mechanics and arsenal using advanced video and training technologies. He emerged as a lefty shoving in the mid-90s with an untouchable slider, and he sliced and diced his way to Double-A by mid-July. He ran into some walk problems up there while trying to reintroduce his changeup, but over the course of the season he pushed his way from non-prospect to the cusp of the majors.

Top Talents 25 and Under (born 4/1/93 or later):

1. Aaron Nola
2. Sixto Sanchez
3. Jorge Alfaro
4. Nick Williams
5. Seranthony Dominguez
6. Adonis Medina
7. Scott Kingery
8. Spencer Howard
9. Alec Bohm
10. Luis Garcia

Aaron Nola is an ace. We no longer need to qualify that. He's just one of the best half-dozen starting pitchers in the game right now. Little more needs to be said here.

The prospect-industrial complex spent much of the past decade arguing about what Jorge Alfaro and Nick Williams would become. Amusingly, they both look like they're settling in as perfectly good regular MLB players—not elite guys, and not busts. Alfaro's defense has developed much more than most predicted, but his bat is only acceptable for the position. Williams was just a touch above a league-average hitter by DRC+, although we have him giving away pretty much all of that value in the field. They are both chugging along on their median projections at the moment.

Seranthony Dominguez entered camp as an oft-injured A-ball pitcher with inconsistent velocity while starting and a breaking ball that flashed; he was the best reliever in the Phillies bullpen by mid-May. He sat 100 or close to it all year, with a devastating low-90s slider and the occasional change at similar velocity. He's never starting again unless it's as part of an opener gambit, but all signs point to a dominant high-leverage reliever into his 30s. If you were ranking the big leaguers just on what they are right now, Dominguez would be at least two spots higher on this list.

Scott Kingery signed by far the biggest contract extension in MLB history for a player with no service time at all before the season, thus eliminating Philadelphia's need to send him down to claw a year back. But Kingery lost all the power he gained in 2017 without any corresponding uptick in contact, leading to a putrid batting line. Maybe he made a good move signing the deal after all. For reasons that never escaped the walls of Citizens Bank Park, the Phillies regularly ran him out at shortstop all year—a position he'd played all of twice in the minors, and one that doesn't suit his defensive talents well. He's still versatile and toolsy, and maybe he'll hit a little more if he's not trying like hell to fight shortstop to a draw.

Some others of note who didn't make it for various reasons: Rhys Hoskins was ineligible by a few weeks, and would've ranked second without much thought for all the reasons you'd think. Zach Eflin was the next-closest to making the list, and would've ranked around or just ahead of Enyel, since you'd take the existing No. 4-type starter over the field of likely No. 4 type starters. Victor Arano was also pretty close, and has an argument if you're more of a believer in the sustainability of his extreme slider-heavy approach. J.P. Crawford likely would've ranked third if he hadn't been dealt for Jean Segura, because I am extremely stubborn.

Pittsburgh Pirates

The State of the System:

I haven't sketched our org rankings out in any sort of detail yet, but man this feels like the fifteenth-best system in baseball.

The Top Ten:

1 Mitch Keller RHP   OFP: 70   Likely: 60   ETA: 2019

Born: 04/04/96 Age: 23 Bats: R Throws: R Height: 6'3" Weight: 195 Origin: Round 2, 2014 Draft (#64 overall)

YEAR	TEAM	LVL	AGE	W	L	SV	G	GS	IP	H	HR	BB/9	K/9	K	GB%	BABIP	WHIP	ERA	DRA	WARP	PF
2016	WVA	A	20	8	5	0	23	23	124^1	96	4	1.3	9.5	131	48%	.284	0.92	2.46	2.86	3.3	95
2016	BRD	A+	20	1	0	0	1	1	6	5	0	1.5	10.5	7	47%	.333	1.00	0.00	2.80	0.2	104
2017	BRD	A+	21	6	3	0	15	15	77^1	57	5	2.3	7.4	64	55%	.248	1.00	3.14	5.75	-0.4	101
2017	ALT	AA	21	2	2	0	6	6	34^2	25	2	2.9	11.7	45	48%	.280	1.04	3.12	3.36	0.8	98
2018	ALT	AA	22	9	2	0	14	14	86	64	7	3.3	8.0	76	55%	.251	1.12	2.72	3.82	1.5	89
2018	IND	AAA	22	3	2	0	10	10	52^1	59	3	3.8	9.8	57	35%	.366	1.55	4.82	3.71	1.1	93
2019	*PIT*	*MLB*	*23*	*2*	*3*	*0*	*8*	*8*	*40*	*37*	*5*	*3.0*	*8.3*	*37*	*44%*	*.304*	*1.26*	*3.96*	*4.54*	*0.4*	*96*

Breakout: 11% Improve: 15% Collapse: 14% Attrition: 30% MLB: 39% *Comparables: J.R. Graham, Nick Martinez, Corbin Burnes*

The Report: Mitch Keller didn't really change much in 2018, which makes him a bit boring to write about. He didn't need to get much better, mind you, and his numbers above reflect that. His fastball/curve combo is one of the best in the minors. The heater is easy-mid-90s cheese, touching 98 at times. The pitch has ample run that can jam righties assuming they even get the bat on it at all. The curve is a potential plus-plus nightmare in the low-80s. Keller has plus command of both offerings, although his fastball command wobbled at times in 2018. Still, the two-pitch combo here is so good that he hasn't needed much of a changeup.

Coincidentally, "not much of a changeup" appears on the scouting sheet after many of his outings. When his third pitch does peek its head out, it looks more like a firm two-seamer around 90. Again, it hasn't been an issue so far, but even a below-average cambio lurking in hitters' minds could make the overall profile here play up more. Keller has an ideal starter's frame and no red flags in his delivery. He's been quite durable and had a heavy workload by early-20s pitching prospect standards. He's still one of the best pitching prospects in the game, even if no news isn't quite good news here.

The Risks: Medium. Keller isn't really risky per se. He's had a couple small, non-arm injuries the past two seasons, but logged 142 frames this year in the upper minors. The FB/CU combo is as major-league-ready as it gets, but I do worry a bit about his lack of true dominance this year. We're quibbling, but you expect more shoving from one of the five or so best pitching prospects in the game.

Bret Sayre's Fantasy Take: Keller may not have the upside of fellow high-end pitching prospects Alex Reyes or Forrest Whitley, but the combination of proximity, ceiling and floor make him an easy top-five dynasty league arm among farmhands. If the change takes a step forward, it's not hard to envision him as a solid SP2 putting up similar numbers to future rotation mate Jameson Taillon—very good but not elite ratios, close to 200 strikeouts and a sprinkling of wins. It's likely we'll see Keller by early summer, and he'll be mixed-league worthy from the jump.

2 Ke'Bryan Hayes 3B OFP: 60 Likely: 50 ETA: Late 2019

Born: 01/28/97 Age: 22 Bats: R Throws: R Height: 6'1" Weight: 210 Origin: Round 1, 2015 Draft (#32 overall)

YEAR	TEAM	LVL	AGE	PA	R	2B	3B	HR	RBI	BB	K	SB	CS	AVG/OBP/SLG	DRC+	VORP	BABIP	BRR	FRAA	WARP	PF
2016	WVA	A	19	276	27	12	1	6	37	16	51	6	5	.263/.319/.393	95	12.4	.304	-1.5	3B(64) 2.0	0.3	96
2017	BRD	A+	20	482	66	16	7	2	43	41	76	27	5	.278/.345/.363	121	18.0	.331	0.8	3B(108) 20.7	3.8	100
2018	ALT	AA	21	508	64	31	7	7	47	57	84	12	5	.293/.375/.444	129	38.7	.344	-0.8	3B(116) 9.0	3.5	92
2019	*PIT*	*MLB*	*22*	*252*	*28*	*10*	*2*	*6*	*23*	*15*	*56*	*4*	*1*	*.219/.267/.354*	*67*	*-3.5*	*.256*	*0.3*	*3B 4*	*0.1*	*96*

Breakout: 25% Improve: 37% Collapse: 1% Attrition: 30% MLB: 39% *Comparables: Taylor Green, Matt Dominguez, Cheslor Cuthbert*

The Report: Charlie's kid passed the Double-A test with flying colors in 2018. The projection hasn't radically changed, but he continues to look like a future major-league regular. The hit tool is plus. Hayes has a frighteningly quick bat with the whip all the kids are talking about, and he can smoke plus velocity over the third base bag. The swing plane is still pretty flat, but he will show plus raw in BP, and if he ever figures out how to lift the ball more consistently, there is 20-home-run potential here. He marries a sweet swing with a strong approach at the plate, so even if he only ends up socking 40 doubles, the bat should play at a corner spot.

Hayes also checks all the boxes for a plus defender at third base, showing good footwork, sure hands, and a plus, accurate throwing arm. Hayes is an average runner whose speed plays up due to good baserunning instincts. The ultimate projection will depend on how many of those doubles turn into home runs at full maturity.

The Risks: Low. Hayes has an advanced hit tool and approach and offers a plus glove at third base. He's hit in the upper minors, and there may be additional pop to come.

Bret Sayre's Fantasy Take: Among the top 20 fantasy options at the hot corner in 2018, only two of them had fewer than 20 homers. It's a position that in many ways demands the kind of pop that Hayes is unlikely to develop. However, one of these two third baseman was Yuli Gurriel, who is a pretty good approximation from a roto sense of what Hayes could be. There's definitely a place in mixed leagues for a corner bat who can hover close to .300 with 10-15 homers and strong counting stats, but it's the limited upside that will keep Hayes towards the back of the Top 101.

3 Travis Swaggerty OF OFP: 60 Likely: 50 ETA: Late 2020

Born: 08/19/97 Age: 21 Bats: L Throws: L Height: 5'11" Weight: 180 Origin: Round 1, 2018 Draft (#10 overall)

YEAR	TEAM	LVL	AGE	PA	R	2B	3B	HR	RBI	BB	K	SB	CS	AVG/OBP/SLG	DRC+	VORP	BABIP	BRR	FRAA	WARP	PF
2018	WEV	A-	20	158	22	9	1	4	15	15	40	9	3	.288/.365/.453	146	12.5	.379	0.9	CF(36) -0.6	0.7	96
2018	WVA	A	20	71	6	1	1	1	5	7	18	0	0	.129/.225/.226	44	-1.2	.159	-0.6	CF(16) 0.7	-0.3	93
2019	*PIT*	*MLB*	*21*	*252*	*23*	*5*	*0*	*7*	*21*	*11*	*84*	*2*	*1*	*.143/.181/.258*	*11*	*-17.4*	*.180*	*-0.1*	*CF -1*	*-2.0*	*96*

Breakout: 1% Improve: 1% Collapse: 0% Attrition: 1% MLB: 1% *Comparables: Abraham Almonte, Xavier Avery, Joe Benson*

The Report: Swaggerty went in the top ten of this year's draft on the overall lack of weaknesses in his game, but there is some tools risk here. On the one hand, you can argue that he's a potential five-tool center fielder. This could be technically correct—the best kind of correct—as all five may grade out as 50 or better, but after a down (by first-round college bat standards) junior year at South Alabama, some warts have appeared in the profile. He has had issues with better fastballs at times, and his load can get a little handsy, lengthening the swing and impacting his bat control. His approach is excellent, but might prove a bit too passive against better pitching. There's plus power potential, but it might play down if the hit tool doesn't play to average. Swaggerty has enough speed to stick in center field for now, but might fit better in a corner in a few years. So we could be looking at a .350 OBP, 15-20 home run right fielder instead. That's still a decent ballplayer, but not necessarily an impact one. The physical profile/projection doesn't line up exactly, but the comp I keep coming back to here is "What if Brandon Nimmo went to college?"

The Risks: Medium. Swaggerty has a broad base of skills, but there are some hit tool questions, some positional questions, and a few levels between him and the majors.

Bret Sayre's Fantasy Take: Swaggerty was on fire to start his final college season and it's been a slow march downhill since then for dynasty leaguers. Yet the outfielder still has plenty of potential—it just hinges on his ability to make contact, which makes him no different than most of the good-but-not-elite toolsy hitting prospects on these lists. If it works, he's a .260-ish hitter with 15-20 homers and 25-30 steals who fares a little better in OBP leagues than standard 5×5 ones. He's in the conversation among the top 50 dynasty prospects in the game, but ultimately I think he falls just short.

4 Oneil Cruz SS

OFP: 60 Likely: 50 ETA: 2021. This might take a little while.

Born: 10/04/98 Age: 20 Bats: L Throws: R Height: 6'6" Weight: 175 Origin: International Free Agent, 2015

YEAR	TEAM	LVL	AGE	PA	R	2B	3B	HR	RBI	BB	K	SB	CS	AVG/OBP/SLG	DRC+	VORP	BABIP	BRR	FRAA	WARP	PF
2016	DDO	RK	17	211	28	18	5	0	23	22	44	11	5	.294/.367/.444	146	14.8	.382	0.0	3B(32) 4.5, SS(13) -0.7	1.7	97
2017	GRL	A	18	375	51	9	1	8	36	28	110	8	7	.240/.293/.342	83	13.5	.323	3.2	3B(47) -9.3, SS(30) 0.2	-0.6	98
2017	WVA	A	18	63	9	2	1	2	8	8	22	0	0	.218/.317/.400	79	3.5	.323	1.0	3B(15) 0.6, SS(1) 0.0	0.1	101
2018	WVA	A	19	443	66	25	7	14	59	34	100	11	5	.286/.343/.488	129	37.7	.346	2.5	SS(102) -5.9	2.1	99
2019	*PIT*	*MLB*	*20*	*252*	*20*	*8*	*1*	*7*	*26*	*8*	*81*	*1*	*1*	*.179/.203/.308*	*34*	*-10.7*	*.231*	*-0.2*	*SS -1*	*-1.2*	*96*

Breakout: 10% Improve: 11% Collapse: 0% Attrition: 4% MLB: 11% *Comparables: Alen Hanson, Andrew Velazquez, Gleyber Torres*

The Report: We suspect that his measurables are now light, and Cruz is one of the most interesting prospects in baseball. In broad strokes, he has a good version of the standard A-ball projectable shortstop skill set: a classic-looking lefty swing geared for contact, good feel for the bat, a plan at the plate, athleticism, soft hands, strong infield instincts and first step, and a real big arm. He also has the monster raw power you'd associate with a guy built like he's two or three years away from playing tight end on Sundays. The downside is that it's basically impossible not to have substantial swing-and-miss when your arms are so long and your strike zone so big. He's shortened up the swing a lot, and yet it's still never going to be less than long just because he's so big.

One of the most frequent conversations I've had with east coast pro scouts over the past year is where the heck Cruz ends up defensively. The easiest guess is right field, since he has a huge arm and might end up with a hulking corner outfield body. But he's improved a lot defensively over the past year, and played a pretty good shortstop in 2018 after spending most of his first two pro seasons at third base.

Could he actually stick at short? If you assume he "only" ends up being something like 6-foot-7 and 220 pounds, he'd be by far the biggest real shortstop in MLB history, but he might still be light and nimble enough for it to work. There's not necessarily any reason a guy that size couldn't play the position if he was appropriately rangy and reliant, especially in the age of aggressive positioning. Having a plus-plus arm can make up for a lot, too.

I'd also suggest the possibility of another unlikely position: center field. I'm not sure he's actually going to get quite as thick as you might guess, and he's a plus runner with good defensive instincts. Doesn't that sound like a center field profile to you? He's far too defensively gifted right now to slide to first base, so he's likely to be among the biggest regulars in history wherever he lands. It is probably going to look weird.

The Risks: We'll default to high, but they're unique and hard to measure. He could be a star and it could take several different forms, from a big power bat at a corner to a well-rounded player up the middle, and we wouldn't be surprised. There's also a real chance he's going to have big problems with velocity or well-located breaking balls due to length, and if he fills out he might fall too far down the defensive spectrum to support the bat. He's so utterly unusual physically that we may be perceiving a higher risk than there actually is, too.

Bret Sayre's Fantasy Take: There's little question that Cruz is a very different kind of prospect than the rest of the folk here. Tall and full of upside, he carries a larger risk profile and more potential power—in our space, we'll almost always take the trade off of the first for the second. A 30-homer bat is a 30-homer bat no matter where he stands, so long as he stands on a major-league field.

5 Calvin Mitchell OF

OFP: 60 Likely: 50 ETA: 2021

Born: 03/08/99 Age: 20 Bats: L Throws: L Height: 6'0" Weight: 209 Origin: Round 2, 2017 Draft (#50 overall)

YEAR	TEAM	LVL	AGE	PA	R	2B	3B	HR	RBI	BB	K	SB	CS	AVG/OBP/SLG	DRC+	VORP	BABIP	BRR	FRAA	WARP	PF
2017	PIR	RK	18	185	17	11	0	2	20	24	35	2	3	.245/.351/.352	123	4.4	.303	-0.9	LF(35) 2.6, CF(3) 0.5	0.3	100
2018	WVA	A	19	495	55	29	3	10	65	41	109	4	5	.280/.344/.427	126	20.4	.347	-4.4	RF(100) 0.5, LF(11) -1.6	0.8	98
2019	*PIT*	*MLB*	*20*	*252*	*18*	*9*	*0*	*6*	*24*	*11*	*76*	*0*	*0*	*.169/.203/.280*	*25*	*-16.0*	*.214*	*-0.6*	*RF 1, LF 0*	*-1.6*	*96*

Breakout: 5% Improve: 6% Collapse: 0% Attrition: 4% MLB: 6% *Comparables: Franmil Reyes, Caleb Gindl, Chris Parmelee*

The Report: My man can hit. Mitchell was assigned to Low-A out of the spring—an aggressive play for a prep in his first full year who just turned 19 and spent the previous summer in the complex. He came out of the chute scorching hot, and continued to hit well enough even as he faded in his first long summer.

Mitchell has a short, effortless swing and the ball jumps off his bat. He's geared to drive the ball, and is already flashing plus power. Throw in an advanced approach and a knack for shooting the barrel with the pitch, and you've got a guy who projects as a 6 hit/6 power bat with room above that. That's the basis for a heck of a player.

We think he'll stick in an outfield corner unless things go bad with the body. He'll probably end up being at least passable out there, if not particularly impressive. He'll never be any sort of stolen base threat or anything, but if you want to be generous, you can even describe him as "sneaky" athletic.

The Risks: Medium. There are always questions about the "hit first, ask questions later" profile until we see it work against MLB pitching, and we're years away from that here. Any hit tool degradation puts his ability to be an above-average hitter into question. Any athletic or defensive degradation slides him to first base, where the bar is much higher.

Bret Sayre's Fantasy Take: And here's the fun guy in the system. A DRC+ of 113 for a teenager in full-season ball is good way to make an impression, and it may catapult Mitchell onto the back-end of the 101 this offseason. There's not much speed in the profile, but his time in West Virginia looked eerily similar to that of current first baseman Josh Bell—and an outfield version of Bell would be a pretty good outcome here, if you believe his talent has yet to quite shine through. There's a .280-25 future, which sadly might be the most valuable realistic ceiling in the organization.

6 Cole Tucker SS

OFP: 55 Likely: 45 ETA: Late 2019

Born: 07/03/96 Age: 22 Bats: B Throws: R Height: 6'3" Weight: 200 Origin: Round 1, 2014 Draft (#24 overall)

YEAR	TEAM	LVL	AGE	PA	R	2B	3B	HR	RBI	BB	K	SB	CS	AVG/OBP/SLG	DRC+	VORP	BABIP	BRR	FRAA	WARP	PF
2016	WVA	A	19	67	9	4	2	1	2	4	9	1	1	.262/.308/.443	107	6.5	.294	0.5	SS(15) 2.8	0.6	91
2016	BRD	A+	19	304	36	12	1	1	25	29	62	5	6	.238/.312/.301	83	3.1	.306	-1.1	SS(61) 12.6	1.3	103
2017	BRD	A+	20	316	46	15	6	4	32	34	70	36	12	.285/.364/.426	139	29.9	.368	1.5	SS(66) -0.4	2.0	100
2017	ALT	AA	20	194	25	4	5	2	18	21	31	11	3	.257/.349/.377	98	11.4	.304	1.3	SS(39) 0.9	0.7	99
2018	ALT	AA	21	589	77	21	7	5	44	55	104	35	12	.259/.333/.356	91	37.5	.310	3.4	SS(131) -0.6	1.3	93
2019	*PIT*	*MLB*	*22*	*32*	*3*	*1*	*0*	*1*	*3*	*2*	*8*	*1*	*0*	*.206/.261/.324*	*51*	*-0.6*	*.250*	*0.1*	*SS 0*	*0.0*	*96*

Breakout: 18% Improve: 33% Collapse: 0% Attrition: 21% MLB: 36% *Comparables: Tyler Wade, Daniel Robertson, Ivan De Jesus*

The Report: Tucker continued to improve at shortstop in 2018, which is a boon for the profile since his bat has not developed at the same pace. While a bit on the tall side for the 6, he moves well on the dirt with above-average lateral range and shows good hands and actions. There's enough arm for the left side, and his quick transfers take some pressure off his throwing. We aren't talking about big shortstop tools here, but Tucker is a "will stick" guy.

At the plate, he's been fine, but not spectacular across two seasons in the Eastern League. Tucker has an athletic frame, but lacks physicality at the plate. There's not much 'oomph.' His hands are good, and the bat control is fine. The bat speed is only average though, and he has struggled at times to identify and deal with Double-A spin. He's not a bad hitter, and you can still bet on some projection in the frame; the profile just lacks the level of impact you could have squinted and seen this time last year.

The Risks: Low. He's a good athlete and a solid shortstop with Double-A time. The bat may not be inspiring at present, but it's the type of skill set that finds itself in the majors even while racking up frequent flier miles to and from Triple-A.

Bret Sayre's Fantasy Take: A quick gander at the steals and you might think this is going to be a more glowing endorsement than it is. Yet Tucker is another good example of why minor league thievery does not translate equitably to the majors. Expectations should be in the 15-20 range over a full season, and when you add that to a meh batting average and middling power (at best), it's a fantasy profile built for 2011.

7 Jason Martin OF

OFP: 50 Likely: 40 ETA: 2019

Born: 09/05/95 Age: 23 Bats: L Throws: R Height: 5'10" Weight: 185 Origin: Round 8, 2013 Draft (#227 overall)

YEAR	TEAM	LVL	AGE	PA	R	2B	3B	HR	RBI	BB	K	SB	CS	AVG/OBP/SLG	DRC+	VORP	BABIP	BRR	FRAA	WARP	PF
2016	LNC	A+	20	462	74	22	7	23	75	55	108	20	12	.270/.357/.533	104	27.8	.310	1.2	CF(54) -8.7, LF(26) -5.8	-1.6	116
2017	BCA	A+	21	198	34	11	2	7	29	20	42	9	5	.287/.354/.494	140	13.7	.333	-1.6	LF(14) 1.1, CF(8) -2.2	0.6	96
2017	CCH	AA	21	320	38	24	3	11	37	19	82	7	6	.273/.319/.483	118	14.1	.343	1.1	LF(57) -6.9	-0.1	100
2018	ALT	AA	22	289	49	13	5	9	34	28	61	7	8	.325/.392/.522	140	31.7	.396	-0.7	CF(62) -2.4, LF(6) -0.6	1.4	93
2018	IND	AAA	22	234	20	5	3	4	21	17	52	5	4	.211/.270/.319	67	-5.5	.261	-0.6	CF(53) -6.5, LF(6) -0.3	-1.2	94
2019	*PIT*	*MLB*	*23*	*37*	*5*	*2*	*0*	*1*	*4*	*2*	*10*	*1*	*0*	*.242/.287/.415*	*77*	*0.0*	*.300*	*0.0*	*RF -1*	*-0.1*	*96*

Breakout: 18% Improve: 44% Collapse: 5% Attrition: 33% MLB: 58% *Comparables: Brett Phillips, Michael Choice, Lewis Brinson*

The Report: The prospect you forgot was in the Gerrit Cole deal—or maybe that was just me—played well in 2018. Martin had a scorching first half of the year in Altoona, followed with some second half struggles for Indianapolis. The overall performance ended up about in line with his 2017, and really his 2016 as well after applying the standard Lancaster adjustment. He's got a very athletic frame—I described him this year as a compact Leody Taveras—but the tools aren't nearly as loud. Martin is merely an average runner with a below-average arm, who's a better fit in left field than center.

The power projection isn't ideal for a corner. He's swing is geared more towards lifting the ball, but he doesn't have the strength to really project for more than average raw, fringy game power. The hit tool is average as well with the added loft, bringing more swing-and-miss. There is some Double-A success here and the ability to at least stand in three outfield spots, so there is likely to be major-league utility as well.

The Risks: Medium. There are strong tweener signs here, and Martin may not hit enough to even "not hit enough for a corner."

Bret Sayre's Fantasy Take: The rest of this system is basically built for undervalued single-digit mono league batters. Unfortunately for those of us in mixed leagues, it leaves a lot to be desired. If you really squint here, you can see something like Harrison Bader. On the bright side, we probably won't have to wait long to find out if he's worthy of a roster spot.

8 Kevin Kramer 2B

OFP: 50 Likely: 40 ETA: Debuted in 2018

Born: 10/03/93 Age: 25 Bats: L Throws: R Height: 6'0" Weight: 200 Origin: Round 2, 2015 Draft (#62 overall)

YEAR	TEAM	LVL	AGE	PA	R	2B	3B	HR	RBI	BB	K	SB	CS	AVG/OBP/SLG	DRC+	VORP	BABIP	BRR	FRAA	WARP	PF
2016	BRD	A+	22	513	56	29	2	4	57	48	63	3	9	.277/.352/.378	119	18.0	.312	0.8	2B(103) 9.7	2.3	101
2017	ALT	AA	23	234	31	17	3	6	27	17	50	7	2	.297/.380/.500	124	20.5	.362	1.7	2B(48) -1.6	0.8	99
2018	IND	AAA	24	527	73	35	3	15	59	38	127	13	5	.311/.365/.492	141	42.2	.392	1.7	2B(82) -6.3, 3B(19) 0.9	3.0	93
2018	PIT	MLB	24	40	5	0	0	0	4	2	20	0	0	.135/.175/.135	56	-3.3	.278	0.5	3B(7) -0.3, 2B(4) -0.6	-0.1	96
2019	*PIT*	*MLB*	*25*	*148*	*19*	*8*	*1*	*5*	*16*	*8*	*41*	*2*	*1*	*.259/.312/.430*	*97*	*4.3*	*.335*	*-0.1*	*2B 0, SS 0*	*0.4*	*96*

Breakout: 8% Improve: 35% Collapse: 8% Attrition: 24% MLB: 53% *Comparables: David Bote, Joey Wendle, Taylor Featherston*

The Report: If you want to dream on these back-end top ten bats adding some badly-needed power to the profile... well, Kramer managed to do it. Stories like this get written every spring, but the proof was in the performance as Kramer more than doubled his career minor league home run total this season in Indianapolis. While Kramer says this wasn't specifically a loft thing, his swing does appear to be more leveraged for pull-side power now, and there's been a corresponding trade-off with an increased K-rate.

Kramer has experience at three infield spots, but his average foot speed and fringy arm play best at second. He's flipped spots among the Pittsburgh prospect Kevins this year, but he will need to strike out in less than 50% of his plate appearances to maintain that. This is probably the last year I'll need to write about them, but I thought that last year too.

The Risks: Low. He's a major-league-ready middle infielder with some pop.

Ben Carsley's Fantasy Take: I'm bored and there are still two more guys left on this list with the exact same boringness as Kramer.

9 Bryan Reynolds OF OFP: 50 Likely: 40 ETA: Late 2019

Born: 01/27/95 Age: 24 Bats: B Throws: R Height: 6'3" Weight: 205 Origin: Round 2, 2016 Draft (#59 overall)

YEAR	TEAM	LVL	AGE	PA	R	2B	3B	HR	RBI	BB	K	SB	CS	AVG/OBP/SLG	DRC+	VORP	BABIP	BRR	FRAA	WARP	PF
2016	SLO	A-	21	171	28	12	1	5	30	11	41	2	0	.312/.368/.500	123	11.7	.391	1.3	CF(33) -4.1	-0.1	114
2016	AUG	A	21	66	11	5	0	1	8	3	20	1	0	.317/.348/.444	113	5.5	.452	0.2	CF(11) 1.5	0.3	97
2017	SJO	A+	22	541	72	26	9	10	63	37	106	5	3	.312/.364/.462	142	35.8	.376	-0.9	CF(50) -4.3, RF(42) -2.9	1.4	100
2018	ALT	AA	23	383	56	18	3	7	46	43	73	4	4	.302/.381/.438	133	33.4	.362	-0.2	CF(43) -3.2, LF(42) -3.6	1.3	92
2019	*PIT*	*MLB*	*24*	*32*	*3*	*1*	*0*	*1*	*3*	*2*	*9*	*0*	*0*	*.234/.278/.374*	*69*	*-0.2*	*.297*	*0.0*	*LF 0*	*-0.1*	*96*

Breakout: 10% Improve: 17% Collapse: 1% Attrition: 21% MLB: 31% *Comparables: Bryan Petersen, Jake Cave, Shane Peterson*

The Report: The Pirates spent much of last offseason trading for corner bats without much power projection; it's a bold strategy, Huntington. Reynolds is fun to watch hit though. He's got a pretty swing from both sides, and despite minimal lower half engagement, he fires and maintains balance well. The BP pop is impressive, flashing above-average raw to all fields, but the game swing is more gap-to-gap. Reynolds marries a good approach with good feel for contact, giving him a potential 55 or 60 hit tool.

The problem is that that's going to have to carry the profile. He's fine in left field, but there won't be much defensive value or game power. If the bat falls short of projection he's more of an up-and-down outfielder unless he finds a way to get more of that raw pop into games. Obviously he wouldn't be the first player to figure that out in the majors, and he has some of the markers we tend to look for among power jump guys, but it's not something we can project until we see it.

The Risks: Low. He's fine. He's hit in Double-A. He's fine.

Bret Sayre's Fantasy Take: It's like we've opened up the kitchen cabinet and a mountain of saltines came flying out. If you were into Billy McKinney, you'll love Reynolds. No, not 2014 McKinney.

10 Kevin Newman SS OFP: 50 Likely: 40 ETA: Debuted in 2018

Born: 08/04/93 Age: 25 Bats: R Throws: R Height: 6'1" Weight: 180 Origin: Round 1, 2015 Draft (#19 overall)

YEAR	TEAM	LVL	AGE	PA	R	2B	3B	HR	RBI	BB	K	SB	CS	AVG/OBP/SLG	DRC+	VORP	BABIP	BRR	FRAA	WARP	PF
2016	BRD	A+	22	189	24	10	1	3	24	17	12	4	1	.366/.428/.494	193	28.1	.375	1.4	SS(38) 1.4	2.4	98
2016	ALT	AA	22	268	41	11	2	2	28	26	24	6	3	.288/.361/.378	111	14.8	.308	2.3	SS(60) 0.3	1.3	109
2017	ALT	AA	23	375	42	18	2	4	30	22	40	4	2	.259/.310/.359	92	14.2	.282	1.4	SS(78) 0.6	0.7	100
2017	IND	AAA	23	178	23	11	2	0	11	7	22	7	1	.283/.314/.373	85	4.9	.324	-1.3	SS(38) 0.4	0.2	95
2018	IND	AAA	24	477	74	30	2	4	35	31	50	28	11	.302/.350/.407	122	32.8	.333	3.2	SS(83) 2.9, 2B(21) -0.6	3.0	94
2018	PIT	MLB	24	97	7	2	0	0	6	4	23	0	1	.209/.247/.231	62	-4.2	.275	-0.6	SS(24) -1.4, 2B(8) -0.7	-0.3	95
2019	*PIT*	*MLB*	*25*	*383*	*40*	*17*	*1*	*7*	*36*	*22*	*59*	*9*	*4*	*.241/.289/.358*	*74*	*2.6*	*.268*	*0.1*	*SS 0, 2B 0*	*0.2*	*96*

Breakout: 15% Improve: 60% Collapse: 1% Attrition: 42% MLB: 72% *Comparables: Brock Holt, Dixon Machado, Brian Dozier*

The Report: The Pirates system could be summarized as "Prospect Fatigue: The List." Newman would top that list; I had my reservations about the profile even back when he was a consensus Top 100 type. He was a plus (or better) hit tool guy without anything else to carry the profile. He didn't hit for power. He was fringy at shortstop. A plus hit tool can take you very far, but it better be a plus hit tool. And as the years went on and the pitching got better, it's looked less like a plus hit tool. Newman hit .300 repeating the International League, but looked overmatched in his late-season major league cameo. He's never been the most physical hitter, and the bat may end up Mark Ellis-ish. Newman still doesn't hit for power. He's still fringy at short, but he's a major leaguer now. So he's got that going for him.

The Risks: Low. He's hit in the upper minors, though not as much as you'd like given the rest of the profile.

Bret Sayre's Fantasy Take: The only thing even mildly interesting about Newman is that his stolen base numbers spiked in 2018—but after nearly reaching 30 in the minors, he was caught on his only attempt in the show. This concludes the test of our emergency broadcast system.

The Next Five:

11 Luis Escobar RHP

Born: 05/30/96 Age: 23 Bats: R Throws: R Height: 6'2" Weight: 210 Origin: International Free Agent, 2013

YEAR	TEAM	LVL	AGE	W	L	SV	G	GS	IP	H	HR	BB/9	K/9	K	GB%	BABIP	WHIP	ERA	DRA	WARP	PF
2016	WEV	A-	20	6	5	0	15	12	67^{2}	50	4	3.7	8.1	61	43%	.254	1.15	2.93	2.87	1.8	99
2017	WVA	A	21	10	7	0	26	25	131^{2}	97	9	4.1	11.5	168	44%	.282	1.19	3.83	2.93	3.6	99
2018	BRD	A+	22	7	6	0	17	16	92^{2}	76	9	3.7	8.3	85	48%	.272	1.23	3.98	3.93	1.5	105
2018	ALT	AA	22	4	0	0	7	7	35^{2}	30	4	5.3	6.3	25	43%	.248	1.43	4.54	4.05	0.5	87
2019	*PIT*	*MLB*	*23*	*1*	*0*	*0*	*21*	*0*	*21^{2}*	*20*	*3*	*4.7*	*8.1*	*19*	*39%*	*.300*	*1.47*	*4.97*	*5.68*	*0.0*	*96*

Breakout: 6% Improve: 14% Collapse: 9% Attrition: 19% MLB: 30% *Comparables: Aaron Blair, Jon Gray, Lucas Sims*

Escobar's strikeouts evaporated some against better hitters in 2018, but the building blocks for a durable backend starter remain. The fastball bumps 95 as a starter, although it generally sits in a more average velo band. It's a heavy pitch with some two-seam run at times as well. Escobar has a fairly long arm action and a high-three-quarters slot so he's not always on top of the pitch and it can sit up in the zone, but even then it can be difficult to elevate. He offers a potentially average curve and change as well. The curve can get a little humpy and ride high as well, but it flashes tight 12-5 action. The change shows some fade, but can be too firm. Escobar is confident enough to throw it early in counts and to both sides though. It's a collection of three averageish pitches, a frame built for logging innings, and the same No. 4/5 starter projection here. Escobar has shown upper-90s velocity at times in short bursts, so there is the potential for a fastball/curve reliever here as well.

12 Lolo Sanchez OF

Born: 04/23/99 Age: 20 Bats: R Throws: R Height: 5'11" Weight: 168 Origin: International Free Agent, 2015

YEAR	TEAM	LVL	AGE	PA	R	2B	3B	HR	RBI	BB	K	SB	CS	AVG/OBP/SLG	DRC+	VORP	BABIP	BRR	FRAA	WARP	PF
2016	DPI	RK	17	190	19	4	1	0	10	24	18	4	8	.235/.359/.275	112	5.7	.265	0.0	CF(42) 3.2	0.8	99
2017	PIR	RK	18	234	42	11	2	4	20	21	19	14	7	.284/.359/.417	126	14.5	.295	-0.9	CF(49) 7.6	1.1	99
2018	WVA	A	19	441	57	18	1	4	34	41	72	30	13	.243/.322/.328	97	14.2	.287	2.7	CF(88) 8.4, LF(19) -2.1	1.3	98
2019	*PIT*	*MLB*	*20*	*252*	*25*	*4*	*0*	*5*	*16*	*10*	*56*	*6*	*3*	*.142/.175/.222*	*0*	*-20.7*	*.159*	*0.4*	*CF 3, LF 0*	*-1.9*	*96*

Breakout: 4% Improve: 4% Collapse: 0% Attrition: 2% MLB: 4% *Comparables: Cedric Hunter, Carlos Tocci, Billy McKinney*

Your typical speed-and-defense center field prospect with a questionable hitting projection. Sanchez is a plus to plus-plus runner with impressive range in the outfield. He was an above-average hitter in Low-A this year, jumping from the GCL while he was still 18. Mitchell is an obvious point of comparison as a similarly-aged outfield mate who we're projecting a lot higher here, and while Sanchez obviously has greater projection everywhere else but the plate than Mitchell, I just don't like the bat path and can't project similar power. If Sanchez can start squaring up and gets more balanced, there's a shot for a regular here with all the secondary skills, but it's a longer shot and this is a deep system as 5/4 types go.

13 Tahnaj Thomas RHP

Born: 06/16/99 Age: 20 Bats: R Throws: R Height: 6'4" Weight: 190 Origin: International Free Agent, 2015

YEAR	TEAM	LVL	AGE	W	L	SV	G	GS	IP	H	HR	BB/9	K/9	K	GB%	BABIP	WHIP	ERA	DRA	WARP	PF
2017	CLE	RK	18	0	3	0	13	10	33	35	4	6.8	7.9	29	48%	.330	1.82	6.00	5.10	0.3	108
2018	CLE	RK	19	0	0	0	8	6	19^{2}	13	2	4.6	12.4	27	60%	.275	1.17	4.58	2.12	0.8	98
2019	*PIT*	*MLB*	*20*	*1*	*3*	*0*	*14*	*7*	*30*	*29*	*4*	*10.5*	*8.9*	*30*	*48%*	*.320*	*2.12*	*6.55*	*7.49*	*-1.0*	*96*

Breakout: 0% Improve: 0% Collapse: 0% Attrition: 0% MLB: 0% *Comparables: Drew Anderson, Michael Feliz, Carlos Estevez*

Thomas appears to be the underlying reason for the Luplow/Gonzalez/prospects swap, at least from Pittsburgh's side. Thomas signed with the Indians as an infielder out of the Bahamas for $200,000 late in his bonus period, but quickly converted to the mound. He's spent two seasons kicking around the complexes, and picked up notoriety in Arizona this year as an athletic arm strength guy with some feel for spin. "Targeting players from emerging baseball markets" and "targeting guys at the beginning of breakouts at the lowest MILB levels" are both trendy plays for aggressive teams, and Thomas fits the bill here. He's still a million miles away from the majors, however: Watch him, while remembering that his future could take nearly any form.

14 Will Craig 1B

Born: 11/16/94 Age: 24 Bats: R Throws: R Height: 6'3" Weight: 212 Origin: Round 1, 2016 Draft (#22 overall)

YEAR	TEAM	LVL	AGE	PA	R	2B	3B	HR	RBI	BB	K	SB	CS	AVG/OBP/SLG	DRC+	VORP	BABIP	BRR	FRAA	WARP	PF
2016	WEV	A-	21	274	28	12	0	2	23	41	37	2	0	.280/.412/.362	156	18.3	.322	-2.7	3B(46) 0.1	1.3	100
2017	BRD	A+	22	542	59	26	1	6	61	62	106	1	3	.271/.373/.371	138	10.8	.335	-7.8	1B(93) 9.4	1.6	100
2018	ALT	AA	23	549	73	30	3	20	102	42	128	6	3	.248/.321/.448	109	28.6	.288	0.6	1B(122) 8.8	1.3	92
2019	*PIT*	*MLB*	*24*	*252*	*25*	*9*	*1*	*9*	*29*	*17*	*67*	*1*	*0*	*.193/.266/.350*	*65*	*-6.1*	*.233*	*-0.4*	*1B 4*	*-0.3*	*96*

Breakout: 2% Improve: 14% Collapse: 0% Attrition: 14% MLB: 19% *Comparables: Mark Canha, Brock Peterson, Lars Anderson*

Craig was a 23-year-old first baseman who hit .248/.321/.448 in Double-A this year. I often like to say that minor-league production, good or bad, exists primarily to be explained. But on rare occasions it is perfectly descriptive in and of itself. The slash line above—with accompanying demographic context—paints a picture in your mind. A hulking slugger with a bit of a stiff swing and commensurate swing-and-miss issues. Plus raw that plays down in games accordingly. I used a "right-handed Rowdy Tellez" comp earlier in the season, and the range of outcomes here is similar. Craig has all the usual pitfalls that we associate with R/R first base types, and there isn't really a role for a right-handed corner dude with that line in 2019. But hey, Rowdy Tellez hit a boatload of doubles last September.

15 Rodolfo Castro 2B

Born: 05/21/99 Age: 20 Bats: B Throws: R Height: 6'0" Weight: 200 Origin: International Free Agent, 2015

YEAR	TEAM	LVL	AGE	PA	R	2B	3B	HR	RBI	BB	K	SB	CS	AVG/OBP/SLG	DRC+	VORP	BABIP	BRR	FRAA	WARP	PF
2016	DPI	RK	17	230	27	15	3	2	29	27	48	2	1	.271/.360/.411	118	15.1	.338	-2.7	SS(52) 5.1, 3B(1) 0.0	1.3	99
2017	PIR	RK	18	211	27	12	4	6	32	16	47	4	3	.277/.344/.479	120	17.7	.338	0.5	SS(19) 1.3, 3B(17) -4.4	0.2	100
2018	WVA	A	19	426	47	19	4	12	50	26	100	6	3	.231/.278/.395	83	10.9	.276	2.9	2B(89) 4.3, SS(12) 1.6	0.6	98
2019	*PIT*	*MLB*	*20*	*252*	*16*	*8*	*0*	*7*	*25*	*5*	*82*	*0*	*0*	*.140/.155/.264*	*3*	*-21.1*	*.171*	*-0.3*	*2B 2, SS 0*	*-2.0*	*96*

Breakout: 9% Improve: 9% Collapse: 0% Attrition: 5% MLB: 9% *Comparables: Nick Noonan, Dilson Herrera, Adrian Cardenas*

And now we have a 19-year-old middle infielder who hit .231/.278/.395 in Low-A this year, and hey, that serves as a serviceable description as well. The shape of the performance gives you the right idea for sure. Castro has a well-developed frame and there is decent raw power here. There's better feel for contact than a .231 batting average in the Sally would suggest, but he tends to swing at far too many pitches out of the zone. That makes him a pesky hitter against A-ball arms, but potentially a windmill against better ones. Castro is a good defender at the keystone, and his arm likely limits him to the right side of the infield. He's a fun enough prospect with a bit to dream on, but likely would be more of a personal cheeseball or low minors sleeper in a deeper system. I should just check the utility infielder box and move on, but sometimes you like a guy more than you should.

Others of note:

Travis MacGregor, RHP, Low-A West Virginia

I had MacGregor on my Sally watchlist when initial rosters came out, and he might've been the buzziest guy coming into the season on a West Virginia roster that turned out to be pretty loaded. I got to see him in their mid-May series in Lakewood, and I spent most of the first two innings of his start perplexed at why his stuff was way down. He exited in the second with an undisclosed arm injury, missed six weeks, came back for a bit, and was shut down again with a forearm problem in August. You can probably already guess that this ended in Tommy John surgery, which Pirates Prospects reported happening in September. Before the injury, he was a tall, projectable righty already sitting in the low-90s from a tough arm angle, with the changeup and curveball flashing as secondaries. We'll see what comes back in 2020.

Braeden Ogle, LHP, Low-A West Virginia

MacGregor's West Virginia rotation mate is also his mirror image in a lot of ways. While not quite as buzzy in Bristol last year, Ogle offers a sneaky-fast low-90s fastball that comes from a tough angle given his low slot and uptempo, crossfire delivery. He can spot the fastball to both sides and it will show good boring action in on righties. He was throwing a slider in April, which had some good short tilt to it; it's a projectable secondary. He has a changeup as well. There's also the shoulder soreness that ended his season in April, which is in some ways even more concerning than actual Tommy John surgery. We'll see what comes back in (hopefully) 2019.

Braxton Ashcraft, RHP, GCL Pirates

Looking above, you might be a bit concerned about the Pirates dearth of pitching prospects. Fair enough. They tried to rectify this in the draft, popping Ashcraft in the second round, and Gunnar Hoglund in the comp round. Hoglund elected to go to Ole Miss, so the Pirates are left betting—like many, many other orgs—on a projectable prep arm from Texas. He added some velocity across the spring—touching the mid-90s—and has the kind of lean, limby frame you can bet on adding some more over the next few years. There's some feel for a breaking ball, although he will slow down and cast it at times. If you like fun facts, he caught 37 touchdowns as a high school senior, so there are gonna be worse athleticism bets out there. We'll see what he shows in 2019.

Top Talents 25 and Under (born 4/1/93 or later):

1. Mitch Keller
2. Ke'Bryan Hayes
3. Travis Swaggerty
4. Keone Kela
5. Oneil Cruz
6. Calvin Mitchell
7. Cole Tucker
8. Jason Martin
9. Kevin Kramer
10. Bryan Reynolds

A comparison between the 2018 and 2019 versions of this list tells you quite a bit about the state of the Pirates. Last year, there were five major-leaguers represented; this year, just one. Josh Bell, Trevor Williams, and Chad Kuhl turned 26 and graduated (along with Joe Musgrove, who hit this milestone a month before his trade from the Astros). These newly minted late-twenty-somethings join an impressive cohort of 27-year-olds—Jameson Taillon, Felipe Vazquez, Gregory Polanco, Nick Kingham, Adam Frazier.

This is good, right? In a vacuum, you want a core of late-twenty somethings, especially given that the two most prominent veterans on the team, Starling Marte and Chris Archer, each just blew out thirty candles in the past few months. With the productive bulk of the roster between 26 and 30, this team should be squarely in its window of contention. The problem, of course, is that the Pirates don't play in a vacuum; they play in the NL Central, where three other teams are loaded to the gills. Given the competition of the Brewers, Cubs, and Cardinals, this is a roster suffering from a relative shortage of both quality and depth.

The lone big-leaguer, former Rangers closer Keone Kela, slots in just after the top three prospects. And, yes, Kela is quite good at what he does, and when his heat-and-hook combo is on, he's well-nigh unhittable. All the same, he's a relief arm. Kela would be the prime candidate to step in for Felipe Vazquez in the case of injury, trade, or banishment from the ninth inning, but it's not like the Pirates don't have other strong bullpen options (Richard Rodriguez, for one) at the ready. Still, Kela is a clear several notches above the only other viable 25-and-under candidate for this list, Michael Feliz, whose first season in Pittsburgh was bogged down by both injury and inconsistency.

One final Yinzer shout-out to Austin Meadows and Tyler Glasnow, who would feature prominently on the front half of this list were they still in the Steel City. They, however, are part of a much more crowded crew of young talent in Tampa Bay, swapped out for Archer in a deadline deal. Certainly, Meadows and Glasnow were prime candidates for changes of scenery, but if Archer doesn't earn that "ace" label quickly, Bucs fans might find their wandering eyes checking out Rays box scores, wondering "what if..."

San Diego Padres

The State of the System:

Their full-slot, top-ten first-round pick from this year's draft is ranked 12th overall. You tell me.

The Top Ten:

1 Fernando Tatis Jr. SS   OFP: 70   Likely: 60   ETA: 2019

Born: 01/02/99   Age: 20   Bats: R   Throws: R   Height: 6'3"   Weight: 185   Origin: International Free Agent, 2015

YEAR	TEAM	LVL	AGE	PA	R	2B	3B	HR	RBI	BB	K	SB	CS	AVG/OBP/SLG	DRC+	VORP	BABIP	BRR	FRAA	WARP	PF
2016	PDR	RK	17	188	35	13	1	4	20	10	44	14	2	.273/.312/.426	117	13.0	.344	2.4	SS(29) -0.1, 2B(8) -1.3	0.3	99
2016	TRI	A-	17	49	4	4	2	0	5	3	13	1	1	.273/.306/.455	110	4.5	.364	0.4	SS(7) -1.4, 3B(3) -0.7	-0.2	91
2017	FTW	A	18	518	78	26	7	21	69	75	124	29	15	.281/.390/.520	150	51.2	.342	0.1	SS(109) -5.6	3.7	106
2017	SAN	AA	18	57	6	1	0	1	6	2	17	3	0	.255/.281/.327	75	0.4	.351	0.9	SS(9) -0.3, 3B(3) -0.5	-0.1	97
2018	SAN	AA	19	394	77	22	4	16	43	33	109	16	5	.286/.355/.507	136	35.8	.370	3.0	SS(83) -1.9	2.4	101
2019	*SDN*	*MLB*	*20*	*287*	*33*	*11*	*1*	*11*	*33*	*15*	*92*	*6*	*2*	*.199/.242/.372*	*59*	*-2.9*	*.254*	*0.5*	*SS -1*	*-0.5*	*100*

Breakout: 15%   Improve: 32%   Collapse: 0%   Attrition: 16%   MLB: 32%   *Comparables: Xander Bogaerts, Addison Russell, Cody Bellinger*

The Report: Tatis Jr. is a special talent. He has a wiry and lean frame with plenty of room to add muscle, but he already has explosive strength in his hips and wrists. Tatis is a plus athlete with top tier quick-twitch movements and an instinctual feel for how to move his body to generate power with fluid grace.

With the bat, this translates into some of the best physical offensive tools in baseball. He has a feel for getting the barrel on the ball consistently with a swing he innately understands how to adjust to location and velocity. When he's on a pitch, he can do damage to all fields. Tatis generates plus bat speed, has double-plus raw power, and a swing that takes advantage of both to the fullest. If the physical parts of hitting were all that mattered, Tatis would be ready to go right now.

There's still a bit of developmental work ahead, however. Tatis will need more reps to improve his pitch recognition and calm his approach. He generally knows the zone and has the patience to eschew offerings off the plate, but he also looks to deal damage on pitches he should stay away from. That, along with trouble recognizing plus off-speed out of the hand, occasionally leads to an ugly at-bat.

Defensively, Tatis uses his quickness and average foot speed to get to the balls he should at short, and he oughta stick at the position for now. He has good hands, doesn't make too many mental errors, and his plus arm can dig him out of trouble. He should be an average defender for now, but may need to move to third as he gets slower and bigger.

With a plus bat and average defense, Tatis should be an all-star caliber shortstop, with a real chance at superstardom if he can refine his approach.

The Risks: Low. The only significant risk is Jr.'s lack of polish against premier pitching, but he has consistently shown he's capable of making in-season adjustments. Over the course of the Texas League season, Tatis went from flailing at average breaking balls to recognizing above-average stuff and making hard contact or letting it go.

The only other thing worth mentioning is he still has plenty of room to put on muscle, which could slow him down enough to push him over to third, where he should be plus.

Bret Sayre's Fantasy Take: An easy top-five overall dynasty prospect, Tatito can be a true five-category superstar at shortstop and soon. You already know this though. We're truly picking nits when I say that it was a good sign Tatis was a more effective base stealer in 2018 because one of the risks here was that he'd only be a 10-15 steal guy, rather than in the 25-30 range. Heaven forbid he not run enough to supplement what could be a .275 average and 30 homers from a middle infield spot.

2 Luis Urias IF

OFP: 70 Likely: 60 ETA: Debuted in 2018

Born: 06/03/97 Age: 22 Bats: R Throws: R Height: 5'9" Weight: 185 Origin: International Free Agent, 2013

YEAR	TEAM	LVL	AGE	PA	R	2B	3B	HR	RBI	BB	K	SB	CS	AVG/OBP/SLG	DRC+	VORP	BABIP	BRR	FRAA	WARP	PF
2016	LEL	A+	19	531	71	26	5	5	52	40	36	7	13	.330/.397/.440	148	41.6	.348	-5.9	2B(80) 6.2, SS(22) -3.2	2.5	96
2017	SAN	AA	20	526	77	20	4	3	38	68	65	7	5	.296/.398/.380	130	40.3	.340	2.6	SS(60) 4.7, 2B(55) -1.1	3.0	94
2018	ELP	AAA	21	533	83	30	7	8	45	67	109	2	1	.296/.398/.447	117	27.3	.373	1.4	2B(90) 10.2, SS(20) 3.4	3.7	114
2018	SDN	MLB	21	53	5	1	0	2	5	3	10	1	0	.208/.264/.354	85	0.6	.216	0.3	2B(12) -0.2	0.1	101
2019	*SDN*	*MLB*	*22*	*410*	*42*	*15*	*3*	*9*	*44*	*42*	*90*	*1*	*1*	*.238/.327/.370*	*91*	*10.4*	*.291*	*-0.3*	*2B 3, SS 0*	*1.5*	*100*

Breakout: 20% Improve: 48% Collapse: 0% Attrition: 27% MLB: 53% *Comparables: Kolten Wong, J.P. Crawford, Steve Lombardozzi*

The Report: We'll start with a mea culpa: The last few prospect list cycles our west coast folks have buzzed around my ear about Urias, and I treated them like a particularly annoying member of the muscomorpha. It's only a hit tool, and is he really gonna hit? What happens if he only hits .270 and pitchers realize he can't hurt them with any sort of power? Yes, he's young, but there's no projection here, he's just small. He's not really a major league shortstop. I swatted them away with every "reasonable" criticism of the profile I had, as it's not one I'm naturally inclined to pound the table for.

I often write that the lifeblood of our prospect lists are the live looks. Naturally we can't see every prospect every year. We'll send our texts or watch video where needed, but then you see a half dozen or so Urias BP swings and "oh... yeah... of course he is going to hit, and also that is at least average raw power, you idiot, next time listen to Wilson."

I wasn't a co-author on the Nathan Report, so I can't tell you if it was the major league balls, but I do know when a dude has that unnatural carry. We've convened a panel earlier this year to discuss the issues with evaluating this profile, and while yes, he's best-suited to second, isn't really a runner, and hasn't hit for anything approaching average power in the minors, so what?

The Risks: Low. He might walk less if pitchers think they can challenge him. He's not gonna offer a ton of athletic/defensive value. We think he's really gonna hit though.

Bret Sayre's Fantasy Take: I am not going to be a popular guy here. Sure, Urias showed *more* power last year, but color me skeptical that he'll be someone you peg for 15 homers in a season even as he matures. The average is great, no question, and he's one of the best bets in the minors to be a .300 hitter, but not too many of you were fawning over Ben Zobrist last year when he put up a realistic Urias line (.305, 9 HR, 3 SB).

3 Francisco Mejia C

OFP: 70 Likely: 55 ETA: Debuted in 2017

Born: 10/27/95 Age: 23 Bats: B Throws: R Height: 5'10" Weight: 180 Origin: International Free Agent, 2012

YEAR	TEAM	LVL	AGE	PA	R	2B	3B	HR	RBI	BB	K	SB	CS	AVG/OBP/SLG	DRC+	VORP	BABIP	BRR	FRAA	WARP	PF
2016	LKC	A	20	259	41	17	3	7	51	15	39	1	0	.347/.384/.531	159	29.7	.388	2.3	C(52) 1.5	2.8	101
2016	LYN	A+	20	184	22	12	1	4	29	13	24	1	2	.333/.380/.488	143	16.8	.366	-0.1	C(35) 0.6	1.1	101
2017	AKR	AA	21	383	52	21	2	14	52	24	53	7	2	.297/.346/.490	131	32.5	.311	1.5	C(71) 1.6, 3B(1) -0.1	2.4	99
2017	CLE	MLB	21	14	1	0	0	0	1	1	3	0	0	.154/.214/.154	78	-1.7	.200	-0.3	C(3) 0.0	0.0	107
2018	CLE	MLB	22	4	0	0	0	0	0	2	0	0	0	.000/.500/.000	69	0.1	.000	0.0		0.0	108
2018	COH	AAA	22	336	32	22	1	7	45	18	58	0	0	.279/.328/.426	101	9.4	.321	-1.2	C(41) 4.6, LF(22) -3.2	0.7	100
2018	ELP	AAA	22	132	22	8	1	7	23	7	25	0	0	.328/.364/.582	122	11.8	.359	0.7	C(26) 1.3	0.9	110
2018	SDN	MLB	22	58	6	2	0	3	8	3	19	0	0	.185/.241/.389	73	-0.3	.219	0.2	C(10) -1.7	-0.1	99
2019	*SDN*	*MLB*	*23*	*306*	*30*	*15*	*1*	*10*	*37*	*14*	*63*	*1*	*0*	*.236/.279/.396*	*79*	*4.8*	*.269*	*-0.4*	*C -3*	*0.2*	*100*

Breakout: 19% Improve: 47% Collapse: 2% Attrition: 21% MLB: 57% *Comparables: Hank Conger, Travis d'Arnaud, Jeff Mathis*

The Report: Last spring, my chat queues were filled with questions along the lines of "What's wrong with Francisco Mejia?" Fair queries given his atrocious start, even if it may have been nothing more than the ol' Triple-A-itis. Once fashionistas could start wearing white, Mejia turned back into the potential .300 hitter with pop that you stashed in your dynasty league two years ago. The slash line looked right in the end, and it matched the eye test. I'm still very confident he will hit.

"Catchers are weird." You might be tired of me writing that by now. So here's another construction: Teams are weird about catchers. I encourage the whole prospect team to write these blurbs—and really, their reports in general—in a vacuum. And my projection for Mejia is "major league catcher." Not a plus one by any means, but a perfectly adequate backstop. He has quite a good arm, and his receiving has improved. He's a bit on the slight side, so durability back there is a fair concern, but Cleveland and now San Diego have demurred when opportunities have presented themselves to make Mejia *the guy*.

Catcher is also the position I am least qualified to evaluate. A lot happens behind closed doors. Teams are just going to know more than I am here, and Yan Gomes and Austin Hedges have justifiably better reps with the glove. But then I see someone try to get in Mejia's kitchen, jam him, and watch him still hit it out, and I wonder if we aren't all overthinking this.

The Risks: High. The funny thing is this risk factor literally just comes down to "Do the Padres think he's a catcher or not?" I've generally been higher on Mejia's glove back there than the organizations that employ him, so ¯_(ツ)_/¯.

Bret Sayre's Fantasy Take: There are two very distinct forces at work in trying to rank Mejia in a dynasty context. The first is that he's a catcher and dynasty league catchers are almost always a bad idea. The second is that the position is so bad that Mejia's upside makes you forget about the first force. Yadier Molina was the second-best fantasy catcher and he hit .261 with 20 homers. Mejia is certainly talented enough offensively to do that if he gets the playing time.

4 MacKenzie Gore LHP   OFP: 70   Likely: 55   ETA: 2021

Born: 02/24/99   Age: 20   Bats: L   Throws: L   Height: 6'3"   Weight: 191   Origin: Round 1, 2017 Draft (#3 overall)

YEAR	TEAM	LVL	AGE	W	L	SV	G	GS	IP	H	HR	BB/9	K/9	K	GB%	BABIP	WHIP	ERA	DRA	WARP	PF
2017	PDR	RK	18	0	1	0	7	7	21^1	14	0	3.0	14.3	34	69%	.333	0.98	1.27	2.99	0.7	101
2018	FTW	A	19	2	5	0	16	16	60^2	61	5	2.7	11.0	74	41%	.354	1.30	4.45	2.81	1.7	105
2019	*SDN*	*MLB*	*20*	*3*	*4*	*0*	*12*	*12*	45^1	*45*	*8*	*4.3*	*9.6*	*49*	*45%*	*.323*	*1.47*	*4.85*	*5.39*	*0.0*	*100*

Breakout: 5%   Improve: 7%   Collapse: 1%   Attrition: 3%   MLB: 10%   *Comparables: Henry Owens, Matt Wisler, Michael Fulmer*

The Report: Gore was periodically sidelined with recurring blister issues throughout 2018. When healthy, he dominated Midwest League hitters with a mid-90s fastball and a knee buckling curve. There are a lot of moving parts to his delivery but he repeats it well and stays balanced and on line. He's athletic, and there's a chance he develops plus command. While he's not the world's hardest thrower, Gore's extreme extension helps the fastball play above its grade. The curveball is already an above-average offering and has the potential to be a true out pitch. It features 1-7 movement with sharp break and Gore has enough confidence to throw it in any count. The other secondaries are still developing but if they become at least average, they will be a nice complement to his top shelf fastball and curve.

The Risks: High. Gore made three trips to the DL during his first full professional season. He has top-shelf ingredients but the blisters could hinder his progress.

Bret Sayre's Fantasy Take: One of my favorite fantasy pitching prospects, Gore pairs stuff and pitchability in a way that shows you a clear path to being an easy SP2. Of course, he is a pitcher and we really don't like pitching prospects in dynasty leagues, but when Ben and I finally shake out our Top 101, don't be surprised to see Gore as one of the top five pitchers gracing that page. He can ride that fastball/curveball combination to 200-plus strikeouts.

5 Chris Paddack RHP   OFP: 60   Likely: 55   ETA: 2020

Born: 01/08/96   Age: 23   Bats: R   Throws: R   Height: 6'4"   Weight: 195   Origin: Round 8, 2015 Draft (#236 overall)

YEAR	TEAM	LVL	AGE	W	L	SV	G	GS	IP	H	HR	BB/9	K/9	K	GB%	BABIP	WHIP	ERA	DRA	WARP	PF
2016	GRB	A	20	2	0	0	6	6	28^1	9	2	0.6	15.2	48	51%	.163	0.39	0.95	0.89	1.4	100
2016	FTW	A	20	0	0	0	3	3	14	11	0	1.9	14.8	23	45%	.379	1.00	0.64	2.51	0.4	104
2018	LEL	A+	22	4	1	0	10	10	52^1	43	3	0.7	14.3	83	47%	.370	0.90	2.24	2.40	1.8	96
2018	SAN	AA	22	3	2	0	7	7	37^2	23	1	1.0	8.8	37	45%	.239	0.72	1.91	2.87	1.1	99
2019	*SDN*	*MLB*	*23*	*2*	*1*	*0*	*5*	*5*	*25*	*21*	*3*	*2.5*	*10.9*	*30*	*42%*	*.312*	*1.11*	*3.21*	*3.55*	*0.5*	*100*

Breakout: 12%   Improve: 29%   Collapse: 13%   Attrition: 19%   MLB: 49%   *Comparables: Drew Smyly, David Paulino, Marcus Stroman*

The Report: A strong, durable frame and easy physicality highlights the basic package for Paddack, a former eighth-rounder and recent Tommy John rehabber. He looked no worse for wear in his first season back from the knife, dominating High-A and holding his own at Double-A on the back of a stellar fastball-changeup combination that he commands with aplomb. The fastball works in the low-90s, up to 95, and he excels at changing eye levels and attacking up with the pitch. Quality extension helps the pitch play up, and with his command, it's a comfortably above-average pitch. He pairs it with an outstanding plus-or-better changeup that tumbles, fades, and cowers consistently out of harm's way. The spin is the least consistent of his offerings at present, though it projects as a solid-average third pitch. How close it gets to that ceiling will determine how far into the middle of a big-league rotation he can rise.

The Risks: Moderate. He's got TJ on his resumé, and three-and-a-half years after he got drafted he hasn't proven that he'll hold up over the long rigor of a full season. The heater's not overpowering and he still needs to develop some consistency with the hook.

Bret Sayre's Fantasy Take: Boy, Paddack sure came back into dynasty consciousness quickly. Don't let the stats fool you; he's pretty unlikely to be more than a solid SP4 in a solid pitcher's park. But he's pretty close to the majors at this point and given his age, the Padres won't hold him down for long in 2019 if there's an opening and he's upright. Don't expect more than 2018 Mike Fiers and you may not be disappointed.

6 Adrian Morejon LHP   OFP: 60   Likely: 50   ETA: 2021

Born: 02/27/99   Age: 20   Bats: L   Throws: L   Height: 6'0"   Weight: 175   Origin: International Free Agent, 2016

YEAR	TEAM	LVL	AGE	W	L	SV	G	GS	IP	H	HR	BB/9	K/9	K	GB%	BABIP	WHIP	ERA	DRA	WARP	PF
2017	TRI	A-	18	2	2	0	7	7	35^{1}	37	2	0.8	8.9	35	41%	.337	1.13	3.57	3.94	0.6	94
2017	FTW	A	18	1	2	0	6	6	27^{2}	28	2	4.2	7.5	23	34%	.321	1.48	4.23	4.83	0.1	102
2018	LEL	A+	19	4	4	0	13	13	62^{2}	54	6	3.4	10.1	70	55%	.302	1.24	3.30	3.86	1.1	98
2019	*SDN*	*MLB*	*20*	*3*	*4*	*0*	*12*	*12*	*55^{2}*	*54*	*7*	*3.9*	*8.7*	*54*	*42%*	*.316*	*1.40*	*4.33*	*4.80*	*0.3*	*100*

Breakout: 2%   Improve: 2%   Collapse: 0%   Attrition: 2%   MLB: 3%   *Comparables: Casey Kelly, Brad Keller, Jeurys Familia*

The Report: The precocious Cuban southpaw more than held his own in the unforgiving California League at age 19, showing advanced feel for his craft along the way. Morejon's frame is mature for his age, and so's his approach to pitching. He'll manipulate his three-pitch mix with an advanced ability to change speeds and land secondaries in the zone to get himself back into counts. His fastball velocity took a big step forward this year, and he's now touching 98 and sitting 93-95 on the regular with quality finish. He'll throw an occasional cut on it and sink it down in the zone, and the pitch shows above-average life. A power curve in the low-80s and a mid-80s change both project to above-average, with the former flashing to plus at its best. There's enough baseline fluidity and athleticism to envision his command becoming an asset at maturity, and the ceiling is impressive if it all comes together.

The Risks: Moderate. There are some health question marks here, as his two-year stateside career now includes multiple minor-but-nagging injuries, including a hip issue that sidelined him for a couple weeks over the summer. His delivery is still inconsistent, and he struggles with his timing enough to suggest that he'll always have much better control than command.

Bret Sayre's Fantasy Take: Despite less flashy numbers, I'd take Morejon over Paddack in a dynasty league right now, and I wouldn't look back. There's sneaky SP2 ceiling with Morejon as his combination of advanced stuff (which keeps looking more advanced) with developing command at such an early stage of his professional career is highly impressive. He'll need to stay healthy, but you could say that about anyone, couldn't you?

7 Luis Patino RHP   OFP: 60   Likely: 50   ETA: 2021

Born: 10/26/99   Age: 19   Bats: R   Throws: R   Height: 6'0"   Weight: 192   Origin: International Free Agent, 2016

YEAR	TEAM	LVL	AGE	W	L	SV	G	GS	IP	H	HR	BB/9	K/9	K	GB%	BABIP	WHIP	ERA	DRA	WARP	PF
2017	DPA	RK	17	2	1	0	4	4	16	11	0	1.1	8.4	15	58%	.256	0.81	1.69	3.72	0.4	96
2017	PDR	RK	17	2	1	0	9	8	40	32	2	3.6	9.7	43	50%	.286	1.20	2.47	3.35	1.1	102
2018	FTW	A	18	6	3	0	17	17	83^{1}	65	1	2.6	10.6	98	45%	.320	1.07	2.16	3.53	1.6	104
2019	*SDN*	*MLB*	*19*	*3*	*5*	*0*	*13*	*13*	*62*	*61*	*10*	*4.3*	*9.2*	*63*	*43%*	*.318*	*1.46*	*4.85*	*5.38*	*0.0*	*100*

Breakout: 8%   Improve: 12%   Collapse: 0%   Attrition: 8%   MLB: 12%   *Comparables: Madison Bumgarner, Jordan Lyles, Roberto Osuna*

The Report: The 18-year-old Patino burst onto the prospect scene this year with a dominant showing in the Midwest League. He pumped mid-90s heat—touching higher—from deceptive, Kershawian mechanics. That, coupled with his ability to spot the pitch at the bottom of the zone or bust it in to righties, would be more than enough on its own to carve up A-ball lineups, but Patino also has advanced off-speed options for his age as well.

His changeup is his best present pitch. Although it can be a bit firm at times, it shows swing-and-miss potential with good tumble. The curve gives him a second potential above-average secondary with consistent 11-5 shape either side of 80 mph. Patino has a developing hard slider as well, although that is more of a work in progress.

Unsurprisingly the Padres were cautious with his development in 2018. He only pitched into the seventh inning once and was hard-capped around 80 pitches an outing. This is now de rigueur for teenage pitching prospects, but it can make projecting and ranking them tricky. We don't know how Patino's stuff will look under a heavier workload.

To compare him with a couple of his talented prospect mates is to recognize the limitations of what we know; we just have more info about Logan Allen and Michel Baez (both good and ill). Allen and Baez both have more traditional pitcher frames—although Patino could certainly add an inch or two and should get stronger in his twenties. The delta here is just going to be higher. Less of a fallback, but more upside, despite the same role grades.

I'm guessing we are looking at a 10 or 15 spot spread on the 101. This order can be argued a number of different ways, but Patino gets the nod for me in the final published version, because once we (hopefully) fill in some of the missing info on him, the upside here could be special.

The Risks: High. Limited pro track record, and given his smaller size, I would like to see him get a 25 start, 150 IP season under his belt.

Bret Sayre's Fantasy Take: One of the most popular pop-up dynasty prospects during 2018, Patino was extremely impressive not just for his age but, like, for the Earth in Low-A. His youth just adds to both his excitement and risk, but the latter is ultimately likely to leave him as just a really interesting top-150 dynasty prospect to watch rather than someone Ben and I juice up the back half of the 101. What would get him on the 101, you say? A bat, for starters.

8 Logan Allen LHP OFP: 60 Likely: 50 ETA: 2019

Born: 05/23/97 Age: 22 Bats: R Throws: L Height: 6'3" Weight: 200 Origin: Round 8, 2015 Draft (#231 overall)

YEAR	TEAM	LVL	AGE	W	L	SV	G	GS	IP	H	HR	BB/9	K/9	K	GB%	BABIP	WHIP	ERA	DRA	WARP	PF
2016	FTW	A	19	3	4	0	15	11	54	48	2	3.7	7.8	47	38%	.301	1.30	3.33	3.85	0.7	99
2017	FTW	A	20	5	4	0	13	13	68^1	49	1	3.4	11.2	85	43%	.294	1.10	2.11	3.86	1.1	104
2017	LEL	A+	20	2	5	0	11	10	56^2	60	2	2.9	9.1	57	50%	.352	1.38	3.97	3.84	0.9	101
2018	SAN	AA	21	10	6	0	20	19	121	89	7	2.8	9.3	125	43%	.269	1.05	2.75	3.35	2.8	102
2018	ELP	AAA	21	4	0	0	5	5	27^2	21	4	4.2	8.5	26	38%	.236	1.23	1.63	6.12	-0.2	107
2019	*SDN*	*MLB*	*22*	*1*	*1*	*0*	*3*	*3*	*15*	*14*	*2*	*3.9*	*8.9*	*15*	*39%*	*.303*	*1.36*	*4.35*	*4.82*	*0.1*	*100*

Breakout: 10% Improve: 19% Collapse: 10% Attrition: 18% MLB: 43% *Comparables: Mike Montgomery, Giovanni Soto, Josh Hader*

The Report: Allen dominated in difficult pitching environments in the upper minors in 2018. He won't blow you away with his stuff like some of the other Padres prospects, and he has the least gaudy radar gun readings among the arms in this Top 10. Allen's fastball sits a couple ticks either side of 90, but there's enough cut to keep it off barrels and the deception in his delivery makes it sneaky fast at times. The delivery has a bit of lefty funk which has impacted his ability to throw strikes at times, but he'll also show you outings where he's pumping the bottom of the zone to both sides.

The major difference maker for him in 2018 has been the development of his slider, which he manipulates between cutter action with deceptive late depth and a more traditional two-plane breaker. It tunnels off the fastball well and could be the bat-misser that he previously lacked. Allen also has a high-70s curve that he struggles to wrangle into a consistent shape and a change he uses sparingly.

The Risks: Medium. Allen dispatched his upper minors assignments without issue, but has had vague elbow problems in the past and it's not exactly plus stuff across the board here.

Bret Sayre's Fantasy Take: Yay, more pitchers. This is nothing against Allen, who's a borderline Top 101 candidate (an impressive feat for a mound dweller), but there are at least 3-4 hitters that I won't get to write fantasy blurbs about who I'd rather own in just about any format. Again, it's a realistic SP4 future without the kind of strikeout numbers to bring him higher. Did you love the 2018 version of Marco Gonzales? Of course you did. What kind of question is that?

9 Michel Baez RHP OFP: 60 Likely: 50 ETA: 2020

Born: 01/21/96 Age: 23 Bats: R Throws: R Height: 6'8" Weight: 220 Origin: International Free Agent, 2016

YEAR	TEAM	LVL	AGE	W	L	SV	G	GS	IP	H	HR	BB/9	K/9	K	GB%	BABIP	WHIP	ERA	DRA	WARP	PF
2017	FTW	A	21	6	2	0	10	10	58^2	41	8	1.2	12.6	82	36%	.264	0.84	2.45	2.60	1.8	108
2018	LEL	A+	22	4	7	0	17	17	86^2	73	5	3.4	9.6	92	37%	.297	1.22	2.91	4.01	1.3	96
2018	SAN	AA	22	0	3	0	4	4	18^1	22	4	5.9	10.3	21	31%	.375	1.85	7.36	3.22	0.5	103
2019	*SDN*	*MLB*	*23*	*5*	*6*	*0*	*16*	*16*	*83^2*	*81*	*14*	*3.7*	*9.4*	*87*	*34%*	*.313*	*1.38*	*4.69*	*5.20*	*0.1*	*100*

Breakout: 9% Improve: 16% Collapse: 14% Attrition: 28% MLB: 41% *Comparables: Aaron Blair, Jon Gray, Jake Odorizzi*

The Report: Baez looks like a cardboard cutout of Dellin Betances; he stands a comparable 6-foot-8 with broad shoulders, but without the same supporting width through his hips and lower half. He leverages that height to generate outstanding plane from an unusual angle, and the combination of a fastball that'll tickle 96 and a tumbling change from on high can give hitters fits when he's consistent through his progressions to slot. He'll work two variants of spin into the mix as well, with a tight slider in the low-80s that'll flash two-plane action and decent bite, along with a mid-70s curve that teases with solid finish and dropping action. The former shows more promise to develop into a solid-average chaser, although there are at present just as many gutters as strikes with both offerings.

The Risks: The above "when he's consistent" disclaimer is a big "if," however. While he indeed flashed better-than-most ability to repeat, the sheer length of his delivery combined with a top-heavy frame lead to periodic struggles maintaining balance and timing through his delivery. There's reliever risk here if his command never comes together, though his stuff and mound presence would make him an excellent option to emerge from a swinging bullpen gate if it comes to that.

Bret Sayre's Fantasy Take: For me, Baez is the clear outlier among the pitchers on this list in that he might not be a top-200 dynasty prospect at this point. It's not really a knock against the stuff, which as you read is more than enough. It's that the odds of him being a starting pitcher are notably lower. If he makes it, he could be a 2008 xFIP superstar, but no one actually projects those pitchers to catch lightning anymore.

10 Hudson Potts 3B

OFP: 55 Likely: 45 ETA: 2020

Born: 10/28/98 Age: 20 Bats: R Throws: R Height: 6'3" Weight: 205 Origin: Round 1, 2016 Draft (#24 overall)

YEAR	TEAM	LVL	AGE	PA	R	2B	3B	HR	RBI	BB	K	SB	CS	AVG/OBP/SLG	DRC+	VORP	BABIP	BRR	FRAA	WARP	PF
2016	PDR	RK	17	195	35	12	2	1	21	9	34	8	4	.295/.333/.399	131	14.1	.356	1.4	SS(14) -1.1, 3B(4) 0.8	0.4	99
2016	TRI	A-	17	72	7	0	1	0	6	9	13	2	1	.233/.352/.267	94	5.0	.298	0.8	SS(10) 1.1, 3B(3) -0.2	0.2	86
2017	FTW	A	18	522	67	23	4	20	69	23	140	0	1	.253/.293/.438	91	9.8	.312	-0.5	3B(116) -6.9, SS(2) 0.2	-0.3	106
2018	LEL	A+	19	453	66	35	1	17	58	37	112	3	1	.281/.350/.498	145	36.6	.348	0.3	3B(99) 0.7, 1B(8) 0.1	2.4	100
2018	SAN	AA	19	89	5	0	0	2	5	10	33	1	0	.154/.258/.231	43	-2.9	.233	-0.2	3B(21) 0.3	-0.4	102
2019	*SDN*	*MLB*	*20*	*252*	*21*	*7*	*0*	*9*	*29*	*6*	*81*	*0*	*0*	*.178/.198/.318*	*36*	*-14.1*	*.221*	*-0.5*	*3B -1, 1B 0*	*-1.6*	*100*

Breakout: 8% Improve: 10% Collapse: 0% Attrition: 3% MLB: 10% *Comparables: Matt Davidson, Rafael Devers, Ryan McMahon*

The Report: The 24th overall pick back in 2016, Potts is another youngin' who acquitted himself quite well in High-A—while playing the whole year at the age of a sophomore in college. His glove at the hot corner was arguably the Cal League's best, as he combines soft hands, solid agility, and a nose for angles and hop trajectory to play himself into good defensive position on most balls. His above-average arm strength holds from multiple throwing positions, and he's smooth and true with his transfers on tough plays. There's a good bit of thunder in his stick as well, and he shows a solid baseline command of the strike zone. While his swing was relatively flat and compact this year, he'll take his lift-and-separate hacks in turn, and there's reason to think he could hit for more power than he's shown down the line.

The Risks: As one might expect of a hitter so young for his level, his approach is still nascent, and there were plenty of at-bats this season where he just got plain overmatched by wily pitchers executing their sequencing. He can be coaxed into expanding the zone, and there's some stiffness to the swing that leaves him vulnerable to in-zone swing-and-miss against good velocity even when he doesn't. Those tendencies are likely to get exploited more against advanced arms, and it may take some time for his game to come together at the plate.

Bret Sayre's Fantasy Take: I think we've finally gotten to the point where Petco isn't a stigma for right-handed batters anymore, but it's not the kind of park that will turn Potts into a top-10 third baseman. Good defense will keep him on the grass, but a .260 average and 20 homers just isn't what it used to be, and it doesn't even look like a top-20 option at the position in this offensive environment.

The Next Five:

11 Cal Quantrill RHP

Born: 02/10/95 Age: 24 Bats: L Throws: R Height: 6'3" Weight: 208 Origin: Round 1, 2016 Draft (#8 overall)

YEAR	TEAM	LVL	AGE	W	L	SV	G	GS	IP	H	HR	BB/9	K/9	K	GB%	BABIP	WHIP	ERA	DRA	WARP	PF
2016	PDR	RK	21	0	2	0	5	5	13^{2}	12	0	1.3	10.5	16	49%	.324	1.02	5.27	2.63	0.5	97
2016	TRI	A-	21	0	2	0	5	5	18^{2}	15	0	1.0	13.5	28	56%	.333	0.91	1.93	1.69	0.8	93
2017	LEL	A+	22	6	5	0	14	14	73^{2}	78	5	2.9	9.3	76	42%	.353	1.38	3.67	3.65	1.4	99
2017	SAN	AA	22	1	5	0	8	8	42^{1}	52	5	3.4	7.2	34	39%	.341	1.61	4.04	3.75	0.7	98
2018	SAN	AA	23	6	5	0	22	22	117	135	12	2.9	7.8	101	45%	.336	1.48	5.15	4.18	1.6	102
2018	ELP	AAA	23	3	1	0	6	6	31	39	4	1.5	6.4	22	50%	.333	1.42	3.48	3.97	0.6	108
2019	*SDN*	*MLB*	*24*	*1*	*1*	*0*	*3*	*3*	*15*	*16*	*2*	*3.5*	*8.1*	*13*	*42%*	*.327*	*1.47*	*4.69*	*5.20*	*0.0*	*100*

Breakout: 11% Improve: 18% Collapse: 5% Attrition: 17% MLB: 24% *Comparables: Scott Diamond, Sam Howard, Wade Miley*

12 Ryan Weathers LHP

Born: 12/17/99 Age: 19 Bats: L Throws: L Height: 6'1" Weight: 200 Origin: Round 1, 2018 Draft (#7 overall)

YEAR	TEAM	LVL	AGE	W	L	SV	G	GS	IP	H	HR	BB/9	K/9	K	GB%	BABIP	WHIP	ERA	DRA	WARP	PF
2018	SDP	RK	18	0	2	0	4	4	9^1	8	2	2.9	8.7	9	69%	.222	1.18	3.86	4.59	0.2	104
2018	FTW	A	18	0	1	0	3	3	9	11	0	1.0	9.0	9	58%	.355	1.33	3.00	4.61	0.1	92
2019	*SDN*	*MLB*	*19*	*2*	*3*	*0*	*9*	*9*	33^2	*37*	*5*	*4.4*	*7.1*	*26*	*50%*	*.319*	*1.59*	*5.39*	*5.99*	*-0.3*	*100*

Breakout: 0% Improve: 0% Collapse: 0% Attrition: 0% MLB: 0% *Comparables: John Barbato, Jaime Barria, Wilfredo Boscan*

Here we have two first-round talents—one of whom made our Top 50 last winter—and yet neither makes the Padres Top Ten. Yeah, this is a historically good system.

With Quantrill, there are some legitimate concerns with the profile now. He has an above-average fastball and a plus changeup, and the minors aren't really supposed to be a challenge for that kind of advanced arm. But his control outpaces his command at present and that was an issue for him at higher levels this year. The fastball can lack wiggle and be just a little too hittable sometimes, and the slider isn't consistent enough to keep righties off the number one. The whole can feel a little less than the sum of its parts. There's still a fair bit of the risk in the profile for an advanced college arm. Petco Park will help though, and Quantrill is likely the best pitching prospect you'll see outside of a team's Top Ten this year.

Weathers is left-handed, unlike his father David, but he did inherit the family physique. He's a shorter, stocky southpaw with a frame that we in the industry refer to as "high-maintenance." That's less of a concern when you are a potential three-pitch lefty. Weathers' fastball sits in the low-90s, but with enough armside movement to keep it off barrels. His curve flashes good 1-7 action, although the shape isn't always consistent, and it can get shorter and flatter. The change is advanced for his age, and I'm not even using it as one of my "damning with faint praise" prep change-up descriptions here. He commands all three pitches pretty well, and while he's not a huge upside play as you might expect from a top ten pick prep arm, he could certainly be Logan Allen in a couple years.

13 Josh Naylor 1B

Born: 06/22/97 Age: 22 Bats: L Throws: L Height: 5'11" Weight: 250 Origin: Round 1, 2015 Draft (#12 overall)

YEAR	TEAM	LVL	AGE	PA	R	2B	3B	HR	RBI	BB	K	SB	CS	AVG/OBP/SLG	DRC+	VORP	BABIP	BRR	FRAA	WARP	PF
2016	GRB	A	19	370	42	24	2	9	54	22	62	10	3	.269/.317/.430	109	10.5	.304	-1.9	1B(81) -2.3	-0.5	97
2016	LEL	A+	19	144	17	5	0	3	21	3	22	1	1	.252/.264/.353	55	-2.9	.276	-0.6	1B(32) -3.4	-1.2	99
2017	LEL	A+	20	313	41	16	2	8	45	27	48	7	1	.297/.361/.452	136	14.6	.333	-0.1	1B(42) -0.6	0.6	100
2017	SAN	AA	20	175	18	9	0	2	19	16	36	2	1	.250/.320/.346	100	0.6	.308	-0.9	1B(40) 1.9	-0.1	96
2018	SAN	AA	21	574	72	22	1	17	74	64	69	5	5	.297/.383/.447	139	27.4	.317	-5.1	LF(89) -20.4, 1B(29) 0.6	-0.4	102
2019	*SDN*	*MLB*	*22*	*252*	*26*	*9*	*0*	*9*	*31*	*16*	*49*	*1*	*0*	*.223/.274/.377*	*74*	*-1.7*	*.244*	*-0.5*	*LF -5, 1B 0*	*-0.7*	*100*

Breakout: 12% Improve: 31% Collapse: 1% Attrition: 19% MLB: 33% *Comparables: Ramon Flores, Dwight Smith, Jake Bauers*

Naylor has long tantalized on account of an outstanding combination of bat speed, strength, and barrel control. In 2018, the 21-year-old showed signs of finally starting to consistently tap into his plus raw power, with more loft in his swing than he had previously. He managed to do that without compromising his high-end bat-to-ball ability, striking out barely more often than he took an increasingly frequent free pass.

After locking up Eric Hosmer last winter, the Padres tried to shoehorn Naylor into left field. But while he's got a sneaky little burst that belies his husky, mature frame, he lacks the agility to muster average defense at the cold corner, and the raw foot speed just isn't going to cut it on the grass. Something's going to have to give, however, as the bat increasingly looks like it can thrive against the sport's best pitchers.

14 Jacob Nix RHP

Born: 01/09/96 Age: 23 Bats: R Throws: R Height: 6'4" Weight: 220 Origin: Round 3, 2015 Draft (#86 overall)

YEAR	TEAM	LVL	AGE	W	L	SV	G	GS	IP	H	HR	BB/9	K/9	K	GB%	BABIP	WHIP	ERA	DRA	WARP	PF
2016	FTW	A	20	3	7	0	25	25	105^{1}	115	5	1.7	7.7	90	48%	.340	1.28	3.93	4.23	1.0	104
2017	LEL	A+	21	4	3	0	11	10	66^{2}	78	5	1.4	6.9	51	48%	.344	1.32	4.32	5.01	0.2	110
2017	SAN	AA	21	1	2	0	6	6	27^{2}	32	0	2.9	7.2	22	45%	.340	1.48	5.53	6.85	-0.6	103
2018	SAN	AA	22	2	3	0	9	9	52^{2}	39	3	1.5	7.0	41	46%	.250	0.91	2.05	3.86	0.9	99
2018	ELP	AAA	22	1	0	0	1	1	6	5	0	0.0	4.5	3	44%	.278	0.83	0.00	4.12	0.1	115
2018	SDN	MLB	22	2	5	0	9	9	42^{1}	52	8	2.8	4.5	21	42%	.306	1.54	7.02	6.94	-0.8	104
2019	*SDN*	*MLB*	*23*	*5*	*7*	*0*	*18*	*18*	*90*	*99*	*14*	*2.9*	*7.0*	*70*	*42%*	*.317*	*1.42*	*4.85*	*5.38*	*-0.1*	*100*

Breakout: 7% Improve: 17% Collapse: 13% Attrition: 25% MLB: 33% *Comparables: Zach Eflin, Blake Beavan, Will Smith*

A groin issue cost Nix the first two months of the season, but he cruised through Double-A and made one Triple-A start before getting pressed into service in the major league rotation. It went… less well. The culprit for Nix was once again his command. His fastball and curve are both above-average pitches. The fastball has some late run down in the zone, but he tends to leave it up. The curve shows good tight downer action, but he can struggle to start it in the zone. The change tends to play below-average. It's a solid fourth-starter profile, but Nix lacks the upside of the arms above him and is at risk of getting squeezed out of rotation consideration in the next season-and-a-half or so. Until then though, the Padres will need to send five dudes out there every five days, so he should get another shot or two.

15 Buddy Reed OF

Born: 04/27/95 Age: 24 Bats: B Throws: R Height: 6'4" Weight: 210 Origin: Round 2, 2016 Draft (#48 overall)

YEAR	TEAM	LVL	AGE	PA	R	2B	3B	HR	RBI	BB	K	SB	CS	AVG/OBP/SLG	DRC+	VORP	BABIP	BRR	FRAA	WARP	PF
2016	TRI	A-	21	231	31	9	4	0	13	22	53	15	5	.254/.326/.337	88	8.3	.338	3.5	CF(50) 3.9	0.4	90
2017	FTW	A	22	347	48	17	8	6	35	23	97	12	8	.234/.290/.396	81	6.1	.315	1.1	CF(85) 1.0	0.1	106
2018	LEL	A+	23	343	54	21	7	12	47	24	84	33	7	.324/.371/.549	137	39.6	.407	6.5	LF(54) -6.1, CF(15) 1.8	1.4	96
2018	SAN	AA	23	195	21	7	0	1	15	12	63	18	3	.179/.227/.235	19	-9.0	.263	2.6	CF(39) 8.1, LF(3) 0.5	-0.3	103
2019	*SDN*	*MLB*	*24*	*252*	*30*	*7*	*1*	*6*	*19*	*10*	*83*	*11*	*3*	*.168/.199/.289*	*22*	*-13.4*	*.219*	*1.9*	*LF -1, CF 2*	*-1.3*	*100*

Breakout: 1% Improve: 1% Collapse: 0% Attrition: 1% MLB: 1% *Comparables: Noel Cuevas, Paulo Orlando, Jared Hoying*

Reed is as impressive an athlete as you'll find on a baseball field, with quick-twitch movements, a flash of a first step, plus-plus straight-line speed, and tapered strength throughout his frame. The physicality has tantalized scouts for many years, and the Padres popped him in the second round despite widespread concerns about his swing and approach. After implementing a series of mechanical adjustments and dominating the Australian League last winter, Reed carried over his success through the first half, when he raked his way through High-A.

A switch hitter with prototypical swing plane differences—more length and loft from the left—his bat crashed back to Earth after a midseason promotion to Double-A, where pitchers exploited his aggressive approach and tendency to get disjointed and off-balance against off-speed pitches. His defensive ceiling—it's an easy plus glove in center with enough arm to play right—and the utility of his blazing speed will keep him on a big-league trajectory even if he never quite hits, but it's the ongoing evolution of his swing and refinement of his approach that will dictate whether he's more than a reserve outfielder at the highest level.

And Five More:

16. Tirso Ornelas, OF, Low-A Fort Wayne

Part of the talented group of teenagers assigned to Fort Wayne, Ornelas got off to a solid start before missing the final month of the season with a wrist injury. His smooth left-handed swing produces plus raw power. Ornelas has an advanced approach at the plate, and shows an ability to recognize secondaries that many young players lack. In the outfield, he has the physical tools to be an above-average defender in a corner. There is still some work to be done on taking efficient routes, but he covers a lot of ground and his arm is more than adequate for right field. His power and defense suggest a future as a corner outfielder. As is often the case, it's just a matter of whether he hits enough for the power to play.

17. Jeisson Rosario, OF, Low-A Fort Wayne

A member of San Diego's large international signing class of 2016, Rosario was at the core of the young 2018 Tincaps team. His youth and rawness showed at times during the season and his power hasn't materialized yet. However, he's a quick-twitch athlete with plus speed. In the field he covers plenty of ground, has a strong arm, and projects to be an above-average center fielder. Rosario's swing is geared for gap-to-gap line drives. He has quick hands and knows the strike zone. The speed and defense will carry him a long way but continued development at the plate is key to reaching his potential as an everyday outfielder.

18. Esteury Ruiz, 2B, Low-A Fort Wayne

Whether it was facing more advanced pitching, a change in approach, or a combination of both, Ruiz's bat took a step back this year. Always aggressive, his strikeout rate climbed to nearly 30 percent and the bat to ball skills that had Arizona League evaluators buzzing disappeared. Ruiz's future is tied to his bat and, being limited defensively to second base, the pressure to hit is huge. There is hope for a rebound next season at Lake Elsinore. He's still very young and he has quick hands and above-average bat speed. There were also times later in the year when he showed glimpses of a more disciplined approach at the plate.

19. Gabriel Arias, SS, Low-A Fort Wayne

Another signing from the Padres' large international bonanza in 2016-17, Arias is already one of the best defensive players in the organization. Thin and athletic, he has plus range, soft hands, and lightning-quick transfers. Combine that with a strong, accurate arm and Arias has the makings of a future plus defender at the highest level. There were some early season struggles at the plate but he showed a more disciplined approach in the second half of the campaign, along with an uptick in power. Arias' premier defense up the middle suggests a future utility role with a chance to become an everyday player if the bat progresses.

20. Edward Olivares, OF, High-A Lake Elsinore

If you like high-waisted, wiry gazelles shagging fly balls in center, you're going to dig Olivares. The Venezuelan oozes physical projection, with lean strength throughout a very athletic frame. He moves well in space and closes hard into the gaps, with straight-line speed that'll push plus and play okaaaay on the bases as well. At the dish there's a nice baseline of hand-eye and directness to the point of contact, and he'll turn around some hellacious line drives along the way. The approach is highly aggressive, however, and he may never get on base enough for everything to come together.

Top Talents 25 and Under (born 4/1/93 or later):

1. Fernando Tatis, Jr.
2. Luis Urias
3. Francisco Mejia
4. MacKenzie Gore
5. Chris Paddack
6. Adrian Morejon
7. Franmil Reyes
8. Manuel Margot
9. Joey Lucchesi
10. Luis Patino

I'll be the first to admit that I did not see last season coming from Franmil Reyes, and certainly not on such a quick timeline. He deserves an enormous amount of credit for making rapid-fire adjustments to drag the full brunt of double-plus power into game action at the highest levels. Thirty-two dingers across Triple-A and the big leagues is a nice accomplishment on which to hang your (massive) hat, and best of all: He accomplished the feat while incrementally improving his approach along the way. There will be constant pressure for him to lose baseballs at a high rate, but so far, so good.

Everything about Margot's game seemed dimmer in 2018, and a couple of those frustrating, linger-y type injuries (bruised ribs in April, a sprained wrist in July) make it difficult to suss out the legitimacy of that backslide. Regardless, there was precious little evidence of improvement amid a disastrous what-actually-happened season. He produced an unholy triumvirate: A well below-average DRC+ fueled by a sub-three OBP, an atrocious success rate on the bases that barely cracked one in two over a not-small sample, and one of the worst defensive seasons by any center fielder in baseball, at least as far as FRAA was concerned. There's still plenty of time for Margot to turn things around, but after 277 big league games (and with arbitration looming next winter), it's getting late early for the former top prospect.

As our intrepid leader Brendan Gawlowski notes, if you're going to be a one-trick pony it is best to have a good trick. Lucchesi's funky delivery and weird pitch movements—a four-seamer with the finish of a two and a cambio that cuts—befuddled big-league hitters enough to rack up whiffs against more than a quarter of the hitters he faced. Sure, hitters deposited his misplaced offerings into the bleachers at an alarming rate, but he managed to minimize enough barreled contact overall to post comfortably above-average indicators in support of a two-plus WARP debut. A much thinner margin for error than most means the jury's out on how long he'll be able to keep the curtain drawn, however.

Beyond that, the bulk of San Diego's youth-oriented optimism still wanders heartland halls a couple years out from impact. Jose Castillo may have the next strongest case for back-end inclusion on this list among the remaining big-leaguers. The Very Large left-hander struck out a whole mess of dudes and looked very much the part of an actualizing high-leverage arm in his 38-odd innings. But in a system this flush with potential (very good) rotation arms, it's just too much of a stretch to shoehorn him in here.

Franchy Cordero's still a bag of obscene tools, but 36-percent whiff rates are also still disconcerting, even in times like these. Eric Lauer's junk didn't lack for utility in his first crack, but he nibbled a lot around the margins and the long-term ceiling questions remain. He commands in-zone pretty well and showed an ability to stay off of barrels with reasonable consistency. But it's tough to envision him threading the needle often enough to hold firm to a rotation spot once the wave of higher-ceilinged arms below him start crashing off Mission Beach. And in this organization, with this system, you have to err on the side of hope for a better tomorrow.

San Francisco Giants

The State of the System:

Joey Bart and Heliot Ramos are really cool. Past that, it's a Giants prospect list.

The Top Ten:

1 **Joey Bart C** OFP: 60 Likely: 55 ETA: Late 2020

Born: 12/15/96 Age: 22 Bats: R Throws: R Height: 6'3" Weight: 220 Origin: Round 1, 2018 Draft (#2 overall)

YEAR	TEAM	LVL	AGE	PA	R	2B	3B	HR	RBI	BB	K	SB	CS	AVG/OBP/SLG	DRC+	VORP	BABIP	BRR	FRAA	WARP	PF
2018	GNT	RK	21	25	3	1	1	0	1	1	7	0	0	.261/.320/.391	83	0.6	.375	-0.1	C(4) -0.1	0.0	101
2018	SLO	A-	21	203	35	14	2	13	39	12	40	2	1	.298/.369/.613	147	21.6	.318	1.2	C(32) -1.0	1.0	118
2019	*SFN*	*MLB*	*22*	*252*	*23*	*10*	*0*	*12*	*32*	*5*	*74*	*0*	*0*	*.157/.192/.346*	*36*	*-9.0*	*.171*	*-0.4*	*C -1*	*-1.0*	*96*

Breakout: 3% Improve: 10% Collapse: 0% Attrition: 8% MLB: 12% *Comparables: J.T. Realmuto, Austin Hedges, Blake Swihart*

The Report: Bart shot up 2018 draft boards on the back of his improving defense. He's a good catch-and-throw guy with a plus arm and he's athletic behind the plate. His receiving is a bit of a work in progress—he can get a little boxy—but should end up at least average. I believe as a prospect writer that I am also contractually obligated to mention that he called his own games in college.

While he's likely to be a solid hand defensively, the real reason Bart went second overall—and had occasional 1.1 scuttlebutt—is the potential with the bat. Only four catchers in 2018 posted an .800 OPS, and Bart has that kind of offensive upside due to his combination of plus bat speed and plus raw. He can still get front-footed on offspeed stuff and the swing can get long in the zone, so there is some hit tool risk that may limit the upside in the profile. But the bar for catcher offense is so low that even a .250, 15-20 HR profile would make him a solid everyday option behind the dish.

The Risks: Medium. His pro debut went extremely well, but an ACC bat mashing in the Northwest League is hardly shocking. There are the usual developmental risks for a prospect who hasn't even seen full-season ball yet, but the glove gives him a strong starting base. Remember though, catchers are weird.

Ben Carsley's Fantasy Take: Catching prospects are the football, reality is Lucy and I am Charlie Brown, but this time I'm just not gonna try to kick the field goal. Bart could very well emerge as a top-10 fantasy backstop capable of putting up 20 bombs a season with a tolerable average. But when do you feel comfortable guessing he'll emerge as that dude? It probably won't happen right when he reaches the major leagues, if the typical learning curve for catchers tells us anything. And again, the upside here is good but not great—we're not talking about a prime Gary Sanchez-type fantasy talent. It's not Bart's fault that he isn't a top-101 prospect, but he's still not. If you really love this profile, go grab Danny Jansen or something. At least he's closer.

2 Heliot Ramos OF

OFP: 60 Likely: 50 ETA: 2021

Born: 09/07/99 Age: 19 Bats: R Throws: R Height: 6'2" Weight: 185 Origin: Round 1, 2017 Draft (#19 overall)

YEAR	TEAM	LVL	AGE	PA	R	2B	3B	HR	RBI	BB	K	SB	CS	AVG/OBP/SLG	DRC+	VORP	BABIP	BRR	FRAA	WARP	PF
2017	GIA	RK	17	151	33	11	6	6	27	10	48	10	2	.348/.404/.645	178	20.8	.500	2.2	CF(28) -2.3	0.7	100
2018	AUG	A	18	535	61	24	8	11	52	35	136	8	7	.245/.313/.396	107	21.5	.319	1.8	CF(113) -4.5	0.7	96
2019	*SFN*	*MLB*	*19*	*252*	*23*	*9*	*2*	*7*	*24*	*3*	*92*	*1*	*0*	*.176/.186/.321*	*27*	*-12.6*	*.241*	*-0.1*	*CF -1*	*-1.5*	*96*

Breakout: 7% Improve: 9% Collapse: 0% Attrition: 3% MLB: 11% *Comparables: Engel Beltre, Nomar Mazara, Gleyber Torres*

The Report: After getting drafted 17th overall in 2017 and signing for $3.1 million, Ramos was the talk of the Giants system last year. An up-and-down initial full-season taste in 2018 tempered some of the excitement and revealed a raw prospect. The big question is how much he'll hit. He shows some feel for using all fields and he barrels the ball consistently when he sees it well, but he's overly aggressive at times and susceptible to basic sequencing. He doesn't turn on the ball enough to utilize his above-average-potential power yet and is more of a gap hitter now. Physically, he's essentially maxed out.

His run tool didn't show up in A-ball as expected: He was average at best down the line, and he'll only get slower. He has the arm for any outfield spot and reads the ball well for his age. Evaluators also wonder whether he'll have the range for center as he gets older (one scout even suggested a move to second base down the road). There are a lot of questions about his ultimate future, but Ramos has the tools to be a major-leaguer, perhaps as more of an average regular than any kind of star.

The Risks: High. Ramos is still getting his feet wet in pro ball, and a full-season assignment unmasked some areas that need improving. He has the tools to be a major-leaguer but also a long way to go before they can actualize. He needs to hit and tap into his power potential.

Ben Carsley's Fantasy Take: Well… at least 2018 has conditioned us to be used to disappointment. Ramos was a BP Fantasy Team favorite heading into last season, so that's a pretty rough report to read all around. He'll still be a top-101 guy because I'm stubborn and there are some loud fantasy tools that remain, but for the time being it seems prudent to knock Ramos down several pegs. Just what this farm system needed…

3 Shaun Anderson RHP

OFP: 55 Likely: 50 ETA: 2019

Born: 10/29/94 Age: 24 Bats: R Throws: R Height: 6'4" Weight: 225 Origin: Round 3, 2016 Draft (#88 overall)

YEAR	TEAM	LVL	AGE	W	L	SV	G	GS	IP	H	HR	BB/9	K/9	K	GB%	BABIP	WHIP	ERA	DRA	WARP	PF
2017	GRN	A	22	3	0	0	7	7	38^{2}	30	2	2.6	8.6	37	52%	.272	1.06	2.56	3.62	0.8	101
2017	SLM	A+	22	3	3	0	11	11	58^{2}	53	6	2.8	7.4	48	43%	.270	1.21	3.99	3.80	1.0	106
2017	SJO	A+	22	3	3	0	6	5	25^{2}	19	1	1.4	7.7	22	51%	.247	0.90	3.51	4.63	0.2	104
2018	RIC	AA	23	6	5	0	17	16	94	93	9	2.1	8.9	93	49%	.316	1.22	3.45	2.88	2.7	95
2018	SAC	AAA	23	2	2	0	8	8	47^{1}	48	5	2.1	6.5	34	47%	.287	1.25	4.18	4.09	0.8	95
2019	*SFN*	*MLB*	*24*	*1*	*1*	*0*	*3*	*3*	*16*	*15*	*2*	*2.8*	*7.9*	*14*	*44%*	*.301*	*1.27*	*4.12*	*4.79*	*0.1*	*96*

Breakout: 11% Improve: 22% Collapse: 20% Attrition: 39% MLB: 51% *Comparables: Walker Lockett, Simon Castro, Matt Andriese*

The Report: This may seem a little bit early to be hitting the polished, older, four-average pitches starter, but this is also the Giants list, so we are running right about on time. Acquired in the Eduardo Nunez deal last Summer, Anderson has actually been a nice development story as a converted starter. You know the dossier by now. It's an average fastball that he can run up to 95 at times, a potentially above-average slider, and improving changeup that gives him an armside option against lefties, and a "fourth pitch," in this case a fringy curve. Add in a frame built to log innings and you've got yourself a fourth starter stew going. The last step for Anderson is to refine his command enough to walk the tightrope against major league hitters. And if Giants Devil Magic exists (light some patchouli), Anderson seems as good a candidate for the Dereck Rodriguez Memorial confusing sub-3.00 ERA season as anyone in the system.

The Risks: Low? Medium? Can I say Smedium? It's not overpowering stuff, it's less command than you'd like with less than overpowering stuff, but he's also just about ready.

Ben Carsley's Fantasy Take: Borrrrrrrrrrrrinnnnnnnnnng. Anderson may be of interest in deep leagues as a spot starter, but that's about it. Thank god we have seven of these guys to go : (

4 Alexander Canario OF

OFP: 60 Likely: 45 ETA: 2023

Born: 05/07/00 Age: 19 Bats: R Throws: R Height: 6'1" Weight: 165 Origin: International Free Agent, 2016

YEAR	TEAM	LVL	AGE	PA	R	2B	3B	HR	RBI	BB	K	SB	CS	AVG/OBP/SLG	DRC+	VORP	BABIP	BRR	FRAA	WARP	PF
2017	DGI	RK	17	274	42	17	4	5	45	33	40	18	10	.294/.391/.464	164	24.0	.335	-1.0	RF(50) 4.0, CF(7) 0.7	2.2	95
2018	GIA	RK	18	208	36	5	2	6	19	27	51	8	5	.250/.357/.403	114	13.2	.317	-0.5	CF(44) 1.0	0.4	97
2019	*SFN*	*MLB*	*19*	*252*	*20*	*8*	*0*	*7*	*23*	*12*	*86*	*3*	*2*	*.152/.190/.270*	*18*	*-15.5*	*.200*	*-0.2*	*CF -1*	*-1.7*	*96*

Breakout: 6% Improve: 8% Collapse: 0% Attrition: 3% MLB: 10% *Comparables: Nomar Mazara, Engel Beltre, Gleyber Torres*

The Report: We started hearing about what a steal the Giants got with Canario when he made his pro debut in the 2017 DSL. That chatter got a lot louder with his 2018 debut stateside. This is a lot of tools and projectability for five figures—a chance at all of them, really. He's got a quick bat, a big swing, and a body that projects out to give him a chance to hit the ball far with that quick bat and big swing. He's athletic, he runs well, and he has a shot to stay in center. It's potentially a big profile.

We don't yet know if he can identify and hit good pitching. He's yet to graduate out of the complex leagues, and as you'll see us point out every now and again, the complex leagues frankly more closely resemble "practice" than "organized baseball." There's some drift and bat wrap in his swing. We've also seen enough big swings on projectable bodies that *didn't* grow into them to be slightly cautious. A likely assignment somewhere between rookie ball and Low-A will be quite telling here, both in how aggressively he's moved and how he handles it.

The Risks: Extreme. He's a complex-league bat and he's going to need to make good on a lot of projection. He could be the best prospect in this system at some point fairly soon, or this could be his high water mark.

Ben Carsley's Fantasy Take: If you're looking to gamble on a high-upside talent that not a ton of people in dynasty circles are super hip to yet, Canario is a solid choice. This will be a slow burn, but once guys like this click they tend to jump into the middle of the top-101 pretty quickly. Also, if you're just here for the fantasy takes, you can pretty much stop reading now.

5 Logan Webb RHP

OFP: 55 Likely: 45 ETA: 2020

Born: 11/18/96 Age: 22 Bats: R Throws: R Height: 6'2" Weight: 220 Origin: Round 4, 2014 Draft (#118 overall)

YEAR	TEAM	LVL	AGE	W	L	SV	G	GS	IP	H	HR	BB/9	K/9	K	GB%	BABIP	WHIP	ERA	DRA	WARP	PF
2016	AUG	A	19	2	3	0	9	9	42	54	7	2.6	6.4	30	57%	.326	1.57	6.21	3.72	0.7	94
2017	SLO	A-	20	2	0	0	15	0	28	26	1	2.2	10.0	31	68%	.325	1.18	2.89	3.10	0.6	100
2018	SJO	A+	21	1	3	0	21	20	74	54	2	4.4	9.0	74	48%	.274	1.22	1.82	6.27	-0.8	98
2018	RIC	AA	21	1	2	0	6	6	30^{2}	30	4	3.2	7.6	26	52%	.289	1.34	3.82	3.80	0.5	93
2019	*SFN*	*MLB*	*22*	*1*	*1*	*0*	*3*	*3*	*15*	*15*	*2*	*3.9*	*8.1*	*13*	*47%*	*.309*	*1.41*	*4.51*	*5.23*	*0.0*	*96*

Breakout: 15% Improve: 21% Collapse: 6% Attrition: 13% MLB: 30% *Comparables: Greg Reynolds, Jonathan Pettibone, Paul Blackburn*

The Report: The Giants bought Webb out of a college commitment back in 2014, but after a nondescript first season he lost big chunks of 2016 and 2017 to Tommy John surgery and subsequent rehab. Last year, he returned to log 20 tightly-guarded starts at San Jose and a half-dozen more in Double-A. The stuff returned with a vengeance, and it is some of the system's best: a riding heater that touches 97 with life in the zone, a low-80s slider that teases two-plane action with solid bite, and a developing mid-80s change that flashes average tumble and fade. He's big and thick, yet athletic and he repeats his balanced delivery with reasonable consistency.

The Risks: High. The Giants have been slow and steady in their rebuilding of Webb after Tommy John, only elevating him to the 80-plus pitch range in his final seven starts of the season. The drive can get inconsistent and there's a bit of effort to the delivery that can joggle his command out of whack. The changeup lags at present, and all of these nicks combined with the red-flag medicals is enough to introduce significant bullpen risk.

Ben Carsley's Fantasy Take: Do you wish Shaun Anderson was worse?

6 Sean Hjelle RHP

OFP: 55 Likely: 45 ETA: 2021

Born: 05/07/97 Age: 22 Bats: R Throws: R Height: 6'11" Weight: 225 Origin: Round 2, 2018 Draft (#45 overall)

YEAR	TEAM	LVL	AGE	W	L	SV	G	GS	IP	H	HR	BB/9	K/9	K	GB%	BABIP	WHIP	ERA	DRA	WARP	PF
2018	SLO	A-	21	0	0	0	12	12	21^{1}	24	4	1.7	9.3	22	49%	.317	1.31	5.06	2.92	0.6	115
2019	*SFN*	*MLB*	*22*	*2*	*3*	*0*	*10*	*10*	*34^{2}*	*38*	*6*	*3.2*	*7.2*	*28*	*39%*	*.316*	*1.47*	*5.21*	*6.03*	*-0.3*	*96*

Breakout: 0% Improve: 0% Collapse: 0% Attrition: 0% MLB: 0% *Comparables: Eric Lauer, Matt Hall, Madison Younginer*

The Report: If Hjelle makes the majors, he will tie Jon Rauch for tallest pitcher in major league history, and he's got a pretty good shot to do that (Philadelphia's Kyle Young may beat him there, though). Despite his long and lean frame, Hjelle has a relatively simple, compact (again—relatively) delivery that he repeats well. He throws strikes, working off a sinking low-90s fastball. His breaker can get a bit slurvy at times, but it flashes as an above-average, tight downer curve around 80. The change is fringy at present, as they so often are. Hjelle's height is gonna create weird angles for hitters, and he's already a very polished arm. If the secondaries don't get all the way there, he has a reasonable fallback profile as... well, it might look a lot like Jon Rauch.

The Risks: High. Limited pro track record, needs further refinement of his secondaries.

Ben Carsley's Fantasy Take: Gun to your head you should probably take Hjelle above Anderson or Webb in fantasy, but why on earth is someone forcing you to draft a guy from the Giants top-10 list?

7 Heath Quinn OF

OFP: 50 Likely: 45 ETA: 2020

Born: 06/07/95 Age: 24 Bats: R Throws: R Height: 6'3" Weight: 220 Origin: Round 3, 2016 Draft (#95 overall)

YEAR	TEAM	LVL	AGE	PA	R	2B	3B	HR	RBI	BB	K	SB	CS	AVG/OBP/SLG	DRC+	VORP	BABIP	BRR	FRAA	WARP	PF
2016	SLO	A-	21	239	37	19	1	9	34	26	50	3	0	.337/.423/.571	176	26.9	.405	1.7	RF(49) 11.2	2.5	111
2017	SJO	A+	22	297	24	9	0	10	29	20	86	0	0	.228/.290/.371	72	-2.6	.294	-2.8	RF(35) -0.5, LF(26) -7.4	-2.2	100
2018	SJO	A+	23	407	53	24	0	14	51	42	98	4	1	.300/.376/.485	143	30.9	.373	0.3	LF(58) -11.4	0.3	98
2019	*SFN*	*MLB*	*24*	*252*	*23*	*8*	*0*	*8*	*29*	*15*	*79*	*0*	*0*	*.197/.246/.340*	*54*	*-7.6*	*.254*	*-0.5*	*LF -7, RF 0*	*-1.5*	*96*

Breakout: 6% Improve: 8% Collapse: 0% Attrition: 9% MLB: 12% *Comparables: Jake Cave, Marc Krauss, Jaycob Brugman*

The Report: 2017 was a lost year for the former third-rounder, as Quinn missed the season's first month recovering from the dreaded broken hamate, then lost a bunch *more* time battling a just-as-dreaded shoulder injury. He wasn't exactly a picture of health again this past season either, but it was a Ripken-esque performance, relatively speaking. And when he was on the field, the big-time raw power that got him drafted resurfaced at High-A. It's an easy plus tool, if not better, and he shows a baseline of plate discipline that helped him bring more of it into games. He's got average wheels for now, along with an above-average arm that should hold serve in right.

The Risks: High. Quinn's medical file is as big as the outfield at AT&T Park. There's enough athleticism and agility that the defensive value should be at least a marginal net positive, but at its core this is a right-handed, bat-first corner profile. Everything needs to click for him to hold a significant role.

Ben Carsley's Fantasy Take: Between the injury history, the future home ballpark, and the modest upside it's tough to get very excited about Quinn. Could he hold some value if he manages to earn an everyday spot? Sure. But he's the type of guy teams are always trying to improve on, and odds are he'll spend as much time on your DL as in your active lineup. Reserve for only the deepest of leagues.

8 Tyler Beede RHP   OFP: 50   Likely: 40   ETA: Debuted in 2018

Born: 05/23/93 Age: 26 Bats: R Throws: R Height: 6'3" Weight: 211 Origin: Round 1, 2014 Draft (#14 overall)

YEAR	TEAM	LVL	AGE	W	L	SV	G	GS	IP	H	HR	BB/9	K/9	K	GB%	BABIP	WHIP	ERA	DRA	WARP	PF
2016	RIC	AA	23	8	7	0	24	24	147^{1}	136	9	3.2	8.2	135	49%	.309	1.28	2.81	3.17	3.4	99
2017	SAC	AAA	24	6	7	0	19	19	109	121	14	3.2	6.9	83	52%	.316	1.47	4.79	5.50	0.2	102
2018	SFN	MLB	25	0	1	0	2	2	7^{2}	9	0	9.4	10.6	9	46%	.409	2.22	8.22	4.22	0.1	98
2018	SAC	AAA	25	4	9	0	33	10	74	82	10	6.8	9.1	75	41%	.346	1.86	7.05	5.04	0.3	105
2019	*SFN*	*MLB*	*26*	*1*	*2*	*0*	*5*	*5*	*25*	*23*	*3*	*4.4*	*8.8*	*24*	*44%*	*.311*	*1.41*	*4.29*	*4.99*	*0.1*	*96*

Breakout: 10% Improve: 17% Collapse: 7% Attrition: 22% MLB: 32% *Comparables: Justin Haley, Tom Koehler, Chris Stratton*

The Report: I started writing about prospects in an official, extremely online capacity in 2011. That summer I popped onto an old internet friend's now defunct pro wrestling podcast (Hola, TH). We happened to record late at night, right after the signing deadline for that year's draft. As we sort of tap danced at the open to the pod, I mentioned that I was up to follow late-breaking draft stuff and the only major draftee who hadn't signed was Tyler Beede, who was popped late in the first round by Toronto. We chatted about the value of a Vanderbilt education, and what the best-case scenario might be for him in three years before launching into a discussion of God knows what, probably Dragon Gate Pro Wrestling. Anyway, this is all to say there is prospect fatigue… and then there is Tyler Beede.

The long and winding road deposited Beede as a spot starter in the Giants rotation in April. It didn't go great. The profile hasn't changed, well, ever really. A low-90s fastball with good two-seam action that he doesn't always command. A four-seamer that'll touch 95. A decent cutter, a change-up that flashes above-average now, a show-me curve. The Giants tried him in the pen back in Sacramento; the stuff didn't really pop, the cutter rounded off and was sliderish, and he still doesn't throw enough strikes or miss as many bats as you (and two different orgs now) would have thought. He's going to age out of the Selective Service soon. TH has two kids now. Dragon Gate is in the midst of a tumultuous transitionary period, it's future uncertain. I'm still thinking (and writing) about Tyler Beede.

The Risks: Low, I guess. I don't feel good about it. I don't feel good about any of this.

Ben Carsley's Fantasy Take: Odds are whatever name value Beede once had doesn't count for much in your league, but if you play with guys and gals who stopped paying attention like three years ago, it couldn't hurt to float Beede's name. Then again, why do you still own Beede?

9 Aramis Garcia C   OFP: 50   Likely: 40   ETA: Debuted in 2018

Born: 01/12/93 Age: 26 Bats: R Throws: R Height: 6'2" Weight: 220 Origin: Round 2, 2014 Draft (#52 overall)

YEAR	TEAM	LVL	AGE	PA	R	2B	3B	HR	RBI	BB	K	SB	CS	AVG/OBP/SLG	DRC+	VORP	BABIP	BRR	FRAA	WARP	PF
2016	SJO	A+	23	160	20	6	0	2	20	14	42	1	0	.257/.323/.340	94	4.7	.350	-1.7	C(41) 1.8	0.3	92
2017	SJO	A+	24	347	43	20	1	17	65	15	73	0	0	.272/.314/.497	115	21.0	.301	-1.3	C(50) 0.7, 1B(17) 0.3	0.8	102
2017	RIC	AA	24	89	11	12	0	0	8	9	21	0	0	.282/.360/.436	120	6.6	.379	1.0	C(20) -0.5, 1B(2) 0.0	0.5	99
2018	RIC	AA	25	328	36	14	1	11	33	20	76	0	1	.233/.287/.395	90	10.4	.272	-2.0	C(69) 10.3, 1B(11) -0.5	1.4	93
2018	SAC	AAA	25	41	5	1	0	0	4	2	12	0	0	.237/.268/.263	60	-1.6	.333	0.3	C(10) 0.5	0.0	107
2018	SFN	MLB	25	65	8	1	0	4	9	2	31	0	0	.286/.308/.492	55	2.9	.500	0.2	1B(10) -0.6, C(7) 0.7	-0.2	96
2019	*SFN*	*MLB*	*26*	*223*	*21*	*9*	*0*	*7*	*25*	*10*	*66*	*0*	*0*	*.213/.253/.361*	*66*	*0.5*	*.272*	*-0.4*	*C 1*	*0.2*	*96*

Breakout: 9% Improve: 17% Collapse: 3% Attrition: 20% MLB: 30% *Comparables: Cameron Rupp, John Hester, Lucas May*

The Report: Look, I don't mean to be pithy or cruel or even sardonic, and I'm (arguably too) often sardonic. Giants fans deserve the same effort as every other team… but Garcia's a backup catcher. That Double-A line reads like a dictionary definition backup catcher. There are only 60 jobs, man. Well, maybe more when Joe Maddon gets a little weird, or somebody, usually Ned Yost I'd guess, wants to carry three catchers.

Garcia will put on the gear and give a decent accounting of himself. He's improved to averagish behind the plate. He'll give you sub-2.0 times on your Accusplit, for all that matters nowadays. His game-calling and receiving have improved enough. At the plate, he'll run into a few, due to his plus raw and loft. He doesn't have Drew Butera's hair or Anthony Recker's ass, but the Royal Fraternity of backup catchers only asks that you have below-average offensive tools. Anything else is a bonus when your poor prospect writer is trying to fill 150 words or so, let alone the poor sucker who has to write the fantasy blurb here.

The Risks: Low. Voros's Law applies to his major league cameo, but it was a major league cameo. The main risk is he gets squeezed out in a catching-rich org, but these rankings happen in a vacuum.

Ben Carsley's Fantasy Take: The Larry David unsure Curb Your Enthusiasm gif, but only the first part where he looks wildly uncomfortable before reconsidering.

10 Chris Shaw 1B OFP: 50 Likely: 40 ETA: Debuted in 2018

Born: 10/20/93 Age: 25 Bats: L Throws: R Height: 6'3" Weight: 226 Origin: Round 1, 2015 Draft (#31 overall)

YEAR	TEAM	LVL	AGE	PA	R	2B	3B	HR	RBI	BB	K	SB	CS	AVG/OBP/SLG	DRC+	VORP	BABIP	BRR	FRAA	WARP	PF
2016	SJO	A+	22	305	47	22	0	16	55	28	70	0	0	.285/.357/.544	156	24.7	.326	-2.4	1B(52) -0.9	0.9	89
2016	RIC	AA	22	256	26	16	4	5	30	20	55	0	0	.246/.309/.414	93	1.6	.299	-3.5	1B(48) -2.3	-1.0	98
2017	RIC	AA	23	154	16	10	0	6	29	18	26	0	0	.301/.390/.511	150	10.5	.333	-1.5	LF(17) -1.1, 1B(16) -0.9	0.4	100
2017	SAC	AAA	23	360	42	25	1	18	50	20	106	0	0	.289/.328/.530	98	13.4	.367	-5.3	LF(76) -14.5	-1.6	100
2018	SAC	AAA	24	422	55	21	2	24	65	21	144	0	0	.259/.308/.505	103	14.4	.345	-2.0	LF(86) -10.4	-0.6	99
2018	SFN	MLB	24	62	2	2	0	1	7	7	23	1	0	.185/.274/.278	65	-1.8	.290	-0.1	LF(15) -1.9	-0.3	98
2019	*SFN*	*MLB*	*25*	*254*	*28*	*13*	*1*	*11*	*34*	*12*	*79*	*0*	*0*	*.227/.267/.432*	*84*	*1.8*	*.287*	*-0.3*	*LF -3*	*-0.2*	*96*

Breakout: 10% Improve: 26% Collapse: 3% Attrition: 27% MLB: 46%   *Comparables: Matt Clark, Andrew Lambo, Daniel Dorn*

The Report: Shaw's strikeout issues became a real problem for him in 2018 despite mashing in the PCL. He has a yoked-up, uppercut swing that allows him to tap into his plus raw power, but it leaves him very vulnerable to stuff moving down or away from him. The bat speed is only average so he has to make decisions quickly, and the decision was rarely to take a pitch, as his walk rate continued to erode. You can manage this profile as a Three True Outcomes slugger, but considering that he's blocked by Brandon Belt at first and a below-average defender in a corner outfield spot, a slugging-heavy .800 OPS isn't that attractive, even if you directly import his Triple-A line. Of course, that's not how baseball works, and major league arms abused Shaw at times in his first taste of the show. All is not lost of course, and he has a long track record of production—and the aforementioned raw power—but the clock starts ticking quickly for corner bat prospects who struggle in the bigs.

The Risks: Medium. So, phrasing risks for these types of profiles is difficult. The actual risk is that he doesn't hit enough and passes into the Quad-A realm that has claimed so many TTO corner mashers before. Even if he does hit pretty close to the projection, you are always looking to upgrade from a Role 5 corner bat.

Ben Carsley's Fantasy Take: *takes deep breath* There's a pretty solid argument to be made that Shaw is the fourth-best fantasy prospect in this system. That does not make him good of course, but we've seen lots of guys with this profile hold short-term value before. We've also seen lots of them tank. Aren't you glad we're done with this system?

Others of note:

Jalen Miller, IF, High-A San Jose

We've been calling Miller a project at the plate since he was drafted, and the Giants finally started to see some deliverables in 2018. We're not ready to declare a minimal viable product here yet; Miller is still hyper-aggressive at the plate. But he had enough hand-eye and bat speed to make it work across a second pass of the Cal League at least. He's an above-average runner and has settled in as a solid defender at second base. The likely range of outcomes here still runs from "good utility player" to "up-and-down utility player," but we'll just roll everything else over into our 2019 Q1 goals.

Jake Wong, RHP

Wong—the Giants third round pick—isn't all that different from Sean Hjelle, minus, oh, nine inches or so. He can pop 95 once in a while with some riding life up, but works more low-90s and the heater can be a bit true. His breaking ball vacillates between a humpy, downer curve that he can change eye levels with, and a tighter backfoot slider option with more gloveside action. These may be two separate pitches but they tend to bleed together a bit, and the middle ground can get slurvy. His changeup is even less of a factor than Hjelle's, and there's more effort in the delivery. The frame looks like a starter's but given the state of the current arsenal, he might be better teasing out a consistent breaking ball he likes and letting it loose in relief.

Mac Marshall, LHP

"The stuff's not that far off Logan Webb" was a thing written in our internal discussion of Marshall w/r/t the Giants list. The health/durability concerns are dead even though, as Marshall was weaned back onto the mound slowly following 2017 elbow surgery. He's never thrown more than 67 innings in a pro season, so as intriguing as the low 90s fastball/high 80s cutter combination is from the left side, you have to wonder if he can hold up under a starter's workload. The third pitch is there, assuming the feel for his potential plus change returns. Marshall might be best off working multi-inning relief where perhaps the fastball will tick up and he can eschew his below-average slider. But we'd like to see a full healthy season before we rank him "not that far off Logan Webb."

Jacob Gonzalez, 3B, Low-A Agusta

Son of Luis, Jacob Gonzalez carries himself on and off the field like a person who has been around a locker room his entire life, which he has. He's a positive clubhouse guy and someone you want in your organization as a person. He also has a tireless work ethic and puts a lot into his defense. It might not keep him at third base long-term, however, because his actions and arm aren't suited for the position. If he moves to left field, he has to max out his hit profile. The bat is quick and he can tap into his above-average power. He's aggressive at the plate and has some swing-and-miss, but the stick is major-league quality, and he might have a future as a bench bat.

Top Talents 25 and Under (born 4/1/93 or later):

1. Joey Bart
2. Heliot Ramos
3. Shaun Anderson
4. Steven Duggar
5. Alexander Canario
6. Logan Webb
7. Sean Hjelle
8. Heath Quinn
9. Tyler Beede
10. Aramis Garcia

Uh... hello? Is this thing on?

We all have our strengths and weaknesses in life, and while building a club capable of peeling off three championships in five years was a strength of Brian Sabean's, integrating the next wave of young players to extend that contention window proved... challenging.

Duggar dipped his toes into big league waters for the first time last season and they were warm enough, before yet another injury—this time a dislocated shoulder—ended his season prematurely. At his healthy best, Duggar will battle through at-bats, take some walks, ambush mistakes, and do a reasonable job covering San Francisco's cavernous centerfield. He should open 2019 with a shot to start in center.

Beyond him, what you see in our prospect list is what you get. You could make a case for Ryder Jones to sneak onto this list at the back, given Beede and Garcia's stagnation. But a return engagement at Sacramento last year didn't go nearly as swimmingly as his first crack, and it was the Panda's Geriatric Belly that got the corner reps when injuries opened up a job, not the young buck. Reyes Moronta has aged out of consideration, and it's a field full of crickets after that.

A new regime and what should be a string of high draft picks over the next couple seasons offers potential for a relatively quick infusion of new blood into these ranks going forward, but given the state of the franchise at present, it feels likely to get darker before that light shines in.

Seattle Mariners

The State of the System:

"Finally there is clarity and there is purpose after all, but every night ends the same as I'm collapsing once more by your side." - Death Cab for Cutie, "Debate Exposes Doubt"

The Top Ten:

1 Justus Sheffield LHP

OFP: 60 Likely: 50 ETA: Debuted in 2018

Born: 05/13/96 Age: 23 Bats: L Throws: L Height: 6'0" Weight: 200 Origin: Round 1, 2014 Draft (#31 overall)

YEAR	TEAM	LVL	AGE	W	L	SV	G	GS	IP	H	HR	BB/9	K/9	K	GB%	BABIP	WHIP	ERA	DRA	WARP	PF
2016	LYN	A+	20	7	5	0	19	19	95^1	91	6	3.8	8.8	93	45%	.321	1.37	3.59	3.57	2.1	102
2016	TAM	A+	20	3	1	0	5	5	26	14	0	3.5	9.3	27	45%	.226	0.92	1.73	2.95	0.7	103
2017	TRN	AA	21	7	6	0	17	17	93^1	94	14	3.2	7.9	82	48%	.293	1.36	3.18	3.54	1.8	94
2018	TRN	AA	22	1	2	0	5	5	28	16	1	4.5	12.5	39	44%	.259	1.07	2.25	3.47	0.6	91
2018	SWB	AAA	22	6	4	0	20	15	88	66	3	3.7	8.6	84	46%	.264	1.16	2.56	4.27	1.2	95
2018	NYA	MLB	22	0	0	0	3	0	2^2	4	1	10.1	0.0	0	55%	.300	2.62	10.12	6.56	-0.1	110
2019	*SEA*	*MLB*	*23*	*4*	*5*	*0*	*13*	*13*	*74*	*65*	*9*	*4.1*	*9.6*	*79*	*43%*	*.288*	*1.33*	*4.29*	*4.62*	*0.7*	*97*

Breakout: 21% Improve: 26% Collapse: 14% Attrition: 33% MLB: 48% *Comparables: Michael Fulmer, Matt Magill, Giovanni Soto*

The Report: We talk a lot about the concept of "prospect fatigue." Sometimes you've seen a guy for years and years and he's fine. He's exactly what you expected him to be at this point in the timeline, no more and no less. You've probably written about him a dozen times over the past few years. He might've been part of a major transaction or two. He was probably a high pick or expensive IFA. And you just get sort of tired of talking about him, so the report comes across lower than it should. Really, there's absolutely nothing wrong.

You're probably not supposed to admit this as a prospect writer, but I do try to be transparent, and Justus Sheffield is the epitome of prospect fatigue for me. Sheffield has been a big name prospect since he was in high school. He has a brother with a similar profile. He's exactly where he "should" be right now. He's ranked at the same basic spot on all of our lists for years. He's got the same grades, the same strengths, the same weaknesses. He's been traded twice, as a primary piece in a major deadline trade and a major winter trade, so we've talked about him a lot in several different evaluative contexts. It feels like I've written a million different Justus Sheffield reports, and it feels like the well is dry on new ways to spin him.

But, hey, this is his first time on Seattle's list, right? So here goes... Sheffield is a fastball/slider/change lefty who debuted in a September relief cameo for the Yankees. He was 94-96 MPH with the fastball then, although he's frequently sat a tick or two little lower as a starter and has also occasionally touched a tick or two higher. The slider is most often a tight mid-80s offering, and it's close to if not already a present plus pitch. He'll also sometimes manipulate it down to a slurve that sometimes gets labeled a curveball, and it is the out pitch he relies on most at present. His changeup flashes plus with a bit less consistency, but it's hard and dives.

Sheffield is short, shows wavering command, and has battled various injuries over his career, so he's often been tipped as a potential impact reliever instead of a potential impact starter. The Yankees didn't appear all that interested in giving him starting reps, passing him over for promotions repeatedly in favor of lesser prospects over the past two seasons. He's now landed in a situation where he will get every opportunity to start over the next few years. The delta is a bit higher than you'd expect for a basically ready upper-minors arm, but with that does come higher upside than most of his cohort.

The Risks: Medium, although there's positive risk here too. If Sheffield can stay in the rotation, increase the consistency of his changeup and command, and avoid injuries, he does have high-end starting potential. But there are a lot of command and durability questions. If this all sounds like the guy he got traded for, well, it might be.

Bret Sayre's Fantasy Take: I really wish I felt better about Sheffield's chances of sticking in a rotation, but even though I'm skeptical, the sneaky SP2 upside gives him plenty of value in dynasty leagues. Of course, it helps that he's slated to throw 120-plus innings this year. The stuff is there for him to strike out 10 batters per nine as a starter and more as a reliever, but the ratios could hold him back due to said command issues. From a purely statistical standpoint, he's got Mike Clevinger upside but without the hair.

2 Jarred Kelenic OF

OFP: 60 Likely: 50 ETA: 2021

Born: 07/16/99 Age: 19 Bats: L Throws: L Height: 6'1" Weight: 196 Origin: Round 1, 2018 Draft (#6 overall)

YEAR	TEAM	LVL	AGE	PA	R	2B	3B	HR	RBI	BB	K	SB	CS	AVG/OBP/SLG	DRC+	VORP	BABIP	BRR	FRAA	WARP	PF
2018	MTS	RK	18	51	9	2	2	1	9	4	11	4	0	.413/.451/.609	184	8.0	.514	-0.1	CF(9) 2.0	0.5	106
2018	KNG	RK	18	200	33	8	4	5	33	22	39	11	1	.253/.350/.431	124	15.2	.300	2.5	CF(43) 5.8	1.3	105
2019	*SEA*	*MLB*	*19*	*252*	*19*	*5*	*1*	*7*	*24*	*12*	*78*	*2*	*0*	*.133/.172/.255*	*10*	*-17.3*	*.155*	*0.4*	*CF 0*	*-1.9*	*97*

Breakout: 5% Improve: 7% Collapse: 0% Attrition: 3% MLB: 9% *Comparables: Engel Beltre, Carlos Tocci, Franmil Reyes*

The Report: Kelenic has more present skills than you might expect from a cold-weather prep bat. The background, drafting organization, and draft position are going to elicit Brandon Nimmo comps as he moves through the minors, but Kelenic is a much more polished product than Nimmo was at 19. He's a better bet to stick as at least an average center fielder too. He can really go get it on the grass, with good instincts and the ability to adjust his routes on the fly. The only thing he really lacks is explosive closing speed on balls, although he is a plus runner at present and I don't see his already mature frame filling out much more.

At the plate Kelenic shows above-average bat speed, covers velo well, and the ball jumps off his bat with backspin. He can get a little handsy during his load and lose some bat control, and the swing will get long at times. He can be exploited early in counts, as he likes to hunt fastballs early. There isn't anything here that screams future plus tool—outside of his arm, which has gotten plus-plus grades thrown on it as an amateur—but all five clock in at average-or-better. That's a nice package in a center field prospect.

The Risks: High. Kelenic hasn't played above rookie-ball yet, and there are some "tweener" warning signs in the profile.

Bret Sayre's Fantasy Take: There's a lot to like from a fantasy standpoint, but not a lot to love here, which means he'll have to max out the sum of his parts in order to be a cornerstone outfielder. He has the potential to hit for average (near .300 if it all clicks), tap into 20-homer power, and steal 20-plus bases, yet the odds of him doing all three are small. He's still a very solid OF3 in the long run if two of those three come together, and he has the potential to move quickly for a prep bat due to his advanced approach. Still, Kelenic found himself on the outside looking in at my top-10 2018 signees and that'll probably be the case on the 101 as well.

3 Evan White 1B

OFP: 60 Likely: 50 ETA: 2020

Born: 04/26/96 Age: 23 Bats: R Throws: L Height: 6'3" Weight: 205 Origin: Round 1, 2017 Draft (#17 overall)

YEAR	TEAM	LVL	AGE	PA	R	2B	3B	HR	RBI	BB	K	SB	CS	AVG/OBP/SLG	DRC+	VORP	BABIP	BRR	FRAA	WARP	PF
2017	EVE	A-	21	55	6	1	1	3	12	6	6	1	1	.277/.345/.532	124	3.7	.250	-0.1	1B(8) -0.6	-0.1	104
2018	MOD	A+	22	538	72	27	7	11	66	52	103	4	3	.303/.375/.458	144	38.3	.363	-0.5	1B(106) 5.5	2.1	94
2019	*SEA*	*MLB*	*23*	*252*	*24*	*7*	*1*	*7*	*29*	*17*	*62*	*0*	*0*	*.222/.276/.360*	*67*	*-5.2*	*.268*	*-0.1*	*1B 1*	*-0.4*	*97*

Breakout: 6% Improve: 15% Collapse: 0% Attrition: 8% MLB: 17% *Comparables: Shane Peterson, Ronald Guzman, David Cooper*

The Report: White's a weird profile, and thus a fun player. The ol' right-hit, left-throw trick's a tough one to pull off, especially for collegiate first basemen who lack prototypical first-base game pop. There's always been plenty of well-founded optimism about the hit tool, and for evident reason: he sees the ball well, works counts effectively, and capably rifles line drives to all fields. There's good torque and bat speed off a deep load, and he's athletic enough to stay back that extra beat and still sync things up to fire at a pitch on time. The club implemented some swing changes over the course of the season to get his legs more involved and help him generate a plane more conducive to lifting and driving pitches, and he did just that down the stretch.

The athleticism is top-shelf for the cold corner. He moves with grace and fluidity around the bag, receives throws with soft hands, and combines quickness, agility, and supreme body control to get after hot hoppers hit his way. He's an efficient runner with a surprising burst, and the body should hang on to above-average or better speed for the foreseeable future.

The Mariners have thus far resisted the obvious temptation to create reps for him in the outfield, but it seems an inevitable outcome in today's game, and he certainly presents the physicality of someone capable of meeting the demands of multiple positions. If it all comes together he can evolve into a versatile player capable of adding value in all three phases of the game.

The Risks: Low but also high? It's complicated. Whether the swing changes and subsequent power burst all holds will have a lot to say about where on the spectrum of a given 25-man roster he winds up. It's really strange to talk about any first baseman's glove as something that sets a reasonably high floor for him, but White's is really, really good, so here we are.

Bret Sayre's Fantasy Take: This is like the profile you would have written for Eric Hosmer nearly a decade ago if you knew he wasn't going to take that step forward in power. And that's not to say Hosmer hasn't been valuable—he's had a few impressive campaigns, sometimes on the back of his thefts and sometimes on the back of a friendly BABIP—yet this is a tough fantasy profile to rely on without a more extreme hit tool. Unfortunately, White's hit tool isn't enough to make him more than a top-150 dynasty prospect.

4 Justin Dunn RHP

OFP: 55 Likely: 45 ETA: Late 2019

Born: 09/22/95 Age: 23 Bats: R Throws: R Height: 6'2" Weight: 185 Origin: Round 1, 2016 Draft (#19 overall)

YEAR	TEAM	LVL	AGE	W	L	SV	G	GS	IP	H	HR	BB/9	K/9	K	GB%	BABIP	WHIP	ERA	DRA	WARP	PF
2016	BRO	A-	20	1	1	0	11	8	30	25	1	3.0	10.5	35	46%	.320	1.17	1.50	2.19	1.1	95
2017	SLU	A+	21	5	6	0	20	16	95^1	101	5	4.5	7.1	75	44%	.322	1.56	5.00	4.27	1.0	108
2018	SLU	A+	22	2	3	0	9	9	45^2	43	2	3.0	10.1	51	42%	.325	1.27	2.36	3.43	1.0	97
2018	BIN	AA	22	6	5	0	15	15	89^2	85	7	3.7	10.5	105	47%	.345	1.36	4.22	3.48	1.9	101
2019	*SEA*	*MLB*	*23*	*6*	*7*	*0*	*21*	*21*	105^1	*102*	*13*	*4.3*	*9.0*	*106*	*40%*	*.305*	*1.44*	*4.57*	*4.92*	*0.7*	*97*

Breakout: 8% Improve: 15% Collapse: 5% Attrition: 15% MLB: 24% *Comparables: Glen Perkins, D.J. Mitchell, Cody Reed*

The Report: After command issues led to a bit of a lost 2017 in the Florida State League, Dunn looked more like a first-round arm in 2018. He still hasn't consistently shown 95+ velocity as a starter in the pros, more often touching 95 while sitting in the average velocity band. The heater can run a little true, showing occasional riding life or cut, but lacking the explosive armside movement he had coming out of BC. The slider projects as above-average, a mid-80s offering with good, late tilt. Dunn's worked on a curveball more this year, but it is difficult to tease out from the slider at times, and he tends to cast it, making it a bit of a slurvy, 11-4 roller. The changeup is still used sparingly and tends to be too firm, although he will usually show one or two a start with good tumble.

Dunn has an athletic delivery, but lacks plane as he's on the short side and uses a three-quarters slot. He throws across his body as well, limiting his command projection to averageish. Dunn has the arsenal to start, but looks more like an "average starter" type, and he might have more impact in relief.

The Risks: Medium. Dunn's had some Double-A success, but there's significant reliever risk here without further command and third pitch gains.

Bret Sayre's Fantasy Take: There's only about a 30-40 percent chance that Dunn becomes even a usable mixed-league starting pitcher, let alone a solid SP4 as further development might portend. There are worse places to work if you don't have a true out pitch against lefties than T-Mobile, but Dunn barely registers as a top-200 name at this point and his movement to the Mariners decreases my confidence that he'll make good on that first-round promise.

5 Logan Gilbert RHP

OFP: 55 Likely: 45 ETA: Late 2020

Born: 05/05/97 Age: 22 Bats: R Throws: R Height: 6'6" Weight: 225 Origin: Round 1, 2018 Draft (#14 overall)

The Report: Stetson University doesn't always produce major-league arms, but when they do, they are Cy Young winners (well, and Lenny Dinardo). Gilbert doesn't have deGrom or Kluber-level stuff, but neither did those two coming out of college (his flow has deGrom potential though). What Gilbert does have is a big 6-foot-8 frame that belies a fairly easy delivery, and a fastball that touches 95. He changes eye levels well with the heater and there is some run and sink at times as well.

Gilbert has a full four-pitch mix, and the curve is his most advanced offering. It flashes plus with tight 12-5 break, but will get loose and humpy at times as well. The slider and change are both potentially average. He does a good job of staying online with his delivery despite a huge frame, but he can get a little "tall and fall" and his command wavers. Gilbert also has yet to throw a pro pitch because he was shut down with mononucleosis. That's a new one.

The Risks: Medium. Gilbert is the kind of polished college arm that usually moves through the minors quickly. "Usually." We have no evidence of that yet though.

Bret Sayre's Fantasy Take: If there's a profile I just genuinely mistrust, it's the tall pitcher without overpowering stuff profile. Give me a tall pitcher who can touch triple-digits and I'll painfully wait through the Tyler Glasnow's of the world, but I'm not inclined to stick around to find out if a pitcher with pretty good stuff figures out of how make use of his long levers. I would not look to him with a second- or third-round pick in dynasty drafts this year, as the odds he gets to his SP4 upside aren't as good as they need to be.

6 Erik Swanson RHP   OFP: 55   Likely: 45   ETA: 2019

Born: 09/04/93 Age: 25 Bats: R Throws: R Height: 6'3" Weight: 235 Origin: Round 8, 2014 Draft (#246 overall)

YEAR	TEAM	LVL	AGE	W	L	SV	G	GS	IP	H	HR	BB/9	K/9	K	GB%	BABIP	WHIP	ERA	DRA	WARP	PF
2016	HIC	A	22	6	4	1	19	15	81^{1}	77	4	2.8	8.6	78	53%	.319	1.25	3.43	3.26	1.7	97
2016	CSC	A	22	0	1	0	5	2	15	14	0	3.0	9.0	15	50%	.333	1.27	3.60	2.65	0.4	84
2017	TAM	A+	23	7	3	0	20	20	100^{1}	115	10	1.3	7.5	84	42%	.344	1.29	3.95	4.34	1.1	104
2018	TRN	AA	24	5	0	0	8	7	42^{2}	22	0	3.2	11.6	55	36%	.253	0.87	0.42	3.54	0.9	87
2018	SWB	AAA	24	3	2	0	14	13	72^{1}	63	10	1.7	9.7	78	37%	.283	1.06	3.86	3.55	1.6	98
2019	*SEA*	*MLB*	*25*	*3*	*3*	*0*	*10*	*10*	*50*	*48*	*8*	*3.0*	*8.9*	*49*	*40%*	*.295*	*1.29*	*4.47*	*4.83*	*0.4*	*97*

Breakout: 11% Improve: 19% Collapse: 13% Attrition: 26% MLB: 36% *Comparables: Sean Gilmartin, Jeremy Hefner, Cory Luebke*

The Report: Not all that long ago, this was one of my favorite sleeper pitching prospects. He's officially too high-profile now to really be called a sleeper, traded twice in significant deals and on the fringes of the 101 discussion, if ultimately a half-grade low. But he might be a pretty good pitcher pretty soon.

Because Swanson—now 25, and in his sixth pro season—has taken some time to ripen as a prospect due to injuries and late development, we think his stuff has been undersold a bit. His fastball can sit as high as the mid-90s and touches 98, and the pitch has plane and life to it. He also throws a hard slider that we like, a developing changeup, and the occasional curveball. He's generally shown strong command and control throughout the minors. He has a big, sturdy-looking frame and looks pretty clean in his delivery, but he's battled injuries over the course of his career and doesn't always hold his velocity through starts. Ultimately, the stuff might pop more in relief.

In other organizations, we suspect Swanson would've gotten a chance during the 2018 season, but the Yankees are perpetually loaded with pitching and always have a crowded 40-man situation. Swanson is now on the 40-man, and Mariners general manager Jerry Dipoto pronounced Swanson as "major-league ready" following the trade. Like Sheffield, he will get every chance to work out in Seattle's rotation over the next few years.

The Risks: Medium. Swanson has a decent amount of relief/injury risk, and has also been generally on the older side for his leagues.

Bret Sayre's Fantasy Take: The argument for Swanson, like Sheffield before him, is centered around his proximity, but accounts for sneaky upside if he can make it through the gauntlet of a full major-league season as a starter. While Swanson may be more SP4 than SP2, he still offers 180-plus-strikeout potential and the ability to register an above-average WHIP. He should be owned in all leagues that roster 200 prospects.

7 Shed Long 2B   OFP: 55   Likely: 45   ETA: Late 2019

Born: 08/22/95 Age: 23 Bats: L Throws: R Height: 5'8" Weight: 184 Origin: Round 12, 2013 Draft (#375 overall)

YEAR	TEAM	LVL	AGE	PA	R	2B	3B	HR	RBI	BB	K	SB	CS	AVG/OBP/SLG	DRC+	VORP	BABIP	BRR	FRAA	WARP	PF
2016	DYT	A	20	389	47	24	1	11	45	44	85	16	3	.281/.371/.457	141	30.7	.346	3.2	2B(82) 2.0, 3B(3) -0.6	2.7	103
2016	DAY	A+	20	159	22	6	4	4	30	10	35	5	1	.322/.371/.503	128	12.2	.393	1.3	2B(38) 3.0	1.0	111
2017	DAY	A+	21	279	37	16	1	13	36	27	63	6	3	.312/.380/.543	147	21.5	.368	-1.1	2B(62) 5.4	1.9	106
2017	PEN	AA	21	160	13	6	2	3	14	19	31	3	1	.227/.319/.362	103	1.9	.271	-2.4	2B(39) -1.7	-0.3	100
2018	PEN	AA	22	522	75	22	5	12	56	57	123	19	6	.261/.353/.412	113	32.1	.333	3.7	2B(123) -1.9	1.4	96
2019	*SEA*	*MLB*	*23*	*65*	*7*	*2*	*0*	*2*	*7*	*5*	*18*	*1*	*0*	*.207/.268/.357*	*63*	*-0.5*	*.256*	*0.1*	*2B 0*	*-0.1*	*97*

Breakout: 12% Improve: 26% Collapse: 4% Attrition: 16% MLB: 36% *Comparables: Brandon Lowe, Carlos Asuaje, Dilson Herrera*

The Report: After struggling some in his initial pass through the Southern League in 2017, Long had a successful consolidation year in 2018. He lacks a standout tool, but he does everything well enough. There's still a bit more swing and miss here than you'd like—Long will do the short-hitter thing where he thinks he can hit pitches at his throat—which may make the hit and power tools only play to average. Long is a good athlete though and still an above-average runner despite the squarish physique. He's fine at second, and could handle a few other spots on the grass or dirt if he's ultimately a bench-piece. But even with the glut of talent at the keystone nowadays, averagish tools across the board are still nice to have at an up-the-middle spot.

The Risks: Medium. It's possible the swing-and-miss issues continue to get worse against better pitching, but there's a broad enough base of skills here to expect some sort of major-league career.

Bret Sayre's Fantasy Take: This was a much more attractive offensive profile before middle infielders started going bananas with the bats. Yet Long continues to trudge along as a potential top-15 second baseman, capable of 15 homers and 15 steals. It's possible GABP could help him sneak beyond the 20 mark in a season or two, but that will likely be the only time he's more than a good MI option in 12-15 team mixed leagues.

8 Kyle Lewis OF

OFP: 55 Likely: 45 ETA: 2020

Born: 07/13/95 Age: 23 Bats: R Throws: R Height: 6'4" Weight: 210 Origin: Round 1, 2016 Draft (#11 overall)

YEAR	TEAM	LVL	AGE	PA	R	2B	3B	HR	RBI	BB	K	SB	CS	AVG/OBP/SLG	DRC+	VORP	BABIP	BRR	FRAA	WARP	PF
2016	EVE	A-	20	135	26	8	5	3	26	16	22	3	0	.299/.385/.530	155	12.1	.344	-1.2	CF(27) -0.9	0.3	103
2017	MRN	RK	21	46	9	2	1	1	7	4	14	1	0	.263/.348/.447	76	4.0	.360	1.4	CF(6) -1.0	-0.1	102
2017	MOD	A+	21	167	20	4	0	6	24	15	38	2	1	.255/.323/.403	109	1.9	.299	-1.5	CF(13) 0.1	-0.1	99
2018	MOD	A+	22	211	21	18	0	5	32	11	55	0	0	.260/.303/.429	104	8.9	.333	0.3	CF(23) -3.1, RF(11) -0.7	-0.3	96
2018	ARK	AA	22	152	18	8	0	4	20	17	32	1	0	.220/.309/.371	90	0.2	.255	-2.0	CF(29) -2.6, RF(1) 0.0	-0.6	103
2019	*SEA*	*MLB*	*23*	*252*	*22*	*7*	*1*	*8*	*28*	*15*	*70*	*0*	*0*	*.181/.230/.321*	*49*	*-6.9*	*.217*	*-0.4*	*CF -1, RF 0*	*-0.9*	*97*

Breakout: 8% Improve: 14% Collapse: 1% Attrition: 7% MLB: 16% *Comparables: Bryan Petersen, Daniel Fields, Jake Cave*

The Report: The greatest success story of Lewis' season was that he had a season at all. It still wasn't a full season, mind you, but it was one that saw him return to more or less full health by the end of it. And that counts for a lot. He's missed a spectacular amount of developmental time battling terrible things in his knee, and the learning curve is only going to get steeper in the months ahead. But the raw tools that got him drafted 11th overall remain readily apparent. He's strong as an ox, with all-fields power and thunder off the barrel. The straight-line speed and elite explosiveness aren't quite there anymore, but the physicality and twitch still are, and the instincts to make those attributes play defensively are, too. It probably makes more sense for everybody if they shuffle him over to right sooner or later, but there's still a shot he can spell up the middle. The bat still has a long road ahead: he struggles to recognize spin, and he'll expand accordingly when fooled. Velocity up can still bite him. But he can catch the latter and leave the junk alone, and the baseball acumen has long been understood as an asset. It's about health and reps now, and he'll need a lot of both to swallow up the kind of growth he's missed and will need.

The Risks: High. He's got a lot of work to catch up on, and the structural integrity of his knee will remain a gaping question mark until it isn't.

Bret Sayre's Fantasy Take: Lewis, at this point in pro career, has both the upside and the knee structure of a 31-year-old Adam Jones and that was not the ceiling that was promised when he was drafted. Yet, like Jones, the bat can still make up for it. Lewis could develop into a .270 hitter with 25 bombs for as long as he can stay on the field, but *could* carries a lot of weight here.

9 Julio Rodriguez OF

OFP: 55 Likely: 40 ETA: 2023

Born: 12/29/00 Age: 18 Bats: R Throws: R Height: 6'3" Weight: 180 Origin: International Free Agent, 2017

YEAR	TEAM	LVL	AGE	PA	R	2B	3B	HR	RBI	BB	K	SB	CS	AVG/OBP/SLG	DRC+	VORP	BABIP	BRR	FRAA	WARP	PF
2018	DMR	RK	17	255	50	13	9	5	36	30	40	10	0	.315/.404/.525	165	33.9	.364	0.6	RF(45) 8.1, CF(6) -0.1	2.5	96
2019	*SEA*	*MLB*	*18*	*252*	*19*	*7*	*5*	*5*	*25*	*14*	*73*	*0*	*0*	*.174/.219/.313*	*39*	*-10.5*	*.223*	*0.6*	*RF 2, CF 0*	*-0.9*	*97*

Breakout: 0% Improve: 0% Collapse: 0% Attrition: 0% MLB: 0% *Comparables: Adalberto Mondesi, Wilmer Flores, Tommy Brown*

The Report: The Mariners signed Rodriguez for $1,750,000 out of the Dominican in July 2017 on the strength of his power stroke. He slugged .500+ in the Dominican Summer League last year, which is at least marginally better than not doing that. There's some length to the swing, but Rodriguez could have plus-plus raw power at maturity with a decent shot to get most of it into games. He's got plenty of arm for right field, which is good because he's already a right fielder at 17. That's less good; you like to at least pretend your top IFAs can play up the middle in their teenage years. Obviously that puts a lot of pressure on the bat, and there's still some uncertainty on how Rodriguez's frame will develop into his 20s. Because he's 17. It's the prototypical right field prospect profile, but with even more risk and uncertainty than your average good right field prospect.

The Risks: Extreme. He's 17, already a right fielder, and not yet stateside.

Bret Sayre's Fantasy Take: This is going to take a while, but man is there a lot to like about Rodriguez's bat. He's got the raw power to hit 30-plus bombs and was reasonably advanced as one of the young-uns in the DSL, especially with the hit tool. You can dream of a 6/7 future here, and while there's plenty of downside from there, Rodriguez probably has the highest potential in this system. He's a sneaky name to invest in this year if he's not owned in your dynasty league—presuming you roster 200+ prospects.

10 Sam Carlson RHP

OFP: 55 Likely: 40 ETA: 2022 or 2023

Born: 12/03/98 Age: 20 Bats: R Throws: R Height: 6'4" Weight: 195 Origin: Round 2, 2017 Draft (#55 overall)

YEAR	TEAM	LVL	AGE	W	L	SV	G	GS	IP	H	HR	BB/9	K/9	K	GB%	BABIP	WHIP	ERA	DRA	WARP	PF
2019	*SEA*	*MLB*	*20*	*2*	*3*	*0*	*7*	*7*	*32*	*31*	*4*	*4.8*	*7.0*	*25*	*53%*	*.274*	*1.50*	*5.66*	*6.11*	*-0.2*	*97*

Breakout: 0% Improve: 0% Collapse: 0% Attrition: 0% MLB: 0% *Comparables: Deolis Guerra, Alex Burnett, Mauricio Cabrera*

The Report: Carlson missed all of 2018 after undergoing Tommy John surgery early in the year. He's likely to miss a fair bit of 2019 as well. When healthy, he was considered a bit of a steal in the second round of the 2017 draft. He's a cold-weather prep arm who popped a few extra ticks on radar guns his senior year and he offers a projectable slider as well. We will see what comes back after rehab, but given the lower slot and high effort delivery, the odds that he's a reliever have only gone up.

The Risks: Extreme. He's in the midst of Tommy John recovery and has three professional innings to his name.

Bret Sayre's Fantasy Take: Carlson was one of my favorite prep pitchers out of the 2017 draft, but this detour just means he'll be available on waivers if he returns in 2020 and starts shoving in full-season ball. Don't burn a roster spot until then.

The Next Five:

11 Braden Bishop OF

Born: 08/22/93 Age: 25 Bats: R Throws: R Height: 6'1" Weight: 190 Origin: Round 3, 2015 Draft (#94 overall)

YEAR	TEAM	LVL	AGE	PA	R	2B	3B	HR	RBI	BB	K	SB	CS	AVG/OBP/SLG	DRC+	VORP	BABIP	BRR	FRAA	WARP	PF
2016	CLN	A	22	284	38	5	1	1	21	25	48	6	1	.290/.363/.331	124	13.8	.355	1.5	CF(40) -0.8, LF(14) -1.1	1.0	97
2016	BAK	A+	22	184	19	6	0	2	22	11	39	2	0	.247/.300/.319	75	4.6	.310	-1.1	CF(34) -3.6, RF(7) -0.8	-0.9	99
2017	MOD	A+	23	412	71	25	3	2	32	45	65	16	4	.296/.385/.400	124	23.2	.356	0.8	CF(70) -1.8, LF(14) 2.1	1.3	99
2017	ARK	AA	23	145	18	9	1	1	11	15	15	6	1	.336/.417/.448	169	14.3	.373	-1.5	CF(31) 1.5	1.2	94
2018	ARK	AA	24	394	70	20	0	8	33	37	68	5	2	.284/.361/.412	139	17.1	.331	-1.9	CF(81) -0.9, RF(2) -0.1	1.7	101
2019	*SEA*	*MLB*	*25*	*32*	*3*	*1*	*0*	*1*	*3*	*2*	*7*	*0*	*0*	*.247/.297/.363*	*66*	*-0.1*	*.294*	*0.0*	*CF 0*	*0.0*	*97*

Breakout: 13% Improve: 44% Collapse: 0% Attrition: 38% MLB: 56% *Comparables: Tim Locastro, Darin Mastroianni, Rafael Ortega*

Bishop was keeping on keeping on, until a pitch fractured his forearm and ended his 2018 season early. The profile here is the same as it was last year, a speed and defense center fielder with questions about how the bat will play against better arms. Double-A is the first real test against "better arms" and Bishop was fine in the Texas League, despite a handsy swing that can limit the quality of his contact at times. He has below-average power at best, but perhaps with enough OBP to carry a second-division starter profile. The clock is ticking some on Bishop—who is already 25—but assuming he comes back from his forearm injury with minimal lingering issues, the Mariners will certainly have major-league outfield openings in 2019. And as a potential plus center fielder, his C.V. stands out in a shallow system.

12 Damon Casetta-Stubbs RHP

Born: 07/22/99 Age: 19 Bats: R Throws: R Height: 6'4" Weight: 200 Origin: Round 11, 2018 Draft (#328 overall)

YEAR	TEAM	LVL	AGE	W	L	SV	G	GS	IP	H	HR	BB/9	K/9	K	GB%	BABIP	WHIP	ERA	DRA	WARP	PF
2018	MRN	RK	18	0	2	0	6	5	6^2	15	0	5.4	9.4	7	46%	.536	2.85	13.50	5.60	0.0	103
2019	*SEA*	*MLB*	*19*	*1*	*3*	*0*	*11*	*6*	*30*	*35*	*5*	*7.1*	*5.9*	*20*	*44%*	*.302*	*1.94*	*7.12*	*7.70*	*-0.8*	*97*

Breakout: 0% Improve: 0% Collapse: 0% Attrition: 0% MLB: 0% *Comparables: Corey Oswalt, Duane Underwood, Joe Musgrove*

The Mariners system is better (read: not the worst), but yeah, an overslot 11th round prep righty still clocks in here. That's not quite as bad as it sounds on paper. His velocity trended up his senior year and he's regularly in the mid-90s now. His slider is a potential plus pitch, and there's some feel for a changeup. The mechanics are going to need some smoothing out, and he looks very much like a fastball/slider reliever at present given the uptempo delivery and lower slot. He's only 19 though, and there is upside worth monitoring.

13 Cal Raleigh C

Born: 11/26/96 Age: 22 Bats: B Throws: R Height: 6'3" Weight: 215 Origin: Round 3, 2018 Draft (#90 overall)

YEAR	TEAM	LVL	AGE	PA	R	2B	3B	HR	RBI	BB	K	SB	CS	AVG/OBP/SLG	DRC+	VORP	BABIP	BRR	FRAA	WARP	PF
2018	EVE	A-	21	167	25	10	1	8	29	18	29	1	1	.288/.367/.534	140	11.6	.309	0.3	C(25) -0.2	0.7	113
2019	*SEA*	*MLB*	*22*	*252*	*22*	*8*	*0*	*10*	*30*	*14*	*68*	*0*	*0*	*.156/.200/.322*	*35*	*-9.8*	*.165*	*-0.5*	*C 0*	*-1.1*	*97*

Breakout: 5% Improve: 14% Collapse: 0% Attrition: 11% MLB: 16% *Comparables: Blake Swihart, Austin Hedges, Christian Vazquez*

The Mariners third-round pick in the 2018 draft, Raleigh is a polished, two-way catcher. While his receiving skills won't have FanGraphs' managing editor erasing Mike Zunino's framing numbers from the cover of her Trapper Keeper any time soon, he's a solid backstop with an average arm who's more athletic and agile than you'd expect given his size, if a bit slow out of a crouch. At the plate Raleigh offers above-average bat speed and potential plus power. An ACC catcher beating up the Northwest League isn't anything out of the ordinary, but the path to playing time behind the plate in Seattle is, uh, clearer now, and Raleigh's polished bat could get him there quickly if the glove comes along as well.

14 Wyatt Mills RHP

Born: 01/25/95 Age: 24 Bats: R Throws: R Height: 6'3" Weight: 175 Origin: Round 3, 2017 Draft (#93 overall)

YEAR	TEAM	LVL	AGE	W	L	SV	G	GS	IP	H	HR	BB/9	K/9	K	GB%	BABIP	WHIP	ERA	DRA	WARP	PF
2017	EVE	A-	22	0	1	2	7	0	7	3	0	3.9	14.1	11	50%	.214	0.86	2.57	3.01	0.2	100
2017	CLN	A	22	0	1	4	11	0	13^1	5	0	4.1	12.1	18	57%	.179	0.82	1.35	4.14	0.1	100
2018	MOD	A+	23	6	0	11	35	0	42^1	29	1	1.9	10.4	49	54%	.277	0.90	1.91	3.59	0.7	100
2018	ARK	AA	23	0	2	0	9	0	10^2	18	0	3.4	8.4	10	42%	.450	2.06	10.12	3.98	0.1	100
2019	*SEA*	*MLB*	*24*	*2*	*1*	*2*	*36*	*0*	*38^2*	*35*	*5*	*4.3*	*9.3*	*40*	*45%*	*.295*	*1.38*	*4.46*	*4.80*	*0.1*	*97*

Breakout: 0% Improve: 0% Collapse: 1% Attrition: 1% MLB: 1% *Comparables: Colton Murray, Adam Kolarek, Branden Pinder*

Mills looks like your typical sidearming righty, beating up on the low minors by throwing from an angle these poor kids haven't seen before. That's not really the narrative here though. First off, all these kids have been seeing low slot dudes for a while; most college and low minors teams have at least two. And Mills' stuff is anything but typical for that profile. He can dial his fastball up to 93 with sink and run, and his low-80s slider should end up above-average or better. The two pitches look the same out of his hand, and he throws strikes with both. There might even be enough changeup to crossover, although Mills' tends to be even flatter than the heater. He has to live at the edges of the zones, and a Double-A cameo showed that better hitters make for finer margins, but there's still a potential Steve Cishekish outcome here, and that's a top-15 prospect in this system.

15 Matt Festa RHP

Born: 03/11/93 Age: 26 Bats: R Throws: R Height: 6'2" Weight: 195 Origin: Round 7, 2016 Draft (#207 overall)

YEAR	TEAM	LVL	AGE	W	L	SV	G	GS	IP	H	HR	BB/9	K/9	K	GB%	BABIP	WHIP	ERA	DRA	WARP	PF
2016	EVE	A-	23	6	2	0	14	8	60^{1}	60	3	2.1	8.7	58	49%	.324	1.23	3.73	3.10	1.4	104
2017	MOD	A+	24	4	2	6	42	1	69^{2}	61	7	2.5	12.8	99	44%	.327	1.15	3.23	2.55	1.9	99
2018	ARK	AA	25	5	2	20	44	0	49	50	6	2.2	12.3	67	47%	.364	1.27	2.76	2.58	1.4	100
2018	SEA	MLB	25	0	0	0	8	1	8^{1}	13	0	2.2	4.3	4	33%	.394	1.80	2.16	7.26	-0.2	98
2019	*SEA*	*MLB*	*26*	*2*	*1*	*0*	*33*	*2*	*34^{2}*	*33*	*5*	*3.4*	*9.6*	*37*	*41%*	*.304*	*1.33*	*4.29*	*4.63*	*0.2*	*97*

Breakout: 13% Improve: 21% Collapse: 8% Attrition: 18% MLB: 33% *Comparables: Evan Scribner, Cody Ege, Jonathan Aro*

Festa became the second East Stroudsburg Warrior to toe a big-league bump when he debuted last June, and he should be in the mix for the middle innings in the year ahead. He more or less abandoned his second breaker, a curveball, on the biggest stage, in favor of a hard four-seam/slider combo. A strong drive and whippy arm action help him propel those pitches effectively to the lower quadrants, and while the velocity backed up a tick last season he's still got plenty of it to get under barrels effectively in the middle innings. The slider has solid late action that minor-league hitters have consistently struggled to find, and if it plays similarly there's a chance for higher-leverage utility here. Is it the sexiest profile in town? No. Could we have waxed poetic in this space about Dan Vogelbach crushing Triple A and knocking on the door of what should finally be a legitimate shot at regular big-league at-bats? Yes. Yes, we could have.

Top Talents 25 and Under (born 4/1/93 or later):

1. J.P. Crawford
2. Justus Sheffield
3. Jarred Kelenic
4. Mallex Smith
5. Evan White
6. Justin Dunn
7. Logan Gilbert
8. Erik Swanson
9. Kyle Lewis
10. Julio Rodriguez

The kids are alriiiight? I guess? This list obviously looks a lot like the names above, and when your prospect list is bottom-third in baseball it's... it's not great. That the only two non-prospects among this group are brand-new acquisitions made this offseason should tell you all you need to know about the organization's recent operating philosophy.

There was a time, not that long ago and across multiple off-seasons, when J.P. Crawford was one of the best prospects in all the land. We comped him to Jimmy Rollins in 2016, and he remained a 7/6-lookin' prospect as recently as our 2017 list iteration. The bat has stalled at the upper echelons of minor-league ball, wet-blanketed further in its development last year by multiple trips to the DL and inconsistent opportunity to test his mettle against the biggest boys. He made some encouraging tweaks in the homestretch, and nothing about the physicality or actions suggests he doesn't still have time to take anticipated strides forward. The Mariners are certainly banking on it after shipping one of their most valuable players to obtain his services.

For his part, Mallex Smith put together a top-line breakout campaign in Tampa last year, albeit one that looked a little less impressive once you climb under the hood. The batting average and stolen-base proclivity may have wowed fantasy baseballers far and wide, but DRC+ was much less impressed with what it deemed a below-average performance at the dish, while defensive metrics roundly agreed that Smith was not a helpful center fielder on balance. On the latter point, he's still young and fast, and defensive metrics are what they are. And on the former, it was a fun, hopefully stepping-stone style offensive campaign for a player in his first season of full-time duty. Another step forward in his development is possible, and the M's are currently committing a significant chunk of their young-player pot to the hope that he takes it.

St. Louis Cardinals

The State of the System:

The Cardinals system has thinned out significantly in recent years, due to graduations and trades, but who knows what plus regular lurks in the lair where Devil Magic is conjured.

The Top Ten:

1 **Alex Reyes RHP** OFP: 70 Likely: 60 ETA: Debuted in 2016
Born: 08/29/94 Age: 24 Bats: R Throws: R Height: 6'3" Weight: 175 Origin: International Free Agent, 2012

YEAR	TEAM	LVL	AGE	W	L	SV	G	GS	IP	H	HR	BB/9	K/9	K	GB%	BABIP	WHIP	ERA	DRA	WARP	PF
2016	MEM	AAA	21	2	3	0	14	14	65[1]	63	6	4.4	12.8	93	42%	.365	1.45	4.96	3.01	1.7	100
2016	SLN	MLB	21	4	1	1	12	5	46	33	1	4.5	10.2	52	44%	.283	1.22	1.57	3.45	0.9	94
2018	SLN	MLB	23	0	0	0	1	1	4	3	0	4.5	4.5	2	40%	.300	1.25	0.00	8.15	-0.1	92
2019	*SLN*	*MLB*	*24*	*6*	*4*	*0*	*16*	*16*	*84[2]*	*64*	*5*	*3.8*	*11.7*	*110*	*40%*	*.312*	*1.18*	*2.80*	*3.30*	*2.0*	*94*

Breakout: 26% Improve: 57% Collapse: 14% Attrition: 20% MLB: 86% *Comparables: Tyler Glasnow, Matt Harvey, Jordan Walden*

The Report: After missing all of 2017 due to Tommy John surgery, it looked like all systems were go for Reyes at the beginning of 2018. The "number-one-prospect-in-baseball" stuff was back and accounted for on rehab. His 2018 MLB debut in May looked fine, despite command issues that aren't uncommon for a pitcher coming off Tommy John. Reyes was then immediately shut down afterwards with a torn lat. He's only 24, and still has potentially the best stuff among all prospect arms, but man we are going to need to see it on the field at some point. The Cardinals might be best served easing him in as a reliever in 2019. That also might be his long term role now.

The Risks: Medium. On the one hand Reyes is literally as "major-league ready" as one can be while maintaining eligibility for a prospect list. On the other, he has functionally missed two full seasons. The lat injury isn't super concerning in and of itself but the larger pattern very much is.

Ben Carsley's Fantasy Take: Honestly, there isn't any one way to value (or devalue) Reyes at this point. If you think he's still a top-10 prospect because of his upside as a starter, I totally get it. If you think he's only a top-50 guy at this point thanks to the injuries and reliever risk, that's fair, too. Personally, I'm hedging my bets a bit and will probably have him somewhere in the 15-to-25 range. To each his own. Good luck if you own him!

2 **Nolan Gorman 3B** OFP: 70 Likely: 55 ETA: 2022
Born: 05/10/00 Age: 19 Bats: L Throws: R Height: 6'1" Weight: 210 Origin: Round 1, 2018 Draft (#19 overall)

YEAR	TEAM	LVL	AGE	PA	R	2B	3B	HR	RBI	BB	K	SB	CS	AVG/OBP/SLG	DRC+	VORP	BABIP	BRR	FRAA	WARP	PF
2018	JCY	RK	18	167	41	10	1	11	28	24	37	1	3	.350/.443/.664	210	25.2	.411	-0.7	3B(33) 7.6	2.2	109
2018	PEO	A	18	107	8	3	0	6	16	10	39	0	2	.202/.280/.426	77	2.3	.255	-0.5	3B(25) 3.9	0.3	102
2019	*SLN*	*MLB*	*19*	*252*	*26*	*6*	*0*	*12*	*28*	*13*	*97*	*0*	*0*	*.145/.188/.319*	*30*	*-15.8*	*.171*	*-0.6*	*3B 5*	*-1.1*	*94*

Breakout: 7% Improve: 9% Collapse: 0% Attrition: 4% MLB: 12% *Comparables: Rafael Devers, Domingo Santana, Nomar Mazara*

The Report: Gorman slid down draft rankings his senior season due to concerns about his hit tool and ultimate defensive home, but the bat sure looked fine in his pro debut. Gorman mashed 17 home runs in 63 games between the Appy and Midwest Leagues and it's not a small sample fluke, as he arguably had the biggest raw power in his draft class. The swing has some stiffness to it, but Gorman has a strong approach for an 18-year-old and should get most of his plus-plus raw power into games. I hate comps, but something like 2017-18 Travis Shaw could be a fair approximation of his bat at peak. Gorman isn't Travis Shaw with the glove though—there's a sentence I never thought I'd type—and there are concerns he might have to move off third base. He's not all that rangy at the hot corner and his arm is only "sufficient."

The Risks: Extreme. There are hit tool issues, perhaps positional ones, and his first taste of full-season ball came with a lot of swing-and-miss.

Ben Carsley's Fantasy Take: Gorman just ranked fifth on Bret Sayre's list of top-50 dynasty league signees from 2018, but he'd be third on my list. I love the power potential and the organizational fit, and those of you who've been along on this ride with me for a few years now won't be shocked that I'm willing to overlook the swing-and-miss to a certain extent. Gorman is a borderline top-50 overall prospect for me already, and he's the type of guy who we could all value the same way we look at Austin Riley right now in a year or two.

3 Dakota Hudson RHP

OFP: 60 Likely: 50 ETA: Debuted in 2018

Born: 09/15/94 Age: 24 Bats: R Throws: R Height: 6'5" Weight: 215 Origin: Round 1, 2016 Draft (#34 overall)

YEAR	TEAM	LVL	AGE	W	L	SV	G	GS	IP	H	HR	BB/9	K/9	K	GB%	BABIP	WHIP	ERA	DRA	WARP	PF
2016	PMB	A+	21	1	1	3	8	0	9^{1}	6	0	6.8	9.6	10	91%	.261	1.39	0.96	3.07	0.2	100
2017	SFD	AA	22	9	4	0	18	18	114	111	5	2.7	6.1	77	58%	.296	1.27	2.53	5.76	-0.8	106
2017	MEM	AAA	22	1	1	0	7	7	38^{2}	36	2	3.5	4.4	19	59%	.272	1.32	4.42	5.27	0.2	97
2018	MEM	AAA	23	13	3	0	19	19	111^{2}	107	1	3.1	7.0	87	59%	.313	1.30	2.50	3.50	2.6	94
2018	SLN	MLB	23	4	1	0	26	0	27^{1}	19	0	5.9	6.3	19	64%	.237	1.35	2.63	6.41	-0.5	93
2019	*SLN*	*MLB*	*24*	*3*	*1*	*0*	*53*	*0*	56^{1}	*49*	*5*	*4.0*	*8.0*	*50*	*56%*	*.293*	*1.32*	*4.09*	*4.78*	*0.1*	*94*

Breakout: 16% Improve: 35% Collapse: 27% Attrition: 44% MLB: 75% *Comparables: Jarred Cosart, Paul Blackburn, Chi Chi Gonzalez*

The Report: As mentioned above, the Cardinals like to debut their starting pitching prospects in the bullpen, but Hudson might be there to stay after showing off a dominant three-pitch mix in his two-month major-league trial. His fastball sits 96-98 with arm-side dive from the two-seamer; the occasional four-seamers show some cut. His cutter is more like a 92 mph slider and it can be patently unfair. His actual slider is the change of pace offering, as it sits in the mid-80s and features more cut that tilt. That doesn't make a lot of sense, but it works. He's shown a curve and change as a starter, but they lag behind and he works best as a three-pitch reliever. Hudson has struggled to harness his repertoire at times, but it's closer stuff, and this may end up more of a Trevor Rosenthal situation than a Carlos Martinez one.

The Risks: Low. He needs to clean up the control and command, but Hudson is ready to be an impact arm in the majors.

Ben Carsley's Fantasy Take: Hudson is a decent add for those of you who are hunting for saves in deep leagues, as he could have a good enough strikeout rate and WHIP to be worth rostering even if he's not closing. He may be the rare reliever who's good enough to sneak onto the back of the top-200 thanks in part his proximity to the majors and the relatively clearish path to closing time in St. Louis.

4 Andrew Knizner C

OFP: 55 Likely: 45 ETA: September 2019

Born: 02/03/95 Age: 24 Bats: R Throws: R Height: 6'1" Weight: 200 Origin: Round 7, 2016 Draft (#226 overall)

YEAR	TEAM	LVL	AGE	PA	R	2B	3B	HR	RBI	BB	K	SB	CS	AVG/OBP/SLG	DRC+	VORP	BABIP	BRR	FRAA	WARP	PF
2016	JCY	RK	21	222	35	12	1	6	42	21	21	0	0	.319/.423/.492	179	18.3	.331	-0.1	C(21) -0.4, 1B(19) -0.9	1.2	105
2017	PEO	A	22	191	18	10	1	8	29	9	22	1	1	.279/.325/.480	125	13.2	.282	0.5	C(26) -0.3, 1B(3) -0.1	0.9	96
2017	SFD	AA	22	202	27	13	0	4	22	14	27	0	1	.324/.371/.462	141	17.7	.355	0.5	C(49) -3.5	1.0	104
2018	SFD	AA	23	313	39	13	0	7	41	23	40	0	1	.313/.365/.434	133	21.9	.339	-1.4	C(74) -7.3	1.0	105
2018	MEM	AAA	23	61	3	5	0	0	4	4	8	0	0	.315/.383/.407	116	3.8	.370	-0.1	C(16) 1.8	0.5	92
2019	*SLN*	*MLB*	*24*	*178*	*16*	*7*	*0*	*5*	*20*	*7*	*34*	*0*	*0*	*.230/.268/.359*	*67*	*0.5*	*.260*	*-0.4*	*C -7*	*-0.7*	*94*

Breakout: 16% Improve: 37% Collapse: 0% Attrition: 21% MLB: 54% *Comparables: Kevin Plawecki, J.T. Realmuto, Willson Contreras*

The Report: Knizner actually has a pretty fun set of offensive tools. He has an excellent catcher's build and there's almost no extra weight on the frame. He has fair quick twitch movements and reacts well both offensively and defensively.

Knizner knows how to hit. He has plus bat speed, excellent weight transfer, a compact swing, and plus hand-eye that allows him to make solid contact around the field. He has a tendency to expand the zone, especially mid-late in counts, and he could benefit from more discipline. He has above-average raw power, but his compact swing and a penchant for going the other way suggests he'll have below-average in-game power. An adjustment to hit the ball out front more could potentially unlock another tier of offensive output.

It's less pretty behind the plate, as Knizner is a below-average receiver. He tends to stab a bit at pitches low in the zone and often won't get calls there. His arm is below-average and even though he can make up for it a bit with his quick transition and good footwork, he'll likely be fringe-average at controlling the run game and decline from there as he ages. He blocks balls well and won't give up too many passed balls, for what it's worth.

The Risks: Low. Outside of the makeup and hit tool, there's just not a ton to add value to the profile. As an offense-first catcher, there's a real chance he won't hit for enough power and get on base enough to start. He is a catcher who can hit though, so overall the risk that he won't at least be able to perform as a bench player is low.

Ben Carsley's Fantasy Take: Knizner may be an intriguing fantasy option down the line if and when he gets regular playing time. But between the fact that all catching prospects are just designed to hurt us and the odds that Knizner ends up as nothing more than a backup, he's not a guy dynasty leaguers need to worry about unless your league rosters 200-plus prospects.

5 Elehuris Montero 3B

OFP: 55 Likely: 45 ETA: 2021

Born: 08/17/98 Age: 20 Bats: R Throws: R Height: 6'3" Weight: 195 Origin: International Free Agent, 2014

YEAR	TEAM	LVL	AGE	PA	R	2B	3B	HR	RBI	BB	K	SB	CS	AVG/OBP/SLG	DRC+	VORP	BABIP	BRR	FRAA	WARP	PF
2016	DCA	RK	17	262	41	14	2	1	26	28	51	2	1	.260/.349/.352	104	4.7	.328	0.5	3B(60) 2.6	0.9	124
2017	CRD	RK	18	208	30	16	1	5	36	22	33	0	2	.277/.370/.468	140	10.3	.305	-0.5	3B(41) 2.8	0.8	109
2018	PEO	A	19	425	68	28	3	15	69	33	81	2	0	.322/.381/.529	163	39.7	.372	0.3	3B(77) 2.7	4.0	101
2018	PMB	A+	19	106	13	9	0	1	13	5	22	1	0	.286/.330/.408	117	5.7	.355	0.6	3B(20) 0.8	0.4	95
2019	*SLN*	*MLB*	*20*	*252*	*19*	*10*	*0*	*7*	*25*	*9*	*70*	*0*	*0*	*.163/.198/.290*	*27*	*-16.8*	*.195*	*-0.5*	*3B 1*	*-1.7*	*94*

Breakout: 13% Improve: 15% Collapse: 0% Attrition: 5% MLB: 15% *Comparables: Matt Dominguez, Rafael Devers, Matt Davidson*

The Report: Relatively unknown outside of prospecting circles, Montero enjoyed a breakout 2018 season. As a teenager, he torched Midwest League pitching to the tune of .322/.381/.522, earning a late season promotion to Palm Beach. He was arguably one of the most advanced bats in the league, featuring a quiet swing and a knack for barrelling the ball. Montero also shows an approach not often seen in someone so young, handling velocity well and rarely getting fooled on secondaries. There is power in his game as well, generated by his natural strength and a swing path that gets leverage.

In the field, Montero is not going to win any awards but he does have the tools to eventually become serviceable. Whether he sticks at the hot corner or not doesn't matter; it's all about the bat. There's a ton of pressure on it, but he has the physical skills to be one of the best hitters in the organization.

The Risks: High. Montero's limited defensively and has only one year above rookie ball under his belt. The quality approach he displayed in Peoria will have to translate against advanced pitching.

Ben Carsley's Fantasy Take: Annnnnnd we've already entered the flier portion of our program for fantasy. Montero's bat makes him interesting, and his lead time isn't too crazy for a dude few knew much about until reading the paragraphs above. That being said, Montero's upside isn't real high, and it's easy to imagine his defensive limitations pushing him to more of a bench-bat role. He might be a top-200 prospect, but just barely.

6 Malcom Nunez 3B

OFP: 55 Likely: 45 ETA: 2024

Born: 03/09/01 Age: 18 Bats: R Throws: R Height: 5'11" Weight: 205 Origin: International Free Agent, 2018

YEAR	TEAM	LVL	AGE	PA	R	2B	3B	HR	RBI	BB	K	SB	CS	AVG/OBP/SLG	DRC+	VORP	BABIP	BRR	FRAA	WARP	PF
2018	DCA	RK	17	199	44	16	2	13	59	26	29	3	0	.415/.497/.774	230	37.1	.437	0.5	3B(30) -1.0, 1B(5) 1.2	2.9	111
2019	*SLN*	*MLB*	*18*	*252*	*26*	*14*	*0*	*10*	*33*	*17*	*68*	*0*	*0*	*.221/.272/.414*	*82*	*-0.3*	*.262*	*-0.5*	*3B -1, 1B 0*	*-0.1*	*94*

Breakout: 0% Improve: 0% Collapse: 0% Attrition: 0% MLB: 0% *Comparables: Adalberto Mondesi, Wilmer Flores, Tommy Brown*

The Report: While the Mesa brothers were the biggest names to sign out of Cuba in 2018, Nunez might be the best long term bet with the bat. We don't normally describe right-handed swings as "pretty" but his qualifies, with advanced feel for the barrel and some present raw pop which might turn into legit juice in the future. He's a potential plus hit/power combination, and that's not scouting the "*Road to the Show* on rookie mode" stat line in the Dominican. He is still just a complex league guy though and the risk here is extreme both with the bat and especially the glove. Nunez is already quite stocky—the listed height and weight look roughly accurate—and he is far from a lock to stick at this corner of the infield. Regardless, the upside in the bat is well worth keeping an eye on his development for the next, oh, half decade or so.

The Risks: Extreme. We hate ranking Dominican complex guys as a rule, so the risk factor here is gonna be top-of-the-scale.

Ben Carsley's Fantasy Take: Nunez is one of my favorite lottery tickets in the low minors, and I'd rather take a flier on him in new player drafts than any of the legion of mid-rotation college arms people start popping once the premier bats are gone. He's only a top-200 guy because of the lead time, but Nunez should be a fun one to watch.

7 Griffin Roberts RHP

OFP: 55 Likely: 45 ETA: Late 2020 as a starter, 2019 as a reliever

Born: 06/13/96 Age: 23 Bats: R Throws: R Height: 6'3" Weight: 205 Origin: Round 1, 2018 Draft (#43 overall)

YEAR	TEAM	LVL	AGE	W	L	SV	G	GS	IP	H	HR	BB/9	K/9	K	GB%	BABIP	WHIP	ERA	DRA	WARP	PF
2018	CRD	RK	22	0	1	1	7	2	8^{2}	6	0	4.2	11.4	11	55%	.300	1.15	6.23	3.43	0.2	103
2019	*SLN*	*MLB*	*23*	*2*	*1*	*1*	*22*	*2*	31^{2}	*31*	*3*	*7.5*	*8.0*	*28*	*47%*	*.312*	*1.79*	*5.61*	*6.54*	*-0.5*	*94*

Breakout: 0% Improve: 0% Collapse: 0% Attrition: 0% MLB: 0% *Comparables: Tanner Anderson, Gerardo Concepcion, Matthew Carasiti*

The Report: Roberts was absolutely dominant his junior year at Wake Forest. He led the ACC in strikeouts, punching out 130 over 96 innings. A lot of those whiffs came off Roberts' slider, arguably the single best breaking ball in the draft class. Despite his low arm slot, he stays on top of the pitch well, and it is a potential wipeout, plus-plus offering with more consistency and refinement. He can dial the fastball up to 95, but usually works more in the low 90s as a starter, and there's the requisite, very occasional mid-80s change.

Roberts could move very quickly as a reliever on the strength of the slider, and the current repertoire, arm slot, and high-effort delivery point to a long term home in the bullpen. The Cardinals do like to stretch this type of arm out as a starter for a while, although Roberts' 2019 campaign will be delayed while he serves a 50-game suspension for a drug of abuse.

The Risks: Medium. Roberts has a major-league quality two-pitch mix right now, but right now is still a year or two away from pitching in the actual majors.

Ben Carsley's Fantasy Take: He's a Cardinals pitching prospect, so who knows? But as a rule, friends don't let friends draft reliever prospects. That's why we gotta pass on Roberts, even if he is among the more intriguing options among a group that shouldn't intrigue us.

8 Evan Mendoza 3B

OFP: 50 Likely: 40 ETA: 2020

Born: 06/28/96 Age: 23 Bats: R Throws: R Height: 6'2" Weight: 200 Origin: Round 11, 2017 Draft (#334 overall)

YEAR	TEAM	LVL	AGE	PA	R	2B	3B	HR	RBI	BB	K	SB	CS	AVG/OBP/SLG	DRC+	VORP	BABIP	BRR	FRAA	WARP	PF
2017	SCO	A-	21	182	34	14	3	3	28	16	33	1	2	.370/.431/.549	187	23.7	.449	0.3	3B(38) 4.8	2.2	107
2017	PEO	A	21	77	9	6	1	1	8	2	15	2	0	.270/.286/.419	98	4.2	.322	1.9	3B(13) -0.8, SS(1) 0.1	0.2	94
2018	PMB	A+	22	162	22	7	0	3	16	9	27	1	0	.349/.394/.456	156	14.7	.412	-2.4	3B(37) -0.4	0.9	96
2018	SFD	AA	22	402	36	12	2	5	26	30	77	1	1	.254/.315/.339	84	1.8	.309	-2.3	3B(88) 3.5, SS(9) -1.3	-0.2	104
2019	*SLN*	*MLB*	*23*	*252*	*22*	*9*	*1*	*6*	*26*	*11*	*60*	*0*	*0*	*.236/.270/.351*	*64*	*-5.2*	*.288*	*-0.4*	*3B 1, SS 0*	*-0.5*	*94*

Breakout: 14% Improve: 20% Collapse: 0% Attrition: 14% MLB: 22% *Comparables: Jefry Marte, Kaleb Cowart, Brent Morel*

The Report: Mendoza has a filled out, average build. He's 6-foot-2 with mostly good weight and average levers for his height. He's an average athlete due to quality body control, but he lacks quick twitch or explosive strength. Mendoza has quality hand-eye coordination, which shows itself both in the field and at the plate.

Mendoza has a compact swing and a good combination of hand-eye coordination and pitch recognition. The bat speed is just average, and he is aggressive on breaking stuff below the zone. Overall, he has the physical markers of an above-average hit tool if he can refine his plate discipline and cut down on the weak contact. He has good strength and average raw power, but the swing doesn't tap into it fully even when he gets out in front and pulls the ball. The lack of length in the swing, along with only fair bat speed, will likely limit his in-game power.

Mendoza has good hands in the field and plays a pretty clean third base. His range is limited by a lack of both quickness and foot speed, but his hands and plus arm still allow him to play an average 3B. He has good baseball instincts and likely won't have much trouble learning first base as well, if it comes to that.

The Risks: Medium. Mendoza has the physical abilities to win a bench role on an MLB roster come spring training 2019. Currently, his raw physical abilities aren't enough to overcome an overly aggressive approach that leads to weak contact and whiffs in bunches. Without improved discipline, MLB pitchers will be able to abuse the combo of a fringy approach and limited bat speed.

Ben Carsley's Fantasy Take: When your ceiling is Brian Anderson we don't have to care about you until you're playing every day.

9 Edmundo Sosa IF OFP: 50 Likely: 40 ETA: Debuted in 2018

Born: 03/06/96 Age: 23 Bats: R Throws: R Height: 5'11" Weight: 170 Origin: International Free Agent, 2012

YEAR	TEAM	LVL	AGE	PA	R	2B	3B	HR	RBI	BB	K	SB	CS	AVG/OBP/SLG	DRC+	VORP	BABIP	BRR	FRAA	WARP	PF
2016	PEO	A	20	378	42	13	1	3	30	19	71	5	4	.268/.307/.336	104	10.0	.325	-1.1	SS(85) 5.1, RF(1) 0.0	1.6	99
2016	PMB	A+	20	35	3	0	2	0	4	1	8	0	0	.294/.314/.412	116	2.2	.385	-0.3	SS(9) -0.3, 3B(1) 1.1	0.2	93
2017	PMB	A+	21	211	25	10	1	0	14	12	34	3	0	.285/.329/.347	105	10.2	.344	2.4	SS(41) 3.1, 2B(7) -1.0	0.9	90
2018	SFD	AA	22	279	34	17	1	7	32	9	52	1	2	.276/.308/.429	92	13.2	.319	1.4	SS(43) -4.8, 3B(11) 1.6	-0.2	104
2018	MEM	AAA	22	209	31	13	0	5	27	13	42	5	2	.262/.321/.408	89	8.4	.310	0.7	SS(28) 1.1, 2B(12) -0.3	0.4	94
2018	SLN	MLB	22	3	1	0	0	0	0	1	1	0	0	.000/.333/.000	84	-0.1	.000	0.0	2B(1) 0.0	0.0	93
2019	*SLN*	*MLB*	*23*	*37*	*4*	*2*	*0*	*1*	*4*	*1*	*9*	*0*	*0*	*.233/.264/.382*	*59*	*-0.5*	*.283*	*-0.1*	*SS 0*	*-0.1*	*94*

Breakout: 35% Improve: 43% Collapse: 3% Attrition: 31% MLB: 47% *Comparables: Wilmer Difo, Trevor Plouffe, Yairo Munoz*

The Report: Sosa is a good athlete with a filled out middle infielder's frame. He has a high waist with strong muscle and strength on his glutes and core. Sosa has some quick twitch and good body control.

The swing has some length to it, but Sosa generates plus bat speed and has good feel for barrel, which allows him to make hard contact around the plate. The swing comes through the zone flat more often than not and he doesn't hit for power unless he gets to the pitch on his front foot. Sosa has average raw power, but the swing doesn't tap into it efficiently and he will likely not hit for much pop in the big leagues. Sosa often gives away plate appearances by swinging at bad pitches and gets more trigger happy the longer the plate appearance goes. Even when he recognizes spin, he'll often throw his hands out and connect weakly. The approach currently limits the profile despite the physical ability for an above-average hit tool.

Defensively Sosa has fringy range at SS with a below-average arm, but he gobbles up everything around him like a 15-year veteran. His motions and footwork are smooth and consistent and the end result is that he can hold his own at SS, even if you wouldn't want him there full time. He has the quickness for 3B and already is an above-average glove at 2B as well.

Overall, Sosa's potential is tied to how much he can tame his free swinging habits and how much power he'll tap into. It's hard to see an everyday player without significant improvement in both areas.

The Risks: Medium. Guys with overly aggressive approaches and good physical hit tools tend to be pretty overrated as a general rule. The tease of what they can do always conflicts with the product they leave on the field at the MLB level. He looks more like a depth guy than an impact talent.

Ben Carsley's Fantasy Take: Watch list at best, dropped off your watch list at worst.

10 Luken Baker 1B OFP: 50 Likely: 40 ETA: 2021

Born: 03/10/97 Age: 22 Bats: R Throws: R Height: 6'4" Weight: 265 Origin: Round 2C, 2018 Draft (#75 overall)

YEAR	TEAM	LVL	AGE	PA	R	2B	3B	HR	RBI	BB	K	SB	CS	AVG/OBP/SLG	DRC+	VORP	BABIP	BRR	FRAA	WARP	PF
2018	CRD	RK	21	28	10	2	0	1	7	3	4	0	0	.500/.536/.708	213	3.9	.550	-0.7	1B(5) 0.1	0.2	109
2018	PEO	A	21	156	16	9	0	3	15	16	31	0	0	.288/.359/.417	144	2.7	.349	-1.4	1B(20) 0.3	0.6	101
2019	*SLN*	*MLB*	*22*	*252*	*23*	*10*	*0*	*6*	*27*	*17*	*63*	*0*	*0*	*.213/.264/.339*	*63*	*-7.1*	*.261*	*-0.5*	*1B 0*	*-0.8*	*94*

Breakout: 8% Improve: 10% Collapse: 0% Attrition: 9% MLB: 10% *Comparables: James Loney, Ronald Guzman, Jose Osuna*

The Report: Baker has a pretty broad range of possible outcomes based on his health and his ability to adjust to improved competition. The offensive tools themselves are massive. His fully filled out 6'4" frame carries elite raw and explosive strength.

Baker has impressive bat speed, despite a long swing. He has above-average hand-eye coordination and has a good feel for getting the barrel on the ball. Baker has a strong understanding of the zone and doesn't chase when he recognizes the pitch. Pitchers can beat him high and in with velocity, especially if there's the threat of a good breaking ball or changeup low in the zone. Baker could also occasionally be enticed into chasing quality off-speed low.

The raw power is double-plus, if not elite, and Baker will regularly put up crazy-high exit velocity numbers. The swing is currently a bit flat and tailored for line drives, but when he gets out in front of a pitch he can hit majestic bombs.

Baker is a liability in the field, as he is flat-out slow. He can make the routine plays at 1B and has an above-average arm to make strong throws to 2B (a shame, as his arm was elite before he got hurt). Baker is locked at 1B. Baker has to hit to provide even average MLB production due to his lack of supporting tools. His power and bat speed provide a large offensive ceiling that will be limited by his ability to adjust against quality breaking stuff and limit his weaknesses up and in against velocity due to his swing length.

The Risks: Medium. He's a first baseman in the low minors. The bat better be great.

Ben Carsley's Fantasy Take: We made it about halfway through, but here is your C.J. Cron comparison: this is a C.J. Cron-ass prospect.

The Next Five:

11 Dylan Carlson OF

Born: 10/23/98 Age: 20 Bats: B Throws: L Height: 6'3" Weight: 195 Origin: Round 1, 2016 Draft (#33 overall)

YEAR	TEAM	LVL	AGE	PA	R	2B	3B	HR	RBI	BB	K	SB	CS	AVG/OBP/SLG	DRC+	VORP	BABIP	BRR	FRAA	WARP	PF
2016	CRD	RK	17	201	30	13	3	3	22	16	52	4	2	.251/.313/.404	113	1.2	.333	-1.6	CF(41) 6.5, LF(9) 0.2	0.6	103
2017	PEO	A	18	451	63	18	1	7	42	52	116	6	6	.240/.342/.347	99	14.2	.323	2.6	RF(79) 0.8, CF(24) 0.1	0.7	97
2018	PEO	A	19	57	5	3	0	2	9	10	10	2	0	.234/.368/.426	135	1.4	.257	-0.7	RF(10) 2.3, CF(4) -0.3	0.4	101
2018	PMB	A+	19	441	63	19	3	9	53	52	78	6	3	.247/.345/.386	113	18.3	.286	1.7	RF(50) 4.7, LF(37) -0.1	1.2	94
2019	*SLN*	*MLB*	*20*	*252*	*19*	*7*	*0*	*6*	*24*	*16*	*76*	*0*	*0*	*.153/.211/.267*	*24*	*-16.3*	*.191*	*-0.5*	*RF -1, LF 1*	*-1.8*	*94*

Breakout: 9% Improve: 11% Collapse: 0% Attrition: 5% MLB: 11% *Comparables: Nomar Mazara, Caleb Gindl, Jesse Winker*

Getting to the Florida State League as a 19-year-old is no mean feat, and Carlson has draft pedigree to boot as the 33rd overall pick in 2017. Rany Jazayerli found that young prep picks have a huge long-term performance advantage over their older peers, so there's plenty of reason to be patient with Carlson. For ranking purposes though, this is a cohort of one, and Carlson hasn't consistently shown enough bat to carry a corner outfield profile so far in his professional career. It's possible that he could, as he is a large human who makes loud contact. He's also very patient at the plate, so perhaps all of our patience will be rewarded with an everyday player. Barring that, there's enough here to be an outfield bench bat at least.

12 Daniel Poncedeleon RHP

Born: 01/16/92 Age: 27 Bats: R Throws: R Height: 6'4" Weight: 185 Origin: Round 9, 2014 Draft (#285 overall)

YEAR	TEAM	LVL	AGE	W	L	SV	G	GS	IP	H	HR	BB/9	K/9	K	GB%	BABIP	WHIP	ERA	DRA	WARP	PF
2016	SFD	AA	24	9	8	0	27	27	151	128	10	3.3	7.3	122	46%	.269	1.22	3.52	4.03	1.9	98
2017	MEM	AAA	25	2	0	0	6	6	29	20	2	4.0	7.8	25	42%	.234	1.14	2.17	5.21	0.2	94
2018	MEM	AAA	26	9	4	0	19	18	96^{1}	69	4	4.7	10.3	110	30%	.272	1.24	2.24	3.89	1.8	92
2018	SLN	MLB	26	0	2	1	11	4	33	24	2	3.5	8.5	31	36%	.259	1.12	2.73	3.52	0.6	94
2019	*SLN*	*MLB*	*27*	*3*	*2*	*0*	*37*	*5*	*58^{2}*	*50*	*8*	*3.9*	*9.4*	*61*	*38%*	*.289*	*1.28*	*4.27*	*4.98*	*0.1*	*94*

Breakout: 3% Improve: 17% Collapse: 10% Attrition: 18% MLB: 36% *Comparables: Tyler Wagner, Chris Heston, Lucas Harrell*

The latest beneficiary of Cardinals Devil Magic, the 26-year-old Poncedeleon dominated the Pacific Coast League and didn't hit many speed bumps during his late-summer call up. The stuff isn't going to wow you here, as you'd probably guess from a 26-year-old ninth-round senior sign. He works primarily off a low-90s fastball with some armside run. He can get it up to 95 and has plus command of the pitch. His cutter has more run than tilt, but coming in around 90, it's an effective armside weapon. He has a potentially average change and curve as well. Poncedeleon can be a bit hittable—despite the plus command he likes to work up in the zone a bit too much at times—but is a ready-now backend starter with upper minors and a bit of major-league success under his belt already.

13 Genesis Cabrera LHP

Born: 10/10/96 Age: 22 Bats: L Throws: L Height: 6'1" Weight: 170 Origin: International Free Agent, 2013

YEAR	TEAM	LVL	AGE	W	L	SV	G	GS	IP	H	HR	BB/9	K/9	K	GB%	BABIP	WHIP	ERA	DRA	WARP	PF
2016	BGR	A	19	11	5	0	23	22	116	110	9	3.7	7.4	96	36%	.305	1.36	3.88	5.65	-0.9	99
2017	PCH	A+	20	4	5	0	13	12	69^{2}	45	3	3.2	7.8	60	39%	.230	1.00	2.84	3.91	1.1	98
2017	MNT	AA	20	5	4	0	12	12	64^{2}	75	6	3.8	7.1	51	37%	.332	1.58	3.62	4.28	0.7	102
2018	MNT	AA	21	7	6	0	21	20	113^{2}	90	11	4.5	9.8	124	35%	.282	1.29	4.12	5.12	0.3	92
2018	SFD	AA	21	1	3	0	5	5	24^{2}	24	3	4.7	7.7	21	37%	.300	1.50	4.74	5.21	0.0	105
2019	*SLN*	*MLB*	*22*	*1*	*0*	*0*	*11*	*0*	11^{1}	*10*	*2*	*4.5*	*9.1*	*11*	*34%*	*.299*	*1.39*	*4.52*	*5.26*	*0.0*	*94*

Breakout: 5% Improve: 10% Collapse: 4% Attrition: 7% MLB: 16%   *Comparables: Chaz Roe, Alex Burnett, Touki Toussaint*

Cabrera was the first of two prospects sent to the Cardinals for Tommy Pham—who already is doing a grand job ingratiating himself with Rays Twitter. It's easy to think of him as a better fit for the Rays, what with The Opener™ and their subsequent willingness to more aggressively pull pitchers before the third time through the order, but it's the rare team that can't use a lefty who bumps 95 with a plus cutter/slider in his locker as well. Given Cabrera's lack of a third pitch and less than ideal command/control, he's likely to end up a late-inning reliever in St. Louis. Ironically, his best chance of "starting" was back in Tampa.

14 Randy Arozarena OF

Born: 02/28/95 Age: 24 Bats: R Throws: R Height: 5'11" Weight: 170 Origin: International Free Agent, 2016

YEAR	TEAM	LVL	AGE	PA	R	2B	3B	HR	RBI	BB	K	SB	CS	AVG/OBP/SLG	DRC+	VORP	BABIP	BRR	FRAA	WARP	PF
2017	PMB	A+	22	295	38	22	3	8	40	13	53	10	4	.275/.333/.472	137	23.4	.313	-2.5	LF(47) 4.3, CF(13) -0.5	1.5	92
2017	SFD	AA	22	195	34	10	1	3	9	27	34	8	3	.252/.366/.380	112	8.2	.299	2.7	LF(40) 0.1, CF(4) -0.9	0.5	102
2018	SFD	AA	23	102	22	5	0	7	21	6	25	9	3	.396/.455/.681	193	15.4	.492	1.0	RF(12) 1.6, CF(6) -0.4	1.3	103
2018	MEM	AAA	23	311	42	16	0	5	28	28	59	17	5	.232/.328/.348	82	9.3	.278	0.8	LF(49) -2.7, RF(18) 0.2	-0.5	90
2019	*SLN*	*MLB*	*24*	*252*	*33*	*10*	*1*	*7*	*23*	*18*	*63*	*9*	*3*	*.218/.291/.356*	*82*	*2.8*	*.271*	*0.5*	*LF 0, RF 0*	*0.2*	*94*

Breakout: 10% Improve: 27% Collapse: 5% Attrition: 21% MLB: 46%   *Comparables: Austin Slater, Chad Huffman, Alex Hassan*

Arozarena follows the bench outfielder recipe to a tee. If there was a baseball version of Ruhlman's Twenty, he'd be first up in the tweener chapter. Arozarena is speedy, but not so speedy, or so instinctual, that he's a regular center field option. He makes contact, but an aggressive approach can limit the quality of it. There is distinctly not enough power for a corner. Marinating time is minimal at least, as Arozarena has 300+ Triple-A plate appearances under his belt now. He's also the kind of prospect who just ends up with a carrying hit tool in St. Louis; perhaps the Cardinals Devil Magic all along was just a good finishing salt, like Himalayan pink.

15 Justin Williams OF

Born: 08/20/95 Age: 23 Bats: L Throws: R Height: 6'2" Weight: 215 Origin: Round 2, 2013 Draft (#52 overall)

YEAR	TEAM	LVL	AGE	PA	R	2B	3B	HR	RBI	BB	K	SB	CS	AVG/OBP/SLG	DRC+	VORP	BABIP	BRR	FRAA	WARP	PF
2016	PCH	A+	20	203	23	11	0	4	31	6	26	0	1	.330/.350/.448	139	8.5	.361	-3.3	RF(43) 3.5	0.7	99
2016	MNT	AA	20	155	20	7	2	6	28	5	30	0	1	.250/.277/.446	87	3.7	.274	0.8	RF(34) -1.7	-0.3	100
2017	MNT	AA	21	409	53	21	3	14	72	37	69	6	2	.301/.364/.489	141	18.7	.334	-2.0	RF(80) -4.8, LF(7) 1.2	1.2	102
2018	TBA	MLB	22	1	0	0	0	0	0	0	0	0	0	.000/.000/.000	83	-0.5	.000	0.0	RF(1) 0.0	0.0	97
2018	DUR	AAA	22	386	41	18	0	8	46	25	81	4	3	.258/.313/.376	97	-4.8	.315	-2.7	RF(80) 13.7, LF(2) 1.0	1.3	98
2018	MEM	AAA	22	76	8	3	0	3	11	5	17	0	1	.217/.276/.391	86	-0.6	.240	-1.1	LF(10) 4.2, RF(7) 0.9	0.4	86
2019	*SLN*	*MLB*	*23*	*252*	*24*	*10*	*1*	*8*	*30*	*12*	*58*	*1*	*1*	*.224/.263/.374*	*68*	*-2.9*	*.261*	*-0.4*	*RF 1, LF 1*	*-0.1*	*94*

Breakout: 15% Improve: 32% Collapse: 1% Attrition: 8% MLB: 33%   *Comparables: J.D. Martinez, Preston Tucker, Tyler Austin*

It seems like a lifetime ago that Arizona drafted Williams in the second round. Now on his third organization after joining Cabrera in the Pham deal, Williams still doesn't regularly tap into his impressive raw tools. He struggles with lefty spin and almost all his power comes against righties. And despite ample raw pop, he doesn't lift the ball particularly often. Like Arozarena, he is basically major-league-ready, and likely a bench outfielder. If you prefer Williams' longside platoon pop potential to Arozarena's speed and glove, fair enough. There's not much to separate the two value-wise despite very different profiles.

Others of note:

Ivan Herrera, C, GCL Cardinals

Signed out of Panama for $200,000 in 2016. Herrera came stateside this summer and mashed. His bat is generally fringy, although his defensive skills are advanced. Herrera is close to physically maxed—oh to be built like a catcher at just 18—and profiles as more of a glove-first backup for now, but if he keeps hitting it doesn't take much to lift a projection in the catching prospect market.

Seth Elledge, RHP, Double-A Springfield

Acquired from the Mariners for sinker/slider relief arm Sam Tuivailala, Elledge is a potential... sinker/slider relief arm; Jerry is going to Jerry. Tuivailala is obviously already established in the majors and Elledge is not, but he isn't that far off. There's a little less fastball here, but Elledge touches 95 with good sink and his slider flashes above-average. So yeah, he's a 95-and-a-slider guy who could help the Cardinals pen by the end of the 2019. Or get traded to the Mariners for the next sinker/slider dude down the line.

Top Talents 25 and Under (born 4/1/93 or later):

1. Jack Flaherty
2. Alex Reyes
3. Paul DeJong
4. Nolan Gorman
5. Harrison Bader
6. Tyler O'Neill
7. Jordan Hicks
8. Dakota Hudson
9. Andrew Knizner
10. Elehuris Montero

The Cardinals' top young player made his first full season count, turning in the best strikeout rate of any rookie starter, the second-best WHIP, and going toe-to-toe with Walker Buehler in two showstopping late-season duels. By all rights and reason, One Year Ago You would have to assume the previous sentence was about Alex Reyes fulfilling his promise, but instead it was Jack Flaherty exceeding his. Strains and tears are piling up on Reyes' track record, and with them a greater and greater chance that he'll be limited to relief or some lesser impact role.

Flaherty, meanwhile, provides something far more tangible at this point: Results. With a 94 mph fastball and a gliding slider that perfectly suits his arm angle, he was one of baseball's 25 best pitchers in 2018—all the while notching an elite zone-contact rate that indicates surprising bat-missing ability and the potential for even more down the line. For so long, Reyes was the ace of the future; that belt now belongs to Flaherty.

Paul DeJong will never be a defensive asset or on-base machine, but Air-Ball Revolution Jhonny Peralta will hit 25 dingers as sure as the sun will rise. The question, then, is whether emerging talents like Harrison Bader can surpass that contribution. Some numbers would tell you Bader already did, but defense is nearly as hard to trust as it is to measure. Not even remotely a contact hitter, Bader's baserunning and center-field prowess won't feel nearly as exciting if a sky-high .358 BABIP and 11 plunkings vanish and turn his average-ish bat into a liability.

Comparing the disparate skills and flaws of corner outfield slugger Tyler O'Neill and potential impact relievers Jordan Hicks and Dakota Hudson feels like a fool's errand, but this fool is here to try. O'Neill, by virtue of not being a relief pitcher, has the highest ceiling. In fact, his minor-league numbers and Bowflex-commercial physique suggest a chance at stardom. The issue is an out-front swing that leads to pretty significant chase issues. At various levels of the minors, he adjusted and exhibited the power that makes him interesting without striking out too often. That process is going to be more difficult in the majors, but it's certainly possible.

Already famous for his triple-digit fastballs, Hicks went through this cycle in 2018: Wildness, followed by obsessive strike-throwing, followed by more walks when hitters just started swinging. As part of that retrenchment, he used his sharp slider more, to good effect. But as the Cardinals' offseason indicates, there is work to do before we can talk about him as a relief ace.

Far less tested at the highest level, Hudson's 27 big-league innings nonetheless look a lot like his time in the minors: Extreme, nearly inexplicable overachievement featuring bushels of walks, few strikeouts, and a sparkling ERA. We know he has a dynamite slider; the rest of the arsenal will likely confine him to the bullpen. Trusting him to beat his peripherals by several runs is not something we're ready to do yet, so the potential setup man falls to the bottom of this very volatile totem pole. For now.

Tampa Bay Rays

The State of the System:

The Rays have built a deep, balanced organization. This is one of the best farm systems in baseball.

The Top Ten:

1 Wander Franco SS   OFP: 70   Likely: 60   ETA: Late 2020 or after Super 2 in 2021

Born: 03/01/01   Age: 18   Bats: B   Throws: R   Height: 5'10"   Weight: 189   Origin: International Free Agent, 2017

YEAR	TEAM	LVL	AGE	PA	R	2B	3B	HR	RBI	BB	K	SB	CS	AVG/OBP/SLG	DRC+	VORP	BABIP	BRR	FRAA	WARP	PF
2018	PRI	RK	17	273	46	10	7	11	57	27	19	4	3	.351/.418/.587	179	35.3	.346	-0.4	SS(53) -5.3	1.6	115
2019	*TBA*	*MLB*	*18*	*252*	*22*	*4*	*2*	*9*	*29*	*7*	*50*	*0*	*0*	*.196/.217/.339*	*47*	*-6.8*	*.205*	*0.1*	*SS -2*	*-0.9*	*99*

Breakout: 0%   Improve: 0%   Collapse: 0%   Attrition: 0%   MLB: 0%   *Comparables: Adalberto Mondesi, Wilmer Flores, Tommy Brown*

The Report: I told the staff at the beginning of this year's list process that I wanted to keep these reports to 150-200 words, so "please try to keep them under 400." But to paraphrase Blaise Pascal, I have only made this report longer because I have not the time to make it shorter. Franco is a potential 6/6 offensive shortstop; those hit and power grades might be light. He has a bit of a dip/hitch to his load, but the bat speed is so good it doesn't matter. It's plus-plus, and he can let pitches really eat before he triggers. He knows the zone well already, recognizes spin, doesn't sell out for power. The raw power is plus. The game power will be plus. The ball makes *that* sound off the bat.

Despite a frame that elicited a scout quote of "he's kind of a block," Franco has enough present athletic tools to project as a shortstop in the majors. He likely won't be a regular at 7:55 PM on ESPN for Web Gems (man, is Baseball Tonight even still on?), but he's a rangy up-the-middle type with good hands and above-average arm strength. The arm grade can play down as he can get a bit scattershot on the move. He struggles with game speed at times, but I expect the defensive issues to get ironed out with further reps. He'd be a plus defender at second base if he does have to move. He's an above-average runner at present although I'd expect him to slow down to average in his 20s. Okay, the second half of this blurb isn't as exciting, so let's circle back to the bat. It makes Franco one of the elite prospects in the game, and as I said in his eyewitness from last summer, stuff him to all your friends.

The Risks: High. There was an argument to go 80/60 extreme on Franco. It's not a grade I really like to use, but we've had internal discussions about using it before; it's on the table. There were two issues with this. (1) I didn't quite see enough from him to go the full OFP 80... yet. (2) I don't see him as an extreme risk. The bat is that good and even a "generous" physical projection coupled with his defensive tools would make him an above-average second base glove. So 70/60 high it is. This may end up looking needlessly conservative too. No question about it, this is a fun gig.

Ben Carsley's Fantasy Take: Seems... pretty good! Given the premium hit tool, the chance for plus power and the fact that Franco will also run a little bit to start his career, it seems the only real flaw in his profile is that he'll grow up to be a Ray (that is one of only three digs I'm allowing myself this article, I promise). It'd be nice if Franco was a year-or-so closer, but he's a no-doubt top-25 dynasty prospect at this point, and he's on the short list of guys who could rank 1-1 a year from now. If visions of a Xander Bogaerts-like outcome are spinning in your head, well, it's tough to blame you.

2 Brent Honeywell RHP OFP: 70 Likely: 55 ETA: 2019

Born: 03/31/95 Age: 24 Bats: R Throws: R Height: 6'2" Weight: 180 Origin: Round 2, 2014 Draft (#72 overall)

YEAR	TEAM	LVL	AGE	W	L	SV	G	GS	IP	H	HR	BB/9	K/9	K	GB%	BABIP	WHIP	ERA	DRA	WARP	PF
2016	PCH	A+	21	4	1	0	10	10	56	43	5	1.8	10.3	64	33%	.279	0.96	2.41	2.35	2.0	95
2016	MNT	AA	21	3	2	0	10	10	59^{1}	51	4	2.1	8.0	53	29%	.287	1.10	2.28	4.70	0.3	99
2017	MNT	AA	22	1	1	0	2	2	13	4	1	2.8	13.8	20	45%	.158	0.62	2.08	0.47	0.7	98
2017	DUR	AAA	22	12	8	0	24	24	123^{2}	130	11	2.3	11.1	152	42%	.366	1.30	3.64	3.37	3.2	98
2019	*TBA*	*MLB*	*24*	*2*	*3*	*0*	*8*	*8*	*40*	*37*	*5*	*2.9*	*9.2*	*41*	*36%*	*.295*	*1.24*	*3.94*	*4.28*	*0.5*	*99*

Breakout: 12% Improve: 27% Collapse: 13% Attrition: 26% MLB: 46% *Comparables: Adam Morgan, Kyle Gibson, Edwar Cabrera*

The Report: Honeywell was one of several high-end pitching prospects to come down with a torn UCL shortly after arriving at camp last February. He was set to compete for a major-league rotation spot (lol j/k he wasn't coming up until the end of April... maybe), coming off a dominant 2017 in the upper minors. He missed all of 2018, but is throwing off a mound again, and should be ready around Memorial Day, depending on how his rehab goes. So there isn't much to change in the report this year. Well, at least we don't have any new info one way or the other. Surgery can change things. But assuming Honeywell's stuff comes back, he will quickly be one of the best pitching prospects in baseball again, and quickly after that, a major-league starter. He's shown plus velocity and five pitches in total that project as average or better, so it doesn't even have to come all the way back for him to be an effective pitcher.

The Risks: High. This is the default "dude hasn't thrown a pro pitch since Tommy John" risk.

Ben Carsley's Fantasy Take: This tends to happen to a few pitchers we rank every year—last year it was Honeywell and A.J. Puk, this year it will be Michael Kopech—but when a great arm like this gets TJ, we basically just lock their value in as-is and add in a half-tick of risk. That means Honeywell should be in the conversation once more for a top-25 spot on our dynasty top-101, although his lack of truly elite fantasy upside may push him a little lower. That being said, assuming he's healthy, he's among the best bets in the minors to at least surface as a reliable fantasy SP3/4, and there's always the chance for a little more.

3 Jesus Sanchez OF OFP: 60 Likely: 50 ETA: Early 2020

Born: 10/07/97 Age: 21 Bats: L Throws: R Height: 6'3" Weight: 210 Origin: International Free Agent, 2014

YEAR	TEAM	LVL	AGE	PA	R	2B	3B	HR	RBI	BB	K	SB	CS	AVG/OBP/SLG	DRC+	VORP	BABIP	BRR	FRAA	WARP	PF
2016	RAY	RK	18	173	25	6	8	4	31	6	31	1	5	.323/.341/.530	145	13.7	.371	-0.9	CF(31) 1.9, RF(10) -1.3	0.6	98
2016	PRI	RK	18	53	8	4	0	3	8	3	12	1	0	.347/.385/.612	175	7.5	.412	0.9	LF(11) 0.5, CF(3) -0.1	0.4	100
2017	BGR	A	19	512	81	29	4	15	82	32	91	7	2	.305/.348/.478	127	29.4	.349	3.4	LF(78) 14.0, RF(19) -0.5	3.6	104
2018	PCH	A+	20	378	56	24	2	10	64	15	71	6	3	.301/.331/.462	133	20.0	.350	-1.5	RF(78) 1.8, CF(7) -1.4	1.2	99
2018	MNT	AA	20	110	14	8	0	1	11	11	21	1	1	.214/.300/.327	93	-0.8	.263	0.7	RF(26) -0.8, CF(1) 0.0	-0.1	94
2019	*TBA*	*MLB*	*21*	*252*	*21*	*10*	*0*	*8*	*28*	*7*	*67*	*1*	*0*	*.200/.219/.340*	*48*	*-9.0*	*.238*	*-0.5*	*RF -1, CF 0*	*-1.0*	*99*

Breakout: 5% Improve: 15% Collapse: 0% Attrition: 9% MLB: 16% *Comparables: Justin Williams, Jorge Bonifacio, Marcell Ozuna*

The Report: Sanchez has one of the most projectable frames in baseball and a potential plus hit/power combo, but the on-field performance didn't quite match the tools in 2018. You'd be forgiven for wanting to continue betting on that sweet lefty swing though, or that a dozen or so of his 30+ doubles will turn into home runs as he fills out. Sanchez's swing has plenty of lift, and there's enough present bat control to project him getting most of that plus raw power into games. He tends to have an overly expansive view of what he actually can hit though, and his aggressive approach got undone in a brief AA cameo. He's also already primarily a right fielder, and while—in 2018 at least—that might have partially been due to wanting to get Joshua Lowe as many of the center field reps as possible, Sanchez is ticketed for a corner regardless. That puts pressure on the bat to play to projection, but it's a bet we're willing to make.

The Risks: Medium. It's a corner outfield profile with a power projection bet and some brief Double-A struggles in 2018. So it's not exactly "safe," as much as we like the bat.

Ben Carsley's Fantasy Take: Sanchez's upside may be a bit oversold in some dynasty circles—he's not the next great outfield prospect—but he's a reasonably safe bet to at least become a fantasy OF4/5, and there's a definite OF3 ceiling to boot. In his early days or off years, Sanchez could hit .270 or so with 15-20 homers and solid but unremarkable RBI/run totals. In his best years, look for 2018 Eddie Rosario (.288/323/.479 with 24 homers) as a solid statistical comp. Add in a reasonable timetable (even factoring in the Rays' conservative approach) and you get a top-50 dynasty prospect.

4 Brendan McKay 1B

OFP: 60 Likely: 50 ETA: 2020; the pitching prospect here will be ready in 2019.

Born: 12/18/95 Age: 23 Bats: L Throws: L Height: 6'2" Weight: 212 Origin: Round 1, 2017 Draft (#4 overall)

YEAR	TEAM	LVL	AGE	PA	R	2B	3B	HR	RBI	BB	K	SB	CS	AVG/OBP/SLG	DRC+	VORP	BABIP	BRR	FRAA	WARP	PF
2017	HUD	A-	21	149	16	4	1	4	22	21	33	2	0	.232/.349/.376	117	3.8	.281	-1.3	1B(21) -1.1, P(6) 0.1	-0.2	93
2018	BGR	A	22	91	12	2	0	1	16	28	13	0	0	.254/.484/.333	175	1.0	.306	-3.1	1B(9) -0.3, P(6) 0.1	0.4	101
2018	PCH	A+	22	139	19	6	1	5	21	16	38	0	0	.210/.317/.403	96	1.6	.260	0.5	1B(18) -0.4, P(11) -0.3	-0.2	101
2019	*TBA*	*MLB*	*23*	*252*	*22*	*4*	*0*	*8*	*26*	*25*	*74*	*0*	*0*	*.141/.228/.268*	*23*	*-19.0*	*.163*	*-0.4*	*1B -2*	*-2.2*	*99*

Breakout: 6% Improve: 17% Collapse: 0% Attrition: 16% MLB: 21% *Comparables: Chris Parmelee, Chris McGuiness, Max Muncy*

YEAR	TEAM	LVL	AGE	W	L	SV	G	GS	IP	H	HR	BB/9	K/9	K	GB%	BABIP	WHIP	ERA	DRA	WARP	PF
2017	HUD	A-	21	1	0	0	6	6	20	10	3	2.2	9.4	21	53%	.159	0.75	1.80	3.10	0.5	93
2018	BGR	A	22	2	0	0	6	6	24^2	8	1	0.7	14.6	40	63%	.167	0.41	1.09	2.63	0.8	103
2018	PCH	A+	22	3	2	0	11	9	47^2	45	2	2.1	10.2	54	39%	.350	1.17	3.21	3.05	1.2	99
2019	*TBA*	*MLB*	*23*	*3*	*4*	*0*	*17*	*12*	*52^2*	*47*	*8*	*3.4*	*9.5*	*56*	*42%*	*.288*	*1.28*	*4.25*	*4.62*	*0.5*	*99*

Breakout: 8% Improve: 11% Collapse: 3% Attrition: 9% MLB: 17% *Comparables: Matt Bowman, Jake McGee, Eric Surkamp*

The Report: Shohei Ohtani came to the majors as a fully-formed two-way threat. With Brendan McKay, we get to watch the actual developmental process on both sides. It's made him, uh, a difficult prospect to grade and rank through our normal channels. The pitching side is fairly easy to deal with. McKay flashed a little more velocity in 2018, making the fastball comfortably plus. He has a major-league ready above-average slider, a potentially average curve and change, and feel and command for everything. While he doesn't have huge upside as a starter, he might be in the majors already if he was solely a pitcher.

As a hitter, it's tough to discern much from a major college bat playing three days a week in A-ball as a 22-year-old. He has the raw power and approach to be a viable 1B/DH option on his off days, but he's unlikely to be an Ohtani-level force at the plate. There's ways to leverage that of course, but he wouldn't be a 101 guy as a hitter. It does save a roster spot, and it's really neat. You can make an argument McKay is one of the most talented baseball prospects in the minors, but we have to project "actual major-league role outside of the talent vacuum" more here than usual.

There's also added development risk and lead time. The oblique injury that sidelined him for six weeks in 2018 is an example. Things you could maybe play through, you can't pitch through. McKay is already 23 and didn't hit so well in Charlotte that you'd move him to Double-A on his performance there alone, even if the arm almost demands it. Perhaps 2019 and the upper minors will clarify things. Perhaps not.

The Risks: Low and High, sort of. He's a very polished pitcher and would be a Top 101 prospect just on the arm, but the dual development path makes things slower and riskier.

Ben Carsley's Fantasy Take: McKay might be a fine MLB prospect, but for my money he's among the more overrated plays in dynasty. Now that we project the bat to be more "nice for a team to have" than "everyday first baseman" quality, we're looking at a fantasy SP4/5 who may be able to occasionally add a little bit of offensive value depending on your league format. Given his proximity to the majors and his floor, that might be enough to get McKay on the 101, but he won't sniff the top-50. If someone still wants to treat him as one of the game's elite prospects thanks to his name value and draft slot, you should be willing to move him.

5 **Lucius Fox SS** OFP: 60 Likely: 50 ETA: Early 2020

Born: 07/02/97 Age: 21 Bats: B Throws: R Height: 6'1" Weight: 180 Origin: International Free Agent, 2015

YEAR	TEAM	LVL	AGE	PA	R	2B	3B	HR	RBI	BB	K	SB	CS	AVG/OBP/SLG	DRC+	VORP	BABIP	BRR	FRAA	WARP	PF
2016	AUG	A	18	331	46	6	4	2	16	37	76	25	7	.207/.305/.277	72	11.4	.273	5.6	SS(70) -4.8	-0.3	95
2017	BGR	A	19	345	45	13	3	2	27	33	80	27	10	.278/.362/.361	110	13.4	.371	0.2	SS(71) -3.8	0.9	105
2017	PCH	A+	19	131	19	3	0	1	12	12	33	3	3	.235/.321/.287	82	1.5	.317	-0.6	SS(29) 4.4	0.4	100
2018	PCH	A+	20	404	54	17	1	2	30	42	79	23	7	.282/.371/.353	124	22.3	.358	2.1	SS(79) -1.5	1.8	98
2018	MNT	AA	20	120	14	3	1	1	9	8	20	6	2	.221/.284/.298	70	1.3	.259	0.6	SS(26) -0.7	-0.1	94
2019	*TBA*	*MLB*	*21*	*252*	*27*	*4*	*0*	*5*	*17*	*15*	*69*	*7*	*3*	*.170/.224/.252*	*28*	*-11.8*	*.215*	*0.6*	*SS -1*	*-1.3*	*99*

Breakout: 4% Improve: 5% Collapse: 0% Attrition: 2% MLB: 5% *Comparables: Tyler Wade, Gavin Cecchini, Jose Pirela*

The Report: I couldn't stop Jarrett from putting a Batman reference in the Annual w/r/t Fox, but we will play it straight here. Fox is a speedy, slick-fielding shortstop, a lock to stick at the 6 and a potential plus glove there. He's a 70 runner who was marginally more efficient on the bases in 2018, even if he's still a bit raw there. He should continue to get opportunities to steal though due to a potential plus hit tool and a good approach at the plate.

The obvious flaw here is—Bahamian Home Run Derby captainship aside—a distinct lack of power. A wide base and simple weight transfer, coupled with a slight, but athletic frame, doesn't bode much for additional power projection either. Upper minors pitching may challenge him more and cut into that walk rate as well. As long as Fox can line enough balls over the infielders' heads, the glove and speed will carry the rest of the profile. If not, he will end up as more of a utility infielder.

The Risks: Medium. As good as that glove is, Fox has to show enough with the stick in the upper minors before we fully buy into a plus everyday profile.

Ben Carsley's Fantasy Take: Fox may not have a very exciting fantasy profile, but he's got a useful one. Even if Fox never truly clicks offensively and becomes a down-the-order slap hitter, his glove and speed should keep him in the lineup often enough to threaten for around 30 steals a year. That'd make him worthy of a bench spot in just about any league, and it makes him a starter in deeper formats. Add in the upside—that Fox may grow into solid averages and play every day—and he's probably a top-101 prospect, albeit more because of the scarcity of stolen bases than anything else. Also, spying on 30 million people isn't part of his job description.

6 **Shane Baz RHP** OFP: 60 Likely: 50 ETA: 2023

Born: 06/17/99 Age: 20 Bats: R Throws: R Height: 6'3" Weight: 190 Origin: Round 1, 2017 Draft (#12 overall)

YEAR	TEAM	LVL	AGE	W	L	SV	G	GS	IP	H	HR	BB/9	K/9	K	GB%	BABIP	WHIP	ERA	DRA	WARP	PF
2017	PIR	RK	18	0	3	0	10	10	23^{2}	26	2	5.3	7.2	19	51%	.348	1.69	3.80	5.57	0.1	96
2018	BRI	RK	19	4	3	0	10	10	45^{1}	45	2	4.6	10.7	54	64%	.344	1.50	3.97	4.64	0.7	98
2018	PRI	RK	19	0	2	0	2	2	7	11	1	7.7	6.4	5	48%	.417	2.43	7.71	10.04	-0.3	111
2019	*TBA*	*MLB*	*20*	*2*	*4*	*0*	*10*	*10*	37^{2}	*39*	*5*	*8.6*	*6.7*	*28*	*52%*	*.298*	*2.00*	*6.50*	*7.06*	*-0.7*	*99*

Breakout: 0% Improve: 0% Collapse: 0% Attrition: 0% MLB: 0% *Comparables: Sandy Alcantara, Wandy Peralta, Clay Holmes*

The Report: Although he has mostly just held serve from his status/report last year as the 12th overall pick and a back end 101 prospect, Baz was a heckuva player to be named later in the Archer deal. He still offers mid-90s heat and a potential plus slider, albeit amidst outstanding questions about his delivery and third pitch. Baz has a full four-pitch mix with both the change and curve having a chance to get to average. The arm action is compact, but high effort, and the delivery has the kind of late torque you associate with fringy command projection, or perhaps a move to the pen. Baz has an electric arm though, and the upside in the profile makes him one of the most intriguing teenage arms in baseball.

The Risks: High. Third pitch and command questions, only a short-season track record.

Ben Carsley's Fantasy Take: We may have been a bit too aggressive on Baz when we ranked him 57th overall in last season's top-101, but Baz still has Great Stuff™ and a promising ceiling as a fantasy SP3/4. The lead time and solid-but-not great ceiling should conspire to lower him in the rankings this time around, but he's still got an outside shot at making our newest iteration of the top-101.

7 Vidal Brujan 2B OFP: 60 Likely: 50 ETA: 2021

Born: 02/09/98 Age: 21 Bats: B Throws: R Height: 5'9" Weight: 155 Origin: International Free Agent, 2014

YEAR	TEAM	LVL	AGE	PA	R	2B	3B	HR	RBI	BB	K	SB	CS	AVG/OBP/SLG	DRC+	VORP	BABIP	BRR	FRAA	WARP	PF
2016	RAY	RK	18	223	41	12	5	1	8	14	15	8	5	.282/.344/.406	140	14.9	.301	1.8	2B(49) 3.8	1.2	98
2017	HUD	A-	19	302	51	15	5	3	20	34	36	16	8	.285/.378/.415	148	20.6	.321	-3.7	2B(65) 14.9	2.6	92
2018	BGR	A	20	434	86	18	5	5	41	48	53	43	15	.313/.395/.427	141	41.0	.351	8.2	2B(88) 4.4	4.0	100
2018	PCH	A+	20	114	26	7	2	4	12	15	15	12	4	.347/.434/.582	165	13.9	.380	1.0	2B(24) 4.5	1.4	101
2019	*TBA*	*MLB*	*21*	*252*	*29*	*7*	*1*	*6*	*19*	*12*	*50*	*9*	*3*	*.180/.220/.294*	*36*	*-9.7*	*.201*	*1.1*	*2B 5*	*-0.5*	*99*

Breakout: 23% Improve: 31% Collapse: 1% Attrition: 13% MLB: 32% *Comparables: Mookie Betts, Jose Ramirez, Jonathan Schoop*

The Report: Brujan's elite speed has been his calling card since signing out of the Dominican Republic in 2015. As a second baseman with no other standout tool, however, he was often overlooked in our world. That changed last season, as the bat took a major step forward and he slashed .320/.403/.459 across two levels.

Brujan is aggressive at the plate but has above-average contact ability and a solid understanding of the strike zone. His swing stays in the zone for a long time and he adjusts well to secondaries. While not a huge part of his game, there is some sneaky power generated by above-average bat speed. He's aggressive on the bases and has double-plus raw speed. Defensively, Brujan is limited to second base. He's raw there but his natural athleticism suggests he'll eventually become adequate. The bat and speed portend a future everyday major-leaguer at the keystone.

The Risks: High. His defensive limitations put pressure on the bat to excel. He made the Midwest League look easy but will have to prove it at every level.

Ben Carsley's Fantasy Take: Wow, my love of speedy middle infielders matches up against my hatred of the Rays. A true unstoppable force vs. immovable object scenario for ya boy here. Honestly, Brujan's profile isn't widely dissimilar to what Jose Peraza's was as a prospect (except Brujan is even more limited defensively), and we all know what I thought of the Brave-turned-Dodger-turned-Red. Peraza may not be lighting the world on fire, but he's actually been a pretty useful fantasy piece thanks to his speed. Brujan could profile similarly, though there's always the risk that his limitations will conspire to push him to a bench role. Overall the profile is limited enough that it may keep him off the top-101, but then again we do love speed...

8 Matthew Liberatore LHP OFP: 60 Likely: 50 ETA: 2022

Born: 11/06/99 Age: 19 Bats: L Throws: L Height: 6'5" Weight: 200 Origin: Round 1, 2018 Draft (#16 overall)

YEAR	TEAM	LVL	AGE	W	L	SV	G	GS	IP	H	HR	BB/9	K/9	K	GB%	BABIP	WHIP	ERA	DRA	WARP	PF
2018	RAY	RK	18	1	2	0	8	8	27^2	16	0	3.6	10.4	32	45%	.258	0.98	0.98	3.07	0.9	98
2019	*TBA*	*MLB*	*19*	*1*	*3*	*0*	*8*	*8*	31^1	*31*	*4*	*6.8*	*8.0*	*28*	*43%*	*.296*	*1.76*	*5.93*	*6.44*	*-0.3*	*99*

Breakout: 0% Improve: 0% Collapse: 0% Attrition: 0% MLB: 0% *Comparables: Jaime Barria, Raul Alcantara, Jason Garcia*

The Report: Liberatore was one of the top players available in last June's draft. He's a big lefty with three potential plus pitches and smooth, if somewhat inconsistent mechanics. He fell to the 16th pick for reasons we can't entirely explain, where the Rays were quite happy to snap him up. If there was a perceived signability problem, it didn't manifest, because he signed for slightly under the slot value even though he was taken a dozen picks later than expected.

Liberatore was in discussion to make the 101 until the very end of the process. We broadly agree that he was the best prep pitcher out of last year's draft right now. This is probably the deepest system in baseball for this particular grade level. And when in doubt, we're going to give the edge to players with more of a substantive track record than high school showcases, some short stints in the complex, and one game in the Appy. The difference between 3-10 in this system isn't huge on talent.

The Risks: Extreme. He's a prep pitcher. His fastball velocity has never been consistent and dipped after the draft, which is both entirely normal for prep pitchers transitioning to pro ball and a reason everyone in the industry has been talking about the volatility inherent in drafting prep pitchers for the last several decades.

Ben Carsley's Fantasy Take: Liberatore has more name value than actual dynasty value right now thanks to his draft slot. If you want to call him a top-150 guy because he's left-handed with solid-average upside, knock yourself out. But don't kid yourself into thinking he's a top-101 (or better) guy yet.

9 Brandon Lowe 2B OFP: 55 Likely: 50 ETA: Debuted in 2018

Born: 07/06/94 Age: 24 Bats: L Throws: R Height: 6'0" Weight: 185 Origin: Round 3, 2015 Draft (#87 overall)

YEAR	TEAM	LVL	AGE	PA	R	2B	3B	HR	RBI	BB	K	SB	CS	AVG/OBP/SLG	DRC+	VORP	BABIP	BRR	FRAA	WARP	PF
2016	BGR	A	21	449	67	15	3	5	42	60	77	6	3	.248/.357/.343	116	14.0	.298	-1.3	2B(88) -9.2	0.1	99
2017	PCH	A+	22	367	62	34	3	9	46	47	65	6	3	.311/.403/.524	166	38.6	.366	2.0	2B(75) -1.1, 3B(2) -0.2	2.7	99
2017	MNT	AA	22	101	8	5	1	2	12	2	26	1	1	.253/.270/.389	73	0.5	.319	-1.3	2B(24) 0.8	-0.3	99
2018	MNT	AA	23	240	37	17	1	8	41	35	55	8	2	.291/.400/.508	158	25.7	.360	2.1	LF(26) 1.8, 2B(24) -3.2	1.7	94
2018	DUR	AAA	23	205	36	14	0	14	35	22	47	0	1	.304/.380/.613	171	24.4	.339	0.4	2B(31) 1.2, LF(13) 0.9	2.1	97
2018	TBA	MLB	23	148	16	6	2	6	25	16	38	2	1	.233/.324/.450	93	6.3	.279	0.8	2B(28) -0.6, LF(11) -0.3	0.3	102
2019	*TBA*	*MLB*	*24*	*340*	*43*	*17*	*1*	*15*	*46*	*29*	*84*	*3*	*1*	*.244/.316/.453*	*106*	*11.7*	*.287*	*-0.3*	*2B -1, RF 0*	*1.2*	*99*

Breakout: 12% Improve: 43% Collapse: 14% Attrition: 34% MLB: 75% *Comparables: Vince Belnome, Rob Refsnyder, Ryan Rua*

The Report: Lowe remains eligible for this list by exactly one at-bat after torching the high minors in 2018 and punching his ticket to TPA. The swing changes he made last year continued to pay dividends with added power to his profile in 2018. It's a leg kick and lift swing from a shorter middle infielder with good knowledge of the strike zone. You know how this can sometimes go. Lowe is stocky and strong and the power can play line-to-line despite only average bat speed. The swing can get a bit stiff as well, and he's going to be susceptible to better stuff down. This may mean more strikeouts and worse overall quality of contact against major-league arms, but Lowe shows enough feel for hitting to get most of this newfound power into games.

Everything else in the profile is average. He's limited to second base as any sort of regular, but should be fine there. The hit tool is going to be the ultimate arbiter of how this all plays out, and that kind of profile can be a bit high variance despite the rather stable skill set. Lowe could have some .260, 25 home runs seasons, but they may be mixed in with years where he's more of a platoon bat.

The Risks: Low(e). The Rays have a very crowded infield, but getting Lowe major-league at-bats should be a priority as any more action in Durham is just a waste of time.

Ben Carsley's Fantasy Take: I'll be honest—I suck at evaluating players with this type of profile. Part of me wants to overcompensate and buy in on Lowe since I've missed on similar guys in the past, but at the end of the day his modest upside doesn't justify any sort of heavy encouragement to buy in dynasty leagues. If you already own Lowe, congrats on getting in on the ground floor of a solid asset. If he's already owned, well, I don't think I'd be banging down the door to acquire him. Let's just all hope for a Scooter Gennett sequel while more realistically preparing for something more akin to off-peak Neil Walker.

10 Ronaldo Hernandez C OFP: 55 Likely: 45 ETA: 2021

Born: 11/11/97 Age: 21 Bats: R Throws: R Height: 6'1" Weight: 185 Origin: International Free Agent, 2014

YEAR	TEAM	LVL	AGE	PA	R	2B	3B	HR	RBI	BB	K	SB	CS	AVG/OBP/SLG	DRC+	VORP	BABIP	BRR	FRAA	WARP	PF
2016	DDR	RK	18	229	34	12	0	6	35	20	12	3	5	.340/.406/.485	175	28.8	.340	-1.2	C(32) -0.3	1.9	93
2017	PRI	RK	19	246	42	22	1	5	40	16	39	2	2	.332/.382/.507	160	23.7	.379	2.5	C(43) 1.1	1.9	109
2018	BGR	A	20	449	68	20	1	21	79	31	69	10	4	.284/.339/.494	132	39.2	.292	-0.8	C(85) 1.2	2.8	100
2019	*TBA*	*MLB*	*21*	*252*	*22*	*10*	*0*	*9*	*30*	*4*	*59*	*1*	*0*	*.204/.215/.353*	*48*	*-5.4*	*.228*	*-0.4*	*C 0*	*-0.6*	*99*

Breakout: 16% Improve: 24% Collapse: 1% Attrition: 19% MLB: 28% *Comparables: Francisco Mejia, Austin Romine, Gary Sanchez*

The Report: My first glimpse of Hernandez came this season during the Midwest League All-Star Game home run derby. He went toe to toe with Cleveland's Will Benson, eventually besting the former first-round pick. Hernandez's plus raw power was on display that night, but it was in my later looks where he showed he's more than just a big bat. He has natural bat-to-ball skills and plate discipline that complements his raw strength and plus bat speed. Relatively new to the position, Hernandez has also made great strides defensively. As the year progressed his comfort level as a receiver appeared to increase, and he looked more and more natural behind the dish. He has a strong arm and the physical tools to eventually become a solid major-league backstop.

The Risks: High. He's a young catcher who has yet to face upper level pitching.

Ben Carsley's Fantasy Take: I refuse to let my heart be broken by catching prospects any more, but Hernandez is a good one. With Danny Jansen and Keibert Ruiz both somewhat likely to exhaust their prospect eligibility in the next 18 months, Hernandez is a solid bet for the top dynasty catching prospect thereafter. We're still quite a ways away from that future, however, and Hernandez's lead time and... well... position will likely keep him from top-101 status. He won't miss by much though.

The Next Five:

11 Shane McClanahan LHP

Born: 04/28/97 Age: 22 Bats: L Throws: L Height: 6'1" Weight: 188 Origin: Round 1C, 2018 Draft (#31 overall)

YEAR	TEAM	LVL	AGE	W	L	SV	G	GS	IP	H	HR	BB/9	K/9	K	GB%	BABIP	WHIP	ERA	DRA	WARP	PF
2019	*TBA*	*MLB*	*22*	*2*	*3*	*0*	*8*	*8*	*33^1*	*29*	*3*	*5.1*	*8.1*	*30*	*45%*	*.271*	*1.45*	*4.54*	*4.93*	*0.2*	*99*

Breakout: 4% Improve: 4% Collapse: 0% Attrition: 2% MLB: 4% *Comparables: Clay Holmes, Edward Paredes, Elvin Ramirez*

A lot of what we wrote above with Liberatore applies to McClanahan as well, except the culprit for his draft-day slide is more obvious. He struggled down the stretch of the college season and already has Tommy John on his resume. He's a lefty who throws 100 with two potential above-average secondaries, but there is some violence in his delivery and he has struggled to consistently throw strikes. He fits broadly into the same range as 3-10 as well, albeit with more health and reliever risk. I would expect the Rays to try to keep him in the rotation as long as possible, but he could move very quickly as a reliever if Tampa were so inclined.

12 Nathaniel Lowe 1B

Born: 07/07/95 Age: 23 Bats: L Throws: R Height: 6'4" Weight: 235 Origin: Round 13, 2016 Draft (#390 overall)

YEAR	TEAM	LVL	AGE	PA	R	2B	3B	HR	RBI	BB	K	SB	CS	AVG/OBP/SLG	DRC+	VORP	BABIP	BRR	FRAA	WARP	PF
2016	HUD	A-	20	285	26	18	2	4	40	30	39	1	0	.300/.382/.437	165	20.7	.338	1.2	1B(65) 2.9	1.8	95
2017	BGR	A	21	269	34	13	0	5	35	36	53	0	1	.293/.387/.415	136	14.0	.356	-0.2	1B(49) 0.2	1.0	105
2017	PCH	A+	21	203	21	10	1	2	24	28	53	1	1	.249/.355/.353	108	0.6	.345	-0.5	1B(51) -1.5	-0.3	99
2018	PCH	A+	22	220	39	15	0	10	44	25	33	0	0	.356/.432/.588	207	22.6	.391	-2.4	1B(35) -2.9	1.7	100
2018	MNT	AA	22	225	36	11	0	13	42	35	30	1	1	.340/.444/.606	211	33.7	.349	1.9	1B(39) -0.4	2.7	91
2018	DUR	AAA	22	110	18	6	1	4	16	8	27	0	0	.260/.327/.460	116	1.4	.319	-1.2	1B(25) -0.1	0.0	99
2019	*TBA*	*MLB*	*23*	*240*	*30*	*10*	*0*	*9*	*28*	*21*	*55*	*0*	*0*	*.233/.302/.408*	*88*	*0.4*	*.268*	*-0.5*	*1B -1*	*0.0*	*99*

Breakout: 10% Improve: 29% Collapse: 5% Attrition: 23% MLB: 47% *Comparables: Ji-Man Choi, Rhys Hoskins, Travis Shaw*

Now we shift gears to a more common archetype of our first twenty lists this year—and really, every list, every year—the slugging first base prospect. Lowe #2 had a breakout year in 2018, slugging 27 home runs and posting a better than 10% walk rate across three levels. He is already 23, and was a 13th round draft pick out of Mississippi State, so his age and pedigree aren't going to wow you. But you can't argue with the production.

With these profiles the question is always: "But will he hit enough in the majors?" It's a length and strength swing to get to his borderline plus-plus raw power, and commensurate stiffness as well. But Lowe isn't merely a one-dimensional slugger, even though I expect any major-league success to look Three True Outcome-ish. He has some feel for hitting and can drive the ball throughout the strike zone. I expect better velocity will beat him more often in the majors, and he's not going to be much more than passable in the field, but he should be able to take up the mantle of league-average Rays first baseman. For a time, at least. They go through them about as often as Spinal Tap cycles through drummers. At least a DFA or trade to Seattle is preferable to being felled by a bizarre gardening accident.

13 Ryan Boldt OF

Born: 11/22/94 Age: 24 Bats: L Throws: R Height: 6'2" Weight: 210 Origin: Round 2, 2016 Draft (#53 overall)

YEAR	TEAM	LVL	AGE	PA	R	2B	3B	HR	RBI	BB	K	SB	CS	AVG/OBP/SLG	DRC+	VORP	BABIP	BRR	FRAA	WARP	PF
2016	HUD	A-	21	186	17	5	1	1	15	10	24	8	9	.218/.280/.276	84	-5.8	.247	-3.0	CF(14) -2.1, LF(13) -0.4	-1.0	91
2017	PCH	A+	22	494	60	22	6	5	62	39	89	23	6	.295/.358/.407	124	24.2	.355	5.1	RF(70) 14.2, LF(21) -1.5	2.3	100
2018	MNT	AA	23	273	40	12	6	7	34	24	58	12	2	.274/.348/.461	131	16.4	.330	-0.4	RF(35) 4.1, LF(18) -2.5	1.1	92
2019	*TBA*	*MLB*	*24*	*252*	*24*	*6*	*2*	*7*	*26*	*11*	*60*	*6*	*1*	*.203/.246/.332*	*48*	*-7.2*	*.243*	*1.0*	*RF 6, LF 0*	*-0.3*	*99*

Breakout: 9% Improve: 19% Collapse: 0% Attrition: 17% MLB: 22% *Comparables: Ben Francisco, Mikie Mahtook, Chris Pettit*

The Rays depth in potential high-end prospect talent is impressive and arguably the envy of the entire league, but we are entering the likely bench outfielder portion of the list—with an interesting exception to come. Boldt is well on his way to fulfilling that destiny. He played all three outfield positions in the Southern League and is average to perhaps a bit above in center field. At the plate, Boldt offers a simple, compact swing that prioritizes contact over power. He has the usual good Rays prospect approach. Neither the bat nor glove alone suggest a slam dunk everyday guy, but the broad base of skills should keep Boldt in the majors well into the 2020s.

14 Carl Chester OF

Born: 12/12/95 Age: 23 Bats: R Throws: R Height: 6'0" Weight: 200 Origin: Round 12, 2017 Draft (#349 overall)

YEAR	TEAM	LVL	AGE	PA	R	2B	3B	HR	RBI	BB	K	SB	CS	AVG/OBP/SLG	DRC+	VORP	BABIP	BRR	FRAA	WARP	PF
2017	PRI	RK	21	145	36	6	4	0	12	20	12	8	4	.345/.455/.462	181	17.2	.380	0.4	CF(28) -0.2	1.1	107
2017	HUD	A-	21	163	26	7	2	0	17	12	31	8	2	.293/.356/.367	129	11.2	.368	3.2	CF(39) 3.4	1.2	94
2018	BGR	A	22	439	61	23	6	5	63	22	67	15	7	.285/.328/.412	114	28.9	.323	2.1	CF(93) 4.7, LF(10) 1.2	2.3	101
2018	PCH	A+	22	55	11	2	1	2	8	0	9	1	0	.346/.345/.538	137	6.0	.372	-0.3	LF(12) 0.9, CF(1) -0.2	0.3	102
2019	*TBA*	*MLB*	*23*	*252*	*24*	*6*	*1*	*5*	*20*	*6*	*59*	*3*	*1*	*.190/.213/.293*	*31*	*-11.3*	*.225*	*0.2*	*CF 2, LF 1*	*-0.9*	*99*

Breakout: 8% Improve: 14% Collapse: 0% Attrition: 9% MLB: 14% *Comparables: Andrew Stevenson, Engel Beltre, Dave Sappelt*

We often like to say that these evaluations happen in more or less a vacuum. "What can a player do?" over "What might the organization do with a player?" The Rays can confound that. Partially because of their organizational creativity (aggressive platooning, the opener, signing every former Mariners shortstop prospect), but they also tend to be very conservative w/r/t development tracks for their prospects. Chester landed on the "next ten" of the 2018 Rays prospect list. That's aggressive for a 12th round college pick in a very good system, but the Penn League reports support it. His bat needs to keep developing, of course, but what can you actually learn from a full season in the Midwest League for a 22-year-old out of the University of Miami? His 2018 season was almost a dead ringer for his 2017 junior year at Miami that triggered concerns about his stick. Is the competition really that much better than Friday nights in the ACC?

This is all philosophy in the end. What we do know is he's still a potential plus glove in center with a bat that makes you worry he's a fourth outfielder in the end. We won't learn a whole lot more in Port Charlotte next year, but we'll keep him on the Next Ten until the reports change or we mercifully get too old for this gig ourselves. In a race between the Rays developmental track and the Heat Death of the Universe, we're all winners in the end.

15 Tanner Dodson RHP

Born: 05/09/97 Age: 22 Bats: B Throws: R Height: 6'1" Weight: 160 Origin: Round 2, 2018 Draft (#71 overall)

YEAR	TEAM	LVL	AGE	PA	R	2B	3B	HR	RBI	BB	K	SB	CS	AVG/OBP/SLG	DRC+	VORP	BABIP	BRR	FRAA	WARP	PF
2018	HUD	A-	21	224	30	7	3	2	19	20	34	8	3	.273/.344/.369	117	9.4	.315	1.9	CF(30) 0.1, P(9) 0.6	0.4	95
2019	*TBA*	*MLB*	*22*	*252*	*22*	*3*	*1*	*6*	*19*	*8*	*61*	*2*	*1*	*.158/.184/.253*	*12*	*-17.5*	*.181*	*0.3*	*CF -1*	*-2.0*	*99*

Breakout: 3% Improve: 3% Collapse: 0% Attrition: 3% MLB: 5% *Comparables: Rafael Ortega, Darrell Ceciliani, Alfredo Marte*

YEAR	TEAM	LVL	AGE	W	L	SV	G	GS	IP	H	HR	BB/9	K/9	K	GB%	BABIP	WHIP	ERA	DRA	WARP	PF
2018	HUD	A-	21	1	0	1	9	0	25	12	0	1.8	9.0	25	57%	.200	0.68	1.44	2.62	0.7	100
2019	*TBA*	*MLB*	*22*	*1*	*1*	*1*	*32*	*0*	*33^1*	*34*	*5*	*4.2*	*7.8*	*29*	*44%*	*.294*	*1.47*	*5.11*	*5.56*	*-0.4*	*99*

Breakout: 0% Improve: 0% Collapse: 0% Attrition: 0% MLB: 0% *Comparables: Drew Smith, Ryan Meisinger, Ian Hamilton*

The other two-way weapon in the Rays system, Dodson isn't quite as good a prospect in either role, but his skill set might actually be easier to leverage full value out of than McKay's. At the plate he's an athletic, switch-hitting, hit over power center fielder. On the mound he can touch the upper-90s and will flash a plus slider.

The swing is a little stiff from the right side, and his bat speed is fringy, but he controls the barrel well. As a hitting prospect, Dodson would be your standard extra outfielder type, and there's a reason he was seen more as a pitcher coming into the draft. But you can Davey Johnson him, sending him to the outfield for your LOOGY. You won't be hiding him there either, so you can get almost all of his fourth outfielder/relief arm value into games using various machinations.

There is more risk here than with McKay that the bat may not get there in a "major-league hitter" sense, leaving him more of your run-of-the-mill 95-and-a-slider guy. Dodson is probably more fun than good, and almost wasted some in the DH league—although the Rays are the right org to get creative here—but it's good to have fun prospects lying around.

Others of note:

Austin Franklin, RHP, Low-A Bowling Green

Franklin was putting together a nice season anchoring the Bowling Green staff until he went down with an elbow injury in July. When healthy, he features a fastball that currently sits 92-94 but could play up a notch with physical maturity. The curve is his best secondary and has the potential to be a plus offering. It features 12-6 movement, has depth, and Franklin will bury it down and away to righties. There are a lot of moving parts to the delivery and it causes the command to waver at times. He's likely to miss most, if not all, of 2019 and if he can return to form it'll most likely be in relief.

Jose Mujica, RHP, Triple-A Durham

Mujica missed some time with a forearm strain in 2018. While there was no structural damage at the time, it's not exactly a surprise that he got Tommy John surgery shortly after the season ended. It's too bad, as Mujica was knocking on the door of the majors on the strength of his mid-90s fastball and potential above-average slider. His delivery has some effort, and his fastball didn't move a ton—although there was good riding life up and occasional run—so he was likely destined for the pen anyway. Now that timetable gets sets back a year or so, and we will have to see what the stuff looks like in 2020.

Resly Linares, LHP, Low-A Bowling Green

Linares did not have Tommy John surgery in 2018, though he did miss about two months with vague shoulder issues. Pitchers, man. Linares came out the other side fine enough, although his slight frame—talk about the uniform *literally* hanging off a player—is going to lead to continued durability concerns until (if?) he fills out some. The fastball runs between the upper-80s and lower-90s but Linares commands it well to all four quadrants and there's a bit of deception as well.

It's a projectable frame with good arm speed so you'd hope he settles more in the average velocity range as he ages. The curve is potentially above-average, a big, low-70s 1-7 breaker with good tilt, although he will snap it off at times when he wants to spot it. He could use a better changeup, and a few more orders of double meat Chipotle burritos on the road, but Linares is still an arm worth keeping an eye on, even if he's been lost in the shuffle a bit in a top-tier system.

Roberto Alvarez, C, rookie-ball Princeton

Getting overly attached to a prep catcher? That's for amateurs. IFA catchers in their second season in rookie-ball? That's the ticket. It was harder to find a low minors sleeper in the Rays system than you'd think despite the overall org depth, but Alvarez caught my eye due to his advanced offensive tools for an 18-year-old.

He's got above-average raw power and can show it off to the oppo gap already. There's loft and above-average bat speed, and although the swing can be a little stiff, he should get to most of his pop. He doesn't sell out for it, and has an idea at the plate. Right-on-right spin is a significant issue at present, but one you can still chalk up to those awkward teenage years for now.

The defense is also a work in progress. Alvarez can get stabby on the backhand and box pitches a bit, but he's a solid athlete for a catcher, blocks balls well, and flashes an average arm. It's gonna be a long while before he's ready, but he's one to watch as a potential role 5 catcher sometime in the 2020s.

Tommy Romero, RHP, Low-A Bowling Green

There was not a lot to choose from in the Mariners farm system when the Rays sent Denard Span and Alex Colome to Seattle in May. While it was not a sexy return, they did net two potential back end rotation types in Andrew Moore and Tommy Romero. Romero, a former 15th-round pick out of Eastern Florida State, has a thick, solid build and is physically mature. The stuff, while not electric, is effective. The fastball sits in the low-90's but is heavy with run and Romero spots it well in the zone. The changeup is his most advanced secondary. Hitters have a hard time with it as Romero replicates his arm action well and it fades away from righties. He doesn't have a high floor, but Romero is a durable, strike-throwing starter who could eventually find his way onto a big-league pitching staff.

Top Talents 25 and Under (born 4/1/93 or later):

1. Willy Adames
2. Wander Franco
3. Tyler Glasnow
4. Austin Meadows
5. Brent Honeywell
6. Jesus Sanchez
7. Brendan McKay
8. Lucius Fox
9. Shane Baz
10. Vidal Brujan

In some ways, this was one of the harder 25 and Under lists to do. Not only are there three fairly recently-graduated top global prospects, but there are another half-dozen players to consider here. Thankfully, the system depth prevents us from having to order them immediately.

Willy Adames is, more or less, what we expected Willy Adames to be right now. He spent years edging up our lists, peaking at No. 14 on the 2018 midseason 50. He mostly just kept drilling in on an above-average outcome every year, and his slash lines have stayed bizarrely consistent across levels and environments, even into the second half of 2018 in the majors. That hides real improvements, because every level is tougher and maintaining your production from Low-A to MLB means you're constantly improving. If he keeps improving in the majors, he could outhit those MILB numbers. Adames edges out Wander Franco by the thinnest of margins in what amounts to a slight stylistic preference for the very good guy who has done it in the majors over the potential superstar who has yet to reach full-season ball yet.

Tyler Glasnow spent the first half of the 2018 season walking too many guys in the Pirates bullpen, and the second half of the season pitching well in Tampa's rotation; DRA suggests that he was actually pretty effective in both roles. He still has an incredible fastball/curveball combination, one of the best in baseball in terms of raw stuff, and absolutely good enough that he can excel in a rotation with little more than a show-me change. All that separates him from a top-of-the-rotation outcome is continuing to throw strikes, but his history throwing strikes is sketchy enough that we want to see it for more than eleven starts before crowning him as such. Glasnow alone has the potential to make the Chris Archer trade look terrible for Pittsburgh.

Austin Meadows is still functionally a prospect, but he accrued a bit too much MLB playing time to remain list-eligible. You know the drill here by now: immense talent, inconsistent results, way too many injuries. Meadows was up-and-down for the Pirates, playing well in MLB stints but struggling in Triple-A, before the Rays picked him up in said Archer trade. He proceeded to torch the International League for the rest of the season and earned his way to St. Pete in September. Meadows is only 23 and he'll probably open the season in the Rays outfield. Like Glasnow, the sky is the limit here.

There are a *lot* of guys who deserve a brief mention here. Former A's first-rounder Daniel Robertson has turned into a really nifty super-utility type, and added a bit of outfield work to his full accoutrement in the infield in 2018. Former Giants first-rounder Christian Arroyo looks like he's headed down the same path, but hasn't quite gotten there yet. Diego Castillo gets it up to 102 MPH and has way more role versatility than we expected he would, everywhere from the first to the ninth. Jose Alvarado touches 101 MPH from the left side and leans on a great slider. Hunter Wood emerged out of obscurity to become a strong bullpen piece who also did some work as The Opener. Jake Faria is a nice back-of-the-rotation type who could be used in a bunch of different roles moving forward. Jalen Beeks came over in the Nathan Eovaldi trade and immediately filled the long relief role that is so crucial for the success of that Opener strategy. Andrew Moore might fill a similar role next year. We haven't even mentioned Anthony Banda yet.

Oh yeah, and AL Cy Young winner Blake Snell only missed this list by four months. The Rays certainly don't lack for young talent.

Texas Rangers

The State of the System:

The Rangers system is back on the upswing, and you will be shocked to learn it is due to an abundance of toolsy up-the-middle bats and young, hard-throwing arms.

The Top Ten:

1 Leody Taveras OF

OFP: 60 Likely: 50 ETA: 2021

Born: 09/08/98 Age: 20 Bats: B Throws: R Height: 6'1" Weight: 190 Origin: International Free Agent, 2015

YEAR	TEAM	LVL	AGE	PA	R	2B	3B	HR	RBI	BB	K	SB	CS	AVG/OBP/SLG	DRC+	VORP	BABIP	BRR	FRAA	WARP	PF
2016	DRN	RK	17	45	6	2	2	0	9	6	5	4	3	.385/.467/.538	199	6.5	.441	-2.1	CF(7) -0.9, RF(2) -0.4	0.0	94
2016	RNG	RK	17	155	22	6	3	1	15	11	24	11	4	.278/.329/.382	117	3.1	.328	-0.3	CF(31) -2.6, RF(3) -0.1	-0.2	107
2016	SPO	A-	17	133	14	6	1	0	9	8	26	3	1	.228/.271/.293	72	2.4	.283	-0.3	CF(26) 2.1, LF(1) 0.0	-0.3	105
2017	HIC	A	18	577	73	20	7	8	50	47	92	20	6	.249/.312/.360	98	17.7	.287	3.3	CF(125) -3.7, LF(3) -0.1	0.7	99
2018	DEB	A+	19	580	65	16	7	5	48	51	96	19	11	.246/.312/.332	91	4.2	.292	0.3	CF(123) 7.0, RF(3) 0.0	0.8	101
2019	*TEX*	*MLB*	*20*	*252*	*23*	*4*	*1*	*5*	*18*	*10*	*59*	*3*	*1*	*.170/.200/.260*	*19*	*-14.8*	*.198*	*0.3*	*CF -1, LF 0*	*-1.7*	*108*

Breakout: 4% Improve: 4% Collapse: 0% Attrition: 2% MLB: 4% *Comparables: Cedric Hunter, Carlos Tocci, Billy McKinney*

The Report: He's dead so we can't be sure Kant wasn't writing about Leody Taveras in his *Critique of Judgement* when he opined: "The judgement of taste is therefore not a judgement of cognition, and is consequently not logical but aesthetical, by which we can understand that whose determining ground can be *no other than subjective.*"

When considering aesthetics, Kant further delves into the beautiful versus the pleasant versus the good.

The Pleasant: "As regards the Pleasant, therefore, the fundamental proposition is valid: *Every one has his own taste.*" The first time I saw Taveras I was running late to the park. Got out of the house tardy, hit traffic on the Garden State, barely got to my seat in Lakewood for the anthem, stuffing rosters into my backpack as I traipsed down the concourse. I don't like to be frazzled. I don't like to miss BP. I caught Taveras in the on-deck circle out of the corner of my eye, taking a couple practice cuts. "One man likes the tone of wind instruments, another that of strings." I like *this.*

The Beautiful: "In all judgements by which we describe anything as beautiful, we allow no one to be of another opinion." Now we touch on universality for a moment. We've never been particularly out of step with the industry on Taveras. The glove, arm, and run tools make him a good bet to at least have Leonys Martin's career. Nor were we the first to sing his praises in particularly hushed tones. Craig Goldstein—I don't know if you remember him—whispered to me about his spring training BPs in 2016.

The Good: "In respect to the Good it is true that judgments make rightful claim to validity for every one; but the Good is represented only *by means of a concept* as the object of a universal satisfaction." I don't remember if it was KG or Parks who said the only goal of a farm system is to convert it into major-league talent. I suppose Kant would call this "purposiveness."

I may lean more towards the transcendental philosopher than the logician end of the spectrum of prospect writing, but I can assure those looking for universality of satisfaction with any prospect, here you will only find pedantry. Oh, and a dude who never gives up on this tools profile.

The Risks: High. His best stateside performance was a .711 OPS in the launching pad of the AZL. All the drool-worthy batting practice swings in the world can't paper over the risk here.

Ben Carsley's Fantasy Take: We've been aggressive in our rankings of Taveras on the fantasy side as well (no. 34 on our midseason top-50), and the tools are still drool-worthy. That being said, I imagine Bret Sayre and I will be butting heads a bit on Taveras when it comes to our 2019 list. I still like Taveras quite a bit, but we're getting to the point where I'm going to value some guys who've actually performed in the high minors above Taveras, who is pretty much still just the idea of a good fantasy prospect at this point. I'm not being alarmist—Taveras is still an easy top-100 and maybe a top-50 guy for me—but he's not the top-25 dynasty prospect I'd hoped we'd all view him as by now.

2 Bubba Thompson OF   OFP: 60   Likely: 50   ETA: 2022

Born: 06/09/98 Age: 21 Bats: R Throws: R Height: 6'2" Weight: 186 Origin: Round 1, 2017 Draft (#26 overall)

YEAR	TEAM	LVL	AGE	PA	R	2B	3B	HR	RBI	BB	K	SB	CS	AVG/OBP/SLG	DRC+	VORP	BABIP	BRR	FRAA	WARP	PF
2017	RNG	RK	19	123	23	7	2	3	12	6	28	5	5	.257/.317/.434	80	3.9	.317	0.8	CF(25) -4.0	-0.6	101
2018	HIC	A	20	363	52	18	5	8	42	23	104	32	7	.289/.344/.446	117	26.0	.396	6.1	CF(67) 1.1, LF(17) 0.7	1.9	99
2019	*TEX*	*MLB*	*21*	*252*	*27*	*7*	*1*	*6*	*19*	*3*	*90*	*7*	*2*	*.162/.174/.276*	*11*	*-16.4*	*.222*	*1.4*	*CF -1, LF 1*	*-1.7*	*108*

Breakout: 0% Improve: 3% Collapse: 0% Attrition: 2% MLB: 3%   *Comparables: Teoscar Hernandez, Joe Benson, Michael Saunders*

The Report: The Rangers have a history of drafting toolsy athletic outfielders from the South who have questionable hit tools, and at first glance Thompson looks the part. He has one of the best body projections in baseball, as he stands at 6-foot-2 with broad shoulders, an athletic build, and lean muscle throughout with room for growth. Thompson is an elite athlete with quick twitch and explosiveness in the hips and wrists. At any given moment he can burst into movement, whether it's into a sprint or firing his hips in a swing.

Unlike the Rangers draft picks of yore, Bubba has an instinctual feel for getting his bat on the ball and the ability to turn on velocity. Thompson generates plus bat speed with a swing plane that generally results in line drives on his hard contact, although he collapses his torso a bit to get a higher launch angle on pitches low and in. Thompson has plus raw power and could grow into more without losing athleticism or flexibility. With his swing, he probably won't tap into all of it, but he still should generate average power at the highest level.

The main concern with the offensive profile is his pitch recognition, as he struggles to pick up off-speed and spin. Thompson is a double-plus runner with a body that suggests he'll stay that way, and he's improving as a baserunner. That speed and a plus arm allow Bubba to make up for his inconsistent reads and routes in the outfield, and with improvement he should be above-average in center or plus in a corner. Ultimately, Thompson profiles as an average center fielder with the upside for much more depending on how much he is able to polish his pitch recognition and zone control at the plate.

The Risks: High. He's young, far away, the power may or may not show up, and he ran a pretty high strikeout rate in A-ball.

Ben Carsley's Fantasy Take: Yes please. See that part about double-plus speed? That means we don't need Thompson to even hit the average power projection to be very invested in him as a dynasty league asset. I realize that the lead time is a little longer than we'd prefer, but Thompson's defense gives him a reasonably high chance of making the majors, and you've got to like the above report about his feel for hitting. One of the most common questions we get every offseason is "which low minor leaguer could make a big jump in value this season?" and Thompson definitely qualifies.

3 Julio Pablo Martinez OF   OFP: 60   Likely: 50   ETA: Your guess is as good as ours. 2020?

Born: 03/21/96 Age: 23 Bats: L Throws: L Height: 5'9" Weight: 174 Origin: International Free Agent, 2018

YEAR	TEAM	LVL	AGE	PA	R	2B	3B	HR	RBI	BB	K	SB	CS	AVG/OBP/SLG	DRC+	VORP	BABIP	BRR	FRAA	WARP	PF
2018	DRG	RK	22	33	10	1	1	1	3	9	7	2	3	.409/.606/.682	160	11.5	.571	2.2	CF(5) 0.4, RF(1) 0.0	0.5	94
2018	SPO	A-	22	273	49	9	5	8	21	34	69	11	6	.252/.351/.436	103	16.4	.323	0.5	CF(55) 1.5, LF(2) 0.1	0.2	105
2019	*TEX*	*MLB*	*23*	*252*	*25*	*4*	*1*	*8*	*22*	*18*	*92*	*3*	*1*	*.124/.186/.255*	*16*	*-15.7*	*.151*	*0.2*	*CF 1, LF 0*	*-1.6*	*108*

Breakout: 3% Improve: 4% Collapse: 0% Attrition: 4% MLB: 4%   *Comparables: Adam Engel, Blake Tekotte, Michael Taylor*

The Report: When you miss out on signing Shohei Ohtani and have a couple million bucks to burn, there are worse places to impulse-buy than the toolsy Cuban outfielder aisle. Martinez fits right into the Rangers system with his plus athletic tools and plus bat speed. He gets more pop out of his smallish frame than you'd expect, but there's some length to get to it and he struggled a bit more than you'd hope for a 22-year-old in the Northwest League, stateside debut or not. But his speed and potential above-average glove in center field will grant him plenty of time to figure out pro pitching, not unlike the two names ahead of him.

The Risks: High. There's a huge delta here until we get a feel for how he will handle better pitching.

Ben Carsley's Fantasy Take: From a fantasy perspective, Martinez profiles pretty damn similarly to Taveras at this point. While the former may have better future projections on the hit tool, the latter has a slightly better ETA. Expect Martinez to rank in middle of the top-101 in some sort of tier of toolsy outfielders, and consider him one of the more attractive additions to the MiLB talent pool for those of you about to hold preseason drafts.

4 Anderson Tejeda SS   OFP: 60   Likely: 50   ETA: He's moving a level a year. 2020

Born: 05/01/98 Age: 21 Bats: L Throws: R Height: 5'11" Weight: 185 Origin: International Free Agent, 2014

YEAR	TEAM	LVL	AGE	PA	R	2B	3B	HR	RBI	BB	K	SB	CS	AVG/OBP/SLG	DRC+	VORP	BABIP	BRR	FRAA	WARP	PF
2016	DRG	RK	18	47	9	2	3	1	7	5	4	5	0	.262/.340/.524	128	5.6	.270	-0.1	SS(8) 1.7, 3B(1) 0.1	0.4	106
2016	RNG	RK	18	142	22	12	6	1	21	8	36	1	0	.293/.331/.496	145	11.8	.392	-0.3	SS(20) -4.0, 2B(12) -0.4	0.0	106
2016	SPO	A-	18	99	15	0	1	8	19	5	33	1	0	.277/.313/.553	72	6.6	.340	0.5	SS(17) -1.9, 2B(3) -0.4	-0.4	109
2017	HIC	A	19	446	68	24	9	8	53	36	132	10	7	.247/.309/.411	94	22.1	.343	2.0	SS(82) -2.0, 2B(30) 0.0	0.7	100
2018	DEB	A+	20	522	76	17	5	19	74	49	142	11	4	.259/.331/.439	120	29.5	.330	3.0	SS(105) 2.9, 2B(12) 1.6	2.9	102
2019	*TEX*	*MLB*	*21*	*252*	*21*	*6*	*1*	*7*	*26*	*10*	*88*	*2*	*1*	*.168/.201/.298*	*26*	*-12.8*	*.223*	*0.1*	*SS 0, 2B 0*	*-1.4*	*108*

Breakout: 4% Improve: 8% Collapse: 1% Attrition: 6% MLB: 9% *Comparables: Trevor Story, Javier Guerra, Nick Franklin*

The Report: That went a bit better. We aggressively placed Tejeda on the 2017 101—perhaps too aggressively—based on strong looks out of the Northwest League. He then struggled in full-season ball, showing typical teenager warts like over-aggressiveness at the plate and mixed reliability in the field. But a strong showing in the High-A Carolina League last year saw Tejeda's stock rise to, and even surpass, where it was two winters ago.

Even now, Tejeda is a Very Rangers Prospect, and we mean that in ways both good and bad. You can probably envision him in your head if you've followed the Rangers system long enough. He's athletic and projectable, but also short. We slap the "good feel for hitting" euphemism on him a lot because we think he'll hit for average eventually, even though he hasn't done so yet. He has plus raw power that he actualized into games this year, as we'd suspected he would for a couple years, and he has really good bat speed. He'll show a strong enough first step and arm to give him a chance to not just stick at shortstop but be pretty good there.

He's also still too undisciplined at the plate, which leads to too much swing-and-miss. It's not as bad as it looked in 2017, and we're optimistic that he'll continue to improve here as he ages. But if it all falls apart for Tejeda offensively against upper-level pitching, well, don't say we didn't warn you.

The Risks: Moderate. As A-ballers go, we're pretty confident Tejeda is a major leaguer, given that the framework for a versatile power-hitting infield reserve is more or less already present. We also think he's got a shot to be a lot more. There's some fuzziness on exactly what type of player he'll be, which mostly depends on whether the hit tool spikes and which way the body goes.

Ben Carsley's Fantasy Take: Shortstop isn't quite the barren wasteland it was for fantasy owners a few years back, but it's still not a very deep position. Consider, for example, that Jose Peraza, Jonathan Villar and Adalberto Mondesi were all top-15 shortstops last year, per ESPN's Player Rater. The catch? All of those guys put up big stolen base numbers, and while Tejeda may run a bit he's not a burner. That means he's gonna have to take more of the 2019 Marcus Semien/Gleyber Torres/ Jurickson Profar path to value, in which well-rounded contributions and non-embarrassing batting averages win the day. This is a long-winded way of saying Tejeda would have to really, really click to become a top-10 shortstop, but top-20 seems well within his grasp if he stays on his current trajectory.

5 Taylor Hearn LHP   OFP: 60   Likely: 50   ETA: Late 2019 as a reliever, 2020 as a starter

Born: 08/30/94 Age: 24 Bats: L Throws: L Height: 6'5" Weight: 210 Origin: Round 5, 2015 Draft (#164 overall)

YEAR	TEAM	LVL	AGE	W	L	SV	G	GS	IP	H	HR	BB/9	K/9	K	GB%	BABIP	WHIP	ERA	DRA	WARP	PF
2016	NAT	RK	21	0	0	0	2	2	6^1	2	1	8.5	11.4	8	55%	.100	1.26	1.42	1.51	0.3	114
2016	HAG	A	21	1	0	0	8	2	22^2	25	3	2.8	12.3	31	39%	.393	1.41	3.18	2.22	0.7	100
2016	WVA	A	21	1	1	0	8	3	22^2	15	2	4.0	14.3	36	47%	.289	1.10	1.99	1.97	0.8	98
2017	BRD	A+	22	4	6	0	18	17	87^1	65	8	3.8	10.9	106	50%	.281	1.17	4.12	3.37	1.9	100
2018	ALT	AA	23	3	6	0	19	19	104	75	6	3.3	9.3	107	41%	.256	1.09	3.12	3.61	2.1	92
2018	FRI	AA	23	1	2	0	5	5	25	29	5	3.2	11.9	33	36%	.375	1.52	5.04	4.29	0.3	114
2019	*TEX*	*MLB*	*24*	*2*	*2*	*0*	*6*	*6*	*30*	*29*	*5*	*4.4*	*9.6*	*32*	*40%*	*.300*	*1.45*	*5.01*	*4.99*	*0.2*	*108*

Breakout: 13% Improve: 26% Collapse: 15% Attrition: 36% MLB: 50%   *Comparables: P.J. Walters, Hunter Wood, Jake Arrieta*

The Report: The first thing that stands out on Hearn's scouting report is, well, the ol' number one. It's a potentially plus-plus mid-90s howitzer with nasty cutting action. He'll bore it into righties with malice of forethought. Hearn will mix in a low-90s two-seamer for an armside look as well. He made strides with his breaking ball, a power 11-6 breaker in the low-80s. It will flash plus, but should settle in as an above-average offering. The change is inconsistent, looking average in some outings, below-average in others.

Hearn generally works off the fastball almost exclusively early in outings, before mixing in the secondaries more as he tries to turn over the lineup multiple times. And that's the open question here: Can Hearn work through a lineup multiple times as a starter? He tends not to hold his velocity deep in games, and the breaker can get rounded and slurvy as he tires as well. The command profile is a bit fringy; while he throws strikes generally, he can be wild within the zone. Hearn is exactly the type of prospect arm who may benefit from changing reliever roles. Where before he may have been either a frustrating starter with command and durability issues or a one-inning power arm, now he could be a multi-inning fireman or an "opener" as well. The stuff is also good enough to close.

The Risks: Moderate. I try to avoid throwing low risk on prospect arms who haven't already bagged a few major-league per diems, but Hearn could get outs in la grande liga with his fastball alone. His command issues require further ironing, but he doesn't need much more refinement to have a long career in the late innings, and there are those on staff who think I'm underselling his chances of becoming an effective starter.

Ben Carsley's Fantasy Take: In general I hate guys with Hearn's profile, but for a long time I've really loved Hearn. I wish he'd been traded, oh, almost anywhere else save for Colorado or Baltimore, as if he was a Padre or a Giant or something I might try to push Bret into sneaking him on to the end of the 101. Alas, Hearn is a Ranger, and that means we may actually want to root for him to move to the bullpen where he could earn some saves. If he stays in the rotation, the WHIP and ERA are likely to hurt too much for you to enjoy the strikeouts.

6 Cole Winn RHP   OFP: 60   Likely: 50   ETA: 2021

Born: 11/25/99 Age: 19 Bats: R Throws: R Height: 6'2" Weight: 190 Origin: Round 1, 2018 Draft (#15 overall)

The Report: Winn isn't your typical first-round righty prep arm, as he doesn't have an overpowering fastball, and instead makes it work with pitchability and a relatively advanced arsenal. He's a plus athlete with a very smooth delivery and clean arm action to top it off.

Winn uses both a four-seamer and a two-seamer, and his fastballs sit from 90-94. He shows a plus 12-6 curveball with a high spin rate with plus depth and good feel in addition to a harder 85-86 slider with gloveside action and dive. He hasn't shown off his changeup much, but when he has it flashes average and should develop into a quality offering.

Winn's delivery and athleticism lead to a better command projection than most prep arms, and his current level of polish suggests he could move fairly quickly. With a four-pitch mix and an average command projection, Winn is a relatively safe bet to become a mainstay in an MLB rotation. Additionally, his well-rounded arsenal and fastball velocity give him a fall-back role as a late-inning bullpen arm if his changeup or command don't progress as expected.

The Risks: High. Even if he's not as risky as the usual prep arm, he's still a prep arm. Pitchers have higher rates of regression of stuff and injury than their position player counterparts and Winn's distance from the big leagues exacerbates the risk.

Ben Carsley's Fantasy Take: As a fan of the game you may enjoy pitchers who survive on pitch mix and command as much as pure stuff. As a fantasy player, you should be more interested in strikeouts. Winn has just enough upside that he's probably worth owning if your league holds 200 prospects, but those of you in shallower formats can drop him on your watch list for now.

7 Brock Burke LHP OFP: 55 Likely: 45 ETA: 2020

Born: 08/04/96 Age: 22 Bats: L Throws: L Height: 6'4" Weight: 200 Origin: Round 3, 2014 Draft (#96 overall)

YEAR	TEAM	LVL	AGE	W	L	SV	G	GS	IP	H	HR	BB/9	K/9	K	GB%	BABIP	WHIP	ERA	DRA	WARP	PF
2016	HUD	A-	19	3	3	0	13	13	61	53	1	4.3	9.0	61	54%	.313	1.34	3.39	3.22	1.5	95
2017	BGR	A	20	6	0	0	10	10	57^1	37	0	3.1	9.3	59	35%	.253	0.99	1.10	4.02	0.8	103
2017	PCH	A+	20	5	6	0	13	13	66	75	6	2.2	6.7	49	47%	.329	1.38	4.64	4.26	0.8	100
2018	PCH	A+	21	3	5	0	16	13	82	85	4	3.3	9.5	87	48%	.343	1.40	3.84	4.03	1.2	100
2018	MNT	AA	21	6	1	0	9	9	55^1	39	2	2.3	11.5	71	37%	.282	0.96	1.95	3.22	1.4	93
2019	*TEX*	*MLB*	*22*	*1*	*1*	*0*	*3*	*3*	*15*	*15*	*2*	*4.3*	*8.6*	*14*	*41%*	*.304*	*1.49*	*5.02*	*5.00*	*0.1*	*108*

Breakout: 7% Improve: 13% Collapse: 11% Attrition: 22% MLB: 30% *Comparables: Luis Ortiz, Keury Mella, Miguel Almonte*

The Report: The "primary" piece in the deal for Jurickson Profar, the Rangers received another high minors arm that has helium going into the 2019 season. The tall athletic lefty has some extreme bend in his torso during the windup which results in a strange look for hitters, especially lefties, who can't pick up the ball until the actual release from an extreme over the top delivery that sees Burke falling off the mound to his gloveside and home plate. The result is a fastball that appears even faster than the 93-95 that he usually sits in games.

To go along with the fastball Burke mixes in an above average 79-80 curveball with 1 to 7 break, a slider that flashes average with average dive, and a below average 82-84 changeup that has some fade, but lacks significant tumble to get consistent whiffs.

Burke is able to stay within and around the zone well, but ultimately has below average command due to being unable to consistently hit spots with the fastball or changeup. When he tries to stay on the outside corner to righties and break the changeup off the plate, the regularly struggles to put it in a location where hitters are tempted. Due to the delivery's noise, it's hard to project much more command as Burke is already a quality athlete with strong limbs and body control.

Burke profiles as a back of the rotation starter who works off his plus 93-95 fastball and utilizes three different secondaries to get through a lineup multiple times. Without improvements to the changeup, Burke may be better suited to a bullpen role, where he could have his fastball play up even further. If Burke can take another step forward with the changeup like he did in 2018, a middle of the rotation spot isn't out of the question.

The Risks: With improved command and a better changeup in 2018, he increased the odds he'd be a productive member of an MLB rotation significantly. The changeup consistency still needs to improve before slotting into a rotation spot. If he stalls out where he is now, he should be able to find a home in a low-setup role where he can brutalize lefties with his fastball/breaking ball combo.

8 Joe Palumbo LHP OFP: 55 Likely: 45 ETA: 2019

Born: 10/26/94 Age: 24 Bats: L Throws: L Height: 6'1" Weight: 168 Origin: Round 30, 2013 Draft (#910 overall)

YEAR	TEAM	LVL	AGE	W	L	SV	G	GS	IP	H	HR	BB/9	K/9	K	GB%	BABIP	WHIP	ERA	DRA	WARP	PF
2016	HIC	A	21	7	5	8	33	7	96^1	71	5	3.4	11.4	122	52%	.287	1.11	2.24	2.49	2.7	96
2017	DEB	A+	22	1	0	0	3	3	13^2	4	0	2.6	14.5	22	58%	.167	0.59	0.66	2.80	0.4	100
2018	DEB	A+	23	1	4	0	6	6	27	24	3	2.0	11.3	34	42%	.304	1.11	2.67	3.01	0.7	102
2018	FRI	AA	23	1	0	0	2	2	9^1	6	0	2.9	9.6	10	39%	.261	0.96	1.93	3.72	0.2	102
2019	*TEX*	*MLB*	*24*	*3*	*3*	*0*	*19*	*8*	51^1	*47*	*6*	*3.9*	*9.9*	*56*	*44%*	*.302*	*1.35*	*4.31*	*4.26*	*0.8*	*108*

Breakout: 15% Improve: 22% Collapse: 3% Attrition: 18% MLB: 30% *Comparables: Glenn Sparkman, Taylor Williams, Glen Perkins*

The Report: Palumbo looked like a promising arm before tearing his UCL in 2017. After the requisite year-and-a-half away from the diamond, he returned to the mound last summer and alleviated many of the concerns evaluators had about his prospects for recovery.

Palumbo is 6-foot-1 with a high waist and long levers on a wiry frame. He is a quality athlete with controlled fluid movements and clean arm action. Palumbo sits 91-94 and tops out at 96 with a high spin rate, but his command of the pitch varies from average to below-average. His best secondary is a plus curveball with an excellent spin rate and plus depth, although his feel for it was inconsistent last summer. His low-80s changeup flashes average with good arm speed and deception with some tumble and armside action. The cambio is his most inconsistent offering, as he occasionally misses up and it can get him into trouble.

Many of Palumbo's current issues aren't surprising after TJS, as his command and feel can vary from inning to inning. His delivery is clean and he could improve his command as he gets further from surgery and adds weight to his slight frame. Currently, Palumbo projects as a back of the rotation starter or a setup arm depending on how his changeup develops. There's mid-rotation upside if his fastball command takes a step forward.

The Risks: Palumbo needs to take small steps forward in command and consistency with all three pitches to actualize. His delivery suggests better command is possible, but he still has to take those strides. Without such improvement, he may wind up in middle relief.

Ben Carsley's Fantasy Take: It's fine to keep Palumbo on your watch list in deep leagues since he figures to get a crack at MLB playing time at some point in 2019. That being said, Texas is among the worst places imaginable for a rookie pitcher, and there's no premium upside here. Basically, remember the name if you end up needing innings, but don't bank on him making super meaningful fantasy contributions.

9 Hans Crouse RHP

OFP: 55 Likely: 45 ETA: 2021

Born: 09/15/98 Age: 20 Bats: L Throws: R Height: 6'4" Weight: 180 Origin: Round 2, 2017 Draft (#66 overall)

YEAR	TEAM	LVL	AGE	W	L	SV	G	GS	IP	H	HR	BB/9	K/9	K	GB%	BABIP	WHIP	ERA	DRA	WARP	PF
2017	RNG	RK	18	0	0	0	10	6	20	7	1	3.2	13.5	30	60%	.176	0.70	0.45	2.04	0.8	103
2018	SPO	A-	19	5	1	0	8	8	38	25	2	2.6	11.1	47	36%	.253	0.95	2.37	3.91	0.6	106
2018	HIC	A	19	0	2	0	5	5	16^2	18	1	4.3	8.1	15	40%	.333	1.56	2.70	6.50	-0.3	104
2019	*TEX*	*MLB*	*20*	*2*	*3*	*0*	*12*	*9*	*37*	*40*	*8*	*5.1*	*8.8*	*36*	*40%*	*.307*	*1.64*	*6.10*	*6.14*	*-0.3*	*108*

Breakout: 0% Improve: 0% Collapse: 0% Attrition: 0% MLB: 0% *Comparables: Carlos Carrasco, Eric Hurley, Anthony Swarzak*

The Report: Crouse is one of the most exciting arms in the system, thanks to three offerings that flash above-average or better, including a double-plus bender. The right-hander is a plus athlete with quick twitch and excellent control of his 6-foot-4 frame. He has a strong lower half with broad shoulders and room for more muscle throughout his torso.

Crouse's delivery is unorthodox and extremely rotational, and he fires from a cross-fire arm slot. He sits 94-96 and tops out at 98 with a high-spin four-seamer that features armside action, though that velocity dips late in games. He has a 70 breaking ball—he calls it a slider, pitch classification systems have their work cut out for them—and a good idea of how to use it. Crouse's mid-80s changeup was one of the early concerns with this profile, but it flashes above-average with quality deception and tumble and he seems to have improving feel for it. Combine it all and he has three separate offerings he can miss bats with.

Crouse currently has below-average command and it's hard to project too much more due to his loud, rotational delivery. The athleticism affords him more command than the motion would suggest and it's possible that it could improve further as he matures, though guys with his delivery and competent command are the exceptions, not the rule.

Crouse fits best in a one time through the order (OTTO) role where he can use his three-pitch mix to maximum effectiveness without suffering any velocity drop late in games. Alternatively, he could fit in a backend rotation spot where he pitches deep into starts on his good days while leaving early in his lesser outings. If he's able to enhance his command, he may even have No. 3 upside.

The Risks: Moderate. Crouse is relatively low-risk in one sense, in that his fastball/breaking ball mix give him a great chance to be productive in the pen in a single-inning role. The below-average command and lack of reliable command projection could keep him from sliding into a rotation spot or as a multi-innings reliever.

Ben Carsley's Fantasy Take: Red flags in his delivery and with his command profile abound, but I'd rather roll the dice on a guy like Crouse figuring it out than go with a lower-ceiling arm like Palumbo. Think of it this way: if Crouse clicks, you may not be able to replicate his production with a guy on the waiver wire. If Palumbo or either of the next two guys click, they'll still be fairly dime-a-dozen.

10 Tyler Phillips RHP OFP: 50 Likely: 40 ETA: 2021

Born: 10/27/97 Age: 21 Bats: R Throws: R Height: 6'5" Weight: 200 Origin: Round 16, 2015 Draft (#468 overall)

YEAR	TEAM	LVL	AGE	W	L	SV	G	GS	IP	H	HR	BB/9	K/9	K	GB%	BABIP	WHIP	ERA	DRA	WARP	PF
2016	SPO	A-	18	4	7	0	13	13	58²	78	2	3.1	8.7	57	53%	.388	1.67	6.44	3.57	1.2	107
2017	HIC	A	19	1	2	0	7	4	25¹	28	2	3.2	5.3	15	47%	.302	1.46	6.39	5.88	-0.2	97
2017	SPO	A-	19	4	2	0	13	13	73	78	6	1.4	9.6	78	52%	.338	1.22	3.45	3.28	1.7	99
2018	HIC	A	20	11	5	0	22	22	128	117	4	1.0	8.7	124	54%	.308	1.02	2.67	3.10	3.2	97
2019	*TEX*	*MLB*	*21*	*5*	*7*	*0*	*19*	*19*	*99²*	*111*	*16*	*3.2*	*7.0*	*78*	*44%*	*.308*	*1.46*	*5.16*	*5.15*	*0.4*	*108*

Breakout: 7% Improve: 12% Collapse: 5% Attrition: 11% MLB: 18% *Comparables: Nick Kingham, Michael Bowden, Jameson Taillon*

The Report: Phillips is significantly thicker than his listed 200 pounds now, and he has the frame of a durable, innings-eating starter. The stuff is a bit light for the "No. 3 or late-inning reliever" prospect class, however. His velocity is averagish, although he will bump 95. It shows occasional run and sink, but gets a bit flat up, and the command isn't so good that it's rarely up.

Phillips will flash a downer, high-70s curve, but the shape is inconsistent. It can be a bit lazy and humpy at times, or look more like an 11-4 slurve. He can struggle to really sell the change, and it will get floaty or cut, though he'll flash a good one with sink and fade. The overall package can be fringy at times, but Phillips throws strikes and is comfortable mixing his pitches. Double-A will be a big test, but he is on track to crack the back of a rotation after a bit more seasoning.

The Risks: Moderate. No upper minors track record, lack of a clear out pitch, but relatively advanced arm who throws strikes.

Ben Carsley's Fantasy Take: Wrong profile, wrong organization, wrong-ish timeline.

The Next Five:

11 A.J. Alexy RHP

Born: 04/21/98 Age: 21 Bats: R Throws: R Height: 6'4" Weight: 217 Origin: Round 11, 2016 Draft (#341 overall)

YEAR	TEAM	LVL	AGE	W	L	SV	G	GS	IP	H	HR	BB/9	K/9	K	GB%	BABIP	WHIP	ERA	DRA	WARP	PF
2016	DOD	RK	18	1	0	0	7	3	13²	17	2	2.0	7.9	12	50%	.375	1.46	4.61	4.54	0.1	101
2017	GRL	A	19	2	6	0	19	19	73²	46	3	4.5	10.5	86	40%	.254	1.13	3.67	3.91	1.2	97
2017	HIC	A	19	1	1	0	5	5	20²	13	3	6.5	11.8	27	37%	.233	1.35	3.05	3.90	0.3	92
2018	HIC	A	20	6	8	0	22	20	108	89	5	4.3	11.5	138	35%	.337	1.31	3.58	4.12	1.4	100
2019	*TEX*	*MLB*	*21*	*4*	*8*	*0*	*19*	*19*	*82*	*83*	*15*	*5.8*	*9.2*	*83*	*36%*	*.305*	*1.66*	*5.93*	*5.96*	*-0.5*	*108*

Breakout: 6% Improve: 6% Collapse: 1% Attrition: 2% MLB: 8% *Comparables: Jake Thompson, Wilmer Font, Edwin Diaz*

The Report: In the 2018 Sally preview, I mentioned Alexy and Alex Speas as a pair of big-armed, high-bonused, projectable 2016 prep arms opening the season with Hickory. Speas pitched 28 2/3 IP out of the Hickory bullpen, alternating dominance with an inordinate amount of walks, and had Tommy John surgery in June; this is why you collect *all* the prep arms.

About as much went right for Alexy as went wrong for Speas. Last offseason, we talked up his projectability a lot, which is what you say for a cold-weather prep arm with a smooth delivery and the makings of a couple good pitches who hasn't done much yet. Now he's done more. The curveball that flashed plus occasionally now gets there pretty often. The fastball ticked up enough that we can no longer describe it as "fringy," and he was touching 97 repeatedly by the end of the season. He threw more strikes over the course of the year, and from June on he was one of the most dominant pitchers in the South Atlantic League. His changeup is behind the rest of the package, but that's true of all but the most precocious Low-A pitching prospect. If you're looking for a sleeper who is a few small improvements from shooting way up in the world, this might be your guy.

The Risks: A bit higher than Phillips. The curve gives him a better chance for an out pitch than Phillips, and would profile him better in relief if it comes to it; that's offset by a lower chance to stick in the rotation. Alexy has struggled in the past to throw strikes and that issue can obviously recur. We're going to need to see the change take another step here too. Still, he's already come a long way since the Darvish trade.

Ben Carsley's Fantasy Take: Wrong profile, wrong organization, wrong-ish timeline.

12 Charles Leblanc 3B

Born: 06/03/96 Age: 23 Bats: R Throws: R Height: 6'3" Weight: 195 Origin: Round 4, 2016 Draft (#129 overall)

YEAR	TEAM	LVL	AGE	PA	R	2B	3B	HR	RBI	BB	K	SB	CS	AVG/OBP/SLG	DRC+	VORP	BABIP	BRR	FRAA	WARP	PF
2016	SPO	A-	20	263	36	12	4	1	15	31	54	1	3	.285/.380/.386	146	20.4	.370	2.9	SS(45) -5.5, 3B(15) 0.1	0.9	106
2017	SPO	A-	21	70	8	4	0	0	2	6	12	2	2	.190/.271/.254	61	0.6	.235	-0.5	3B(10) 1.5, SS(4) 1.5	0.0	101
2017	HIC	A	21	217	27	7	0	4	19	19	33	3	0	.262/.327/.359	112	11.7	.294	1.3	3B(51) 4.6, 2B(1) -0.1	1.3	99
2018	DEB	A+	22	533	65	27	4	10	72	56	120	7	3	.274/.349/.412	115	21.0	.342	-1.7	2B(60) 0.8, 3B(52) -3.0	0.8	102
2019	*TEX*	*MLB*	*23*	*252*	*20*	*6*	*0*	*6*	*24*	*15*	*68*	*0*	*0*	*.182/.229/.286*	*38*	*-11.9*	*.225*	*-0.4*	*2B 1, 3B 1*	*-1.1*	*108*

Breakout: 7% Improve: 12% Collapse: 0% Attrition: 8% MLB: 14% *Comparables: David Adams, Phil Gosselin, Jayson Nix*

"Chuck The White" remains sneaky young for a 2016 college pick due to an oddball situation (his last year as a Quebec prep was technically a post-grad year) that saw him popped as a draft-eligible sophomore out of Pitt just a few days after his 20th birthday. Still just 22, he had an age-appropriate minor breakout in the Carolina League after we pegged him as a guy to watch last spring. He has a quick bat and knows what he wants to do in the box. He'll frequently get his money's worth swinging that quick bat and can get a little out of control, which leads to more swing-and-miss than you'd like for a guy with his polish. He spent most of the first half of the season at third and most of the second half at second, and he's athletic enough to profile at either position. He played both positions in the Arizona Fall League, but also added his first pro experience at first. He profiles as a potential regular at second or third, with a strong utility fallback if the bat winds up a bit short.

13 Jonathan Hernandez RHP

Born: 07/06/96 Age: 22 Bats: R Throws: R Height: 6'2" Weight: 175 Origin: International Free Agent, 2013

YEAR	TEAM	LVL	AGE	W	L	SV	G	GS	IP	H	HR	BB/9	K/9	K	GB%	BABIP	WHIP	ERA	DRA	WARP	PF
2016	HIC	A	19	10	9	0	24	22	116^{1}	110	14	3.8	6.6	85	49%	.279	1.37	4.56	3.64	1.9	99
2017	HIC	A	20	2	5	0	9	9	46^{1}	55	5	2.5	8.9	46	48%	.370	1.47	4.86	3.21	1.1	102
2017	DEB	A+	20	3	6	0	14	13	65^{1}	66	2	4.3	8.8	64	47%	.350	1.48	3.44	4.00	1.0	92
2018	DEB	A+	21	4	2	0	10	10	57^{1}	37	6	2.7	12.1	77	52%	.263	0.94	2.20	2.39	2.0	100
2018	FRI	AA	21	4	4	0	12	12	64	58	6	5.1	8.0	57	51%	.299	1.47	4.92	4.46	0.7	107
2019	*TEX*	*MLB*	*22*	*5*	*7*	*0*	*19*	*19*	96^{2}	*92*	*12*	*4.6*	*8.9*	*95*	*44%*	*.305*	*1.47*	*4.70*	*4.67*	*0.9*	*108*

Breakout: 14% Improve: 21% Collapse: 6% Attrition: 24% MLB: 34% *Comparables: Jordan Walden, Sean Reid-Foley, Jake Thompson*

You could argue that Hernandez should be a bit higher on this list, but he tends to split evaluators, due to a rotational cross-fire delivery and the inconsistent fastball command that comes with it. That said, there's a lot to like in his profile. Hernandez is an athlete with good feel for his body and more ability to repeat his release point than most who pitch like he does. Hernandez throws a fastball that sits 96-98 with armside life, a hard 86-88 mph plus slider with sharp dive and gloveside movement, a high-70s curveball that flashes above-average with a big spin rate, and an above-average changeup with quality deception and tumble. The main problem lies in his fastball command, which often puts him behind in counts and makes it difficult for him to get to his bevy of secondaries. Hernandez appears to be a strong "pitch backwards" candidate and it would be interesting to see how effective he was on a team more comfortable with that pitching philosophy.

14 Mason Englert RHP

Born: 11/01/99 Age: 19 Bats: B Throws: R Height: 6'4" Weight: 205 Origin: Round 4, 2018 Draft (#119 overall)

The overarching theme of this Rangers list is that the organization is "leaning into their strengths," so here we have a tall, athletic Texas prep arm who was pumping an easy 95 post-draft from a compact arm action. The #brand is strong. The Rangers went overslot in the fourth round, giving Englert one million smackers to buy him out of a Texas A&M commit. The fastball has run and sink, and he offers a full four-pitch mix at various stages of development. The slider is very projectable, and this is the exact type of profile Texas gets to jump in their first full pro season, so keep an eye out.

15 Pedro Gonzalez OF

Born: 10/27/97 Age: 21 Bats: R Throws: R Height: 6'5" Weight: 190 Origin: International Free Agent, 2014

YEAR	TEAM	LVL	AGE	PA	R	2B	3B	HR	RBI	BB	K	SB	CS	AVG/OBP/SLG	DRC+	VORP	BABIP	BRR	FRAA	WARP	PF
2016	DRO	RK	18	30	3	0	1	0	6	2	4	4	1	.222/.300/.296	93	0.0	.261	-1.0	CF(7) 0.3	0.0	107
2016	GJR	RK	18	248	32	15	8	2	19	14	77	6	7	.230/.290/.394	43	8.6	.336	1.8	CF(57) 2.5	-0.7	106
2017	GJR	RK	19	209	28	16	6	3	28	18	53	11	6	.321/.388/.519	96	13.6	.432	0.9	CF(41) -3.9	-0.1	120
2018	HIC	A	20	371	47	17	5	12	46	28	110	9	5	.234/.296/.421	92	11.7	.307	1.7	CF(60) 4.7, LF(20) -1.1	1.0	100
2019	*TEX*	*MLB*	*21*	*252*	*22*	*7*	*1*	*6*	*20*	*6*	*89*	*2*	*1*	*.151/.170/.270*	*7*	*-19.2*	*.201*	*0.1*	*CF 0, LF 0*	*-2.1*	*108*

Breakout: 0% Improve: 1% Collapse: 0% Attrition: 1% MLB: 1% *Comparables: Teoscar Hernandez, Keon Broxton, Daniel Fields*

It seems appropriate that Gonzalez is now a Rangers prospect. The org has a type after all, so it's not a shock that Gonzalez was the player to be named later in the Lucroy deal. He's a toolsy center fielder (for now) with plus raw, a plus arm, and a potential plus glove in a corner. If Gonzalez does grow off center, there will be a lot of pressure on the bat to play to its full potential, and he is still a bit raw at the plate. It's a long and strong swing with just average bat speed, and he struggled to make consistent quality contact in the Sally. Our Rangers prospect lists from the last decade are littered with dudes with swing-and-miss issues in Hickory. But when they hit, they hit big.

The Injured Guys

Cole Ragans, LHP

The southpaw's season ended before it began, thanks to a UCL tear. Pre-injury Ragans was lauded as a bit of a Cole Hamels development kit, given his easy mechanics, clean arm action, a low-90s fastball, and a plus changeup that he had good feel for. Ragans did struggle with his command during the season, which is a common issue for pitchers who have problematic wear on their UCL, but he still managed to clean through hitters on the strength of his changeup. Before the injury, he was often mentioned as a pitcher who would likely be able to use fastball location, his changeup, and an average curveball to solidify himself into the middle of an MLB rotation. We'll just have to see how it all looks once he's back on the mound.

Chris Seise, SS

Seise missed the entire 2018 season due to shoulder surgery. The projection is still appealing though, as Seise has a premium build with athletic movements. Pre-surgery, Seise was seen as a good bet to be at least an average defender at short due to his quick reactions and strong arm, but arm strength and consistency will be something to watch as he comes back. The bat is a bigger question, as his approach is still fairly raw. He has a big-leaguer's coordination and bat speed, but he'll need to find a way to tap into more of his average raw power while improving his patience and pitch recognition; if he can't, he'll be more of a utility guy than a starting SS.

Kyle Cody, RHP

Arguably the biggest disappointment for the Rangers came when Kyle Cody's partially strained UCL rehab turned into Tommy John surgery after a short rehab stint. Pre-injury Cody was making a major push up this list, and perhaps had a chance to work his way onto the 101 as well. Cody uses his 6-foot-7 frame to deliver a mid-high 90's fastball on an extreme downhill plane, a consistently plus curveball, and a developing changeup that was regularly flashing average during his breakout. At the very least, Cody appeared on track for a spot in the back of the Rangers rotation or as a late-inning reliever.

Unfortunately he's 24 and he will likely miss all of next season, which makes him hard to rank. He will likely be close to turning 26 the next time he takes the bump and two years removed from a start against age-appropriate competition. At that point the best option for the Rangers and Cody may be to have him work strictly fastball/curveball out of the pen to see what he can do there.

Others of note:

Sam Huff, C, Full-season-A Hickory

It also seems appropriate that the Rangers have a prospect who sounds like a Sun-Records-era Johnny Cash protagonist. Huff is a big dude with big raw and better defense behind the plate than you'd expect for a 20-year-old catcher listed at 6-foot-4, 230 lbs. But a swinging he will go, he will go, and that was an issue in his first taste of full-season ball. Despite his large frame, there are questions about his durability behind the plate, and he's playing more first base and DH at this point in his pro career than you'd like. So we have a good collection of tools, a chance to stick behind the plate, and another very Rangers prospect. Check back in when he kills a ball in Reno, just to watch it die.

Tyreque Reed, 1B, Full-season-A Hickory

Reed was drafted in the 8th round of the 2017 MLB draft out of Itawamba Community College, where he spent a season completely tearing through overmatched pitchers. At 6-foot-2, 260 pounds, Reed is about as large-bodied as large body first baseman come and he hits like it. He has plus bat speed and double-plus raw power, but he has little experience against quality competition. He struggled to pick up spin and off-speed early on in professional ball, but adjusted to put up gargantuan numbers down the stretch. In the second half of the season, Reed put up a .424 wOBA while maintaining a 10.8% walk rate with manageable strikeout numbers. The coordination and bat speed are both there to take advantage of his raw strength if he's able to continue improving against quality secondaries.

Jonathan Ornelas, SS, AZL Rangers

Pre-draft Ornelas was viewed primarily as a stereotypical toolsy athletic body who needed to be taught how to hit. In the AZL, he changed those perceptions quickly. He moves like a premium athlete with quick twitchy bursts and he has an instinctual feel for getting pop from his still-immature build. He generates plus bat speed and has quality bat-to-ball skills that allow him to make consistent contact on fastballs around the zone. Ornelas should be able to gain weight without losing foot speed or flexibility and he could develop above-average raw power. He's also fairly patient at the plate, as he walked 25 times in 203 plate appearances this summer.

Mike Matuella, RHP, Advanced-A Down East

This seems like a good time to point out that we don't use the 101 spot strictly for the 101st best prospect in baseball—it's more for a player we want to highlight or one we like better than anyone else. Regardless, Matuella didn't exactly reward our ranking in 2018. He struggled with his command before getting moved to the pen to manage his innings. He still has a plus fastball, and can touch higher. He's added a slider which he doesn't really have a feel for yet, and will still flash a power change. Matuella will be 25 next year and may never return to the starting rotation. We'll keep an eye on the stuff in 2019, because... well, we did like him more than anyone else, but for now he's yet another reason I still want to end every pitcher risk entry with: "Also, he's a pitcher."

Top Talents 25 and Under (born 4/1/93 or later):

1. Rougned Odor
2. Joey Gallo
3. Jose Leclerc
4. Nomar Mazara
5. Leody Taveras
6. Ronald Guzman
7. Bubba Thompson
8. Julio Pablo Martinez
9. Anderson Tejeda
10. Taylor Hearn

The Rangers' 25 and under list features many of the names you're used to, including a young core of big-leaguers. Leading that group is Odor. Though Odor missed a significant amount of time at the beginning of the season due to a hamstring injury, he compiled 2.4 WARP and finished the year with a 97 DRC+ and a career-high 7.5 FRAA. After a rough 2017, Odor's rebound confirms that he's still an integral part of this Rangers roster.

Gallo again makes the list after having a similar-ish season to the previous one. You look at his numbers and think that maybe, just maybe, his hitting ability is sustainable. He had another 40 homer season, and even though his DRC+ dropped a bit, the dip wasn't alarming. He posted 2.7 WARP this season—lower than the 3.1 he put up in 2017—but a 2+ WARP player who can hit 40-something home runs is a good thing to have.

Jose Leclerc makes the list for the first time after coming off a very, very strong 2018. He posted a 2.87 DRA and also improved his walk and strikeout numbers considerably. After fanning 85 hitters in 58 innings, he'll return as the Rangers closer in 2019.

Dropping from first to fourth is Mazara. Mazara turns 24 in April, and is coming off another 20 home run season, one in which he raised his DRC+ to 98. Defensively, he produced the worst FRAA numbers of his career, though it's worth mentioning that he spent most of the season nursing a thumb injury. Mazara was the headliner of the Rangers 25 and under list the last two years, but after three seasons of middling production, it's getting harder to imagine him as a star. Perhaps this is just who he is as a major leaguer.

Sixth on the list is Ronald Guzmán, who made his debut in April. He's still young and hasn't reached his full potential. His walk and strikeout numbers are concerning, but he has time to adjust.

The remainder of the list features the toolsy "hey those guys might be good let's see what they can do" type of prospects this organization loves to cultivate. They didn't hit on a ton of those types in their last cycle—which is one of the reasons why Texas is looking up at their division mates from the AL West cellar.

Toronto Blue Jays

The State of the System:

Okay Mark, it's probably a top five system.

The Top Ten:

1 Vladimir Guerrero Jr. 3B OFP: 80 Likely: 70 ETA: Whenever Shapiro deigns to make a phone call

Born: 03/16/99 Age: 20 Bats: R Throws: R Height: 6'1" Weight: 200 Origin: International Free Agent, 2015

YEAR	TEAM	LVL	AGE	PA	R	2B	3B	HR	RBI	BB	K	SB	CS	AVG/OBP/SLG	DRC+	VORP	BABIP	BRR	FRAA	WARP	PF
2016	BLU	RK	17	276	32	12	3	8	46	33	35	15	5	.271/.359/.449	134	19.2	.283	1.5	3B(50) -10.7	-0.2	108
2017	LNS	A	18	318	53	21	1	7	45	40	34	6	2	.316/.409/.480	172	26.9	.336	0.8	3B(61) -2.6	2.9	110
2017	DUN	A+	18	209	31	7	1	6	31	36	28	2	2	.333/.450/.494	182	17.1	.365	-2.4	3B(41) -1.5	1.5	108
2018	NHP	AA	19	266	48	19	1	14	60	21	27	3	3	.402/.449/.671	192	37.4	.402	-2.9	3B(53) 1.0	2.9	107
2018	BUF	AAA	19	128	15	7	0	6	16	15	10	0	0	.336/.414/.564	185	11.5	.323	-4.8	3B(25) 4.3	1.4	97
2019	*TOR*	*MLB*	*20*	*457*	*62*	*23*	*1*	*20*	*66*	*38*	*69*	*1*	*1*	*.304/.368/.510*	*139*	*31.4*	*.325*	*-0.9*	*3B 0*	*3.4*	*105*

Breakout: 24% Improve: 39% Collapse: 1% Attrition: 6% MLB: 41% *Comparables: Jason Heyward, Mike Trout, Jurickson Profar*

The Report: A scout once told me that 8 reports are just 2 reports, but longer. How much is there to explain? The usual language of baseball scouting is insufficient. Vladito "came back to earth" in Buffalo, which means that the 19-year-old didn't quite manage to hit [expletive deleted] .400 for a full season in the upper minors. Shruggie face. I spent a soupcon of tortured prose on him already this year. What else is there to say? I shouldn't be writing this blurb. Vladito should belong to the MLB scribes now; let them consult their muses and thesauruses to try to come up with something novel.

He's 7 hit/7 power. Well, that might be low. It's what I can *responsibly* put down on the page. He's a below-average third baseman, but playable there for now if you were so inclined. Get his bat into the lineup however you [expletive deleted] want. This is the best prospect in baseball, the best pure bat in the minors. And the only reason we aren't calling him one of the best pure bats in the majors is we've codified a bunch of sabermetric writing by dudes from 2009 who thought they were smarter than Brian Sabean as "good process." The only good process here is watching Vladito hit majestic dingers on the biggest possible stage. That's what's best for the Blue Jays and best for the game.

The Risks: Low. Yeah, I know. But it's low.

Ben Carsley's Fantasy Take: Listen, writing about fantasy prospects makes one prone to hyperbole. Because everyone is always looking for The Next Star (seriously we were getting "who is the next Ronald Acuna?" questions last February), you feel pressure to exaggerate how good or how impactful guys can be. But the reality of the situation is the established elite tier at pretty much every position is considered elite for a reason. There isn't always an Acuna or a Juan Soto waiting in the wings. Sometimes it's smarter to preach caution and be realistic, even if it's less fun. Sometimes.

This is not that time. Vlad's fantasy ceiling is legitimately as the next Miguel Cabrera. His floor probably looks something like your median Anthony Rizzo year. He's gonna win you a few championships if you're lucky enough to have him/don't suck at roster construction. Let's party.

2 Bo Bichette SS

OFP: 70 Likely: 60 ETA: Well, I expect he will be ready by late 2019

Born: 03/05/98 Age: 21 Bats: R Throws: R Height: 6'0" Weight: 200 Origin: Round 2, 2016 Draft (#66 overall)

YEAR	TEAM	LVL	AGE	PA	R	2B	3B	HR	RBI	BB	K	SB	CS	AVG/OBP/SLG	DRC+	VORP	BABIP	BRR	FRAA	WARP	PF
2016	BLJ	RK	18	91	21	9	2	4	36	6	17	3	0	.427/.451/.732	264	19.5	.484	-0.4	SS(16) 1.7, 2B(6) 0.3	1.5	98
2017	LNS	A	19	317	60	32	3	10	51	28	55	12	3	.384/.448/.623	209	48.4	.452	3.0	SS(51) 0.2, 2B(14) 0.3	5.0	110
2017	DUN	A+	19	182	28	9	1	4	23	14	26	10	4	.323/.379/.463	146	12.5	.360	-0.2	SS(35) -0.3	1.1	107
2018	NHP	AA	20	595	95	43	7	11	74	48	101	32	11	.286/.343/.453	125	40.6	.331	3.2	SS(116) -4.0, 2B(9) 0.6	3.1	105
2019	*TOR*	*MLB*	*21*	*252*	*32*	*15*	*2*	*7*	*26*	*11*	*61*	*7*	*2*	*.249/.280/.416*	*87*	*6.2*	*.301*	*0.6*	*SS 0, 2B 0*	*0.7*	*105*

Breakout: 21% Improve: 38% Collapse: 10% Attrition: 28% MLB: 51% *Comparables: Franklin Barreto, Addison Russell, Alen Hanson*

The Report: Dante's kid wasn't quite the same inferno at the plate this year, but Double-A wasn't much of a challenge for him either. Bichette combines elite bat speed and hand/eye to produce a laser show only matched by Pink Floyd Night at your local Planetarium. I don't really buy Bichette's listed height/weight, as his frame looks smaller than listed, but regardless, the plus raw is legit. The ball jumps off his bat and the power plays foul line to foul line. He has so much bat speed that he can really let the ball eat and drive it the other way, and if he does end up at his listed size, there might be more power coming.

Bichette's swing is unorthodox, featuring a long load behind his back shoulder with a near armbar and hitch, but he makes it work and tracks pitches well. He can get too aggressive and pull-happy at the plate, but the raw material is certainly here for a plus-or-better major-league hit tool. At shortstop, Bichette grinds it out to get to fringe-average, but he grows on you there. He has good hands and instincts, but the range is a little light and puts pressure on a merely solid-average arm. Everything just feels a half-grade short for the 6, but then you will see him make a plus play and talk yourself into him sticking there for a while. If he slides over to the keystone, he will be an above-average defender there. But really, you're here for the bat, and there's all-star upside in the profile if Bichette continues to rake in the majors.

The Risks: Medium. I believe in the bat here—although it took a little cajoling—but any swing this unorthodox may allow major league pitchers to suss out holes.

Ben Carsley's Fantasy Take: Did you enjoy Xander Bogaerts' 2018 season? Yes? Good, because that's the type of upside Bichette brings to the table. It's tough to say whether Toronto's absurd… let's call it "caution" with Vladito means they'll hold Bichette down too long as well. But regardless of when Bichette gets the call, he'll be an immediate fantasy factor and potential top-7 fantasy shortstop. He gets lost a bit because he's not the best dynasty prospect in his own organization (Vladito) or at his position (Tatis Jr.), but Bichette is a no-s*** top-10 fantasy prospect right now in his own right. Get excited.

3 Nate Pearson RHP

OFP: 60 Likely: 50 ETA: 2020

Born: 08/20/96 Age: 22 Bats: R Throws: R Height: 6'6" Weight: 245 Origin: Round 1, 2017 Draft (#28 overall)

YEAR	TEAM	LVL	AGE	W	L	SV	G	GS	IP	H	HR	BB/9	K/9	K	GB%	BABIP	WHIP	ERA	DRA	WARP	PF
2017	VAN	A-	20	0	0	0	7	7	19	6	0	2.4	11.4	24	40%	.158	0.58	0.95	4.39	0.2	103
2019	*TOR*	*MLB*	*22*	*2*	*4*	*0*	*9*	*9*	*33*	*38*	*8*	*3.9*	*7.5*	*28*	*38%*	*.308*	*1.59*	*6.16*	*6.39*	*-0.3*	*105*

Breakout: 0% Improve: 1% Collapse: 0% Attrition: 1% MLB: 1% *Comparables: Elvis Araujo, Braden Shipley, Austin Voth*

The Report: One of the absolute best arms in the minors. He hits 100 MPH with some frequency as a starter, and was famously up to 103-104 with the fastball for a short burst in this year's Fall Stars Game. He's got one of those low-90s sliders that should be a physical impossibility, and a slower curve and change that both flash average-to-plus. It's not just a starter's arsenal, it's a straight-up ace arsenal. The stuff comes packaged in a starter's frame and a pitching motion that doesn't scream reliever. If Pearson fully actualizes, he'll look a lot like another Blue Jays late-first rounder: Noah Syndergaard.

That's the positive side. The negative side starts with some simple math: 20 1/3 of his 42 professional innings were in this year's Arizona Fall League. As a pro, he's been unavailable to pitch far more often than he's been available; before wowing everyone in the AFL, he had a lost 2018 season, with an oblique injury followed by a fractured right forearm from a comebacker in his only regular season start. The delivery isn't totally clean, with a head whack and a fairly hard landing. The fastball can get kind of flat—Peter Alonso turned around one of those 104s for a monster home run. He is going to need one of those offspeed pitches to jump. He's thrown less than two innings in full-season ball, so it isn't like there's a track record of pro success here… yet.

The Risks: Extreme in both directions. Pearson already had significant reliever and injury risks when he was drafted, and a traumatic injury to his pitching forearm didn't reduce those. He has a screw in his pitching elbow from surgery during high school. He could go a lot of different ways in 2019, including paths where the above roles look silly in either direction.

Ben Carsley's Fantasy Take: Eovaldi isn't just a good comp for Pearson's MLB value; it works for his fantasy value as well. That means some years you could be getting a dominating, strikeout-heavy SP3, while other years you could be signing up for an occupied DL slot. In general fantasy owners root for pitchers to remain starters, but in Pearson's case, a future as a closer may be most lucrative.

4 Danny Jansen C

OFP: 60 Likely: 50 ETA: Debuted in 2018

Born: 04/15/95 Age: 24 Bats: R Throws: R Height: 6'2" Weight: 225 Origin: Round 16, 2013 Draft (#475 overall)

YEAR	TEAM	LVL	AGE	PA	R	2B	3B	HR	RBI	BB	K	SB	CS	AVG/OBP/SLG	DRC+	VORP	BABIP	BRR	FRAA	WARP	PF
2016	DUN	A+	21	217	18	7	0	1	23	22	40	7	1	.218/.313/.271	84	0.6	.268	-0.2	C(50) -1.3	0.0	109
2017	DUN	A+	22	136	19	6	0	5	18	8	14	0	0	.369/.422/.541	183	17.1	.385	-0.7	C(25) -2.0	1.1	104
2017	NHP	AA	22	210	23	15	1	2	20	22	19	1	0	.291/.378/.419	119	15.5	.311	-1.4	C(50) -0.9	0.8	103
2017	BUF	AAA	22	78	8	4	1	3	10	11	7	0	0	.328/.423/.552	165	11.2	.333	-0.1	C(21) -0.4	0.7	92
2018	BUF	AAA	23	360	45	21	1	12	58	44	49	5	1	.275/.390/.473	137	32.9	.292	0.2	C(56) -6.0	1.7	96
2018	TOR	MLB	23	95	12	6	0	3	8	9	17	0	0	.247/.347/.432	100	6.6	.274	0.9	C(29) 1.0	0.7	106
2019	*TOR*	*MLB*	*24*	*412*	*48*	*18*	*1*	*13*	*47*	*42*	*75*	*2*	*0*	*.228/.329/.389*	*100*	*18.5*	*.259*	*-0.5*	*C -10*	*0.9*	*105*

Breakout: 12% Improve: 39% Collapse: 7% Attrition: 23% MLB: 74% *Comparables: Josh Bell, Conor Jackson, J.R. Towles*

The Report: Warby Parker would struggle to find a better celebrity endorser than Danny Jansen. Besides having some of the most fashionable specs in pro ball, the new lenses sparked a 2017 breakout that continued throughout 2018. It's a striking infomercial before and after: from org guy to borderline Top 101 prospect. Jansen has a bit of an unorthodox swing, where he drops his hands by his hip during setup, followed by a minimal load and a slight uppercut plane. His hand-eye is good enough now that he can still cover just about everything. The quality of contact is inconsistent, but hard enough to project average hit and power tools, which would make him one of the better hitting catchers in today's game. His glove behind the plate has improved to averageish as well. There are no real weaknesses in his defensive profile, but it's possible he might end up in more of a timeshare if his org prefers a backstop with a plus glove.

The Risks: Low. The balanced profile and 2018 major league performance makes him a fairly safe bet to have a significant major league career.

Ben Carsley's Fantasy Take: I've written at length about how trusting catching prospects to make immediate impacts is a poor strategy. It's through the lens of those lessons learned–and not through any particular fault of Jansen's–that I'm going to urge caution in projecting big 2019 production. Yes, he's close to the majors, and yes, the power tool looks real. But Russell Martin is still going to get plenty of playing time, and the learning curve for young catchers is especially steep. Eventually, Jansen can be a top-10 option and routine 20-homer threat at the position. Just don't confuse his MLB ETA (pretty much right now) with his fantasy impact ETA (2020 or beyond).

5 Kevin Smith IF

OFP: 55 Likely: 50 ETA: 2020

Born: 07/04/96 Age: 22 Bats: R Throws: R Height: 6'1" Weight: 188 Origin: Round 4, 2017 Draft (#129 overall)

YEAR	TEAM	LVL	AGE	PA	R	2B	3B	HR	RBI	BB	K	SB	CS	AVG/OBP/SLG	DRC+	VORP	BABIP	BRR	FRAA	WARP	PF
2017	BLU	RK	20	283	43	25	1	8	43	16	70	9	0	.271/.312/.466	94	18.0	.337	3.9	SS(58) 8.3	1.4	102
2018	LNS	A	21	204	36	23	4	7	44	17	33	12	1	.355/.407/.639	190	33.7	.397	3.1	SS(24) 1.7, 3B(21) 0.7	3.2	104
2018	DUN	A+	21	371	57	8	2	18	49	23	88	17	5	.274/.332/.468	125	23.3	.319	4.6	SS(63) 6.9, 2B(13) 1.0	3.0	102
2019	*TOR*	*MLB*	*22*	*252*	*25*	*11*	*0*	*9*	*30*	*6*	*76*	*4*	*1*	*.196/.213/.362*	*45*	*-7.6*	*.238*	*0.4*	*SS 4, 3B 0*	*-0.4*	*105*

Breakout: 12% Improve: 35% Collapse: 1% Attrition: 17% MLB: 40% *Comparables: Franklin Barreto, Derek Dietrich, Trevor Story*

The Report: If not for Vladito, you could make the case that Smith had the most impressive 2018 season among all Blue Jays farmhands. He put to bed the notion that he was a glove-first guy who lacked an approach at the plate by slashing .302/.358/.528 over two levels. The former Maryland star has quick hands, above-average bat speed, and a swing that gets leverage. It's a strong enough bat with above-average raw power that will play at any spot in the infield.

Smith is fluid and balanced defensively, with good instincts and adequate arm strength. It's not flashy but he should stick at short for the foreseeable future. Vladito and Bichette are the future stars of the organization, but Smith is an important cog in the rebuild as well.

The Risks: Medium. He's yet to face advanced pitching in the upper minors and there is bound to be a learning curve there. He has a broad base of skills, however, and that should carry him to the major leagues.

Ben Carsley's Fantasy Take: Smith may be a better IRL prospect than a fantasy one thanks to his defensive profile, but he's still got plenty of value in our world, too. The hope is that Smith continues to hit as he climbs the MiLB ladder and that we eventually view him somewhat similarly to how we see Luis Urias today. Even if the hit tool falls a bit short of those levels, Smith is a nice grab for those of you in deeper leagues today and could hit the back of the top-101 in 2020 if he keeps performing and has as clear a path to playing time as he does at present.

6 Eric Pardinho RHP   OFP: 60   Likely: 45   ETA: 2023

Born: 01/05/01 Age: 18 Bats: R Throws: R Height: 5'10" Weight: 155 Origin: International Free Agent, 2018

YEAR	TEAM	LVL	AGE	W	L	SV	G	GS	IP	H	HR	BB/9	K/9	K	GB%	BABIP	WHIP	ERA	DRA	WARP	PF
2018	BLU	RK	17	4	3	0	11	11	50	37	5	2.9	11.5	64	47%	.274	1.06	2.88	3.62	1.3	108
2019	*TOR*	*MLB*	*18*	*1*	*3*	*0*	*7*	*7*	*32^{1}*	*35*	*6*	*5.3*	*8.2*	*29*	*44%*	*.310*	*1.68*	*5.92*	*6.12*	*-0.2*	*105*

Breakout: 0% Improve: 0% Collapse: 0% Attrition: 0% MLB: 0%   *Comparables: Mike Soroka, Martin Perez, Roberto Osuna*

The Report: Pardinho rose to fame as an interesting curiosity in September 2016, when he was the 15-year-old ace of the Brazilian national team in WBC qualifying. Besides being a fun story, he's also a legitimate prospect. Pardinho's signing bonus in the 2017-18 international pool was lower than you might expect for a higher-end J2 with name value, likely because of perceived limited projectability due to his small stature and questions about the level of competition he faced in Brazil. His 2018 pro debut couldn't have been more splendid, with a dominant age-17 season in the Appalachian League against much older batters (Wander Franco excepted). He's incredibly advanced for his age, with significantly better command than you'd expect to see out of his age cohort—high school juniors—and the makings of a full four-pitch mix. He's not a finesse pitcher, either, as he's already running his fastball into the mid-90s. And he's so young.

The Risks: Extreme. He's a 17-year-old short righty in rookie ball. He's here because the stuff profile is so advanced, but he's still a 17-year-old short righty in rookie ball. He might get hurt, he might not be a starter, etc. Quite a lot happens developmentally to young pitchers between rookie ball in the majors.

Ben Carsley's Fantasy Take: Watch list. The top part of your watch list that you fill with players you check in on every 10-or-so days, but still, watch list.

7 Sean Reid-Foley RHP   OFP: 55   Likely: 45   ETA: Debuted in 2018

Born: 08/30/95 Age: 23 Bats: R Throws: R Height: 6'3" Weight: 220 Origin: Round 2, 2014 Draft (#49 overall)

YEAR	TEAM	LVL	AGE	W	L	SV	G	GS	IP	H	HR	BB/9	K/9	K	GB%	BABIP	WHIP	ERA	DRA	WARP	PF
2016	LNS	A	20	4	3	0	11	11	58	43	2	3.4	9.2	59	52%	.277	1.12	2.95	3.51	1.1	105
2016	DUN	A+	20	6	2	0	10	10	57^{1}	35	2	2.5	11.1	71	49%	.254	0.89	2.67	2.90	1.7	107
2017	NHP	AA	21	10	11	0	27	27	132^{2}	145	22	3.6	8.3	122	42%	.318	1.49	5.09	5.63	-0.7	104
2018	NHP	AA	22	5	0	0	8	8	44^{1}	27	3	4.1	10.6	52	55%	.240	1.06	2.03	3.65	0.9	110
2018	BUF	AAA	22	7	5	0	16	16	85^{1}	76	5	3.2	10.3	98	43%	.318	1.24	3.90	3.19	2.3	96
2018	TOR	MLB	22	2	4	0	7	7	33^{1}	31	6	5.7	11.3	42	36%	.312	1.56	5.13	4.95	0.1	104
2019	*TOR*	*MLB*	*23*	*4*	*5*	*0*	*13*	*13*	*74*	*68*	*9*	*3.8*	*9.6*	*79*	*43%*	*.300*	*1.34*	*4.30*	*4.40*	*0.9*	*105*

Breakout: 22% Improve: 33% Collapse: 16% Attrition: 34% MLB: 64%   *Comparables: Michael Fulmer, Zach Davies, Lucas Giolito*

The Report: The Top 101 version of Reid-Foley showed up more often in 2018, although he remains a frustrating pitching prospect. He'll show a tick-above-average fastball velocity, but it can take him a bit to ramp up to it. Reid-Foley will cut and run the pitch, but it's not always effective movement. He still struggles to show even average command with it, as he tends to lose his release point despite relatively simple mechanics.

Both his breaking balls project as average but will flash better. The slider sits in the mid-80s and will flash good tilt, but it's built to entice grounders rather than swings and misses. The curve comes in around 80 and can bleed into the slider in the low-80s, but Reid-Foley will flash a tight downer version as well. He commands both breakers better than the fastball. His change is used sparingly and can lack deception, but will flash good velo separation and fade. His 2018 major league cameo didn't really answer the main question with the profile, which is "will he throw enough strikes, or enough quality strikes to turn over a lineup multiple times?" The stuff is more solid-average than plus, so Reid-Foley will need to limit the self-inflicted damage to stick in the back of a rotation over the long haul.

The Risks: Low. Reid-Foley finally conquered the upper minors and missed bats everywhere. How much further he refines his command will determine the ultimate major league outcome here. I'd bet he'll always be a little bit frustrating though.

Ben Carsley's Fantasy Take: If Reid-Foley had even marginally better stuff or marginally better command, it'd be a lot easier to get excited about him. As he stands currently, he'll bring much more value to the Jays than he will to fantasy owners. He should be owned in TDGX-sized leagues (800-plus players), but he's a spot starter in shallower formats.

8 Anthony Alford OF

OFP: 55 Likely: 45 ETA: Debuted in 2017

Born: 07/20/94 Age: 24 Bats: R Throws: R Height: 6'1" Weight: 215 Origin: Round 3, 2012 Draft (#112 overall)

YEAR	TEAM	LVL	AGE	PA	R	2B	3B	HR	RBI	BB	K	SB	CS	AVG/OBP/SLG	DRC+	VORP	BABIP	BRR	FRAA	WARP	PF
2016	DUN	A+	21	401	53	17	2	9	44	53	117	18	6	.236/.344/.378	107	15.0	.327	2.3	CF(84) 2.6, LF(6) 1.7	1.3	109
2017	TOR	MLB	22	8	0	1	0	0	0	0	3	0	0	.125/.125/.250	65	-0.8	.200	0.0	LF(3) -0.2, RF(2) 0.0	0.0	106
2017	NHP	AA	22	289	41	14	0	5	24	35	45	18	3	.310/.406/.429	135	22.0	.360	2.5	CF(32) 5.1, LF(13) 1.0	2.1	101
2018	BUF	AAA	23	417	52	22	1	5	34	30	112	17	7	.240/.312/.344	96	9.0	.327	4.5	CF(43) 2.9, LF(31) -1.7	0.8	96
2018	TOR	MLB	23	21	3	0	0	0	1	2	9	1	0	.105/.190/.105	75	-0.9	.200	0.7	LF(7) 0.2, RF(3) -0.1	0.1	105
2019	*TOR*	*MLB*	*24*	*107*	*11*	*5*	*0*	*2*	*10*	*7*	*30*	*3*	*1*	*.221/.288/.341*	*72*	*0.4*	*.296*	*0.2*	*CF 1, LF 0*	*0.2*	*105*

Breakout: 11% Improve: 22% Collapse: 1% Attrition: 16% MLB: 30% *Comparables: Reymond Fuentes, Drew Stubbs, Brian Goodwin*

The Report: It's been quite a road. The Blue Jays drafted Alford back in 2012 as a multi-sport star planning to play football at Southern Miss, where he became a part-time starter as a true freshman option quarterback. He transferred to Ole Miss to play defensive back after being charged in a campus altercation, and didn't play much baseball for three seasons until he quit football in the fall of 2014. He quickly re-established himself as a top prospect on the diamond, making the 101 in each of the last three seasons. He has the incredible all-around athletic ability you'd expect of a guy who saw substantial playing time as an FBS true freshman option quarterback.

Alford's baseball career has been marred by a series of injuries, including a severe concussion, a broken hamate, recurring knee problems, and this year's entry, a hamstring strain in spring training. With only 430 pro games under his belt, frankly, he just hasn't played all that much. His hitting performance has been inconsistent, and despite call-ups in each of the last two years, he's yet to master Triple-A. He hasn't hit for much game power to date, although we still think he has enough raw to have a shot at average or even above-average power later on. At times the hit tool has looked like a plus, and at times he's hit in the .230s. His defense is more than good enough for center currently and he can play the corners well, too.

The Risks: High, especially considering that he's spent parts of the last two seasons in the majors. He might not hit and he might not be healthy enough. We're basically giving Alford a pass from his lost 2018 because of his overwhelming athleticism, the history of prior success, and the hamstring injury, but maybe this is what he is now.

Ben Carsley's Fantasy Take: Fool me three times, shame on you, but fool me four times... There's an argument to rank Alford in the Top 101 again based on his speed and proximity to the majors, but I'm out. He can't stay healthy, and I'm not totally convinced he can hit. Will Alford sneak in a few seasons where he swipes 20-plus bases and makes me look dumb? Yep. Will he have even more years where he's a total fantasy non-factor? Also yep.

9 Jordan Groshans SS

OFP: 55 Likely: 45 ETA: 2022

Born: 11/10/99 Age: 19 Bats: R Throws: R Height: 6'3" Weight: 178 Origin: Round 1, 2018 Draft (#12 overall)

YEAR	TEAM	LVL	AGE	PA	R	2B	3B	HR	RBI	BB	K	SB	CS	AVG/OBP/SLG	DRC+	VORP	BABIP	BRR	FRAA	WARP	PF
2018	BLJ	RK	18	159	17	12	0	4	39	13	29	0	0	.331/.390/.500	148	14.7	.387	-0.8	3B(16) -1.2, SS(15) 0.6	0.6	103
2018	BLU	RK	18	48	4	1	0	1	4	2	8	0	0	.182/.229/.273	34	-0.6	.194	0.1	SS(6) 0.9, 3B(5) 0.0	-0.1	103
2019	*TOR*	*MLB*	*19*	*252*	*12*	*2*	*0*	*6*	*20*	*1*	*74*	*0*	*0*	*.103/.105/.182*	*-33*	*-33.4*	*.114*	*-0.5*	*SS 1, 3B -1*	*-3.6*	*105*

Breakout: 4% Improve: 6% Collapse: 0% Attrition: 3% MLB: 7% *Comparables: Adalberto Mondesi, Gleyber Torres, Elvis Andrus*

The Report: The first of two Magnolia High alums taken by the Jays in last summer's draft, Groshans is a big ol' Texas country boy with country strength to match (yes, yes Magnolia is a sleepy Houston suburb, but let's not let that get in the way of scouting cliches, I have a word count to hit). For now, Toronto has him splitting time between shortstop and third base. The former seems... optimistic given his frame, but his strong arm will play at either spot on the left side of the infield and he has solid enough hands for the hot corner. The body might not cooperate there in five years either, but further physical projection might also allow Groshans to grow into even more raw power. It's plus at present, although he struggles to get to it at times due to a fairly flat swing plane. There's a bit of length to the swing, and an occasional bat wrap sporadically lengthens it further. The profile will require more basting than your average high-pick prep bat, but Groshans could be an above-average regular when the timer goes off.

The Risks: High. Hit tool questions, positional questions, limited pro track record, basically the Full Monty.

Ben Carsley's Fantasy Take: Groshans may not be among the first 10 guys you pop in dynasty first-year player drafts, but he should probably be among the next 10. A three-plus season lead time isn't wonderful, but Groshans has the power and hit projections needed to turn into a top-12 fantasy third baseman in time. Factor in how well the Jays have developed guys like this lately, and there's more to like here from a fantasy perspective than first meets the eye.

10 T.J. Zeuch RHP

OFP: 55 Likely: 45 ETA: Summer 2019

Born: 08/01/95 Age: 23 Bats: R Throws: R Height: 6'7" Weight: 225 Origin: Round 1, 2016 Draft (#21 overall)

YEAR	TEAM	LVL	AGE	W	L	SV	G	GS	IP	H	HR	BB/9	K/9	K	GB%	BABIP	WHIP	ERA	DRA	WARP	PF
2016	VAN	A-	20	0	1	0	6	6	23	21	1	2.0	8.6	22	70%	.317	1.13	3.52	3.79	0.4	99
2016	LNS	A	20	0	1	0	2	2	8	10	1	2.2	15.8	14	65%	.474	1.50	9.00	2.68	0.2	103
2017	BLJ	RK	21	0	2	0	3	3	7	9	1	2.6	6.4	5	60%	.333	1.57	5.14	4.15	0.1	94
2017	DUN	A+	21	3	4	0	12	11	58^2	63	3	2.6	7.1	46	64%	.312	1.36	3.38	3.97	0.9	103
2018	DUN	A+	22	3	3	0	6	6	36^1	34	4	2.2	5.9	24	63%	.273	1.18	3.47	5.91	-0.2	102
2018	NHP	AA	22	9	5	0	21	21	120	120	7	2.3	6.1	81	56%	.298	1.26	3.08	4.02	1.8	105
2019	*TOR*	*MLB*	*23*	*1*	*1*	*0*	*3*	*3*	*15*	*16*	*2*	*3.3*	*6.6*	*11*	*53%*	*.301*	*1.45*	*5.01*	*5.15*	*0.1*	*105*

Breakout: 24% Improve: 35% Collapse: 11% Attrition: 26% MLB: 52% *Comparables: Paul Blackburn, Chad Kuhl, Jarred Cosart*

The Report: So this fellow is a giant former first-rounder who throws a plus sinker and flashes three offspeed pitches at above-average or better, and has useful command often enough. What is he doing all the way down here? Well, there's a hard reality about the modern game, in that you can have a 60 fastball and two average offspeed pitches without really having a swing-and-miss offering. This has already manifested in Zeuch's poor strikeout rates. The other issue is that his command profile, slider, curve, and change all come and go from look-to-look. He's consistently shown enough to get outs but he hasn't been dominant as often as you'd like. Tall pitchers do sometimes develop late, and there are enough individual pieces here for optimism.

The Risks: Moderate, in that he could just be a sixth starter or middle reliever. There's also more positive risk than you'd think for a 23-year-old college pitcher—there are worse upside bets than the tall dude with this kind of pitch profile.

Ben Carsley's Fantasy Take: Zeuch has just enough upside to be more interesting than most mid-to-backend starter prospects, but that's damning with faint praise. Toronto is not a good place to pitch, Zeuch looks likely to kill your WHIP at present and wins may be hard to come by as a Jay for a good little while. He's a watch list player at best.

The Next Five:

11 Cavan Biggio IF

Born: 04/11/95 Age: 24 Bats: L Throws: R Height: 6'1" Weight: 203 Origin: Round 5, 2016 Draft (#162 overall)

YEAR	TEAM	LVL	AGE	PA	R	2B	3B	HR	RBI	BB	K	SB	CS	AVG/OBP/SLG	DRC+	VORP	BABIP	BRR	FRAA	WARP	PF
2016	VAN	A-	21	238	24	11	3	0	21	29	28	9	3	.282/.382/.366	128	13.1	.324	-0.4	2B(49) -3.0	0.0	99
2016	LNS	A	21	42	3	1	0	0	5	4	7	2	0	.222/.310/.250	84	-0.3	.267	-0.8	2B(9) 0.6	-0.1	106
2017	DUN	A+	22	556	75	17	5	11	60	74	140	11	7	.233/.342/.363	95	10.2	.304	1.1	2B(116) 6.4, 3B(6) -0.4	0.8	105
2018	NHP	AA	23	563	80	23	5	26	99	100	148	20	8	.252/.388/.499	135	44.8	.307	3.6	2B(68) 1.5, 3B(34) -1.1	3.5	105
2019	*TOR*	*MLB*	*24*	*252*	*32*	*7*	*1*	*9*	*26*	*30*	*73*	*4*	*2*	*.182/.282/.348*	*74*	*-0.5*	*.221*	*0.2*	*2B 1, 3B -1*	*0.0*	*105*

Breakout: 8% Improve: 19% Collapse: 2% Attrition: 22% MLB: 32% *Comparables: Drew Robinson, Alex Blandino, Darnell Sweeney*

The other, other, other bloodlines guy at New Hampshire this year, Biggio may not have the upside of Bichette or Vladito, nor the major league time under his belt of Gurriel, but his 2018 was a bit of a minor breakout. While he'd be far from the first lefty to have a power spike playing his home games at Northeast Delta Dental Stadium, Biggio was actually better on the road in 2018. He tweaked his swing to tap into his solid-average raw power and has turned into a potential three-true-outcomes infielder. Where he ends up on the dirt is an intriguing question. He'd be fringy at second or third, but could handle either spot (the aforementioned existence of Vladito, Bichette, and Gurriel meant he played a fair bit of first as well), and while it's not out of the question that he slugs and walks his way to a second-division starter role at one of those spots, Biggio might be best suited as a Swiss Army knife lefty bench piece with some pop. The Blue Jays have started getting him some corner outfield reps as well, perhaps with an eye toward that outcome.

12 Adam Kloffenstein RHP

Born: 08/25/00 Age: 18 Bats: R Throws: R Height: 6'5" Weight: 243 Origin: Round 3, 2018 Draft (#88 overall)

YEAR	TEAM	LVL	AGE	W	L	SV	G	GS	IP	H	HR	BB/9	K/9	K	GB%	BABIP	WHIP	ERA	DRA	WARP	PF
2019	*TOR*	*MLB*	*18*	*1*	*3*	*0*	*6*	*6*	*29^{2}*	*28*	*3*	*9.3*	*7.8*	*26*	*47%*	*.285*	*1.99*	*6.30*	*6.53*	*-0.4*	*105*

Breakout: 0% Improve: 0% Collapse: 0% Attrition: 0% MLB: 0% *Comparables: Mike Soroka, Deolis Guerra, Aaron Sanchez*

Groshans' high school teammate got 2.5 million bucks to forgo TCU. Unlike most prep arms, Kloffenstein doesn't need any late-night runs to Raising Cane's to fill out his frame. He's already built like a rotation stalwart, and most of the rest of the profile fits the "third-round overslot prep arm" mold. He's got a fastball that can touch the mid-90s and features wicked two-seam action at times. He has two breaking balls that bleed together a bit, but he'll flash a tight power slider. The change-up is a "work in progress." There's some reliever risk here; compact arm action, Kloffenstein has significant effort in his delivery. Still, given the present stuff and frame, he's a fairly "safe" prep arm—which is to say, not safe at all, but relatively safe.

13 Griffin Conine OF

Born: 07/11/97 Age: 21 Bats: L Throws: R Height: 6'1" Weight: 200 Origin: Round 2, 2018 Draft (#52 overall)

YEAR	TEAM	LVL	AGE	PA	R	2B	3B	HR	RBI	BB	K	SB	CS	AVG/OBP/SLG	DRC+	VORP	BABIP	BRR	FRAA	WARP	PF
2018	VAN	A-	20	230	24	14	2	7	30	19	63	5	0	.238/.309/.427	93	2.2	.304	-1.5	RF(46) 10.1	0.4	103
2019	*TOR*	*MLB*	*21*	*252*	*18*	*10*	*0*	*9*	*27*	*8*	*91*	*0*	*0*	*.126/.155/.276*	*8*	*-21.3*	*.150*	*-0.5*	*RF 4*	*-1.9*	*105*

Breakout: 1% Improve: 2% Collapse: 0% Attrition: 2% MLB: 2% *Comparables: Destin Hood, Kyle Waldrop, Moises Sierra*

The other, other, other, other bloodlines guy in the Jays system, Conine was a potential first-round pick coming into his junior year at Duke, but struggled a bit the first half of the season as he sold out for power too much. When you have plus-plus raw, fair enough, but the strikeouts mounted. While he toned it down and his overall line ended up quite robust, concerns about the—at times—controlled violence in his swing may have led to a bit of a draft day slide. The K's and bombs continued apace in his pro career, and he's limited to an outfield corner, so the bombs will have to come pretty regularly. But there's enough juice in the bat to project a potential regular with time. Conine will also miss the first 50 games of 2019 after testing positive for a banned stimulant.

14 Hector Perez RHP

Born: 06/06/96 Age: 23 Bats: R Throws: R Height: 6'3" Weight: 190 Origin: International Free Agent, 2014

YEAR	TEAM	LVL	AGE	W	L	SV	G	GS	IP	H	HR	BB/9	K/9	K	GB%	BABIP	WHIP	ERA	DRA	WARP	PF
2016	TCV	A-	20	2	0	0	7	3	28^{2}	19	0	3.8	11.3	36	44%	.275	1.08	1.57	3.02	0.7	106
2016	QUD	A	20	2	1	0	7	7	31^{1}	28	1	6.3	12.6	44	49%	.380	1.60	4.60	2.97	0.8	101
2017	QUD	A	21	1	1	0	4	3	18	9	2	5.5	12.0	24	51%	.200	1.11	2.50	2.20	0.6	103
2017	BCA	A+	21	6	5	2	21	14	89^{1}	69	6	6.8	10.5	104	55%	.300	1.52	3.63	5.02	0.1	95
2018	BCA	A+	22	3	3	2	17	11	72^{2}	50	5	5.0	10.3	83	48%	.263	1.24	3.84	3.28	1.7	98
2018	CCH	AA	22	0	1	0	4	2	16^{2}	12	0	4.3	9.7	18	49%	.279	1.20	3.24	3.20	0.4	109
2018	NHP	AA	22	0	1	0	6	5	25^{2}	17	1	5.6	11.2	32	37%	.276	1.29	3.86	4.07	0.4	108
2019	*TOR*	*MLB*	*23*	*1*	*0*	*0*	*15*	*0*	*16^{1}*	*15*	*2*	*6.4*	*10.0*	*18*	*43%*	*.300*	*1.61*	*5.09*	*5.24*	*-0.1*	*105*

Breakout: 11% Improve: 23% Collapse: 3% Attrition: 22% MLB: 34% *Comparables: Antonio Bastardo, Jose Cisnero, Luke Jackson*

Hey, it's a 95-and-a-slider dude! Perez can actually touch higher in short bursts which might portend more consistent upper-90s velo if he moves to the bullpen, which… he probably will. The arm action is compact but a bit violent, and he's struggled with both his control and command as a starter. He pairs the fastball with a tight, power slider that also carries plus projection. It's potential impact stuff in relief, and Perez could hit the majors in 2019, assuming he can get the walk rate even marginally more under control.

15 Thomas Pannone LHP

Born: 04/28/94 Age: 25 Bats: L Throws: L Height: 6'0" Weight: 195 Origin: Round 9, 2013 Draft (#261 overall)

YEAR	TEAM	LVL	AGE	W	L	SV	G	GS	IP	H	HR	BB/9	K/9	K	GB%	BABIP	WHIP	ERA	DRA	WARP	PF
2016	LKC	A	22	5	5	0	17	17	89^1	73	7	2.5	8.5	84	39%	.269	1.10	3.02	3.33	1.8	103
2016	LYN	A+	22	3	0	0	8	7	43^2	31	1	3.3	7.8	38	40%	.254	1.08	1.65	3.81	0.8	101
2017	LYN	A+	23	2	0	0	5	5	27^2	10	0	2.3	12.7	39	48%	.212	0.61	0.00	2.91	0.8	93
2017	AKR	AA	23	6	1	0	14	14	82^1	67	5	2.3	8.9	81	37%	.281	1.07	2.62	3.73	1.4	99
2017	NHP	AA	23	1	2	0	6	6	34^2	31	9	2.1	7.5	29	38%	.232	1.12	3.63	4.15	0.4	105
2018	NHP	AA	24	0	0	0	2	2	9	9	1	5.0	12.0	12	29%	.348	1.56	3.00	3.84	0.2	96
2018	BUF	AAA	24	0	3	0	6	6	36^2	40	8	1.7	9.8	40	24%	.327	1.28	4.91	5.29	0.1	97
2018	TOR	MLB	24	4	1	0	12	6	43	37	7	3.1	6.1	29	36%	.234	1.21	4.19	5.89	-0.3	106
2019	*TOR*	*MLB*	*25*	*5*	*7*	*0*	*16*	*16*	*91^1*	*92*	*17*	*3.3*	*8.0*	*81*	*35%*	*.287*	*1.37*	*5.25*	*5.42*	*0.1*	*105*

Breakout: 15% Improve: 30% Collapse: 19% Attrition: 34% MLB: 60% *Comparables: Michael Bowden, Scott Lewis, Eric Skoglund*

I should know better by now than to buy-in to another strike-throwing southpaw sitting in the high-80s with average secondaries after some upper-minors (and even major-league) success. And that's even before we consider that Pannone will have to get by with that profile in the AL East, playing his home games in the Rogers Centre. This profile has fine margins, and while some of these dudes have real major league careers, they also account for a plurality of starters in the upper minors. So your hit rate isn't going to be good.

But I've always liked Pannone more than I should. Some of these guys do make it for a few years after all, and he can hit all four quadrants with the fastball. He hides it a bit, runs it a bit. He's got a big, slow, sweepy curve in the low-70s that he can manipulate, spot or bury. There's good feel for an average change. Pannone might give up a million home runs in the majors, but he's already in the majors, and for whatever reason I think he can be a backend starter or swing guy for a while. These aren't really pref lists, except when they are kinda sorta pref lists.

Others of note:

Logan Warmoth, SS, High-A Dunedin

Certainly on pedigree Warmoth deserves to be ahead of Pannone (and arguably a few other names in the next five), but it's hard to describe his 2018 with anything more polite than "well, it was a lost season." You would expect a polished, 22-year-old college bat to make easy work of the Florida State League, but Warmoth struggled badly. We don't scout the statline of course, but production will matter with this profile, as he doesn't offer much in the way of tools or physical projection. So it would be nice if he'd hit a bit.

The power was always likely to play as below-average, but one home run in a half-season in High-A isn't great, Bob. Warmoth projects as a below-average runner who will have to grind it out at short, and may fit better at third, so an average over .250 would improve our confidence interval w/r/t his being a major-league starter. And yes, Warmoth missed time with hamstring issues, that could be a factor, but he does seem to get hurt a lot. So performance isn't the be all and end all, but it does have to be explained. And none of the explanations I can come up with here are going to be more comforting than "well, it was a lost season."

Jordan Romano, RHP, Triple-A Buffalo

Hey, another 95-and-a-slider dude! Romano is a fine example of how this profile comes from everywhere now—an underslot 10th-rounder out of Oral Roberts in this case. You know the drill: Romano is a big dude who throws in the mid-90s with good command and an average hard slider that flashes better. There's a tad more upside here than you'd think for a guy who just spent the season being good but not great in Double-A at age-25; it took him a few seasons to really get going as a pro due to Tommy John surgery the spring after he was drafted. Whether or not he stays in the rotation depends on the development of his change, which is still fringy. Not the world's most exciting profile, but he's probably going to pitch in the majors for awhile.

Forrest Wall, OF, Double-A New Hampshire

The return from the Rockies for Final Boss, Wall is a former first-round pick who wasn't a disaster in Double-A and was acquired for a pretty good (and cheap) reliever with an additional year of control. He was then not added to the Blue Jays 40-man for Rule 5 protection purposes. Could he stick on another team? Perhaps. He's a plus runner who's still rough in center at times, but he has the range for it.

The swing still looks good. It's a classic, rotational left-handed stroke, although he looked lost at times against Double-A stuff. He lacks physicality... wait, do I just see Carlos Tocci in every prospect now? That's not a great comp, but it might be what Wall does if he's jumped to the majors. And you may not get more than a fourth outfielder at the end of his now-disrupted development process. Unless you are 95-with-a-slider (his arm is fringy and would force him to left if he can't stick up the middle), teams are going to try and sneak you through an extra year now.

Top Talents 25 and Under (born 4/1/93 or later):

1. Vladimir Guerrero Jr.
2. Bo Bichette
3. Nate Pearson
4. Danny Jansen
5. Kevin Smith
6. Ryan Borucki
7. Lourdes Gurriel
8. Eric Pardinho
9. Sean Reid-Foley
10. Anthony Alford

In each of the last two years, this space has led off by noting that hey, the Blue Jays sure are old. It would be poor storytelling for me to not complete the trilogy; at an average of 30.3 years of age, Toronto was indeed old as all heck in 2018. They were also, for the second consecutive year, bad. Old and bad are perhaps the two worst conjoined traits for a baseball team, and fortunately, Mark Shapiro and company have been busy behind the scenes.

Like the planet of Tatooine, the view of Toronto's 25U talent is dominated by the beauty and scorching heat coming off twin stars. Vlad Guerrero Jr. is maybe the only teenager in the history of the game for whom hitting .330 in Triple-A feels anticlimactic, while Bo Bichette is just your standard 20-year-old handling Double-A with aplomb. For some franchises, having either of the two would be a once-a-decade kind of developmental coup. The Blue Jays have both, and the ceiling of the franchise's next era feels inexorably linked to their two stud prospects.

Below the headliners, Toronto's youngsters flash talent across positions and levels. Nate Pearson is a huge arm attached to a huge body, coming off a lost season. Kevin Smith is a slick fielding shortstop whose bat serves as another encouraging sign of the org's ability to develop talent. Ditto Danny Jansen, who in two years has progressed from organizational afterthought to Russell Martin's successor-in-waiting.

The last half of the list darts all over the map. Ryan Borucki harnessed his spectacularly whelming profile into spectacularly whelming big-league results, which is worth more than most fans give it credit for. Lourdes Gurriel was the most difficult talent to rank on this list. His prospect hype has waned, and his defense doesn't make him enough of an asset to offset the fact that he walks and dingers just a bit less than needed to be anything more than adequate with the bat. Still, he's a big leaguer, and given that MLB stalwarts like Aaron Sanchez and Marcus Stroman have aged out of consideration for this list, Gurriel settles in at seven here.

Eric Pardinho is barely old enough to drive, and won't reach Toronto until well into the next decade, but his international pedigree and signing bonus, coupled with the faces his fastball melted off in rookie ball, squeak him onto the list. Sean Reid-Foley climbed through three levels in 2018, including Toronto, and missed bats at every level. Anthony Alford has showcased droolworthy tools for years, but has yet to put it all together. His ceiling as a plus CF and accompanying athleticism is all that keeps him on this list—and less athletic players like Billy McKinney, and Reese McGuire off of it.

Fans of the Legion of Adult Large Sons will scream for Rowdy Tellez to be on here, and it's an understandable ask; barrel-shaped boys finding barrel is an aesthetic delight. However, Tallez's underwhelming performance in two seasons of Triple-A make his marginal success in the bigs last September look flukier than we'd like, and his defensive and baserunning skills are, uh, not great.

The 2015-16 Blue Jays were the most entertaining and successful Canadian team in decades, but they were an old club with a short shelf life. The stagnation and ultimate dissolution of that talent stings; saying goodbye to heroes always does. But while 2019 will be a rebuilding year, the farm system looks ready to graduate at least one, and perhaps two legitimate stars. With unrivaled top end prospect depth, and some fun guys coming up behind them, next year's Blue Jays will at least let fans dream of the future, a welcome improvement over mourning the death of their recent past.

Washington Nationals

The State of the System:

How bad can a system be with two OFP 70s and another likely 101 guy? Let's find out!

The Top Ten:

1 Victor Robles OF

OFP: 70 Likely: 60 ETA: Debuted in 2017

Born: 05/19/97 Age: 22 Bats: R Throws: R Height: 6'0" Weight: 190 Origin: International Free Agent, 2013

YEAR	TEAM	LVL	AGE	PA	R	2B	3B	HR	RBI	BB	K	SB	CS	AVG/OBP/SLG	DRC+	VORP	BABIP	BRR	FRAA	WARP	PF
2016	HAG	A	19	285	48	9	6	5	30	18	38	19	8	.305/.405/.459	144	31.6	.346	6.2	CF(63) 11.9	3.6	101
2016	POT	A+	19	198	24	8	2	3	11	14	32	18	5	.262/.354/.387	111	10.3	.304	-1.0	CF(40) 5.9	0.9	99
2017	POT	A+	20	338	49	25	7	7	33	25	62	16	7	.289/.377/.495	146	30.8	.345	0.7	CF(70) 16.1	3.8	98
2017	HAR	AA	20	158	24	12	1	3	14	12	22	11	3	.324/.394/.489	136	17.0	.368	2.7	CF(30) 4.1, RF(1) 0.1	1.5	100
2017	WAS	MLB	20	27	2	1	2	0	4	0	6	0	1	.250/.308/.458	79	-0.6	.333	-0.8	RF(6) 1.2, CF(3) -0.3	0.0	96
2018	SYR	AAA	21	182	25	9	1	2	10	18	26	14	6	.278/.356/.386	100	9.9	.318	1.2	CF(39) -0.8	0.4	96
2018	WAS	MLB	21	66	8	3	1	3	10	4	12	3	2	.288/.348/.525	103	5.2	.311	0.7	CF(14) 0.1, LF(2) 0.0	0.3	106
2019	*WAS*	*MLB*	*22*	*445*	*53*	*19*	*2*	*11*	*45*	*36*	*89*	*19*	*9*	*.230/.303/.370*	*80*	*7.2*	*.266*	*0.7*	*CF 10, LF 0*	*1.8*	*100*

Breakout: 13% Improve: 52% Collapse: 0% Attrition: 21% MLB: 59% *Comparables: Gregory Polanco, Andrew McCutchen, Dalton Pompey*

The Report: We 8'd him last year, and there's a good argument to do it again. Robles's skills are unchanged, but he keeps getting hurt. Last year, he screwed up his elbow diving for a ball in April and sat out most of the season. In the past, he's also missed time with a hand injury and a few different leg injuries. It's the slightest of knocks, but we hold the role 8 projection in such esteem that we're withholding it this year, even recognizing that we're not going to get another shot to put it out there before he exhausts his eligibility.

Still, Robles is the truest five-tool prospect in baseball, with four tools that could reach 7 or higher, and the power "only" projecting as above-average. He's a natural hitter, combining feel for the barrel with a whip-fast swing. Considering his age-relative-to-league, he's shown excellent discipline and pitch recognition. He's a sure-shot center fielder, with fantastic range, a knack for the big acrobatic play, and a cannon arm. He posts consistent plus-plus times down the line, and will be a major stolen base threat in his twenties; the Nationals carried him more or less as a pinch-running specialist in the 2017 playoffs.

We've been projecting the power to tick up for years now, and it might've finally arrived last September. He should be in Washington's Opening Day lineup and could stay there into the 2030s. Along with division rival Peter Alonso, he's a clear favorite for NL Rookie of the Year.

The Risks: Low, and it would be basically non-existent if not for injuries. He's already had bursts of MLB success, and the profile has an extremely high floor. Unless he's just completely sapped by injuries or something bizarre, he's almost certainly a budding long-term regular. Something to watch for: Although it abated a bit last year, and is a positive skill so far as it affects his OBP, Robles gets plunked really often—he got drilled more times in the minors in 2016 than Brandon Guyer has ever been hit in any MLB season, for example. That increases the injury risk a touch more.

Ben Carsley's Fantasy Take: Don't let prospect fatigue get the best of you; Robles remains a no-doubt top-5 fantasy prospect who could win you leagues as soon as this season thanks to his speed. The injuries are mildly concerning but most are of the freak accident variety, and honestly Robles wouldn't even have to play 162 games every season to have a ton of value. It bears repeating that only 10 players swiped more than 30 bags last season, and only three stole more than 40. Robles can join their ranks, and it wouldn't be too shocking to see him post a line similar to Trea Turner's 2018—.271/.344/.416 with 19 homers and 43 SB—during his peak seasons. Buy, buy, buy.

2 Carter Kieboom SS

OFP: 70 Likely: 60 ETA: Late-2019 or early-2020

Born: 09/03/97 Age: 21 Bats: R Throws: R Height: 6'2" Weight: 190 Origin: Round 1, 2016 Draft (#28 overall)

YEAR	TEAM	LVL	AGE	PA	R	2B	3B	HR	RBI	BB	K	SB	CS	AVG/OBP/SLG	DRC+	VORP	BABIP	BRR	FRAA	WARP	PF
2016	NAT	RK	18	155	22	8	4	4	25	12	43	1	2	.244/.323/.452	84	5.1	.319	-0.3	SS(31) 0.6	-0.1	110
2017	HAG	A	19	210	36	12	0	8	26	28	40	2	2	.296/.400/.497	159	20.4	.344	-0.7	SS(45) 1.4	2.0	100
2018	POT	A+	20	285	48	15	0	11	46	36	50	6	1	.298/.386/.494	157	31.4	.332	0.5	SS(56) -0.4	2.3	101
2018	HAR	AA	20	273	36	16	1	5	23	22	59	3	1	.262/.326/.395	107	13.3	.324	0.5	SS(62) 2.6	1.3	100
2019	*WAS*	*MLB*	*21*	*252*	*25*	*10*	*0*	*8*	*24*	*14*	*75*	*1*	*0*	*.178/.226/.318*	*40*	*-9.4*	*.222*	*-0.4*	*SS 1, 2B 0*	*-0.9*	*100*

Breakout: 17% Improve: 30% Collapse: 5% Attrition: 18% MLB: 38% *Comparables: Franklin Barreto, Willy Adames, Addison Russell*

The Report: Kieboom goes the prospect dynamite. It was quite a good year for House Kieboom, with Carter's prospect stock soaring in a healthy, fine season and brother Spencer finally joining the international fraternity of backup catchers.

Kieboom's offensive profile is hit-tool oriented, which does bring in some variance. In part, that's because hit tools are inherently variant, but it's also the toughest attribute for scouts to evaluate. He does have plus raw power, which started showing up in games, and he has the sort of bat speed you associate with good averages and plenty of doubles. His performance in Double-A looks sort of ugly on the triple-slash, and he does need to improve his pitch recognition to succeed in the upper minors and majors. Yet by DRC+ he was still close to a league-average bat as a 20-year-old in his first taste of Double-A. That's not a negative, especially if he improves during his second spin through the Eastern League.

Out in the field, we have greater hope that he might stick at shortstop than we used to. He's retained more athleticism and nimbleness than we thought, and migrated from the "probably not" bucket to the "maybe" bucket at shortstop. We also now suspect that he might end up moving to second instead of third if he slides down the spectrum, which would be slight added value in a vacuum and might matter a ton if the Nats re-sign Anthony Rendon.

The Risks: Medium. We'd like to see him hit for average at higher levels. Health has been an issue. He could still slide down the defensive spectrum.

Ben Carsley's Fantasy Take: Kieboom has a bit of an odd profile as a guy who's perhaps a safer bet to hit .280-plus than he is to hit 20-plus bombs yearly, but that's not necessarily a bad thing as long as he remains shortstop-eligible. There's no true fantasy star upside here, but Kieboom could be a top-10 producer at the position through much of his 20s before perhaps settling in as a top-15 third baseman (and hopefully growing into a bit more pop) later in his career. He's hardly an unknown at this point, but I still think he's a bit undervalued in dynasty circles.

3 Luis Garcia SS

OFP: 60 Likely: 50 ETA: 2020

Born: 05/16/00 Age: 19 Bats: L Throws: R Height: 6'0" Weight: 190 Origin: International Free Agent, 2016

YEAR	TEAM	LVL	AGE	PA	R	2B	3B	HR	RBI	BB	K	SB	CS	AVG/OBP/SLG	DRC+	VORP	BABIP	BRR	FRAA	WARP	PF
2017	NAT	RK	17	211	25	8	3	1	22	9	32	11	2	.302/.330/.387	97	7.3	.353	1.7	2B(25) -3.0, SS(17) 0.7	-0.2	105
2018	HAG	A	18	323	48	14	4	3	31	19	49	8	5	.297/.335/.402	110	16.4	.343	0.7	3B(36) -4.6, SS(27) 0.4	0.4	98
2018	POT	A+	18	221	34	7	2	4	23	12	33	4	1	.299/.338/.412	116	9.8	.337	-0.3	SS(40) -2.7	0.4	101
2019	*WAS*	*MLB*	*19*	*252*	*21*	*4*	*1*	*5*	*20*	*1*	*61*	*1*	*1*	*.187/.188/.273*	*16*	*-17.5*	*.221*	*-0.1*	*SS -1, 3B 0*	*-2.0*	*100*

Breakout: 5% Improve: 6% Collapse: 0% Attrition: 3% MLB: 8% *Comparables: Carlos Triunfel, Elvis Andrus, Adalberto Mondesi*

The Report: I've sat on Garcia often enough that I should have a good handle on him, as he rolled through Lakewood twice while with Hagerstown. But if I'm being entirely honest, I didn't "see" it. He only played shortstop once between the two series, and while he was fine everywhere and even flashy sometimes, you usually don't project guys as MLB shortstops if they're playing more third than short in the Sally. His swing looked a bit stiff and I just didn't see him as more than a garden variety good prospect.

What could I have missed? Garcia was often playing out of position to increase his versatility and to let Yasel Antuna take shortstop reps. Maybe he didn't show great for me because of minor injuries. Maybe he was working on something specific, trying out a swing adjustment for a few weeks. Maybe he just had a bad group of games—it happens, and sometimes we don't think about that enough when filing.

The rest of the story should color this too: Everyone else I have talked to about Luis Garcia likes his offensive potential. You know the terms: a quick bat, a smooth stroke, some power projection, advanced ability for his age, that sort of stuff. He turned 18 a month into a season in which he played well at both full-season A-ball levels. The defensive consensus is still that he sticks at shortstop, but even if he lands elsewhere he still projects to add real defensive value. He's quite athletic and the body has good projectability. He's a seven-figure former IFA, and while bonus numbers aren't necessarily important, they are a good indicator that he was a well-regarded 14-year-old. This isn't a pref list based on my live looks and little else, and the preponderance of the evidence points to Garcia as a 101 candidate and the clear third-best guy in this system.

The Risks: Low, considering his age. The Nationals have been well-served by moving prospects extremely aggressively, and Garcia has responded to it well already. He has a real shot to be in the majors as a teenager.

Ben Carsley's Fantasy Take: Hey Jarrett, how about you fight me? Garcia is one of my absolute favorite dynasty prospects: I was so unreasonably high on him in the first draft of last off-season's top-101 that BP podcast personality Craig Goldstein genuinely questioned my sanity (for not the first or last time). But if you listened and went all-in on him a year ago, you're pretty happy right now. Garcia's MLB ETA may be a bit more generous than his fantasy impact ETA, but in his prime we're talking about a well-rounded top-10 shortstop who could challenge for 20/20 status. I am Brick in the "do you really love lamp" scene, and Garcia is lamp.

Mason Denaburg RHP   OFP: 55   Likely: 45   ETA: 2023

Born: 08/08/99   Age: 19   Bats: R   Throws: R   Height: 6'4"   Weight: 195   Origin: Round 1, 2018 Draft (#27 overall)

The Report: We normally try to avoid ranking prep arms who don't pitch much before or after the draft because of bicep problems, but this isn't a very good system and Denaburg's arm is more interesting than most. Once a candidate to be the first prep hurler selected, the righty never pitched after signing, although he did throw in instructs. (You'll be shocked to hear that the Nationals drafted a Boras client who fell due to injuries, I'm sure.)

As an amateur, Denaburg ran his heater up into the mid-90s. He combines the fastball with a big hook, and you can see the outlines of an impressive two-pitch mix there. His changeup lags far, far behind, and the command isn't there yet either. There's obviously a lot of reliever risk here until he shows a functional third pitch and durability. 2019 will tell us a lot about what the shape of his career will look like; for now he's an interesting live arm.

The Risks: Maximum. He's a prep arm with reliever risk who spent much of last season dealing with an arm injury. Do I need to say more?

Ben Carsley's Fantasy Take: Bubba Thompson is the Most Rangers prospect, Brendan Rodgers is the Most Rockies Prospect, Kyle Lewis is the Most Mariners prospect, and Denaburg is the Most Nationals prospect. His upside is such that he bears consideration in deeper dynasty leagues—it's not like the Nats haven't gotten the most out of guys like this before—but the risks are high enough that he'll be kept a ways away from the top-101. He'd be in the next 100, though.

5 Yasel Antuna IF   OFP: 55   Likely: 45   ETA: 2023

Born: 10/26/99   Age: 19   Bats: B   Throws: R   Height: 6'0"   Weight: 170   Origin: International Free Agent, 2016

YEAR	TEAM	LVL	AGE	PA	R	2B	3B	HR	RBI	BB	K	SB	CS	AVG/OBP/SLG	DRC+	VORP	BABIP	BRR	FRAA	WARP	PF
2017	NAT	RK	17	199	25	8	3	1	17	23	29	5	5	.301/.382/.399	138	10.5	.352	-1.9	SS(21) -0.7, 3B(15) 1.4	0.5	106
2018	HAG	A	18	362	44	14	2	6	27	32	79	8	7	.220/.293/.331	84	2.4	.269	-0.6	SS(67) -8.8, 2B(9) 0.2	-0.9	97
2019	*WAS*	*MLB*	*19*	*252*	*21*	*5*	*0*	*5*	*18*	*10*	*71*	*2*	*1*	*.141/.174/.229*	*3*	*-20.7*	*.171*	*-0.4*	*SS -4, 2B 0*	*-2.6*	*100*

Breakout: 6%   Improve: 7%   Collapse: 0%   Attrition: 4%   MLB: 9%   *Comparables: Gleyber Torres, Adalberto Mondesi, Elvis Andrus*

The Report: The adjective I want to use here is "smooth." He's smooth in the field. He's smooth at the plate. He's a five-tool athlete and things just look easy for him, even if we think he'll grow off shortstop.

You can tell by the statistical line that they weren't easy, obviously. Antuna struggled early and often, and then disappeared to the disabled list for the last six weeks of the season. He assembled a line so bad from the right side of the plate (.165/.252/.214) that it's closer to a decent-hitting pitcher than a bad-hitting hitter.

Indeed, it is the comparison to Garcia that makes Antuna look bad. Consider that Antuna jumped straight out of the complex and didn't face a single pitcher all year that he was older than, and suddenly the season looks okay. Not good, but far from disastrous.

The Risks: High. He might just not hit, and the defensive profile is still unclear. Something intuitively tells me to like him more than I should, though.

Ben Carsley's Fantasy Take: While Kieboom and Garcia may be slightly undervalued fantasy assets, Antuna has been a bit overrated in our circle. The ceiling remains somewhat enticing, and he should be rostered in most TDGX-sized leagues with 200-plus prospects kept, but those in shallower formats can look to players with higher upsides or more favorable ETAs for the time being. Perhaps most damningly, I keep reading his name in Andy Bernard's voice.

6 Seth Romero LHP

OFP: 55 Likely: 45 ETA: 2021

Born: 04/19/96 Age: 23 Bats: L Throws: L Height: 6'3" Weight: 240 Origin: Round 1, 2017 Draft (#25 overall)

YEAR	TEAM	LVL	AGE	W	L	SV	G	GS	IP	H	HR	BB/9	K/9	K	GB%	BABIP	WHIP	ERA	DRA	WARP	PF
2017	AUB	A-	21	0	1	0	6	6	20	19	0	2.7	14.4	32	40%	.404	1.25	5.40	1.57	0.9	108
2018	HAG	A	22	0	1	0	7	7	25^1	20	3	2.8	12.1	34	45%	.279	1.11	3.91	2.52	0.8	98
2019	*WAS*	*MLB*	*23*	*2*	*3*	*0*	*9*	*9*	35^2	*33*	*5*	*3.8*	*9.5*	*37*	*38%*	*.311*	*1.35*	*4.16*	*4.72*	*0.2*	*100*

Breakout: 3% Improve: 5% Collapse: 1% Attrition: 3% MLB: 6% *Comparables: Frank Garces, Steven Matz, Christian Friedrich*

The Report: If you're ever sad about your favorite prospect's bad year, just come back and read this blurb. Romero was sent home from spring training due to repeated missed curfews, wasn't assigned to an affiliate until June, suffered an elbow injury while ramping up, and had Tommy John surgery in September after a failed comeback. He was fine if a bit inconsistent when he pitched, still flashing three potential plus offerings: fastball, slider, and changeup. The command was still inconsistent when the injury struck.

Romero repeatedly found trouble before entering pro ball, with publicly-reported incidents and suspensions including more missed curfews, low effort during conditioning drills, a failed marijuana test, and posing with a bong in his uniform. He was ultimately dismissed from his college team for decking a teammate. So the suspension by the Nationals, which we normally wouldn't care much about, is a continuation of an alarming trend. Teams will ultimately ignore this if you can play, of course, but Romero's not there yet. His stock has dropped a lot more than the one spot on this list and half-grade of roles might suggest.

The Risks: Extreme. I usually don't ding guys for makeup without cause, but Romero's now missed large chunks of two straight seasons for tomfoolery. Now he's going to miss another season for Tommy John and, if all goes well, pop back up in 2020 as a 24-year-old with 47⅓ pro innings, all at Low-A or below. You can't stay a top prospect if you're never on the field.

Ben Carsley's Fantasy Take: Does this seem like the type of prospect you really want to invest in? No no, not the bad attitude part—the pitcher with injuries and non-elite upside part? I didn't think so. He and Jon Denney would've made a great battery.

7 Wil Crowe RHP

OFP: 55 Likely: 45 ETA: Late 2019 as a reliever, 2020 as a starter

Born: 09/09/94 Age: 24 Bats: R Throws: R Height: 6'2" Weight: 240 Origin: Round 2, 2017 Draft (#65 overall)

YEAR	TEAM	LVL	AGE	W	L	SV	G	GS	IP	H	HR	BB/9	K/9	K	GB%	BABIP	WHIP	ERA	DRA	WARP	PF
2017	AUB	A-	22	0	0	0	7	7	20^2	18	3	1.3	6.5	15	52%	.250	1.02	2.61	5.93	-0.2	107
2018	POT	A+	23	11	0	0	16	15	87	71	6	3.1	8.1	78	47%	.267	1.16	2.69	3.35	2.0	101
2018	HAR	AA	23	0	5	0	5	5	26^1	31	4	5.5	5.1	15	44%	.325	1.78	6.15	4.71	0.2	99
2019	*WAS*	*MLB*	*24*	*5*	*7*	*0*	*18*	*18*	83^2	*88*	*16*	*3.9*	*7.1*	*66*	*43%*	*.302*	*1.48*	*5.31*	*6.01*	*-0.7*	*100*

Breakout: 4% Improve: 5% Collapse: 4% Attrition: 9% MLB: 13% *Comparables: Daniel Poncedeleon, James Houser, Scott Barlow*

The Report: Crowe started to make up for lost time in 2018—like almost every Nationals pitching prospect, Tommy John is on the resume already—getting to Double-A by the end of his first full professional season. The results were decidedly mixed. Crowe looks like the kind of durable, mid-rotation starter that I have long since run out of new ways to describe in the Annual without resorting to medieval poetic forms. There's above-average fastball velocity, a power slider, a change that needs a grade jump or more, the usual boxes ticked. But Crowe struggled badly at times with his control and command in 2018 and the culprit was not hard to identify. The delivery is extremely high effort and upper-body heavy with late timing. In other words, it all ends up looking more like a 95-and-a-slider relief arm. Given that he's already 24, the Nationals might consider making that conversion sooner rather than later, although getting Crowe more professional innings might take priority for now.

The Risks: Medium. The command and control may wobble too much for him to be effective in the majors even as a reliever. He has a history of arm issues.

Ben Carsley's Fantasy Take: Christ, Daredevil thinks this system fell off quickly.

8 Jose Sanchez SS OFP: 55 Likely: 40 ETA: 2023

Born: 07/12/00 Age: 18 Bats: R Throws: R Height: 5'11" Weight: 155 Origin: International Free Agent, 2016

YEAR	TEAM	LVL	AGE	PA	R	2B	3B	HR	RBI	BB	K	SB	CS	AVG/OBP/SLG	DRC+	VORP	BABIP	BRR	FRAA	WARP	PF
2017	NAT	RK	16	178	22	3	0	1	20	14	26	0	2	.209/.280/.247	55	-4.0	.242	2.1	SS(18) 2.8, 3B(15) 2.8	0.1	105
2018	AUB	A-	17	239	20	9	1	0	23	24	56	1	0	.230/.309/.282	78	1.7	.310	-1.0	SS(63) 7.0, 2B(1) -0.2	0.4	102
2019	*WAS*	*MLB*	*18*	*252*	*14*	*1*	*0*	*5*	*17*	*8*	*82*	*0*	*0*	*.104/.131/.165*	*-29*	*-30.4*	*.130*	*-0.5*	*SS 2, 2B 0*	*-3.0*	*100*

Breakout: 0% Improve: 0% Collapse: 0% Attrition: 0% MLB: 0% *Comparables: Adalberto Mondesi, Wilmer Flores, Tommy Brown*

The Report: Here's where the system noticeably thins out. Sanchez is a potential impact defender at the 6, with fantastic instincts and a knack for making the quick and correct first step. We were concerned about his arm some in 2017, but he was playing through an injury and it showed much better in 2018. His hands are strong too, and we're now reasonably confident as 18-year-olds go that he'll stick at shortstop all the way up, and be pretty good there.

The bat... well, if I ever fail to mention a position player's stick in the first paragraph, there's probably a reason. Sanchez has no present power and not much projection. In general, physical projection is the problem here—we're just not seeing it yet. He has some feel for contact, if you want to be nice about things, and he's been extremely young for his levels, so maybe there's more offensively than he's shown so far.

The Risks: Extreme. A lot of things can cause a guy who is a defensively-minded shortstop this low to stop being a defensively-minded shortstop, and not all of them are controllable. He might, for example, just grow a lot more than we think.

Ben Carsley's Fantasy Take: Maybe if he starts hitting or running? Those seem like important qualifiers for fantasy?

9 Tim Cate LHP OFP: 50 Likely: 45 ETA: 2021

Born: 09/30/97 Age: 21 Bats: L Throws: L Height: 6'0" Weight: 185 Origin: Round 2, 2018 Draft (#65 overall)

YEAR	TEAM	LVL	AGE	W	L	SV	G	GS	IP	H	HR	BB/9	K/9	K	GB%	BABIP	WHIP	ERA	DRA	WARP	PF
2018	AUB	A-	20	2	3	0	9	8	31	34	1	2.9	7.5	26	45%	.333	1.42	4.65	3.82	0.5	101
2018	HAG	A	20	0	3	0	4	4	21	23	4	2.6	8.1	19	44%	.306	1.38	5.57	6.82	-0.4	106
2019	*WAS*	*MLB*	*21*	*2*	*3*	*0*	*8*	*8*	*37*	*42*	*7*	*3.9*	*6.5*	*27*	*37%*	*.311*	*1.56*	*5.59*	*6.33*	*-0.4*	*100*

Breakout: 0% Improve: 0% Collapse: 0% Attrition: 0% MLB: 0% *Comparables: Ranger Suarez, Clay Buchholz, Wilking Rodriguez*

The Report: Cate had first-round buzz coming into the 2018 college season as UCONN's Friday night starter. Working with perhaps the best curveball in the draft class, he began the season well, but the stuff and velocity were a bit inconsistent and he was eventually shut down for "precautionary reasons." Cate returned for the College World Series and the low-90s velocity and 12-6 hammer curve were back. Anyway, the Nats never met a pitcher with questionable medicals who they wouldn't draft, and they popped Cate in the second round.

Cate worked primarily off his fastball as a pro, and the pitch shows some life up with occasional cut. The curve still looks like a plus offering, flashing higher. Cate can manipulate the pitch, and spot or bury it. He doesn't have ideal height, but his near over-the-top slot gives him some plane on his fastball. There isn't much of a changeup here at present, although it dives tantalizingly at times. Cate might be best deployed as a lefty crossover guy out of the pen where he can max out the velo and spam the curve, but the curve might also end up good enough on its own that he can spam it as a starter. He also might get hurt again. Pitchers, man.

The Risks: High. Cate is a shorter lefty without a major-league-quality third pitch and mysterious arm issues in his recent past.

Ben Carsley's Fantasy Take: Can I go home now?

10 Israel Pineda C

OFP: 50 Likely: 40 ETA: 2024ish? Catchers are weird, man.

Born: 04/03/00 Age: 19 Bats: R Throws: R Height: 5'11" Weight: 190 Origin: International Free Agent, 2016

YEAR	TEAM	LVL	AGE	PA	R	2B	3B	HR	RBI	BB	K	SB	CS	AVG/OBP/SLG	DRC+	VORP	BABIP	BRR	FRAA	WARP	PF
2017	NAT	RK	17	65	10	5	2	0	12	4	13	0	0	.288/.323/.441	104	5.9	.354	0.3	C(16) -0.1	0.1	105
2018	AUB	A-	18	185	25	7	0	4	24	12	35	0	0	.273/.341/.388	112	8.6	.320	-1.2	C(30) 0.2	0.1	102
2019	*WAS*	*MLB*	*19*	*252*	*15*	*8*	*0*	*6*	*23*	*3*	*79*	*0*	*0*	*.147/.157/.251*	*-1*	*-20.6*	*.184*	*-0.5*	*C 0*	*-2.2*	*100*

Breakout: 5% Improve: 7% Collapse: 0% Attrition: 3% MLB: 9% *Comparables: Francisco Pena, Gleyber Torres, Adalberto Mondesi*

The Report: Pineda was one of the second-tier prospects the Nationals picked up when they busted their 2016 bonus pool for Antuna, Garcia, and Sanchez. Reports are mixed, but there isn't a lot of offensive impact here at the moment; the bat speed isn't there yet and the present power is muted. If you want to be optimistic, you can point to power potential and some hit tool projectability, and he's hit decently so far. Reports on his glove are stronger, and he has a shot to make the majors as a backup catcher even if he doesn't hit much.

Finding a tenth prospect for this list to replace Daniel Johnson was not fun. You'll see some of the other candidates for that below, and they're not great either. So we're going to go with a high-variance short-season catcher whom we have mixed reports on. It is what it is.

The Risks: High, in the sense that he might not be very good. He's a short-season catcher who we think might be a glove-first backup. He could top out as a Double-A player, or even a Double-A coach.

Ben Carsley's Fantasy Take: Love 2 roster the prospect version of Christian Vazquez for my successful dynasty fantasy baseballing leagues.

Choose Your Own Adventure: Should Any Of These Guys Actually Be 10th?

Two years ago, we had a "pick the tenth-best prospect in the Phillies system" section, because they were so deep that you could make a case for a half-dozen guys at 10. This is, well, the opposite of that—a system bad enough that I was cross-checking names to make sure they didn't declare MILB free agency.

Telmito Agustin, OF

Our first contestant is a 22-year-old hitter from the Virgin Islands. Agustin is a big, strong youngster who we've liked for awhile with the stick, and he hit .300 with some pop as an age-appropriate player in the High-A Carolina League. He runs well and can fake all three outfield spots with varying levels of competence. On the other hand, he's often on the shelf—a dislocated finger cost him almost two months this past summer—and he was just passed up by the 29 other teams in the Rule 5 Draft.

Nick Banks, OF

Bachelor number 2 is a contact-oriented outfielder out of Texas A&M who hasn't made particularly great contact yet. Banks has a nice swing and a decent idea of what he's doing at the plate, but doesn't hit the ball with much authority and probably never will. He does play fine defense at all three outfield spots. This profile passes for interesting in this system because you can see the outline of a defense/contact fourth outfielder or marginal starter here.

Joan Baez, RHP

One of the best-named prospects in baseball, Baez is a fastball/curveball "starter" who throws in the mid-90s and has no idea where anything is going. His command has never taken any kind of leap forward. He has obvious reliever mechanics anyway, with a hard landing and difficulty repeating. The Nationals have stubbornly kept running him out there in various A-ball rotations, although you have to assume the conversion is coming since he still walks five per nine every year. Baez also went unprotected and unpicked in Rule 5.

Jackson Tetreault, RHP

We sort of like Jackson Tetreault and have occasionally touted him as a sleeper. He's a nice get for a JUCO seventh-rounder, a guy with a heavy sinker in the low-90s and a breaking ball that flashes. He had a decent first full campaign in Hagerstown. A reasonable upside projection is a back-of-the-rotation starter or a seventh-inning type reliever, and every system has several pitching prospects of this type. We rarely write them up.

James Bourque, RHP

He has a rockin' mustache! He had a great season in the minors! They actually bothered to put him on the 40-man! He's... ah, crap, it's a 25-year-old reliever in Double-A. Bourque was a struggling starter coming off Tommy John who converted to relief before last season and started getting results off a velocity bump to the mid-90s. He'll probably pitch in the majors in a setup or middle relief role.

Tanner Rainey, RHP

Our last bachelor was plucked out of the Reds system in the Tanner-for-Tanner salary dump. Rainey tops out at 101 MPH and mixes in the exact hard slider you'd expect a guy with that arm strength to throw, also adding in the occasional firm change. That's way better than anyone else we've talked about, right? Well, the kicker is that he turned 26 at the end of December and walked a ton of batters between Triple-A and a few short MLB stints last season.

So, that's how we ended up with a likely backup catcher at the ten-spot...

Top Talents 25 and Under (born 4/1/93 or later):

1. Juan Soto
2. Trea Turner
3. Victor Robles
4. Carter Kieboom
5. Luis Garcia
6. Joe Ross
7. Mason Denaburg
8. Yasel Antuna
9. Koda Glover
10. Seth Romero

Sure, it's a really crappy system. But when you have two young MLBers as good as Soto and Turner, it makes up for a crappy system and then some.

Soto had one of the greatest teenage hitting seasons in the history of baseball. We absolutely adored him as a prospect, even ranking him a spot ahead of Vladito on the 2017 midseason list, and we still didn't see *this* coming. He's already one of the best hitters in baseball and he has another season left before he can legally drink. Enjoy him.

Turner is an above-average hitter, one of the best baserunners in the league, and he's settled in as a capable shortstop after jaunts in center field and second base. 2018 was his first fully-healthy season and he very quietly accrued 5.3 WARP. If he can keep playing every day, we'd expect him to have a few seasons where he contends for batting titles and MVPs.

Surprisingly, Joe Ross is still eligible for this list. He emerged as a quality mid-rotation starter way back in 2015 but missed most of the past two seasons recovering from Tommy John. He was injury-prone even before the surgery, so we're not fantastically optimistic that he's ever going to be a consistent 30-start guy. If your glass is half full, his stuff did look pretty much normal in a September cameo, and he used his changeup as a third pitch far more than in the past.

I don't have the slightest idea what to do with Koda Glover, who came back late in the season from shoulder surgery without his best fastball. I think the slider is still good enough for late-inning relief, but he turns 26 right after Opening Day and between injuries and underperformance, he's yet to establish himself in the majors.

Organization Rankings

by Jeffrey Paternostro

"Right Here Waiting" by Richard Marx playing through speakers

30. Boston Red Sox

29. Milwaukee Brewers

28. Chicago Cubs

Flags fly forever, and there is no pennant for topping our organizational rankings. Boston flew another World Series banner last year, Milwaukee won only their third division title ever, and the Cubs made the playoffs for the fourth straight season. All have leveraged their farm system heavily in recent years to create playoff-caliber major league rosters, and this was the inevitable result. I'm sure Dombrowski, Stearns, and Epstein sleep pretty well at night. (Mind you, we can quibble about how well Epstein should be sleeping nowadays).

These rankings may eventually be an issue for the big club, although Boston and Chicago could easily just keep spending their way out of it (nudgenudgeMannyMachadoBryceHarper). The Red Sox didn't have a single prospect really even in contention for the 101, and it's a shallow system, full stop. Milwaukee has one of the best prospects in the game—Keston Hiura—but their farm drops off almost as quickly as the Red Sox. The Cubs are deeper than either, but not exactly deep. They are at least the most likely to improve by 2020 given the lack of impending graduations and some potential 2019 breakout guys (Hoerner, Amaya, Ademan, Marquez).

Better luck next time.

27. San Francisco Giants

26. New York Mets

25. Washington Nationals

Oh San Francisco, fancy meeting you here. A top-five pick in Joey Bart helps at the top, but Heliot Ramos struggled in his first exposure to full-season ball, Marco Luciano hasn't actually played an organized baseball game yet, and the rest of the system is very Giants.

The Mets were closer to mid-table before Franklyn Kilome felt a twinge in his elbow and Jarred Kelenic and Justin Dunn were shipped out to Seattle. Since Steven Matz—the last in the pipeline of high-end Mets pitching prospects—graduated, the system has slowly gotten shallower in part due to an overly conservative draft strategy. New York does continue to do well in the international market though, and either Ronny Mauricio or Shervyen Newton could make the 2020 Top 101 and lead off the next incarnation of the Mets team list.

A lot of what I wrote in the opening paragraph of the tier above also applies to the Nationals, but they still have potential impact major league talent on the farm in Victor Robles and Carter Kieboom. Also, Luis Garcia is a backend 101 name and a potential 2019 breakout, but it's going to take a few years to reload the organization in the nation's capital.

So sorry for eternally dooming you.

24. Baltimore Orioles

23. Detroit Tigers

Our first tier of actively "rebuilding" teams. There's a lot of "rebuilding" teams nowadays, which, well, makes it harder to rebuild. The Orioles have spent all their MLB player capital in trades already and didn't radically reshape their system or anything. It's a *better* version of what it was last year, but it still lacks for both depth and impact talent. Baltimore does have the first overall pick in this year's draft—and are the clear chalk to "earn" another 1.1 for 2020—but this one is going to take some time.

The Tigers are in the middle of their rebuild and in a division that is a little less competitive than the AL East. Still, you would have liked to have seen more progress, even considering how arm-heavy the system is. Recent first round arms Alex Faedo and Matt Manning have struggled at times in the pros. Faedo's stuff has gone backwards from college, while Manning's mechanics are still very much a work in progress, and his stuff inconsistent. A Michael Fulmer trade could bolster the system some more, but he might never again be as valuable as he was this time last year. The best prospect they returned for Justin Verlander (Franklin Perez) has had injury issues. Pitchers, man. Daz Cameron and Isaac Paredes don't have a ton of upside past solid regular, but are at least close to helping the major league club. 2018 first round pick Casey Mize might not be far behind.

Well, I've narrowed it down to two possibilities: yes and no.

22. St. Louis Cardinals

21. Colorado Rockies

20. Cleveland Indians

19. Miami Marlins

18. Philadelphia Phillies

17. Seattle Mariners

The mushy lower-middle class of organizations:

There's a mix of rebuilding teams that did better in their trades (Miami, Seattle), orgs sliding down due to graduations and/or going for it (Rockies, Phillies) and just run-of-the mill fringy systems (St. Louis, Cleveland).

You could argue the Cardinals are more in line with the graduations/going for it group, but somehow Alex Reyes is still eligible for this list and they haven't really gone for it. Or at least haven't used their "farm system" that way (neither piece in the Goldschmidt deal was technically prospect-list eligible). A tetrarch of interesting hot corner prospects keeps them in this tier for now, but how the four fare in 2019 could move the system one way or the other.

Colorado is down here for the right reasons, having graduated two-fifths of a playoff rotation (German Marquez and Kyle Freeland) and two major lineup pieces (David Dahl and Trevor Story) in recent seasons. Brendan Rodgers and Garrett Hampson should join the homegrown core this year, but past them the system thins out quickly.

Cleveland has upside to spare—Luis Oviedo, Nolan Jones, George Valera, Brayan Rocchio... [deep breath]...Noah Naylor, Ethan Hankins, and Lenny Torres all could end up above-average major leaguers—but there's little help for a win-now 2019 major league squad. Triston McKenzie had an arm issue in 2018, and Sam Hentges has a Tommy John surgery on his resume, but both could hypothetically make the major league rotation at some point I suppose. Yu-Cheng Chang might get pressed into major league service as well depending on how Francisco Lindor's recovery from a recent calf injury progresses this Spring. Past the above names, there's some interesting relief arms, but not much else. And there's a lot of risk in the above names.

The gap between the Phillies and Marlins systems narrowed quickly once Sixto Sanchez changed uniforms. While we certainly consider overall organization health in these lists. Impact talent is premium. You can find a role 4 reliever or bench outfielder easily enough outside your org. You ain't getting Sixto. The Marlins got him. The Phillies still have the edge on both overall depth and surety in the notable names. However Philadelphia is starting to feel the effects of less than stellar high-first-round picks in recent years, while in 2018 Miami got the sharp end of the variance stick from their prospects acquired in their tear down deals.

The Mariners would have been at the bottom of our org rankings had this exercise been done in October. They remade their system quickly, acquiring half of their current top ten prospects in offseason maneuvers. While it's not a good system yet, it's the best Mariners system in a long while. Alas, it is probably not to last as Justus Sheffield, Erik Swanson, and Justin Dunn all have a decent chance of graduating off the list in 2019.

Hey, I'm on kinda a self-improvement kick.

16. Kansas City Royals

15. Arizona Diamondbacks

14. Cincinnati Reds

13. Los Angeles Dodgers

The Royals and Diamondbacks systems are on the rise. The Royals improvement comes via a strong draft class featuring six of the first 100 selections last June. They also have a trio of high upside bats in A-ball (Matias, Lee, Melendez), and this system should only improve in 2019. Meanwhile, the Diamondbacks have made hay in the international market, adding tools up-the-middle types, Jazz Chisholm, Kristian Robinson and Gerardo Perdomo most notably, but keep an eye out for Jorge Barrosa next year as well.

The Reds traded from some of their prospect depth to acquire Sonny Gray, Yasiel Puig, and Alex Wood, and now sit near the median in both our org rankings and PECOTA projections for 2019. They still have Nick Senzel and Taylor Trammell though.

The Dodgers system has backslid the last couple seasons as they haven't really backfilled for graduations and trades. So they don't technically fit in this tier, but on the other hand their whole player development and front office staff should probably look into that self-improvement kick.

Don't mind if I do.

12. New York Yankees

11. Oakland Athletics

10. Pittsburgh Pirates

9. Texas Rangers

8. Houston Astros

Five pretty good systems that don't quite have the right recipe for their organizational cocktail yet. The Yankees are in transition. They have their usual supply of diamond in the rough pitching finds and toolsy IFAs, but haven't turned this batch into their next generation of top prospects yet. And they traded two of their last generation for James Paxton. I'd expect them to be back amongst the top systems in baseball by next year's org rankings.

The Athletics were in better shape until their first round baseball pick played himself into being a first round football pick, but both they and the Pirates lack depth in future regulars despite a top five in both orgs that would comfortably fit in the next tier up.

I think the Rangers system is designed to rank five spots higher in our rankings than anyone else's. I love the kind of athletes they bring in, and while they had downright awful injury luck in 2018, they also saw a few notable breakouts (Bubba Thompson, Anderson Tejeda) and acquired some names that seem destined to be mentioned as next year's notable breakouts (Julio Pablo Martinez, Cole Winn).

The Astros have more two-pitch arms with command questions than olives in Derek's martini. They tend to get more out of these guys than your league-average player development staff, but we can't really *project* that, and they lack for plus regular projections past Whitley and Tucker.

I don't know about you guys, but I am definitely the best version of myself.

7. Minnesota Twins

6. Los Angeles Angels

5. Chicago White Sox

4. Toronto Blue Jays

We move onto the "really good" systems now. The Twins have three potential impact major league players at the top of their prospect list. The Angels organization continues to rapidly improve under Billy Eppler and Mike Gallego and now boasts impressive depth to go along with...well, Jo Adell. We love Jo Adell in case you didn't know. The White Sox system is still strong, but entering a bit of a transition period. They likely have a couple more high draft picks coming to fill in as more top prospects graduate. However, it's about time for the rebuild to end, and the competition cycle to start. This won't be the first or last time in this piece I mention a team should maybe sign Manny Machado or Bryce Harper. Simply because it's unlikely even a "really good" farm system produces a player of that level.

Well, unless you are the Blue Jays that is. This system isn't just Vladito though. Bo Bichette is a potential all-star middle infielder, who would get more headlines in a system that didn't also have the best prospect in baseball. Nate Pearson has arguably the best stuff in all of the minors, and there's a bevy of Role 5 types beyond the top names.

You have a rippin' bod and you can literally do anything!

3. Atlanta Braves

While discussing the Tigers, I alluded to the risks in building your system around arms. That said, if you acquire enough good arms, a few are bound to work out, right? The Braves have far more than a few, clocking in with five Top 101 pitchers, plus one that just missed (Kyle Muller) and one that made it last year (Joey Wentz). The bats aren't bad either with Austin Riley almost ready to take over the everyday third base spot and sure shot centerfielders Cristian Pache and Drew Waters lurking in A-ball. Oh yeah, and they already have the core of a playoff team in place. Hopefully this time they don't break it up after one down year.

Two thumbs up!

2. Tampa Bay Rays

1. San Diego Padres

Pretty much any other year the Rays would be the number one system in baseball. They have built a remarkably deep system with seven top 101 prospects and three or four more that easily could have made it. It's balanced between arms and bats, upside and surety, and the pipeline runs from Brandon Lowe—barely eligible for the list on at-bats—to Wander Franco, who spent 2018 in the Appalachian League. Every affiliate in between is stocked. And it could be even better next year.

But this year it comes in second to the Padres. This is the best system I've ranked in my time as BP's lead prospect writer. I don't think it's all that close (frankly, you could argue the next best is this year's Rays). Impact talent at the top, a dozen or more potential future regulars in the bigs, high upside plays in the low minors, depth for days. I started out insisting that there is no pennant for topping these rankings, but both Tampa and San Diego are well-positioned to turn their minor league organizational health into future major league success (either team should still sign Bryce Harper or Manny Machado, mind you).

—Jeffrey Paternostro is an author of Baseball Prospectus.

Top 101 Prospects

by Jeffrey Paternostro and Jarrett Seidler

1. Vladimir Guerrero Jr., 3B, Toronto Blue Jays

An occasional topic of conversation on Jason Parks and Kevin Goldstein's *Up and In* podcast was what an elite hitter would do if he hypothetically had to spend a full season in the minors. One time it was Miguel Cabrera, perhaps another time Mike Trout. There are limitations to the statistical ceiling here, of course—whether it's the vagaries of balls in play or the occasional slider good enough to get you out every once in a while. But overall you'd expect a pretty ludicrous triple slash across the course of five months. Vladito hit .381/.437/.636 in 95 games between Double and Triple-A. He's only 19. Cabrera and Trout would beat that, but perhaps not by all that much. That tells you what the offensive potential is here. The younger Guerrero is by far the best pure bat in the minors this year (or most any other year), and the best prospect in baseball, full stop. This was not controversial. There were no long email threads, no heated DMs among the BP prospect team. The only real bone of contention was whether or not a .300 batting average with 30 bombs was too conservative a median seasonal outcome for our number one prospect.

2. Jo Adell, OF, Los Angeles Angels

There are plenty of seasons where Adell would clock in as the top prospect in the land. He certainly looks the part. He's built like an NFL wideout with speed to match. He's a sure-shot center fielder. There's plus-plus raw power that a previous author of this list would have called "abnormal" in a slightly bewildered Texas drawl. And Adell has a remarkably advanced feel for hitting as a teenager. Oh, he was also 97 with a projectable slider off the mound in high school, so there's your fifth tool checked off. It's also another indication of just how good he was as a *hitting* prospect for him not to have ended up as a pitcher. We do love our five-tool center fielders here at Baseball Prospectus, and Adell is a particularly impressive specimen. You can't quibble with the performance either. He raked across three levels in 2018 as a 19-year-old, only a thumb injury and brief, initial Double-A struggles keeping him from going full Acuna on the minors. So while we now may have to wait a little longer for him to go full Acuna on the majors, we assure you: It will be worth the wait.

3. Fernando Tatis Jr., SS, San Diego Padres

Can you imagine if Rick Hahn never made the June 2016 James Shields trade? Right before starting their rebuild, the White Sox moved Tatis, then a recent international signing of moderate tout most notable for his bloodlines, at the head of a package for a fading and heavily subsidized Shields. It was the last desperate gasp of a failing contention cycle. Nine times out of ten, this trade is forgotten by 2019, but here on Earth-10, Tatis is now one of the three best prospects in baseball. He tore up the Double-A Texas League, and might've reached the majors as a teenager if it wasn't for a thumb injury and the usual service time shenanigans. He's been in the shadow of Vladito since they signed, both sons of Dominican All-Stars coming of age in the same July 2 class. But the gap is closing, even though Guerrero is the best offensive prospect of recent memory. Tatis is that good.

4. Eloy Jimenez, OF, Chicago White Sox

Acquiring cheap control of a pitcher may have cost the White Sox dearly in 2016, but *trading* a much better version of the same was a windfall in 2017. Jimenez has continued mashing at all levels since migrating across the Second City in the Jose Quintana trade. Sometimes we forget about him because he's not a teenage destroyer of worlds, in a weird sort of prospect fatigue where he's been around for awhile and is limited to outfield corners and points right on the defensive spectrum. We shouldn't. This is his third-straight top ten ranking, and he ended 2018 with a half-season as one of Triple-A's best hitters at just 21. Jimenez is a limitless bundle of offensive upside that should be directly entering the middle of the lineup by the beginning of this summer at the absolute latest.

5. Victor Robles, OF, Washington Nationals

Robles was our "1b" last year behind Ronald Acuna. Both were graded out as OFP 80/Likely 70. Acuna—as you are no doubt aware—went onto have a 70-grade major league campaign while Robles missed most of the year after hyperextending his left elbow on a diving catch attempt in Syracuse. Dropping him to fifth this year might be a bit of undue caution, though. Robles was already major-league-ready in 2017, and he was quite good in his brief 2018 cameo with the Nats. There's still three potential plus-plus tools in his hit, run, and glove, and we have been projecting above-average game power since we first laid eyes on him. The speed and defense make him a likely solid regular even if the bat doesn't play to projection, and he won't turn 22 until six weeks into the 2019 season. While we are worried enough about the injury and lost development time to bump the OFP down to 70 this time around, that might end up another bit of undue caution on our part.

6. Keston Hiura, 2B, Milwaukee Brewers

The known unknown of the 2017 Draft was Hiura's injured elbow. He spent his entire junior campaign at UC-Irvine at designated hitter. There was real concern that his elbow might force him to left field or first base, or even a permanent move to DH. It took him about a year to slowly transition back to full-time play in the field, but by this past summer he was playing second base regularly and doing it without complication. He's even pretty good out there, not that it terribly matters when you're in an organization that just made a pennant run with Travis Shaw standing in the vicinity of the keystone. If you ignored the medical and defensive flags, Hiura was already the best college bat in that class, and you can see how quickly and how high he's risen with a clean bill of health. You rarely hear us talk about a right-handed swing in whispers and high appellations. This swing is perfect.

7. Forrest Whitley, RHP, Houston Astros

There was serious discussion among the BP prospect team this year whether we should just drop every pitching prospect 20 spots or so. They are just so volatile when compared with the position players. And while a quick glance at our DRA-based WARP leaderboard does show several former elite pitching prospects near the top, they're mixed in with names like Jacob deGrom, Corey Kluber, and Patrick Corbin. There's just so many ways it can go wrong for a top prospect arm, even past the more predictable elbow-based ones. Forrest Whitley's arm is fine—as of publication—but plenty went wrong in his 2018 season. He missed the first 50 games after being suspended for using a banned stimulant in the offseason. Then a tweaked oblique limited him to just 50 innings between Double-A and the AFL. But he looked every bit a potential top-of-the-rotation starter during those scant outings. Whitley sits in the mid-90s with four potential plus pitches—and not in the Joe Kelly sense—with advanced command of the whole arsenal. There's ace upside, and he could help the Astros rotation as soon as this summer. Even if we did move every pitching prospect down 20 spots, Whitley would still be an easy choice for #1.

8. Royce Lewis, SS, Minnesota Twins

If it's possible for the first overall pick to be underrated as a prospect, Lewis might be. Most of the heat in the mock drafts in 2017 were on two-way prospects Hunter Greene and Brendan McKay. Lewis was the other prep shortstop. Since draft day, Jo Adell and Keston Hiura have gotten bigger headlines and higher rankings. And look, we obviously really like Adell and Hiura, but all Royce Lewis did in his first full pro season was hit .292/.352/.451 while flashing all five tools. We're more confident he's a shortstop long term now—although still curious about how the profile would look in center. We're more confident he can *really* hit, and he's starting to grow into an average-or-better power projection. That's a monster shortstop prospect. And while the tools might not be quite as loud as Adell's, nor is he as sure a bet with the stick as Hiura, Lewis is still one of the ten best prospects in baseball and a potential perennial All-Star. So let's give him the ink he is due.

9. Nick Senzel, 3B/2B/SS?/OF?, Cincinnati Reds

Could we finally have the new Ben Zobrist? We typically attach the Zobrist sobriquet to prospects without role 7 projections or players nowhere near as good as Zobrist. Zobrist was, of course, a role 7 himself for most of his career, so if you wanted to actually create a Zobrist, you'd have to get that kind of defensive versatility with a prospect that good. Enter Nick Senzel, role 7 potential third base prospect with strong defensive instincts and good athleticism. Right after Senzel was drafted with the second pick in 2016, Eugenio Suarez morphed from a young shortstop filling in at third base to a two-way star third baseman. The Reds eventually locked Suarez up through 2025, and thus the search for a new position for Senzel began. Except they didn't just pick a new position and stop, and he started sliding up the defensive spectrum instead of down. Senzel got experience at shortstop last spring, spent most of his injury-marred 2018 regular season campaign at second base, and tried his hand at left and center field in fall instructs. He may yet settle in somewhere permanently, but the trials around the diamond went well enough for the jack-of-all-trades star possibility to emerge too.

10. Wander Franco, SS, Tampa Bay Rays

One of the prospect team's favorite maxims is that the short-season leagues are "barely organized baseball." Oh, you'll still hear John Fogerty's "Centerfield" during batting practice, and your local pizza place will sponsor some sort of dizzy bat race between innings, but the level of play is so far removed from the majors that it can make evaluating prospects a bit trickier. They aren't seeing major league quality velocity or spin. They might not even see a pitch anywhere near the plate some at-bats. Philosophies can vary on how to deal with this. Some evaluators might just start a mental rolodex, a catalog of what a prospect can do. Others might look for a moment—a swing, a play, a throw—that wouldn't look out of place in the majors. Some don't even bother with these levels at all. That last one is a mistake—for several reasons—but mostly because they would have missed out on seeing Wander Franco. Nothing looks out of place here. Franco is a potential five tool shortstop with particularly loud ones at the plate. As a 17-year-old he posted a 1.000 OPS with more walks than strikeouts for Princeton, and nothing about it seemed unsustainable. There is star upside with the bat and a good chance to stick at the 6. You don't want to miss this, and in the future if you need lunch recommendations in Western Virginia or East Tennessee, hit us up.

11. Taylor Trammell, OF, Cincinnati Reds

Playing baseball is incredibly hard—tell 'em Wash—and the guys that are really good at it often know exactly how good they are. We don't mind a little swagger in our top prospects, and nothing encapsulates that more than Taylor Trammell flashing two fingers towards the Team USA dugout when he thought he'd hit his second home run of the Futures Game this past July. Unfortunately for Trammell, he'd hit a laser beam to the deepest part of Nationals Park and merely hit the fence. He did turn on the jets and still managed to cruise in for a triple on his way to the game's MVP award, but that moment is likely to show up for a few years on "During this commercial break here are some highlights from MLB.com." The Futures Game was a great showcase for Trammell, displaying the premium tools that get him ranked this high, but his performance in the Florida State League was more muted. No matter: Prospect evaluation is in part about what is possible, and for Trammell those possibilities land him back playing exhibition baseball in July for many years to come.

12. Bo Bichette, SS, Toronto Blue Jays

We never want to like Bo Bichette. His swing has a weird-looking hitch that shouldn't work, which we usually describe with the "unorthodox" euphemism. His approach can collapse in a hurry when he gets too aggressive, and that happens more than you'd hope for. He might be a second or third baseman pretty soon. His brother was one of the more infamous first-round busts of recent memory. His father was one of the more overrated MLB players of the Steroid Era. We thought he might have real trouble with advanced pitching, and he certainly stopped putting up the ridiculous averages he did in A-ball. But he made the adjustments as the summer went along and had a strong season as a 20-year-old in Double-A. Ultimately, the bat speed and wrists just play so long as he isn't trying to yank low-and-outside pitches 600 feet down the line. Bichette has all the pieces for a well-rounded offensive game, and he's likely to hold substantial defensive value somewhere or another. Give him a shot to make you like him.

13. Jesus Luzardo, LHP, Oakland Athletics

We really wanted to push Luzardo further up the 2018 incarnation of this list, trust us. But that's a tough sell on a 19-year-old in short-season who already has a Tommy John surgery in his medical history. Even our soothsayers didn't see this level of a breakout coming in 2018. The now 20-year-old crushed three levels of the minors, finishing in Triple-A, striking out 10+ batters per nine and flashing three plus pitches from the left side. The fastball sits around 95, touching higher, with wicked armside left and present above-average command. There's a potential plus change with 10+ mph of velocity separation and impressive tumble. The breaker can get slurvy, but tightened up as the year went on and could be the third 60-grade offering here. The Jesus Lizard is just about ready for a mainstage show at the top of Oakland's rotation, and this version is far less likely to leap into the crowd and start licking fans. Too bad the Bay Area has priced out all the crust punks.

14. Kyle Tucker, OF, Houston Astros

Our evaluations happen in a vacuum. You just evaluate the player, not the situation. Organizational needs can change rapidly, and heck, a prospect can change organizations at any time too. This is to say that the evaluation on Kyle Tucker hasn't really changed. He's a potential plus hit/plus power corner outfielder who has been young for every level he's played at and hit at every level he's played at. He did struggle across a series of major league call-ups, but his playing time was intermittent. That doesn't seem to be a situation that's going to rectify itself soon either. The Astros are at the top of their contention cycle and will rightfully value surety everywhere on the diamond. Tucker's 2019 playing time might get siphoned off to new signing Michael Brantley, who has always hit in the majors when healthy. But as we said, prospects can change organizations too, and perhaps Tucker will find himself with a clear path to playing time outside of the Lone Star State. He certainly has nothing left to prove in the minors.

15. Nick Madrigal, 2B/SS, Chicago White Sox

You can always count on us here at Baseball Prospectus to not shy away from the extreme skill set, and Nicklaus Madrigal has the most extreme skill set of any top prospect in the minors by a mile. Madrigal was generously listed at 5'8" in college. He hit three home runs as a junior—and that was with ping bats. He was pushed off shortstop at Oregon State by Cadyn Grenier. He still went with the fourth pick in the nation, and we are ranking him ahead of every other 2018 draftee. That's how good his hit tool is. Madrigal is the first player in a long time that we've talked internally about grading as an 8 hitter without significant upper-minors or MLB experience. His contact ability might be unmatched in the minors or majors, with the exception of fellow unicorn Willians Astudillo. The White Sox shifted him to shortstop in instructs, and he has the skills to handle the position, especially in the modern age of positioning. We can't reasonably project him to hit for a lot of home run power, but he's far from a punch-and-judy hitter. The swing is short, already geared for line drives, and generates quite a bit of bat speed, so if he somehow adds loft, watch out.

16. Carter Kieboom, SS, Washington Nationals

Kieboom hasn't shown quite enough game power yet for us to just unleash a series of bad puns in this 150-word blurb, but everything else is going well for the Nats prospect. He mashed in High-A and held his own as a 20-year-old in Double-A. He's a potential .300 hitter who has started to lift the ball more. Kieboom has also improved enough at shortstop that there's a non-zero chance he sticks there, although it's more likely he ends up an above-average second baseman. The raw power is plus, and Kieboom still has some room to fill out, making him a decent bet to drop the...well...uh...boom on the Eastern League in a return engagement in 2019. Looks we just said it wouldn't be a *series* of bad puns.

17. Luis Urias, 2B, San Diego Padres

As a prospect evaluator, sometimes you just have to concede the point. In the past, we've hedged on Urias because we know that our greatest weakness in evaluating prospects is the hit tool. Basically, we weren't sold that he was a potential 7 hit guy. We're there now. Urias combines high-end bat-to-ball ability and barrel control with a hair-trigger quick bat, and that's created a lot of offensive potential. Despite a small frame, he has some loft in his swing and generates surprising pop; it might manifest more in gap power than over-the-fence power in the majors, but at the very least he's going to hit a lot of doubles. He's also finally settling in at second base, the defensive home where it was long predicted he would eventually excel. Urias already made his MLB debut in August, and has bigger upside than you might think looking at his measurables.

18. Mitch Keller, RHP, Pittsburgh Pirates

Keller is a weird choice to be another "prospect fatigue" entry, but here we are. This will only be his third appearance on the 101, so he still has a half-decade to go to catch Jorge Alfaro. And he's been a very good pitching prospect, year-over-year since he first burst onto the radar in 2016. There's just nothing new to write about him in 2019. Keller threw 140 good upper minors innings. He's always been durable and efficient. He still has a mid-90s fastball with above-average movement and command, a potential plus-plus curve, and a crude changeup used sparingly. We could wonder aloud again if the lack of an armside weapon against lefties might limit his upside, but he's gone another year against better hitters without really needing it. Keller did have the occasional command/control blip in 2018, but it's hardly a worrying pattern or anything. He's just a very good pitching prospect about ready for the majors, a potential number two starter, and there isn't much more to write at this time.

19. Alex Verdugo, OF, Los Angeles Dodgers

We've repeated the same process for Verdugo for three straight offseasons now. We always start with him being ranked way lower than he ends up. It's not hard to figure out why. He has some tweenerish tendencies. We always wonder more about hit tool projections. He's been up in the majors four separate times now without getting a real opportunity to establish himself. Despite a contact-heavy offensive approach and the ability to play all three outfield positions, he's never cracked a postseason roster. He's been connected to every trade rumor under the sun, and we're honestly not sure he's still going to be on the Dodgers when you read this. Yet every fall during the rankings breakout process, we come to the same realization that he's better than a half-dozen similar players listed ahead of him, and we have to move him up. Maybe we subconsciously underrate boring competence. He's both high floor and high delta despite two seasons of Triple-A, which seems like a paradox, but really isn't. We're pretty sure he's on the Monopoly board as a MLB player; he could reasonably land from about St. Charles (good fourth outfielder or platoon type) to Marvin Gardens (contending for batting titles), or anywhere in between. Having Reading Railroad always returns good surplus value, right?

20. Francisco Mejia, C, San Diego Padres

Jeffrey's column is titled "The View Behind the Backstop" and that's the best vantage point to evaluate most prospects. It does make things tricky for catchers, though. Heck, a lot of the work of the major league catcher happens before he even steps in between the foul lines. The stuff on the diamond isn't much easier. Evaluating gamecalling is tricky from any vantage point: Your view of receiving isn't going to be much better from the scout seats. We've always thought Mejia was a fine, viable, if not above-average major league catcher. Cleveland seemed to disagree, trying him at third and corner outfield before dealing him for a pair of relievers at the deadline. The Padres have one of the best defensive catchers in baseball in Austin Hedges. He doesn't have Mejia's bat—we can see that fine from behind the backstop—which projects as .300 with 15-20 bombs. That's an All-Star catcher if he can stick behind the plate, and somebody, somewhere should give him the chance to prove it one way or the other.

21. Alex Reyes, RHP, St. Louis Cardinals

Two years ago we ranked Alex Reyes as the best prospect in baseball. Since then he has thrown 23 innings. His torn UCL got announced the day we published the 2017 Top 101 on the website. We regret nothing, but we may have to lower our expectations a little in 2019. Everything looked fine in 2018 right up until he tore his lat in his first major league appearance. There's certainly top pitching prospects that have recovered from essentially two years off and turned into good major league starters. Jameson Taillon—whose lost time we grappled with on that ill-fated 2017 list—comes to mind, but that kind of Play Index search will turn up far more Hunter Harveys, and names even more obscure than Hunter Harvey. What we do know: Reyes' stuff all came back from the Tommy John surgery. He might have the best two-pitch combo on this list, and the change is potential plus as well. There were always lingering concerns he might be a reliever, and those voices are only going to grow louder now, but with triple-digit heat and a plus-plus curve, he'd be a heckuva reliever.

22. Brendan Rodgers, SS, Colorado Rockies

Our upper-minors Rodgers reports continue to be a touch less enthusiastic about his ultimate outcome as a player than our older, lower-minors Rodgers reports. There's nothing inherently wrong here—the big tools are still there and his Double-A performance has been good. To the extent that there's a serious knock here, it's that he remains very aggressive at the plate and as a result has sometimes struggled to make consistent, hard contact. He has power, overall feel for hitting, and time still on his side, but they're less on his side than they were a few years ago. The narrative is similar on defense, where he has a decent shot to remain at shortstop but has also been exposed to second and third base as potential alternative positions. The story might end in something looking a lot like, well, Trevor Story.

23. Sixto Sanchez, RHP, Philadelphia Phillies

Sixto missed most of the 2018 season with "elbow inflammation." That can mean a host of different things, most of them ranging from "bad" to "extremely bad." A planned assignment to the AFL was scuttled after a "setback." We are using a lot of air quotes as scare quotes here, but we haven't seen the MRIs so we're mostly guessing. We'll start ranking the dudes that are in the midst of Tommy John recovery a little bit lower, but you'd have to place the odds on Sixto going under the knife point at "higher than you'd like." But he *hasn't* had surgery yet, and when he was on the mound in 2018 he was still Sixto bleepin' Sanchez, owner of arguably the best arsenal in minor league baseball. He was due to be promoted to the Eastern League—where he would have been one of the youngest players in Double-A—before his elbow started barking. He still throws triple-digit heat with movement, offers a cavalcade of potential plus secondaries, and features some of the best pitchability in the prospect world. He's incredibly risky now, but also closer to the majors than you think. He's a conundrum, a potential ace, a potential closer, a potential surgery candidate. He might be Sixto different things to six different prospect writers, but this is a long term value list, and on a long enough timeline we like our chances with Sixto.

24. Michael Kopech, RHP, Chicago White Sox

Kopech continued to restrain himself in 2018, keeping the heater mostly dialed back to the upper-90s while throwing more strikes and reintroducing a plus curveball. (Yes, 95-99 MPH qualifies as dialed back for him.) On the one hand, it was a success in that he carved through Triple-A and reached the majors in August. On the other hand, it didn't matter, as the Tommy John Gods felled him four starts in. It was unfortunate timing for Kopech, who will miss most or all of 2019, and even more unfortunate for the White Sox, who will lose a full year of team control while he's on the disabled list, unlike...

25. Brent Honeywell, RHP, Tampa Bay Rays

...the Rays, whose decision to leave Honeywell down late in 2017 "paid off" huge when Honeywell tore his own UCL early in spring training, if you ignore the utter absurdity of counting your then-top prospect's Tommy John surgery as having positive benefits. Had the Rays called Honeywell up when he was actually ready two summers ago, he'd have spent 2018 on the MLB disabled list, and would have accrued two-plus years of service time by the end of 2019. As it stands, the Rays were able to option him in 2018, and will almost certainly do the same to open 2019. He'll come up later in the spring or summer and won't accrue a season of service time until 2020. Ultimately, that delayed call-up will likely cost Honeywell tens of millions of dollars over the course of his career. Whether you view that as a bug or feature of the system depends on which side of the labor debate you're on. Pending a clean return—and he was already throwing off a mound at press time in December—Honeywell retains top-of-the-rotation potential, just like Kopech.

26. Dylan Cease, RHP, Chicago White Sox

We've been waiting for years for Cease to make the big leap into prospectdom's upper tier. 2018 *finally* brought a measure of durability to go with the elite fastball/breaking ball combination, with Cease spinning 124 dazzling innings in High-A and Double-A. He's improved the secondary offerings and command enough that he's likely to stay in the rotation so long as his health allows. Of course, his medical history contains enough red flags for a DSA meeting, most arm-related. This section of the list contains a ton of pitchers who could front a good rotation if they can get to 200 innings. The distribution of outcomes here means that it's likely that some will, but you might as well get out the ouija board if you want to predict which ones.

27. Dustin May, RHP, Los Angeles Dodgers

We didn't have any sort of nominative determinism in mind when we bestowed the *nom de plume* of "The Gingergaard" on Dustin May after he was drafted. It was merely an aesthetic comp. But a certain—albeit tiny—percentage of those projectable Texas prep arms do develop into Norse Gods. And while May isn't there yet, he was at least a jötnar in 2018. The towering redhead developed a flaming fastball to match in 2018, bumping from the low-90s to the mid-90s and touching as high as 99 with sink and run. His powerful, high-spin curveball is a potential plus-plus offering, so as with Mitch Keller above, you are less concerned with the lack of a changeup at present. May has added a cutter as well for another look, although it is very much a work in progress at present. So yeah, you never comp Noah Syndergaard, but that sure sounds like a Noah Syndergaard starter kit. And the *plume* is particularly impressive as well.

28. MacKenzie Gore, LHP, San Diego Padres

If you agree with Jarrett that the fastball/curveball lefty is the most aesthetically pleasing prospect in baseball, come get your mans. Gore has one of the best curves in the minors, a gorgeous big hook that he can manipulate as a freeze or chase pitch. It works well paired with a lively mid-90s fastball, and it all comes out of a deceptive motion with a classic big leg kick. The changeup also flashes plus but needs greater consistency, which is a sentence that could be applied to 80 percent of the prospects on the list. Just like the rest of the crop, there's a durability concern already present and accounted for. Gore battled blister and fingernail problems all season, which limited him to just 60 2/3 innings. At least the particular worry is about his hand instead of his elbow or shoulder.

29. Ian Anderson, RHP, Atlanta Braves

There's usually a prospect every year where we look up from our locked Top 101 list and blink once or twice while wondering "Wait, how did *he* end up so high?" We shouldn't be so surprised honestly. While Anderson's 2018 season was among the quieter breakouts, it was certainly a breakout, as he struck out nearly 11 per nine while dominating High-A and Double-A. His pedigree has never been as issue, Anderson was the third overall pick in 2016. As a cold-weather arm out of New York State, the stuff was likely to be a slow burn, but it showed up white hot in 2018. He flashed three potential plus pitches, a mid-90s fastball with sink, a tight, swing-and-miss 12-6 curve, and a high-80s change with good arm speed. The control is ahead of the command at present, and the "plus" change is far more projection than present, but you don't have to project too much to see Anderson as a number two starter in reasonably short order. That's how you end up so high on the 101.

30. Austin Riley, 3B, Atlanta Braves

When is a prospect ready? Austin Riley has about a season-and-a-half in the high-minors. He dominated Double-A in the second half of 2017 and especially the first half of 2018, and he continued to be very good at Triple-A in the second half of 2018. Way back in A-ball, he had a risky profile and we legitimately didn't know whether he'd adjust to tougher pitching. There's still too much swing-and-miss, which is just going to be a fact of life with his size, swing, and power, but he's consistently shown the ability to hit MiLB pitching. He's good enough defensively at third base now that he deserves a shot to stick there. And yet despite all of that, Atlanta tipped that they didn't think Riley was ready for permanent MLB work when they signed Josh Donaldson to man third base for 2019. Riley will still likely make his MLB debut soon—Donaldson's health record recently is a disaster, and Riley can probably play other corners if it comes to it—and this does present a convenient rationale for some service time manipulation. But should we care as evaluators that Riley looks ready to play and Atlanta blocked his clear path to playing time for a year anyway?

31. Keibert Ruiz, C, Los Angeles Dodgers

By Baseball Prospectus' WARP—which has the most robust catcher defensive metric—Yasmani Grandal has been at worst the second-best catcher in baseball during his time in Dodger blue. The Dodgers do not seem particularly inclined to sign him to a long-term deal. Yes, he's on the wrong side of 30, but Los Angeles also arguably has the most catching prospect depth in the majors. Catchers are weird, but if you collect enough of them you can mitigate some of the individual weirdness. The best of the crop is Ruiz, a 20-year-old who more than held his own in the Texas League this year while getting rave reviews for his defense and pitcher handling. The offensive tools may only play to average in the end, but even that would make him one of the five or so best *hitting* catchers in the game, and he could be a plus defender behind the plate. That's not quite Yasmani Grandal, but it might be close enough for the Dodgers.

32. Jesus Sanchez, OF, Tampa Bay Rays

In last year's Annual we ranked Sanchez as the 60th best prospect in baseball, while expressing concerns about whether the bat would carry a corner outfield profile. Well, we still have concerns, but we are always going to have concerns about corner bats. Sanchez hit .300 in the Carolina League before scuffling in August after a promotion to Double-A. This is still very much a projection bet as the ideal corner outfield power doesn't always show up after sundown. It's a great frame to make the bet on though, and Sanchez already shows enough bat speed and barrel control to project a plus hit tool. If it all comes together there's All-Star potential in the bat, but we are going to have to wait until at least 2019 to see it all come together, so carry your concerns accordingly.

33. Brusdar Graterol, RHP, Minnesota Twins

A 6'1" righty with reliever red flags and a body like a catcher is not the traditional Top 101 pitching prospect demo here at Baseball Prospectus. When you touch 101 with movement, however, we don't really care how many synonyms for "stocky" we'll have to come up with before Graterol makes the majors. He pairs the triple-digit sinker with a potential plus-plus slider, as well as a curve and change with some projectability. The control and command might never be plus—although that's less of an issue when you hit 100 with regularity—but there's front-of-the-rotation upside coming off a dominant A-ball season as a 20-year-old. And if Graterol does end up a reliever, arms like his fit in there just fine.

34. Nolan Gorman, 3B, St. Louis Cardinals

Often your best third base prospects are presently playing shortstop, but this year's 101 has a bumper crop of hot corner options. Gorman was the other big bat in the Appalachian League this past Summer, and you might wonder how an 18-year-old putting up video game numbers in his first taste of pro ball lasted to the nineteenth pick in the draft. Well, sometimes your third base prospects are your best first base prospects, and there are concerns that he might grow off the hot corner—where he already isn't super-rangy. There's concerns the swing might have holes that upper minors pitchers can exploit, and he did strike out a fair bit in 2018 when he wasn't hammering the ball. But Gorman had arguably the most raw power in his draft class and you saw plenty of that last season too. You hope with time and reps he develops into...well, Austin Riley. Stay tuned, but we like his chances as you might have gathered from this ranking.

35. Jonathan India, 3B/SS, Cincinnati Reds

It might feel a little aggressive to list India as a shortstop, but given what the Reds have done with Nick Senzel, he may actually be headed there for real. India played a handful of games at the six spot after the draft, and focused on it even more during fall instructs. Not all that long ago, moves up the defensive spectrum like this would've been scoffed at, and yet you keep reading about them for highly-regarded infielders in this section. The traditional way to find a prospect's position was to start every promising right-handed throwing infielder off at shortstop and let them migrate right on the spectrum from there, like an inverted application of the Peter Principle. For example, Miguel Cabrera and Miguel Sano both played a goodly amount of short in their first two pro seasons, as unfathomable as that may seem if you're familiar with their later defensive profiles. But more and more, stigmas have changed, and players have started picking up shortstop at higher levels. In the most extreme example we can imagine, Scott Kingery went from playing two games at shortstop over his entire minor-league career to starting 101 games there as a major-league rookie. India certainly has the defensive chops to make a more permanent transition to shortstop plausible, and he now has the same Eugenio Suarez roadblock in his way that Senzel does. Credit the Reds with thinking ahead to turn a potential problem into increased flexibility.

36. Casey Mize, RHP, Detroit Tigers

We haven't ranked the first-overall pick as the top prospect from his draft class in the following winter's top 101 list since Gerrit Cole placed 9th on our 2012 list. (As you may have heard, the writer of that list has since won a World Series ring as a scouting director.) This year is no different, as 2018's 1.1 ranks behind the players taken 4th, 19th, and 5th, respectively. It's probably not entirely a coincidence that Cole was taken in the last draft under the old soft-slotting system; the current system encourages teams to cut an underslot deal up high to pick up more top talents later. Mize was hardly a reach, and got the highest bonus in the draft class and the second-highest bonus ever under the current system. He *still* came in nearly $600,000 under the slot value, savings that allowed the Tigers to draft and sign high-upside prep outfielder Parker Meadows in the second round. On his own merits, Mize is a prototypical top-of-the-draft college righty: a polished craftsman already showing three above-average pitches, all flashing a shot for plus or more. There are more red flags than you'd like for a polished college starter—we're concerned about a history of elbow injuries, and he throws with some effort—and that's why he's not up there fighting with Madrigal for the top ranking amongst 2018 draftees. If he can handle the rigors of a full workload, he's likely to be quite good.

37. Chris Paddack, RHP, San Diego Padres

Paddack has been comically dominant everywhere he's ever pitched, to the point that we can't stop PECOTA from grouping him amongst the best ***MLB*** pitchers. Parts of the scouting report even support that. His changeup is one of the best pitches of any prospect in the game. His fastball "only" gets to the mid-90s, but he manipulates and sequences it brilliantly, and has high-end command to boot. And yet there are two concerns on him which are just major enough that we capped his OFP at 60 and ranked him down here. More significantly, he just hasn't shown the ability to stay on the mound enough. Tommy John surgery cost him the second half of 2016 and all of 2017, and he was surely on a limited count of bullets in 2018. Yet we can't ignore that the 17 starts and 90 innings he did throw last year both represent more than half of his total pro output since being drafted in 2015. We have no clue if he can start yet, basically. Adding to the reliever concern is that he's close to a fastball/changeup only guy at present, with an inconsistent breaking ball that only projects to around average. This is a profile where adding a hard slider to throw a fifth of the time might cause the entire thing to take a huge step forward, and a lot of pitchers have added such in the high-minors or majors, but we can't actually project that until he does it. This ranking could look supremely low if he ends up being a 180-200 inning pitcher with a good third pitch. While those are legitimate huge problems to surmount, there's still less standing between Paddack and the top of a rotation than most.

38. Andres Gimenez, SS, New York Mets

Gimenez has developed a reputation as a low-to-medium upside, higher probability prospect. Based on the relative lack of physicality he showed through 2017, that was more than a reasonable take. We even wrote him up that way in last year's book. He's still a bit small of stature, but the physicality popped in 2018 in ways we weren't entirely expecting. He added significant strength to his upper core and gained some loft in his swing. Suddenly, instead of merely poking the ball around, he started driving it for gap power. He also gained speed, and now projects as a significant stolen base threat. While the football-style offseason workouts organizationally preferred by the Mets have been frequently derided, they have been associated with unexpected strength and speed gains for certain prospects in the past—Amed Rosario is another example. Gimenez looks like the latest, and he's retained the preternatural feel for the game that got him on last year's list. He's closer to the majors than you might think, and he's got a chance to be an impact player instead of just a steady hand.

39. Alex Kirilloff, OF, Minnesota Twins

Every offseason, we have one prospect that generates nearly as much ranking discussion as every other prospect on the list combined. Kirilloff was that prospect this year. We had passionate arguments for him to be significantly higher *and* lower than this. If you aren't this high on him, you can point to timing mechanisms in his swing that might be exploited by upper-level pitchers and the historical profile issues of hit-first prospects who don't generate elite bat speed. His swing is leveraged without showing a lot of lift. If you think we have him way too low, you can point to a rare combination of offensive upside and polish. He's a first-round prep bat with an advanced approach and big raw power who demolished both levels of A-ball in his full-season debut, and there are evaluators that believe in a high hit tool outcome. Risk can run both positively and negatively, and this ranking splits the middle on a prospect none of us truly agree on, recognizing that there's probably some truth to both sides.

40. Peter Alonso, 1B, New York Mets

The top of this list is loaded up with players who just shouldn't be eligible for prospect lists anymore. Some of them are still here in part due to injuries, sure. It's also true that the majority of MLB teams have gotten insanely conscious of service time machinations, and that's resulted in more aggressively holding down prospects who are otherwise ready and have clear paths to playing time. More than anyone else on this list, Alonso is here as a victim of service time manipulation. There was little reason for the Mets to keep him in the minors for all of 2018. Adrian Gonzalez won the first base job out of camp and was cut two months later. Wilmer Flores took the bulk of the playing time from there through August, and was non-tendered this offseason. Jay Bruce took most of the September reps before being unceremoniously salary dumped on Seattle. There was plenty of time available for Alonso if the Mets wanted to, at any point, find out important things like "can he excel against right-on-right MLB sliders" and "will his defense be acceptable." Instead, they prioritized long-term financial considerations—ones that won't even matter much unless Alonso is a star. The ironic part is that new general manager Brodie Van Wagenen has been talking up Alonso's shot to win the Opening Day first base gig all winter, a possibility which would make the previous regime's service silliness all for naught.

41. Joey Bart, C, San Francisco Giants

We think the Mike Zunino comp most often made for Bart is supposed to be a pejorative and represent his downside. Except Zunino, even through long bouts of minimal contact and brutal OBPs, was worth 11.4 WARP to the Mariners during his four-plus seasons in Seattle. That's an undeniably good prospect outcome, even for a top-three pick, as Zunino and Bart both were. The first major factor in Zunino's hidden value also applies to Bart. The catching position is extremely weak now, and if you can play adequate defense and provide any sort of offensive value, you're already as ahead of the curve as Zunino's swing often gets. The second factor—Zunino's framing excellence—may or may not apply to Bart, who has a good reputation but hasn't shown whether he can regularly steal strikes. If all goes well, the Giants may have decades straight of high-end catching production, because Bart should be ready at right about the same time Buster Posey is going to be shedding the tools of ignorance. But he's a catcher, so all might not go well.

42. Brendan McKay, 1B/LHP, Tampa Bay Rays

McKay is perhaps the single trickiest prospect to rank this year. As a left-handed pitching prospect, he's a better version of Logan Allen. That prospect would perhaps rank in the 60s somewhere. As a first base prospect, he's Evan White, a just-missed. If he can be both at times, well, we guess he's the 42nd-best prospect in baseball. We at Baseball Prospectus may not know the meaning of the universe, but definitely would settle for figuring out how McKay is going to get deployed by the boundlessly, uh, creative Rays. Adding to the problem is the dual development has slowed his timetable, leaving a polished college bat (and arm) in A-ball for a full season. We—and he—aren't going to learn much there. The universe is full of questions, of course, we just wish there were fewer open queries about McKay at the moment. He's the string theory of baseball prospects. A third starter/average first baseman outcome is still on the table though, which could arguably give him one of the most valuable skill sets in baseball. A wise man once wrote: "the chances of finding out what's really going on in the universe are so remote, the only thing to do is hang the sense of it and keep yourself occupied." McKay should keep us busy for a while.

43. Triston McKenzie, RHP, Cleveland Indians

McKenzie continues to be a confounding prospect. He was easy to love as a "projectable" 18-year-old, dreams of mid-90s velocity dancing in your head, but two years on he might just be "skinny" and the velocity still hasn't really jumped. It also hasn't mattered, as he dominated Double-A much like he did every other level. He spots the fastball well, and works in a potential plus-plus hook and developing change. A forearm injury—gulp—delayed the start of his 2018, but he's generally been extremely durable given his Christian-Bale-in-*The-Machinist* frame. He doesn't really fit any of our leitmotifs for pitching prospects. This would all be a lot easier if he was left-handed, but for now we will more or less hold serve with a little bit of added risk after the whole "forearm injury" thing.

44. Yusniel Diaz, OF, Baltimore Orioles

Diaz certainly became more famous this past summer as the centerpiece prospect of the Manny Machado deadline deal, but the Cuban outfield prospect has long been on our radar. Any return was going to feel a bit underwhelming to Orioles fans after watching six-plus seasons of Manny freaking Machado, and Diaz in particular isn't going to wow you with big tools. The PR here is a little bit tougher. There is plenty to like though: He has a broad set of baseball skills, everything is solid across the board. He's fine in right field, and could stand in center for you. He's likely to be an above-average hitter with above-average pop. That's an above-average everyday regular, and a good prospect to add to a below-average system in a rebuilding organization. It's just not Manny Machado, so Diaz is always going to unfairly suffer by comparison.

45. Luis Robert, OF, Chicago White Sox

One of these years we'll solve this riddle. That year wasn't 2018. A string of injuries delayed the start of Robert's season, and then interrupted it a few more times. He ultimately only got into 50 regular season games, and reports and results were mixed throughout them, although he did impress in the Arizona Fall League. Of course, even that was interrupted when he pulled his hamstring. Robert retains an impressive upside profile, with potential to hit for average, hit for power, and run while playing a cromulent center field. Yet he's only shown what we think is his true talent in short bursts, and has yet to put it together at the same time. We're also becoming worried there's a risk of his injuries affecting his talent, more specifically his speed and range. It hasn't happened yet, but the leg injuries are starting to add up.

46. Josh James, RHP, Houston Astros

For the last few decades, we've talked about health as an abstract "skill" for the purpose of evaluation. At the core, though, these are human individuals who sometimes have very human health problems that aren't covered within our usual scope. We can't know about them. Sometimes the players themselves don't. Josh James was drafted in the 34th round in 2014 as a redshirt sophomore out of a junior college you've probably never heard of, after landing there as a D2 transfer infielder. He signed with the Astros for a measly $15,000. He spent the first few years of his pro career as a very minor prospect, a generic minor-league swingman with middling stuff and an organizational soldier future. What we didn't know was that James constantly felt tired and lethargic, and his roommates frequently complained about his loud and restless sleep. Eventually, he was diagnosed with sleep apnea and started using a CPAP machine. Finally rested and healthy, James greatly improved his mechanics and body, and his velocity subsequently jumped about eight ticks over the course of the 2018 season. He struck out 171 hitters in 114 1/3 innings in the minors while laying complete waste to tough Double-A and Triple-A environments. By the time he was called up to the majors on September 1st, he was sitting 97-99 and touching 101, accenting it with a plus changeup and flashing a devastating slider. He was so impressive in September that he forced the team's hand and cracked a ridiculously loaded Astros playoff staff. This is, bar none, the most impressive prospect breakout we can remember. We aren't remotely equipped to handle what any of this means going forward for a role or projection because it's so far out of the norm, other than to tell you that James will likely be an incredible force for as long as he can stay healthy.

47. Leody Taveras, OF, Texas Rangers

Public metrics continue to move forward. We measure everything, project everything a bit better than we did a decade ago. One of the areas we still fail to accurately model is minor league performance. The talent level is too wide, the prospects too volatile, still developing. This is one of the reasons we can justify putting Leody Taveras in the top 50 after posting a .246/.312/.332 line in High-A. Here, "don't scout the statline" is more plea than counsel. Taveras was one of the youngest players in the Carolina League, spending the whole season as a 19-year-old, and he will still put on a show in batting practice that will assuage the doubts of even the most cynical of gray-haired scouts. There's also the matter of the plus center field tools across the board. Eventually Taveras will have to produce a .700 OPS at a full-season level, but we'll ignore the metrics for now and focus on the tools. The unstoppable engine of progress doesn't cover as much ground in the outfield as he does anyway.

48. Bubba Thompson, OF, Texas Rangers

Just one level and one spot on this list behind Taveras is his long-term competition. Thompson is an incredible athlete that chose a baseball career over offers to play quarterback at some FBS powers, including Tennessee, UCF and Ole Miss. We have been sold on the overall profile since he was drafted, but he showed up in Low-A with a much better feel for hitting than we thought. Mind you, better is not necessarily great—he struck out over a quarter of the time, and we have major concerns about his ability to recognize spin. Still, it's always nice to see an elite athlete show up to play full-season baseball and show a broader base of skills than you thought might be there. Defensively, Thompson may grow out of center field on his own, and Taveras may push him out one of these years even if he doesn't. There's five-tool upside here, with a wide range of outcomes below that.

49. Yordan Alvarez, 1B/OF, Houston Astros

We're slowly warming to first base prospects here at Baseball Prospectus. Alvarez can more credibly stand in the outfield than most of his cold corner brethren, but his is probably not the lower-half of a long term left fielder. Functionally it doesn't *reaaaaally* matter anyway, the point is he is going to have to hit a lot regardless. He sure hit a lot in 2018. He couldn't legally drink on Opening Day, and ended the year with a .900 OPS across the upper minors. He's close to major-league-ready—although like Tucker, the Astros may not have an obvious spot for him—with a plus hit/ plus power projection. That's about the bare minimum for this profile to make the 101, but despite occasional stiffness in the swing to get the ball in the air, Alvarez profiles as a safe, above-average corner guy. I didn't say we were in love with the profile or anything, did I?

50. Justus Sheffield, LHP, Seattle Mariners

A lefty prospect turned 22
He made the majors, and got traded for James Paxton
It's getting hurt again while lighting up the radar gun
It's finding your fastball command, two minutes too late
Isn't it ironic, don't you think?

It's like being ranked in the 50s here for three straight years
It's a conversion to relief for the playoff roster you didn't make
It's the opportunity in the Yankees rotation that you just didn't take
And who would have thought you'd end up on the Mariners?

51. Ryan Mountcastle, 3B, Baltimore Orioles

Defensive profiles are becoming more amorphous by the year. Radical positioning and aggressive strategies have let players stick at positions that we'd have never guessed they'd stick at, without doing the harm they'd have done in previous generations. Mountcastle is a big dude who doesn't throw well, which makes him a tough fit at the positions where he could be an offensive star even though his hands and instincts are fine. The Orioles tried shortstop for awhile, which went poorly. Third base has gone a little better, but it's always going to be a stretch. Outfield might be worth a shot at some point, but he has no professional experience out there and we're not sure he'll be rangy enough. If we're talking an ideal defensive home, a larger player with soft hands and good defensive feel is a natural for first base, but that starts to put an enormous strain on his offensive profile. Mountcastle turned in a quality Double-A campaign after missing the first month of the season with a broken hand, shaking off a bad cameo there at the end of 2017. He remains far too aggressive at the plate, which has placed an upper bound so far on big hit and power potential. If the light goes on at the plate and he can play reasonable defense somewhere, he'll be a star. He'll still be pretty good if one or the other happens. If neither occurs...well, he could be C.J. Cron.

52. Seuly Matias, OF, Kansas City Royals

Some tools are almost trivial to grade. Run a stopwatch on a home-to-first dig or a stolen base play at second and consult your chart—congratulations, you've graded run and catcher arm. Raw power is not quite that simple. There's some nuance, and you do have to keep your eyes open during batting practice, but Seuly Matias makes it an easy scout. This is 80-grade raw folks, and while his five o'clock show might not be quite as majestic as Joey Gallo or Miguel Sano's, it's damn impressive. The return engagement at game time isn't bad either, as Matias socked 31 home runs in 94 games at Low-A. Oh yeah, he was 19 all season. It's not just a one-tool profile either: Matias wields a cannon for an arm, which will cover for the deficiency of his range. He's a better *hitter* than you'd think. He isn't a grip it and rip it guy, but it's not easy power per se, and there's significant swing-and-miss issues thus far. You're here for the power though, and Matias just needs to get enough of it into games to be a middle-of-the-order monster.

53. Mike Soroka, RHP, Atlanta Braves

The one constant in Soroka's prospect profile over the years has been his remarkable durability—and Atlanta's willingness to let him throw a lot of innings—as a prospect. So of course he missed most of 2018 with "right shoulder inflammation." Pitchers, man. Soroka was well on his way to a very good rookie campaign—and list ineligibility—before he hit the shelf. He has a full collection of solid-average-or-better offerings. The fastball velocity ticked up—he's a more consistent 92-94 now—while retaining its above-average movement. The slider looks like a real plus pitch as opposed to just flashing, and the change is above-average as well. All the elements are here for a top-five pitching prospect in baseball, but if he had been healthy, we wouldn't be ranking him. He wasn't healthy and shoulders make us very nervous. The profile was always "safe number three" and it's not safe anymore—although "number three" might now be light. So this year we have to rank Soroka's among the risky guys like...

54. Nate Pearson, RHP, Toronto Blue Jays

This is the best stuff in the minors. It's also about as risky a profile as you can get. Pearson can sit in the triple-digits and touched 104 MPH in a short outing in the Arizona Fall League's Fall Stars Game. As you might guess for a guy with that arm strength, he has a wicked low-90s slider, and a curveball and changeup also flash plus. Before the Fall League, his 2018 was lost to a spring oblique injury and a summer fractured forearm from a hard comebacker off his pitching arm. Injuries have been a recurrent drag here, and he was a known medical red flag in the 2017 Draft over a screw in his pitching elbow from high school. Pearson's mechanics have enough violence to be an issue on their own. What we ultimately have right now is an ace starter's arsenal and no idea about what role—if any—he can stay healthy in. The career path of another, similar Nate hints that this could take up to a decade to play out, although we suspect that Pearson would be happy to eventually get Eovaldi's recent $67.5 million contract.

55. Ke'Bryan Hayes, 3B, Pittsburgh Pirates

Last summer at Baseball Prospectus we published a roundtable discussion that considered—in part—if there is a way to figure out if certain prospects are more likely to develop additional power once they reach the majors. The idea was to see if it were possible to identify the next Chris Taylor or Ozzie Albies. If we had an actual methodology for that, we'd all have different jobs than "prospect blurb writer," but we did come up with a few useful criteria: (1) Good contact ability, (2) plus bat speed, (3) an advanced approach, (4) above-average raw power. Despite hitting just 15 home runs across three pro seasons, Ke'Bryan Hayes checks all four boxes. (1) He hit .290 in Double-A and rarely struck out, making consistent, high-quality line-drive contact. (2) A lot of those hits were absolute laser beam doubles over the third baseman's head, so yeah, he can cover velocity. (3) He'll spit on spin away, work walks, foul off tougher stuff; he's pesky. (4) Go dig up batting practice video of Hayes from the Futures Game where he put pitch after pitch ten or twenty rows back in the left field bleachers, it's in there. But even if the power doesn't come, he's a plus defender at the hot corner that will give you the good Cesar Hernandez seasons at the plate. That's a nice everyday player. But we think there might be more in the bat. Although I suppose if we *really* thought that he'd be 40 spots higher. How's that for a hedge?

56. Griffin Canning, RHP, Los Angeles Angels

You might be aware that the Angels spent years with a terrible, awful, no good farm system. A major part of the turnaround was betting on big upside with injury concerns on their first two picks in 2017. Jo Adell had a dead arm before the draft, and that pick has turned out gangbusters. The even riskier selection was Canning—an early-to-mid first-round talent who fell due to bad medicals and huge college pitch counts—in the second round. He roared back to his talent level with a vengeance in 2018, with a velocity spike under lighter usage while still making 25 starts and reaching Triple-A in his pro debut. Durability and health concerns may yet limit him to a mid-rotation outcome, but he does have better stuff than the usual mid-rotation starting profile. Popping Canning might pay off pretty big, too.

57. Adonis Medina, RHP, Philadelphia Phillies

Oh yeah, we are deep in the mid-rotation starter woods now. Medina's long been an exemplary example of the "number three starter or late-inning reliever" projection. His 2018 was almost a carbon copy of his 2017. He was at High-A instead of Low-A, so that's good. The slider is improving and closer to its plus projection, that's also good. He lacks ideal height, ideal command, and an ideal changeup. That's good for our overarching profile purposes, though less good for Medina's prospect status. Double-A is often where these type of arms separate out more clearly into the mid-rotation starter and late-inning reliever buckets, so Medina's 2019 Eastern League campaign will be one to watch. But *note bene*, don't pay too much attention to the top line stats; Reading remains one of the worst parks in the minors to pitch.

58. Kyle Wright, RHP, Atlanta Braves

Wright made his MLB debut in a relief cameo at the end of his first full pro season, and he's still down a dozen-plus spots from where he ranked after the draft. He remains a polished, healthy, advanced college arm, and a pretty good bet to be headed for the middle of a rotation. To the extent that there is an issue, the issue is that almost everything in the profile is a hair lighter than you hoped for out of the draft, and the slight nitpicks do add up come rankings season. The command and control are fine, but a little worse than we hoped for. The velocity is fine, but a little worse than we hoped for. The breaking balls are fine, but a little worse than we hoped for. The changeup consistency is more than adequate for a fourth offering, but it's a little worse than we hoped for. As the sign on *The Good Place* reads, everything is fine. It's just not *great*.

59. Will Smith, C/IF, Los Angeles Dodgers

The "catcher who can play other positions" is in vogue right now as benches get shorter and positioning gets closer to radar precision. Smith has improved enough behind the plate that you could just play him there everyday and hope that his 2018 power spike turns him into a plus backstop. But the Dodgers love their positional fluidity—see Max Muncy, second baseman—and Smith has experience at second and third as well (Smith, like so many of the dudes on the 101, was a shortstop in high school). The value of this defensive flexibility doesn't always show up in raw WARP totals—although it will if it gets Smith an extra 20-30 starts a year—but as baseball changes so must our prospect lists. Though if anything this ranking might be a bit low for a more traditional starting catcher with 20-home-run pop.

60. Bryse Wilson, RHP, Atlanta Braves

Atlanta has had a lot of volatility in their pitching prospect stock. Wilson is one of the big risers, jumping from A-ball to a major-league debut at just 20, beating many of his previously more touted (and older) org mates to The Show. He's not all that different from Soroka and Wright; if he seems like a revelation while they seem like a disappointment, that's mostly an artifact of draft positions and old rankings. Wilson is extremely advanced as prep pitchers of his age and experience level go, without the typical level of concern over things like command, third pitch consistency, and ability to handle a full workload. There's still the usual "he's a pitcher" concerns, of course, and he doesn't have the extreme upside that most of his age cohort ranked in this general area possesses. Having a bunch of high-probability third starter types in your system is a good way to develop a rotation, especially since there's always a shot one of these arms moves forward unexpectedly too.

61. Khalil Lee, OF, Kansas City Royals

Lee was a three-true-outcomes hitter in Low-A in 2017, a bit like Seuly Matias but with "only" plus raw power. He cut his K-rate in 2018 across two levels while maintaining his strong approach, but sacrificed a chunk of game power in the process. This isn't uncommon for hitting prospects trying to figure out the balance between contact and lift, hit and pop. It's easy to suggest that Lee just marry the two approaches, and much harder to execute as the pitching gets better. His ultimate defensive home is unknown as well. He has the athletic tools for center field, but his instincts and routes are still a bit raw. He's the most nebulous prospect on the 101, and that includes the short-season ones. Lee continues to look the part of a major league outfielder, but what exact role we are casting for is still an unknown unknown.

62. Cristian Pache, OF, Atlanta Braves

Pache might be the best defensive center fielder in the minors. That's */checks notes*...yes, extremely valuable. He's a plus-plus runner with a plus-plus arm and has good enough instincts on the grass to project as a plus-plus glove. That's...six pluses! That's a lot! The superlatives don't flow quite as easily during his at-bats though. Pache has an aggressive approach and takes his hacks like a man who thinks he has two additional grades of raw power than he actually does. The swing can get long, and he can get out of balance in the box. If Pache can tone all this down a bit and manage even an average hit tool, the complementary skills here are more than enough to make him a plus regular, perhaps even an occasional All-Star, but we probably wrote that opening line about Manuel Margot a few years ago too.

63. Jarred Kelenic, OF, Seattle Mariners

There was some significant prospect-industrial complex hype around Kelenic when he was traded by the Mets. This list was written by two ancestral diehard Mets fans, so we certainly get the urge to do a LOLMETS. Kelenic is a very good prospect, and in a year or two might be the sort of prospect the Mets will sorely wish they still had. But he's not there yet, and a stroll down memory lane will reveal more highly drafted prep outfielders who didn't work out than you'd think, many of them of broadly similar skills and post-draft sheen as Kelenic. As for this one right here, right now, he projects to have a broad base of offensive and defensive value, but may lack a carrying tool. If there is a carrying ability, it'll probably be that he hits for a higher average generally reaches first more than we'd expect right now. Of course, the downside risk is largely the same variance in the other direction, and his swing has some length and leverage to it. Projecting the future of teenage bats is nearly as tough in baseball as projecting teenagers is in real life. (Also, Edwin Diaz is a lot better than you may realize.)

64. Jonathan Loaisiga, RHP, New York Yankees

That happened fast. Loaisiga's second full-season pitcher appearance in his minor league career—he had one in Low-A in June 2016 before undergoing Tommy John surgery—was on April 7th, 2018 for High-A Tampa. Just ten starts later, on June 15th, he made his MLB debut by firing five shutout innings in Yankee Stadium. It was a hell of a long road before 2018, though. Originally signed by the Giants in 2012, Loaisiga never made it out of the complex levels as he battled shoulder issues, and was released in May 2015. He went home to Nicaragua, and pitched in winter ball and for the national team early in 2016, where he was discovered by Yankees scout Ricardo Finol shortly before departing to play the summer in Italy. Upon recovering from the torn UCL, he was brilliant in the Gulf Coast and New York-Penn Leagues late in 2017, brilliant enough in fact that we wrote him up on a loaded team list after the season and the Yankees had to add him to the 40-man despite their perpetual Rule 5 crunch. So it really wasn't out of nowhere, just way faster than we thought. He had more shoulder problems later on in the summer, his command is inconsistent, and he's small of stature, all of which may be tipping a bullpen future. If he can somehow stay in the rotation, it'd be premium upside, with a fastball and breaking ball that both flash plus-plus and an average changeup that might get a notch higher.

65. Drew Waters, OF, Atlanta Braves

As part of the MLB investigation into the Braves illegal bonus manipulations under John Coppolella, Atlanta was docked a third-round pick for offering Waters "extra benefits" as part of his signing bonus. Waters—himself a second round pick—remained a Brave, likely because MLB didn't want the precedent of that high a draftee being made an unrestricted free agent. All the IFA players that were granted free agency were still subject to international bonus pool restrictions. Despite losing an entire IFA class, the Braves remain one of the healthiest farm systems in baseball, mostly because some of the players from their suspect machinations remain in the system, and many have turned into top prospects (or the 2018 Rookie of the Year). We don't know if any lessons have been learned by anyone involved. Anyway, Waters had a breakout season in Low-A, is a potential five-tool center fielder, and instead gets a prospect blurb that is about everything but that.

66. Estevan Florial, OF, New York Yankees

One of our favorite cliches around these parts is "a year is a lifetime for a prospect." Well, Florial's 2018 was the dril tweet: "awfully bold of you to fly the Good Year blimp on a year that has been extremely bad thus far." The culprit here was mostly injury: Florial had to have hamate surgery during the season, and that's one of the worst injuries in terms of lingering effects on offensive performance, especially power. The tools are loud enough, and the ceiling remains high enough, that we are mostly willing to give Florial a pass for his bad 2018, but the clock is ticking now and 2019 will be a very important year for the Haitian-Dominican outfielder.

67. MJ Melendez, C, Kansas City Royals

You have to evaluate each prospect on their own individual merits, but the world doesn't exist entirely in a vacuum either. Melendez was taken with the 52nd pick in the 2017 Draft out of a Miami prep school. The last prep catcher to be drafted in the early rounds to have a significant MLB career was Wil Myers in 2009. Unless you hold Devin Mesoraco's All-Star year in great esteem, the last one to be both a good player and stick as a starting catcher for any length of time was Brian McCann way back in 2002. No matter which way you count, dozens and dozens of high school catchers have been taken since then, we've ranked many of them in this space, and essentially none of them have turned into good MLB backstops as yet. Dating back decades, sabermetric research has consistently shown high school catchers as a group to be the absolute worst investments in the Rule 4 Draft. And yet there's still a bunch of prep catchers drafted in the first few rounds every year, and here we are again, telling you that this time it will be different and MJ Melendez is going to be the one to break the streak. We have to write what we see, and we see a strong two-way catching prospect. But if you're reading this book, we presume that you are interested in the metagame of baseball, and the history of this class of prospect is bad.

68. Jahmai Jones, 2B, Los Angeles Angels

This is Jones' third straight year on the 101, but first entry as a second baseman. It's a bit of a weird positional switch, as usually players with his physical tools go from the dirt to the grass, rather than vice versa. He's developing fine at the keystone, but it will take some time, and he did project as at least an average defensive center fielder. The continued existence of Mike Trout in Angels Stadium might be influencing things here, as could be the emergence of Jo Adell, but it's added some weird developmental risks into the profile that weren't there before. Jones still has an athletic swing and a quick bat, married with an advanced approach he showed going back to the draft year reports. And he still projects for above-average hit and average power, but the overall offensive performance did suffer a bit in 2018. How much of that is his first taste of Double-A and how much might be his main focus being on learning a new position is an open question. For our part, we held Jones more or less steady with his 2018 ranking, but hopefully more will become clear this year.

69. Jazz Chisholm, SS, Arizona Diamondbacks

Thelonious Monk once said that "the piano ain't got no wrong notes." There weren't any wrong notes in 2018 for Jazz Chisholm either. His glovework was never in doubt; he is a potential plus-or-better shortstop who handles tough chances in the field as adroitly as Coltrane maneuvering through the opening chord changes of "Giant Steps." Jazz's power at the plate this year was unexpected, a John Zorn heavy metal EP, but it's married with an approach that's a bit more Charlie Mingus, dissonant and only rarely restrained. If his chops hold up at higher levels, he could end up a true classic of the toolsy shortstop genre, but many a potential jazz cat ends up just another birdbrain once they suit up in Double-A. If that does happen at least we won't have to flog these references again for the 2020 Annual. We aren't exactly the baddest hipsters in the barrelhouse, after all.

70. Touki Toussaint, RHP, Atlanta Braves

Baseball is rapidly becoming a de facto salary cap sport, even if it isn't a de jure one quite yet. In any capped sport with guaranteed contracts, you're going to get aggressive salary dumping. To that end, teams have created surplus value calculations to place monetary values on prospects. For over a decade, the public analytics community has followed suit, with the most recent extensive research published late last year by Craig Edwards at FanGraphs. It's a necessity if you're going to make "salary cap trades" instead of "baseball trades," and yet at the same time it is radically dehumanizing. On his 19th birthday, Toussaint was functionally sold by the Diamondbacks to clear about $10 million left on Bronson Arroyo's contact. It was the harbinger of things to come, the beginning of a trend that is taking clearer shape four years later. There was no baseball rationalization for this move at the time, only a financial one, and it looks even worse in retrospect with Toussaint's raw potential now close to actualizing as a good pitcher. But unlike most similar moves, we can't say the money went to debt service, investors, or ownership pockets, because Arizona did sign Zack Greinke the next offseason.

71. Victor Victor Mesa, OF, Miami Marlins

The world is changing. Not that many years ago, the story of the Mesa brothers coming stateside would've been much uglier. It'd have involved a harrowing journey involving human trafficking elements, and perhaps even foreign warlords. It'd have been scandalous for father Victor, who is Cuban baseball royalty and would've been forced to pick between blood and country. These days, they just left, seemingly with tacit approval, to seek American contracts (shortly after the Mesas signed, MLB, the MLBPA and the Cuban Baseball Federation announced a formalized posting system similar to Japan and Korea, although it faces uncertain political prospects in the States) and Victor Sr. plans to split his time between Miami and Cuba. Like Luis Robert last year, Victor Victor hasn't played baseball in awhile, and we'll get a much better idea what kind of prospect he is when he gets in competitive game situations this spring. Industry chatter has frequently compared Victor Victor to Cubs outfielder Albert Almora both offensively and defensively, if you want a hint of the shape of things to come.

72. Adrian Morejon, LHP, San Diego Padres

Morejon was our "third starter poetry entry" last year, and the second verse isn't all that dissimilar from the first. He had a successful season pitching in the tough climes of the Cal League as a teenager, although he was limited to around 70 innings by a hip injury. His fastball bumps 98 now, and sits comfortably in the plus velocity range. He has two potential above-average secondaries in his curve and change, with the breaker ahead of the cambio and both ahead of his command. He's an undersized lefty and lacks projection, but the present arsenal is good enough, that he doesn't have to improve all that much in his early 20s to be a mid-rotation starter.

73. Sandy Alcantara, RHP, Miami Marlins

Unlike most of the other prospects the Marlins acquired in their latest firesale, at least Alcantara is holding steady. Alcantara still throws really hard and still has a three-pitch profile. He's also still not really striking that many batters out in the high-minors, he's still a work-in-progress on command, and still an injury risk in frame and history. If you guessed that he might end up in the bullpen eventually, congratulations for having already read the other dozen reports above with this same broad stroke profile, though he's likely to get more shots than most to start because of lack of organizational depth. He'll certainly face little in the way of competition for space in Miami's rotation over the short term, and he showed flashes of readiness in September.

74. Luis Patino, RHP, San Diego Padres

We have internal conversations a lot about what to do with pitching prospects that we just don't yet know enough about to put into a role box. We know enough about Patino to strongly suspect that he's one of the 101 best prospects in baseball. He throws pretty hard. The command, deception, and changeup are all unusually advanced for a teenager. He will likely end up with three or four usable pitches. These are all building blocks for a future good rotation piece. We also know enough to know that the delta on his set of outcomes is enormous, making this an impossible ordinal ranking. He's on the smallish side. The Padres kept the reins firmly attached in 2018, only letting him make 17 starts at Low-A and never allowing him to throw more than 84 pitches. We have nothing to go on for his durability either way, just vague concerns and general industry trends. Over the next year or two, this will surely play out one way or another, and we'll probably have several chances to revisit this topic in future books.

75. Hunter Greene, RHP, Cincinnati Reds

Jeffrey and Jarrett were in a Lyft with some friends in Cambridge, MA early last August, heading to our Saberseminar presentation, when we heard that Hunter Greene's MRI came back with a UCL sprain in his elbow. We both talked about Tommy John surgery as a fait accompli, since it so often is from there, and mentally filed him as returning in 2020. A few months later we started researching Reds prospect reports and we found out that Greene had yet to have surgery and that his rehabilitation was going well. In late-October, Greene himself reported on Twitter that he'd been given a clean bill of health. We're going to maintain a bit of skepticism until he throws in some games, but it's a special arm talent, if a bit raw around the edges.

76. Dane Dunning, RHP, Chicago White Sox

A potential third starter, frame sturdy and strong
The fastball low-90s, moves wayward and steep
Oh, I write these same blurbs through all winter long

No ballad composed about his breakers, nor song
Average for both, hey the arsenal's deep
A potential third starter, frame sturdy and strong

He commands the curve well, I say to the throng
The slider may cut, sometimes it will sweep
Oh, I write these same blurbs through all winter long

The change flashes plus, you knew all along
His face on the mound won't make batters weep
A potential third starter, frame sturdy and strong

We're almost to the end, the meter's all wrong
The audience bored on the verge of deep sleep
Oh, I write these same blurbs through all winter long

Can he mix his stuff well and limit the dong?
Could one of the breakers perhaps take a leap?
A potential third starter, frame sturdy and strong
Oh, I write these same blurbs through all winter long

77. A.J. Puk, LHP, Oakland Athletics

The most dangerous time of year for a pitching is ramping up before the season. Every year, we get a handful of high-profile UCL tears as everyone stretches their arm out. Puk was one of the 2018 Cactus League casualties. It was especially unfortunate because he was seemingly beginning the leap early in spring, and likely would've been in the majors no later than midseason. This wasn't a great season developmentally for Puk to miss, and the command and repeatability issues that we were already concerned about can be exacerbated during Tommy John recovery. The hope is that he'll be back sometime around when spring turns to summer, and if all goes well he might be a MLB candidate again later in the season.

78. Julio Pablo Martinez, OF, Texas Rangers

The Rangers have always had a fondness for toolsy Cuban outfielders. Well, any toolsy outfielder really. Or toolsy shortstop for that matter. Martinez is runner up to Victor Victor for this year's Luis Robert Memorial "We have no real idea what to do with this guy." We do have a bit more stateside info at least. After signing for $2.8 million, Martinez spent a bit of time in the Northwest League and Arizona Fall League where he was fine, but maybe a bit underwhelming for a 22-year-old with four years under his belt in Serie Nacional. The seven-figure tools were all accounted for, though. Martinez is a good bet to be an above-average defender in center and gets more pop than you'd expect out of his five-foot-nine frame. We'll have a lot more info on him after a proper full-season debut in 2019. For now, this is a bit of a dart throw.

79. Lucius Fox, SS, Tampa Bay Rays

More of a field man than a bat man, but with the fall of Matt Harvey, he's Gotham's best chance for a new savior. Fox actually has his own interesting backstory, as he attended three years of high school in South Florida before moving back to his family home in the Bahamas. That got him reclassified from the Rule 4 Draft to the international signing pool, and he cashed in as a $6 million bonus baby with the Giants in 2015. He was moved along to Tampa Bay in a 2016 deadline package for mercurial lefty Matt Moore, the top prospect on this list seven years ago. Puns aside, Fox is a plus-plus runner and a silky smooth defender, and there's some feel for hitting present too. He has limited gap power, but it's a very playable athleticism and defense profile even if the bat never begins to shine.

80. J.B. Bukauskas, RHP, Houston Astros

A nice thing about the Arizona Fall League is the availability of Statcast data, and before that PITCHf/x data. Because of that data and our partner site Brooks Baseball, I can give you an accurate picture of what JBB was throwing in October, without the variability of inconsistent radar guns or spotty private information. He was sitting 95-96 with the fastball and touching 98, leaning on one of the minors' best sliders as his out pitch, and flashing a hard change at 90-91. This is a bit of a velocity bump from what he'd shown previously, and most importantly it all confirms that he's healthy (and then some) after a back injury from a car accident cost him a large chunk of the regular season. We don't put much stock in AFL *performance*, but when there's a profile jump that seems sustainable, that does matter. And that AFL jump—and our ability to confirm it with reasonably reliable data—got Bukauskas onto the final draft of this list.

81. Luis Garcia, SS/3B, Washington Nationals

He's likely to soon be the best of baseball's many, many Luis Garcias—there are at least five currently active in the American minors, including fellow top infield prospect Luis Garcia of the Phillies, plus major-league reliever Luis Garcia, who was traded from the Phillies to the Angels this past offseason, and several more playing internationally. This particular Luis Garcia was born in 2000 (don't you feel old right now?) and has already hit at both full-season levels of A-ball. He also has a better chance to stick at short than you'd expect for a guy who was already picking up other positions as a 17-year-old. The Nationals sometimes move prospects very aggressively, and Garcia is already moving quickly. He has a shot to be in the majors before he turns 20 in May 2020.

82. Travis Swaggerty, OF, Pittsburgh Pirates

We're ranking ten 2018 draft picks on the 101 this time around. That's low even for us, who tend to be a bit more conservative with evaluating recent draftees. There are a few reasons for that: It was a slightly down draft class. A couple high first-round picks didn't sign. A few high first-round arms have injury concerns. A few more picks ended up between 102 and 110. But it's worth noting that as more teams ~~tank~~ move their contention window a few years down the road, that the recent successful rebuilds had less to do with high draft picks than you'd think. In baseball you are never getting the immediate impact of a franchise quarterback or a LeBron James anyway. The Pirates were still nominally competing in 2017 when they underperformed enough to have the tenth overall pick in 2018. Swaggerty is a fine prospect, a college center fielder with average-to-above tools across the board and a good approach at the plate. He's unlikely to be a franchise-altering piece, nor is their 18th overall pick next year. You need good regulars to compete, but too many teams are trading their present ones on for the hope of cheaper ones somewhere down the line in the vast medium term.

83. Anderson Tejeda, SS, Texas Rangers

He's back! Two years ago, we made an aggressive call on Tejeda, including him on the bottom of the 101 based on big reports from various complex and short-season levels. He had some typical full-season adjustment issues in 2017, most obviously an overly aggressive plate approach. But he started popping again for us in 2018, improving his pitch recognition and tapping into significant game power. We still aren't giving up the ghost on the hit tool, either; it's a sweet swing with a lot of bat speed. He's not a stone cold lock to stick at shortstop, but he has a good shot, and even if he moves off it would probably be to another premium position. Can you tell we like him a lot?

84. Logan Allen, LHP, San Diego Padres

Earlier we referred to Brendan McKay as "better Logan Allen," but actual Logan Allen is a very good prospect in an organization stuffed to the gills with very good prospects. His 2018 statistical dominance does overstate the stuff a bit. The fastball is low-90s with command to both sides and the ol' lefty funk and deception. The slider is cutterish, but an effective bat misser. There's a potentially average change and curve as well. He's left-handed. He's already in Triple-A. He's another third-starter prospect. The Padres have collected so many of these that the law of averages—or if you prefer, percentile projections—suggests that one of them will over-perform our spate of 6/5 grades. The stuff suggests it's less likely to be Allen, but perhaps…

85. Michel Baez, RHP, San Diego Padres

We have more info about Baez than we had last year for good and for ill. He threw 105 innings, proving that he can get stretched out—at least by prospect arm standards—and keep the big fastball/change combo. The slider is slowly improving and should give him a needed gloveside option against righties. He did struggle in his first taste of Double-A however, and continues to have issues keeping all six-foot-eight of his frame on line to the plate. He's far more likely to be a reliever than Allen, but also more likely to have serious impact if he sticks in the rotation. He gets the same 6/5 grade despite a much larger delta/risk. Sometimes more info doesn't help as much as we'd like.

86. Nico Hoerner, SS, Chicago Cubs

Here's the other player who vaulted into the list from shining reports in the Arizona Fall League. For many years now, we've viewed college hitting prospects from Stanford with early suspicion because of the "Stanford swing." In short, Stanford tended to teach their hitters, no matter what their offensive skills, to use a flat, pokey swing geared for opposite-field contact. This was a reasonable strategy for college baseball with metal/composite bats, lousy fielders, and a lot of turf fields. If you've paid any attention to the recent "launch angle revolution" in pro ball, you already know that this is a terrible idea for certain classes of professional hitters, who often maximize by gaining greater lift to their swing to optimize their launch angle. Legion have been the talented Stanford hitters who got to the minors and couldn't make the adjustment to wood bats. That might be changing with a new coaching staff, and Hoerner looks like he's not going to fall into that bucket, anyway. He takes a healthy rip and has a history of hitting well with wood bats, including on the Cape in the summer of 2017. We'll be hearing terrible Hoerner/horny puns in Wrigleyville sooner than you may think.

87. Heliot Ramos, OF, San Francisco Giants

We covered the "injury lost season" with Florial above. His toolsy compadre in the Bay Area—well, technically the Augusta area—had the "performance lost season." That can be more troubling, or at least less explicable, but full-season ball was always going to be a slightly aggressive assignment for Ramos. The power/speed combo still flashed, but he was too often undone by an ultra-aggressive approach at the plate. The South Atlantic League is likely the first place he saw even fringy breaking balls. The results weren't great, but it's hardly a disaster considering he spent the whole season as an 18-year-old. He will likely get another shot at Low-A in 2019, and hopefully some adjustments will unlock the plus potential in the bat. We are always going to be the last ones to give up on toolsy center fielders regardless.

88. Shane Baz, RHP, Tampa Bay Rays

The Rays have almost as many very good prospects as San Diego, but it sure didn't hurt that they added Baz late in the year as the player to be named later in the Chris Archer deal. Often these PTBNL end up as straight cash, homie. Sometimes it's even a player being traded for himself. The Rays instead got a high upside arm, albeit one that spent 2018 in the Appalachian League. Baz offers mid-90s heat, a potential plus slider, and a developing changeup, the usual prep arm package one year out from being a first round pick. He is a riskier version of the same third-starter prospect we've pontificated about over the last 50 spots or so. But we are almost to the last of them now. As Leonard Cohen sang: *"And other forms of boredom advertised as poetry / I know you need your sleep now / I know your life's been hard / But many men are falling / Where you promised to stand guard."*

89. Danny Jansen, C, Toronto Blue Jays

"Catchers are weird" is one of our favorite mantras here at Baseball Prospectus. Two offseasons ago, Jansen got prescription glasses. Suddenly able to see, he immediately jumped from a lightly-regarded potential backup catcher to one of the better catching prospects in the game. He consolidated the 2017 breakout in 2018, performing well in Triple-A before claiming the bulk of the catching time in the majors over the last six weeks in the season. He has a solid but unspectacular defensive reputation, very likely good enough to remain at catcher, which is half the battle. The other half is framing, and we'll have to see where he lands in the majors on that. The bar is so low at catcher now that he has potential to put up big value just by being average to above-average in all phases, and unless things get notably weird again, he should do that starting in 2019.

90. Jon Duplantier, RHP, Arizona Diamondbacks

The injury bug that Duplantier avoided in 2017 struck in 2018, with a bout of biceps tendinitis costing him much of the summer. He was very good when he pitched, and has the usual bunch of red flags for the maybe mid-rotation/maybe bullpen profile that dots the second half of this list and many of the next few dozen that miss: a checkered injury history, effort in the delivery, inconsistent command, and further development needed on the third pitch. He also has one fairly unique one: he's a pitcher from Rice. "Rice pitcher" has an even worse track record than "high school catcher" or "Stanford hitter," owing to chronic overuse under the coach that retired shortly after Duplantier entered pro ball. The inflection point for the third starter-or-short reliever game is getting close here.

91. Oneil Cruz, SS, Pittsburgh Pirates

Yes, seriously, shortstop. Pittsburgh slid one of baseball's largest humans over to shortstop after picking him up from the Dodgers in the Tony Watson trade. It is quite the strange visual to see a man of Cruz's giant frame—he's been listed at 6'6", 175 pounds since he signed, but is likely a few inches taller and at least a few dozen pounds heavier now—in the middle infield. Yet he's currently adequate there, even if he's likely going to have to find another defensive home down the road if he fills out as he might. He has monster raw power and an arm to match it, and a more advanced feel for hitting and approach than you might expect from a giant with these tools. The downside of all these tools and physicality is that swing-and-miss could be a real problem due to a naturally long swing. There's huge upside here, in a lot of different forms.

92. DL Hall, LHP, Baltimore Orioles

What a blessing it is for a prospect writer under deadline crunch to get write about an Orioles pitching prospect named "DL." We won't be the first nor last to make that wisecrack, and the 19-year-old southpaw was healthy throughout 2018, although his workload was managed quite conservatively in his full-season debut. You can't quibble with his results, as he struck out better than a batter per inning on the strength of his mid-90s fastball, heavy with occasional cut, and potential plus power curve. There's a slider and a change too, although both lag behind along with his control and command. The delivery needs to be smoothed out in places, and we need to see him perform like this across longer outings, but Hall could be a pretty good third starter or late inning reliever in a few years. He's gotten comps to Scott Kazmir, which is both pretty good company and also extremely unlikely to help with all those "DL" jokes.

93. Luis Oviedo, RHP, Cleveland Indians

Amongst our research into the masses of mid-rotation starters we occasionally stumble on a nice surprise. Signed out of Venezuela for $375,000 in 2015, Oviedo dominated the Penn League this year as a 19-year-old. It's big stuff out of a still-projectable six-foot-four frame. His fastball already scrapes the upper-90s, and he flashes a plus-or-better breaking ball. The cambio and command need work, so okay, he's not *all* that different from the third starter reports that dot the second half of this list. But Oviedo is at least a new name, and while we aren't quite ready to go higher than 6/5 on him, there are scouts out there who are.

94. Brandon Marsh, OF, Los Angeles Angels

As we hinted at earlier, the Angels spent several years as one of the worst systems in baseball, basically from the moment Mike Trout lost prospect eligibility. The system is on the rise again, and Marsh is the fourth of five Top 101 names. He's a potential plus hit/plus power outfielder who is passable in center for now, but likely ends up in right field long term, where his plus arm will be an asset. The Angels have bet on athletes in recent years in the draft, and Marsh is another hit for a system almost ready to supplement the best player in baseball, since it's become pretty clear in recent years he can't do it all on his own.

95. Sean Murphy, C, Oakland Athletics

Murphy is a prototypical good catching prospect. We are in the range of the list now where things get very fuzzy. The difference between Murphy and the 125th best prospect in baseball—oh, let's say Freudis Nova—just isn't that significant. The difference between him and the next best catching prospect, Miguel Amaya, even less so. So why Murphy? Well, he does everything pretty well. Despite a stiff swing he makes enough quality contact to get most of his plus raw into games. He's a solid defensive catcher with a big arm and good receiving skills. Everything here grades out as average or better—well, except speed—which makes him an above-average catcher. And even if he falls short in one tool or another, the bar for catchers is such that he could still be an average backstop. There's only 30 everyday jobs, and Murphy is about ready to grab hold of one of them.

96. Vidal Brujan, 2B, Tampa Bay Rays

Last year, we had Brujan as one to watch after his short-season campaign in Hudson Valley. While the profile hasn't radically changed, the full-season performance this year will certainly make you stand up and take notice. His approach and potential plus hit tool didn't find any speed bumps at either A-ball level. There's big bat speed here, if not a ton of power projection, since Brujan likes to swing from the heels and can get off-balance. He's a plus-plus runner and passable, if still a bit raw, at the keystone. The hit tool and speed will have to carry the profile and Double-A will be a good test of the bat, but by 2020 Rays fans could be humming "mmm, must be the season of the witch."

97. Calvin Mitchell, OF, Pittsburgh Pirates

We've been making a concerted effort to flag more of the "hit first, ask questions later" prospects for our readers when we really like their offensive potential. Like with pitchers, there's a natural inclination to recoil a bit from this class of prospects. There's inherent added risk that we're overestimating the hitting ability, and there's inherent profile risk that becomes obvious when you consider how teams value decent regulars here. Every year, established league-average hitters without significant defensive utility are freely available as budget free agent options. Sometimes you can pick them up for just the waiver price, or in trade for a prospect you don't really care about. For all the C.J. Cron jokes we make, he was a first-round pick and pretty decent prospect that turned into a solid hitter, usually around league-average or a little bit above. His 2018 campaign was perhaps his best yet. It was book-ended by being salary dumped before the season and claimed off waivers after it. The industry just doesn't value these guys unless they *hit*. So when we rank a guy like Mitchell, who might be a corner outfielder and might be a first baseman, it's because we *really* like the bat. Mitchell showed well enough as a 19-year-old in the Sally that we think he has a shot at the elusive 6 hit/6 power projection that is the general baseline for his archetype. Now he just has to get there.

98. Garrett Hampson, 2B/SS, Colorado Rockies

Ben Franklin helpfully covered death and taxes, but there are three other certainties in life: Jose Mourinho's third season in charge will always be a disaster, a Murakami protagonist will always encounter a mysterious cat, and Baseball Prospectus will always rank a bunch of shortstops on the 101. Hampson is the final one on this year's list, and he's a bit of an outlier for us. While we do enjoy the dirty uniform types that max out their talent, the scout's favorites, we tend to write them as 45s. We prefer the Anderson Tejedas and Lucius Foxes. But Hampson just wins you over. He's not without tools. He's a plus-plus runner who weaponizes his speed with aggressive base running that inevitably, well, gets his uniform dirty. He gets everything out of his defensive game, and while he's a better fit at second, he's average at short and showed better there in 2018 than the more-heralded Brendan Rodgers. He's a pesky hitter that fouls off pitches, works walks, and makes quality contact despite a swing with a lot of moving parts. There's not much power, although he will absolutely take an extra base on any ball in the gap if he can. He's a prototypical dirt dog, and maybe he's only a 50, but that's good enough for us.

99. Jordyn Adams, OF, Los Angeles Angels

Adams was a highly-recruited wideout, set to head to North Carolina where his father is also a coach, before the Angels went well over 17th-pick slot to get him to play baseball exclusively. Early specialization in baseball has made this kind of two-sport prospect more of a *rara avis* lately, but we see it as a positive marker for baseball development. Premium athleticism can play in more facets of the game than just straight-line speed on the bases or in the outfield—though Adams certainly doesn't lack for either. There's body control and the ability to repeat. Does that portend a more consistent swing and more offensive projection? The sample size is never going to be large here, but anecdotally the guys with "stiff" swings don't tend to look like Adams. His first pro summer went fine, and he will head to full-season ball next year. Although with all apologies to the Iowa tourism board, Burlington isn't exactly the Triangle in terms of things to do. There is baseball to be played though.

100. Kristian Robinson, OF, Arizona Diamondbacks

There are no players from the Bahamas currently in the majors. The best player the chain of islands has ever produced was Andre Rodgers, an eleven-year journeyman shortstop who played in the 1950s and 1960s. Both of those are about to change. Robinson is the third Bahamian prospect on this list, along with Jazz Chisholm and Lucius Fox. An additional crop of high-upside players is percolating in the lowest levels of the minors, and surely some of them will be making our lists over the coming years. Six-figure bonuses are now commonplace, and there have been a handful of millionaire signees too. Robinson is one of them, a $2.5 million signee from the 2017 international class. He picked up buzz out of the complex circuit long before ever making his debut in game action, and wowed with explosive athleticism and raw hitting ability. He's a long, long way from the majors, but the potential here is unlimited.

101. Kyler Murray, OF, Oakland Athletics

Murray became the second Heisman Trophy winner currently in organized baseball when he won college football's highest honor in December. Unlike Mets outfielder Tim Tebow, Murray did it the old-fashioned way, playing both sports at the same time. His draft deal with Oakland contained a contractual exception allowing him to play his redshirt junior season at Oklahoma. That type of deal used to be more commonplace, but has fallen out of favor as sports have become more compartmentalized. At the time Murray signed his baseball contract, he was pegged as top NFL pick Baker Mayfield's possible replacement, but he faced a camp competition at quarterback and wasn't seen as having a major NFL future himself. He won the job, and then ripped off one of the greatest dual-threat seasons in college football history more or less out of nowhere. More relevantly, Murray's NFL Draft stock shot up amidst a thin quarterback crop, and he started pontificating about playing both sports professionally, in contravention with the deal agent Scott Boras cut with the A's. On the diamond, he has five-tool athleticism but is unusually raw for a college outfielder because of lack of reps. The outside shot that he's this generation's Bo Jackson or Deion Sanders makes him one of the most interesting athletes in the world right now. The downside risk is that he could be this generation's Chad Hutchinson or Drew Henson and never reach pro excellence on either side. For now, we'll enjoy the ride.

Trust, Buckets and Prospect Evaluation Frameworks

by Craig Goldstein

Given that the basic framework of our prospect lists hasn't been altered very much since at least the Jason Parks-era format, it might seem that we don't spend a lot of time thinking about how to best convey the information within them to our audience. I promise this is not the case—Jeffrey Paternostro, Bret Sayre, and I take time every year to create a wish list of items we'd like to see on the top-10 lists, or tweaks we'd like to make to it. We then argue over whether any of those items actually enhance or compromise our ability to communicate the evaluations, and the concepts on which those evaluations are based.

An offseason discussion with Jason Wojciechowski regarding the A's list gave me reason to question the effectiveness of our current setup. There are two prospects who appear at the back end of the list who couldn't be more different in terms of player type, and yet both received the same 55/45 OFP/Likely grade. While Sean Murphy (ranked 10th) earned those grades with a more standard distribution of skills and risk, James Kaprielian checked in one spot above him with a much more... eclectic mix of present talent, projection, and risk.

To refresh, here is what we had to say on each.

Kaprielian:

The Good: At his best, Kaprielian runs a big fastball into the upper-90s, pairs it with three offspeed pitches with potential to be above-average, and has strong command and a feel for pitching. The fastball is only sometimes that hot on velo, and he was a low-90s guy out of the draft, so it could be fool's gold. On the other hand, the slider is showing up plus already and the change and curve both flash potential. Four-pitch potential with good stuff usually leads to writers bestowing their ace blessings on a young man. Why not here?

The Bad: Well, he had Tommy John surgery in April 2017 after barely pitching in 2015 and 2016 due to recurring elbow problems. He'll return sometime in 2018 as a 24-year-old with 29 pro innings in three seasons, all in A-ball. He's also never maintained the high-end velocity without his elbow barking nearly immediately after.

The Role: OFP 55—Mid-rotation dude with tantalizing velocity/good Nate Eovaldi; Likely 45—Dude bouncing between roles with tantalizing velocity/normal Nate Eovaldi

The Risks: We have absolutely no idea whether he can stay healthy throwing a baseball, let alone whether it's as a starter, a reliever, or somewhere in between. Since the improvement in stuff was so closely correlated with his elbow problems, we also have little idea what he's going to look like as a healthy pitcher. There's way more upside than the ranking indicates, but there's also major concern he'll never pitch effectively again.

Murphy:

The Good: Murphy is an excellent defender, with all of the building blocks you look for in a future above-average catcher. The arm is among the better ones currently in the minor leagues, with strong velocity that holds its line, and he maxes it out with fluid pops that will register plus-plus times on the regular. He controls the zone at the dish, demonstrating a clear plan of attack with a swing built to bring above-average power potential into games.

The Bad: It's a strength swing that can get rigid through the zone, and he was exposed a bit by the more advanced arms of the Texas League, with loads of rolled-over ground ball contact the most frequent result. He puts the ball on the ground so often it's unclear just how much of his power will play at higher levels, and while he's not a black hole of running speed like some of his catching compatriots, he's also not going to make it a habit of beating out too many of those left-side grounders, either.

The Role: OFP 55—Above-average catcher; Likely 45—Solid second-division catcher

The Risks: The bar for catcher offense is so low, and Murphy's defensive baseline high enough, that it's not hard to envision him hitting enough to produce comfortably above-average value behind the dish. It's wise to temper expectations for the offense panning out to ceiling, but the fundamentals here are such that Murphy's a higher likelihood prospect than most.

As you can see, Kaprielian poses a problem within our valuation framework: by all accounts, when he's healthy he projects as a potential top-of-the-rotation starter, with an upper-90s fastball and the potential for *multiple* above-average breakers. That type of ceiling generally earns an OFP (Overall Future Potential) of higher than 55—even if OFP isn't representative of a true ceiling. Conversely, the health issues he's already endured put his realistic floor well below that of a back-end starter, especially factoring in that even if he returns to the mound, it could be with diminished stuff.

So we see that Kaprielian and his high-beta outcomes pose a particular problem that his neighbor to the South, Murphy, does not. A more honest accounting of Kaprielian's OFP might be a 60, or even a 70, when he's healthy and at his finest. A more honest representation of his floor might read: "60-day disabled list." But these honest representations belie the complexities of projecting the probabilities of the various permutations of a player's career. Those complexities are present across every OFP/Likely grade we generate, but players like Kaprielian push the framework we employ close to its breaking point.

So, we're left with a few options: switch to a different framework—perhaps one with an all-encompassing grade, such as Future Value; create an entirely different framework that better explicates the ways in which these probabilities shake out; or live with what we've got and understand there are going to be some guys who just won't fit the system well.

We've seen the usage of one singular grade, that bakes in the good, the bad, the risks, and so forth. We have our current system that demonstrates a strong developmental outcome, as well as a likely one, hopefully demonstrating the distance in risk that some players have relative to others in more than just words. But there's another way, that I'd argue both the singular figure produced in Future Value and the OFP/Likely both draw upon, but don't state explicitly.

In fact, it might well be the best way for us to convey this information on a guy like Kaprielian, and arguably on every prospect—and that is clearly delineating our estimates of their likelihood to land in each grade bucket from 20-80.

For Kaprielian that could look like:

Name	20	30	40	45	50	55	60	70	80
Kaprielian	25%	5%	10%	10%	15%	15%	15%	5%	<1%

Whereas for someone like Murphy, it could look like:

Name	20	30	40	45	50	55	60	70	80
Murphy	<1%	5%	15%	35%	25%	15%	5%	<1%	<1%

The exact percentages aren't the point so much as recognizing the way the distributions are so starkly different, and that's without getting into the notion that Kaprielian's likelihood of being a "20" is probably misleading because he's probably either better than that or just not on the field (thus, not even an organizational player).

The reason we don't (or haven't) presented the information in the above format to our readers isn't because they wouldn't get it—we have some of the smartest, sharpest readers on the planet—but rather because there's a significant element of false precision in this framework. False precision is something I worry about a lot. There's already a fair amount of it baked into our current model, and opting to choose something that would introduce more of it has always concerned me, even if I think the above better represents how my prospect team and I go about thinking of these players.

So, for the same reason that I shy away from using grades such as 35 and 65 (yes, this is a real point of contention within the community—some do not consider them "real" grades), I shy away from adopting this approach for every player. Sometimes the broader view (OFP/Likely) allows for better signal, as the details are obscured and the bucketing of percentages and outcomes and projection provides a cleaner presentation and a cleaner take away. The granularity that the percentage approach exposes is a better way to understand potential prospect outcomes, but it also allows someone to be right no matter the outcome.

Spread the possible outcomes over the different percentages and you're never wrong—this version of reality just played out a certain way, which "you" already conceded was a possibility. The OFP/Likely approach bakes in the more granular effort, while also forcing one to a decision point: What do you believe the ceiling version of this player is, incorporating the risks involved with health, development, and so forth. Furthermore, what do you believe a realistic outcome is for that profile? How do you think those same risks are *likely* to play out?

I used the term "honest" before, when describing the bucketing approach. While that is the most accurate approach, I'm not sure that the OFP/Likely designations don't force us to be more *honest* in our assessments of those likelihoods, or at the very least, more useful to our readers as long as they trust us to be honest in the first place.

—Craig Goldstein is an author of Baseball Prospectus.

True Outcomes

by Jarrett Seidler

Over at the BP Prospect Team, we spend a lot of time writing scouting reports, making rankings, and talking largely in vernacular that feels like it could be inscrutable. All of these lists and reports have grades called "OFP/likely" on the 20-80 scale. We just sort of assume you know what it means or can glean it from context.

But what can you, the reader, actually tell me about OFP? You might know that it stands for Overall Future Potential. We have a section in our glossary at BaseballProspectus.com defining it, but that section was written more than a decade ago and uses the term in a fashion slightly different than how we use it today.

I suspect everyone subscribed to BP is at least somewhat familiar with PECOTA, our longtime statistical player projection system. What you might not be familiar with unless you've clicked around a lot on our player cards is that PECOTA doesn't just spit out "a projection." I mean, it does—that's the weighted mean projection, the one that shows up in the depth charts, projected standings, and fantasy product. But it also spits out projections every 10 percentiles, starting with the 10th-percentile outcome all the way up to a 90th-percentile outcome.

Although each individual evaluator will have a slightly different interpretation, I've always viewed our grades and terminology in something of a percentile outcome form. They're a range of projections—OFP/likely covering a particular slice of the most important outcomes for you to know. We'll get to those shortly, but let's start all the way at the bottom because there are some points about prospect failure that we don't get to make often.

1st-Percentile Outcomes

This is essentially the "acts of god" section. A tiny slice of guys in their late-teens through mid-twenties will have something absolutely horrible happen to them that leaves them unavailable to play our great and glorious game, or so diminished that they might as well be. Oscar Taveras died. Brian Cole died. Nick Adenhart died. Greg Halman died. Ryan Westmoreland had a cavernous brain malformation. Matt Imhof lost his eye. Brien Taylor punched with his pitching hand. Mike Olt had a terrible concussion. Jason Neighborgall couldn't throw a strike. It feels heartless to talk about, and you can't worry about or predict horrible outliers other than to know that they happen and it totally blows.

10th-Percentile Outcomes

These are the bad outcomes we can worry about. Wade Townsend never recovered from heavy usage at Rice, destroyed every part of his pitching arm worth destroying, and became an online poker pro living in Mexico and later a YouTube blogger. Bad luck, but not really an act of god, and frankly not all that unforeseeable. Brett Wallace's bat ended up being too slow. Jesus Montero couldn't make good enough contact. Fernando Martinez never figured out the difference between fastballs and breaking balls amidst injuries. Joel Guzman couldn't control a wild and long swing. Plenty of pitchers destroyed their arms after warning signs and were never the same.

Essentially everyone who hasn't established themselves as a decent player in the majors has a 10th-percentile outcome of having no MLB career, or a career so insignificant it might as well have never happened. From an evaluative standpoint, all we can do is talk about guys who have extreme cases or risks, really—think a guy like Hunter Harvey, who can't stay healthy and who has much more than a 1-in-10 chance of getting struck down like this. But you should remember that prospect analysts once declared Mark Prior the perfect pitching prospect with perfect mechanics and perfect everything, and his arm fell off, too, albeit aided by a collision with Marcus Giles and a bad comeback liner. It can happen to anyone.

25th-Percentile Outcomes

When we talk about a "reasonable floor" or a "fallback role," this is usually what we mean. A guy with a likely mid-rotation starter projection can "miss" and still be a useful back-end starter or reliever. A guy projected to be a first-division position player can "miss" and still be a useful utility player or fourth outfielder. We often debate whether these players were technical busts or not, but does it really matter? They made it, a little.

Joba Chamberlain will never live up to ranking one spot ahead of Clayton Kershaw once upon a time, but he had a few great relief seasons, a few okay starting seasons, and some other flashes of usefulness in a decent-enough career. Jose Tabata feels like an eternal disappointment and was out of organized baseball by his late-twenties, but he still had a six-year MLB career as a perfectly fine fourth outfielder. These are usually somewhere around your one-in-four bad outcomes for good prospects.

50th-Percentile Outcomes

These are the likeliest group of outcomes. We literally call them a "likely role." This is right around the midpoint, where half the outcomes should be better and half the outcomes should be worse if we're doing our jobs right.

This seems like a good place to note that prospect grades just aren't normally distributed. There are way more projected role 2s and 3s than anything else, because there are way more minor-league-quality players than major-league-quality ones. There are more 4s than 6s for the same reason.

Tool grades don't track on a normal distribution either. In any given season, we can give out dozens of 80 speed or fastball grades, whereas we might only project a hit tool to 80 a time or two a decade. I don't think this is a failure of the system, per se, but I've seen wide disagreement on that through the years, along with countless analyses that try to normalize things and end up missing the mark.

75th-Percentile Outcomes

Here's where I peg OFP to, at least in the context of how we at BP use it on reports and lists. I suspect I may get a little technical blowback on this; there are versions of scouting vernacular that combine OFP and likely into one number that is something much closer to the likely number, and sometimes that is called OFP. (This may not be immediately apparent to the reader, but the grading of prospects can take many, many technical forms; for example, there are MLB organizations that don't use the 20-80 scale at all.)

If I'm casually saying "Joe Dude is a 6" in a conversation with a scout, that's probably closer to what I mean, and he'd be a "OFP 70/likely 60" on our scouting report. However, in our likely/OFP setup, OFP is definitionally a higher outcome than likely, and this is around where I aim to be on it. We threw OFP 80s on two prospects this year, Ronald Acuña and Victor Robles. I feel pretty confident that at least one out of every four future Ronald Acuñas and one out of every four future Victor Robleses will be a role 8 player if we got to run their careers out multiple times from here.

Of course, this isn't a Texas hold'em cash game and you can't run it multiple times to reduce variance, and in saying that we think there's about a 25 percent chance for either of them, we're also saying there's a better than 50 percent chance that neither of them will become that player. And yet, we'll all still have dudes in our mentions if they don't quite get there.

90th-Percentile Outcomes

When we talk about "upside," this is usually around where we mean. Most legitimate prospects have star upside. Top prospects have superstar upside. To bring Acuña and Robles up again, it feels right that about one out of every ten times, one of them will become a high-end 8, perennial MVP type. It'd take a bit of unexpected development—Acuña would need to absolutely maximize his immense hitting potential, and Robles would need to develop significant power—but it's something you can see if you squint right. It's how you can watch Sixto Sanchez on the mound and see Pedro Martinez. There's a chance.

99th-Percentile Outcomes

These are literally the 1-in-100 best-case scenarios, tougher to hit than runner-runner to a backdoor flush. What's your personal 1-in-100 best-case scenario? You get the job of your dreams, marry your soulmate, become wealthy enough so you don't have to work unless you want to and neither do your kids, and die happy at the age of 104? Sometimes prospects develop like that, too.

What's every half-decent prospect's 99th-percentile outcome? It's at least MLB superstar. Think Jacob deGrom, Dallas Keuchel, and Justin Turner. They were projected to be fringe, below-average types right until they got to the majors or even after they initially made it, but developed late into role 7 or 8 types, some of the best in the game. Someone has to vastly overperform even late projections or player development would be far too easy and predictable: known unknowns and all that. Hell, Turner got claimed on waivers and non-tendered before he turned into one of the game's best hitters. You couldn't hit that one without guessing so wildly that you miss on dozens of other calls.

What's the 1-in-100 high-side outcome for a true top global prospect? Are we living it right now? Mike Trout is 26 years old. He ranked in the top three of the BP 101 twice, in 2011 and 2012. By Jay Jaffe's JAWS system, using Baseball-Reference's formulation of WAR, which likes Trout exactly as much as BP's formulation of WARP does, he's already the 10th-best center fielder in the history of baseball, and he hasn't had his seventh full season to fill out the peak score of JAWS.

At 26, Trout has already had a median Hall of Fame career by the best metric we have to evaluate such things. Barring life-altering injury or unexpected collapse, there are few outcomes where Trout doesn't ultimately retire as one of the greatest players in baseball history; he showed up as a 10-win player in May 2012 and has never been much less than that since. Simply continuing his present pace until his mid-thirties will stamp him as arguably the greatest player who ever lived.

—Jarrett Seidler is an author of Baseball Prospectus.

Dynasty Top 101

by Bret Sayre and Ben Carsley

"We always think we'll end up disagreeing more than we end up disagreeing." That's how we began the 2018 installment of this annual list after a ranking process that found us on the same page a vast majority of the time. Did we have minor quibbles with each other's lists? Sure. Did we each win and lose a few arguments around player placement? Sure. Ben still liked fast middle infielders a little too much, and Bret's hatred of pitchers was still pretty extreme. Death, taxes and what not. But in the end, we were about as aligned as you can ask two prospect rankers to be.

But 2019? Turns out 2019 is a different year. Compiling the top 40 names on this list wasn't too bad, though we had some differences in order outside the top 15-or-so guys. But once we got past the top 40, well, it took a lot more discussion and negotiation than in years past. Maybe that's a positive—the no. 1 thing we always worry about is amplifying instead of compensating for each other's blind spots—or maybe it's just indicative of a larger trend among minor leaguers right now: much of who you prefer comes down to personal preference.

Yes, there is a very clear elite tier of prospects and another two-dozen-or-so who most people would agree are strong fantasy assets. But after that it sure gets murky. Perhaps that's because 32 players on this year's version of the list were eligible for but unranked on last year's edition. Another 13 on the 2019 rundown were not eligible for our list last year. For those math majors at home, that means nearly 50% of the names on the 2019 Dynasty 101 are newcomers, at least when it comes to us ranking them. And that left us lots and lots of room for discussion.

A few minor adjustments we made from last year: one, we finally took our own advice about catchers a bit more seriously. Only four are on this list, and two of them come at the very end. Second, we got a little more comfortable rolling the dice on "our guys"—in fact, there's a meaty section around the 50s and 60s of players we just couldn't come to a consensus on, so we took a "shoot your shot" approach before going back to a consensus ranking system. And finally, we eased up *slightly* on dinging pitchers in these rankings. There still aren't that many—only 26 among our top-101, to be exact—but we became ever slightly more liberal in sprinkling the good-but-not great SP4 types into the back-half of this list.

There aren't really any other themes this year. The minors are wide open, and whether you want to roll the dice on the next group of potential stars or play it safer with the crop of near-MLBers depends on your risk tolerance, your league size and your contention cycle. Remember those key points and use this list as a guide rather than a bible, and you should get some useful information out of it. We know we sure did.

~Our Annual Disclaimers~

As always, there are a few list-specific disclaimers to go over before we jump in. These rankings are for fantasy purposes only, and do not directly take into account things like an outfielder's ability to stick in center or a catcher's pop time. That being said, these factors matter indirectly as they affect a player's ability to either stay in the lineup or maintain eligibility. Additionally, we factor in home parks and organizational strengths, just as when we are talking about a major-league player. We can't pretend that these prospects operate in a vacuum, unaffected by park factors. Of course, there's no guarantee that they will reach the majors with their current organization, so while it is reflected, it's not a heavy ranking factor. Most importantly, the intention of this list is to balance the upside, probability, and proximity of these players to an active fantasy lineup.

Within the list below, you'll find important information about each prospect, including their potential fantasy value (in dollars) at their peak and the risk factor associated with reaching their projected output. Also, you will find a fantasy overview, which summarizes how many categories each player will be useful in, along with any that carry impact. For this exercise, we defined "impact" has having the potential to be in the top 15-20 players in a given category. For instance, impact in home runs roughly equates to the potential to hit 30, impact in steals is 25, and impact for strikeouts is the potential to punch out 200. Then you'll see a realistic ceiling and floor for each prospect, purely in terms of rotisserie value. The comments are brief because we've already written fantasy-specific comments on each of these players in the individual top-10 lists.

Previous Rank correlates to where repeat entrants placed on the 2018 Top 101. The "NR" key means the player was not ranked, while "N/A" means they were not eligible. Ages listed are as of 4/1/2019.

With the fine print out of the way, let's dive right in. We hope you enjoy!

The Man With No Tier

1. Vladimir Guerrero Jr., 3B, Toronto Blue Jays (Age: 20, Previous Rank: 3)

Potential Earnings: $35+
Risk Factor: Super Low
Fantasy Overview: Four-category contributor; Impact potential in AVG, R, HR, RBI
Fantasy Impact ETA: Should'f Been Late 2018
Realistic Ceiling: Miguel Cabrera
Realistic Floor: "Only" a top-5 first baseman

Tier 1: Future Fantasy Cornerstones

2. Fernando Tatis Jr., SS, San Diego Padres (Age: 20, Previous Rank: 7)

Potential Earnings: $35+
Risk Factor: Low
Fantasy Overview: Five-category contributor; Impact potential in R, HR, RBI, SB
Fantasy Impact ETA: Mid 2019
Realistic Ceiling: Not too far off from Manny Machado
Realistic Floor: More like Peak Didi Gregorius

3. Victor Robles, OF, Washington Nationals (Age: 21, Previous Rank: 2)

Potential Earnings: $35+
Risk Factor: Medium
Fantasy Overview: Five-category contributor; Impact potential in AVG, R, SB
Fantasy Impact ETA: Right now
Realistic Ceiling: When we first started comparing him to Starling Marte it was more of a compliment…
Realistic Floor: Faster Ender Inciarte

4. Eloy Jimenez, OF, Chicago White Sox (Age: 22, Previous Rank: 5)

Potential Earnings: $35+
Risk Factor: Low
Fantasy Overview: Four-category contributor; Impact potential in AVG, R, HR, RBI
Fantasy Impact ETA: Early 2019
Realistic Ceiling: J.D. Martinez with the prospect pedigree
Realistic Floor: A power-heavy OF2

5. Jordon Adell, OF, Los Angeles Angels (Age: 19, Previous Rank: 33)

Potential Earnings: $35+
Risk Factor: Medium
Fantasy Overview: Five-category contributor; Impact potential in R, HR, RBI, SB
Fantasy Impact ETA: 2020
Realistic Ceiling: 90% of Mookie Betts
Realistic Floor: Something like Matt Kemp's career

Tier 2: Prospects You Want to Take Home to Mom

6. Keston Hiura, 2B, Milwaukee Brewers (Age: 22, Previous Rank: 17)

Potential Earnings: $25-30
Risk Factor: Low
Fantasy Overview: Four-category contributor; Impact potential in AVG, R, RBI
Fantasy Impact ETA: Mid 2019
Realistic Ceiling: A less powerful Robinson Cano
Realistic Floor: Peak Daniel Murphy without the speed

7. Kyle Tucker, OF, Astros (Age: 22, Previous Rank: 10)

Potential Earnings: $25-30
Risk Factor: Low
Fantasy Overview: Five-category contributor; Impact potential in AVG, R, RBI
Fantasy Impact ETA: Early 2019
Realistic Ceiling: 110% of Andrew Benintendi
Realistic Floor: 90% of Andrew Benintendi

8. Nick Senzel, 3B/OF, Cincinnati Reds (Age: 23, Previous Rank: 8)

Potential Earnings: $25-30
Risk Factor: Low
Fantasy Overview: Five-category contributor; Impact potential in AVG, R, RBI
Fantasy Impact ETA: Early 2019
Realistic Ceiling: What if Anthony Rendon was always healthy?
Realistic Floor: What if Anthony Rendon was often hurt *and* an outfielder?

9. Taylor Trammell, OF, Cincinnati Reds (Age: 21, Previous Rank: 28)

Potential Earnings: $30-35
Risk Factor: Medium
Fantasy Overview: Five-category contributor; Impact potential in R, SB
Fantasy Impact ETA: 2020
Realistic Ceiling: Once again we tried to get more creative than Carl Crawford, but…
Realistic Floor: Tim Anderson in the outfield

10. Wander Franco, SS, Tampa Bay Rays (Age: 18, Previous Rank: NR)

Potential Earnings: $35+
Risk Factor: High
Fantasy Overview: Four-category contributor; Impact

potential in AVG, R, HR, RBI
Fantasy Impact ETA: 2021
Realistic Ceiling: 1-1 on this list a year from now
Realistic Floor: Mid-50s on this list a year from now

11. Royce Lewis, SS, Minnesota Twins (Age: 19, Previous Rank: 22)

Potential Earnings: $30-35
Risk Factor: Medium
Fantasy Overview: Five-category contributor; Impact potential in AVG, R, RBI, SB
Fantasy Impact ETA: 2021
Realistic Ceiling: The best version of Jean Segura
Realistic Floor: A toolsy Twins first-rounder would never fail to meet expectations!

12. Bo Bichette, SS, Toronto Blue Jays (Age: 21, Previous Rank: 15)

Potential Earnings: $20-25
Risk Factor: Low
Fantasy Overview: Five-category contributor
Fantasy Impact ETA: Late 2019
Realistic Ceiling: We'll stick with Prime Ian Kinsler
Realistic Floor: Brian Dozier with ~20 more points of batting average

13. Brendan Rodgers, SS, Colorado Rockies (Age: 22, Previous Rank: 4)

Potential Earnings: $30-35
Risk Factor: Medium
Fantasy Overview: Four-category contributor; Impact potential in AVG, R, RBI, HR
Fantasy Impact ETA: Late 2019
Realistic Ceiling: A top-7 shortstop for the next decade
Realistic Floor: A top-15 second baseman for the next five years

14. Alex Kirilloff, OF, Minnesota Twins (Age: 21, Previous Rank: NR)

Potential Earnings: $25-30
Risk Factor: Medium
Fantasy Overview: Four-category contributor; Impact potential in AVG, R, HR, RBI
Fantasy Impact ETA: 2020
Realistic Ceiling: A borderline OF1 who marries his hit tool with his power
Realistic Floor: An OF3 who only figures out how to do one or the other

15. Austin Riley, 3B, Atlanta Braves (Age: 21, Previous Rank: 70)

Potential Earnings: $20-25
Risk Factor: Low
Fantasy Overview: Three-category contributor; Impact potential in R, HR, RBI
Fantasy Impact ETA: As soon as Josh Donaldson hits the DL
Realistic Ceiling: 40 homers and a tolerable average
Realistic Floor: 25-plus homers but while hitting .240

Tier 3: Well Worth the Gamble

16. Forrest Whitley, RHP, Houston Astros (Age: 21, Previous Rank: 23)

Potential Earnings: $25-30
Risk Factor: Medium
Fantasy Overview: Four-category contributor; Impact potential in W, K, ERA, WHIP
Fantasy Impact ETA: Mid 2019
Realistic Ceiling: An actual, in-the-flesh SP1
Realistic Floor: Even the best pitching prospects are more likely to be SP3s than SP1s

17. Peter Alonso, 1B, New York Mets (Age: 24, Previous Rank: NR)

Potential Earnings: $20-25
Risk Factor: Low
Fantasy Overview: Three-category contributor; Impact potential in R, HR, RBI
Fantasy Impact ETA: Early 2019
Realistic Ceiling: Bret will never shut up about it
Realistic Floor: Ummmm Bret would never overrate a Mets first baseman, no siree

18. Jesus Luzardo, LHP, Oakland Athletics (Age: 21, Previous Rank: 92)

Potential Earnings: $25-30
Risk Factor: Medium
Fantasy Overview: Four-category contributor; Impact potential in W, K, ERA, WHIP
Fantasy Impact ETA: Early 2019
Realistic Ceiling: The Good (and healthy) James Paxton
Realistic Floor: Eduardo Rodriguez

19. Francisco Mejia, C/OF, San Diego Padres (Age: 23, Previous Rank: 13)

Potential Earnings: $20-25
Risk Factor: Low-ish
Fantasy Overview: Four-category contributor
Fantasy Impact ETA: Now
Realistic Ceiling: A bona fide top-5 catcher for quite some time
Realistic Floor: An OF4 who has you cursing front offices

20. Alex Reyes, RHP, St. Louis Cardinals (Age: 24, Previous Rank: 11)

Potential Earnings: $25-30
Risk Factor: Medium
Fantasy Overview: Four-category contributor; Impact potential in W, K, ERA, WHIP

Fantasy Impact ETA: 2017
Realistic Ceiling: A tried and true fantasy SP1
Realistic Floor: Dellin Betances (but with some saves)

21. Carter Kieboom, SS, Washington Nationals (Age: 21, Previous Rank: 47)

Potential Earnings: $20-25
Risk Factor: Low
Fantasy Overview: Four-category contributor; Impact potential in AVG, R, RBI
Fantasy Impact ETA: Late 2019
Realistic Ceiling: A Vegas-quality Corey Seager impersonation
Realistic Floor: An A.C.-quality Kyle Seager impersonation

22. Nick Madrigal, 2B/SS, Chicago White Sox (Age: 22, Previous Rank: N/A)

Potential Earnings: $25-30
Risk Factor: Medium
Fantasy Overview: Five-category contributor; Impact potential in AVG, R, SB
Fantasy Impact ETA: 2020
Realistic Ceiling: Dustin Pedroia's career, plus a few more steals
Realistic Floor: A .290 hitter with 25 steals and little else

23. Garrett Hampson, 2B/SS, Colorado Rockies (Age: 24, Previous Rank: 84)

Potential Earnings: $20-25
Risk Factor: Low
Fantasy Overview: Four-category contributor; Impact potential in R, SB
Fantasy Impact ETA: As soon as the Rockies capitulate
Realistic Ceiling: Not too many players steal 30 bags and hit .300 these days
Realistic Floor: Ryan Theriot in Coors, basically

Tier 4: Mostly Familiar Faces

24. Luis Robert, OF, Chicago White Sox (Age: 21, Previous Rank: 19)

Potential Earnings: $25-30
Risk Factor: High
Fantasy Overview: Five-category contributor; Impact potential in SB
Fantasy Impact ETA: 2021
Realistic Ceiling: A five-category OF2
Realistic Floor: Another reason to throw shade on future Cuban prospects

25. Yordan Alvarez, OF/1B, Houston Astros (Age: 21, Previous Rank: 68)

Potential Earnings: $20-25
Risk Factor: Low
Fantasy Overview: Four-category contributor; Impact potential in R, HR, RBI
Fantasy Impact ETA: 2020
Realistic Ceiling: 2017 Josh Bell
Realistic Floor: 2018 Josh Bell

26. Ryan Mountcastle, 3B, Baltimore Orioles (Age: 22, Previous Rank: 35)

Potential Earnings: $20-25
Risk Factor: Medium
Fantasy Overview: Four-category contributor; Impact potential in HR, RBI
Fantasy Impact ETA: 2020
Realistic Ceiling: Nick Castellanos with more power
Realistic Floor: What's another C.J. Cron comp?

27. Sixto Sanchez, RHP, Philadelphia Phillies (Age: 20, Previous Rank: 30)

Potential Earnings: $25-30
Risk Factor: High
Fantasy Overview: Four-category contributor; Impact potential in W, K, ERA, WHIP
Fantasy Impact ETA: 2020
Realistic Ceiling: The best fantasy starter in baseball for a year or two
Realistic Floor: Hurt, or a reliever, or both

28. Brent Honeywell, RHP, Tampa Bay Rays (Age: 24, Previous Rank: 29)

Potential Earnings: $20-25
Risk Factor: Medium
Fantasy Overview: Four-category contributor; Impact potential in W, K, WHIP
Fantasy Impact ETA: As soon as his elbow will permit
Realistic Ceiling: A very solid all-around fantasy SP3
Realistic Floor: Makes 30 starts but with, like, 160 IP

29. Luis Garcia, SS, Washington Nationals (Age: 18, Previous Rank: 76)

Potential Earnings: $20-25
Risk Factor: Medium
Fantasy Overview: Five-category contributor; Impact potential in AVG, R
Fantasy Impact ETA: 2021
Realistic Ceiling: We will never shut up about being so early on this top-50 stud
Realistic Floor: We may have seriously overhyped the next Jhonny Peralta

30. Trevor Larnach, OF, Minnesota Twins (Age: 22, Previous Rank: N/A)

Potential Earnings: $20-25
Risk Factor: Medium
Fantasy Overview: Four-category contributor; Impact potential in AVG, R, RBI
Fantasy Impact ETA: 2020

Realistic Ceiling: We're really trying to avoid the Michael Conforto comp, but...
Realistic Floor: A nondescript OF4

31. Yusniel Diaz, OF, Baltimore Orioles (Age: 22, Previous Rank: 50)

Potential Earnings: $15-20
Risk Factor: Low
Fantasy Overview: Five-category contributor
Fantasy Impact ETA: Mid 2019
Realistic Ceiling: What if Peak Melky Cabrera played in Camden Yards?
Realistic Floor: Kevin Pillar (again, offense only)

32. Jesus Sanchez, OF, Tampa Bay Rays (Age: 21, Previous Rank: 54)

Potential Earnings: $20-25
Risk Factor: Medium
Fantasy Overview: Four-category contributor; Impact potential in HR, RBI
Fantasy Impact ETA: 2020
Realistic Ceiling: Eddie Rosario with more power
Realistic Floor: Post-peak Jay Bruce

33. Andres Gimenez, SS, New York Mets (Age: 20, Previous Rank: NR)

Potential Earnings: $20-25
Risk Factor: Medium
Fantasy Overview: Five-category contributor; Impact potential in SB
Fantasy Impact ETA: 2020
Realistic Ceiling: The guy we still think Amed Rosario can be
Realistic Floor: The guy Rosario is now

34. Luis Urias, 2B/SS, San Diego Padres (Age: 21, Previous Rank: 69)

Potential Earnings: $15-20
Risk Factor: Low
Fantasy Overview: Three-category contributor; Impact potential in AVG, R
Fantasy Impact ETA: Right now
Realistic Ceiling: A .300 hitter who pushes for 15/15 seasons and bats second
Realistic Floor: A .280 hitter who's more of a 10/10 guy and bats eighth

35. MacKenzie Gore, LHP, San Diego Padres (Age: 20, Previous Rank: 42)

Potential Earnings: $25-30
Risk Factor: High
Fantasy Overview: Four-category contributor; Impact potential in W, K, ERA, WHIP
Fantasy Impact ETA: 2021
Realistic Ceiling: A regular borderline SP1
Realistic Floor: An SP4 who can't quite put away righties

36. Mitch Keller, RHP, Pittsburgh Pirates (Age: 22, Previous Rank: 25)

Potential Earnings: $20-25
Risk Factor: Medium
Fantasy Overview: Four-category contributor; Impact potential in W, ERA
Fantasy Impact ETA: Mid 2019
Realistic Ceiling: Honestly, not too dissimilar from Jameson Taillon
Realistic Floor: More of a SP4/5 whose results don't match his stuff

37. A.J. Puk, LHP, Oakland Athletics (Age: 23, Previous Rank: 26)

Potential Earnings: $25-30
Risk Factor: High
Fantasy Overview: Four-category contributor; Impact potential in W, K, ERA
Fantasy Impact ETA: 2020
Realistic Ceiling: Patrick Corbin with even more strikeouts
Realistic Floor: Josh Hader with better tweets

38. Michael Kopech, RHP, Chicago White Sox (Age: 22, Previous Rank: 12)

Potential Earnings: $25-30
Risk Factor: High
Fantasy Overview: Four-category contributor; Impact potential in W, K, ERA
Fantasy Impact ETA: 2020
Realistic Ceiling: Chris Archer
Realistic Floor: Wade Davis with Josh Hader's tweets

39. Keibert Ruiz, C, Los Angeles Dodgers (Age: 20, Previous Rank: 49)

Potential Earnings: $20-25
Risk Factor: Medium
Fantasy Overview: Four-category contributor; Impact potential in AVG
Fantasy Impact ETA: 2020
Realistic Ceiling: Jason Kendall with less speed
Realistic Floor: 101_Pic1

Tier 5: Fast Risers and Steady Climbers

40. Alex Verdugo, OF, Los Angeles Dodgers (Age: 22, Previous Rank: 40)

Potential Earnings: $15-20
Risk Factor: Low
Fantasy Overview: Four-category contributor; Impact potential in AVG, R
Fantasy Impact ETA: Early 2019
Realistic Ceiling: Jesse Winker with 90 percent of the OBP
Realistic Floor: Jesse Winker with 87.5 percent of the OBP

41. Bubba Thompson, OF, Texas Rangers (Age: 20, Previous Rank: HM)

Potential Earnings: $25-30
Risk Factor: High
Fantasy Overview: Five-category contributor; Impact potential in SB
Fantasy Impact ETA: 2022
Realistic Ceiling: The next Taylor Trammell, hopefully
Realistic Floor: One could argue we've misjudged toolsy Rangers outfielders in the past

42. Drew Waters, OF, Atlanta Braves (Age: 20, Previous Rank: NR)

Potential Earnings: $25-30
Risk Factor: High
Fantasy Overview: Five-category contributor
Fantasy Impact ETA: 2021
Realistic Ceiling: #bathtime
Realistic Floor: "Explain to me how he is not fancy dog Blake Rutherford?" – Ben

43. Khalil Lee, OF, Kansas City Royals (Age: 20, Previous Rank: 97)

Potential Earnings: $20-25
Risk Factor: Medium
Fantasy Overview: Five-category contributor; Impact potential in R
Fantasy Impact ETA: 2020
Realistic Ceiling: The good-but-not great Shin-Soo Choo years
Realistic Floor: The good-but-not great Alex Gordon years

44. Jahmai Jones, 2B, Los Angeles Angels (Age: 21, Previous Rank: 39)

Potential Earnings: $20-25
Risk Factor: Medium
Fantasy Overview: Five-category contributor
Fantasy Impact ETA: 2020
Realistic Ceiling: A Brandon Phillips you can believe in
Realistic Floor: A Cesar Hernandez you waited way too long for

45. Cristian Pache, OF, Atlanta Braves (Age: 20, Previous Rank: 95)

Potential Earnings: $20-25
Risk Factor: Medium
Fantasy Overview: Five-category contributor; Impact potential in web gems
Fantasy Impact ETA: 2020
Realistic Ceiling: A top-25 prospect if the bat holds up against high-minors pitching
Realistic Floor: Potentially off this list if it doesn't

46. Vidal Brujan, 2B, Tampa Bay Rays (Age: 21, Previous Rank: NR)

Potential Earnings: $25-30
Risk Factor: High
Fantasy Overview: Five-category contributor; Impact potential in AVG, R, SB
Fantasy Impact ETA: 2021
Realistic Ceiling: A 40-steal middle infielder
Realistic Floor: "What if Tony Kemp couldn't hit?" isn't a great proposition

47. Ian Anderson, RHP, Atlanta Braves (Age: 20, Previous Rank: NR)

Potential Earnings: $20-25
Risk Factor: Medium
Fantasy Overview: Four-category contributor; Impact potential in W, ERA
Fantasy Impact ETA: 2020
Realistic Ceiling: The middle class Aaron Nola
Realistic Floor: Julio Teheran (sorry Braves fans)

48. Tyler O'Neill, OF, St. Louis Cardinals (Age: 22, Previous Rank: 93)

(Side note: We use IP/AB and not service time for eligibility, so yes, he's eligible)
Potential Earnings: $20-25
Risk Factor: Medium
Fantasy Overview: Three-category contributor; Impact potential in HR, RBI
Fantasy Impact ETA: Sometime in 2019
Realistic Ceiling:
Realistic Floor:

49. Nolan Gorman, 3B, St. Louis Cardinals (Age: 18, Previous Rank: N/A)

Potential Earnings: $25-30
Risk Factor: High
Fantasy Overview: Four-category contributor; Impact potential in R, HR, RBI
Fantasy Impact ETA: 2022
Realistic Ceiling: A regular 40-homer threat at the hot corner
Realistic Floor: A wind turbine

50. Alec Bohm, 3B, Philadelphia Phillies (Age: 22, Previous Rank: N/A)

Potential Earnings: $25-30
Risk Factor: High
Fantasy Overview: Four-category contributor; Impact potential in R, HR, RBI
Fantasy Impact ETA: 2021
Realistic Ceiling: Rhys Hoskins at third base
Realistic Floor: Who Bret and Ben originally thought Rhys Hoskins would be (oops)

51. Jonathan India, 3B, Cincinnati Reds (Age: 22, Previous Rank: N/A)
Potential Earnings: $20-25
Risk Factor: Medium
Fantasy Overview: Five-category contributor
Fantasy Impact ETA: 2021
Realistic Ceiling: A third baseman who approaches 20/20 a few times
Realistic Floor: Fancy Dog Brian Anderson

Tier 5.5: Ben's and Bret's Guys

52. Oneil Cruz, Skyscraper, Pittsburgh Pirates (Age: 20, Previous Rank: NR)
Potential Earnings: $25-30
Risk Factor: High
Fantasy Overview: Five-category contributor; Impact potential in HR, RBI
Fantasy Impact ETA: 2021
Realistic Ceiling: Both a literal and metaphorical high one
Realistic Floor: Jabari Blash was big, too

53. Victor Victor Mesa, OF, Marlins (Age: 20, Previous Rank: NR)
Potential Earnings: $20-25
Risk Factor: Medium
Fantasy Overview: Five-category contributor; Impact potential in AVG, R, SB
Fantasy Impact ETA: 2020
Realistic Ceiling: Lorenzo Cain without the injury risk
Realistic Floor: I mean, 75 percent of the industry already thinks he's Albert Almora

54. Dylan Cease, RHP, Chicago White Sox (Age: 23, Previous Rank: 80)
Potential Earnings: $25-30
Risk Factor: High
Fantasy Overview: Four-category contributor; Impact potential in W, ERA, K
Fantasy Impact ETA: Late 2019
Realistic Ceiling: Gerrit Cole
Realistic Floor: A high-strikeout, oft-injured reliever

55. Estevan Florial, OF, New York Yankees (Age: 21, Previous Rank: 18)
Potential Earnings: $25-30
Risk Factor: High
Fantasy Overview: Four-category contributor; Impact potential in HR, RBI
Fantasy Impact ETA: 2021
Realistic Ceiling: The really good version of Marcell Ozuna
Realistic Floor: The really good version of Jose Osuna

56. Colton Welker, 3B, Colorado Rockies (Age: 21, Previous Rank: 99)
Potential Earnings: $20-25
Risk Factor: Medium
Fantasy Overview: Four-category contributor; Impact potential in AVG, RBI
Fantasy Impact ETA: 2021
Realistic Ceiling: Ben gets his Garin Cecchini re-do ... in Coors!
Realistic Floor: Colin Moran without the hype

57. Leody Taveras, OF, Texas Rangers (Age: 20, Previous Rank: 34)
Potential Earnings: $20-25
Risk Factor: Medium
Fantasy Overview: Five-category contributor
Fantasy Impact ETA: 2021
Realistic Ceiling: A speed-based borderline OF1 in his best years
Realistic Floor: The worst gamble on Tool Time since someone resurrected Tim Allen's career

58. Jordyn Adams, OF, Los Angeles Angels (Age: 19, Previous Rank: N/A)
Potential Earnings: $30-35
Risk Factor: Extreme
Fantasy Overview: Five-category contributor; Impact potential in R, SB
Fantasy Impact ETA: 2022
Realistic Ceiling: A 20/40 outfield stud
Realistic Floor: You name it, he could fall short of it

59. Kristian Robinson, OF, Arizona Diamondbacks (Age: 18, Previous Rank: NR)
Potential Earnings: $30-35
Risk Factor: Extreme
Fantasy Overview: Five-category contributor; Impact potential in R, HR, RBI
Fantasy Impact ETA: 2022
Realistic Ceiling: Ronald Acuña with a touch less power
Realistic Floor: You name it, he could fall short of it

60. George Valera, OF, Cleveland Indians (Age: 18, Previous Rank: NR)
Potential Earnings: $30-35
Risk Factor: Extreme
Fantasy Overview: Five-category contributor; Impact potential in AVG, R, RBI
Fantasy Impact ETA: 2022
Realistic Ceiling: Juan Soto with a touch less power
Realistic Floor: He's literally had 18 pro at-bats

Tier 6: Where We Finally Got Comfortable Ranking Pitchers

61. Mike Soroka, RHP, Atlanta Braves (Age: 21, Previous Rank: HM)

Potential Earnings: $20-25
Risk Factor: Medium
Fantasy Overview: Four-category contributor; Impact potential in W, ERA, WHIP
Fantasy Impact ETA: 2019
Realistic Ceiling: Zack Greinke's pitchability with Rick Porcello's stuff
Realistic Floor: He's a pitcher with a shoulder injury on his record, so

62. Brusdar Graterol, RHP, Minnesota Twins (Age: 20, Previous Rank: NR)

Potential Earnings: $25-30
Risk Factor: High
Fantasy Overview: Four-category contributor; Impact potential in W, ERA, K
Fantasy Impact ETA: 2021
Realistic Ceiling: It's lazy, but Jose Berrios isn't a terrible fantasy comp
Realistic Floor: You know who else has Great Stuff?

63. Ke'Bryan Hayes, 3B, Pittsburgh Pirates (Age: 22, Previous Rank: NR)

Potential Earnings: $20-25
Risk Factor: Medium
Fantasy Overview: Five-category contributor; Impact potential in AVG, R
Fantasy Impact ETA: 2019
Realistic Ceiling: Remember that time Bill Mueller won the batting title?
Realistic Floor: Remember all those times he didn't?

64. Casey Mize, RHP, Detroit Tigers (Age: 21, Previous Rank: N/A)

Potential Earnings: $25-30
Risk Factor: High
Fantasy Overview: Four-category contributor; Impact potential in W, K, WHIP
Fantasy Impact ETA: 2021
Realistic Ceiling: One of the 25-or-so best pitchers in baseball
Realistic Floor: A generic SP4 who seems worse because of the pedigree

65. Jazz Chisholm, SS, Arizona Diamondbacks (Age: 21, Previous Rank: NR)

Potential Earnings: $25-30
Risk Factor: High
Fantasy Overview: Five-category contributor; Impact potential in HR, RBI
Fantasy Impact ETA: 2021
Realistic Ceiling: A Love Supreme
Realistic Floor: Christian Rock Album Chisholm

66. Travis Swaggerty, OF, Pittsburgh Pirates (Age: 21, Previous Rank: N/A)

Potential Earnings: $25-30
Risk Factor: High
Fantasy Overview: Five-category contributor; Impact potential in R, SB
Fantasy Impact ETA: 2021
Realistic Ceiling: If A.J. Pollock traded a few hits for walks
Realistic Floor: JBJ without the Gold Gloves

67. Joshua James, RHP, Houston Astros (Age: 26, Previous Rank: NR)

Potential Earnings: $20-25
Risk Factor: Medium
Fantasy Overview: Four-category contributor; Impact potential in ERA, K
Fantasy Impact ETA: Right now
Realistic Ceiling: Mike Clevinger
Realistic Floor: Seranthony Dominguez

68. Yusei Kikuchi, LHP, Seattle Mariners (Age: 27, Previous Rank: N/A)

Potential Earnings: $15-20
Risk Factor: Low
Fantasy Overview: Four-category contributor
Fantasy Impact ETA: Opening Day
Realistic Ceiling: A solid fantasy SP4
Realistic Floor: A solid fantasy SP5

69. Dustin May, RHP, Los Angeles Dodgers (Age: 21, Previous Rank: NR)

Potential Earnings: $20-25
Risk Factor: Medium
Fantasy Overview: Four-category contributor; Impact potential in W, WHIP
Fantasy Impact ETA: 2020
Realistic Ceiling: The ideal embodiment of a solid all-around fantasy SP3
Realistic Floor: Not as nice as this ranking

70. Nate Pearson, RHP, Toronto Blue Jays (Age: 22, Previous Rank: NR)

Potential Earnings: $25-30
Risk Factor: Extreme
Fantasy Overview: Four-category contributor; Impact potential in W, ERA, K
Fantasy Impact ETA: When the stars align
Realistic Ceiling: A fantasy SP2
Realistic Floor: Brandon Morrow's career

Tier 7: Last of the Consensus

71. Brandon Marsh, OF, Los Angeles Angels (Age: 21, Previous Rank: 96)

Potential Earnings: $20-25
Risk Factor: High
Fantasy Overview: Five-category contributor; Impact potential in R
Fantasy Impact ETA: 2021
Realistic Ceiling: The Good Josh Reddick
Realistic Floor: The Other Josh Reddick

72. Seuly Matias, OF, Kansas City Royals (Age: 20, Previous Rank: 85)

Potential Earnings: $20-25
Risk Factor: High
Fantasy Overview: Three-category contributor; Impact potential in HR, RBI
Fantasy Impact ETA: 2021
Realistic Ceiling: Basically Khris Davis
Realistic Floor: A really good Double-A slugger

73. Heliot Ramos, OF, San Francisco Giants (Age: 19, Previous Rank: 45)

Potential Earnings: $25-30
Risk Factor: Extreme
Fantasy Overview: Five-category contributor; Impact potential in HR, RBI
Fantasy Impact ETA: 2021
Realistic Ceiling: Who we thought he was last year, just slower
Realistic Floor: Rymer Liriano

74. Kyle Wright, RHP, Atlanta Braves (Age: 23, Previous Rank: 81)

Potential Earnings: $15-20
Risk Factor: Medium
Fantasy Overview: Four-category contributor
Fantasy Impact ETA: 2020
Realistic Ceiling: Good enough to earn and keep a spot in the crowded Braves rotation
Realistic Floor: A very talented set-up man

75. Adrian Morejon, LHP, San Diego Padres (Age: 20, Previous Rank: 78)

Potential Earnings: $20-25
Risk Factor: High
Fantasy Overview: Four-category contributor; Impact potential in W, WHIP
Fantasy Impact ETA: Late 2020
Realistic Ceiling: A solid SP2 in the mold of the good Jose Quintana
Realistic Floor: A solid SP5 in the mold of a near 2018 Jon Lester

76. Chris Paddack, RHP, San Diego Padres (Age: 23, Previous Rank: NR)

Potential Earnings: $20-25
Risk Factor: High
Fantasy Overview: Four-category contributor; Impact potential in W, WHIP
Fantasy Impact ETA: 2020
Realistic Ceiling: The Good Michael Wacha in Petco
Realistic Floor: A streaming option in shallow leagues/SP6 in deeper formats

77. Gavin Lux, SS/2B, Los Angeles Dodgers (Age: 21, Previous Rank: NR)

Potential Earnings: $15-20
Risk Factor: Medium
Fantasy Overview: Five-category contributor
Fantasy Impact ETA: 2020
Realistic Ceiling: Is he really all that different from Luis Urias?
Realistic Floor: Is he really all that different from Christian Arroyo?

78. Julio Pablo Martinez, OF, Texas Rangers (Age: 23, Previous Rank: NR)

Potential Earnings: $20-25
Risk Factor: High
Fantasy Overview: Four-category contributor; Impact contributor in SB
Fantasy Impact ETA: 2021
Realistic Ceiling: Jeffrey will stop calling him Juan
Realistic Floor: A spare outfielder who teases but never puts it together

79. Jarred Kelenic, OF, Seattle Mariners (Age: 19, Previous Rank: N/A)

Potential Earnings: $20-25
Risk Factor: High
Fantasy Overview: Five-category contributor; Impact potential in AVG, R
Fantasy Impact ETA: 2021
Realistic Ceiling: Jeff McNeil, if you're an optimist
Realistic Floor: Brodie, you sly dog

80. Hunter Greene, RHP, Cincinnati Reds (Age: 19, Previous Rank: 56)

Potential Earnings: $25-30
Risk Factor: Extreme
Fantasy Overview: Four-category contributor; Impact potential in W, ERA, K
Fantasy Impact ETA: 2022
Realistic Ceiling: Becomes a pitcher
Realistic Floor: Stays a thrower

81. Justus Sheffield, LHP, Seattle Mariners (Age: 22, Previous Rank: HM)
Potential Earnings: $15-20
Risk Factor: Medium
Fantasy Overview: Four-category contributor
Fantasy Impact ETA: Early 2019
Realistic Ceiling: A high-strikeout, high-WHIP SP5 who teases more
Realistic Floor: We still think he might be a reliever TBH

82. Anderson Tejeda, SS, Texas Rangers (Age: 20, Previous Rank: NR))
Potential Earnings: $20-25
Risk Factor: High
Fantasy Overview: Five-category contributor
Fantasy Impact ETA: 2021
Realistic Ceiling: Turns out we were just 18 months too early on him!
Realistic Floor: Turns out we shouldn't have believed in his comeback

83. Danny Jansen, C, Toronto Blue Jays (Age: 23, Previous Rank: NR)
Potential Earnings: $15-20
Risk Factor: Medium
Fantasy Overview: Four-category contributor
Fantasy Impact ETA: Right now
Realistic Ceiling: A real-life 20-homer catcher
Realistic Floor: Would you burn a prospect roster spot on Welington Castillo?

84. Joey Bart, C, San Francisco Giants (Age: 22, Previous Rank: N/A)
Potential Earnings: $20-25
Risk Factor: High
Fantasy Overview: Three-category contributor; Impact potential in HR, RBI
Fantasy Impact ETA: 2021
Realistic Ceiling: A real-life 25-homer catcher
Realistic Floor: I don't think we've ever seen an elite catcher from Georgia Tech fail before, right? Right??

85. Triston McKenzie, RHP, Cleveland Indians (Age: 21, Previous Rank: 43)
Potential Earnings: $15-20
Risk Factor: Medium
Fantasy Overview: Four-category contributor
Fantasy Impact ETA: Late 2019
Realistic Ceiling: The new posterboy for "pitchability"
Realistic Floor: Mostly only good for "he's a crafty righty!" commentary

86. Calvin Mitchell, OF, Pittsburgh Pirates (Age: 20, Previous Rank: NR)
Potential Earnings: $20-25
Risk Factor: High
Fantasy Overview: Four-category contributor; Impact potential in AVG, RBI
Fantasy Impact ETA: 2021
Realistic Ceiling: An exciting OF2/3 who hits .280-plus with 20-plus homers and a few steals
Realistic Floor: A generic OF5 who hits .260-plus with 15 homers

87. Xavier Edwards, SS, San Diego Padres (Age: 19, Previous Rank: NR)
Potential Earnings: $25-30
Risk Factor: Extreme
Fantasy Overview: Three-category contributor; Impact potential in R, SB
Fantasy Impact ETA: 2022
Realistic Ceiling: Dee Gordon with some semblance of on-base skill
Realistic Floor: A really fun pinch runner who fantasy owners won't quit

88. Isan Diaz, 2B, Miami Marlins (Age: 22, Previous Rank: 64)
Potential Earnings: $15-20
Risk Factor: Medium
Fantasy Overview: Four-category contributor
Fantasy Impact ETA: Mid 2019
Realistic Ceiling: 85% of Good Rougned Odor
Realistic Floor: Bad Rougned Odor

Tier 8: Throwing Darts... While Blindfolded

89. Tirso Ornelas, OF, San Diego Padres (Age: 19, Previous Rank: NR)
Potential Earnings: $20-25
Risk Factor: High
Fantasy Overview: Four-category contributor; Impact potential in HR, RBI
Fantasy Impact ETA: 2021
Realistic Ceiling: The version of David Peralta with 30-homer power
Realistic Floor: The hitter formerly known as David Peralta

90. Michael Chavis, 3B, Boston Red Sox (Age: 23, Previous Rank: 48)
Potential Earnings: $20-25
Risk Factor: High
Fantasy Overview: Four-category contributor; Impact potential in RBI
Fantasy Impact ETA: 2020
Realistic Ceiling: An annual source of 25 homers for, like, the

Mariners
Realistic Floor: Ummmm Ben would never overrate a Sox third baseman, no siree

91. Sandy Alcantara, RHP, Miami Marlins (Age: 23, Previous Rank: 88)

Potential Earnings: $20-25
Risk Factor: High
Fantasy Overview: Three-category contributor; Impact potential in SV
Fantasy Impact ETA: Early to Mid 2019
Realistic Ceiling: A solid all-around SP4/5 who peaks a bit higher
Realistic Floor: A mid-tier fantasy closer some years

92. Alek Thomas, OF, Arizona Diamondbacks (Age: 18, Previous Rank: N/A)

Potential Earnings: $20-25
Risk Factor: High
Fantasy Overview: Five-category contributor; Impact potential in AVG, R
Fantasy Impact ETA: 2021
Realistic Ceiling: Adam Eaton with more steals
Realistic Floor: A second-generation Strength and Conditioning Coach

93. D'Shawn Knowles, OF, Los Angeles Angels (Age: 18, Previous Rank: NR)

Potential Earnings: $25-30
Risk Factor: Extreme
Fantasy Overview: Five-category contributor; Impact potential in AVG, R, SB
Fantasy Impact ETA: 2022
Realistic Ceiling: Truly D'Lightful
Realistic Floor: A real D'Sappointment

94. Luis Garcia, SS, Philadelphia Phillies (Age: 18, Previous Rank: NR)

Potential Earnings: $25-30
Risk Factor: Extreme
Fantasy Overview: Five-category contributor; Impact potential in AVG, R
Fantasy Impact ETA: 2023
Realistic Ceiling: The next Jean Segura
Realistic Floor: The next Everth Cabrera

95. Nathaniel Lowe (Nate/Nat?), 1B, Tampa Bay Rays (Age: 23, Previous Rank: NR)

Potential Earnings: $20-25
Risk Factor: High
Fantasy Overview: Four-category contributor; Impact potential in HR, RBI
Fantasy Impact ETA: 2020
Realistic Ceiling: We've had a blind spot for these late-blooming sluggers before
Realistic Floor: There's a reason we generally avoid this profile

96. Brandon Lowe, 2B/OF, Tampa Bay Rays (Age: 24, Previous Rank: NR)

Potential Earnings: $10-15
Risk Factor: Low
Fantasy Overview: Four-category contributor
Fantasy Impact ETA: Now, if he makes the Opening Day roster
Realistic Ceiling: A grilled cheese sandwich on white bread
Realistic Floor: Someone holding an elevator for you at the end of a long day

97. Nico Hoerner, SS, Chicago Cubs (Age: 21, Previous Rank: N/A)

Potential Earnings: $15-20
Risk Factor: Medium
Fantasy Overview: Four-category contributor
Fantasy Impact ETA: 2020
Realistic Ceiling: A 25-homer bat at shortstop
Realistic Floor: The generic Jed Lowrie years

98. Hudson Potts, 3B, San Diego Padres (Age: 20, Previous Rank: NR)

Potential Earnings: $20-25
Risk Factor: High
Fantasy Overview: Three-category contributor; Impact potential in HR, RBI
Fantasy Impact ETA: 2021
Realistic Ceiling: Matt Chapman
Realistic Floor: Christian Villanueva

99. Nolan Jones, 3B, Cleveland Indians (Age: 20, Previous Rank: NR)

Potential Earnings: $20-25
Risk Factor: High
Fantasy Overview: Three-category contributor; Impact potential in HR, RBI
Fantasy Impact ETA: 2021
Realistic Ceiling: Matt Chapman
Realistic Floor: Christian Villanueva

100. Wander Javier, SS, Minnesota Twins (Age: 20, Previous Rank: 77)

Potential Earnings: $25-30
Risk Factor: Extreme
Fantasy Overview: Five-category contributor; Impact potential in HR, RBI
Fantasy Impact ETA: 2022
Realistic Ceiling: A top-40 fantasy prospect at this time next year
Realistic Floor: All we are is Dusty in the wind

101. Touki Toussaint, RHP, Atlanta Braves (Age: 22, Previous Rank: NR)

Potential Earnings: $15-20
Risk Factor: Medium
Fantasy Overview: Three-category contributor; Impact potential in K
Fantasy Impact ETA: Early 2019
Realistic Ceiling: Patience is a virtue
Realistic Floor: Patience sucks

So, About Brendan McKay... Consider McKay prospect no. 102 on this list. Is he a better pure fantasy prospect than some of the last 15-or-so names on this list? You could certainly make the argument. But we decided to leave him off to help illustrate the point that he is being wildly overvalued in dynasty leagues right now. When McKay was drafted, the dream for dynasty owners was that he'd emerge as a fantasy SP2/3 *and* a borderline top-20 first baseman, or at least a usable CI/UT on the days he'd hit. But McKay now looks more like a suped up Michael Lorenzen than a baby Shohei Ohtani. Could he be a fantasy SP4/5? Sure, but so could lots of other guys who didn't quite make this list. It was the bat that made him special, and well, the bat just doesn't look special. Like we said, if you prefer him to Alcantara or Touki or any of the teenagers in our final dozen-or-so dudes, we can't blame ya. But he doesn't belong with the Kellers or Andersons of the world either.

So, About Kyler Murray... Let's pretend for a minute that Murray is going to play baseball. If so, his calling card from a fantasy perspective is speed—genuine potential 50-steal speed. He's also got more pop than you'd think from a smaller dude, and obviously the overall athleticism is beyond reproach. Can he hit though? We don't really know yet, and we won't have a way of knowing until we see him against low- and mid-minors arms. If he plays, he could be Ender Inciarte. Or Lorenzo Cain. Or Byron Buxton. Or Kevin Pillar. Or Terrance Gore. You get it: very high risk, very high reward. He'd probably be in the 60s on this list as a result. The problem, of course, is that it sure seems like Murray wants to play football. You're stuck with him for now if you drafted him; don't drop him unless he officially declares for football. But don't look to buy in on him right now either, because the tea leaves aren't being read in our favor.

So, About Marco Luciano... No, we didn't forget him. We just think the hype is a little out of control at present. He'd be in the next 50 names for sure, but so would 49 other guys.

Honorable Mention

- Austin Beck, OF, Athletics
- Daz Cameron, OF, Tigers
- Griffin Canning, RHP, Angels
- Antonio Cabello, OF, Yankees
- Lucius Fox, SS, Rays
- Monte Harrison, OF, Marlins
- Adam Haseley, OF, Phillies
- Spencer Howard, RHP, Phillies
- Brendan McKay, LHP, Rays
- Matt Manning, RHP, Tigers
- Jonathan Loaisiga, RHP, Yankees
- Ronny Mauricio, SS, Mets
- Adonis Medina, RHP, Phillies
- Elehuris Montero, 3B, Cardinals
- Josh Naylor, 1B, Padres
- Luis Patino, RHP, Padres
- Buddy Reed, OF, Padres
- Esteury Ruiz, 2B, Padres
- Blake Rutherford, OF, White Sox
- Antonio Santillan, RHP, Reds
- Taylor Widener, RHP, Diamondbacks
- Bryse Wilson, RHP, Braves

Dan Vogelbach Mention

- Dan Vogelbach, 1B, Mariners

—Bret Sayre and Ben Carsley are authors of Baseball Prospectus.

Top 50 Signees

by Bret Sayre

The easiest way to know that it's a new calendar year, besides all that time you've been spending at the gym, is another iteration of ranking the players who enter our dynasty-league player pools. It's a beautiful thing—a new wave of fresh-faced youth who haven't been around long enough to disappoint us yet. Yet, ultimately they will (on the whole). What we're attempting to do here is to give you the best chance at making the most of your drafts in the aggregate, and that requires a combination of both picking the right players and making the most of your draft spots.

There are years when it's better to have high-end picks in dynasty drafts, and there are years when it's better to have more picks. This year is the latter. I may personally adore the player who graces the top spot on this list, but he might be the weakest to occupy it since I started putting together these lists nearly a decade ago. What's going to end up happening due to this flattening is that this year's drafts are going to be unpredictable. It's not hyperbole to say that you could talk yourself into taking any of the first 15 names below with a top-three pick. In fact, if you sample enough leagues, you'd probably find that to be true in practice. And it doesn't get much clearer after that. The depth of this draft class is strong, but it's incredibly fluid.

Before we get to the most exciting part, it's the paragraph that frames the list and its utility. The below is intended for dynasty leagues of approximately 14-16 teams, with one catcher. It assumes a separate farm team, and if your league does not have a separate farm team, feel free to bump up the players with faster timetables. If you're in a deeper league, prioritize safety. If you're in a shallower league, load up on risk. And, finally, each player's situation is factored into their values. This can mean organizational history of developing players and/or future home ballpark (though the latter is discounted a bit since these players are generally pretty far away and park factors are not constants). You know your league best, and now you know how to translate what is about to come to your individual circumstances.

Now, the part of the article you actually came for (though I do appreciate you either reading the intro or lying to me about it): the 50 best players who entered professional baseball during the 2018 calendar year:

1. Nick Madrigal, 2B, Chicago White Sox

If we've learned anything over the last few years of baseball, it's that power comes both from the traditional and non-traditional places. Sure, the top of the leaderboard looks as muscular as always—with Khris Davis, J.D. Martinez and Joey Gallo—but Jose Ramirez, Francisco Lindor, Mookie Betts and Alex Bregman all eclipsing 30 bombs? That's the power of quality contact, and it ties in with why Madrigal sits at the top of the list this year. There's no one better in this class at making quality contact than the diminutive second baseman from Oregon State. I mean, he only struck out five times in 173 plate appearances in his pro debut across three levels. In a previous life, we'd assume that with his height and relatively linear swing, Madrigal would top out at around five homers a year. That, combined with the ability to hit over .300 and steal 30-plus bases, would be attractive enough without the power. Add 15-homer potential to that, though, and you basically have Whit Merrifield with a pedigree. Madrigal has the raw power to get there, despite his small frame, and we know the frame is no longer the impediment it once was.

2. Trevor Larnach, OF, Minnesota Twins

This is the first time I've ever seen the top two players available in dynasty drafts come from the same school—not surprisingly the team that won the NCAA Championship last spring. (They also have a candidate for next year's top spot, but I digress.) The big question around Larnach heading into his junior season was whether he could turn his strength into over-the-fence power, and boy did he. Larnach hit 19 homers after just three in his previous two seasons, and kept it going with a .200 ISO in his pro debut. He'll get compared to fellow Beaver Michael Conforto more than he should, but from a fantasy sense, it's not far off.

3. Victor Victor Mesa, OF, Miami Marlins

This is a tier unto itself, and there are a lot of similarities between these two players. Some of the excitement around Lewis comes not only from the fact that he has plenty of upside (he could steal 30-40 bases, while also pushing 20 homers if everything coalesces), but also from his extreme youth when compared with his level. He held his own in an 18-game sample at the end of 2017 in the Midwest League. That is a data point. Yet, we don't have to go back very far to see the same exciting things about Robert. In his last season in Serie Nacional, a then-18-year-old Robert hit .401/.526/.687, with 12 homers and 11 steals in just 53 games. That's more impressive than any player we've seen come to the majors from Cuba at that age. Robert may not have the upside of a Yoan Moncada, but a fast-moving 20/20 outfielder capable of hitting for strong averages (and high OBP, if you're into that sort of thing) is a real possibility.

4. Jordyn Adams, OF, Los Angeles Angels
5. Nolan Gorman, 3B, St Louis Cardinals

The two best prep bats in this draft, Adams and Gorman couldn't be much more different. The former is the prototypical Angels outfield prospect: dripping with tools including plus-plus speed and the potential to reach average or better in both hit and power. There are multiple paths for Adams to be a high-end fantasy outfielder, even if all of the above don't come together (they likely won't), which makes him a little less risky than the typical "athlete" profile would suggest. On the other hand, Gorman has more thunder in his bat than any other player on this list, and is likely the only one who could one day hit 40-plus bombs in the majors. Of course, like you'd expect, it comes with a lot of swing and miss—yet it wasn't egregious in the Appy League and it's foolish to judge an 18-year-old on how much he struck out in full-season ball during his draft year. There's no wrong way to order these two, and it's reasonable that they might both be available in the second half of the first round in most dynasty drafts.

6. Alec Bohm, 3B, Philadelphia Phillies
7. Travis Swaggerty, OF, Pittsburgh Pirates
8. Jonathan India, 3B, Cincinnati Reds

This is a natural tier here, as it's three college bats with more question marks than the two who sit at the top of the list. Bohm hints at an above-average hit tool and plus power, which could lead him to a few .270-30-100 campaigns at Citizens Bank Park. On the other hand, he'll turn 23 during the 2019 season and he hasn't seen a single at-bat in full-season ball. Swaggerty has the most athletic profile of this group and he's a potential 20/20 contributor, with more upside in steals than that, but offers more swing-and-miss than fantasy owners are quite comfortable with. Not to mention that he doesn't have a long track record of high-end performance. India is the safest of this group, but he's also the most boring. It's average tools across the board, and if any aspect of his game drops below average, the whole profile becomes much less palatable, regardless of what position he ultimately plays.

9. Casey Mize, RHP, Detroit Tigers

And we finally get to the first-overall pick in the draft. Going from pitching prospect to SP2 is really hard while keeping your arm in one piece, and while Mize certainly has that upside, so did Kyle Wright, A.J. Puk, Dillon Tate, Carlos Rodon, Mark Appel, and Kevin Gausman. What do all those pitchers have in common? They were the first college arms selected in their respective drafts going back to 2012. Buyer beware.

10. Yusei Kikuchi, LHP, Seattle Mariners

This isn't a Darvish or Ohtani situation, where Kikuchi pushes himself up to the top of draft lists due to top-of-the-rotation upside. Instead, he offers immediate production and reasonable mixed-league certainty. In terms of landing spots, Seattle certainly isn't ideal, especially in the short term. Their defense is shaping up to be below-average, but the kicker is Omar Narvaez and his bottom-of-the-barrel framing. Expect an ERA north of 3.50, a WHIP around 1.20 and 170-ish strikeouts if he can pitch a full season. He's talented enough to be a top-30 starter, but sometimes it takes more than just talent.

11. Xavier Edwards, SS, San Diego Padres

As the two of the most impactful (yes this is a word, Craig) speedsters in the draft, it's natural to compare Adams and Edwards. The Padres supplemental pick has 40-plus steal potential and showed off an extremely strong approach in his pro debut, walking more times than he struck out across the Arizona League and the Northwest League. The thing that keeps Edwards out of the top-10 for me is his limited pop, and while he could add strength and approach double-digit homers, it would likely come at the expense of some of those steals. Nits, they must be picked.

12. Kyler Murray, OF, Oakland Athletics

There's no question who the most famous person on this list is, as Murray won the Heisman Trophy (it's a football thing). And while he's saying all the right things about committing to baseball and the Athletics, there's always going to be the risk he ends up in the NFL instead. Murray's speed is his calling card, but he's strong enough to muscle more than a few out of the park as well—he hit 10 homers in his final season at Oklahoma and could get to 20-plus as a pro. He'll have plenty of eyes on him as he starts his baseball career in 2019.

13. Julio Pablo Martinez, OF, Texas Rangers

While Martinez will be 23 before Opening Day this season and he stands a paltry 5-foot-9, he's dripping with tools and the Rangers should move him relatively quickly through the minors so long as he can hold his own in 2019. His strong defensive profile will continue to get him looks and opportunities to work through the swing-and-miss and tap into his 25-homer power.

14. Jarred Kelenic, OF, Seattle Mariners

The lone player on this list who's already been traded, Kelenic will look for a strong hit tool to carry his profile in Seattle but complements that nicely with 20-homer pop and even some speed to get to 10-15 steals. It's not the sexiest profile, but the sum of its parts could make him a strong OF3 in time.

15. Joey Bart, C, San Francisco Giants

The only thing more frustrating than pitching prospects are catching prospects. Bart hit *checks notes* a billion homers in the Northwest League after being drafted second overall last year, and he's a good bet to stick behind the plate. Yet, the track record of catching prospects is just brutal—with Buster Posey standing tall as the lone college catcher to go from the first round of the draft to a consistent top-10 option at the position. Maybe Bart can break the trend, but, well, you know the definition of insanity.

16. Alek Thomas, OF, Arizona Diamondbacks
17. Connor Scott, OF, Miami Marlins

For those of you counting at home, this now makes eight first names in a row. The only things that separate Thomas and Scott are 50 spots in the draft and five inches. Both carry speed-hit profiles leaving them capable of hitting .280-plus with 30 steals. The power lingers behind, but neither are scrubs in the department—and you wouldn't need to flinch much to see one of them developing 20-homer pop. It's just a starter kit at this point, as they're both unlikely to reach the majors until 2022, but if you're going to pick a starter kit, might as well be the Andrew Benintendi one.

18. Brice Turang, SS, Milwaukee Brewers
19. Matthew Liberatore, LHP, Tampa Bay Rays

Both Turang and Liberatore were potential top-five picks early last spring before ultimately settling into the back half of the first round. Turang can work a count and steal a base, but he'll have to develop some power in order to be a starting fantasy shortstop. Liberatore may not have traditional overpowering stuff, but he throws four pitches that can be above-average and shows advanced command and pitchability for his age. If he can tick up his fastball velocity like some scouts believe he can, he'll make this ranking look low.

20. Grant Lavigne, 1B, Colorado Rockies
21. Triston Casas, 3B, Boston Red Sox
22. Jordan Groshans, 3B/SS, Toronto Blue Jays
23. Seth Beer, DH, Houston Astros

For the power-hungry of you out there, this group is for you. Lavigne is a cold-weather prep bat with a great approach and very strong raw power. Plus, it won't hurt that he'll call Coors home in a few short years. Casas is forgotten about a little because he only got five plate appearances in before a season-ending injury in his pro debut, but if Gorman had the most power in the prep ranks, the Sox first-rounder falls right behind him in line. He'll have to fight some potential contact issues, but he won't be the first or last prep bat to do so. Groshans has a chance to be a more balanced hitter between his average and power than the two players he is sandwiched between, but don't race him up your draft board just because the Blue Jays are experimenting with him at shortstop. Unless you're a catcher, positions don't matter anymore. The same applies to Beer, who profiles best as someone who should never pick up a glove, save to hand it to a teammate in a friendly fashion. His biggest problem is that there's a lot of concern the power he showed in college won't transfer to wood, and it's also going to be long road if he wants to hit lefties. In a perfect world, he's Schwarber-esque. In most realistic worlds, he'll top out as a Logan Morrison type.

24. Bo Naylor, C/3B, Cleveland Indians

The thing about fantasy catching prospects is that their bats have to be able to carry them at another position, and they ideally should be athletic enough to play somewhere other than the cold corner. Naylor fits both of these descriptors as he projects for a plus hit tool and has the arm/range for third if Cleveland moves him out from behind the plate.

25. Nico Hoerner, SS, Chicago Cubs

The Cubs' first-rounder is a scrappy hitter with underrated strength, and while that gives him limited upside in our circles, a strong showing in the AFL has his name on more tongues this winter than expected. He's another who is a better selection in deeper leagues, as he's more of a .290-15-10 ceiling type.

26. Mike Siani, OF, Cincinnati Reds
27. Marco Luciano, SS, San Francisco Giants
28. Brady Singer, RHP, Kansas City Royals
29. Mason Denaburg, RHP, Washington Nationals
30. Merrill Kelly, RHP, Arizona Diamondbacks

The Reds may not have taken Siani until the fourth round, but he didn't fall on talent, he fell on price tag. His strong center field skills will give him lots of opportunity to develop with the bat, and his plus-plus speed will provide him many chances with fantasy owners as well. Luciano is the top traditional J2 signee from 2018, and while he may not have the polish that Vladito or Wander Franco had, he's got power, speed and a good approach at the plate. Singer was a potential 1-1 pick at the start of the spring and he had a strong showing at Florida in his junior season, but lacks the ceiling of the arms before him (all three of them). He's hurt the most by my unease about investing in pitchers early in dynasty drafts. The Nationals love to draft pitchers with injury questions, and while Denaburg doesn't have the lofty ceiling of a Lucas Giolito or Jesus Luzardo, they have a strong track record here. He has the talent to ride a strong fastball/curve combo to SP3 status with the potential for 200 strikeouts, if he's healthy. Kelly is a fun story, but expecting him to be the next Miles Mikolas is extremely far-fetched. That said, he's only 30 and he could be a reasonable SP5 this year in mixed leagues, and that has value in its own right.

31. Malcom Nunez, 3B, St Louis Cardinals

32. Ryan Weathers, LHP, San Diego Padres

33. Jameson Hannah, OF, Oakland Athletics

34. Jeremiah Jackson, SS, Los Angeles Angels

35. Logan Gilbert, RHP, Seattle Mariners

36. Ethan Hankins, RHP, Cleveland Indians

37. Blaze Alexander, SS, Arizona Diamondbacks

38. Greyson Jenista, OF, Atlanta Braves

39. Jackson Kowar, RHP, Kansas City Royals

40. Grayson Rodriguez, RHP, Baltimore Orioles

This is the part of the draft where you should be taking pitchers—in the third through fifth rounds. Some of these arms will end up being strong major-league contributors, but there's so much development necessary between draft day and a major-league debut both in terms of physical strength and coaching—and that's in addition to figuring out which of these guys holds their stuff while pitching every fifth day. Among these arms, Hankins has the highest ceiling and greatest risk—his fastball before the shoulder injury that caused him to drop in the draft was a true 80 pitch. Gilbert, on the other hand, has the highest floor if such a thing existed among pitching prospects. Rodriguez would probably be inside the top 30 were he drafted by almost any other organization, as I don't trust the Orioles to develop a roll of film. Nunez set the Dominican Summer League ablaze after signing with the Cardinals in the spring, but he's a true bat-only profile and though the Cardinals have had some success here, it's tough to push him much higher than this. He may seem out of place here as an 11th-round pick, but Alexander was a top-100 name pre-draft and got a bonus five times slot. He'll get chances to hit based on his defense (his arm at short was probably the best in the draft class), and he got off on the right foot in the Arizona and Pioneer Leagues.

41. Nick Schnell, OF, Tampa Bay Rays

42. Cole Winn, RHP, Texas Rangers

43. Noelvi Marte, OF, Seattle Mariners

44. Tristan Pompey, OF, Miami Marlins

45. Jeremy Eierman, SS/3B, Oakland Athletics

46. Griffin Conine, OF, Toronto Blue Jays

47. Diego Cartaya, C, Los Angeles Dodgers

48. Shane McClanahan, LHP, Tampa Bay Rays

49. Joe Gray, OF, Milwaukee Brewers

50. Gabriel Rodriguez, SS, Cleveland Indians

Schnell is a fun name to keep an eye on late, if he falls in drafts, but the overall ceiling is what drops him to this tier despite having average, power, and speed at his disposal. Winn is another arm who would push the top 30 if he'd been drafted elsewhere, as Rangers have had almost as good of a time developing pitching prospects as the Orioles. Pompey, Eierman and Conine were strong college bats with limited upside—though they balance it by having slightly more advanced timelines. (Of course, Conine went and messed that latter part up a bit by getting suspended for PEDs.) Pompey, the brother of oft-injured Jays prospect Dalton, has already gotten 101 PA in High-A, showing strong on-base skills and flashing some speed. I know I shouldn't put a J2 catching prospect on here, but Cartaya is extremely advanced in his approach and the Dodgers have a pretty good track record with catching prospects.

Honorable Mention (in alphabetical order):

- Luken Baker, 1B, St Louis Cardinals
- Richard Gallardo, RHP, Chicago Cubs
- Sandy Gaston, RHP, Tampa Bay Rays
- Cadyn Grenier, SS, Baltimore Orioles
- Adam Kloffenstein, RHP, Toronto Blue Jays
- Victor Mesa Jr., OF, Miami Marlins
- Jake McCarthy, OF, Arizona Diamondbacks
- Misael Urbina, OF, Minnesota Twins
- Steele Walker, OF, Chicago White Sox
- Cole Wilcox, RHP, Washington Nationals

—Bret Sayre is an author of Baseball Prospectus.

Index of Names